Seeing the Forest and the Trees

Seeing the Forest and the Trees
Human-Environment Interactions in Forest Ecosystems

edited by Emilio F. Moran and Elinor Ostrom

The MIT Press
Cambridge, Massachusetts
London, England

MIT Press books may be purchased at special quantity discounts for business or sales promotional use. For information, please email special_sales@mitpress.mit.edu or write to Special Sales Department, The MIT Press, 5 Cambridge Center, Cambridge, MA 02142.

This book was set in Sabon on 3B2 by Asco Typesetters, Hong Kong.
Printed and bound in the United States of America.

Library of Congress Cataloging-in-Publication Data

Seeing the forest and the tree : human-environment interactions in forest ecosystems / edited by Emilio F. Moran and Elinor Ostrom.
p. cm.
Includes bibliographical references and index.
ISBN 0-262-13453-5 (alk. paper) — ISBN 0-262-63312-4 (pbk. : alk. paper)
1. Deforestation. 2. Forest management. 3. Forest ecology. 4. Nature—Effect of human beings on. I. Moran, Emilio F. II. Ostrom, Elinor.
SD418.S44 2005
333.75—dc22 2004062122

Printed on recycled paper.

10 9 8 7 6 5 4 3 2 1

Contents

Preface and Acknowledgments

This book is the result of research carried out by a team of scientists representing the biological, physical, and social sciences. It is made possible by the substantial support of the National Science Foundation (NSF), through its support for Centers on the Human Dimensions of Global Environmental Change, in grant SBR 95-21918 from the Directorate for Social and Behavioral Sciences. We have been privileged during this period to have worked with outstanding program officers at NSF, particularly Cheryl Eavey and Thomas Baerwald. They not only have been managers of the grant that funded the Center for the Study of Institutions, Population, and Environmental Change (CIPEC) at Indiana University but they have been outstanding sounding boards for the ideas we have generated, and they have encouraged us to develop an external advisory board of world-class scholars who, through their annual visits, pushed us continuously to achieve ever more ambitious goals. We wish to thank members of the board over these years: Robert Costanza, Diana Liverman, Michael F. Goodchild, Gary Libecap, Bobbi Low, Bonnie McCay, Jerry Melillo, João M. F. Morais, Michael J. White, and Oran Young. Oran Young served as chair of the board over this entire period, and we are particularly thankful for his constructive leadership that always sought to ensure that our work was significant. We also benefited greatly from regular interactions with members of our Indiana University Scientific Advisory Board: George Alter, Dennis Conway, Hendrik Haitjema; Jeffrey Hart, Kerry Krutilla, J. C. Randolph, Robert Robinson, Jeanne Sept, and James M. Walker. The thoughtful input of our former and current associate directors Jon Unruh and Tom Evans has improved our research productivity immensely as well as helping to keep a complex organization going smoothly.

The inspiration for this book came from conversations with board members, who felt that while peer-reviewed journal articles achieve a certain degree of visibility and reach a variety of audiences, books also are needed to advance new and emerging fields of science, and in teaching graduate courses in these new areas where the literature tends to be widely dispersed and where instructors only control part of the scope of knowledge. With that in mind, the CIPEC co-directors, and the co-editors of this book, sought to provide readers with what we felt were important fundamental concepts and literature that would help teachers and students in getting access to the field of land-use/land-cover change, within the larger field of human-environment interactions in forest ecosystems. We also wished to share in a comprehensive book some of the lessons we have learned from a rare, broad-scale, big science project cutting across the physical and social sciences in the hope that the case studies and lessons will be instructive in guiding the field's future.

In the process of working on the center's research, outreach, and in the preparation of this book, we have many people to thank. Besides NSF and our external and internal advisory boards, Indiana University, particularly through the Office of the Vice-President for Research and the College of Arts and Sciences, made the work of the center not only possible but a true model of how to build up an interdisciplinary field at a U.S. university. The close collaboration of the college with the office of research led to a commitment of six tenure-track positions for the work of the center that has built up a very healthy core of young scientists to take the work well into the future. Space and computing support provided by the university further enhanced the work of the center over the past several years.

The center has been blessed with outstanding staff who have made the science flow uninterruptedly over the past several years, and deep friendships have resulted. The contributors to this book have been blessed with an extraordinarily talented support staff. Particularly enriching contributions have been made by Joanna Broderick, Carol Buszkiewicz, Rich Caldanaro, Laura Carlson, Julie England, Teena Freeman, Robin Humphrey, Mark Mangrich, Aaron Manire, Nat McKamey, Sean Sweeney, and Dave Terret, as well as many student part-time staff members across the years. In addition to the chapter authors, we have had the wonderful opportunity to work with a variety of postdoctoral scholars and research associates who have added greatly to the quality of our work at CIPEC, including Krister Andersson, Fábio de Castro, David Dodds, Nives Dolšak, Clark Gibson, Matthew Hoffmann, Marco Janssen, Philip Keating, Fabrice Lehoucq, and Steve McCracken.

The book that is before you has benefited from the careful attention in organization and editing that Joanna Broderick has brought to it. The subject is at times quite technical, but we hope it is more accessible than the same subject may be in professional journals of a specialized nature, and that it provides a good opening for learning the complexities of arcane topics such as remote sensing, geographic information systems (GIS), and biomass estimation. We are grateful to the anonymous reviewers selected by The MIT Press, who provided us with thorough and very detailed reviews of an earlier draft, resulting in a much improved manuscript. We are thankful also to Senior Acquisition Editor Clay Morgan at MIT Press, and the very able staff at MIT Press, for their support and help in the production of the book.

The authors could not have done their work as well as they have if they had not had an army of first-rate graduate students with whom they worked in the laboratory and in the field, and who contributed significantly to the collection of data, the analysis of the data, and to thinking together about the ideas that are before you. We are very grateful to all of them; many of them are already independent researchers at other institutions carrying out the work they started with us at CIPEC. From our former and current research assistants, the contributions of Ryan Adams, Chetan Agarwal, Bryn Bakoyéma, Mateus Batistella, Bruce Boucek, Cynthia Croissant, Shanon Donnelly, Kathleen Dowd-Gailey, Sugato Dutt, Salvador Espinosa, Alejandro Flores, Célia Futemma, Min Gong, Julie Hanson, Mark Hanson, Tanya Hayes, Lindan Hill, Derek Kauneckis, Tei Laine, Lilian Marquez-Barrientos, Jake Matthys, Tun Myint, Diego Pacheco, Ajay Pradhan, David Reeths, Ashok Regmi, Maria Clara da Silva-Forsberg, Neera Singh, Cynthia Sorrensen, Wenjie Sun, Angelica Toniolo, Paul Turner, Sameer Uplenchwar, Sandra Vasenda, Nathan Vogt, David Welch, and Abigail York are deeply appreciated.

The views expressed in this book are the sole responsibility of the authors and do not necessarily represent those of the agencies that funded the work reported here.

Contributors

Jonathon Belmont is a graduate of the Ph.D. program in the School of Public and Environmental Affairs at Indiana University and program manager for Charis Corporation, an environmental science, engineering, and program management company in San Bernadino, California.

Eduardo S. Brondízio is an assistant professor in the Department of Anthropology, assistant director for research at the Anthropological Center for Training and Research on Global Environmental Change, and a faculty research associate in the Center for the Study of Institutions, Population, and Environmental Change at Indiana University in Bloomington.

Theresa Burcsu is a Ph.D. candidate in the School of Public and Environmental Affairs at Indiana University and currently is an assistant scientist in the Department of Geography at the University of Florida (UF) in Gainesville and a research scientist in the UF Land Use and Environmental Change Institute.

Tom P. Evans is an assistant professor in the Department of Geography at Indiana University in Bloomington and associate director of the Center for the Study of Institutions, Population, and Environmental Change in Bloomington.

Glen M. Green is a research associate of the Center for the Study of Institutions, Population, and Environmental Change at Indiana University in Bloomington and a satellite remote sensing specialist in Edmonds, Washington.

Eric Keys is assistant professor in the Department of Geography at Arizona State University in Tempe.

Dengsheng Lu is an associate research scientist in the Center for the Study of Institutions, Population, and Environmental Change at Indiana University in Bloomington.

Paul Mausel is emeritus professor of geography in the Department of Geography, Geology, and Anthropology at Indiana State University in Terre Haute.

William J. McConnell is the science officer of the Focus 1 Office of the Land Use/Cover Change Project of the International Geosphere-Biosphere Programme and the International Human Dimensions Programme on Global Environmental Change and an associate research scientist in the Center for the Study of Institutions, Population, and Environmental Change at Indiana University in Bloomington.

Vicky Meretsky is an associate professor in the School of Public and Environmental Affairs and faculty research associate in the Center for the Study of Institutions, Population, and Environmental Change at Indiana University in Bloomington.

Emilio F. Moran is co-director of the Center for the Study of Institutions, Population, and Environmental Change; director of the Anthropological Center for Training and Research on Global Environmental Change; professor in the Department of Anthropology and the School of Public and Environmental Affairs; and adjunct professor in the Department of Geography at Indiana University in Bloomington.

Darla K. Munroe is an assistant professor in the Department of Geography at Ohio State University in Columbus and a research associate in the Center for the Study of Institutions, Population, and Environmental Change at Indiana University in Bloomington.

Harini Nagendra is the Asia research coordinator in the Center for the Study of Institutions, Population, and Environmental Change at Indiana University in Bloomington and lives in Bangalore, India.

Elinor Ostrom is co-director of the Center for the Study of Institutions, Population, and Environmental Change; co-director of the Workshop in Political Theory and Policy Analysis; professor in the Department of Political Science; and adjunct professor in the School of Public and Environmental Affairs at Indiana University in Bloomington.

Dawn C. Parker is an assistant professor in the Departments of Geography and Environmental Science and Policy at George Mason University in Fairfax, Virginia, and a research associate in the Center for the Study of Institutions, Population, and Environmental Change at Indiana University in Bloomington.

J. C. Randolph is director of the Ph.D. Programs in Environmental Science; director of the Midwestern Regional Center of the National Institute for Global Environmental Change; professor in the School of Public and Environmental Affairs and the Department of Biology; and a faculty research associate in the Center for the Study of Institutions, Population, and Environmental Change at Indiana University in Bloomington.

Charles M. Schweik is an assistant professor in the Department of Natural Resource Conservation and the Center for Public Policy and Administration at the University of Massachusetts in Amherst and a research associate in the Center for the Study of Institutions, Population, and Environmental Change at Indiana University in Bloomington.

Jane Southworth is an assistant professor in the Department of Geography at the University of Florida in Gainesville and a research associate in the Center for the Study of Institutions, Population, and Environmental Change at Indiana University in Bloomington.

Catherine M. Tucker is an assistant professor in the Department of Anthropology and a faculty research associate in the Center for the Study of Institutions, Population, and Environmental Change at Indiana University in Bloomington.

Jon Unruh is associate professor in the Department of Geography at McGill University in Montreal, Canada, and a research associate in the Center for the Study of Institutions, Population, and Environmental Change at Indiana University in Bloomington.

Leah K. VanWey is an assistant professor in the Department of Sociology and a faculty research associate in the Center for the Study of Institutions, Population, and Environmental Change at Indiana University in Bloomington.

Nathan Vogt is a Ph.D. student in the School of Public and Environmental Affairs and a research associate in the Center for the Study of Institutions, Population, and Environmental Change at Indiana University in Bloomington.

David Welch is a Ph.D. student in the School of Public and Environmental Affairs and a research assistant in the Center for the Study of Institutions, Population, and Environmental Change at Indiana University in Bloomington.

I

Human-Environment Interactions

1

Human-Environment Interactions in Forest Ecosystems: An Introduction

Emilio F. Moran

All around us today we see evidence of environmental change. There is clear evidence of a buildup of earth-warming gases that threaten to change our climate by changing the circulation of air and water. Among the most important of these changes is the buildup of carbon dioxide and methane. The buildup of both of these earth-warming gases is a result of human activities: through fossil fuel use and tropical deforestation in the case of carbon, and from the raising of vast populations of animals and irrigated rice that result in large methane emissions. We see evidence of large changes in biodiversity and loss of species as a result of human modification of natural landscapes, particularly conversion of forests and savannas into agropastoral uses. Changes in climate associated with changes in Earth's atmosphere and air and water cycles threaten, in turn, the viability of agriculture in some marginal areas, while resulting in devastating losses in other regions due to the increasing variability of rainfall events in an increasingly patchy environment (Steffen et al. 2004).

Of all these changes, clearly one seems to have the greatest consequence, both for humans and for other species: changes in land cover, particularly changes in forest cover. Forests provide a large number of ecological services that stabilize climate, protect plant and animal species, and can sequester vast amounts of carbon due to the constant turnover of plant biomass and plant senescence. For a very large part of human history, forests may have changed in spatial coverage and composition due to natural climatic changes occurring commonly over long periods of time. The changes that occurred during the Pleistocene are one example that resulted in the drying up of the Amazon basin. This led to reduced areas of tropical moist forest that became "islands" in a desiccated basin. It is believed this change may have been responsible for changes in speciation patterns during that period, resulting from isolation of species in these islands of forest vegetation. What is different is not the fact of land-cover change but its acceleration through the growing human capacity to transform vast areas of the landscape through agriculture, the building of dams and roads, and the rise of cities with vast areas asphalted, thereby changing albedo and water infiltration. We know that it took several centuries for the monasteries of the Middle Ages to deforest a substantial portion of the west European landscape. Palynological data obtained in recent years show a devastating impact on forests from the agricultural activities based in monasteries in the early to late Middle Ages. By the nineteenth century, it was possible for homesteading farmers to move across the forested lands of North America and cut down most of the existing forests in less than a century. Comparable deforestation is now possible in a matter of decades, due to much higher technological capacity, favorable government policies, and much larger populations acting simultaneously to make forests into agropastoral and urban areas.

In this book, the authors examine why some forested areas seem to be thriving and growing back, while other areas seem to be experiencing rapid losses of forests or degradation. This is a question of more than academic interest. Given the role of human action, and human institutions, it behooves us to understand the variables that account for forest restoration, as well as forest loss. Since human populations and human institutions play such a key role, we need to understand how different human groups organize, or not, to achieve their goals of balancing their needs to produce food and income from forested areas with their need to conserve forests. Forests play important roles in protecting the very landscapes upon which humans depend (see chapter 5). Forests transpire vast amounts of water vapor that creates the moisture conditions favorable to rainfall. Forest canopies provide interception of rainfall and facilitate the penetration of water into the soil and the water table, thereby abating or preventing rapid runoff, soil erosion, and loss of this precious resource to plants, animals, and people in local areas. Forests near streams protect water resources and ensure that streams are relatively permanent, rather than only seasonal, sources of water. Forests provide a habitat for many species of economic interest, besides preserving ecosystem structure and function. Forests provide large amounts of valuable nutrients for farmers when they clear forests through slash-and-burn methods, thereby making poor and mediocre soils produce a bountiful yield for a year or two. When practiced at low population densities, the slash-and-burn method of land preparation provides a sensible, low-cost way to obtain vital produce from otherwise low agricultural yield regions. Forests in North and South America, Africa, and Asia have undergone cycles of slash-and-burn activity that only became destructive and unproductive when fallows were shortened due to high population pressure, and natural restoration was not allowed to complete an adequate cycle of regrowth of secondary vegetation (M. Williams 2003).

The authors of the chapters in this book have been associated with the research of the Center for the Study of Institutions, Population, and Environmental Change at Indiana University (CIPEC), which is funded by the National Science Foundation (NSF). The center is dedicated to advancing research on land-use/land-cover change and the human dimensions of global environmental change (HDGC), a research program that began to be articulated in 1989 at the request of scientists studying atmosphere and climate who recognized that the human dimensions of the processes they were studying in the physical sciences were not receiving adequate attention despite the clear impact of human actions on Earth's climate and atmosphere.

History of the Development of the Human Dimensions Agenda

Until 1988, the study of global environmental change was carried out largely by earth science disciplines such as meteorology, atmospheric chemistry, atmospheric sciences, and geology. The focus of this work, under the aegis of the International Geosphere-Biosphere Programme (IGBP) was on documenting the extent of biosphere change and projecting at global scale the likely consequences of changing atmospheric conditions on Earth. Models, particularly global circulation models (GCMs), were heavily used given the absence of many important data points and the ambition of understanding the global environment—but scientists also identified, and lobbied for, research in areas needed to better run the GCMs. Among the many achievements of this effort, for example, was the creation of a vast network of buoys in Earth's oceans to measure changing temperatures, which over time led to the current ability of atmospheric and marine scientists to forecast El Niño and La Niña events many months in advance of human populations feeling their terrestrial impact. Scientists accurately predicted the onset of the 2002–2003 El Niño Southern Oscillation almost a year in advance. This was done by observing the warming and cooling of the waters over the northern Pacific and following its circulation around the globe. But something was missing. The coarse spatial scale of these early GCMs did not allow for any meaningful role for what human behavior does within the Earth system, which ran at very coarse spatial (several degrees of latitude) and temporal (decades to centuries) scales with broad assumptions, like what might happen if all tropical forest cover were removed and replaced by pasture. While the results of such models were informative, they did not realistically represent anything likely to be done by humans, who are apt to desist from the total elimination of tropical forest cover by information dissemination and feedback processes.

At the request of scientists associated with the IGBP, the International Social Science Council (ISSC) was asked to consider assembling a working group to develop a human dimensions (social and economic sciences) agenda to parallel the ongoing work of atmospheric and climate scientists studying global environmental change. The ISSC met and recommended that it would be desirable to begin to create national panels to undertake such a discussion and write up research plans that would articulate well with the IGBP research. This led to the creation of a group parallel to the IGBP, named the Human Dimensions Programme (HDP) and composed of a panel of social scientists from around the globe, to discuss how best to proceed. In the United States, both the National Research Council (NRC) and the Social Science Research Council (SSRC) created expert panels of scientists to discuss research priorities for the human dimensions as well.

Interestingly, the SSRC, the NRC, and the HDP developed research priorities (energy, industrial metabolism, health, environmental security, institutions, decision making, land-use/land-cover change), and of these topics one that quickly became a research area likely to best articulate with the work of the IGBP, and to which social scientists could make the strongest contributions in the short term, was to study land-use/land-cover change. The logic was that there was a preexisting community in the social sciences concerned with cultural ecology, agrarian studies, and agricultural and resource economics whose work approximated the likely areas of interest of a land-centric research program. This led to the creation of the Land-Use and Land-Cover Change (LUCC) core project, a joint activity of IGBP and HDP, with support from groups such as SSRC and NRC. A panel of scientists began to meet and produced over the next several years a science plan to guide the work of the international community (Skole and Turner 1995). The science plan had several major science questions that they deemed central to the core project:

- How has land cover changed over the last 300 years as a result of human activities?
- What are the major human causes of land-cover change in different geographic and historical contexts?
- How will changes in land use affect land cover in the next 50 to 100 years?
- How do immediate human and biophysical dynamics affect the sustainability of specific types of land uses?
- How might changes in climate and biogeochemistry affect both land use and land cover?

• How do land uses and land covers affect the vulnerability of land users in the face of change, and how do land-cover changes in turn impinge upon and enhance vulnerability and at-risk regions?

Similar but varying in some degree were research priorities defined by the NRC and SSRC. The first major guiding document to appear from these expert panels was the "rainbow book," *Global Environmental Change: Understanding the Human Dimensions* (NRC 1992). This book defined a broad set of priorities that identified land-use/land-cover change as one of the top research priorities along with other important questions that deserved attention, such as environmental decision making, integrative modeling, environmental risk analysis, and studies of population and environment. Many of the recommendations of this book served as guidance to funding agencies and have since been implemented, such as the creation of human dimensions centers of excellence by NSF, land-use/land-cover change research programs at the National Aeronautics and Space Administration, human dimensions of global change programs at the National Oceanic and Atmospheric Administration, and population and environment programs at the National Institute of Child Health and Human Development.

The following year, the NRC published a smaller and more accessible document entitled *Science Priorities for the Human Dimensions of Global Change* (NRC 1994). This document reaffirmed the priorities of the 1992 book and added several new areas of interest: land-use/land-cover change, decision-making processes, energy-related policies and institutions, impact assessment, and population dynamics. By 1995, the NSF announced a competition for national centers of excellence on the human dimensions of global environmental change. Carnegie Mellon and Indiana Universities received center-level awards, while Harvard, Yale, Pennsylvania State, and the University of Arizona received substantial group project awards. An informal consortium of these institutions functioned in the early years to ensure communication, common learning, and advancement of the still fledgling agenda on human dimensions. Of the two centers, Indiana University focused more on land-use/land-cover change, and in particular on forest ecosystems, while the Carnegie Mellon center focused on integrated assessment issues.

Since that period considerable advances have taken place. These are summarized at some length in an NRC book, *Global Environmental Change: Research Pathways for the Next Decade* (NRC 1999a). The Human Dimensions Programme became the International Human Dimensions Programme (IHDP) in 1996 when it moved from Geneva to Bonn, Germany. IHDP has played a growing role in coordinating the work of national human dimensions panels and creating IHDP-based research groups on the institutional dimensions of global environmental change, industrial metabolism, and human security.

One of the important activities of the LUCC program has been to stimulate the generation of syntheses of what we know about land-use/land-cover change processes, such as tropical deforestation (e.g., Geist and Lambin 2001), agricultural intensification (see chapter 13), desertification (Geist and Lambin 2004), and urbanization (Seto and Kaufmann 2003) to provide input to a larger synthesis for Earth system science (Steffen et al. 2004). These syntheses rely heavily on the scholarly community working on issues of land-use/land-cover change. CIPEC has contributed to this community effort by focusing on understanding the human-environment interactions in forest ecosystems presented in this book, in publications cited throughout the book, and available online at http://www.cipec.org.

Other interesting research areas in the HDGC agenda include social dimensions of resource use, perception of environmental change, how people assess environmental changes and environmental risks, the impact of institutions, energy production and consumption, industrial ecology, environmental justice, and environmental security. These and many other topics will grow in importance as findings from the work on land-use/land-cover change advances. Recent expert panels from the NRC came up with eight *Grand Challenges in Environmental Sciences* (NRC 2001) that defined key priorities. The eight priorities share one common denominator: they require joint work by biophysical and social scientists. A similar recommendation came from the National Science Board, which developed similar but not equivalent priorities but also gave multidisciplinarity across the biophysical and social sciences a strong nod.

Characteristics of Research on the Human Dimensions

Research on the human dimensions, or as it is more commonly known today, human-environment interactions, differs from disciplinary research in a number of ways. Global change research must be inherently multidisciplinary given the complexity of factors that must be taken into account. No discipline offers an adequate array of theories, methods, and concepts to provide integrative modeling. Because it is global, the work must be multinational in scale; otherwise one is likely to erroneously think that what one sees as processes in one country applies to the globe. This forces an agenda oriented toward comparative research wherein one must collect comparable data in a number of nations and regions to sample the diversity of biophysical and social processes. Spatially explicit research methods provide powerful tools for the study of complex systems such as the Earth system. Spatially explicit techniques allow human-environment interactions to be studied across multiple scales and to anchor the work precisely on Earth's surface and understand what is site-specific and what is generalizable. Because the agenda is driven by a concern with changing dynamics, the work must be multitemporal and have some historical depth. The depth will vary with the questions and processes of interest, so that some scientists operate in temporal scales of millennia (paleoclimatologists and palynologists), while others work in terms of centuries and decades. Because the disciplines' methods vary, it is likely that the processes examined will vary, not just in time and spatial scales but also in the scale of analysis (from local to regional to national to global). It is well-known but rarely analytically addressed that explanations for processes vary by the scale at which they are studied. Thus, specificity of what scale is being explained is essential, but also it is necessary that each analysis make an effort to scale both up and down from the scale of interest so that the effort and investment is useful to other scientists in the community working at other scales. Finally, because the work is about an impending environmental crisis of global and local proportions (i.e., exponential carbon dioxide and methane emissions, loss of biodiversity), the work must keep in mind the relevance and importance of the research in informing policies that might reverse current negative outcomes and favor sustainability of human-environment interactions.

Antecedents in the Social Sciences

The work on HDGC has deep roots in the social sciences. Greco-Roman, Arab, Enlightenment, and later philosophers laid the basis for our ideas about the impact of the environment on people (Thomas 1925; Alavi 1965; Glacken 1967; E. Moran 2000). Three main themes can be observed in Western intellectual history up to the 1950s that sought to explain human interactions with nature: environmental determinism, possibilism, and adaptationism. The first view overemphasized the influence of nature, while the second view overemphasized the role of culture. The third view bridged the gap between these two and emphasized the mutual interactions of people with nature as they co-adapted from this mutual interaction (E. Moran 2000, 27).

Environmental determinism was a dominant view from at least Greco-Roman times to well into the twentieth century. This view arose from observations of the apparent link between psychological tendencies and climate. However, it is curious that while the views of Greco-Roman and Arab thinkers credited their superior achievements in their heyday to the superb dry Mediterranean climate (and the inferiority of northern temperate peoples to the beastly cold of the north), in later centuries when temperate countries were ascendant politically, temperate climates were viewed as explaining their great imperial achievements, while warmer climates were viewed as a reason for the lesser power of those peoples (E. Moran 2000, 28–32). This view still occasionally makes an appearance under the guise that, for example, a given poor soil dooms a people to poverty, or that oppressive heat saps people of their energy for work and achievement. Environmental determinism, however, is mostly discredited today.

The possibilistic view is mostly gone as well, but it persists among neo-Malthusians who regularly raise the specter of the limited capacity of Earth to support the natural growth of populations. It persists in notions such as the analogy of Spaceship Earth, which views the planet has having very limited resources. Possibilism takes many forms intellectually, but they all share a common characteristic: that the environment sets limits but does not determine the direction and character of human decisions. In the case of neo-Malthusian views, the notion is that Earth has limited productive capacity and the specter of famine is just around the corner (Malthus [1803] 1989). This view has persisted over a century despite impressive achievements in food production that have kept up with the dramatic increase in the human population. However, this view has increasingly become informed by the dominant view today, that of the mutual interaction of people with their physical environment.

In this latter view, that is, the adaptationist view, which is today represented by a number of theories and approaches, among them human-environment interactions, the population interacts with the environment, faces its limitations, adapts to them sometimes, and at other times modifies, if possible, those environmental conditions to favor human objectives. This view has its roots in the nineteenth century. The work of George Perkins Marsh, that of German anthropogeographers such as Friedrich Ratzel, and the work of historians of the American frontier such as Frederick Jackson Turner begin to formulate ideas that closely connect the environment to social outcomes, regional character or personality type, and even the potential for development and change. In the first half of the twentieth century, the work of anthropologists such as Franz Boas (who started in anthropogeography and physics), Alfred Kroeber, and Julian Steward, and the work of geographers such as Carl Sauer began to emphasize what seemed to be correlations between environmental features (biogeography or natural areas) and cultural characteristics. The great leap achieved by Steward was in seeing that it was neither nature nor culture-bearing humans but, rather, the process of resource utilization that was the object of study. Thus he began to focus attention of the interactions of people in obtaining resources, in getting organized to use them effectively, and in defining what to exploit at their level of technology and organization (Steward 1938, 1955).

In the second half of the twentieth century, a rich number of theoretical approaches proliferated, variously called cultural ecology, human ecology, ecosystem ecology, ethnoecology, political ecology, and historical ecology. While they differed in emphasis, they were all trying to define what would best characterize the key variables that account for human-environment interaction. These emphases reflected the larger context of what was going on in society and went along with other trends in the biophysical sciences (Siniarska and Dickinson 1996). Among the most promising trends that favor interdisciplinary integration is the work that is the focus of this book (human-environment interactions) and related topics such as historical and population ecology, the study of institutions, regional analysis, and ecological economics.

To think in historical ecological terms is to bring attention to the fact that a complete explanation of ecological structure and function must include the actual sequence and timing of events that produce an observed structure or function (Butzer 1990; Winterhalder 1994; Harrison and Morphy 1998; Batterbury and Bebbington 1999; Redman 1999). One powerful way to achieve this is through historical demography, as demonstrated by Netting (1976, 1980, 1990) in a study of demographic change in a Swiss village over several centuries. At first, he was inclined to present the village as a system in equilibrium but later revised his views as he discovered that the apparent stability was maintained by dynamic movement of people out of the ecosystem. The age-gender structure of human populations is a summation of their historical experience and can provide powerful ways to examine environmental events, such as deforestation, in light of the changing structure of households.

Regional analyses provide a powerful approach to the processes of human adaptation. A regional study tends to emphasize historical and economic factors and takes into account historical forces that affect the human and environmental system (Geertz 1963; J. Bennett 1969; Braudel 1973). One advantage of regionally scaled studies is that they make it more viable to carry out comparative analyses. Locally based studies tend to be rich in detail but not always well nested within the range of variability commonly observed. A set of local studies nested within a regional analysis is more likely to provide the kind of rich multiscaled information that can provide inputs to regional and global analyses for HDGC.

The human-environment interactions research community has given considerable attention in the past decade to what seem to be the chief responses of human populations: adaptation and mitigation. Adaptation speaks to the effort of human populations to adjust themselves to changes as they occur. These can take the form of behavioral changes, such as clothing to meet changes in heat and cold, or physiological changes that are reversible, such as acclimatory adaptations like increased red blood cell formation with reduced oxygen pressure (hypoxia) at high altitudes. Further, populations who live in areas that undergo long-term changes may even experience some developmental adaptations that are irreversible but improve the efficiency of adaptation to their environment, such as larger lung volume at high altitudes. Mostly, we seem to rely on social and behavioral adaptations such as scheduling changes and moving to a different area to avoid exposure to reduced air quality, even if for only part of the day (E. Moran 2000).

Mitigation, on the other hand, speaks to the efforts of human groups to change the current conditions so that exposure to poor air quality is eliminated through regulation, by reducing carbon emissions from fossil fuels through a change in consumption patterns, and, like the Kyoto protocol aims to do, setting a goal that reverses changes that we have come to accept as being unstoppable. Mitigation and adaptation are not only strategies individuals pursue, they also are political choices around which major debates in both developing and developed countries are taking place, with some countries wishing to reverse current trends and even current levels, while others seem to prefer a wait-and-see attitude and trust that technology will offer solutions that are not currently available (NRC 1992, 1998, 1999b).

Disciplinary Aspects of Human Dimensions Research

Participation in human dimensions research offers a number of advantages to the advancement of social science theory, particularly theories on human-environment interactions. The questions posed by the human dimensions agenda are new questions that reach beyond the traditional disciplinary concerns and thus extend the value of social science to all of society. The disciplines bring important theories to this kind of research: anthropology and geography have contributed cultural ecology, which remains an important paradigm in understanding human use of resources; biology and ecology have contributed ecosystem and evolutionary ecology; political science has contributed theories about institutions and collective action. Unlike traditional disciplinary research, however, human dimensions research demands a multiscaled approach to research. This is rarely the case with discipline-based research and is thus a broadening of the way the social sciences can contribute to the understanding of the world around us. The work on human dimensions links the biological, physical, and social sciences, thereby making social sciences centrally important not only to other social scientists but to the rest of the sciences. It is important to recall that it was the physical sciences that recognized the role of human actions and that felt the need to encourage the social science community to join them in an effort to understand global environmental changes. While much remains to be done to achieve this integration, there has been progress.

Work on human dimensions requires comparison and multidisciplinary approaches. This offers the potential for more robust tests of the applicability of site-, region-, or nation-specific findings. By testing things cross-nationally, cross-regionally, and cross-locally, the results are more likely to be robust and strengthened by theory. The human dimensions research agenda challenges most of the social sciences (except geography, which already is sensitive to this) to develop new spatially explicit ways to select cases for comparative analysis, to determine sampling frames in a spatial context, and to model results that are spatially informed. This is true as much for the social sciences as for ecology, which only now, too, is developing spatial ecology as a field of study and thereby revolutionizing the way ecologists think about population ecology and community ecology.

Undertaking these challenges is an awesome task. It requires that we work in large teams of scientists, rather than work alone, as is more common in the social sciences. As noted earlier, the work should be multinational, multidisciplinary, multiscalar, multitemporal, spatially explicit, and policy relevant. To be successful, it requires that we leave our "weapons" at the door, and that we choose the right tools, theories, and methods for the questions that are being asked (without regard for what disciplines they come from). The goal is to pick the right ones for the job at hand, even if it means that team members will need to learn all sorts of new approaches that were not part of their earlier academic training. It is a challenging and exciting task, one that ensures continuous growth in one's skills and perspectives; an open approach to research, without sacrificing rigor; and research that speaks to the questions society needs answers to, not just the academic scientist. These challenges have been faced by the authors of the chapters in this book, and the reader will be the judge of the degree to which they have succeeded in integrating their disciplinary skills with the demands of interdisciplinary environmental research.

The Challenge of This Book

This book brings together some of the findings from the first five years of research at CIPEC. CIPEC is an HDGC center within which anthropologists, geographers, economists, sociologists, political scientists, environmental scientists, and biologists have worked together to understand why some forests are thriving while others are declining and becoming degraded. The center aims to contribute to the human dimensions research agenda, and in particular to land-use/land-cover change research. One of the first tasks faced by any research group tackling such a topic is to define and delimit the object of study. In this case, we chose to focus on forest ecosystems—and in particular tropical moist, tropical dry, and midlatitude deciduous temperate forests. We originally planned to also tackle boreal and temperate rain forests, but wise advisors convinced us that we had undertaken a challenging enough task by tackling the other three forest ecosystems. These three types of forest ecosystems account for a significant percentage of the total forest cover of the planet, and for a substantial proportion of the world's biodiversity.

We also defined our task as focusing on the interactions of people with those three forest ecosystems as mediated by a variety of institutional arrangements, namely privately held forests, communally held forests, and federal- and state-held forests. How people define rights of use is defined by their institutions to regulate access and use of forest resources. It is commonly thought that private tenure is a form of resource management superior to all others, that communal tenure can lead to a tragedy of the commons, and that government lands are poorly managed due to lack of popular interest and limited government capacity to regulate users. This is one of the puzzles that we have tried to test rigorously by examining for each type of forest ecosystem a set of cases of private, communal, and government institutional arrangements to assess the effectiveness of managing forest resources. As we will see in this book, the answer is more nuanced than some would like, but it is also more satisfying in that it shows that the existence of formal institutions alone does not effectively constrain behavior.

CIPEC has emphasized social science questions and methods in its work, given its focus on trying to link and understand how human institutions and population factors interact with forest ecosystems. Thus, the work on the biophysical dimensions gave emphasis to methods such as land-cover analysis using remotely sensed data (aerial photos and satellite data), attention to landscape variables such as slope and aspect, and soil quality. The center during this phase of its work did not go into topics such as soil microbiology, climate variability, hydrology, biodiversity assessment, and other important topics relevant to forest ecology. We hope in the coming decade to undertake such work as more colleagues in the biological sciences join our team and we are able to obtain funds sufficient to undertake this type of work, which requires considerable and highly diverse laboratory facilities and personnel.

Finally, we also wanted to address the role of population, which is often suggested by policy makers and many scientists as being the major driver of forest loss. To do so, we sought to examine a number of cases in the three types of forest ecosystems, and along a variety of institutional arrangements, as noted above, wherein we could test the extent to which population density or its distribution is associated with loss of forest, or its recovery. Here, again, the findings from the work of the center are nuanced. Population does indeed show an association with deforestation at aggregate scales, but at local to regional scales it does not. Moreover, some of the most successful cases of management of forests occur at the highest population densities.

To carry out these tasks we began with extended discussions on methods and measures that we could agree would have broad applicability across our forest ecosystem types and across different cultural and national boundaries, and would facilitate the eventual task of comparison. We gave considerable weight to the availability of remotely sensed data (from aerial photos to Earth-observing satellites such as Landsat), since this permitted work at a variety of spatial and temporal scales, could be scaled up and down from small areas to large regions, and made the task of spatially explicit research clear from the start. To choose sites for research, therefore, we insisted that those candidate areas, besides fitting within our three forest ecosystem types, must have a cloud-free time series of remotely sensed data that can be obtained to facilitate land-cover change analysis over large areas to complement the local studies that would be undertaken. These remotely sensed data, mostly Landsat data at 30-m resolution, would be further enhanced by data overlays using geographic information systems (GIS) developed to handle data layers such as soil class information, vegetation types, hydrologic network, topography, and other information coming from sources such as a census.

Since this work is fundamentally concerned with the human dimensions, we developed instruments, or protocols, to obtain data from people on a range of issues such as demography, forest uses, local institutions, economy, history of land use, and their relationship to other user groups in the ecosystem and local region. All these data were collected in a spatially explicit fashion using global positioning system (GPS) instruments to locate precisely on the ground the data that were obtained.

To ensure accurate classification of the land-cover analysis using satellite data, a large number of "training samples" were obtained for each land-cover class of interest. Training samples are detailed descriptions of a land-cover type, with a precise geolocation using a GPS that can be used to train the computer to recognize like classes on the image. A substantial number of these are reserved for later use to arrive at an accuracy assessment of the land-cover classification.

One challenge we faced in working with remotely sensed data was to integrate this type of analysis with extensive field studies and survey research so that both kinds of information interactively informed the other. The other challenge was how to compare satellite data collected at different locations at different points in time, given the different atmospheric conditions present at those various places at various times. This meant moving away from the use of digital numbers provided by the satellite data and converting this information to actual reflectance so we would have a standard that was understood and clear across sites (see chapter 6 for details on these procedures; see also Lu et al. 2002b).

The challenge of working with social science data in a comparative framework was no less daunting. Comparative research has been widely touted as one of the important goals of social science, but there are just a handful of studies that have been able to undertake the systematic collection of data across a variety of national boundaries using common protocols. We were fortunate to have had experience in our team with the work of the International Forestry Resources and Institutions (IFRI) research program, which had already developed and tested cross-nationally ten protocols that focused on forest-related institutions and their management of forests. We used these protocols as a basis for our own and made modifications to fit the particular focus of our work—such as collecting the data in spatially explicit fashion, linking the data to satellite time-series data, using GIS data layers, and including, when possible, data at the household level, in addition to the community level, that had been the focus of IFRI research.

Theory is central to the work of all scientists, but differences in theory have proved in many cases to be obstacles to communication across disciplines. We worked very hard to become familiar with each other's theories in a wide variety of disciplines, from biology and ecology to anthropology, geography, sociology, and political science. We created reading groups to read and discuss a range of theories that offered potential in guiding our research (many of these are discussed in chapter 2). The goal was to force all members of the group to become familiar with the work of disciplines and theories other than their own, and to learn what they might offer to the research tasks we had defined for ourselves. This was largely successful and it was a lovely sight to see political scientists talking about soil types, ecologists talking about common-property institutions, and anthropologists examining demographic data such as life course tables.

Lessons Learned

The bulk of the book that is before you focuses on the efforts to compare data across sites, and it offers considerable detail about how we carried out our work so that the experience of these efforts may assist others wishing to undertake similar interdisciplinary scientific work. Some of the chapters focus on sites within a region, like the Amazon or Mexico. Here the differences may lie in biophysical factors such as soil quality, but one can hold the forest type somewhat constant, as well as the political economy that affects forests in that one region or country. Others constitute comparisons across national boundaries that allow for the examination of processes wherein national policies may play roles in differentiating management of forests but which may be comparable in, say, forest type or institutions. Other parts of the book focus on related issues such as modeling land-cover change, defining the future of studies of forest ecosystems, and helping define a future research agenda for the human dimension of global change. Despite our best efforts, the entire work of the center could not be included in a single volume. Readers who remain curious, and unsatisfied, may find additional material of interest in other publications by members of the center listed at the center's website and in the references cited throughout the book. It is our sincere wish that our work stimulates readers to think of further ways in which we can undertake the challenge posed by our human-environment conundrum: in solving the puzzle of how to move toward a sustainable world lie our hopes for human life on Earth.

A number of *lessons* were *learned* from the work reported in this book. Readers will find many others not highlighted here as they examine the chapters. They can be divided into methodological lessons, empirical findings, and theoretical lessons.

Methodological Lessons

- It is possible to develop an integrative biophysical–social science set of standardized research protocols, but the costs in terms of time are substantial and it requires flexibility in theory and method at all times. However, it is a task that needs to be undertaken if we expect case study data to be broadly useful to the global change research community.

• GIS and other geospatial approaches are tools that enable disparate data sources to be integrated, fostering communication across disciplines and thus leading to richer data analysis. GIS and spatial analysis are critical tools because of the scale dependence of social and biophysical phenomena and the scale dependence of complex human-environment relationships. Working at a single spatial scale risks misrepresenting the processes at work in a location. Analysis of spatially explicit data is one of the few ways to address the scale issues inherent in these systems.

• Scale matters even if processes at one scale frequently do not emerge at other scales as having the same significance. This needs to become an object of study in itself, as it may result in no small part from the way data are collected at different scales, and from the lack of forethought in these different empirical traditions to the challenge of cross-scale analysis.

• Remote sensing provides a robust dataset for human dimensions research, but for comparative research across time and space, this requires dealing with complex ways to eliminate sources of variability in the images to ensure that the changes being observed are a result of land-cover change and not of atmospheric and other sources of variability (sensor, seasonality, interannual climate variability).

Empirical Findings

• Context matters: Comparative research can be carried out but requires great discipline in execution, given substantial differences in ecosystems, societies, cultures, and institutions.

• Researchers need to be very careful in defining what they mean by "a forest," particularly for the purposes of exploring dynamics and comparison. The definition of what a forest is can vary, and having a clear definition is essential to making progress in assessing how humans are influencing forests. Using standardized forest mensuration techniques ensures that comparisons between forest stands adhere to rigorous standards.

• Datasets have spatial and temporal scale limitations, and multiple datasets from different sources rarely cover the same temporal and spatial scales. This requires that selection of data sources take into account these limitations and that modeling efforts be cognizant of these limitations.

• We find no evidence to support the notion that a given tenure regime is superior in ensuring forest well-being. The evidence is that rules-in-use associated with resource management shape forest conditions whether in private, communal, or government-owned tenure regimes. Evidence is that property owners under any tenure regime can design successful institutions.

• Comparative analysis of forests in Guatemala and Honduras found that the forests were far more dynamic in land cover over the nine-year study interval than anticipated based on reports from other studies. The concurrent processes of vegetation regrowth and deforestation, as well as significant areas that remain unchanged, suggest that studies that focus on a single issue, like deforestation, can easily miss the dynamic processes of change, and stability, in forest ecosystem regions.

• Biophysical limitations, such as steep slope and difficulty of access, can provide considerable protection to forests, but they provide only a necessary but not sufficient degree of protection. Institutions play a major role, in combination with biophysical limitations, in protecting these limited areas from deforestation and erosion.

• Estimation of biomass and carbon is surrounded by considerable uncertainties due to a wide array of estimation procedures and a limited set of baseline destructive sampling datasets (i.e., actual measurements of biomass rather than estimates). Remotely sensed data can be used if methods are tailored to the differences in forest structure present from place to place (see chapter 11).

• Cross-national meta-analyses suggest that there is a pervasive lack of agreement on what data should be collected, even among investigators working on land-use/land-cover issues. This impedes the advancement of theory and of practical understanding of the dynamics of land-use/land-cover change. Particularly glaring omissions are data on climate (temperature and precipitation), soils, demography, and details of crops cultivated and reasons for leaving an area (see chapter 13).

Theoretical Lessons

• Population growth is not necessarily correlated with loss of forest under local conditions. We have found that population density is associated in several cases with improved management of forests and restoration of forest cover. In areas with low population density, there is a common perception that forests are unlimited in supply. This tends to result in widespread deforestation and lack of institutions to regulate access to forest resources. Advances in population-and-environment theories can help us get a better handle on the role of population size and its distribution.

• Processes of forest change vary by the scale of analysis used. Dramatic changes in a locality may hardly be noticed at a larger scale and be invisible at regional to global scales. Multiple scale analyses are possible but require rigorous monitoring of the scale-dependent processes. This complexity needs to be taken into account in policy making and decision making, given the many different levels at which decisions are made about forest resources, and the often conflicting foundations for those decisions.

• Forest transition theory: Viewed over long temporal periods, forests go through cycles of growth, deforestation, agricultural use, and regrowth as a result of cycles in the political economy, population movement, and in the patterns of human settlement coupled with human understanding of the natural growth of these forests (knowledge of growth rates of trees, their composition over time, and the potential uses of the resources within them). Understanding the triggers for cycles of deforestation, the drivers or factors that sustain the cycle of deforestation, and the emergence of negative feedbacks that begin to play a role in slowing down and eventually reversing deforestation with effective ways to reforest is critical to the use and conservation of these multiple-use forest ecosystems. Forest transition theory helps us see the forest and the trees as dynamic entities profoundly coupled with people and their institutions.

Road Map to the Book

These lessons, and many others, are elaborated on in the chapters of this book. The book is written with two readerships in mind: scholars in the global change community, and students and faculty who want to gain access to the theories, methods, and practice of human-environment interactions research as applied to land-use/land-cover change. Thus, readers who are already familiar with the methods of this type of research on land-use/land-cover change may wish to skim through part II of this book, which provides access to those who are not fully initiated into the combination of methods that are used routinely—forest mensuration, GIS, and remote sensing. Part II will be useful to faculty, students, and researchers who are familiar with only some but not all of these methods. While it does not provide full discussion of these methods, the chapters provide core knowledge to get readers familiar with elements from these methods and direction on where to go for further knowledge. In short, scholars in this field already may wish to read parts I and III, and use part II as a reference if needed.

Novices, and those familiar with either the social or the physical but not both types of methods, may wish to work their way through the book systematically. Part I focuses on theories of human-environment research. Part II focuses on methods used in human-environment research, particularly those appropriate for study of land-use/land-cover change in forested ecosystems. Chapter 3 focuses on the challenges presented by consideration of multiple scales, chapter 4 introduces readers to institutional analysis, chapter 5 provides a brief introduction to forest ecology, chapter 6 introduces readers to some key considerations in remotely sensed data acquisition and analysis, and chapter 7 sensitizes readers to the challenge of spatially explicit analysis.

Part IV is constituted of case studies from a broad range of research carried out by the center, most of them looking at more than one site. The scholarly community familiar with human dimensions and land-use/land-cover change will find this section particularly interesting as it is here that advances at linking theory and method through empirical cases are to be found in detail. Some of them may choose to go straight to this part of the book first, and then read in parts I and II if they need to refer to particular theories or methods. We hope readers will find this road map useful in navigating through these rich materials which represent the work of a very substantial group of researchers over several years. We welcome comments and suggestions from readers, and readers should check the website at http://www.cipec.org, where they can find other useful materials not found in this book, and where they can go to communicate with any of the authors.

2

Theories Underlying the Study of Human-Environment Interactions

Leah K. VanWey, Elinor Ostrom, and Vicky Meretsky

Understanding environmental change in the early years of the twenty-first century is a major challenge. Research teams composed of scholars from multiple social and biophysical disciplines face the problem of having a plethora of theories that can inform their work. Further, some of the theories accepted in one discipline have been challenged and rejected in others. Which theories should form the foundation for broad, multidisciplinary, cumulative research is a puzzling, and at times, contestable issue. Most traditional theories of population-environment relationships tried to posit the simplest models to explain phenomena at a national or international level. An extensive review by Lambin and a large number of informed scientists from multiple disciplines (Lambin et al. 2001) argues that almost all of the simple models positing only a few factors determining land-use/land-cover change have been disproved by serious empirical research. Previously accepted theories positing population and poverty as the major causes of environmental change have turned out to be myths rather than empirically supported theories.

In this chapter, we first review some of these traditional theories about relationships between population and environmental change. Then, we discuss more general theories of social and ecological change and how they can be applied to questions of environmental change, specifically land-use change. The past decade has seen a proliferation of research on other issues related to how human actions affect the global environment (e.g., consumption, industrial emissions of greenhouse gases, automobile usage). A review of this literature is both beyond the scope of this chapter and less appropriate as a foundation for the following chapters. Thus, we focus on theories relevant to land-use/land-cover change. We divide these theories into those that posit a unidirectional deterministic relationship between one key set of independent variables and environmental degradation (primarily deforestation), and those that assign agency to individual actors as they affect environmental change. These theories are brought together in the multiscalar approach that we use to study relationships among social and biophysical variables. We end this chapter with a discussion of bringing together and building on these many theories to inform empirical research.

Our multiscalar approach and our evaluation of the utility of existing theories owe much to the empirical research undertaken in the past half-century of work on human-environment relations. In their efforts to examine the simple theories, scholars have executed careful, replicable research projects. Two broad conclusions have been derived from this research: scale matters and context matters. First, relationships that exist at one scale frequently do not exist at other scales. On the other hand, some theories operate at multiple scales. Thus, researchers must be extremely careful about the theories and measurements they use to be sure they operate at the scale of the question being pursued and the measurements made. In our discussion we consider four scales of social and environmental factors. Social forces are observable at global, regional or country, local (community), and household or individual scales. These forces include the demographic, cultural, economic, and political characteristics of units at a given scale of observation. The corresponding four scales of environment that we consider are global, ecosystem, community, and individual parcels of land. Two issues are important to keep in mind as we discuss these scales in describing theories of human impact on land-use/land-cover change. No hard-and-fast boundaries exist between scales; for example, the distinction between local and regional varies depending on the particular research question. A one-to-one correspondence does not exist between social and environmental units in either size or boundaries. For example, one human community might impact an area smaller than a complete watershed, but this impact might cross the boundaries of several local government units.

Second, not only do we find that relationships verified to exist at one scale are not present at other scales, we also find that the same relationship may exist in settings A, B, and C at one scale, but not in D, E, and F at the same scale. These relationships are contingent on certain key contextual variables. Sorting out what variables constitute the context for changes in relationships and how they change the patterns of relationships within a particular scale is another major challenge facing contemporary scientists. For example, substantial research has assumed that human population size and its level of affluence are the most important factors affecting environmental conditions. Repeated tests of this presumed relationship have shown that institutions are an important contextual factor that mediate whether the size, rate of growth, and poverty of a population directly affect land-use/land-cover change (Kaimowitz and Angelsen 1998; Lambin et al. 2001). In our discussion here, we use the insights from many theories to construct a model that identifies the important contextualizing variables in models of land-use decision making.

In conceptualizing our multiscale approach, we stand on the shoulders of many giants in the social and natural sciences. We structure the remainder of this chapter to show the development of our work and the work of others from early and more recent giants. We begin by discussing the traditional approaches to human impacts on the environment. From there we proceed to more general theories of social and environmental change in which (1) socioeconomic structure or biophysical conditions determine the effects of human actions on land use and land cover; or (2) impacts are determined by individual or collective actors responding to structural constraints, but also changing the structure within which they act. We follow these sections with two sections covering the theoretical development of our approach and the empirical uses of our approach.

Traditional Approaches to Population-Environment Relationships

The theories in this section are traditional in two ways. First, they are primarily theories that have been around for a long time. These perspectives have spurred extensive research and policy on population and the environment, in part because of their elegance. As of 1998, Kaimowitz and Angelsen were able to synthesize the results of more than 140 models of deforestation of which over 90 percent had been produced since 1990. Because of the simplicity of these models and their applicability to a wide range of settings, these theories remain current despite their age. Second, these theories explicitly focus on the relationship between population (generally population size and density) and the biophysical environment, mediated through land use. The theories we discuss in the next sections apply to a wide variety of human behaviors, not just to those behaviors that impact the environment.

Malthus

The Reverend Thomas Robert Malthus, writing at the turn of the nineteenth century, was perhaps the first population and environment theorist (Malthus [1803] 1989). Without explicitly considering a level of analysis, he formulated a theory of population and environment (with a focus on the ability of the environment to produce food) that is applicable to any human population, from a community all the way up to all of humanity. His first observation was that without starvation, disease, or fertility limitation, human populations necessarily increase in a geometric series (e.g., 1000 people each having two children leading to 2000 people in the next generation, 4000 people in the next generation, etc.). His second observation was that the productivity of agriculture increases linearly over time. Yields increase by a standard amount per increment of time, producing a steady linear increase. Malthus pointed out in book 1, chapter 1 of his *Essay on the Principle of Population*, that he foresaw no limit to the potential expansion of productivity. Rather, he saw a limit to the rate of increase in productivity. The key determinant of the living standards enjoyed by humans is the ratio of population to agricultural yield. Without detrimental external factors, this ratio will increase at an increasing rate over time, leading to declining standards of living.

Malthus studied ways to avoid population growth's outpacing the growth of productivity and described preventative checks on population's outpacing agriculture, including social customs that governed fertility (e.g., age at marriage, proportion of women marrying, norms assigning responsibility to fathers), infanticide, and out-migration. He also described population checks resulting from population growth's outpacing agriculture—famine, disease, and conflicts over land. The essential components of Malthus's argument are (1) population growth will outstrip the ability of the environment to provide, and (2) lack of sufficient resources will cause a decrease in population.

Malthus's theory has two essential flaws that carry through many subsequent and related theories. First, he did not allow for the possibility of nonlinearities in the growth of agricultural productivity, such as large jumps in productivity associated with new agricultural technologies. Second, and related, Malthus did not include agricultural innovation among the possible reactions to scarcity. In his consideration, population pressure on limited resources will lead instead to population reduction. The "green revolution" in staple crops is the clearest example of how wrong Malthus's assumptions were. In this case, anticipated and actual population pressure led to rapid agricultural technological innovation.

IPAT versus PPE

Several of the better-known recent efforts to understand how population and other variables affect the environment are simple multivariable models in which population in one form or another plays the role of villain. Ehrlich and Ehrlich (1991), for example, adopted Commoner's (1972) earlier three-variable IPAT causal model: $I = P \times A \times T$. In this approach, I is defined as the impact on the environment, $P =$ population, $A =$ affluence measured by levels of consumption, and $T =$ technologies employed. Grant (1994) developed an alternative model called the PPE model. Population growth and poverty—the two Ps in this model—are viewed as two types of reinforcing pressures that jointly impinge on *E*, or environmental conditions. All three factors—population, poverty, and environment—are affected by and affect political instability. Grant's PPE model was written for UNICEF and focused on processes he thought were occurring primarily in developing countries. As with Malthus's model, these two models can be applied to any size of human population, from a small community to the entire globe. They are most commonly applied in country-level analyses, given the easy availability of data measuring key variables and the immediate policy relevance of studies at this level.

Comparing the IPAT and PPE models illuminates the substantial knowledge gap that exists in understanding human-ecological processes. First, they disagree on the sign of the relationship between poverty and environmental variables. Grant sees poverty as a major cause of adverse environmental impact whereas the Ehrlichs see affluence as a major cause. It is understandable that UNICEF focuses attention on developing countries, but is the Ehrlich model only intended to explain environmental degradation in industrialized countries? That is highly doubtful. Or, should one expect poverty to adversely affect environment in developing countries and affluence to have a similar impact in developed countries? Grant focuses on population growth while the Ehrlichs focus on population size. Technology appears in one model and political instability in the other. How public policy should intervene depends on which model one might accept.

Billie Lee Turner II et al. (1993b) also examined the question of how humans affected the environment in the proposal made to create a land-use/land-cover change effort within the International Geosphere-Biosphere Programme on the human dimensions of global environmental change. They generated the general framework (shown in figure 2.1) that linked the human dimensions with the physical dimensions of global change. This framework forms the foundation for considerable work on human-environment aspects of global change and on land-use/land-cover change. Four human driving forces are identified that are similar to aspects of the IPAT and PPE models. Mertens et al. (2000, 984) recently characterized these forces as (1) variables that affect demand (e.g., population), (2) variables that determine the intensity of land use (technology), (3) variables that reflect access to resources (political economy), and (4) variables that create incentives (political structure).

Boserup

While neo-Malthusian theories have focused largely on population as the driving force of negative environmental change (Hopfenberg 2003), scholars broadly following the work of Boserup (1981, 1983, 1990) have focused more on how scarcity

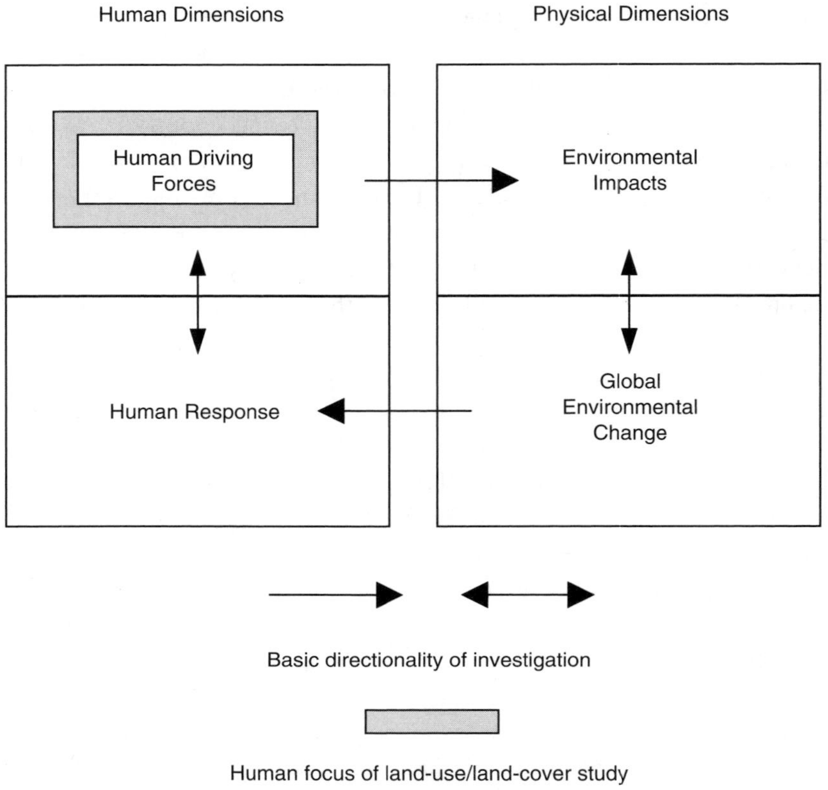

Figure 2.1
International Geosphere-Biosphere Programme framework for understanding the human dimensions of global environmental change. (From B. Turner et al. 1993b, 10.)

may stimulate changes in technology, which in turn, lead to positive rather than negative impacts on the environment. This is a more subtle theory than Malthusian theories or the variations on IPAT theories. Boserup challenged the presumption that either population or technology was the dominant engine of agricultural change and development. Rather, Boserup posited that increases in population density leading to land scarcity could be seen as a trigger that may stimulate agricultural intensification (increasing the yields on land already under cultivation). She did not try to explain population change but rather examined some of its likely consequences.

Basically, Boserup argued that farmers who faced little scarcity were not motivated to search for ways of increasing productivity. When faced with increased population density, however, farmers would be motivated to increase the amount of effort they invested in land by terracing, building irrigation systems, and carrying crop residues and forest litter to fertilize their land. Because of this focus on farmers and their immediate experience of scarcity, Boserup's work has been applied most successfully in studies at the community level. Considerable research has shown that some farming groups have devised intensive agricultural technologies that are dramatically more efficient and less harmful to the environment than extensive technologies (Netting 1986, 1993; B. Turner et al. 1993a). While some scholars have viewed this theory and Malthusian theories as similarly mechanistic, more sensitive interpreters of Boserup's work point to the complexity of the processes involved. Changing technology in particular environments requires considerable experimentation and investment in new tools and techniques. Some groups may therefore be faced with such rapid changes in population and scarcity of resources that they cannot adjust fast enough. On the other hand, groups that have invested heavily in intensive agriculture do not shift away from this technology if population densities fall (Brookfield 1972).

One of the permanent lessons of the exploration of Boserup's theory is recognition that there is no "agrarian ceiling" or "natural carrying capacity" for a particular environmental region. The level of productivity that is achievable in a particular environmental zone depends on the technology or physical capital available or invented as well as the available human and social capital. Her work is also consistent with viewing actors more broadly as decision makers trying to improve their well-being by choosing among the productive options that appear to be available to them or, when necessity calls for it, inventing new options.

Multiphasic Response

The principle of the multiphasic response to population pressure was first put forth by K. Davis (1963) and more recently was revived by Bilsborrow (Bilsborrow 1987; Bilsborrow and Ogendo 1992). In many ways, Bilsborrow's multiphasic response formulation can be seen as an adaptation of several previous theories, including Malthus's writings on checks to population growth, the Ehrlichs' focus on the role of technology as a mediating factor, and Boserup's work on agricultural intensification. Although Davis's original formulation of a theory of multiphasic response was applied at the country level, applications in the population and environment literature focus on communities. Following Bilsborrow, human populations respond to population pressure (land scarcity for a given population size) in one of four ways. Individuals and populations first increase food production to keep pace with population growth, either by agricultural extensification (bringing new lands under cultivation), intensification, or both. If these strategies prove insufficient, three demographic responses can ensue. First, temporary labor migration of individuals from their rural homes to other rural areas, or to urban areas, allows households to maintain a primary residence in their rural home while generating enough income to subsist in the face of insufficient available land. Households next engage in more permanent migration strategies, where individual members leave the household entirely to take up residence elsewhere, lessening the pressure on the local land resources. Only after the failure of these initial strategies does fertility reduction occur (Bilsborrow and Carr 2001). Fertility control can reduce the size of the next generation, lessening the fragmentation of land among heirs and lessening the overall population pressure on limited land resources.

Von Thünen and Agricultural Location Theory

Another early and major influence on contemporary research on land use was the work of von Thünen, whose first installments of *The Isolated State* were originally published in 1826 (see P. G. Hall 1966). As both a working farmer and a budding geographic economist, von Thünen tried to uncover basic empirical laws that related agricultural prices, distance to markets, and land uses. Much of the contemporary study of land-use/land-cover change owes a deep intellectual debt to the early work of von Thünen and the stream of work in agricultural location theory that has been pursued by both economists and geographers during the past century (e.g., see Croissant 2001). The concept of a central place hierarchy and much of contemporary spatial economics that are used extensively in regional and urban research also have direct links back to von Thünen (Samuelson 1983; Krugman 1995).

One of the core questions von Thünen asked was how location affected potential land uses. In an oft-quoted passage, he described an isolated terrain that enabled him to set up a mental model that has been an amazingly productive tool:

> Imagine a very large town, at the center of a fertile plain which is crossed by no navigable river or canal. Throughout the plain the soil is capable of cultivation and of the same fertility. Far from the town, the plain turns into an uncultivated wilderness which cuts off all communication between this state and the outside world. There are no other towns on the plain. The central town must therefore supply the rural areas with all manufactured products and in return it will obtain all its provisions from the surrounding countryside (P. G. Hall 1966, 7).

By focusing only on the distance from a central place on a homogeneous plain, von Thünen and hundreds of other scholars have examined how land value and rents would be related to distance to a central place (effectively adding transportation costs to production costs in the maximization decisions of farmers). Numerous studies have provided strong empirical support for the proposition that the types of crops planted are strongly determined by transportation costs and that changes in external market value or cost of transportation are reflected relatively rapidly in the spatial allocation of agricultural activities (e.g., see Muller 1973; O'Kelly and Bryan 1996).

Related to the work of Boserup, scholars in this tradition also have studied how spatial factors affect the intensity of agricultural production using a variety of specifications for the production function, for the number of crops, and for scale economies (see particularly Webber 1973; Visser 1982). Researchers have found that even among individual fields, farmers make substantial, differential investments so they invest less labor and capital in fields located a greater distance from a central place (de Lisle 1978). "Although gross income declined with increasing distance from the farmstead, the adjustments in the organization and intensity of farming offset the effects of distance on net income" (O'Kelly and Bryan 1996, 464). Thus, one should expect that the level of deforestation that occurs as a result of agricultural expansion will be directly related to the presence of roads and the transportation costs that farmers face for the crops that they may invest in (E. Moran 1976, 1981; Chomitz and Gray 1996).

Structural Theories of Population Change and Environmental Change

In this section and the next we describe theories that come from multiple academic disciplines, from core social science disciplines to ecology. These are general theories of human behavior and ecological change that are not specific to the relationship between humans and land use or land cover. As general theories, they provide a more complex picture of the impacts of social and economic behaviors on land use than the above theories. Theories of this sort are necessary to understand the conflicting results of research undertaken with simpler models. In their review of economic models that include population effects on deforestation, Kaimowitz and Angelsen (1998) conclude that population (and migration) "affect deforestation rates, but in a complex fashion that cannot simply be reduced to saying population growth promotes deforestation" (p. 5). Kolstad and Kelly (2001), for example, examine the possibilities of change based on a stable population rather than the geometrically increasing population posited by Malthus. In addition, the general nature of these theories (and the fact that researchers subscribe to them) means that they have proved robust across the wide variety of settings in which they can be and have been tested.

The theories in this section describe factors across geographic areas that form the structure within which individuals act. We start our discussion with theories at the most macrolevel, and progressively move to theories that cover smaller geographic areas, concluding with a theory of household structure as determining household land use. As these theories are formulated, they describe individual and aggregate behaviors (land use) and environmental characteristics (land cover) changing directly as a result of structural conditions. Individual people, households, or communities carry out the changes, but they act simply in accord with structural factors. In our own work we reject the notion of structural determinism, whether the structure be social or biophysical. These theories are invaluable, however, because they provide a rich understanding of the constraints and opportunities inherent in changing social and economic structures and varying biophysical contexts (Kolstad 2000).

Dependency Theory/World Systems Theory

In line with the PPE theory described above, we briefly describe another (more general) approach that lays the blame for land-use/land-cover change not on population per se, but rather on the organization of the world political economy (Ehrhardt-Martinez 1998; Ehrhardt-Martinez et al. 2002). This theory has been termed dependency theory by development economists (e.g., see Frank 1967) and world systems theory by sociologists (e.g., see Wallerstein 1974; Chase-Dunn 1998). We focus here on the sociological variant. Key variables determining environmental change are measured at the country level, even though there is clear heterogeneity in the extent of environmental degradation within countries. The nations of the world are organized into a "world system" based on capitalism and market connections (Wallerstein 1974; Chase-Dunn 1998). Nations are unequally advantaged in this system, with the "core" nations having the most power in the market and in the political organization of the world. Core nations use their power to maintain their privileged position through the exploitation of "peripheral" and "semiperipheral" countries. Core countries are more developed (economically), contain the headquarters of most transnational corporations, and wield considerable political influence over peripheral and semiperipheral countries. As core countries export capitalism, peripheral and semiperipheral countries are drawn into world economic markets. This unequal organization and the diffusion of capitalism affect a whole host of economic outcomes. When considering land-use change, it is particularly important to consider the role of world food markets. Less developed countries enact programs of export agriculture for these markets and consequently develop unsustainable agricultural practices in order to produce enough cash crops to allow them to purchase other goods on the world market.

The entry of peripheral and semiperipheral countries into world markets leads to poverty and population growth, and to unsustainable land-use change (Rudel 1989). The decline of traditional subsistence agriculture and entry into world economic markets from a disadvantaged position lead to poverty among the populations of developing countries. This poverty leads to population growth as children represent a net (economic) benefit to families in the absence of mandatory education and child labor laws. The entry into world economic markets simultaneously causes conversion of land from forest and traditional agriculture to commercial agriculture by increasing the value of land for agriculture and introducing capital-intensive methods of cultivation. The transition from traditional to commercial agriculture in early developing regions of a country leads also to the dislocation of farmers from traditional employment and modes of living (Sassen 1988; Massey et al. 1993). This population of dislocated farmers is highly mobile and in turn contributes to environmental change in frontier areas and other migration destinations. Thus, any relationship observed between population growth and environmental degradation is spurious. Population growth and land-use change both result from the penetration of capitalism into less developed countries and the unequal nature of the world system.

Economic Forces and Government Policies

A different body of theory focuses on economic factors as they affect land use and levels of deforestation. Kaimowitz and Angelsen (1998) have undertaken the most exhaustive review of economic models of deforestation, including in their analysis over 140 models. The most general source of deforestation in tropical areas that they identify is the expansion of cropped areas and pastures. They point out, as will be discussed in part IV of this book, that pasture expansion is especially important in Latin America. These findings are consistent with the type of general equilibrium models posited by leading economists such as Deacon (1994, 1995). General equilibrium models explore the cumulative effects of decisions by actors in an economy under diverse taxes and inducements. If there are no government policies related to land-use changes from forested land to agriculture or pasture uses, general equilibrium models posit that an inefficient equilibrium will exist, since standing forests—and the ecosystem services produced by them—are not given any value in such a setting. Further, when ownership rights to property are insecure, deforestation rates have been shown to be higher (Bohn and Deacon 2000).

Once taxes and inducements are introduced, the results can be either better or worse, depending on the particular pattern of taxation and subsidy undertaken by a government. Some developing countries adopt policies that have the effect of reducing the overall return to agricultural production (see Repetto 1989), but in other developing countries the "net force of government policy runs in the opposite direction and subsidizes agricultural production. The leading example is the system of tax credits, tax exemptions, and loan subsidies provided by the Brazilian government for cattle ranching in the Amazon" (Deacon 1995, 11). This is certainly relevant for the discussions in chapters 9 and 11, which illustrate the substantial land-use changes in the Amazon.

Demographic Transition

Concern over a direct effect of population growth on land cover is at least implicitly based on an understanding of how population growth rates change over time. Demographers describe the typical changes in vital rates of birth, death, and growth experienced by a population over the course of development as the "demographic transition" (see Kirk 1996 for a description and history of the theory of the demographic transition). For the majority of the long course of human history, populations were in the first stage of the demographic transition, experiencing high death and birth rates. These rates balanced each other and population growth was minimal. As communities, countries, and regions developed modern public health programs, and to a lesser extent modern medicine, death rates began to fall.

During this second stage of the demographic transition, death rates fall rapidly while birth rates remain high and stable, leading to increasing rates of population growth. The growth rate of the population, in the absence of migration, is the birth rate minus the death rate. As countries or regions enter the third stage of the demographic transition, death rates stabilize at a relatively low level (not quite the level achieved by today's developed countries, but quite low compared to earlier rates) and birth rates begin to fall. Population growth rates are maximized on the cusp between the second and third stages, when death rates have fallen and birth rates are just beginning to fall. During the third stage, birth rates fall, with death rates low and stable, leading to declining growth rates. Once birth rates have fallen to the same low level as death rates, marking entry into stage 4 of the demographic transition, population growth is minimal. The distribution of countries across these stages, with many of the world's largest countries still in stage 3, creates understandable alarm among theorists positing a direct negative effect of population size or growth on the environment.

Falling death rates are driven by the discovery and adoption of public health practices (sanitary sewers, landfills, etc.), as well as by the adoption by later-developing countries of modern medical techniques (particularly vaccination) (Livi Bacci 2001). The declining death rates, and corresponding economic development, are often associated with high rates of urbanization. Changes in birth rates are then driven by a variety of factors pertaining to the changing costs and benefits of children in urban areas and in nonagricultural lifestyles (Szreter 1996).

The demographic transition most accurately describes the experience of northern and western Europe, the sources of the data on which it was based. Both the ordering of declines in birth rates and mortality rates and the time elapsed between stages vary across other regions of the world, and indeed even within northern and western Europe (Coale and Watkins 1986). Early demographic transition theorists considered the mortality decline to be a necessary cause of the birth rate decline, while later research called into question this assertion (Chesnais 1992; Mason 1997). The experiences of today's developing countries, which were able to import rather than develop many of the drivers of mortality decline, point to the causal disconnect between mortality rate declines and birth rate declines. For population and environment researchers, the demographic transition theory serves as an organizing principle for thinking about geographic variation in human growth rates, and in the potential for future growth of human populations, by distinguishing between countries likely to have declining growth rates and those likely to continue to have high growth rates.

Regional Ecological Variability

Human communities (e.g., villages, cities, counties) affect and interact with landscapes, so it is useful to consider the characteristics of the ecological units they inhabit as determinants of the environmental change they bring about. We focus here on the characteristics of ecosystems because of our focus on the determinants of land-use/land-cover change.

We first briefly note the importance of topography in determining both the ecological characteristics and the social characteristics of an area. Topography affects how human communities use the land and determines the location of roads, water-based transportation networks, and other transportation networks. As discussed above, these factors in turn affect the profitability of various land uses by increasing the costs of transporting agricultural or forest products to markets for communities that are separated from transportation networks because of topography (Hanink 1997). Slope affects the costs (primarily labor costs) of farming in certain areas; farming on steeper land is more difficult and less productive. Topographic variability shapes watersheds and affects distribution of ecosystems on the land.

Ecosystems are usually delineated on the basis of an identifiable vegetation community, defined on the basis of structure and composition (e.g., grassland, forest, marsh). In addition to the plant community, an ecosystem includes the other living components of the community (e.g., animals, fungi), as well as the nonliving components of the system (soil, bedrock, water) and the processes that bind them together (nutrient cycles, hydrologic cycle, climate) (Whittaker 1975).

Different ecosystems offer different products and services to human communities, and human impacts therefore vary among ecosystems. Grasslands have been the most extensively altered due to their suitability for grazing and agriculture (WRI et al. 2000). In grasslands, grazing in the form of nomadic pastoralism may more closely mimic prehuman grazing pressures and more nearly preserve original plant communities than would conversion to large-scale monocultural farming. However, even nomadic pastoralism can severely stress a desert grassland (Rea et al. 1997). Forested ecosystems can be converted to grassland, pasture, or agriculture, or can be managed as forest. Uneven-aged forest management more closely mimics some kinds of forest succession than plantation agroforestry based on non-native tree species. However, even when land remains in forest or returns to forest, vegetation composition and structure are often altered purposefully by extractive human activities (grazing, timber, and nontimber forest product harvest, etc.) or inadvertently, as a side effect of human activities (e.g., "escaped" fires; introduction of non-native species; elimination of pollinators, herbivores, or other ecosystem components) (WRI et al. 2000). In contrast to grasslands and forest ecosystems, desert and tundra systems are less obviously altered, although anthropogenic activities are known to have altered desert plant communities even in prehistory (Rea et al. 1997).

Our ability to make generalized predictions about human impacts on ecosystems is improving with our understanding of the nature of the forces that maintain ecosystems. The early ideas of equilibrium and climax vegetation suggested that ecosystems were relatively unchanging and, if perturbed, would return to some equilibrium state through the process of vegetation succession (Wu and Loucks 1995).

In recent years, the notion of equilibrium resilience of ecosystems—the ability of an ecosystem to return to its original condition after an event such as a fire or hurricane—has matured, and we now recognize that disturbances are merely one of the processes that define ecosystems (Spies and Turner 1999). Instead of conceiving of forests as unbroken stands of ancient trees, we now expect that even forests that have been undisturbed by humans will exist as mosaics of patches of different ages, depending on the disturbance history of the forest. In addition, we understand that ecosystems vary in their ability to withstand (resistance) and recover from (resilience) disturbance. For example, fire may remove almost all the aboveground vegetation of a fire-adapted grassland, but recovery is swift—the system shows resilience in response to fire. In contrast, fire may remove relatively little aboveground vegetation in a fire-adapted woodland—this system is resistant to fire. Finally, fire occurring after a series of droughts in a normally wet forest may destroy almost all the aboveground vegetation and recovery to previous conditions may take centuries—this system is neither resilient nor resistant to fire.

Our more nuanced understanding of equilibrium resilience has been joined by the notion of ecosystem resilience (Holling 1973; Ludwig et al. 1997). Whereas equilibrium resilience pictures ecosystems as entities with a strong tendency to exist in a particular state, ecosystem resilience acknowledges that sufficiently strong stressors can entirely change the "default" ecosystem on a particular piece of ground. Natural resource management regimes can be such a stressor. We know, for example, that grasslands can be overgrazed to the point of converting to shrublands (Cross and Schlesinger 1999). Restoring the original ecosystem, or something like it, is not always possible. Theoretical work on equilibrium resilience has now been applied to linked human and ecological systems (Berkes and Folke 1998; Gunderson and Holling 2002). The quest here has been to develop and test theories that focus on the processes that lead to major changes in human systems and the ecological systems to which they are linked (Anderies et al. 2004).

Household Life Cycle

The key elements of the household life cycle as applied to household land-use decisions have their roots in mid–twentieth-century anthropology and economics. The anthropologist Goody (1958) described households as the locus of social reproduction, and described the cycle followed by all households over time. Households pass from an expansion stage (where birth rates are high and the family is growing) through a dispersion stage (where children are leaving the household) to a decay stage (when the original household head dies and is replaced by a son or daughter). The economist Chayanov ([1925] 1966), writing much earlier, had described the household-farm economy of Russian peasants. According to Chayanov, the extent of agricultural cultivation by individual households depends on the demographic characteristics of the household. Available household labor is a limiting factor, but the consumption needs of the household are what ultimately determine the behavior of the household. Combining the theoretical ideas of Goody on changing household demographics over the life cycle and the work of Chayanov on how household demographics determine land-use decisions, recent population and environment researchers have modeled land use as a function of stage in the household life cycle (Walker and Homma 1996; S. McCracken et al. 1999; E. Moran et al. 2001; Perz 2001).

Figure 2.2 shows the idealized trajectory of household composition and land use first published by S. McCracken et al. (1999) to explain patterns among in-migrants in the Brazilian Amazon. Households move down along this figure, from nuclear households with small children through nuclear households with children aging

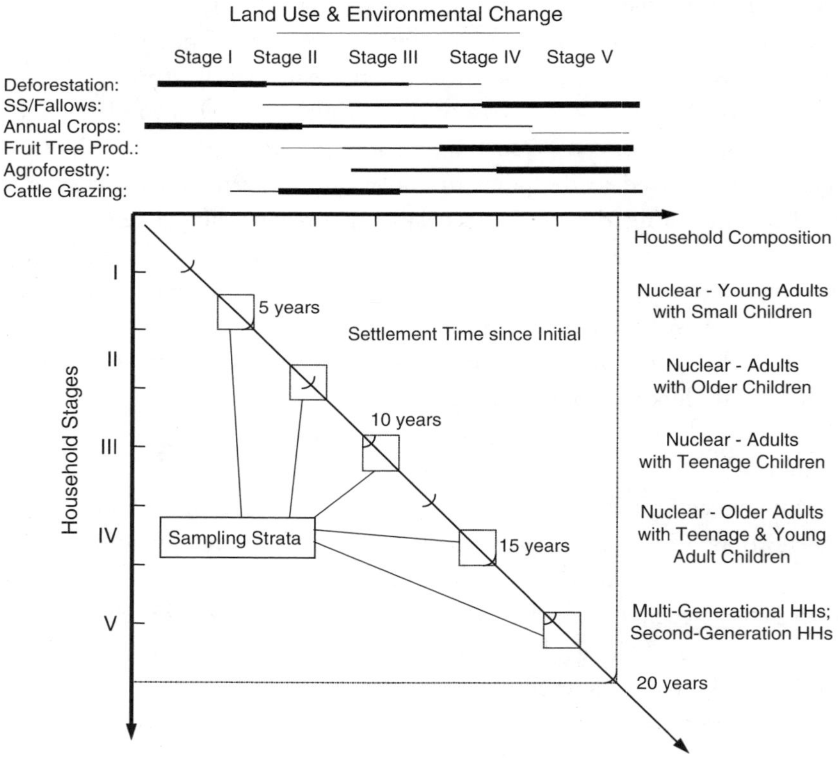

Figure 2.2
Land-use trajectory across the household (HH) life cycle. SS, secondary succession. (From S. McCracken et al. 1999, 1313.)

and leaving the household to multigenerational or second-generation households. As they move along this trajectory, the consumption needs of the household (determined by the number of household members, particularly by the number of dependents) and the available labor in the household (determined by the number of working-age household members) change. Corresponding to these changes, the household first concentrates on clearing (deforesting) land and on growing annuals, and later concentrates on land uses that provide lower short-term and higher long-term rewards. This theoretical perspective argues that land use, particularly the extent of deforestation, varies across households (within communities) primarily as a function of household size and composition.

Putting Decision-Making Actors Back In

In most of the theoretical approaches reviewed above, relationships among variables were presented in a mechanistic manner. Demographic "pressures" or "driving forces" affect land-use/land-cover change without human agency playing more than an incidental role. In presuming that increases in demographic pressures may lead to agricultural intensification, Boserup (1981) does envision a role for human actors who face definite costs and benefits of continuing or changing their agricultural technology. Much of the research in this tradition, however, has continued to look at changes in population density as a driving force rather than as a change in the incentives facing individuals who then make choices about future actions. Similarly, von Thünen focused on farmers' maximizing decisions, but simply increased the number of variables that could be viewed as determining causes of a location or production decision. Because he saw the goal as determining the equilibrium of a system, decision makers at equilibrium had little or no strategic input (P. G. Hall 1966).

A contrasting tradition starts from models of social and environmental change that view actors (whether they are individuals, households, or larger collectives) as making real decisions after taking into account the strategies available to them in a particular setting. In this sense, actors are the ultimate drivers of change. They do act within certain constraints, commonly those identified in structural theories, but also have an independent impact on environmental change. Theories involving individual actors initially get us out of the box of structural determinism, allowing us to explain the microlevel changes that make up any macrostructural change. However, we must guard against considering individuals as simply economically rational actors seeking to maximize personal rewards at the expense of any other potentially desirable outcomes.

Individual Actors: Early Focus on Equilibrium Analysis with Fully Rational Actors and Recent Work with More Broadly Conceptualized Rational Actors

Theories that overtly examine the decision processes and outcomes of individuals and households vary among themselves in the specific models of human behavior that they use. For neoclassical economists and economic geographers, the individual actor weighs the material benefits and costs of making particular choices and makes decisions to maximize short-term private returns. When this model of human behavior is used to explain behavior of actors embedded in a highly competitive environment, such as an open competitive market, predictions from the theory assuming individual, maximizing, self-interested returns have been supported by extensive field and experimental research. As Alchian (1950) long ago addressed, however, this success can be largely attributed to the strong selection pressure of the institutional environment leaving those who maximize profits as the survivors rather than to the internal decision-making calculus of the individual actor.

The narrow model of rational behavior and a heavy emphasis on finding the equilibrium of a static situation dominated economic approaches to the study of human-environment interactions until quite recently. Resource economics and economic geography textbooks tended to presume that individual maximizers were driven to particular production and location decisions by factors in their environment. This work was therefore highly consistent with the "driving forces" literature that focused primarily at a more macrolevel. Further, unless individuals had secure private property tenure, they would not take into account the long-term consequences of their use of natural resources (Demsetz 1967; Welch 1983). Consequently, the presumption was that rational decision makers would take actions that adversely affect the environment (see Dales 1968; Dasgupta and Heal 1979). Institutions designed to curb these strategic actions were viewed as necessary changes that would have to be imposed by external authorities on local resource users.

As a result of the theoretical challenge of Simon (1985, 1997) and the growing work in behavioral economics (see Camerer 1998, 2003), contemporary microtheories of human action affecting natural resources are less likely to view humans as mechanically and narrowly rational—pursuing their own immediate and material ends. Contemporary theoretical work on human choice related to land use often may presume that actors have a broader set of values that they take into account, access less complete information, and have weaker calculation prowess (e.g., see E. Ostrom and Walker 2003 for multiple papers examining how and why individuals trust one another when rational actors should not extend trust). As we discuss in the next section, substantial empirical research has challenged the theoretical predictions that individuals confronted with the problems of providing or managing public goods and common-pool resources will not engage in voluntary activities to achieve their own long-term benefits. Behavioral economics shares many theoretical insights with the work of sociologists (particularly Coleman 1990), political scientists (Young 1999), and institutional economists (North 1990). For example, recent demographic work revisiting the causes of fertility decline has focused on the role of social networks in regulating the flow of information and indeed in determining the way in which information is evaluated (Mason 1997; Kohler 2000). One finds a mixture of these approaches among those who have been interested primarily in explaining the human causes of land-use/land-cover change.

Thus, recent research focusing on how decisions made by individual actors affect resource conditions tends to recognize that there is a family of models that can be used when theorizing about individual choice. The theorist must make at least three key decisions about (1) whether to assume that actors have as much information as exists in the environment, (2) how their preferences reflect outcomes for themselves and others, and (3) what type of calculation they undertake (full analysis vs. some kind of heuristic). As described in chapter 8, one of the advantages of using agent-based models of individual choice is that researchers can vary the model of individual actors and ascertain which submodels of this broad family of models are more consistent with observed changes in land use over time.

One recent strand of land-use/land-cover change research which relaxes the assumption of perfect information explores the role of experience in the decisions of landowners. The interaction of individual experience or knowledge and the biophysical characteristics of the environment can play a significant role in the environmental impact of landowner choices. The suitability of land for growing certain crops or certain rotations of crops, both for a single year and year after year, is constrained by the topography, the precipitation, and the soil characteristics of the land (as discussed in several chapters of part IV). Because of the variability in these characteristics across parcels, even within the same community, parcel-specific knowledge can allow farmers to most effectively manage land. This is evident in economic models of landholder behavior (e.g., see Rosenzweig and Wolpin 1985 on the higher value to sons of inherited land and the relative infrequency of market transfers of land in agricultural areas characterized by small farmers). In areas of high in-migration, this parcel-specific knowledge may be lacking, and landholders may make unsustainable choices as a result. When knowledge is unavailable, or comes from an unfamiliar source (e.g., indigenous people), human impacts are likely to increase. This issue is explored by Brondízio in chapter 9.

Collective-Action Theory

Collective-action theory has become a core theory across all of the social sciences used to explain the costs and difficulties involved with organizing cooperation to achieve collective ends, such as the reduction of harvesting rates and the protection of habitats. The theory has many roots. In the 1950s, H. Gordon (1954) and Scott (1955) analyzed simple common-pool resources—in this case, open-access fisheries—to show that fishermen would always overharvest. In 1965, Olson published a path-breaking book, *The Logic of Collective Action*. In it, he conceptualized individuals facing such problems as making decisions independently without an external enforcement agency to make them keep agreements. In this setting, Olson predicted that unless individuals were in very small groups or had established selective incentives, they would not cooperate to achieve these joint benefits. In 1968, Hardin published a major article in *Science*, "The Tragedy of the Commons," in which he envisioned individuals jointly harvesting from a commons as being inexorably trapped in overuse and destruction. Drawing on a simple view of a resource (a common pool) and of the users (the self-seeking, maximizers of short-term gains in the prevalent model of rational behavior of the time), he argued that there were only two solutions to a wide variety of environmental problems: the imposition of a government agency as regulator or the imposition of private rights.

Until recently, the possibility that the users themselves would find ways to organize themselves had not been seriously considered in much of the environmental policy literature. Organizing to create rules that specify the rights and duties of participants creates a public good for those involved. Anyone who is included in the community of users benefits from this public good, whether they contribute or not. Thus, getting "out of the trap" is itself a second-level dilemma. Further, investing in monitoring and sanctioning activities to increase the likelihood that participants follow the agreements they have made also generates a public good and, thus, represents a third-level dilemma. Since much of the initial problem exists because the individuals are stuck in a setting where they generate negative externalities on each other, it is not consistent with the conventional theory that they solve a second- or third-level dilemma in order to address the first-level dilemma under analysis.

Evidence from both experimental and field research challenges the generalizability of the earlier accepted theory (E. Ostrom et al. 1994). While it is generally successful in predicting outcomes in settings where users are alienated from each other or cannot communicate effectively, it does not provide an explanation for settings where users are able to create and sustain agreements to avoid serious problems of overuse. Nor does it predict well when government ownership will perform well or how privatization will improve outcomes. Scholars familiar with the results of field research substantially agree on a set of variables that enhance the likelihood of users organizing themselves to avoid the social losses associated with open-access, common-pool resources (Schlager 1990; McKean 1992a; Tang 1992; E. Ostrom 1992; Wade 1994; Baland and Platteau 1996; NRC 2002). Consensus is growing that key attributes of a resource, of the users, and of higher levels of government provide a strong context within which individuals may or may not self-organize to protect resources (Libecap 1995; Dietz et al. 2003). The resource attributes have to do with its size, its predictability, the presence of reliable indicators, and the existence of damage to the resource that can be repaired. The attributes of users have to do with their dependency on the resource, their time horizons, the trust they have developed, their autonomy, their organizational experience, and the distribution of interests within a community (E. Ostrom 1999).

The key to further theoretical integration is to understand how these attributes interact in complex ways to affect the basic benefit-cost calculations of a set of users using a resource (E. Ostrom 2001). Each user has to roughly compare the expected net benefits of harvesting while continuing to use the old rules to the benefits he or she expects to achieve with a new set of rules. Further, users must estimate three types of costs: (1) the up-front costs of time and effort spent devising and agreeing on new rules, (2) the short-term costs of adopting new appropriation strategies, and (3) the long-term costs of monitoring and maintaining a self-governed system over time (given the norms of the community in which they live). If the sum of these expected costs for each user exceeds the incentive to change, no user will invest the time and resources needed to create new institutions. In field settings, no one is likely to expect the same costs and benefits from a proposed change. Some may perceive positive benefits after all costs have been taken into account, while others perceive net losses. Consequently, the collective-choice rules used to change the day-to-day operational rules related to harvesting and use affect whether an institutional change favored by some and opposed by others will occur. For any collective-choice rule, such as unanimity, majority, ruling elite, or one-person rule, there is a minimum coalition of users that must agree prior to the adoption of new rules. New rules are established when a winning coalition perceives expected benefits to exceed expected costs.

This theoretical approach, however, is relatively difficult to implement empirically because of the need to obtain substantial field data. To understand patterns of environmental change, one needs considerable information about users at many levels, about the attributes of the resource itself, and about institutional arrangements assigning authority to change day-to-day rules over time. The relations between collective action, institutions, and land-use/land-cover patterns are explored further in chapters 4 and 10.

This approach to institutions has guided our work on the management of collectively owned resources. However, we note the promise of recent alternative institutionalisms in sociology (Powell and DiMaggio 1991) and political science (March and Olsen 1984; P. A. Hall and Taylor 1996; Peters 1999) for the study of land-use decisions. This work has blurred the line between culture and institutions by focusing on how culture shapes behavior in ways that are not rational. Culture both enforces irrational behavior and limits the menu of behavioral options. Individuals are posited as adopting orientations to others that affect their perception of appropriate ways of relating to each other (e.g., fatalistic, individualistic, hierarchical, or egalitarian) and to risk (Douglas 1986, 1992; but see Ellis and Thompson 1997). Actors draw on organizational forms with which they are familiar (rather than forms which are necessarily the most efficient) in structuring new organizations. This approach has not been used in the study of land-use decision making. However, it has the potential to provide explanations for why effective collective management of natural resources might develop in some communities or countries and not in others, and to explain the importance of past experience with collective action for future collective management of resources.

Landscape Ecology

Landscape ecology is the study of patterns of land cover, their causes, and their implications (M. Turner et al. 2001). Land cover may refer to vegetation communities and other natural features, such as sand dunes, or to human communities and other human constructions, or, most usefully, to all of these. By considering the processes underlying these patterns, landscape ecology points to the importance of context in the study of human-environment relations. Whereas humans once existed in islands of homes, pastures, and fields set within forests and grasslands, the reverse is now often true. Forests and uncultivated grasslands exist as islands within urban, suburban, and agricultural landscapes. Yet these patterns do not occur universally, even within zones of largely similar biophysical endowments. The focus on the different processes that lead to different outcomes within similarly endowed areas, or that lead to similar outcomes in differently endowed areas, points our attention to the interactions between variables leading to land-cover change.

Processes Lead to Patterns Initially, landscape ecologists tended to treat human communities and their roads, cattle, and other accessories as exogenous disturbances, and focused their efforts on understanding how biophysical processes shaped landscape patterns—for example, how underlying patterns in soil or topography affect the distribution of vegetation types. As social sciences have been incorporated into landscape ecology (NRC 1998), human actions and processes have joined the list of factors that produce landscape patterns. In the development of the field of global change, the interacting impacts of human and biophysical processes on landscape patterns are at last being fully explored and modeled (see chapter 8). In this book, researchers document the impacts of government policies on rates of deforestation (see chapter 10), as well as the impact of anthropogenic factors such as livestock grazing on forest health. Scale of analysis affects the degree to which forest change is observed in these studies. Brondízio (chapter 9) reviews considerable research from the Brazilian Amazon showing links between a variety of human processes and landscape patterns. Among other results, economic processes (labor, production, control of capital) are linked to land use, and land cover. Soil characteristics affect fallowing practices, rates of abandonment of farmland, and rates of regrowth following abandonment or during fallowing, and, once again, scale of observation and analysis affects the perception of pattern. The effect of soil factors and land-use history result in patterns of forest biomass that can be detected even with satellite data (see chapter 11).

The conservation and sustainable development communities rely on the fact that differences in human processes result in different landscape patterns. Unruh, Nagendra, Green, McConnell, and Vogt (chapter 12) discuss programs in Asia and Africa that study land-cover change, particularly deforestation, under different ownership regimes to determine what regimes are most consonant with sustainable forest use. This issue becomes particularly important in management of parks and other areas in which policy makers may assume that forest cover is maintained due to institutional status, when, in fact, land use is more extractive and deforestation more extensive than a fully protected institutional status would predict.

Fragmentation and Habitat Loss Although landscapes are affected by human decisions at many levels of society, the physical processes that produce landscape change (e.g., clear-cutting, grazing, home construction) most often involve communities and individuals. The decisions of individuals acting either individually or collectively are impacted by local ecology, but they also determine the local ecology. Human actors have the ability to choose among patterns of land use that have similar social and economic characteristics, but which may have very different ecological impacts.

From the landscape perspective, a major result of community and individual land-use decisions is that natural or seminatural habitats no longer exist in large patches, but now are reduced to fragments. The decreasing size of natural patches creates a situation in which the ratio of area on the edge of the patch (and consequently exposed to areas with different characteristics) to the area in the center of the patch is substantially higher than prior to human impact. As a result, greater area is at increased risk of invasion by nearby livestock, hunters and gatherers who would find it difficult or inconvenient to travel to the center of a larger patch, and so on. Because of increased disturbance at the edges, small patches lose more species than their small size alone would suggest. Edge areas also are at increased risk of accidental fire, are at increased risk of invasion by non-native plant species, are more accessible to predators from surrounding habitat patches, and experience more damage from wind than interior areas. Changes in temperature, humidity, and light along patch edges can further change the characteristics of a small patch and alter the plant communities and animals that depend on them (Schelhas and Greenberg 1996; Laurance and Bierregaard 1997; Bierregaard et al. 2001).

Connectivity, the capacity of a landscape to support movement by any given species across the landscape, is of increasing concern for conservation biologists (Meffe and Carroll 1997). As the connectivity of a landscape increases from the human perspective (generally through increases in road networks), connectivity decreases for many other species (With and King 1999). Although we may see many species of animals moving across human landscapes (e.g., deer, wolves, and turtles crossing roads or wandering through our backyards), landscapes substantially altered for human use act as barriers to movement of both animal and plant species. In some cases these barriers are incomplete—many turtles die on roads, but some make it across. In other cases, passage is essentially impossible—cities along landscape corridors such as river valleys can effectively eliminate genetic exchange between previously connected plant and animal populations; dams can permanently halt spawning of fish by blocking travel to their breeding grounds. Thus, edge effects and lack of connectivity can decrease the conservation value of remaining habitat below what its mapped area might suggest, increasing the impact of fragmentation (Debinski and Holt 2000).

A Multiscalar Approach

The above discussion foreshadows our application of theoretical principles in empirical work. We first considered structural theories of population change and environmental change, and then considered theories which incorporated individual (or household or collective) actors' making strategic decisions in the face of structural constraints. These theories lead us to consider the importance of social and biophysical structures at several levels of aggregation and the individual decision-making process in determining environmental change. Indeed, previous empirical research also points to the need for a theoretical approach that explains variation across scales. At the local level, many studies find no relationship between population growth and loss of forest cover (Fox 1993b; Agrawal 1995; Fairhead and Leach 1996; Varughese 1999, 2000; Debinski and Holt 2000). At a regional or national level, however, more studies tend to find that population growth is positively related to deforestation (see Rudel 1989). On the other hand, afforestation appears to be occurring primarily in those countries that already have achieved considerable affluence, such as Sweden and Switzerland (Hägerstrand and Lohm 1990; Pfister and Messerli 1990), even though population levels there are neither growing nor shrinking. Forest regrowth is also occurring in developing countries where previous agricultural fields are reverting to forest (Rudel et al. 2000, 2002).

We term the approach described here a *multiscalar approach*. Multiscalar studies allow us to address the following key questions:

- How do the characteristics of individual actors affect land-use decisions? In particular, how do these characteristics affect whether land is managed individually or collectively?
- How do regional- and country-level policy, cultural patterns, and socioeconomic forces mediate the relationship between characteristics of actors and their land-use decisions?
- How do local policy and socioeconomic and environmental characteristics mediate the relationship between characteristics of actors and their land-use decisions?

In addition to facing challenges in the implementation of multiscalar studies (discussed further in the following chapters), we faced an initial challenge to develop a multiscalar approach in finding a common understanding of what multiscalar means and what the important levels are. The term *multiscalar* is itself multivalued, as notions of scales differ among disciplines (Gibson et al. 2000b). Social scales of interest vary from the individual to household, community, state, and international levels. Ecological scales of interest, however, might be individual to population, community, ecosystem, or planet, or, alternatively, might be patch to local landscape, region, continent, or planet. Even the term *scale* has different meanings across disciplines, with geographers applying scale to the ratio of map distance to land distance, and social scientists considering scale as the level of aggregation (see chapter 3). To further complicate matters, social and ecological scales are both cross-cut by temporal duration. Different social processes are more evident from year to year than from decade to decade or from one century to the next. Ecological history is affected both by human history and by the history of other forms of disturbance that may occur on the same or vastly different temporal durations: forest fires, ice ages, continental drift.

Simply having an idea that drivers of land-use change (as well as the land-use change itself) are observed at various scales is insufficient for the design of effective research. We must have some conception of how processes across levels are related to each other. In designing and conducting analyses involving propositions and data from multiple levels, we acknowledge the complexity of human-environment interactions. In any complex system, phenomena (sometimes called emergent phenomena) exist at coarser scales or higher levels that cannot be predicted on the basis of what is known only from finer scales or lower levels (Mayr 1982; Lansing and Kremer 1993). For example, the rules of social systems cannot be formulated on the basis of information about individual humans (or ants or antelope). Studies of complex systems are therefore often multiscalar (Holland and Mimmaugh 1995; Levin 1998). Koestler (1973) stressed that hierarchical organization is the sine qua non of stable complex systems composed of living or inanimate subsystems. By hierarchical, Koestler meant that all organized systems have organized subsystems within them, many having considerable autonomy. They affect higher-level systems as well as being affected by them.

The concept of wholes and parts rarely exists in an absolute sense. "What we find are intermediary structures on a series of levels in ascending order of complexity, each of which has two faces looking in opposite directions: The face turned toward the lower levels is that of an autonomous whole, the one turned upward, that of a dependent part" (Koestler 1973, 290). The crucial point, however, of this view of the world is that it is appropriate to study different levels as relatively autonomous systems as long as scholars are aware of the larger systems in which they are embedded, as well as the smaller systems that are contained at any one particular level.

Koestler (1973) proposed the term *holons* for these "Janus-faced sub-assemblies." He meant by this term to quiet the debate between advocates of atomism and those of holism and to replace the notion of parts and whole by a multilevel, hierarchical view of organized systems. He argued that a "hierarchically organized whole cannot be 'reduced' to its elementary parts; but it can be 'dissected' into its constituent branches while the holons represent the nodes of a tree, and the lines connecting them the channels of communication, control, or transportation as the case may be" (p. 291).

We take this idea of holons, of relatively autonomous levels, to guide our analyses at one level with data from multiple levels. By considering each level as relatively autonomous, a daunting analytical task involving endogenous variables at multiple levels and cross-level feedback loops can be simplified to tractable models of the decision making of actors at a single level influenced by exogenously determined forces at that and higher levels.

Gibson et al. (2000b) identified four theoretical issues related to scale that affect all sciences: (1) the effect of scale (level of interest of study), extent (size of study area), and resolution (size of sampling unit) on the identification of patterns; (2) the manner in which explanations of specific phenomena vary across levels; (3) the generalizability of propositions derived at one level to other levels; and (4) optimization of processes at particular points or regions. In a multiscalar approach, conducting analyses of the same basic process (e.g., deforestation) at household/parcel levels, as well as at community or higher levels, allows the researcher to address these four issues. Descriptively, one can identify scales at which certain processes are more or less evident (addressing issue 1). In predictive models, one can model the optimization processes operating at various levels (issue 4). By modeling the various inputs into the optimizing decisions of actors, one can examine differences in the drivers of land-use change at various levels. This allows one to address issue 2. Finally, by conducting analyses in a theoretically informed manner, by using the results of a given analysis (combined with existing theory) to generate propositions for subsequent analyses at the same or different levels, one can address issue 3.

Because much of the earlier work of the Center for the Study of Institutions, Population, and Environmental Change (CIPEC) focused on subnational areas, communities, and households or individuals, we initially focus on household or individual theoretical models. Factors above these levels affecting land-use decisions (and land-use change) have been treated as exogenous. That is, we have yet to address empirically the bidirectional causality between individual, household, and community characteristics (both social and land-use) and national- or international-level policy or environmental change.

These household- and individual-level decisions about individual parcels, or about all the land area owned, are influenced by various higher-level factors. In this multilevel schema, community characteristics include such variables as the history of a location, its geographic location in relation to large urban centers or major roads, socioeconomic factors, demographic trends, cultural norms shared by most community residents, degree of cultural heterogeneity, types of educational opportunities available, number and types of local business and philanthropic organizations, and structure of local government. Further, the kind of shared information present in a community about the value of the forest as a generator of ecological services, about various agroforestry technologies, and about their political efficacy and authority also affect decisions made at this level. As described above, a variety of these factors change the value of children, which changes household demographics. These changing demographics then change the ability of households to enact various land uses and the desirability of various land uses. The proximity of the community to markets and the availability of nonfarm employment change the rewards associated with agriculture relative to other income-generating strategies. Following collective-action theory, many of these factors also affect the ability of a community to create and maintain effective institutions for the management of resources (Gibson et al. 2000a).

Above the community level, regional, national, or international policy regimes or economic forces impact the decisions of actors by changing the incentive structure within which decisions are made (Barbier 2000). The location of a community within a country that is disadvantaged in the world economy affects the tradeoffs between agriculture and nonfarm employment. For example, the decision to grow certain crops has very different meanings for landholders in Indiana and landholders in the Amazon. National subsidies and their potentially perverse incentives (Myers and Kant 2001) and international inequalities lead to less risk and higher return associated with farming in the United States. The level of the development of the country affects the decision making of farmers indirectly by affecting access to education, access to high-paid and stable off-farm employment, and the functioning of various markets. Aside from government subsidies, one reason that certain types of agriculture are more feasible and less risky in the United States is that fully functioning credit, insurance, and futures markets exist. Landholders are able to access credit to purchase inputs to increase productivity, are able to purchase insurance against crop failure, and are buffered against the volatility of the international market by internal futures markets. Because of the case-study nature of most population and environment research, most of these forces are controlled in any given analysis. We do not directly estimate the effect of these forces. Rather, they provide the context within which we interpret results and make cross-national comparisons between the results of multiple case studies.

Formulating Testable Hypotheses

Given these disparate theories, we face the task of developing hypotheses that are both testable and explicit with regard to the level at which the dependent and independent variables are measured. The multidisciplinary nature of our research, as well as disagreement within disciplines, provides us with the rich theoretical literature briefly reviewed above. The multiscalar nature of our research, combined with the fact that many of the theories we consider are explicitly at a given scale, leads to a multiplicity of testable hypotheses that are not necessarily incompatible. We now briefly outline some points of complementarity and disagreement between the theories described above and focus further on our multiscalar approach. Empirical research points to the deficiencies of traditional approaches, as well as to the importance of scale. While many studies have been published, they do not produce a clear set of findings regarding the impact of population, poverty, technology, and political instability (see Meyer and Turner 1992). And, most important for the work in this book, patterns of relationships depend substantially on the scale at which processes occur and observations are made.

One initial note on formulating testable hypotheses pertains to the issue of scale in empirical research. Theories at the highest levels of aggregation have proved difficult or impossible to test. We have only one planet, with one population, and one growth rate at any given point in time. Changing rates of environmental degradation or food scarcity can never be completely attributed to changing population size or growth rates. We can never rule out the possibility that both are caused by some third factor since one world at any given point in time allows us only one predictive variable. Nothing else can be controlled. As we move down levels of aggregation, our potential degrees of freedom increase, making the causal arguments in lower-level studies more persuasive. By then combining these lower-level studies using a comparative approach, we can test the effects of higher-level variables.

Figure 2.3 shows the causal relationships posited by the groups of theories described above. In illustrating traditional theories of population and environment relationships (*a*) and structural theories of human behavior that can and have been applied to land-use/land-cover change (*b*), we indicate the scale at which these theories implicitly or explicitly posit a relationship. Our multiscalar approach (*c*) combines the basic relationship between actors and outcomes posited by general theoretical models incorporating strategic actors with structural forces shown to be important in other theories.

The traditional theories (*a*), and their arguments about the relationship between population and environment, can be brought together under a single model that includes a unidirectional causal relationship between population (size, density, or location) and the extent of environmental degradation. Each of these theories applies to any human population, whether global, regional, or local. Malthus's basic arguments about a productivity increase relative to population size increase, as well as the IPAT model, apply at the global, regional, and local levels. These models are complementary in the sense that each tells a portion of the story. Malthus's arguments about population growth outpacing agricultural productivity and leading to food scarcity are modified and updated in the IPAT model. Malthus did not foresee the role of technology in increasing the ability of the environment to provide and did not specify the role of heterogeneity in consumption. The IPAT model thus expands on Malthus's initial model, both by specifying more causal factors and by generalizing the adverse consequences to any environmental impact, not only those associated with food.

Other traditional approaches might well apply at the global and regional levels but have more commonly been applied to the local level. In contrast to the IPAT model and to Malthusian approaches, both Boserupian approaches and the multiphasic response consider population density (or land scarcity) to be the key driving force. These models posit a more complex set of population-environment relationships, allowing population pressure on natural resources to lead to agricultural intensification and modification of social behavior. However, in the end, the effect of population density simply acts through these intervening factors to determine the extent of environmental degradation.

Von Thünen's agricultural location theory includes a different independent variable, but is a theory with much the same form. The location of agricultural land relative to urban agglomerations is an exogenous force determining the profitability of various land uses. Thus, the extent of environmental degradation (a function of land-use decisions) is determined by the location of human settlement.

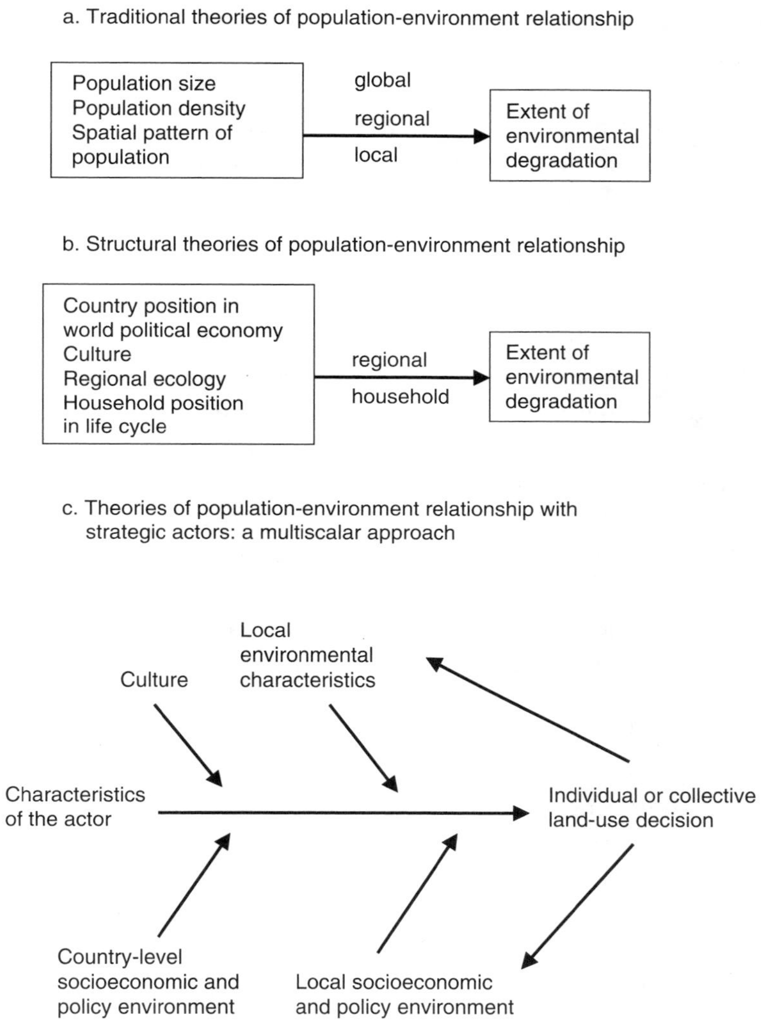

Figure 2.3
Schematic representation of theories of population-environment relationship.

The structural theories of human behavior (see *b* in figure 2.3) operate at regional and household levels. Dependency theory points to the position of an entire country in the world political economy in determining changes in population and socioeconomic organization within the country. Similarly, microlevel political-economic theories point to the position of the household or community in a national or international economy, as well as the structure of that economy, as determinants of the behaviors of household or community actors.

At a suprahuman level of analysis, variability in the ecology of an area affects the amount of human degradation of the environment (because some ecosystems are more amenable to human uses and because some ecosystems are more resilient). While we expect that the proponents of these theories allow population size and density to have an effect on environmental degradation, the approach argues for the primary cause of environmental degradation to be the characteristics of the ecosystem itself. Some ecosystems are simply more likely to be overused by humans by virtue of their higher level of attractiveness for human uses. These theories are therefore not in conflict with traditional theories, but are also not entirely satisfactory for reasons addressed below.

The final structural model that speaks to the causes of environmental degradation is the household life-cycle model. Using this model, we can argue that the changing size and structure of households as they move through their life cycle determine the extent of environmental degradation on an associated parcel of land. This theory is not inconsistent with any of the other approaches. It does not argue that there is no role of population growth or density, or that there is no role of country-level socioeconomic characteristics, but rather that all of these larger forces act through the demographic composition of the household. The forces identified by theories pertaining to higher levels of aggregation simply act as antecedent variables to the size and composition of the household, which directly determines land use.

The household life-cycle and regional ecological variability approaches, as well as the other structural theories reviewed, however, prove unsatisfactory to us for two reasons. First, because they are structural theories, they do not allow for individual (or household, or collective) agency in land-use decisions. Structural forces completely determine the behavior of individuals. Second, these theories frequently posit a unidirectional, causal relationship between one independent variable and an environmental outcome. We propose instead an approach that improves on previous approaches in three ways. First, we consider land use (and environmental change) to be the outcome of decision making by actors who seek complex goals given the information they have about the situation they find themselves in or try to change.

Second, we consider environmental and socioeconomic context not as antecedent variables but rather as mediating variables. Third, our approach allows for some reciprocal causation, or feedback, in the system. We recognize that additional feedbacks between variables, particularly between levels, exist. Indeed, we could probably draw bidirectional arrows between most of the variables in the diagram. However, we focus here on land-use decisions as the dependent variable and on the key relationships that we seek to model in our empirical work.

We note that there are many excluded causal relationships between the large categories of variables shown in the simplified model diagram of our theoretical approach (*c* in figure 2.3). We do not argue that the causal arrows in our figure are all the possible arrows, but rather they are the most important for understanding individual or collective land-use decision making. This diagram is not entirely inconsistent with the arguments represented in the other diagrams (*a* and *b*), because it points to the importance of country-level cultural, socioeconomic, and policy characteristics and to the importance of local-level socioeconomic, policy, and environmental characteristics. All of these are key causal factors identified by more deterministic theories identified above. Where we differ is in how these important causal factors enter the picture. In our model, these factors determine the context within which actors make decisions. Instead of directly causing the land-use changes, they mediate the relationship between the characteristics of the actor and the ultimate decision. The direction and existence of the relationship between actor characteristics and land use depend on these contextual variables. Our consideration of local and country-level characteristics as mediating variables follows directly from our commitment to an actor-based approach as opposed to a deterministic structural approach. The one theory addressed above that does not enter into the model in this way is the household life-cycle approach. In our model, the household position in the life cycle is a characteristic of the actor (with the actor being the household) that interacts with the local and country-level context to determine the ultimate land-use decision.

The focus on actors also leads us to a more nuanced understanding of the dependent variable under consideration. Decades of theorizing and research on collective action have shown us that environmental degradation differs based on whether a group of actors can manage a resource collectively rather than each acting individually. Taking the insights from this theoretical and empirical perspective, and the insights from landscape ecology described above, we specify a complex dependent variable. For example, the pattern (edge-to-interior ratio, existence of wildlife corridors, etc.) of deforestation on an individual parcel or on the land managed by a community is as important a measure of environmental impact as simply the percent or total area deforested.

The final addition made by our approach (shown in *c* of figure 2.3) is the explicit recognition of reverse causation. Local characteristics are not exogenous to land-use decisions. The local biophysical environment affects the decision-making process of actors, but is also itself affected by these decisions. Past land-use decisions determine current environmental conditions as well as current socioeconomic conditions and public policy. These instances of reverse causality are the simplest to model and arguably the most theoretically important, but are by no means the only possible instances. For example, we might argue that the characteristics of the actor were themselves either caused by past land-use decisions or at least jointly determined with land-use decisions. In particular, the household size and composition, its assets, and the current land use are likely to be jointly determined. We do not deny the possibility of this and other modifications to our basic model, but rather argue that we have struck a balance between complexity and parsimony.

This model provides a structure for designing empirical studies of human impacts on the environment, including those presented in the remainder of this book. By focusing our attention on the relationship between the characteristics of individual actors and their land-use decisions, we focus on the effects in the model that are the most straightforward to estimate. For example, in a study examining households in a single community, we control for the culture, country-level socioeconomic and policy environment, the local environmental characteristics, and the local socioeconomic and policy environment. By examining households that share all of these characteristics, we can focus on the effects of the household characteristics that do vary (household composition, wealth, etc.). Similarly, we can examine the relationships between community-level actors (e.g., forest user groups) and community-level land-use decisions. When examining an individual community, we control for any higher-level variables. When examining a set of communities in a single country, we control for country-level variables while estimating the effect of community-level variables.

The three chapters in part II provide an essential discussion of key concepts used in a multiscalar approach and some preliminary evidence regarding our approach. The chapters in part III are written to give the reader a solid foundation on the diverse methods and models needed to understand human-environment linkages at multiple temporal and spatial scales, and part IV provides evidence from case studies of these diverse patterns. Chapter 14 provides a conclusion to our work conducted through spring 2004 and a look ahead to future work.

II

Conceptual Foundations of Human-Environment Analyses in Forest Ecosystems

The chapters in part II are intended to provide the reader with the basic conceptual foundations for understanding research on human-environment interactions in forest ecosystems. Chapter 3 by Glen Green, Charles Schweik, and J. C. Randolph focuses on the challenge of understanding these interactions across time and space. One cannot study land-cover change more generally and forest dynamics more specifically without spatial and temporal dimensions to the study. These dimensions, so crucial to our work, are particularly challenging in the conduct of multidisciplinary research, since the core disciplines involved in this research define and use these concepts differently. Thus, how temporal and spatial concepts are used in multiple disciplines is discussed, as well as how key terms are used in the rest of the book. The chapter provides a basic grounding for the work in parts III and IV.

In chapter 4, Catherine Tucker and Elinor Ostrom address another concept that is used in multiple ways across disciplines: institutions. They provide a conceptual definition of institutions as the formal and informal rules defining what individuals may, must, or must not do within any particular situation. Rules are the "dos and don'ts" that parents teach their children. More important, any system of forest governance must find a way of "teaching" those using a particular forest what activities they are permitted to do, what obligations they face, and what actions are forbidden under what circumstances. The authors describe the approach used in the rest of the book to combine data obtained from forest users, officials, and archives, as well as from the use of remotely sensed data and geographic information systems. Drawing on research conducted by Center for the Study of Institutions, Population, and Environmental Change (CIPEC) scholars, they illustrate how institutional analysis helps us to understand the incentives and behavior of key actors as they affect forest ecosystems.

Chapter 5 then turns to a more specific focus on forest ecosystems as they are used by humans. J. C. Randolph, Glen Green, Jon Belmont, Theresa Burcsu, and David Welch provide the essential concepts developed in forest ecology on the nature and extent of forests that researchers studying human-forest environment interactions must know. Chapter 5 is a primer of the core concepts used to describe and analyze biophysical processes occurring in forested ecosystems around the world. The chapter also provides an overview of the three forest types included in CIPEC research and reported on in the remainder of the book.

Many readers of this book already will be familiar with *some* of the concepts presented in part II. Not all readers, however, will be familiar with a literature that consistently uses concepts across *all* of the disciplines represented by the authors of these chapters, by participants in the CIPEC research program, and by serious students of human-environment interactions. Thus, readers may find some sections of each of these three chapters to be elementary. We invite you to scan the pages that present familiar concepts rapidly. Readers who find a particular section to be elementary should be aware that other readers of this book will be introduced to terms defined for the first time in their academic life. We think that most readers will find some sections of part II to be informative and a good foundation for parts III and IV of the book.

3

Linking Disciplines across Space and Time: Useful Concepts and Approaches for Land-Cover Change Studies

Glen M. Green, Charles M. Schweik, and J. C. Randolph

This chapter develops concepts and approaches in which contrasting disciplines, and more specifically the fields of remote sensing, geographic information systems (GIS), and institutional analysis, can be appropriately integrated to advance our understanding of the human dimensions of land-cover change. While we have specifically applied these approaches to study how humans influence forest cover, they also may help direct the study of terrestrial vegetation change in general. We first discuss the dimensions of space, time, and human decision making and then examine how different aspects of the human-related land-cover change processes that affect woody plants vary across these dimensions. Finally, from this examination we present several simple graphical diagrams that help illustrate these complex relationships and thereby clarify the concepts presented here for readers who are unfamiliar with these approaches. These diagrams also can help researchers and students effectively display diverse datasets together and plan more robust strategies for land-cover change studies.

Dimensions of Space and Time: Maps and Timelines

Common understandings shared across disciplines help advance interdisciplinary land-cover change research programs, especially those that attempt to link the social and physical sciences. Yet the diverse vocabularies, contrasting research methods, and diverse datasets used by different disciplines can hinder the development of commonalities. Since most of the phenomenology of land-cover change is thought to exist within the four dimensions of space and time, perhaps we can help bridge our disciplinary differences by exploiting this fundamental connection. Any two analyses, regardless of disciplinary focus, have at least these four dimensions in common. Thus, this approach may help facilitate the development of a common set of

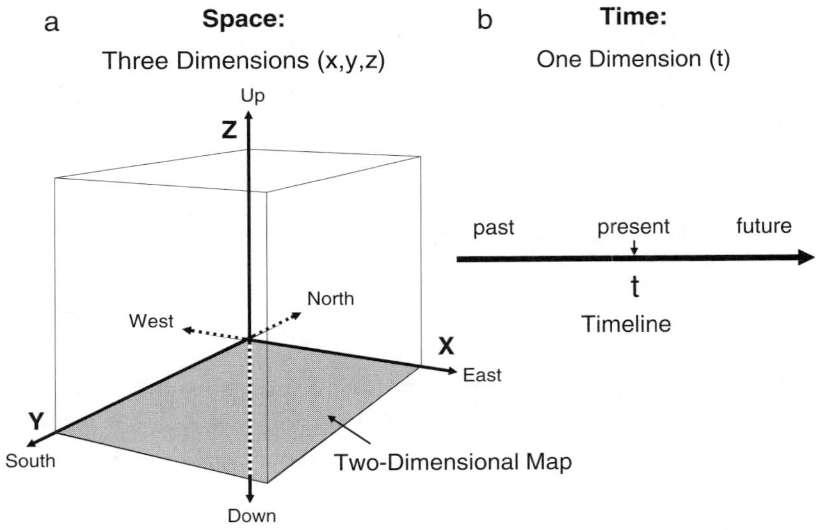

Figure 3.1
(*a*) Space can be depicted by three perpendicular axes: x, y, and z. The surface of Earth is often simplified in maps by using only the x and y axes, and is conventionally positioned such that north is to the top of the map. (*b*) Time can be depicted as a single axis (*t*) laid horizontally with the future positioned to the right.

basic nomenclature and conventions about how land-cover change processes manifest themselves across space and time.

The four dimensions of space and time in which land-cover change processes exist are depicted in figure 3.1. Three perpendicular dimensions are often used to define volumetric space, commonly known as the x, y, and z axes. One can, at least theoretically, travel forward and backward along all three of these spatial dimensions. Depiction of Earth's surface often uses only two dimensions because variability in the z-direction (elevation or height) is usually small relative to the other two dimensions. Thus, a "map," shown in *a* of figure 3.1, usually depicts variability in the x and y dimensions, although variability along the z-dimension is sometimes added as contours on topographic maps or as differential coloring of elevation of cells in a digital elevation model (DEM). Typically, the x and y axes are oriented such that the direction of geographic north is toward the top of the map.

Time, in contrast, varies only along one dimension, and, unlike travel along the three dimensions of space, one can travel in only one direction through time (into the future), since travel into the past is not possible. All states of land cover and the changes that affect them can be positioned along a timeline based on when in the sequence of time they occur (*b* in figure 3.1). Typically, timelines are drawn horizontally such that positions to the left are older than (occur before) those to the right. Thus, the map and the timeline together comprise two fundamental, graphical diagrams through which we can display measures of land-cover change. A third important, though less common, graphic will also be introduced later in the chapter.

In several major disciplines, emphasis is placed on one dimension over another. History, for example, traditionally places more emphasis on time (the temporal aspects under study) and less on spatial aspects. Geography, more than most other disciplines, emphasizes the spatial dimensions over the temporal one. Other disciplines, such as geology and ecology, contain more of a mix of both dimensions. Certain social sciences (e.g., political science, sociology, and anthropology) traditionally emphasize space or time when needed. For example, political scientists do, at times, undertake research that emphasizes the temporal aspects in longitudinal studies. Geographic studies within political science are less prevalent, although they are becoming more common as the technologies of GIS are applied more readily (see chapter 7). The emerging interdisciplinary field of land-cover change research, however, emphasizes all four dimensions of space and time. Both spatial and temporal variability are at the core of this important field.

With the diverse vocabularies of separate disciplines, it is no wonder that land-cover change processes can appear extremely complicated. Aggravating this is a sense of urgency often felt by researchers, students, policy makers, and land managers because of the inherent complexity in understanding land-cover change processes, and the feeling that our understanding lags severely behind the processes involved. Land-cover change specialists also may feel like they are caught up in a race—simply put, a race between land-cover change itself and our collective ability to document past and current land-cover change episodes and understand the human-environment relationships behind them. If our collective monitoring and understanding of land-cover change continues to lag severely behind those changes, how can humanity mitigate any negative consequences of land-cover change and try to prevent avoidable future problems? While individual examples of sustainable use of forests, for example, are plentiful in both developing and developed countries, the study of land-cover change currently would profit from strategies to apply the lessons of these individual positive examples over a greater area. Also, many local studies are currently unrelated to broader spatial and temporal trends, so the relevance of these studies is questioned (especially by policy makers) even though they contain a wealth of detailed information. Remote sensing combined with directed multidisciplinary field studies may offer one strategy to "catch up" with land-cover change.

Regardless of how one chooses a geographic area of interest, the land-cover change community faces a tremendous challenge related to discerning the relationship between information generated over a wide range of spatial extents and temporal durations. Inherent in many land-cover change studies is the goal of relating detailed studies of a small area, such as those at the plot, site, or landscape level (see the section on spatial patterns of change in this chapter for our definitions of these) to those conducted over larger spatial extents at the regional, continental, and global levels. One crucial puzzle we face is how to take advantage of the wealth of detailed work by individual researchers of different disciplines studying in contrasting geographic areas and relate the information from each of these cases to larger areas.

How can this synthesis be accomplished? What strategies can we use to help integrate all the varying analytical "lenses" used by scholars from a variety of social and physical science disciplines? Is it possible to build a geographic "quilt" of individual case studies such that it ultimately spans a large geographic area? Can we make individual case studies more comparable and compatible with each other such that we can identify significant trends manifest across all cases? While each land-cover researcher moves forward in his or her individual research endeavors, the broader land-cover change community as a collective group would probably benefit by generating a library of compatible studies (e.g., see chapter 13). Studies that are well documented with respect to their spatial and temporal dimensions can inform and build on one another. Specific articulation of the spatial and temporal parameters in each land-cover change study would significantly ease case-to-case integration and compatibility. While this proposition is simple, it is a collective-action problem, yet it may yield synergistic results that are critical for land-cover change research to progress. Moreover, diverse spatial and temporal perspectives will help the student and researcher understand how contrasting processes relate to each other and will help place a given case study in a broader context.

Human Decision Making

We propose a framework to aid in assessing land-cover change based on three critical attributes for categorizing and relating processes of human-environment dynamics. We stated earlier that space and time provide a common setting in which all biophysical processes operate. In addition, we can emphasize the important human

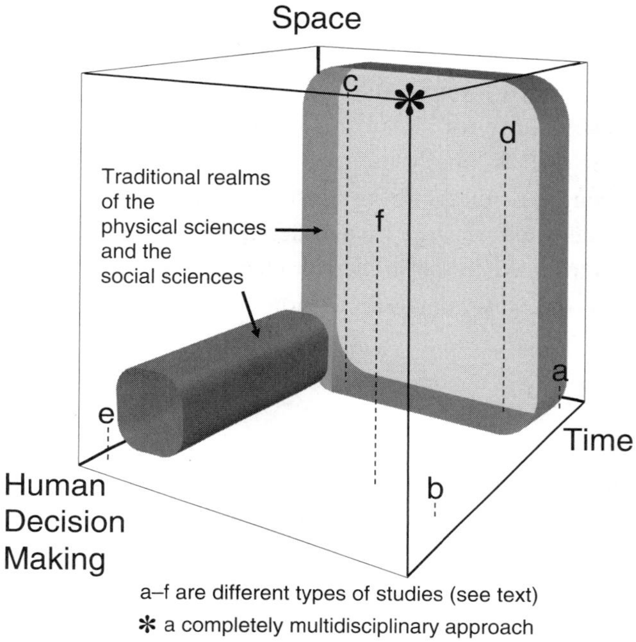

Figure 3.2
A three-dimensional framework, using space, time, and human decision making, can be used to distinguish the traditional realms of the natural and social sciences and different types of land-cover change studies.

aspects of land-cover change, a central theme throughout this book. When land-cover change processes incorporate human activities (NRC 1998), human decision making also becomes important. We can visualize this in figure 3.2 using three axes: space, time, and human decision making (Agarwal et al. 2002; Grove et al. 2002). This figure links together three important attributes in land-cover change research. The traditional, contrasting realms of the natural and social sciences also can be depicted in this framework, as well as categories of research or individual studies.

A robust understanding of land-cover change requires a multidisciplinary approach including an understanding of both biophysical phenomena, generally in the realm of the natural sciences, and phenomena involving human decision making, generally in the realm of the social sciences. Specific contrasting types of studies important to land-cover change research also can be seen in this figure: time-series studies and dynamic models with no human component (*a*); dynamic studies with human decision making explicitly incorporated (*b*); most traditional GIS studies (*c*);

GIS studies with an explicit temporal component and models such as those using cellular automata (*d*); econometric and game-theoretic studies (*e*); and recent multidisciplinary, dynamic, spatially explicit studies and models such as those using agent-based approaches (*f*). The space-vs.-time plane of the framework depicts strictly biogeophysical phenomena, traditionally the realm of the natural sciences, while phenomena mainly involving human choice and institutions, generally in the realm of the social sciences, are depicted near the human decision-making axis. The asterisk in figure 3.2 marks the ultimate goal of land-cover change research—a synthesis incorporating spatial, temporal, and human dimensions.

Scale: A Problematic Word

Both social and ecological processes can operate at different spatial extents and temporal durations (Allen and Hoekstra 1992; Ehleringer and Field 1993). Finding significant variance between study findings is in part hindered by a lack of a clear articulation of measures used in various studies and the lack of a vocabulary that crosses disciplinary boundaries (E. Moran 1984b, 1990). A glossary of terminology would facilitate communication of this information across disciplines.

The word "scale" is often heard in the context of land-cover change. Unfortunately, as described in Agarwal et al. (2002) and M. Turner et al. (2001), "scale" is often a confusing term in land-cover change research because it has conflicting meaning across disciplines. Notably, geography and the other social sciences, core disciplines in land-cover change studies, often use "scale" to infer opposite meanings. Geographers define "scale" as the ratio of length of a unit distance (scale bar) on a paper map to the length of that same unit distance on the ground (Greenhood 1964). Thus, a large-scale map usually shows more detail but covers less area (e.g., a paper map of a small town, produced at a 1:10,000 scale—the ratio between a given distance measured on the map [1] and the same distance measured on the ground [10,000] using the same ruler), while a small-scale map usually shows less detail but covers more area (e.g., a paper map of the entire United States, produced at a 1:6,000,000 scale). To the geographer the scale bar itself is what is large or small. Unfortunately, most other social scientists give opposite meanings to the terms large-scale and small-scale. For example, in these disciplines, a large-scale study generally means it covers a large spatial extent, and a small-scale study is a more detailed study covering a small area. Used in this way, the word "scale" can generally be dropped completely with little change in the meaning of the sentence.

To clarify this confusion, Agarwal et al. (2002) propose two other terms that carry more intuitive meaning—"fine-scale" and "broad-scale"—and, interestingly, M. Turner et al. (2001) independently proposed similar terms. In this book, we have made the decision to use other more specific and clearly defined terms in place of "scale" whenever possible and if they are available. For example, by substituting spatial extent, spatial resolution, temporal duration, or temporal interval (all defined in detail later in the chapter) in place of "scale," we feel multidisciplinary communication is strengthened.

Terms that describe the spatial and temporal characteristics of land-cover features or processes are critical for land-cover change research, yet these adjectives often have conflicting or ambiguous meanings. For example, terms like "long" and "short" can describe both distance and time, while space can refer to an area or a volume. Overcoming incongruent and ambiguous language presents an important challenge as land-cover change studies strive to link disciplinary studies of human-environment relationships.

Spatial Patterns of Change

Fortunately, we already have many words that are widely used across all disciplines and differentiate various temporal durations: day, week, month, year, decade, century, and millennium. However, different terminologies have been developed and employed in various disciplines to help communicate differences in spatial extents. After numerous sessions of trying to come to a common understanding among our affiliated anthropologists, geographers, political scientists, forest ecologists, demographers, historians, and others at our research center, we settled on several terms depicting various levels of spatial extent: globe, continent, region, location, landscape, site, and plot. Figure 3.3 illustrates how processes that affect forests can vary at different levels of spatial extent.

We use "globe" (in the context of land-cover change) to mean the terrestrial surface of Earth (about 150×10^6 km^2). "Continent" is at first glance also rather self-explanatory, referring to the seven great land masses on Earth (which range in area from 10×10^6 to 50×10^6 km^2). While this may be clear at present (though, on closer examination, the Europe/Asia division seems rather arbitrary and politically motivated), it is important to remember that plate tectonics has moved and rearranged the continents through past ages. A "region" is a subdivision of a continent, though it may comprise islands in one area of ocean (ranging from 100,000 to

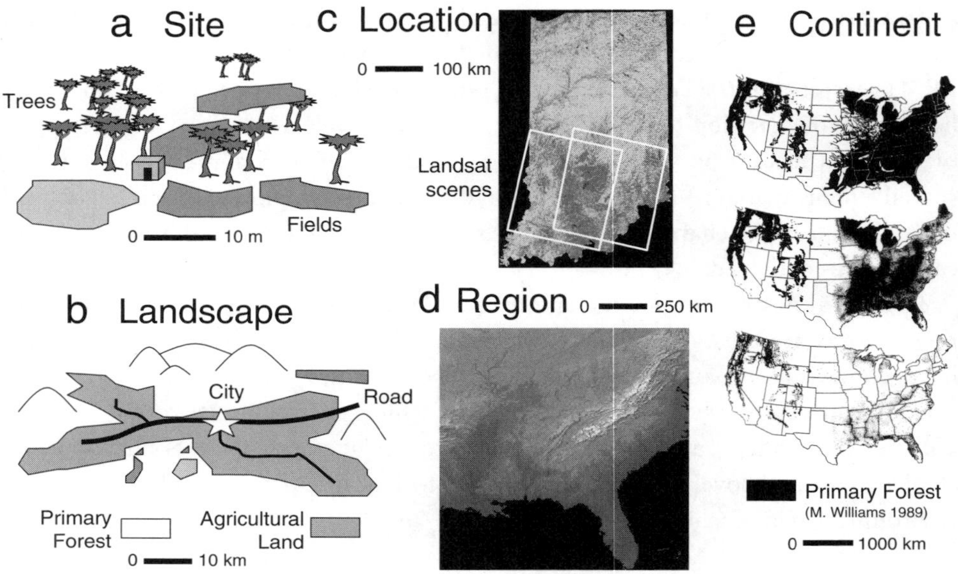

Figure 3.3
Anthropogenic land-cover change processes vary at different levels of spatial extent. Different factors influence land-cover change at different levels (see text for a more detailed explanation). (*e* from M. Williams 1989.)

10×10^6 km^2). A region may encompass one or multiple countries, or only a fraction of a country in the case of larger ones, such as the Midwest of the United States containing Ohio, Indiana, Illinois, Michigan, and so on. Alternatively, we can consider a region to be multiple countries, such as the region comprising the countries of Central America. The term "location" is defined in more detail in chapter 6, but we use it to designate the area captured within a time series of Landsat satellite images (from 15,000 to 30,000 km^2). The term "landscape" designates a fraction of a location and it can range from 100 to 10,000 km^2. We use the term "site" to describe a relatively small geographic extent (from 10 to 10,000 hectares) within which ecological and social fieldwork might be conducted by an individual or team of researchers. Therefore, a site is a local area that can be traversed on foot. Sites have been historically important to land-cover change research because it is at this spatial extent that household interviews and community surveys are conducted and at which institutional analysis usually takes place. Moreover, sites are particularly important as we strive to connect theory and empirical data on individual and community decision making to broader measures of space, time, and human decision making. Plots are the smallest level of spatial extent (from a fraction of a square meter to 10,000 m^2) and are usually used in the context of the direct measurement of vegetation in the field (see chapter 5). Plots, sites, landscapes, and locations are the levels at which land-cover change studies tend to collect field-based data relevant to forests and how they change.

A difficult problem facing researchers of land-cover change is that human-induced forest change processes (e.g., deforestation) exhibit different dynamic patterns, or "space-time footprints," at different levels of analysis (see figure 3.3). It is apparent that one simply cannot add up, or aggregate, observations of changes at the site level and generate those observed patterns at larger extents, such as at regional and continental levels. We can illustrate this with a simple example. Let us assume we observe at a particular site a large old-growth tree being cut in a single day, thereby clearing an area of about 100 m^2 (*a* in figure 3.3). At first glance, a simple linear extrapolation may suggest that to clear primary forest from a continent, an area of about 1×10^{12} m^2, it would take more than 27 million years, an obviously fanciful estimate. History shows that the eastern United States (see *e* in figure 3.3) was almost completely cleared of primary forest in a period of around 300 years (M. Williams 1989). One obvious problem uncovered by this example is that the deforestation of the eastern United States was a complex process. It started in the early seventeenth century as several hundred colonists using medieval technologies cleared fields near Boston and Jamestown, two of the earliest colonies. By 1800, hundreds of thousands of colonists were clearing forest, and firewood supplied virtually all of the country's energy needs. In the late 1890s, the last large expanses of old-growth forest were being cleared from the Midwest for agricultural use and export wood products. Today, few, if any, of the last remaining small patches of primary forest (now accounting for less than 0.01 percent of the original area) are experiencing clearing (M. Davis 1996).

Diverse patterns of forest change are apparent across a wide range of spatial extents (see figure 3.3). Therefore, it is important that researchers clearly articulate the spatial extent of their respective studies so this diversity can be identified and any trends documented. At the site level, patterns of forests and fields (*a* in figure 3.3) may be affected by household economics, available family labor and technologies, land tenure, local institutions, cultural practices, ethnic backgrounds, and microclimates. At the site level (in an open-access situation), for example, optimal foraging theory would predict that certain tree species used for important products would be diminished in areas closer to households and along trails than in less accessible areas (Schweik 2000). At broader spatial extents at the landscape level (*b* in figure 3.3), land-cover change patterns may be a function of topography, proximity to city and road, city population, urban demand, and the institutional landscape (county/district institutional differences). At the location level, topographic relief, urbanization, population density, transportation infrastructure, and county institutional differences may play a role (*c* in figure 3.3, based on Indiana Gap data; see also chapter 6).

A regional spatial analysis may exhibit forest and deforestation patterns that are the result of factors such as topographic relief, regional climate, soils, population density, state institutional differences, and broader intrastate political differences (*d* in figure 3.3, a shaded relief image of topography from the Satellite Radar Topography Mission data [http://www2.jpl.nasa.gov/srtm/p_status.htm]). A continental analysis may highlight patterns in forest cover that are the result of broader spatial and temporal physical and human processes such as climate, historical human migrations and technological development, as well as state, national, and global institutions (*e* in figure 3.3).

Institutional Landscapes

Elinor Ostrom and others define "institutions" as the rules that humans follow, or the "rules-in-use," and as the mechanisms established to monitor and enforce those rules (E. Ostrom 1990; E. Ostrom et al. 1994; Schweik et al. 1997). Institutions can be formally designated by national, state, or local legislation, such as environmental statutes, but also can exist in a variety of other forms, such as the standard operating procedures of an organization, or informal social norms established by communities of people. Institutions, like the forests they govern, frequently carry spatial and temporal attributes and often change shape and composition over time. Schweik (1998) refers to these spatial and temporal distributions as "institutional landscapes."

Institutions are human-crafted mechanisms designed to alter human behavioral response in a given physical and social setting. Humans use rule configurations and monitoring and sanctioning mechanisms in an attempt to change their behavior. The incentive structure that institutions create raises the costs of undertaking certain actions while reducing the cost of other actions. Effectively enforced institutions can be just as important an influence on how humans impact land-cover change as biophysical factors, such as topographic attributes, or portions of the built environment (e.g., transportation infrastructure). Institutions, therefore, can be an important factor determining forest patterns across all the levels presented in figure 3.3.

Institutional landscapes vary with spatial extent and temporal duration. At the broader spatial levels of the location, region, or continent, international treaties are often negotiated (with varying degrees of success) with the goal of placing restrictions on the actions of organizations (e.g., companies and government agencies) associated with one or more countries. More common are the broad national laws that may place requirements or limitations on the actions of organizations or individuals. Similarly, environmental laws which affect forests are often created at other levels of governance, such as state or city zoning ordinances. Similarly, less formal institutions can be created, and these often have spatial attributes. Organizations, such as the U.S. Department of Agriculture Forest Service, sometimes create standard operating procedures that designate how and where operational-level actions may take place, for example, restricting forest cutting within certain distances of riparian areas. At the site or landscape level, social norms within communities may establish less formal (unwritten) rules for private property or communal ownership through which activities are required, permitted, or prohibited. Institutions also have a temporal dimension. A particular rule may be long-lived or, alternatively, may depend on political cycles and exist for only a brief period of time. For example, Schweik (1998) describes three different institutional configurations that governed the Hoosier National Forest between 1985 and 1992.

Temporal Patterns of Change

Human-induced land-cover changes can be portrayed on a timeline. Figure 3.4 shows two episodes of forest change in Indiana: (1) the progressive elimination of the primary forests from the state by colonists during the nineteenth century and (2) the regrowth of secondary forests during the twentieth century on less than a quarter of the state's area. Both episodes probably followed some type of logistic, or S-shaped curve. The figure shows that deforestation rates probably have varied widely, starting slowly, progressing to a maximum in the 1860s, and then slowing as the last remnants of primary forest were cleared in the early years of the twentieth century. Surveyed in the early 1800s, Indiana was 87 percent forested (the remainder of the state was covered with wetlands and prairie; see *b* in plate 4) before settlement by colonists, yet by 1870 and 1900 primary forest covered 30 percent and 6.5 percent of the state, respectively. The initial deforestation was largely the result

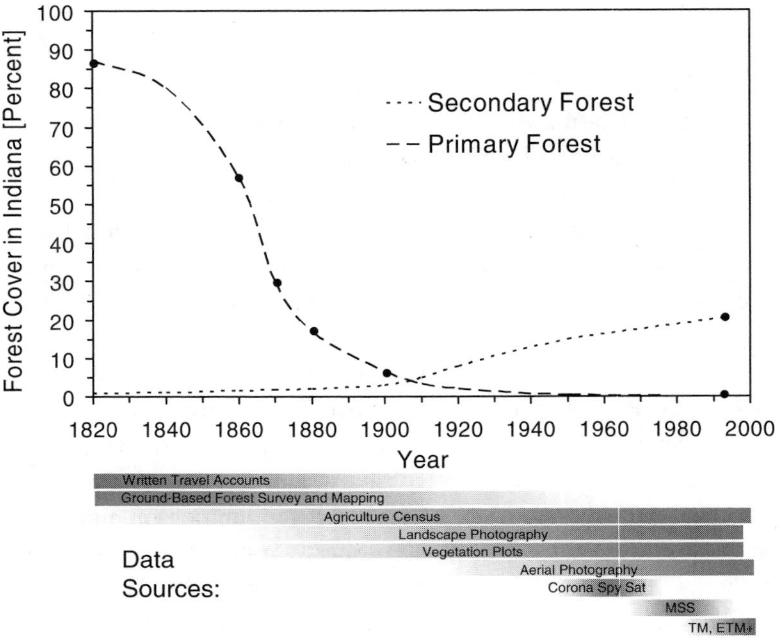

Figure 3.4
A timeline showing two distinct episodes of land-cover change affecting Indiana's forests. MSS, TM, and ETM+, Landsat Multispectral Scanner, Thematic Mapper, and Enhanced Thematic Mapper Plus.

of clearing by colonists for crops and grazing. Only a few dozen small patches of uncut forest remain today (M. Davis 1996). Secondary forest cover expanded during the 1900s and covered more than 20 percent of the state in 1992 (mostly on lands of higher topographic relief; see *a* and *c* in plate 4). Now, however, little secondary forest cover is currently being added. Today, an estimated 4.5 million acres of forested land, mostly secondary forest, exist in Indiana, covering about 20 percent of the state (IDNR 1997). Estimated areas at particular dates were taken from Indiana Department of Natural Resources data (IDNR 1997), Jackson (1997), and G. Parker (1997). The data sources available to document these land-cover changes also vary greatly through time (see figure 3.4). The availability of a particular dataset is restricted by the history of the technology that is used to generate it. For example, satellite images from the Landsat Multispectral Scanner (MSS) instrument are mostly available from 1972 to 1992.

Space-Time Diagram

Anthropogenic processes affect trees and forests over a wide range of spatial extents and temporal durations. Figure 3.5, a modified Stommel diagram (Stommel 1963), shows that processes that affect woody plants vary across a wide range of extents and durations. The diagram is constructed such that the spatial extent of a land-cover change process, measured in units of square meters, is plotted along an exponentially scaled y-axis, and the temporal duration of the process, measured in units of days, is plotted along an exponentially scaled x-axis. The figure employs log-log scales of time (on the x-axis in keeping with the timeline's orientation) and area (on the y-axis). The log-log plot is useful in accommodating a wide range of durations and areas on the same plot. Conventional subdivisions (levels) of time are labeled, and corresponding levels of area are given. This space-time diagram is a third key graphic in land-cover change studies (together with the map and timeline). It uses relative scales of space and time (how large or small an area is, or how long or short a time duration is) as opposed to the absolute scales used in maps (geographic coordinates, such as latitude and longitude) and timelines (year A.D. or B.P.). The ovals in figure 3.5 represent our "best-guess" estimates of the range in extent and duration of each episode in which those processes take place; the actual boundaries of these processes in the figure are debatable until actual measures are compiled.

The forest-change processes in figure 3.5 range from felling an individual tree, which might typically take place in one day's time and affect an area of 100 m^2, to the deforestation of a continent, which might take place over several hundred years and affect an area of millions of square kilometers. A forest-change zone (bounded by dashed lines) marks the general range of extents and durations of these processes. The distribution of processes along the diagonal of figure 3.5 reveals that, typically, processes that cover small areas happen during short periods of time (processes of lesser magnitude; see inset in figure 3.5), while processes that affect large areas take longer times to occur (processes of greater magnitude). In general, processes that involve gases (atmospheric phenomena) are located in the upper left portion of the diagram; processes that affect solids (geologic phenomena) are located in the lower right portion; and processes that affect liquids, such as water (hydrologic phenomena), are found along the diagonal. Therefore, process dynamism increases to the upper left of the diagram and decreases to the lower right (see inset in figure 3.5).

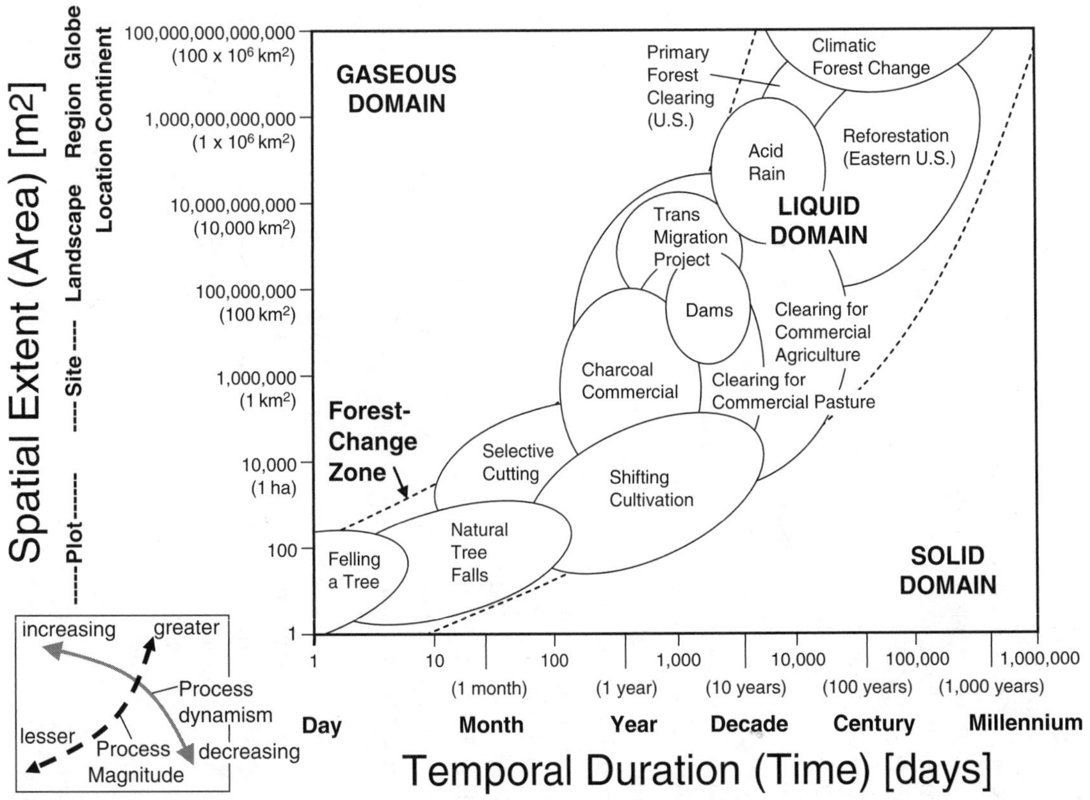

Figure 3.5
A space-time diagram shows how various human-influenced processes that affect woody plants and forests vary across a wide range of spatial extents (in square meters) and temporal durations (in days). Ellipses circumscribe the general range in extent and duration of some examples of land-cover change processes that affect trees and forests (see text for a more detailed description).

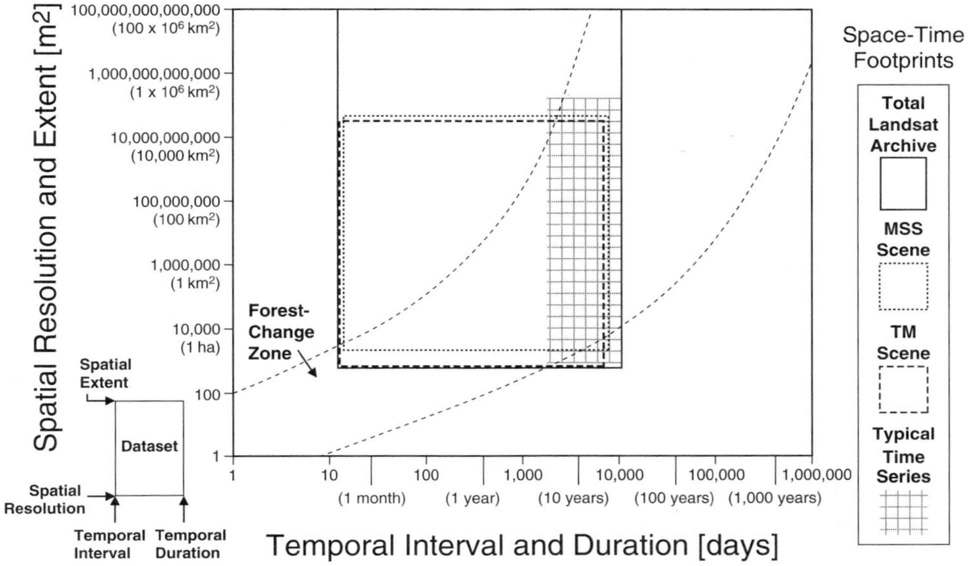

Figure 3.6
Many different datasets can be described by using four important parameters plotted on a space-time diagram: spatial extent, spatial resolution, temporal duration, and temporal interval. The four values determine the dimensions of a space-time footprint of a particular dataset (rectangular areas). The cross-hatched pattern shows the footprint of a typical Landsat image time-series dataset used in a land-cover change study.

Plotting Datasets on a Space-Time Diagram

Space-time diagrams also can be used to explore what datasets would be particularly relevant in examining a given land-cover change process. Figure 3.6 shows an example of how a widely used remote-sensing dataset (Landsat satellite images; see chapter 6) is plotted on a space-time diagram.

Four parameters are particularly useful in describing a dataset (see inset in figure 3.6): (1) *spatial extent* describes the extent of the area it covers; (2) *temporal duration* describes the length of time over which it was collected, such as the time between the oldest and newest images of a satellite image time series; (3) *spatial resolution* describes the smallest spatial unit that makes up the dataset; and (4) *temporal interval*, or sampling frequency, describes the smallest time step used to describe it.

Figure 3.6 shows how these four parameters can be used to describe the Landsat dataset. Each value determines the dimensions of a "sampling footprint." The resulting rectangle in the figure thus represents the spatial and temporal dimensions of the dataset. The figure shows four such footprints for Landsat datasets: (1) the MSS archive for a single location, (2) the Landsat Thematic Mapper (TM) archive for a single location, (3) the entire Landsat archive, and (4) a typical Landsat time series used in a land-cover change study. The spatial extent of the dataset controls the top boundary of the dataset sampling footprints. For example, a single image acquired by the TM covers an area of 170 × 185 km, while the total Landsat system of satellites has acquired images that have inventoried almost the entire extent of Earth's terrestrial surface. The bottom boundary of each rectangle is controlled by the spatial resolution of the dataset. For example, a single picture element, or pixel, of a Landsat 4 TM image covers an area of 28.5 × 28.5 m on the ground, while an MSS image pixel from Landsat 1 is 56 × 79 m. The left boundary of the rectangle corresponds to the temporal interval or sampling frequency of the dataset. For example, Landsat satellites return to a given location and acquire an image as frequently as every 16 or 18 days (see chapter 6). Finally, the right boundary of each rectangle in figure 3.6 represents the temporal duration of the dataset. Landsat data have been collected from 1972 to the present, a period of more than thirty years. These temporal duration and interval values are theoretical maxima, since cloud cover or lack of a receiving station in a particular location, for example, may further restrict image availability (see also figure 6.6). Lack of funds in a given study for images or processing may further restrict a dataset's space-time footprint, often making the duration of a given image time series shorter and the interval between individual images in a time series longer. The cross-hatched pattern in figure 3.6 shows the space-time footprint of a typical Landsat image time-series dataset used in a land-cover change study (sampling every four to five years from 1972 to 2003, in two adjacent locations).

A particular dataset can inform a study on those land-cover change processes (see figure 3.5) whose extents and durations are coincident with that dataset's time-space footprint (see figure 3.6). Landsat satellite images often are important to land-cover change studies because they inform over a significant portion of spatial and temporal parameters that are important when studying forest changes (the forest-change zone in figures 3.5 and 3.6). The sampling footprint of a given Landsat image time series in figure 3.6 may be appropriate to inform how certain land-cover change processes affect woody plants in figure 3.5 (such as building a hydroelectric dam), but that same dataset may be too coarse in resolution and too infrequently sampled to measure other processes (such as a particular farmer felling an individual tree).

Similarly, Landsat data may not be appropriate to study many broader-level atmospheric phenomena.

Temporal duration and interval are analogous to spatial extent and resolution, respectively. The terms *resolution* and *extent* often are used to describe both temporal and spatial levels; however, we have attempted to make these distinctions more explicit so readers will not be confused by which dimensions we are referring to in any particular discussion, and we think these careful distinctions in terminology are important for enhancing future dialogue involving land-cover change.

Land-Cover Change Data Sources

Processes of interest to the land-cover change community occur at spatial extents as small as a fraction of a square millimeter (e.g., the exchange of gases in a leaf) and extend to the entire surface area of the Earth (roughly 510 million square kilometers). A researcher interested in forest change may determine that a Landsat image provides an appropriate spatial extent to capture that phenomenon, or alternatively, a researcher interested in phenomena related to leaf structure (such as gas exchange) might choose to work with a spatial resolution of 10^{-6} m (to view individual cells) and a spatial extent of roughly 20 cm. The same approach applies with respect to time. A researcher interested in studying the climate of a particular region may decide to collect precipitation data at a monthly temporal interval and use data collected over the duration of a year. In contrast, a researcher interested in investigating leaf respiration might choose a shorter sampling interval, such as a minute, and collect measurements for the duration of a day. Figure 3.7 illustrates how some commonly used datasets in land-cover change research may appear when plotted on a space-time diagram. Each dataset informs within a certain region of the space-time continuum, and it is often necessary to use several different datasets in combination to examine a particular land-cover change process. Setting one dataset within the context of another broader-level dataset (overlapping) may help to address questions related to the significance of a given finer-level piece of information in a broader context.

Each rectangle in figure 3.7 is associated with a different data source. The spatial extent of the dataset controls the top boundary of any rectangle in the figure. Sun-synchronous weather satellite images, collected by the advanced very high resolution radiometer (AVHRR), for example, are collected across the entire globe (both land and oceans) and hence have the largest spatial extent of the examples shown. The Landsat dataset, as a whole, has inventoried nearly the entire extent of Earth's

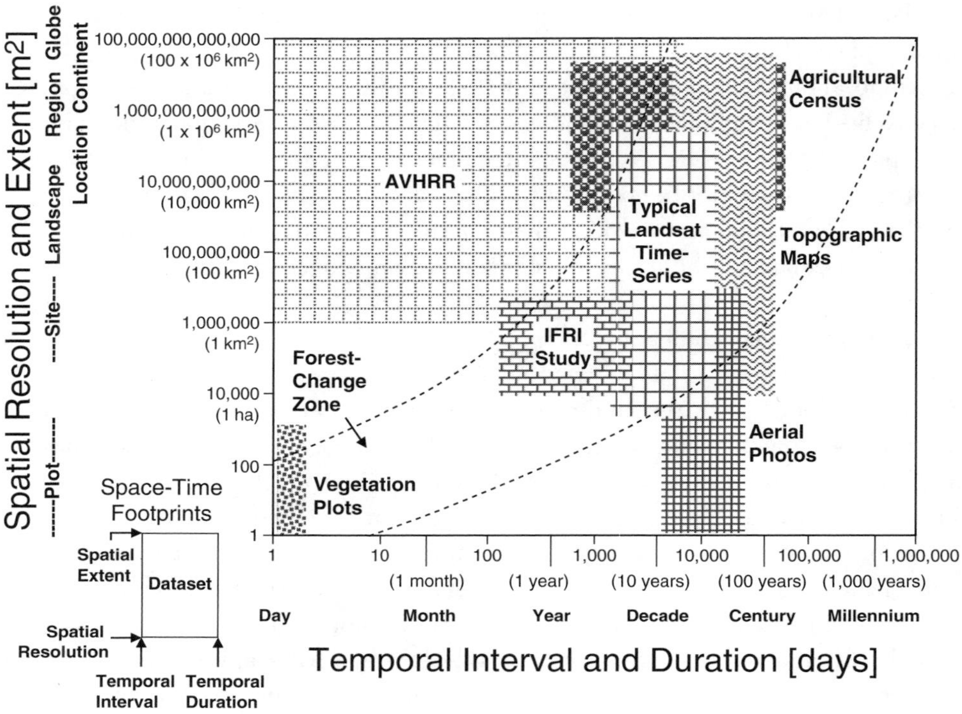

Figure 3.7
The space-time footprints of various datasets commonly used in land-cover change studies. Landsat images provide an important dataset because they cover a central range of both space and time, and can be used to efficiently position the collection of more detailed but costly data, such as vegetation plots or institutional analyses. AVHRR, advanced very high resolution radiometer; IFRI, International Forestry Resources and Institutions. (For IFRI studies, see chapter 4.)

terrestrial surface. Individual agriculture census datasets often cover entire states. The bottom boundary of each rectangle in figure 3.7 is controlled by the spatial resolution of the dataset. For satellite images a convenient measure of resolution is the area of an individual picture element. For example, acquired AVHRR images have a spatial resolution (at nadir) of 1.1 × 1.1 km. In contrast, most bands in a Landsat TM image contain pixels that measure 28.5 × 28.5 m on the ground. Topographic maps sometimes provide resolutions of one hectare or less, and aerial photography often provides resolution of a meter or less. The left boundary of any given rectangle shows the temporal interval of a dataset. Weather satellite images are collected many times in one day. Agriculture census data are commonly collected once a year, and aerial surveys are conducted about once every ten years. This temporal interval is similar for population census data. Landsat satellites return to a location and record data as frequently as every sixteen days. Finally, the right boundary of each rectangle in figure 3.7 represents the temporal duration of a dataset. For example, the duration of the Landsat data archive is more than thirty years. Agricultural censuses in the United States have been collected for well over one hundred years, for example, in Indiana since 1860.

The datasets shown in figure 3.7 are not inclusive of all possible datasets by any means but are used to illustrate how spatial and temporal attributes of a dataset may be displayed and compared and may help the researcher consider what datasets are appropriate to address a particular research question and phenomenon of interest. Researchers can consider the spatial and temporal dimensions of the datasets available to them and consider which ones apply to various levels of analysis. Landsat images provide an important dataset because they cover a central range of both space and time. Landsat data have a relatively fine spatial resolution and temporal interval, yet Landsat images still cover a relatively broad spatial extent, and image time series can have a duration of thirty years or more. However, no one dataset, including Landsat, can inform at every spatial extent or temporal duration; therefore a multidisciplinary approach using several different datasets in combination can be advantageous. Also, datasets which cover larger extents and longer durations can be used to efficiently position (as in a map) the collection of more detailed but costly data, such as vegetation plots or institutional analyses (International Forestry Resources and Institutions studies; see chapter 4). We also have shown that space-time diagrams can be used to plot contrasting land-cover change processes (see figure 3.5). Though not often stated, one of the keys to effective land-cover change research is ensuring that the dataset one uses to inform a study has the same spatial and temporal dimensionality as the process one is trying to understand. This can be accomplished rather simply, for example, by overlaying figures 3.5 and 3.7.

Conclusions

We feel it is important for researchers to articulate the spatial extent and temporal duration of an analysis clearly to place a particular study in a broader context of space and time. We hope our discussion will help diverse disciplines understand one another better and facilitate more multidisciplinary collaboration. We have presented a short description of three key diagrams: the map, the timeline, and the space-time diagram. For readers planning a research program, approaches like those described in this chapter may help them think through their scientific research strategies—strategies that hopefully will be cognizant of how land-cover change processes change across spatial and temporal levels and which datasets may be appropriate for studying particular processes. We also encourage readers to be particularly careful in their use of terms like "scale" so the results of their future research can cross disciplines more readily and with less confusion. Finally, we present these concepts and approaches because we think they can help to better leverage those resources available to the land-cover change scientist (or student) to produce significant results.

4

Multidisciplinary Research Relating Institutions and Forest Transformations

Catherine M. Tucker and Elinor Ostrom

In 1986, the Mexican government created the Monarch Butterfly Special Biosphere Reserve, and severely restricted use rights for the residents who had long depended on the forested mountains for their livelihood (Chapela and Barkin 1995; Merino 1999). People questioned why they should protect the forests when they had lost their legal rights. In a context of local resistance, overlapping responsibilities, unclear regulations, and limited resources, government authorities experienced difficulties administering the reserve (C. Tucker 2004). Rates of forest degradation and clearing increased, and researchers declared that the reserve had failed (Brower et al. 2002).

In 1998, a private landowner in southern Indiana felled many trees on his steeply sloped, forested lot on a reservoir shoreline, despite ordinances restricting clearing on the reservoir (Van der Dussen 1998a,b). Despite local outcry, judicial proceedings, and fines levied against the accused party, unauthorized tree-cutting occurred on other private parcels on the same reservoir in 2001–2002 (Van der Dussen 2002a,b).

For generations, the Kuna people of southern Panama have maintained their tropical rain forests through customs that limit extraction. They practice fishing and agroforestry, sell crafts, and exchange products with traders to benefit from markets as well as subsistence production. Their land tenure entails private fields, family holdings, and several types of communal property, all of which contribute to their livelihood (Ventocilla et al. 1995). In recent years, new roads into the region have facilitated the settlement of people from other parts of Panama, and an agricultural frontier has been advancing into the forests. The Panamanian government has considered the possibility of building an intercontinental highway through the region to Colombia. Although this plan is currently shelved, the ongoing migration to the region poses no less of a threat to the future of the Kuna and their highly biodiverse forests.

The above examples illustrate a few of the dilemmas and struggles that relate to the management of forest resources. Integral to all of these cases is the role of institutions, and the difficulty of crafting and maintaining effective institutions in a context of diverse, often conflicting interests and stakeholders. As a fundamental aspect of human social organization, institutions have been studied by researchers for a long time. Yet the study of institutions for natural resource management represents a new and dynamic field. Intense debates exist over the kinds of institutions, arrangements, and approaches that offer the greatest promise of desirable outcomes given the diversity of political economic, cultural, and environmental conditions that shape the world's forests. Therefore, the challenge is to conduct research that permits the identification of the patterns and relationships in successes (or failures) of forest management. By this means, we aim to discover the principles associated with effective institutions.

We define *institutions* as the formal and informal rules, the "dos and don'ts," that people recognize in a given situation (Dietz et al. 2002, 21). Formal rules-in-use include legislation, executive decisions, court decisions, and private contracts that are respected and enforced. If formal rules are widely ignored or unknown, they are not rules-*in-use*. Rules-in-use include formal rules that are generally followed, as well as customary rules that may evolve over time or be designed in settings where they are not legally recognized. The rules that people follow have direct and indirect ramifications for forests (or any natural resource), and shape conditions and processes of change. If institutions to govern forests are absent, unenforced, or poorly defined, the result is open access, leaving the forest in an unrestricted state. Degradation of the forest is then likely if an open-access forest contains commercially valuable species or the area around a forest experiences population growth leading to heavy use of the forest for subsistence or for other land uses.

The challenge of effective governance of forests relates to their attributes as common-pool resources. By definition, common-pool resources are those that are subtractable (subject to depletion) and for which exclusion is difficult (McKean 2000, 28–29). Common-pool resources include forests, watersheds, oceans, fisheries, and the stratosphere. These resources are important for humanity and planetary ecosystems, but overuse threatens their integrity. The future of these resources depends largely on human ability to craft new institutions, or improve existing ones, for sustainable resource management from local to regional to global scales.

Even clearly defined institutions are not always successful in stemming forest degradation. Therefore, researchers are faced with the challenge of identifying the circumstances in which sustainable forest management can be achieved and what types of institutional arrangements are most conducive to this goal. Given that ecological factors and social, political, and economic processes shape the outcomes of institutions for forest management, interdisciplinary research is needed to address the various relationships among variables that shape forest conditions.

This chapter highlights an approach to institutional analysis relevant to research on forest-change processes. The discussion also explores the importance of institutional analysis for multidisciplinary research on forest transformations as explored throughout this book. The discussion recognizes that institutional analysis benefits from the experience of other disciplines in the natural and social sciences in analyzing environmental processes and social conditions. While ecologists have tended to overlook the role of institutions in shaping the environment (Gibson et al. 2002), it is also the case that social scientists have sometimes overlooked the ways that biophysical conditions may influence how institutional arrangements affect outcomes (cf. Doornbos et al. 2000).

The importance of including variables related to both biophysical and social processes becomes apparent when institutional arrangements are evaluated. A recent study of the effectiveness of national parks concluded that they worked surprisingly well at reducing land-cover change within park boundaries as compared to the immediately surrounding landscape (Bruner et al. 2001). The study did not, however, note whether the differences between the protected area and the adjacent area had emerged prior or subsequent to park creation. This leaves open the possibility that the noted differences also reflected underlying biophysical conditions and not simply institutional arrangements. It also leaves open the possibility that use has shifted from within the parks to the immediate surroundings of the parks.

The challenge of analyzing institutions with reference to the natural environment becomes acute when the goal is to achieve sustainable use and management of a resource. Oakerson (1992) notes, "The analysis of the commons, therefore, should specify as precisely as possible the 'limiting conditions' that pertain to natural replenishment or maintenance of the resource. Physical limits established by nature or technology provide critical information for devising rules to maintain jointly beneficial use ..." (p. 44). Yet, evaluating and quantifying the limiting conditions relevant to a resource base is a nontrivial matter. Efforts to define and establish sustainable levels of extraction for renewable natural resources typically involve uncertainty. Institutional analysts, as well as ecologists, find that some of the critical information needed for management decisions and institutional design is unavailable. To deal with uncertainties that may include environmental fluxes and social change, institutional design implies a need for flexibility and adaptive capacity.

Major Questions

The problems of managing forests and the implications for global environmental change draw attention to a major question: Under what circumstances can common-pool resources be managed sustainably? Successful institutional design and implementation for management of global commons, such as the atmosphere and the oceans, have yet to emerge. Yet studies of resources with a smaller extent, including forests, alpine pastures, and hydrologic resources, have shown that it is possible for groups to manage them effectively over long periods of time (Netting 1976; E. Ostrom 1990; McKean 1992a,b). These studies raise two general questions: (1) What factors facilitate the development of effective institutions for common-pool resource management? (2) What factors facilitate the persistence of effective institutions for common-pool resource management?

When we turn to understanding how institutions specifically affect the incentives of various actors who affect forest transformations over time, we ask more specific questions, including

- How do institutions affect the incentives facing forest users (forest dwellers, timber corporations, transhumant populations, etc.)?
- How do these incentives encourage forest users to engage in the sustainable development or the destructive use of forests?
- Why do forest users establish collective-choice arrangements or continue to pursue independent strategies?
- How are forest users affected by government-driven development activities and policies?

These questions complement empirical analyses undertaken at higher-level (meso- and macrolevel) analyses to understand the patterns of forest change. Data collected at the local level also provide a critical dimension for informing multiscale and cross-scale analyses of the institutional, political, socioeconomic, and ecological factors associated with forest change. As we mentioned above, these questions must be addressed in light of good knowledge about the biophysical structure of a forest and the likely forest dynamics over time, independent of the incentives induced by institutions at multiple levels.

Ecologists and biologists already have learned the importance of an inclusive hierarchy of terms ranging from the most general level (e.g., animal, plant, and nonliving entities), through graduations (general types of animals, plants, and nonliving entities), down to very specific entities such as a particular species or subspecies. Only a few scientific explanations can be made at the most general level, such as those related to the basic differences between living and nonliving entities. Most scientific findings are established for specific entities, and efforts are made to establish over time whether the findings fit more general groupings of entities and all subclasses of the entity studied.

Recent Developments in Understanding Institutions

Social scientists are in the midst of a major theoretical and conceptual revolution to rethink basic institutional concepts. This dynamic process has resulted in new perspectives and efforts in institutional analysis and its closely linked corollary, policy analysis. The productivity of diverse researchers and approaches has led to what one scholar characterized as "Mountain islands of theoretical structure, intermingled with, and occasionally attached together by, foothills of shared methods and concepts, and empirical work, all of which [are] surrounded by oceans of descriptive work not attached to any mountain of theory" (Schlager 1997, 14). Our discussion here presents a coordinated effort to connect islands of theoretical structure to foothills of methods and concepts by means of comparable, rigorously empirical, and descriptive work.

Several decades ago, the concept of property rights was divided into two broad categories—well-defined property rights and poorly defined property rights. Private property and government property were grouped together as well-defined property rights. Poorly defined property rights included a vast array of possibilities embracing the total absence of any rights, rights that were under contest, and various forms of common property (all of which were presumed to be poorly defined). With this simple scheme, public policies were developed in many settings to declare all forests that were not already clearly privately owned to be government forests so as to ensure that all forests in a country had well-defined property rights (Arnold and Campbell 1986). With the substantial discoveries of common-property regimes that had clearly demarcated the rights and duties of many resource users in Europe (Netting 1976, 1982; Dahlman 1980; Maass and Anderson 1986) and Asia (Coward 1979; Siy 1982; McKean 1992a,b) over centuries of intensive use, common-property regimes were added to private and government property regimes as encompassing potentially well-defined right systems. A wide variety of property rights enable users to overcome collective-action problems, but none of them is guaranteed to work in all situations (Libecap 1995).

As scholars have continued to undertake extensive research on the impact of institutional arrangements on environmental resources, simply adding one more very broad category (common property) to government and private properties still has proved too coarse to be useful in making clear predictions and explanations about the effect of institutions on resource characteristics. The examples at the opening of this chapter indicate that all public, private, and communal forests may experience degradation related to inadequate or conflicting institutions (see also Dietz et al. 2003). Consequently, developing research protocols that dig into the rules actually used to determine who is an authorized user of a resource; what forest products can be harvested when, where, and for what use; how forest users will be monitored; what sanctions will be applied for nonconformance with rules; and how a local governance regime is nested in higher-level regimes has been an essential step in developing an appropriate set of research methods to address the core questions identified above. Fortunately, property-rights theorists have provided useful analytical tools that can be adopted in the conduct of empirical research (see Libecap 1989; Sandler 1995).

We begin from basic hypotheses derived from case studies. We expect that the effective institutions for conserving forests will be evident by the maintenance of forest cover and total forest area over time, and that ineffective or weak institutions will be associated with diminishing forest cover and area (Devlin and Grafton 1998). Similarly, we draw on existing research to hypothesize that a growing population does not necessarily lead to forest destruction (Tiffen et al. 1994). Rather, we hypothesize that population growth may be associated with forest users becoming more aware of forest scarcity and developing new institutions to cope more effectively with the problem of overharvesting. Unfortunately, we cannot assert this to be a regular outcome since increased population has been shown to lead to both better and worse forest governance (Fox 1993a; Agrawal 2000; Varughese 2000). We anticipate that institutional arrangements may develop when people realize that important resources are becoming scarce and have the local resources needed to increase their vigilance regarding forest use. We examine the current state of research on these hypotheses further below.

Approaches and Methods for Institutional Analysis

Methods for analyzing institutional arrangements draw on a broad set of theories and encompass diverse data collection methods commonly employed by social scientists. These include, but are not limited to, surveys, informal and formal interviews, censuses, and polls. More recently, researchers have incorporated remotely sensed image analysis and geographic information systems (GIS) (see chapters 6 and 7) as a means to study land-cover change through time, and thus analyze institutional outcomes (Southworth and Tucker 2001; Schweik and Thomas 2002). Two approaches that have been developed specifically to examine institutions within a multidisciplinary perspective include the Institutional Analysis and Development (IAD) framework and the International Forestry Resources and Institutions (IFRI) research program. Many scholars working in the Americas, Africa, Asia, and Europe have incorporated these approaches for institutional analysis as components of multidisciplinary projects.

The Institutional Analysis and Development Framework

The IAD framework presents a set of elements that are present in any type of institutional analysis. It has roots in the theories of rational choice, collective action, common property, and social capital. As a framework, however, it does not depend on a specific theory, but directs researchers toward certain questions about human interaction and institutional functions and processes. The focus of IAD is the action situation, which is composed of participants, positions, actions that respond to information and relate to potential outcomes, and the costs and benefits associated with actions and outcomes. Actors who participate in action situations have preferences, information-processing capabilities, selection criteria for making decisions, and individual resources that shape their range of feasible options. The framework recognizes that action situations are in turn shaped by the attributes of the physical world, the human community, and rules-in-use. Ultimately, action situations influence patterns of interaction and outcomes (E. Ostrom et al. 1994).

International Forestry Institutions and Resources Research Program

The IFRI research program is an interdisciplinary, rigorously comparative methodology for investigating the social and biophysical factors that influence forest conditions and shape resource use and management through time. The program incorporates principles of the IAD framework for recognizing multidisciplinary dimensions that relate to institutional arrangements. Thus, it integrates institutional analysis with approaches from the natural and social sciences to facilitate analysis of the interrelationships among the many variables that shape forest conditions and institutional arrangements. It addresses the activities and results of community, government, and nongovernment organizations (NGOs) dealing with forest issues, and the influence on sustainability of socioeconomic, political, and legal dimensions (E. Ostrom and Wertime 2000, 243). The research focuses on the local level because it bears great potential for shedding light on the contexts of human choices that most intimately shape forest conditions and their ties with macrolevel processes (Arizpe et al. 1994; Schmink 1994).

The IFRI program grew out of a concern to address the many knowledge gaps that exist in our understanding of how human choices impact processes of forest change (E. Ostrom 1998b). The program aims to collect comparable data in numerous sites that will assist communities, policy makers, and scientists in analyzing and addressing the factors that shape human action and forest conditions, and to provide policy recommendations based on comparative analyses (E. Ostrom and Wertime 2000). Many of the studies reported in this book include the methodology as part of the data collection strategy as the methods have been integrated into the overall research methods used by colleagues at the Center for the Study of Institutions, Population, and Environmental Change (CIPEC) in their field research.

The program derives "from an examination of diverse policy processes rather than from a model of a specific problem such as deforestation" (E. Ostrom 1998b, 16). It lends itself to testing the numerous models and hypotheses that exist concerning the relationships between humans and forests. By including a wide range of questions drawn from many disciplinary perspectives, IFRI has the potential to address new questions as they emerge. This program is among the first to collect reliable forest measurements from plot data in association with systematic, detailed data collection on socioeconomic, demographic, institutional, and biophysical characteristics in multiple sites across time.

Data Collection Methods and Protocols

The IFRI methodology used in many field sites incorporates ten protocols (table 4.1). Researchers in the natural and social sciences collaborated to develop these protocols, which address a broad range of socioeconomic, demographic, and biophysical variables, as well as institutional dimensions that may influence the relationships among people, forests, and institutions. The protocols were designed to apply to forests and forest users throughout the world. The questions require specific quantitative data and capture qualitative assessments and perceptions concerning forests, their stakeholders, and relevant organizations, as well as relationships among them.

To collect data, researchers arrange in-depth group discussions with a variety of respondents (e.g., residents, authorities, members of formal and informal groups that use the forests, representatives of national organizations and NGOs, and other knowledgeable sources) during the process of completing the protocols. The goal

Table 4.1
Data Collection Forms and Information Collected

IFRI Form	Information Collected
Forest form	Size, ownership, internal differentiation, products harvested, uses of products, changes in forest area, appraisal of forest condition
Forest plot form	Tree, shrub, and sapling size; density and species type within 1-, 3-, and 10-m circles for a sample of plots at each site
Settlement form	Demographic information, relation to markets and administrative centers, geographic information about the settlement
User group form	Size, socioeconomic status, attributes of forest user groups
Forest–user group relationship form	Products harvested by user groups and their purposes
Forest products form	Details on three most important forest products (as defined by user group), amount and market value of products harvested, uses of products, changes in harvesting patterns, alternative sources and costs of substitutes, harvesting tools and techniques, harvesting rules
Forest association form	Institutional information about forest association (if one exists at the site), including association's activities, rules, structure, membership, record keeping
Nonharvesting organization form	Information about organizations that make rules regarding a forest(s) but do not use the forest, including structure, personnel, resource mobilization, record keeping
Organizational and inventory form	Information about all organizations (harvesting or not) that govern a forest
Site overview form	Site overview map, local wage rates, local units of measurement, exchange rates, interview information

IFRI, International Forestry Resources and Institutions.
Source: from Ostrom 1998, 19.

is to obtain reliable, representative data (cf. H. Bernard 1995). Data collection methods include participatory rural appraisal, formal and informal interviews, archival research, and participant observation. Respondents are selected primarily through purposive sampling methods; the team endeavors to identify key stakeholders and knowledgeable individuals, and to speak with each individual or group that is likely to provide relevant knowledge or perspectives. In some cases, researchers also use random sampling methods to select additional individuals and households to interview or survey. These methods work well to address the social structure and the institutions as well as the many demographic, political-economic, and cultural aspects. Moreover, they provide flexibility to adapt to any cultural context.

Whenever possible, a research team incorporates researchers from the region and local assistants. The inclusion of team members who know the culture and the environment facilitates the research process, generally easing integration into the locale and reducing the risks of misinterpretation of events and social gaffes that may occur when outside researchers first enter a community. Moreover, it can increase the transparency of the research process.

Two of the protocols specifically focus on forest conditions and changes through time. A summary of the forest notes the current conditions, characteristics, and rules-in-use for the forest. It includes a forester's assessment of current forest conditions relative to similar forests in the area (biodiversity, commercial value, subsistence value) and residents' perceptions of recent forest changes and the suitability of the existing rules-in-use. Forest mensuration takes place in plots distributed randomly through study forests. Forest data include species composition, tree diameter at breast height, tree height, and observations of plot conditions. In recent years, many researchers also have adopted the use of global positioning systems to record the coordinates of the forest plots to locate plots on maps and remotely sensed images.

Protocols for collecting data on communities (settlements) provide historical, demographic, political-economic, and geographic contexts for understanding the relationships between the residents and their forests. Data on the user groups include consideration of group composition (demography, ethnic and religious characteristics), economic activities, and background. Where users are organized into formal groups (associations), a protocol collects information on the characteristics of the organization.

The forest products and institutional arrangements recognized by user groups receive attention in a general form that overviews the relationships between a certain group and a specific forest (forest–user group relationship form). Another protocol captures information about the three most important products for each group, including quantities harvested, their uses, and availability. These protocols are also adapted to reflect important nonconsumptive products valued by user groups, such as recreation, nature appreciation, and worship in sacred areas. Further information is collected on organizations that influence forest uses and institutions, but do not utilize resources themselves (nonharvesting organizations). These groups may include NGOs and government oversight and enforcement agencies. A site overview form records basic information on site selection, sampling methods, and team composition. A summary, organizational inventory form delineates the relationships and institutional arrangements that characterize the formal and informal groups, organizations, and entities that relate to the forest and potentially influence its conditions.

The protocols enable researchers to collect information on institutional arrangements at multiple levels in relationship to the forest, the user groups, user group associations, and product exploitation. Achieving an informed analysis of rules and the roles of institutions presents a number of challenges for researchers. When rules exist as formal institutions, such as written legislation or legal precedents enforced by authorities, researchers can readily identify them. It is more difficult to ascertain informal rules that affect how people relate to forest resources, as when unwritten rules exist as norms, values, and shared understandings that influence people's behaviors. Both formal and informal rules present issues for research. Informal rules may be invisible and difficult for outsiders to discern. Formal rules can be easy for researchers to discover through examination of documents and legislation, but written rules and regulations do not necessarily translate into rules-in-use. In the absence of enforcement, people may blatantly ignore legislation, or they may lack knowledge of the formal rules. Therefore, researchers need to use multiple techniques to gain reliable information about rules-in-use that govern how people use forest resources or prevent them from exploiting these resources.

The combination of protocols allows researchers to examine the interrelationships among forest conditions, institutional arrangements, and social, economic, and political processes. To capture changes through time, return visits to study sites are planned at regular intervals to see how forests and the social contexts are transforming. Return visits are projected to occur at five-year intervals. They now have begun to revisit a number of sites, and incorporate additional questions to explore changes since previous fieldwork. Through these return visits, researchers expect to gain important data on the longitudinal relationships among the factors that shape forest conditions.

While this methodology provides a basis for the collection of comparable data over time, the data are not exhaustive or equally relevant for all sites. Researchers frequently augment the protocols with surveys, censuses, and additional interview questions to address specific research questions and incorporate issues that are of particular concern to a project or a particular field site. Household surveys and censuses provide detailed information that may be critical in regions where private property arrangements dominate forest ownership. Household surveys are an effective complement to community-level protocols when trying to determine why members of a community use private-property arrangements for some parcels of land

and move to common-property arrangements for organizing the use of other parcels of land (see Futemma et al. 2002). In addition, remote sensing and GIS can be used to identify anomalies that may indicate the presence (or absence) of effective institutions (Schweik et al. 2003).

For those who desire more information on the principles and methods of collecting social data, H. Bernard (1995) provides an excellent discussion of methods for scientifically rigorous social sampling, interviews, surveys, and participant observation. E. Moran (1995) offers a well-rounded set of essays that propose standards for the collection of social and environmental data. Both of these resources provide helpful information for beginning and experienced researchers who aim to collect comparable environmental, social, and institutional data.

Integration of Remote Sensing, GIS, and Landscape Characterization Techniques

The fieldwork protocols provide excellent data on a site at a single point in time, but as discussed in chapter 2 it is difficult to project backward or forward in time based solely on the fieldwork data. Integration of advanced techniques for quantifying land cover and its change over time, through remote sensing, GIS coverages, and landscape fragmentation analysis (typically using a software program such as FRAGSTATS), opens the possibility of quantifying spatial characteristics over time. Quantifiable estimates of trends in land-cover change provide a means to verify interview data, add a perspective on change over time to forest mensuration data, and give evidence for evaluating institutional effectiveness.

The interpretation of remotely sensed data and fragmentation analyses depends on data from forest mensuration, training samples, and interviews. Weak institutions may lead to degradation in the understory or in species composition that is not readily evident from remotely sensed data, but will be apparent from forest mensuration. Environmental or biophysical variables (e.g., poor soils, unfavorable climate, steep slopes, distance from roads) may constrain human activity, and ameliorate institutional shortcomings. Higher-level policies or market pressures may undermine strong institutions; the interview questions explore this possibility. Thus the conjunction of fieldwork data with techniques for multitemporal, spatial analyses permits researchers to investigate the interactions among institutions, biophysical parameters, and sociopolitical and economic processes.

Challenges Facing Comparative, Over-Time Analyses

Conducting comparative, over-time research on forest conditions and processes of change presents challenges for researchers beyond the usual difficulties encountered by fieldwork. The challenges can be broadly grouped as pertaining to (1) the acquisition of comparable data in the face of missing, inaccessible, or nonexistent sources and (2) the comparable assessment of forest conditions and changes across diverse ecozones and climates.

The acquisition of comparable data poses a constant challenge for researchers. Although training and shared protocols provide the context for the collection of comparable data, the information needed is not always available. Historical data on settlements, demographic change, and forest changes do not exist in many rural and developing areas of the world. In some cases, records have been damaged or lost, or the information was never recorded in the first place. Archival research and interviews with knowledgeable elders can help to approximate social and demographic histories. Quantitative data simply may not exist, which presents difficulties for understanding how past processes have shaped current circumstances. Many questions about forest change require information on past forest conditions. Interviews with local observers can assist with the analysis, and additional data can be gained through the use of remotely sensed images (aerial photographs and satellite images). Remotely sensed images can provide valuable quantitative data over time for forest-cover estimates even in the absence of other data sources; however, these data do not prove very helpful for estimating changes in biodiversity or species composition.

Achieving a reliable assessment of forest conditions that allows comparison across diverse forests represents a notable issue. Our major questions require that researchers assess how institutional, economic, and political contexts shape forest conditions across sites, but in many cases the forests are not comparable. Quantitative forest measurements, such as total biomass, species richness, and measures of dominance, relate primarily to the forest type and biophysical factors (soil fertility, precipitation, temperature regimes, elevation, slope, and aspect). The characteristics of tropical rain forests cannot be compared directly with those of temperate deciduous forests, yet if research is to ascertain whether systematic relationships exist among social, institutional, and economic factors as they influence forests, then a reliable basis for comparative assessment is needed. To control for variation, some comparative research projects focus on a certain forest type. With this strategy, relationships among social and institutional contexts and their impact on forest conditions can be more readily evaluated because environmental differences in forests are held relatively constant. When possible, the optimal means of evaluating forest conditions is to compare each study forest with a reference forest of comparable type and biophysical characteristics that has experienced minimal human interference.

Unfortunately, pristine forests do not exist for every forest type, but if relatively undisturbed forests can be identified, then the extent of human-caused transformations and the effectiveness of institutional arrangements are more readily estimated. In a few cases, researchers have been able to find a suitable representative. For example, research in a Bolivian tropical rain forest was able to compare the area with a large protected area in Peru (Becker and Leon 2000). In the absence of reference forests, foresters assess the study forest relative to similar forest types in the region.

To investigate whether relationships among variables persist or vary across forest types and biophysical factors, foresters and user groups are asked for their perceptions of forest conditions and the changes that are occurring. Although these qualitative assessments cannot entirely substitute for comparable, quantitative measures, they provide interpretations of status and the directions of change based on the evaluations of the people who best know the actual conditions and processes occurring in the forests.

User evaluations of the conditions of their local forests were a valuable source of information in an effort to examine hypotheses commonly held, but rarely tested, regarding the impact of social heterogeneity on the likelihood of effective collective action to reduce deforestation in Nepal. Varughese and Ostrom (2001) found that the level of collective action related to forest resources did vary substantially across communities, as did various forms of social heterogeneity. Heterogeneity was not, however, consistently associated with either higher or lower performance. When users crafted rules that took into account various forms of heterogeneity, they were able to undertake substantial levels of collective action and improve their forest conditions, in contrast to their neighbors.

User evaluations appear to be related to measured forest conditions. Varughese (1999) was able to ask whether user assessments and perceived trends were positively associated with measures (e.g., average diameter, stems per hectare, and species richness) obtained from a random sample of forest plots in six forests. In all six sites, revisits had occurred that enabled Varughese to make this comparison. He found a close correlation between actual measures of changes in forest conditions and the perceived trends in five of the six sites. In the sixth site, forest users evaluated the trend more negatively than a sample of the entire forest revealed. Close attention to the spatial distribution of data from the forest plots revealed, however, that the users were reflecting changes occurring at the margin of the forest where recent encroachments were noticeable to those living nearby and reflected in the plot data for these plots in contrast to the plots measured farther from the daily view of the users. Thus, the knowledge that users have about their forests appears to correlate well with measures derived from careful forest mensuration. Further, the evaluation of local users of their own forests is valuable information for understanding user behavior. These multiple methods for measuring forest conditions do not overcome all of the challenges to institutional comparisons across multiple forest types and across time, but they represent a solid context for comparative analysis, particularly when combined with data from GIS analysis and remotely sensed images.

Advances and Issues in Institutional Analysis

The linkage of institutional analysis with multidisciplinary studies strengthens researchers' ability to explore the relationships among institutions, individuals, and the natural environment. The resulting information suggests that researchers may identify circumstances propitious for collective action, recognize institutions that are successful in maintaining forests, evaluate the effectiveness of institutions for common-pool resources, and improve knowledge of factors correlated with institutional failures (NRC 2002). Research incorporating multidisciplinary methods and institutional analysis as discussed here has contributed to advances studying (1) the incommensurability of property type with successful institutions for forest management, (2) the interplay between the environmental-biophysical context and institutional arrangements, and (3) environmental outcomes under weak institutions.

Incommensurability of Property Regime and Successful Institutions for Forest Management

Policy makers have tended to look at property rights as a means to arrest degradation of common-pool resources. The establishment of secure property rights appears to be a critical enabling factor for wise resource management, but this often has been conjoined with a conviction that there must be one form of tenure that consistently promotes wise resource management. Strong proponents exist for private, public, and common property. Policy makers have tended to identify a single property type as *the* universal remedy for all contexts. Increasing evidence suggests, however, that no type of formal tenure—private, common-property, or public ownership—assures wise management of forests and other common-pool resources. Rather, the evidence indicates that the *specific* rules-in-use, not the *general* type of tenure regime, shape forest transformations.

Comparative analyses of contrasting property rights illustrate the importance of specific sets of rules, as contrasted to the general tenure status. In Uganda, a study of four government forest reserves and one private forest showed that illegal harvesting activities were pronounced in three government reserves with open-access conditions. But a reserve monitored by an indigenous group presented very few signs of illegal exploitation; relative inaccessibility also helped to protect that reserve. The private forest had rules-in-use that permitted local villagers to practice traditional harvesting, but forest guards effectively limited illegal activities (Banana and Gombya-Ssembajjwe 2000). In addition, a growing literature shows that common property can be managed sustainably (Netting 1976; McKean 1982; McCay and Acheson 1987; E. Ostrom 1990; Bromley et al. 1992), at times even better than private property (Gibson 2001).

A cross-sectional study of private and communal forests in western Honduras found no statistically significant differences in forest characteristics by tenure (C. Tucker 1999). All of the forests experienced heavy grazing, but private forests had lower levels of firewood collection because owners limited trespassing. In theory, the private forests should have presented better conditions, but forest mensuration and the observations of the research team did not discern significant differences. Subsequently, a time-series analysis using Landsat Thematic Mapper (TM) images did find that the private forests were experiencing more regeneration than the communal forests (Southworth and Tucker 2001). The dynamic process could not be documented with a single time point of forest mensuration but became evident in the analyses using remotely sensed data. Thus the results underscore the thesis presented in chapter 2 of the importance of both cross-sectional measurement (to examine spatial patterns) and over-time analyses (to examine the temporal patterns).

When forests managed under similar formal tenure are compared, notable differences also emerge. Two communities that own communal land in southern Indiana share values for living close to nature and conserving forest. Their forests are comparable in terms of species diversity, structural characteristics, and vegetative abundance (Gibson and Koontz 1998). Yet the communities differed markedly in the types of institutions they had designed. One of the communities required a trial membership period, significant membership dues, and a formal membership agreement that specified restrictions on forest use. The other community lacked formal documentation of a commitment to conserve the forest, had a minuscule membership fee, and permitted members to partition the forest for private use. The latter community had experienced periods of conflict and dissension, forest fragmentation with the creation of private house lots, and a dramatic fluctuation in membership over the years. In one instance, a member clear-cut his lot, and the community lost a court case against that individual because a written agreement did not exist.

Thus, contrasting institutional arrangements—despite similar tenure and expressed community values—contributed to differences in community stability, adherence to community values, and the degree to which the original forest area was maintained. The results conform to the findings of Agrawal and Gibson (1999), who note that it is the institutions within communities that determine the success of community-based resource management.

A comparison of two government forests in Indiana—one a national forest and one a state forest—provides further evidence concerning the differences among forest regimes that are grouped together in overly general concepts. Using spectral mixture analysis of Landsat Multispectral Scanner (MSS) images from 1972 to 1992 to develop rigorous measures of land use and land-use changes, Schweik (1998) was able to show that the internal policies of national vs. state forests do make a difference in the types of land uses that occur in these forests. He found that the legislative-based incentive structures that encourage state forest property managers to harvest from state forests to generate income did generate more timber production in the state forest compared to the national forest during these two decades (see also Koontz 2002). Also, national legislation since the 1980s has led to increased transaction costs for harvesting from national forests. However, the intensity of environmental group activities during the 1990s brought more attention to, and eventual reduction in, harvesting activities in state forests. Schweik also was able to show that the overall timber stands in state forests were showing increasing signs of maturation, reflecting the change in internal policy to increase the importance of conservation over management for timber production.

The evidence presented in this section indicates that property owners under any tenure regime may design successful institutions. It is equally possible, whatever the formal property rights, that owners may design inadequate or inappropriate institutions. They may choose profit maximization or face policies and contexts that inhibit the emergence or effectiveness of institutional arrangements for forest management.

As the above discussion also indicates, the standard conceptualization of three tenure types (private, common, or public) oversimplifies a complex reality. Property regimes are embedded within larger social systems that attempt to balance individual and social interests. As a result, the bundle of rights associated with ownership is distributed among many stakeholders. Even private property owners usually must comply with constraints on what may be done with their land, and governments around the world reserve the right of eminent domain regardless of property ownership (Geisler and Daneker 2000; Singer 2000).

Interplay between the Environmental-Biophysical Context and Institutional Arrangements

Research has recently paid closer attention to the interrelationships among institutions, biophysical conditions, and resource management outcomes. Forests that persist or regenerate often exist in regions that discourage human interventions. Therefore, analyses of institutional arrangements must be joined with evaluation of ecological and biophysical variables to explain forest conservation, regeneration, or degradation. Studies of the distribution of forested land in Indiana show that the majority of forest cover occurs in areas with complex topography and poor soil fertility. By the beginning of the twentieth century, much of the privately owned land in the state was cleared, but many farms failed during the 1920s and 1930s due to rapid erosion, infertile soils, or poor drainage under the challenging economic conditions of the time. These failed farms eventually became the core areas of national and state forests (S. McCracken et al. 1997). Substantial regrowth has occurred in these government forests. Very substantial regrowth also has occurred on private land in the hilly southern part of the state (Evans et al. 2001a).

An examination of land-cover change in Celaque National Park (Honduras) through time revealed that the park appeared to be effective in limiting land-use/land-cover change within its boundaries (Southworth et al. 2002; Nagendra et al. 2003). A notable factor in Celaque's conservation is its relative unsuitability for maize production, which has limited human settlement in the cloud forest. The borders of the park are visible from space; they mark not only an institutional boundary but an ecological transition zone. Often, protected areas are created to conserve specific natural resources that are endangered, distinct from their surroundings, or representative of threatened ecosystems. The Monarch Butterfly Special Biosphere Reserve, for example, is designed to protect rare fir forests found only on high mountaintops where monarch butterflies hibernate during winter months (Chapela and Barkin 1995; Brower 1999).

The design and implementation of institutions to manage natural resources occur in diverse situations and for diverse reasons; successful institutions tend to be rules specifically designed to cope with the local context (E. Ostrom 1990). Elinor Ostrom (1998b) points out that the emergence of collective action for common-pool resource management depends in part on the attributes of a resource. A number of studies have shown that common property institutions tend to occur in association with resources that are sparse, low in productivity, or dispersed in time and space. Areas that present conditions favorable for high productivity tend to be held privately (Netting 1976, 1982; Runge 1986). Gibson and Koontz (1998) argue that people develop new rules to control resource use when they perceive resources to be scarce and salient. In one site, a community possessed extensive ownership rights over a distant, ecologically fragile cloud forest. Not recognizing the environmental services the cloud forest provided to their local water supply, members of the community allowed degradation to occur (Gibson and Becker 2000). When the community learned about the connection between the native vegetation in their forest and water collection for their local streams, they created a reserve within the forest to halt the conversion of the native species to a commercially valuable crop (Becker 1999).

Studies of the interplay between institutions and biophysical factors offer the potential to reveal patterns in the kinds of rules that are effective under certain environmental conditions. Such an integrated, multidisciplinary focus also may avoid misconceptions and oversimplifications of factors that contribute to, or complicate, institutional success. Ultimately, biophysical conditions represent only one set of relevant factors that interact with institutional arrangements, albeit one that has frequently been slighted by the social sciences. By contrast, population processes, market incentives, infrastructure (e.g., roads), and policy incentives are widely recognized to influence forest transformations and institutional outcomes (Repetto and Gillis 1988; Binswanger 1991; E. Moran 1992; Geist and Lambin 2001). Yet the direction of these relationships is not consistent; for example, increasing population is not necessarily associated with forest degradation, as it may provide incentives for improved forest management (Tiffen et al. 1994; Varughese 2000). Similarly, a given set of biophysical conditions or constraints may have contrasting ramifications for institutional arrangements from place to place, depending on interactions with other variables. Ultimately, institutions emerge, flourish, or fail within social, biophysical, and political fluxes that shape motivations, incentives, and perceptions of costs and benefits.

Ramifications of Ineffective or Absent Institutions for Common-Pool Resources

The importance of institutions for the management of common-pool resources may be revealed best by cases in which institutions are ineffective or absent. According to theory, open-access resources (for which no rules-in-use exist) will suffer overexploitation and degradation. This prediction is largely supported, but the processes of resource exploitation are more nuanced than the proverbial pasture described by Hardin (1968) in which the entire area suffers overgrazing. Studies in Nepal and Guatemala show that in a context of weak or nonexistent institutions, people tend to follow an optimal foraging strategy. In other words, people invest the least possible effort to exploit a resource. Patterns of exploitation then relate to distances from roads and settlements, slope, elevation, and avoidance of areas governed by institutions. The result is a pattern of overexploitation of highly desired products in the most easily accessible areas (Schweik 1996; Gibson 2001). Under this scenario, the least accessible areas of a forest may retain relatively good conditions even without institutions, but only until the resources are expended from the readily accessed areas. The progressive deterioration of a resource under optimal foraging, and the increasing effort associated with exploitation, may in some cases provide incentives for users to undertake collective action for resource protection.

Future Directions

Large *N* Studies

Individual case studies contribute greatly to our understanding of institutions and their variability, but in order to develop coherent theory and inform policy, it is necessary to conduct comparative research. One of our longer-term plans is to slowly accumulate sufficient cases whereby it may be possible to undertake multivariate statistical analyses of a large number of forests that are governed by diverse property regimes. This is a very challenging task for many reasons. First, one cannot create a random sample of forest regimes. A list of all forest regimes existing within a country does not exist in any country of the world—let alone a list that would enable one to develop a random sample across countries. Complete inventories of government-owned forests usually do exist but not of forests owned by private households or corporations or by diversely structured communal groups. As discussed in chapter 1, many of the sites we are studying have been chosen primarily on availability of satellite imagery and an effort to ensure that within a site there are at least two types of ownership present.

Another problem with any effort of this type is selection bias. An important hypothesis of our own work is that well-crafted rules lead to an improvement in forest conditions. In order to examine this hypothesis statistically, however, one cannot manipulate the rules that are used to govern forests. We also hypothesize that users will not self-organize to create effective rules unless they also face some deterioration in the condition of their forest. Thus, poor forest conditions should lead to better organization and rules that, in turn, should lead to better forest conditions. Cross-sectional studies of a large number of forests have to use very precise statistical techniques to try to cope with this problem.

Using such techniques, Gibson et al. (in press) have undertaken an initial analysis of 112 forests in Africa, Asia, and the Western Hemisphere. Their central hypothesis is that regular monitoring of rules—regardless of the specific rules-in-use—is a necessary condition associated with better forest conditions. Without some form of regular monitoring, both formal and informal rules may become meaningless within a short period of time. In this initial analysis, the authors found a strong and consistent relationship between consistent monitoring of rules (in contrast to sporadic monitoring) and user perceptions of forest conditions. We have considerable confidence in this finding because the importance of monitoring is well documented in many of our more detailed case studies and is consistent with considerable theoretical work.

In a related effort, Hayes (2004) conducted a preliminary analysis of 158 forests to investigate whether legally protected forests (parks) differ significantly in forest conditions from forests under other types of institutional arrangements (nonparks). Parks in the sample do not prove to have significantly better conditions (as determined by a forester's evaluation of vegetation density) than forests managed under private and community ownership. All types of property regimes presented a range of conditions. Where users had rights to design rules, however, forest conditions proved to be significantly better. Indeed, in a majority of cases where users had rights to design rules, they exercised these rights. Very few parks allow users to participate in designing the rules. These early results imply that participation of users in rule formation may be integral to compliance and contributes to consistent monitoring when users are also monitors. Further work is planned for the next several years.

Multiscalar, Multilevel Institutional Analyses

The analysis of interrelationships among institutional arrangements, social factors, and environmental variables requires integration of data across varying spatial extents, spatial resolutions, temporal durations, and levels of analysis. The complexity of this endeavor represents a fundamental challenge for understanding forest transformations and for broadly understanding human-environment interactions, particularly because processes tend to exhibit different patterns at different levels of analysis (see chapter 3). A multiscalar, multilevel approach provides the context in which integrative analyses can be accomplished.

While ecology has long focused on relationships of scale in ecosystems, the use of scale has been less well defined or consistently applied in the social sciences. In general, social scientists tend to focus on a specific level of analysis associated with their subdiscipline or research topic. Although geography has paid particular attention to spatial relationships, institutional arrangements have not been a focus. While political science has looked closely at institutional arrangements, few theories or approaches have looked explicitly at linkages across levels and scales. Exceptions to this include federalism, polycentricity, and the IAD framework (e.g., see Tocqueville [1840] 1945; E. Ostrom et al. 1994; McGinnis 1999; V. Ostrom 1999; Gibson et al. 2000a).

Evaluating multiscalar, multilevel institutional interactions and the ramifications for environmental processes requires identification of the variables and processes relevant to the question at hand. Many variables interact with institutions that operate across different spatial extents, temporal durations, and levels of analysis. There is still much to learn about the interactions of social, biophysical, political, and economic variables with institutional arrangements, even within a single study site or at one level of analysis. Moreover, the variables and processes that are important tend to vary across scales and levels of analysis. For example, if forest change is taken to be a dependent variable indicating the institutional effectiveness of forest management, then the challenge is to define the geographic and jurisdictional levels at which forest change and institutional impacts will be measured. Forest processes have scale-dependent aspects; local reforestation and conservation may be obscured by national deforestation trends, yet it is important to understand how local institutional arrangements and their interactions with higher-level institutions can foster reforestation in some cases and deforestation or relative stability in others (e.g., see Southworth and Tucker 2001). As Young (2002a) notes, "... institutions generally operate as elements in clusters of causal forces. There is little prospect of identifying simple generalizations about the roles that institutions play without regard to the effects of other drivers that interact with institutions" (p. 3).

As a result, a fundamental prerequisite of multiscalar, multilevel institutional analysis is interdisciplinary collaboration that permits the exchange of data and the incorporation of multiple perspectives to evaluate institutions with respect to other variables involved in environmental change. Much of the research conducted by CIPEC to date analyzes relationships across spatial extents at local and regional levels and temporal durations of years and decades—for example, with studies of forest change through time (S. McCracken et al. 1997; Nyerges and Green 2000; Southworth and Tucker 2001; Nagendra et al. 2003; E. Moran et al. in press). As discussed in part I, globalization, market integration, and decentralization processes, each of which entails institutional arrangements, are widely recognized as influencing regional and local land-cover change processes (see also Wei 2002). Recently, several studies have applied rigorous, comparative research to systematically examine interrelationships among institutions and the natural environment at different levels of political jurisdiction. Decentralization has become a widespread approach to motivate improved natural resource management; the interactions across national to local levels provide a critical context to interpret the ramifications for natural resource management. Gibson and Lehoucq (2003) examine the effects of decentralization on municipal forest management decisions in Guatemala.

Andersson (2003a,b), in another example, explored the impact of a very substantial decentralization of formal authority regarding land and forest resources in Bolivia to a municipal level. He found substantial variation in the level of activities undertaken by municipalities across Bolivia in regard to forests within their jurisdictions. The performance of the decentralized system depends to a substantial extent on efforts expended at a smaller and at a larger level than just that of the municipality. Where forest users, local NGOs, and municipalities engage in extensive discussions and negotiations concerning the rules to be used for forest use and management, and how these rules are to be implemented and monitored, policies emerge that lead to more sustainable use. Further, municipalities that interact effectively with national agencies also have undertaken more effective local policies. Thus, decentralization has the *possibility* of reducing unsustainable harvesting practices and enhancing the viability of local land-use practices, but whether the possibility is realized depends on whether local officials expend extensive time and effort working out common agreements about particular rules to be crafted, implemented, and enforced. Andersson found that the motivation of local officials to invest in such a process was highly variable from one municipality to another, and that this variability explained a great deal of the mixed outcomes of the decentralized regime.

Work in progress and future endeavors will include comparative studies of institutions across spatial and temporal scales and diverse levels of analysis, where institutional dimensions are recognized as significant in environmental change. A number of studies will be needed to discover what kinds of institutions and arrangements work best across global, national, regional, and local levels for sustainable forest management outcomes. But it is already recognized that the successful design of institutions is unlikely to result from implementing a standard set of rules and procedures (Young 2002b). Institutions that work well result from a process of crafting arrangements that fit specific situations and are flexible to processes of change.

5

Forest Ecosystems and the Human Dimensions

J. C. Randolph, Glen M. Green, Jonathon Belmont, Theresa Burcsu, and David Welch

Changes in land cover, most notably those affecting forest ecosystems, are occurring at an unprecedented rate (Goudie 2002). The research discussed throughout this book is focused on how humans, organized in various ways and using a variety of institutional structures and processes, have affected and will continue to affect the nature and extent of forests. To do this carefully, we have used a wide variety of methodologies, as discussed in some detail in the various chapters devoted to methodology. To fully understand this research, and the work of many other scholars studying forests, we need to (1) provide background information about the nature and extent of forests; (2) examine how humans interact with forests, as well as the products and services humans derive from forests; (3) discuss the forests that the Center for the Study of Institutions, Population, and Environmental Change (CIPEC) researchers have studied and the concept of "forest condition"; and (4) describe the basic methodologies CIPEC researchers have used in forest mensuration and evaluation.

Most of the concepts defined and methodologies explained in this chapter are well-known to ecologists. Social scientists who are not yet familiar with concepts related to the measurement of forests (so as to assess how human actions affect forests) are encouraged to read this chapter first, before reading later chapters that use the concepts and methods described here. Forest ecologists may find this chapter to be rather elementary—but should recognize the interdisciplinary audience intended for this book.

Nature and Extent of Forests

Types, Amounts, and Spatial Distribution of Forests

By the simplest definition, a *forest* is a biotic community dominated by tree species. The U.S. Department of Agriculture (USDA) Forest Service defines *forested land* as land that is at least 16.7 percent stocked (contains a *basal area* of at least 7.5 sq ft per acre, or 1.72 m^2/ha) with trees of any size, or that formerly had such tree cover and is not currently developed for nonforest use. Forest trees are woody plants that have a well-developed stem and usually are more than 12 ft (3.69 m) in height at maturity. The minimum area for classification of forested land is 1 acre (0.4047 ha) (Birch 1996, 21). Using this definition, forested land can have little or no above-ground woody growth if recently harvested, as long as the land has the potential for growth of trees.

Both forest ecologists and foresters typically use the concept of a "stand" as the working unit of a forest. A stand is a group of trees growing in a specific locale and having sufficient uniformity in species composition, age, density, and other spatial arrangements to be distinguishable from adjacent stands. Stand boundaries may be delineated by tree species composition, hydrologic or topographic features (e.g., streams, ridge tops), ownership or management, or some combination of these. Stands vary considerably in size, ranging from about one hectare up to several hundred hectares. A forester would not consider a small group of trees to be a stand, nor would a stand include many thousands of hectares of forest. Multiple stands typically constitute a forest.

Stands usually are described by the dominant or codominant tree species (e.g., a *Quercus-Carya* or oak-hickory forest). Larger regions of forests are described by either taxonomic or morphological characteristics such as coniferous, needle-leaf evergreen, deciduous, broadleaf evergreen, or by climatic and geographic characteristics such as tropical moist forest. Table 5.1 presents a summary of the areal extent, total biomass, and total annual net primary productivity (NPP) estimated for all major terrestrial ecosystems on Earth. The estimates of Saugier et al. (2001) were made about twenty-five years after those of Whittaker and Likens (1975). The two sets of estimates are similar for several ecosystem types, but the Whitaker and Likens estimates are somewhat higher for forests. Different estimates of areal extent for a given ecosystem type likely result from differences in the classification used, as well as any actual changes over the time period. Biomass and NPP values are expressed in units of carbon, using the average value that dry plant biomass is 50 percent carbon.

Forests, not including savanna and shrubland, make up 24.5 to 27.9 percent of Earth's terrestrial surface. Tropical forests have by far the largest total biomass of any ecosystem type. Forests represent 82.2 to 91.5 percent of Earth's terrestrial biomass and have 52.1 to 66.8 percent of the total annual NPP. Dividing the

Table 5.1
Area, Total Carbon, and Total Annual Net Primary Productivity for Terrestrial Ecosystems

Ecosystem Type	2001 Area[a] (10^6 km^2)	1975 Area[b] (10^6 km^2)	Total Carbon[a] (Pg)	Total Carbon[b] (Pg)	Total NPP[a] (Pg C y^{-1})	Total NPP[b] (Pg C y^{-1})
Tropical forests	17.5	24.5	340	513	21.9	24.7
Moist[c]		17.0		383		18.7
Seasonal[c]		7.5		130		6.0
Temperate forests	10.4	12.0	139	193	8.1	7.5
Evergreen		5.0		88		3.3
Deciduous[c]		7.0		105		4.2
Boreal forests	13.7	12.0	57	120	2.6	4.8
Shrublands	2.8	8.5	17	25	1.4	3.0
Savanna	27.6	15.0	79	30	14.9	6.8
Grasslands	15.0	9.0	6	7	5.6	2.7
Tundra	5.6	8.0	2	2.5	0.5	0.5
Deserts	27.7	18.0	10	6.5	3.5	0.8
Crops	13.5	14.0	4	7	4.1	4.5
Ice/rock/sand	15.5	24.0	0	0	0	0
Total Terrestrial	149.3	149.0	652	903	62.6	55.4

NPP, net primary productivity; Pg, pedagram = 10^{15} g.
[a] Source: from Saugier et al. 2001; summary data for subcategories of tropical forests and temperate forests are not given.
[b] Source: from Whittaker and Likens 1975.
[c] Forest types studied by CIPEC researchers.

value of total carbon by the total area for a given ecosystem type gives the carbon standing crop in kilograms of carbon (kg C) per square meter of land surface area.[1]

Most of Earth's forests occur in two broad bands. Plate 1 provides a map of the distribution of Earth's forests. Boreal forests occur in a circumpolar band extending from approximately 45° N to the Arctic Circle. Tropical forests occur primarily between the tropic of Cancer and the tropic of Capricorn on all continents. In the mid-latitudes, the interiors of all continents have physiographic features that result in drier climatic zones; thus, shrublands, grasslands, and deserts are the dominant ecosystem types. Consequently, temperate zone forests are much more patchily distributed at mid-latitudes.

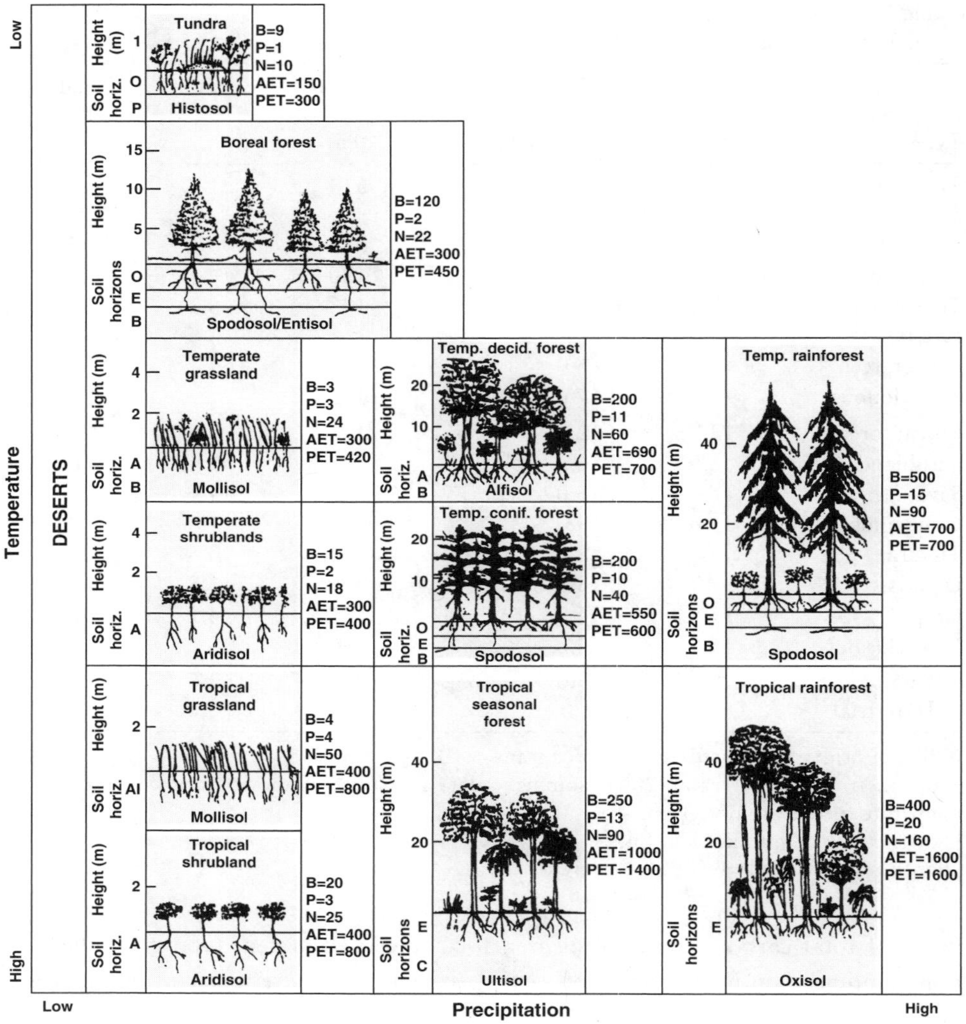

Figure 5.1
Classification of major ecosystem types in relation to climate regimes. Predominant ecosystem types are noted at the top of the cells, and predominant soil classes are at the bottom. Heights of dominant vegetation and depths of soil horizons are shown. The precipitation scale increases from Low to High, but the temperature scale decreases from High to Low. B, total plant biomass in Mg/ha (multiply by 0.5 for an estimate of carbon); P, total ecosystem productivity above ground in Mg/ha y^{-1} (multiply by 0.5 for an estimate of carbon); N, nitrogen uptake by plants in kg N/ha y^{-1}; AET, actual evapotranspiration in mm of water per year; PET, potential evapotranspiration in mm of water per year. Soil horizons are indicated

Biophysical Factors Influencing Forest Type

At the global level, climate is most important in determining vegetation composition and, subsequently, soil formation and characteristics. Solar radiation, temperature, precipitation, and evapotranspiration are important factors that influence the photosynthetic process and the duration of the growing season, thus controlling the NPP of a given ecosystem. Ambient temperature and water availability influence metabolic rates of all organisms and control the rate of decomposition of dead organic matter. Both the amount of water available and the chemistry of that water influences carbon and nutrient dynamics and, consequently, soil formation and structure.

Climate, soils, and vegetation interact to produce regional-level patterns of distinguishable terrestrial ecosystems which can be characterized broadly, as seen in figure 5.1. As a result of high annual precipitation, tropical rain forests have the highest actual evapotranspiration (AET), which is the annual sum of the water evaporated to the atmosphere from soil and other surfaces plus the water transpired by plants. In climates where precipitation is abundant, the AET value will be the same as the potential evapotranspiration (PET) value, which is the amount of evapotranspiration that would occur with unlimited water availability. In dry climates, AET is limited by water availability and is significantly lower than PET. In those fairly dry climates, dominant vegetation types are grasslands and shrublands. Slightly greater annual precipitation allows development of more robust grasslands and shrublands, as well as savannas in warmer climates, and tundra and boreal forests in colder climates. In temperate and seasonal tropical climates, AET is typically 70 to 95 percent of PET, water availability to vegetation is higher, and both coniferous and broadleaf forests flourish. In wet, cool climates, AET and PET are similar, but less solar radiation and cooler temperatures reduce evaporation and PET is lower. Coniferous tree species are typical dominants in the resulting temperate rain forests. Tropical rain forests have the most abundant precipitation and solar radiation resulting in year-long growing seasons with little or no water stress on vegetation. Broadleaf evergreen trees are the typical dominants in those ecosystems.

by O, organic horizon contains partially decomposed litter and organic matter; P, permafrost in arctic climate of the tundra; A or A1, upper layer of mineral soil altered by mixing of organic matter from the O horizon; E, eluviation zone, the mineral soil horizon altered mainly by weathering and leaching of minerals (many soils show either an A or an E horizon depending on the relative importance of chemical weathering vs. the biological incorporation of organic matter); B, lower layer of mineral soil altered by the chemical deposition or precipitation of material leached from the overlying horizon; C, deepest soil horizon consists of mineral material not affected by soil development. (From Aber and Melillo 2001, 18.)

Spatial and Temporal Distribution of Forests

Chapter 3 provides a discussion of the spatial and temporal levels relevant to the study of the human dimensions of global environmental change. However, some specific aspects of the temporal and spatial characteristics of forests are discussed in more detail here. First, and most important, is the recognition that forests are comprised of a myriad of living organisms representing many different taxa with species having vastly different morphologies, physiologies, and life histories. Some of these organisms have rapid life cycles and live for only a few days or weeks, while some species have life spans of a century or more. Individual trees of some species, such as the bristlecone pine (*Pinus aristata*), can live for several thousand years. Organisms also respond to other temporal cycles as well, such as the diurnal cycle, seasonal changes in precipitation and temperature, and interannual climatic variability.

Different processes in forests operate at different temporal durations:

- *Daily and shorter*: photosynthesis, respiration, nutrient uptake, herbivory
- *Seasonal*: growth, reproduction, senescence, mortality, decomposition
- *Annual*: changes in species composition; interannual variability in many seasonal processes, such as net primary productivity, result of interannual climate variability
- *Decadal*: succession, changes in physiognomy, canopy gap creation and filling
- *Millennial and longer*: evolution

More rapid processes usually occur at smaller, local spatial extents (e.g., photosynthesis in chloroplasts of individual leaves), whereas seasonal and annual durations are relevant to growth of individual trees and decadal durations are relevant to the species composition of the forest ecosystem.

Forest components also occur at different spatial extents in a hierarchy:

- *Cells*: in leaves: palisade and mesophyll cells with gaps for gas exchange
- *Organs*: for trees: foliage, boles and branches, roots, flowers, fruits
- *Organisms*: individual plants, animals, and microbes
- *Populations*: reproductive groups of a single species in one locale
- *Biotic communities*: groups of species coexisting in one locale
- *Ecosystems*: groups of biotic communities and their physical environment
- *Landscapes* (or *biomes*): recognizable groups of similar ecosystems
- *Regions*: groups of landscapes or biomes
- *Earth*: the entire biosphere

Figure 5.2 shows a space-time diagram that includes multiple processes which affect forests. Chapter 3 has additional discussion of spatial and temporal processes and presents several analogous figures. Many factors, including human activities,

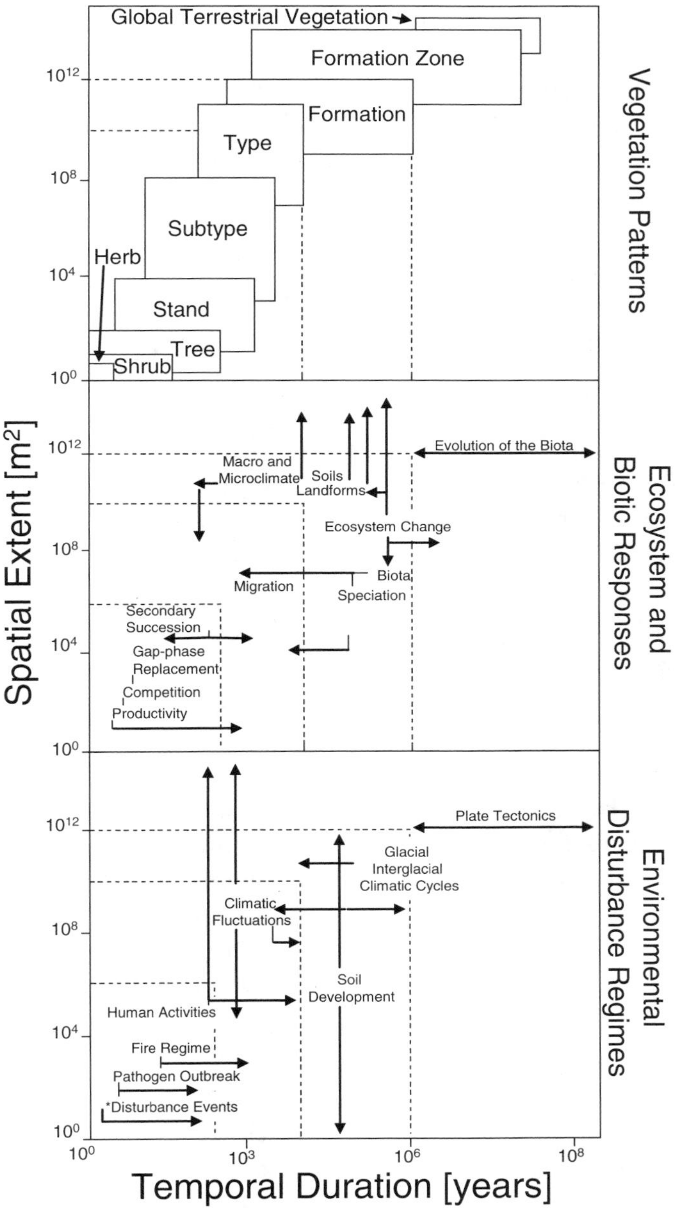

Figure 5.2
Environmental disturbance, ecosystem responses, and vegetation patterns. (Adapted from Barnes et al. 1998, 23.)

can impact forest productivity and stability, and these disturbance regimes vary with both space and time. In turn, forests respond through different mechanisms and processes at different spatial extents and temporal durations. The resultant vegetation patterns are thus complex and dynamic. However, attention to what level these processes operate on helps our understanding of the causal relationships between forest conditions at any given time and the factors characteristic of that geographic area.

Carbon Dynamics of Forests

Forests constitute only about 28 percent of Earth's land cover, yet they include about 82 percent of the terrestrial biomass and about 52 percent of all terrestrial productivity (calculated from table 5.1). Plants use the photosynthetic process to convert water and atmospheric CO_2 to carbohydrates, primarily cellulose, the principal constituent of cell walls in most plants. Plant biomass is 46 to 50 percent carbon (dry mass basis); thus, forests have an enormous influence on the global carbon cycle. Because of the well-documented increase in the CO_2 concentration of Earth's atmosphere and the subsequent changes in global climate patterns, study of all aspects of the carbon cycle have become paramount.

The carbon balance of individual plants is controlled by the quantity of CO_2 fixed by photosynthesis and the rate at which fixed photosynthate is returned to the atmosphere by respiring tissues. Solar radiation, temperature, and availability of water and nutrients all influence plant physiological processes that, in turn, influence the productivity of individuals and thus the productivity of the ecosystems in which those plants occur. Woody plants partition fixed carbon into growth and maintenance of foliage, branches, stems, fine and coarse roots, and reproductive structures.

Most herbaceous plants (annuals) produce seeds as a mechanism for survival during unfavorable seasonal conditions such as excessively dry or cold periods. Seeds can exist in a stasis more resistant to those conditions and, when favorable conditions return, can germinate and allow the plant to grow rapidly. However, the living cells of perennial woody plants must be able to survive variable temperature and water availability across all seasons. Each year woody plants fix more CO_2, make more cellulose, and add more carbon to their growing structures throughout their life span. These contrasting life strategies make forests a much greater sink of fixed CO_2 than ecosystems dominated by herbaceous plants and grasses. The patterns of carbon allocation to growth, storage, and the production of defensive compounds to reduce herbivory are genetically controlled and vary widely among plant species. Although the carbon dynamics of individual trees is important, other organisms and processes also play significant roles in the carbon dynamics of a forest ecosystem.

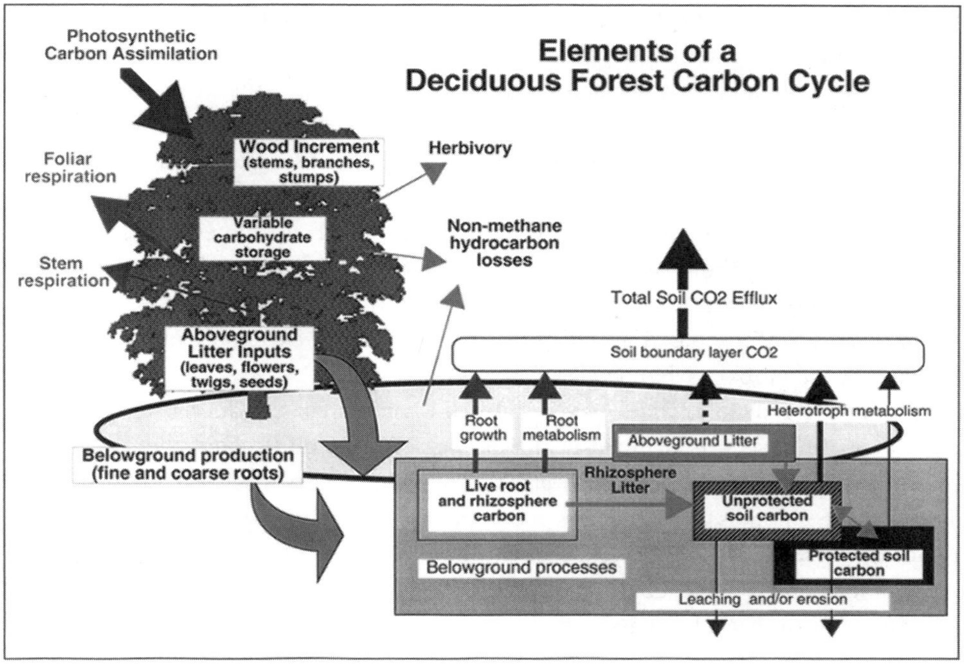

Figure 5.3
Elements of a deciduous forest carbon cycle. (From Hanson 2001.)

Figure 5.3 illustrates the more important carbon pools and fluxes in a deciduous forest ecosystem.

Net ecosystem production (NEP) is positive when carbon inputs to the biota of the ecosystem exceed carbon losses to the atmosphere and is negative when carbon losses exceed inputs. Consequently, any given ecosystem can be a significant sink of atmospheric CO_2, a significant source of atmospheric CO_2, or neutral. For example, high-latitude forest ecosystems can be a net carbon source in warm years and a net carbon sink in cool years because heterotropic respiration responds more to temperature than photosynthesis does in cool climates.

During the past decade, new methodologies for measuring and estimating NEP have been developed. Perhaps the most widely used approach requires a tower to be constructed through and above the vegetation to measure atmospheric CO_2 fluxes with a technique called eddy covariance analysis (Baldocchi et al. 1996). Net ecosystem CO_2 exchange (NEE), measured using eddy covariance methods, integrates CO_2 fluxes from vegetation and soil and provides a measure of net carbon exchange on a subhourly basis, which then can be summed for daily, seasonal, and annual estimates. For annual and shorter durations, in the absence of erosion and deposition and assuming that the leaching loss of carbon to groundwater is minimal, NEE is an integrative measure of NEP. Several studies (Barford et al. 2001; Curtis et al. 2002; Ehman et al. 2002b) have found that NEP estimates of forests using biometric methods compare well with NEE estimates using eddy covariance methods in the same location. No matter which methods are used, there now are ample data (several examples are summarized in Barnes et al. 1998 and Chapin et al. 2002) indicating that forest ecosystems are extremely important components of the global carbon cycle.

Although no detailed data about biomass, ecosystem productivity, or carbon dynamics of forests are included in this book, several CIPEC researchers are working on these topics in various projects. Chapter 11 discusses several techniques for assessing tree biomass and presents a comparison of techniques primarily based on remotely sensed images. Both chapter 6, discussing remote sensing, and chapter 7, discussing vector-based geographic information systems (GIS), are relevant to the measurement of forest biomass and productivity.

Biodiversity of Forests

There are high-biodiversity forests on every continent, but the greatest diversity occurs in South American forests (Gentry 1992). Observations of higher-diversity forests in tropical areas have led to hypotheses that ecosystems in lower latitudes typically have higher biodiversity because of consistent wetter and warmer conditions at these latitudes. However, the relationship between latitude and biodiversity is far from simple (Connell and Lowman 1989; Hart et al. 1989). Rather, topographic and edaphic variation within latitudes, as well as variation in local and regional climate, can produce areas of both low and high diversity at all latitudes. For example, within the United States, areas with the highest diversity of forest tree species are in the southern regions of the Appalachian Mountains, a relatively central location in terms of latitude. A complex relationship between available resources and environmental conditions exists that affects diversity. Physiography, soils, disturbance regimes, and vegetative succession all play a role in determining the number of species in an area (Barnes et al. 1998).

Variation in forest biodiversity across latitudes and continents is best explained as a function of spatial extent. The measurement of biodiversity changes with the extent of the study area and at the local level involves counting species richness within a single area (also referred to as alpha diversity). Species count or richness is one of several levels of biodiversity conceptualized by researchers. By defining the level of analysis, one can look at the relationship between biodiversity and ecological gradients (e.g., beta diversity), where plant and animal communities might differ dramatically due to extreme changes in altitudes over short distances. A mountain, for instance, might have high beta diversity due to many different assemblages of species taking advantage of steep moisture and temperature gradients due to a rain shadow effect or changes in altitude. Over larger areas, diversity within a landscape (called gamma diversity), or over a group of landscapes (epsilon diversity) are also important measures of biodiversity (Whittaker 1975). Rarity is also an important descriptor of biodiversity. A rare species might be locally abundant, but globally rare, such as many of the endemic species on the Galapagos Islands. Rarity also might be due to a species that is never abundant in any single location, but is found over a wide geographic area. The alarming rate of species extinctions has spurred scientists and policy makers to focus on efforts to conserve rare species. Conservation of biodiversity is one of the most important issues for the coming decade (see chapter 14).

Natural and Human Disturbances

Disturbance has been defined as a discrete event that affects ongoing processes or produces a change in the state of a system (Sousa 1984; Begon et al. 1996). The state changes may be observable in a forest ecosystem as changes in species composition (e.g., replacement of a dominant species by another), forest structure (e.g., increased density of downed trees), or ecosystem function (e.g., decrease in stored biomass and carbon) (Barnes et al. 1998; see also figure 5.2). More simply, the result of a disturbance can be viewed as a change in the availability of resources, such as food and space (Pickett and White 1985). Disturbance varies as a function of both spatial extent and temporal duration. Examples of disturbances range from short-lived but acute events, such as droughts or tornados, to chronic and long-term conditions, such as smog and continuing exposure to acid rain events (Forman 1995).

Since disturbances are defined as a deviation from some norm or process, it is helpful to also define theoretical reference points. Equilibrium theory and nonequilibrium models in ecology provide these references (Begon et al. 1996). Equilibrium theory proposes that there is an ideal state toward which any system tends. However, it is generally considered that such an equilibrium state is not truly achievable; instead, systems fluctuate around that state. Nonequilibrium models focus on the dynamics and transient behavior of a system from a reference point, usually an equilibrium state. These have been especially useful in understanding change across time and space (e.g., patch dynamics).

Concepts that are important for understanding disturbance are spatial extent and disturbance duration, frequency, and intensity. These concepts can be used to define any disturbance event and understand the response of an ecosystem to that disturbance. Here, we refer to the size of a disturbance as its spatial extent, or the area that is directly affected. Duration is the length of time (ranging from seconds to millennia) over which the actual disturbance occurs, but does not include any period of recovery. Frequency refers to the disturbance's recurrence interval (i.e., how frequently it occurs). The intensity of the disturbance refers to the severity of the event and sometimes is evaluated as the fraction of biomass damaged or removed during the event.

Disturbances can be generally categorized as natural or human-induced. Natural disturbances include both biological and physical mechanisms. Natural biological disturbances such as greatly increased herbivory and predation may affect competition dynamics between organisms as well as change the species composition and richness in an ecosystem. Invasive plant and animal species frequently are the source of such disturbance. Perhaps the most commonly occurring natural biological disturbances to forests involve pests, such as gypsy moths, or pathogens, such as Dutch elm disease. Natural physical disturbances predominantly result from extreme meteorological conditions; wind movements, such as hurricanes, tornados, and intense gusts; water movements, such as floods, snow, and ice damage; or lack of water, droughts. Other major types of natural physical disturbances include fire and land movements, such as earthquakes, landslides, and volcanic eruptions.

Perhaps the most common human-induced disturbance to forests is timber harvesting and extraction of forest products, using a wide variety of methods. Another major type of disturbance to forests is clearing for construction of buildings, roads, and other structures; surface mining; and agriculture (whether permanent cash-cropping, shifting agriculture, or pasture). The unplanned consequences of some human technologies, such as agricultural and industrial processes, also have led to forest disturbance. Many of these unintended forest disturbances take place spatially and temporally removed from the human activity that ultimately produced them. For example, acid rain can result in forest mortality many hundreds of kilometers downwind of the electric generating facilities that lead to its production. Also, forest disturbances may be temporally displaced from those human activities that caused them. For example, change in species composition of forests as a result of global climate change may occur decades after the burning of fossil fuels or land-cover changes that produced the greenhouse gases.

Threats to Biodiversity

The harvesting of forests for timber, clearing of forests for agricultural land use, and mining for mineral resources are among the most obvious threats to forest species. Not all intensive human uses of forests necessarily lead to declines in biodiversity; for example, traditional systems of coffee cultivation provide important habitats for fauna (Moguel and Toledo 1999). Similarly, agroforestry systems focused on the açai fruit or other systems of agriculture provide structural diversity that may support more species than other land uses (see chapter 9). The relationship between human systems and forest biodiversity is not clear, in part because our knowledge of species richness in forests is incomplete (E. Wilson 1988).

Efforts to curb the loss of endangered or threatened species have come from institutions at the international, national, and subnational levels. International treaties dedicated to the regulation of trade in threatened species are formal manifestations of this concern; for example, the Convention on International Trade in Endangered Species of Wild Fauna and Flora (CITES) or institutions at the country level (e.g., the Endangered Species Act of 1973). Other efforts have focused on preserving and managing species habitats because without adequate habitat, species cannot continue to survive. Parks and other protected areas that can support rare species are examples of such efforts. The effectiveness of such parks and preserves depends on their ability to reduce human impact on local ecosystems, because human activities such as tropical forest clearing are known to result in loss of species (Lugo 1988). However, recent studies of human land use have revealed that impacts on various taxa occur at several different spatial extents (Mensing et al. 1998). Therefore, parks may be a limited solution at best because enforcement occurs only within the park boundaries and even there is often difficult or lax.

A failure to understand and conserve remaining biodiversity poses threats at many different levels and is best exemplified by the fact that direct impacts are sometimes foreseeable, but indirect effects often are not. Conservation of biodiversity, as both a scientific concept and a management goal, extends beyond mere numbers of species or changes in biotic community composition.

Human Benefits and Uses of Forest Resources

Table 5.2 summarizes the most important direct benefits and uses of forest resources by humans. Although metal and stone products also are used, lumber and related

Table 5.2
Consumptive Human Uses of Forests

Human Action	Utility or Product
Clear forests for space	Transportation conduits: canals, railroads, roads, pipelines, power lines Settlements and industry: urban, suburban, rural Surface extraction: mining, oil, gas
Clear forests for space and water	Dams: flood control, irrigation, power generation
Clear (and burn) forests for space, water, soil, and nutrients	Agricultural production of Woody plants: plantation, woodlot, secondary forest Herbaceous plants: commercial and subsistence crops Pasture for grazing: commercial and subsistence Illicit drugs: coca, khat, poppies, marijuana
Capture of resources required by forest	Diversion of water for other human needs; diversion of animal nutrients for human needs; diversion of forest litter for human needs
Use forest components directly	Wood and leaves Material: construction (buildings, transportation) Material: small products (furniture, chips) Fiber: cardboard and paper products (pulp) Fuel: charcoal (transportation, cooking, heating) Food: fodder for ungulates and other browsing animals Fruits and nuts: human consumption, animal feed, baits Bark: cork, landscaping material Fluids: saps, latex, oils, water Chemicals: pharmaceuticals, fertilizers Genetic material: seeds, rhizomes, cuttings Animals: human consumption, fur, feathers, hides, ornamental uses
Use of whole live trees	As ornamentals, horticultural production, or fencing in a different location
Destruction of forest to deny its use by others	Eliminate forest to remove enemy combatants' protection (use of defoliants); eliminate forest to disrupt forest peoples; eliminate forest or trees to remove habitat of animal or plant considered a pest

Table 5.3
Nonconsumptive Human Uses of Forests

Services	Type Provided	Benefits
Ecosystem	Climate system stabilization	Water vapor production; CO_2 storage and sink; temperature buffering; lowers surface albedo
	Hydrologic system stabilization	Water drainage and flow stabilization and seasonal buffering of floods; water quality control; water temperature control; detoxification of some pollutants
	Soil system stabilization	Erosion control; soil creation
	Ecosystem stabilization	Biodiversity; pest control; disease control; wildlife habitat
Social	Cultural	National heritage; communal heritage; local heritage
	Scientific	Knowledge is intrinsically valuable; education
	Philosophical/spiritual	Richer, more complex world better than simpler, more uniform one; wrong to kill nonhuman life; incorporated into some religions
	Aesthetic/symbolic	Proximate • Sensing: seeing likenesses of forests (paintings, photography, video) • Knowledge of existence Distal • Sensing (seeing vistas) • Experiential (outdoor recreation) Security buffer (reassuring that resources are not scarce); surrounded by biological entities; look of nature: old growth has a more natural appearance

Source: Adapted from Borza and Jamieson 1991 and Reid et al. 2002.

timber products provide most of the materials used in construction of many types of buildings and other structures. Hardwood timber with certain desirable characteristics is the basis for much furniture manufacturing. Paper and cardboard products are other important direct benefits from pulpwood and wood chips. In many parts of the world, wood and other cellulosic materials, often converted to charcoal, are a primary fuel for both cooking and space heating. Many species of trees, often grown in plantations, produce a wide variety of fruits and nuts. Various kinds of leaves, barks, saps, and oils are other forest products useful to humans.

In addition to providing timber and nontimber forest products, forest ecosystems provide additional nonconsumptive services from the local to the global level, as summarized in table 5.3. Ecosystem services are the benefits supplied to human societies by natural ecosystems (Daily et al. 1997). Ecosystem services are processes which influence and stabilize the climatic, hydrologic, edaphic, and ecological systems upon which humans depend. Like ecosystem services, forests provide important social services, which also are more difficult to quantify than the consumptive use of forest products. Benefits of forests, such as tourism and recreation, are more tangible than other social services.

Outdoor recreation provides other examples of nonconsumptive uses of forests. Many persons enjoy viewing forested landscapes from a vista, while others enjoy hiking, horseback riding, bird or mammal watching, camping, or hunting in most types of forests.

Forests Examined by CIPEC Research

Forest Types

CIPEC researchers have studied three forest types that together account for 21 percent of the areal extent of Earth's terrestrial surface and 65 percent of the area covered by forests (see table 5.1). These are (1) temperate deciduous forests, dominated by broadleaf trees that drop their leaves during cold weather; (2) tropical seasonal forests, which are deciduous or semideciduous during dry weather; and (3) tropical moist forests, characterized by broadleaf evergreen trees.

The most detailed discussion of forest conditions (defined in the next section) is presented in chapter 10, which presents a case study of several pine-oak–dominated forests in Guatemala and Honduras. Chapters 9 and 12 provide some additional case studies from Brazil, Uganda, Madagascar, and Nepal.

Forest Conditions

In each of the forest types studied, we undertook an assessment of forest conditions. The term "forest conditions" has been used in scientific literature for well over a century (Scientific 1888; Whitford 1901) and has been used to categorize or qualify the generalized state of a forest with regard to its "sustainability, productivity, aesthetics, contamination, utilization, diversity, and extent" (Riitters et al. 1992, 22–23). The term also has been used in reference to a variety of disturbances such as fire (C. Miller and Urban 2000), acidic deposition (Loucks 1992; Reams and Peterson 1992), and pollution (Kubin et al. 2000; Nordlund 2000). It is frequently (and incorrectly) used as a synonym for describing forest health (Gorte 2002; Ferretti et al. 1999; McLaughlin and Percy 1999). And the term has been used simply as a means to put biological indicators of forest assessments into context (Canterbury et al. 2000; Riitters et al. 1992).

Although most definitions of forest conditions have been ambiguous (Skelly 1989), numerous examples of studies and programs designed to examine forest conditions do exist. Some of these focus on the health of individual trees (which actually is an assessment of forest health), whereas others consider forest species composition or forest productivity, or both. For example, according to Innes and Boswell (1990), "all European countries now monitor the condition of their forests" (p. 790). However, they comment that "techniques [to monitor forest conditions] vary slightly from country to country" (p. 790). In the United Kingdom, for example, the Forestry Commission collects data on crown discoloration, crown density, needle retention, premature leaf loss, flowering, shoot mortality, leaf rolling, branching density, extent, and location to examine forest condition. In Italy, the Ministry for Agricultural Policy's forest ecosystem management program measures crown transparency, crown discoloration, and the occurrence of a series of damaging agents. Even though some aspects of these and other programs do seem to be similar, or at least overlap, there are further differences in sampling intensity, frequency, and spatial extent.

Recent interest in global climate change has intensified interest in examining forest conditions. In Finland, the effects of climate change (more specifically, weather changes) from 1980 to 1995 were studied in regard to tree damage. Tree height, needle and leaf browning, damage to phloem and woody tissues, nutrient pools, insect damage, premature needle or leaf shedding, and number of leaves were all examined under the context of changes in temperature, moisture, and growing season (Raitio 2000).

Riitters et al. (1992) describe some indicators to detect changes in forest conditions. These key indicators include landscape patterns (connectivity, dominance, contagion, and fractal dimensions), visual symptoms (how the trees in the forest appear), foliar nutrients (micro- and macronutrient pools and dynamics in vegetation), soil nutrients (micro- and macronutrient pools and dynamics in the soil), and growth efficiency (the ratio of actual tree growth to capacity for growing, as suggested by Waring 1983).

Lundquist and Beatty (1999) state that forest conditions are assessed by comparing the current ecological state to a range of values specified for a number of variables. Unfortunately, there is a lack of consensus concerning which variables should be examined, how they should be examined, and at what frequency and intensity (both temporal and spatial) to describe forest conditions. Our research group developed its own set of "most useful" variables in providing a quantitative assessment of forest conditions, as described below. Our group currently is undertaking an

Box 5.1
Variables and Methods of Forest Mensuration

Variables measured or observed in the field:	Variables calculated from field data or measured in the laboratory:
Diameter at breast height (dbh) of tree boles by species	Basal area by tree species
Total height of trees by species	Basal area of stand
Density of trees by species	Relative dominance (basal area of species/basal area of stand) by tree species
Distribution (frequency) of trees by species	Age, size, taxonomic, or functional classes of vegetation
Estimate of successional age of forest	Biomass or carbon content of vegetation
Evidence of invasive, non-native plants affecting forest	Biodiversity estimates by taxonomic or functional classes
Evidence of pests or diseases affecting forest	Soils: physical properties (texture, structure); chemical properties (C, N, P, K)
Evidence of pollution affecting forest	
Evidence of fire or timber harvesting	
Evidence of livestock grazing or erosion	

in-depth study of the most appropriate variables for comparisons between a "reference" (typically old-growth, largely undisturbed) forest and various forests of the same type in the same (or very similar) physiographic and climatologic environment but that have been subjected to natural or human disturbance. Such quantitative comparisons of "forest conditions," both within various forests of the same type and among forest types, will be useful in assessing the effects of various disturbances.

Geographic Locations, Site Selection, and Traverses

At most CIPEC research locations, before beginning fieldwork, prints of multispectral color composites (see chapter 6) derived from subset areas of Landsat Thematic Mapper (TM) satellite images are prepared at scales of 1:25,000 or 1:30,000 with a 1-km grid overlay using the Universal Transverse Mercator (UTM) coordinate system. These prints are highly useful in selecting potential sites for analysis and in interviews with landowners. In-depth interviews are conducted with each landowner or occupant at each site. Information about past land use and forest management practices are obtained for each site, and initial observations of several potential sites are made. The goal is to select a forested area that is representative of the forests in the location of interest.

Traverses are prescribed, repeatable methods for locating sampling points in field research. Traverse methods vary according to topography and vegetation density. Regular grids and the use of randomly chosen coordinates provide a statistically robust method of locating plots. However, in irregular topography and dense vegetation, establishing a grid is infeasible. Linear traverses along topographic features, such as ridges, with plots dispersed from the transect line, are often a good choice. When the forest stand is sufficiently large, using the random distance and random bearing method provides an excellent way to locate plots. A global positioning system (GPS) receiver is used to determine UTM or latitude/longitude coordinates for all plots. Plot locations that are not representative of the stand are not sampled.

Sample Plots and Measures of Individual Plants

A nested plot design is used: larger plots are used to sample large trees (dbh >10 cm), medium-sized plots to sample small trees and saplings (dbh >2–<10 cm), and smaller plots to sample understory vegetation, coarse woody debris, and fine litter. Plots may be either circular or square; CIPEC researchers have used both geometries. For circular plots, large plots have a 10-m radius (315 m^2 area), medium plots have a 3-m radius (28.3 m^2 area), and small plots have a 1-m radius (3.1 m^2 area). For square plots, large plots are 18 × 18 m (324 m^2 area), medium plots are 5 × 5 m (25 m^2 area), and small plots are 1 × 1 m (1 m^2 area). Circular plots work well in less dense vegetation and regular, flatter terrain, whereas square (or rectangular) plots are preferable in dense vegetation and irregular terrain. At least twenty plots are sampled at each site.

In the large and medium plots, individual trees are identified by species, and dbh and total height are measured. Species identification is facilitated by using experienced local botanists in the field. Also in large plots, careful observations are made to estimate the successional age of the stand and for evidence of past forest management practices (timber harvest), disturbances such as fire or livestock grazing, or the presence of invasive species, pests, or pathogens. In the small plots, seedlings and saplings of trees are identified to species and, when possible, herbaceous plants and grasses are identified. Chapter 10 provides an example of how these forest mensuration data are used in a CIPEC case study in Guatemala and Honduras.

Soil Samples

In some CIPEC sites, soil samples are taken using an auger at 20-cm intervals to a depth of 1 m in at least three plots at each site. In a few sites, a soil pit 25 × 25 cm in area is excavated at 20-cm intervals to a depth of 60 cm. Roots are sieved from the excavated soil samples, divided into categories of fine root (<2 mm in diameter) and coarse root (>2 mm), weighed, and collected. Also, in a few sites bulk density sampling rings are used to take soil samples in each 20-cm depth interval and used to calculate bulk density and the carbon content in soils. Soil samples are placed in sealed plastic bags and stored in a freezer until chemical and physical analyses are completed.

Training Samples

Training samples are areas of known land-cover types and composition used to develop and verify remotely sensed image-processing techniques such as spectral analysis and classifications. The term "training sample" is used to refer to (1) a selected area of pixels representative of a specific land cover in a remotely sensed image and (2) the actual land cover observed on the ground for that location. For the former to have high validity, observations of the latter must occur. Sometimes the field observations are referred to as "training sites." Chapter 6 provides more background information about the various remote-sensing instruments and techniques mentioned here.

CIPEC researchers developed and have used a detailed protocol for conducting the actual observations of selected areas developed from an initial analysis of the remotely sensed image. Prior to going to the field, researchers review the Landsat TM (or Multispectral Scanner) images of a specific area, often using two multispectral color composites of the area: one from the TM infrared bands (bands 4, 5, and 7 set to red, green, and blue, respectively, called an "all infrared" composite) and a second displaying the visible TM bands (bands 1, 2, and 3 set to blue, green, and red, respectively, called a "natural color" composite). For image classification all areas that appear to be "pure" samples in the image are identified. These include areas that have homogeneous reflectance values within a block of pixels, such as a 3×3 pixel area. Examples typically include agricultural fields, open water, mature forests, grass and pasture, and urban and suburban areas and other built features (such as roads, highways, airport runways, dams).

Individual point sampling is used to provide statistically representative information about the characteristics of land cover within specified pixels. Relatively inexpensive and accurate GPS receivers have greatly facilitated this analysis. Researchers note the coordinates of a group of pixels in the image and use a GPS receiver to find that location on the ground. Although this method is based on methods used for measuring plant communities, they are not ecological sampling techniques. Images show very coarse pictures of land cover and cannot distinguish between different plant communities except at a broad level; therefore training samples are not a replacement for ecological sampling. Thus, the collection of training samples requires a balance between information that a satellite may observe and detailed data that can be observed only on the ground.

Field data forms are used to assure a standard set of information about training samples on the ground. Using UTM coordinate positions developed from the image analysis, specific areas of representative land-cover types are selected for field observation. Although the specific details of the observation vary greatly among land-cover classes, the overall objective is to obtain a detailed, quantitative dataset for the target area. For forests, dominant tree species are identified and some measures (dbh, height) of individual trees are made. For agricultural areas, the specific crop and its stage of development are observed. For built features, details about the nature, size, and approximate age of the structure are observed.

Concluding Remarks

Climate, topography, soils, and vegetation interact to produce regional-level patterns of distinguishable ecosystems. Those patterns occur even in the complete absence of humans. Until fairly recently humans impacted forest ecosystems primarily at the local level, typically by the use of vegetation and manipulation of soil nutrients. With technological developments, humans continue to modify vegetation and soils, but now have begun to modify topography and climate as well. In some areas, these human modifications of the biophysical world are strikingly apparent. In many areas, both the nature of the human modifications and their consequences on forest ecosystems, both intentional and unintentional, are complex and fairly subtle. Thus, in order to understand the consequences of human modifications on forest ecosystems it is necessary to (1) understand the biological and physical factors that influence the nature and composition of the forest and (2) make the most appropriate observations of variables describing "forest conditions." Studies of how human behaviors and institutions influence forest ecosystems conducted in the absence of considerable knowledge of those ecosystems will be largely meaningless.

Note

1. Multiply that value by 10 to get units of Mg C/ha. Similarly, dividing the total NPP by the total area for a given ecosystem type gives NPP in units of kg C/m^2 per year, and multiplying that value by 10 gives units of Mg C/ha per year.

III

Methods

The chapters in part III focus on some critical methods that are used widely by the land-use/land-cover change and human-environment interactions research community. Attention to methods is no less important than attention to theoretical and conceptual rigor. Methodological rigor should not be confused with methodological inflexibility. Rather, the chapters that follow point to the importance of fitting methods to the questions asked, and to the tradeoffs between using one method vis-à-vis another. A key point the authors make is that these methods are not disciplinary by their nature, even if perhaps historically they may have been started in one discipline. They are now widely used across the social and physical sciences, and, because of this broad use, applications are rich over a range of environmental problems.

Chapter 6, by Glen Green, Charles Schweik, and J. C. Randolph, focuses on remote sensing, and particularly on the challenge presented to researchers by a variety of sources of data variation deriving not from land-cover changes by themselves, but from atmospheric, sensor, and illumination effects. This is never a simple task, but it is particularly challenging in those cases where a researcher wants to make comparisons across sites and across time. In those cases, the number of sources of variability increases across that many satellite images and can lead to significant errors in interpretation. The key is to determine a way to keep things as constant as possible, so the analysis can focus on the actual changes in land cover. To do so requires complex techniques for converting the data from the way they are collected, as digital numbers, and converting them to a more common framework, such as surface reflectance. The authors explain the reasons why this is important to those delving into remotely sensed data collected by satellites—Landsat, SPOT, ASTER, IKONOS, and the newer families of submeter resolution satellites (e.g., Quickbird)—and how to choose the right method to process the images to achieve effective comparisons. Readers who are specialists in remote sensing may not find this chapter as interesting as those who are less familiar with remote sensing and who may welcome the technical introduction to the physics involved.

In chapter 7, Tom Evans, Leah VanWey, and Emilio Moran discuss the ways in which human-environment research can benefit from the use of geographic information systems (GIS) approaches. GIS is just one of a family of approaches to making one's data spatially explicit, that is, making data collection always include a precise location in latitude/longitude or some equivalent system, such as UTM (Universal Transverse Mercator). Many scientists in the past seemed concerned with the preciseness of the temporal occurrence of events, but less often with precisely locating events in both space and time. Geography has shown the rest of the sciences the importance of place, and we now have sophisticated ways in which to spatially locate on Earth anything and anybody at any time with the use of global positioning system (GPS) devices. They are now becoming widely used in automobiles, camping, and research. By taking advantage of the twenty-four satellites that make up the network that informs GPS devices, it is possible to locate oneself anywhere on the planet with great accuracy, sometimes to within a meter or less. This provides researchers with great power for analysis of the relationship of people to the land and to forests by permitting a very close linkage between landscape features and the people who act on it through land use within particular boundaries, whether they are private or communal tenure systems. The authors provide examples of some of the challenges our group faced in making these interactions have analytical power, given the range of variation in the ways in which people constitute themselves on the landscape. The chapter is not an advanced discussion of GIS, so readers who are specialists in this field may wish to browse it quickly, but the great majority of readers who are not familiar with the analytical use of GIS (it is a lot more than making maps!) will want to read it carefully for insights into relevant applications to their work.

Chapter 8, by Tom Evans, Darla Munroe, and Dawn Parker, focuses on the use of modeling in land-use/land-cover change research, and particularly on our experience with three types of modeling approaches: dynamic simulation models, agent-based models, and econometric modeling. The authors highlight the importance of examining data availability, the level of complexity desired in relation to these data, and concern with issues of temporal and spatial scale before choosing the appropriate modeling approach. Like the other chapters, this one points to the advantages and disadvantages of each modeling approach, and when and where to use each one. Readers who are modelers may not find much new here, but other readers will find the discussion a balanced assessment, peppered with our practical work using these models, of some use in making their own choices. The balance between completeness and reductionism is a common one in modeling and one for which there is no simple solution. The only complete model of a system is the system itself; thus, modeling must try to simplify the complexity of systems to a reduced number of variables. Choosing correctly is a constant challenge.

6

Retrieving Land-Cover Change Information from Landsat Satellite Images by Minimizing Other Sources of Reflectance Variability

Glen M. Green, Charles M. Schweik, and J. C. Randolph

During the past century, human activities have had a devastating effect on Earth's biota and ecosystem functions (Costanza et al. 1997; Houghton et al. 2001). They have modified a significant proportion of Earth's terrestrial ecosystems (Vitousek et al. 1997), and the resulting land-cover modifications have led to significant losses of plant and animal species (E. Wilson 2002).

Our Center for the Study of Institutions, Population, and Environmental Change (CIPEC) research group examines how humans affect and manage some of Earth's forest lands. We restrict our analysis to land occupied by three forest types: moist tropical forests, dry tropical forests, and temperate deciduous forests (see chapter 5). Even in restricting ourselves to three types of forest cover, the study of land-cover change is a very complex undertaking. The spatial extent of these three forest types dwarfs what an individual researcher could possibly examine alone. Interdisciplinary teams of researchers are needed to address the scope of such studies. Human impacts on forests often involve long durations compared to an individual human life span. Also, researchers may endeavor to study episodes of forest change that began years before they commence their study. Land-cover change often involves both anthropogenic and nonanthropogenic processes and thus falls within the intersection of the social and natural sciences—an intersection that has suffered from traditional academic divisions.

In overcoming these hurdles, land-cover change studies may benefit by investigating datasets, analytical methodologies, and theories which incorporate (1) broad levels of space and time (large spatial extents and long temporal durations), (2) numerous processes that act across various spatial distributions and at various temporal frequencies, and (3) different disciplinary perspectives. While the scope of the problems facing the global community is great, our experiences and work with rigorous interpretation of Landsat satellite images may provide helpful guidance and suggest productive approaches and methods for other scholars to use (see chapter 3 for an introduction to these concepts).

Many publications exist that demonstrate how remotely sensed satellite images can provide a unique and robust dataset to understand land-cover change processes across a critical range of spatial extents and temporal durations (e.g., see chapter 11 and its citations). However, land-cover change scientists have begun to realize that many other processes, both physical and social, other than those directly related to land-cover change, also must be considered (e.g., changes associated with seasonal differences in climate or those associated with the day-night cycle). While many of these processes may not involve anthropogenic land-cover change, many of them, unfortunately, can significantly influence what is detected by a remote-sensing satellite such as Landsat. As a result, the other sources of image variability can confound the retrieval of land-cover change information from remotely sensed images. There is a real danger that the unwanted image variability will obscure land-cover change information that is actually present in the images or, worse, that the variability may be incorrectly identified by the researcher as evidence of land-cover change itself. This chapter examines several specific methodologies and underlying scientific principles that can be employed to help remove or at least minimize the sources of satellite image variability not directly associated with land-cover change. We believe these strategies also will help facilitate comparative land-cover change studies among sites, locations, landscapes, and regions.

We will accomplish this by addressing four main topics: (1) strategies and methods that facilitate the integration of satellite image data into land-cover change studies, paying particular attention to issues involving image sampling in both space and time; (2) methods needed to minimize variability in image reflectance associated with seasonal weather effects and interannual climate variability; (3) normalization methods needed to minimize variability in image reflectance associated with differences in satellite sensor instrumentation, illumination, and atmospheric conditions; and (4) strategies to minimize variability associated with strictly biogeophysical differences across the landscape to more thoroughly isolate land-cover change processes related to social and institutional differences.

Integrating Remote Sensing across Space and Time

While employing remote-sensing techniques to land-cover change studies has many advantages, it is not without costs. Remote-sensing analyses, especially those that involve comparisons across space and time, often require significant investments in labor and equipment. Major investments in the early part of project planning and image database construction (i.e., image processing) may account for much of a project's budget. Many of these costs must be incurred long before the results of a project begin to emerge. Thus, an adequate budget and effective management are required for the long-term success of a complex land-cover change project.

One of the earliest challenges a multidisciplinary research effort faces is developing a common vocabulary. With respect to remote sensing, this may involve some training for collaborators who lack prior satellite image experience and some training for remote-sensing personnel in the phenomenologies they will be asked to identify, for example, forest ecology for those involved with forest mapping. All parties may benefit from learning to avoid disciplinary jargon.

Broad comparative projects often demand more consistency in data collection methods even though individual researchers encounter pressing local site demands. Like any dataset, satellite images must share similar spatial extents and resolutions as well as temporal durations and intervals with those processes under study. Also, any images must be coincident in both space and time to produce interpretable and significant results to answer the questions being addressed. Chapter 3 discusses how space-time diagrams, maps, and timelines can be used to check the synchronization of these parameters.

The Landsat System

The Landsat satellite system, its image data archive, and the body of analytical literature that has developed from it, can address many questions involving land-cover change processes (USGS 1979, 1984, 2003). Landsat satellites detect electromagnetic radiation reflected by Earth's surface features at visible and infrared wavelengths and regularly monitor the land areas between 81° N and 81° S latitude. Table 6.1 gives a chronology of the Landsat series of satellites, starting with the launch of Landsat 1 in 1972 through Landsat 7, which was launched in 1999 and continues to operate.

One of the greatest advantages of the Landsat image archive is its long duration—over thirty years. Many satellite remote-sensing platforms exist today, yet none can match the Landsat system's duration. Therefore, while another satellite may offer a better current match to a researcher's particular requirements, land-cover change studies often require datasets spanning many decades. Thus, many projects often incorporate Landsat images, since they may be the only data available for the past. For these reasons, Landsat played the prominent role in our use of satellite image analysis for land-cover change detection.

Table 6.1
Landsat Satellite Parameters

Satellite	Launch Date	Out of Service	Instruments	Orbit Altitude	WRS no.	Repeat Interval
Landsat 1[a]	7/23/1972	1/6/1978	RBV, MSS	920 km	1	18 days
Landsat 2[a]	1/22/1975	2/25/1982	RBV, MSS	920 km	1	18 days
Landsat 3[a]	3/5/1978	3/31/1983	RBV, MSS	920 km	1	18 days
Landsat 4	7/16/1982	6/1/2001[b]	MSS, TM	705 km	2	16 days
Landsat 5	3/1/1984	12/31/1999	MSS, TM	705 km	2	16 days
Landsat 6[c]	10/5/1993	—	ETM	—	—	—
Landsat 7	4/15/1999	Operational[d]	ETM+	705 km	2	16 days

WRS, World Reference System; RBV, Return Beam Vidicon; MSS, Multispectral Scanner; TM, Thematic Mapper; ETM, Enhanced Thematic Mapper; ETM+, Enhanced Thematic Mapper Plus.
[a] Named Earth Resources Technology Satellites (ERTS) until the launch of Landsat 4.
[b] Decommissioned in 1993.
[c] Failed to achieve orbit.
[d] Scan Line Corrector failed May 31, 2003.

Landsats 1, 2, and 3 had a temporal sampling interval (frequency or repeat cycle) of the same area every eighteen days, while images from Landsats 4, 5, and 7 were acquired every sixteen days. Although more frequent image acquisition intervals (daily) are available from other satellites, eighteen- and sixteen-day sampling intervals usually are adequate for land-cover change studies. Because of adequate image frequency and other good matches of the dataset to the process under study (see figures 3.5, 3.6, and 3.7), we present examples using only Landsat images.

The primary sensor instruments of the Landsat system include the Multispectral Scanner (MSS) on Landsats 1 through 5, the Thematic Mapper (TM) on Landsats 4 and 5, and the Enhanced Thematic Mapper Plus (ETM+) on Landsat 7. Figure 6.1 depicts the spectral and spatial resolution characteristics of the instruments and shows that several wavelength bands from different instruments provide comparable information, even though image resolution changes. Understanding the spectral characteristics of land cover, while technically described by a spatial dimension (in micrometers, or 10^{-6} m), is often very useful for monitoring change. An individual Landsat image can capture information across a wide range of spatial levels: from as fine as an individual picture element (pixel), through an entire scene (185 × 170 km for TM or ETM+), to larger extents when multiple adjacent scenes are combined. Regional and even continental extents can be achieved by using mosaics of multiple Landsat images (Sussman et al. 2003; Jensen and Hodgson 2004).

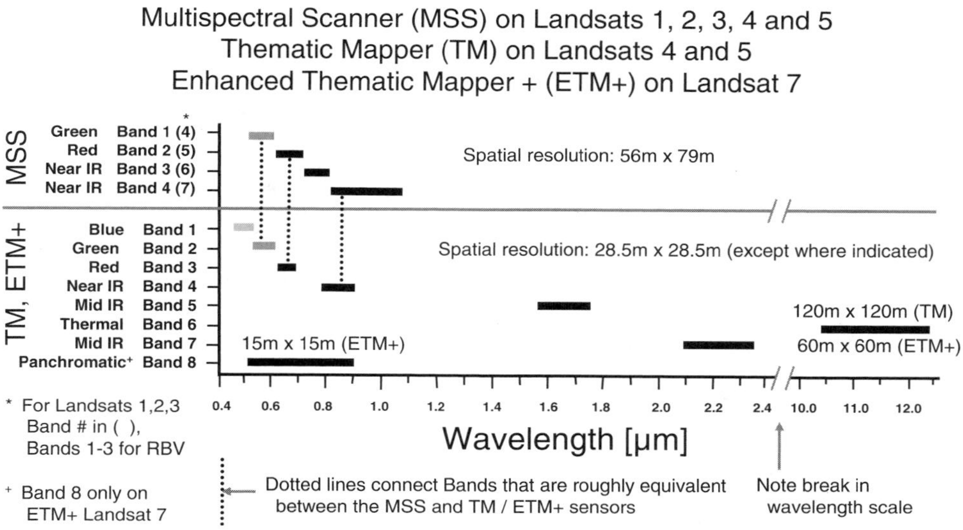

Figure 6.1
The spectral characteristics and spatial resolutions of the different Landsat satellite sensor instruments (see also table 6.1).

Since land-cover change studies often involve images acquired from several Landsat satellites, we use the term *location* (see example in figure 6.2) to refer to the spatial extent of the overlap between the footprints captured by a Landsat 1, 2, or 3 satellite image (World Reference System-1, WRS-1) and the corresponding footprints acquired from a Landsat 4, 5, or 7 image (WRS-2). The two coordinate systems (WRS-1 and WRS-2) resulted from lowering the satellite orbit altitude from 920 km to 705 km between Landsats 3 and 4 (see table 6.1). This change often creates a shift in many Landsat footprints when constructing a time series of Landsat images (figure 6.2). The orbits of the later Landsat satellites were lowered to permit space shuttles to service them. While no Landsat satellites were serviced in this way due to the closing of the Vandenberg shuttle launch facility following the *Challenger* accident, many Landsat change-detection analyses must now accommodate these shifts.

Landsat images are acquired in the morning (local time) as the satellite traces an orbital path from north to south in a swath 185 km wide (see *b* in figure 6.3). The WRS coordinate systems divide these north-south paths into approximately 170-km-long image segments called rows (see *c* in figure 6.3). Thus, a given Landsat scene is located by a unique pair of path and row coordinates for WRS-1 or WRS-2,

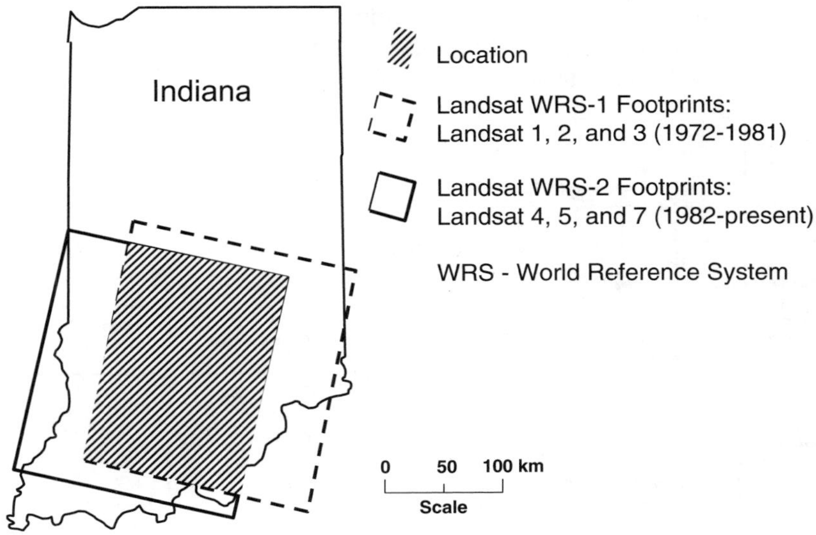

Figure 6.2
Due to a change in Landsat satellite orbit elevation between Landsats 1, 2, and 3 and Landsats 4, 5, and 7, the ground footprints of images acquired from these two groups of satellites often do not align. As a consequence, for a given area there are two Landsat image World Reference System (WRS) path and row coordinates: WRS-1 (for Landsats 1, 2, and 3), and WRS-2 (for Landsats 4, 5, and 7). The overlap between the two WRS footprints is termed a "location."

depending on which satellite acquired it. Landsat WRS maps are available from the U.S. Geological Survey (USGS) Earth Resources Observation Systems (EROS) Data Center.

Research Questions and Associated Research Designs

Landsat data can be used to help answer three general land-cover research questions. First, What are the spatial extent and distribution of land cover at specific locations? This question can be addressed using one of three research designs (*a*, *b*, and *c* in figure 6.3) that examine one location at one time. Strategy *a* shows the simple case of a single Landsat scene, while designs *b* and *c* involve multiple but spatially proximate scenes. Strategy *b* illustrates the use of multiple scenes that are adjacent or close and acquired along the same path. Landsat MSS, TM, and ETM+ sensors use side-sweeping scanners that produce a continuous swath of diurnal image data along a single orbital path. This continuous image is divided by rows

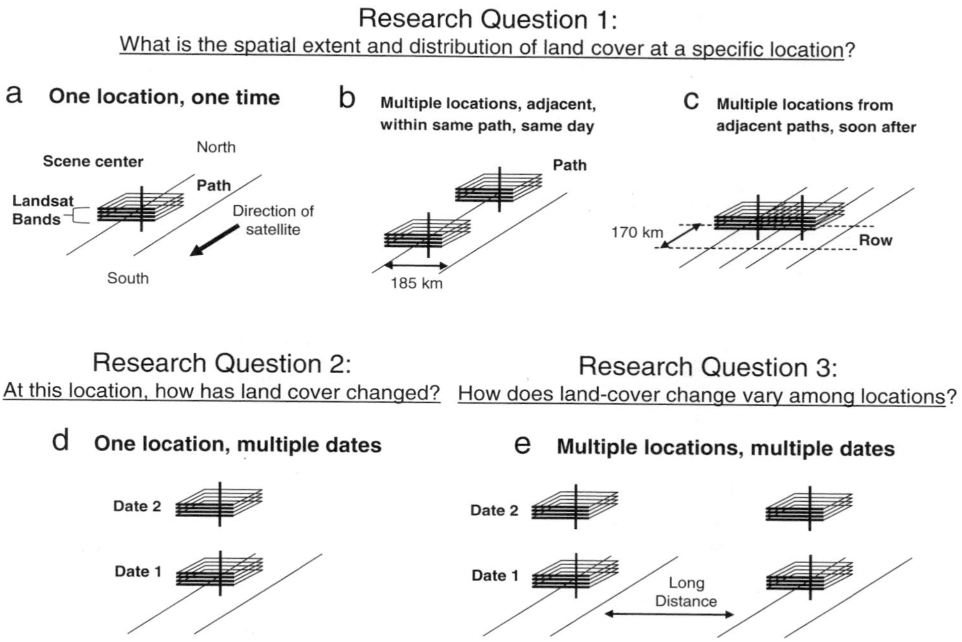

Figure 6.3
Land-cover change research questions and research designs using Landsat images.

into individual Landsat scenes for distribution. Thus, adjacent or close scenes along the same path acquired on the same day could be considered contiguous portions of a larger image. Strategy *c* involves multiple scenes acquired along overlapping paths on the same row. The amount of overlap, or sidelap, between adjacent paths varies as a function of latitude, from 85 percent at 80° N and 80° S to 14 percent at the equator (Freden and Gordon 1983). While adjacent image paths for Landsats 1, 2, and 3 are acquired on successive days, adjacent paths for Landsats 4, 5, and 7 are acquired at seven- or nine-day intervals (Freden and Gordon 1983). Therefore, with MSS scenes from adjacent rows acquired with Landsat 1, 2, or 3, it is possible to increase the spatial extent of a study while maintaining nearly equivalent times of acquisition. This advantage increases toward the equator.

The second general land-cover research question that Landsat data can be used to address is, At a specific location, how has land cover changed? Multiple Landsat images acquired at the same location have been used in many change-detection studies. Research design *d* in figure 6.3 represents this type of land-cover change comparison at one location across several dates. Due to swath convergence in adjacent paths toward the poles (Freden and Gordon 1983), design *c* in figure 6.3 also can be used to investigate this question at high latitudes.

A third land-cover research question, and one gaining in importance, is, How do the nature and extent of land-cover change differ among locations? Research design *e* in figure 6.3 can address this question by examining images from multiple dates at multiple locations. For example, in this book we describe the study of deforestation through time in three different forest types as influenced by different institutions. Studies that attempt to link broad-level land-cover change phenomena with multiple site-level data also are facilitated by this research design. Some previous studies have investigated these types of questions but have not incorporated a remote-sensing component (e.g., see Agrawal 1996; Gibson and Koontz 1998; E. Ostrom and Wertime 2000). Other studies (see chapter 9) have begun such comparative endeavors (Skole and Tucker 1993; E. Moran and Brondízio 1998; E. Moran et al. 2003).

Let us now look at an example of research question 3 in figure 6.3. Our work at CIPEC asks why some forested areas are thriving while others are experiencing major degradation, and still others suffer rapid losses. The online supplement to Dietz et al. (2003) presents Landsat image composites (explained in the image product section later in this chapter) at five different locations derived from three Landsat images acquired on different dates for each location. These multitemporal color composites show that all forms of ownership—government, private, and communal—can succeed or fail to halt deforestation. We have found both extremes occurring together in small geographic areas. The supplement to Dietz et al. (2003) shows how some communities and groups manage to meet their needs by producing food and income from forested areas and conserve their forests, while others fail to achieve these two objectives. We find that public policies, private actions, and human institutions all play key roles in forest loss and regrowth. This study provides a good example of how research design *e* in figure 6.3 can be employed in land-cover change studies.

A Strategic Cyclical Scaling Approach

The selection of where to conduct a land-cover change study can enhance our ability to pose and answer significant land-cover change questions, yet often an ad hoc process is used in their selection. For example, a researcher might examine a satellite image that includes areas that match her or his previous research. While this approach might enhance earlier research, it may not take full advantage of available satellite remote-sensing products. An alternative, potentially useful approach may be to select locations for remote-sensing analysis (and subsequent fieldwork) that maximize the variability associated with the processes under study while at the same time trying to minimize the variability associated with other sources. Typically, two types of research designs compare ecological processes across a range of spatial extents: (1) top-down approaches that move from analysis of large extents to analysis of smaller extents (e.g., from regional to site level) and (2) bottom-up approaches that move from small to larger extents. When used in isolation, neither technique offers an ideal predictive model (Jarvis 1993). Top-down approaches, such as the Monteith model (Monteith 1977), are not useful for making predictions outside the range of variation incorporated in the model development and typically aggregate detailed information. Bottom-up approaches can model ecological phenomena at the process level; however, they are usually quite complex and highly sensitive to initial conditions (Jarvis 1993). Furthermore, variables that serve as good predictors of system function at the site level, for example, may not be appropriate at broader levels (Jarvis 1993). To mitigate these problems, some researchers have advocated a combined approach (Jarvis 1993; Vitousek 1993; Root and Schneider 1995).

The authors of this book have tried to employ a research approach grounded in the ideas of Root and Schneider (1995), which take advantage of both the large spatial extent of satellite images as well as detailed site-level ecological and institutional field research. Root and Schneider proposed the "strategic cyclical scaling" (SCS) paradigm in which top-down and bottom-up "approaches are cyclically applied and strategically designed to address practical problems" (p. 337). Relationships, trends, or associations identified at large spatial extents are used to focus more site-level investigations to ensure that the phenomena at the site level really are generating the broader relationships. The SCS approach advocates a continual cycling between top-down and bottom-up approaches, with "each successive investigation building on previous insights obtained from all scales" (p. 337).

To apply these ideas to the study of land-cover change, particularly in the context of forested landscapes, the first step in our analytical process may be to consider the broadest level of biophysical processes that influence the distribution of forest vegetation. The analyst might begin at the continental or regional spatial level and consider general climatic and physical conditions that have existed for long periods. At these broad levels, climate, geomorphology, geologic parent material, and soil are biophysical factors that influence the distribution of vegetation. A significant literature exists to help the researcher identify broad climatic influences (Breckle 2002). Biomes (see chapter 5) represent the largest geographic areas where similar climate and soils result in distinguishable patterns of vegetation. A simplified example of

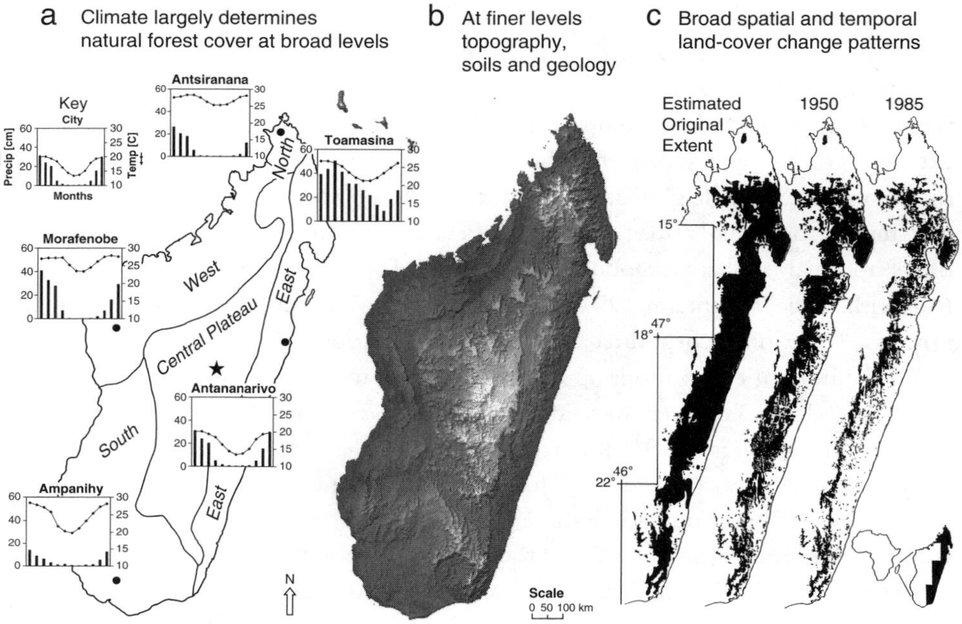

Figure 6.4
Deforestation in the eastern tropical moist forests of Madagascar. Multiple factors can affect the distribution of forests. At regional and continental levels, the natural distribution of forests is mainly controlled by climate (*a*). Two second-order factors more important at location, landscape, and site levels are topography (*b*) and historic human land-cover changes (*c*). (From Green and Sussman 1990.)

two broad-level vegetation classes (tropical moist forest and tropical dry forest) in Madagascar is shown in figure 12.2. At this broad level, the distribution of the two forest types is associated with seasonal weather patterns shown in a simplified way in *a* of figure 6.4 (Wernstedt 1972; FTM 1985). Such continental- or regional-level maps can help the researcher understand these broad biophysical factors in a particular geographic area of interest.

Next, differences in the distribution of topographic relief (*b* in figure 6.4), surface geology, and soils can be used to further explain the distribution of vegetation biomes (Breckle 2002). This shaded relief image of topography in Madagascar is derived from Shuttle Radar Topography Mission data (JPL 2003). Hilly or mountainous regional topography, for example, is an important factor in determining where forests occur in our U.S. and Madagascar sites (Green and Sussman 1990; Sussman et al. 1994; Evans et al. 2001a).

Next, the researcher may move to a regional spatial level using existing literature or datasets that reveal historical land-cover change patterns and the processes that affected them. A time series of regional maps of land cover from given dates can be used to investigate where these anthropogenic processes have occurred or are occurring. For example, a regional analysis of deforestation of the tropical moist forests of eastern Madagascar is shown in *c* of figure 6.4 (Green and Sussman 1990). The patterns might be used to sample finer-level areas based on their relationship to the advancing deforestation front. Also, Emilio Moran and colleagues (E. Moran and Brondízio 1998; E. Moran et al. 2002a) used broad differences along a gradient of soil fertility to create a sampling transect of Landsat locations across the Amazon basin, all located within a single forest type (moist tropical forest) and with similar topography characteristics. The sampling of location-level studies also could be guided, for example, by using the deforestation history of the eastern deciduous forest of the United States (see *e* in figure 3.3) (M. Williams 1989). Other factors, such as population density, migration patterns, roads, rivers, and political boundaries, also are known to influence where forests occur at regional spatial levels, and their distribution often can be determined from existing maps.

Spatial Sampling

Aided by an understanding of the broad spatial processes (at the continental or regional level), the land-cover change researcher can use this information to stratify sampling at the location level, collecting specific parameters thought to influence land-cover change. Using these relationships and Landsat WRS coordinate maps, the researcher might select Landsat locations that capture the central trends identified. In addition, this analysis might identify some anomalies where the general trends (e.g., forest cover distribution) do not appear to hold, and the researcher could examine why these anomalies exist. We return to the discussion of anomalies later in the chapter and in chapter 12.

Other considerations related to the choice of study location are also important: transportation, lodging, logistic support, and safety of field personnel. Having access to an existing research facility, if only a small field station, can be extremely valuable. Nearby offices of local government agencies and nongovernment organizations often can assist with local arrangements. Adequate lodging for the research team should be located within a reasonable distance from the potential study sites so most of the daylight hours are not used getting to and from the sites. Dependable transportation is also important. Finally, and perhaps most important, the safety of the field sites, from both natural hazards and human conflicts or crime, is critical.

After locations are identified, the researcher can begin image processing and analysis, to identify potential field sites within the locations. Ideally, the preliminary image processing and generation of image-based map products together with topographic maps can be used to guide site-specific sampling during fieldwork, which in turn provides ground-truthed measurements for more refined Landsat-based land-cover mapping (E. Moran et al. 1994a; E. Moran and Brondízio 1998; Schweik and Green 1999). Sussman et al. (2003) give an example from recent fieldwork in Madagascar of methods used in the preparation of image products, the choice of study sites, and logistical considerations for the field. This study employs the sampling approach described above by using Landsat-derived multitemporal image products to identify broad deforestation patterns in southern Madagascar, and these broad patterns are subsequently used to identify sites to be investigated in the field.

Simple Landsat-Derived Image Products

An example of two image products derived from Landsat data is shown in plate 2. The area is 25 km on a side and includes a forest located in Madagascar. The top row in the figure shows multispectral color composites, each generated from the three different dates of Landsat images used in this particular study: a 1973 MSS color composite uses bands 1, 2, and 4 colored in blue, red, and green, respectively; a 1985 TM composite uses bands 2, 3, and 4 colored in blue, red, and green, respectively; and a 2000 ETM+ composite uses bands, 2, 3, and 4 colored in blue, red, and green, respectively (see also figure 6.1 for comparability of bands). Each of the multispectral composites is generated using bands that correspond to the same wavelengths and depicts forest as green and the surrounding savanna as tan or brown. The figure shows that forest present in 1973 and 1985 has been cleared from the central portion of the 2000 multispectral composite.

The second row in plate 2 shows single-band images from each of the image dates: band 2 from the 1973 MSS scene, band 3 from the 1985 TM scene, and band 3 from the 2000 ETM+ scene, each acquired in the red wavelength. At this wavelength, forested land is dark and nonforest (largely savanna) is depicted in shades of gray or white. Differences in brightness in the savanna-covered areas between the dates probably are caused by year-to-year climatic variability and different burning histories. These three single-band images from each date can be combined to form a multitemporal color composite (bottom of plate 2). For this composite, the three single bands are combined such that the 1973 band is set to blue, the 1985 band is set to green, and the 2000 band is set to red. Combined in this way, the colors of the multitemporal composite depict land-cover change. Dense forest that remained stable for the three dates is black, while many of the savanna areas are white (other areas of savanna are depicted in light pastel colors caused by slight differences in grass cover and burn scars between the three dates). Red areas of the composite depict forest that was cleared between 1985 and 2000. Multitemporal color composites probably provide the most cost-effective means of retrieving land-cover change information from a time series of Landsat scenes.

Applying the cyclical scaling approach to the landscape and site levels (see chapter 3), for example, may involve the selection of one or more sites within a location, an examination of human-environment relationships in the field at each site, and consideration of how much variability at the location level is explained by information gathered during fieldwork. After land-cover change at a site is reasonably well understood, the spatial extent of the study may be broadened by adding more sites in the location (resources permitting). It then may be appropriate to change to a bottom-up approach and investigate other candidate locations.

Temporal Sampling

Any research design also requires appropriate consideration of temporal sampling. We use a similar approach to maximize the variability associated with the process being studied while simultaneously trying (through appropriate temporal sampling) to minimize the variability not associated with that process. Different biogeophysical and social processes can act over different temporal durations and thus contribute to differences in Landsat image reflectance (figure 6.5). For example, the day-night cycle produces huge differences in brightness but has nothing directly to do with land-cover change. Although the Landsat system was designed to minimize diurnal illumination differences by acquiring images at similar times of day, other sources of temporal variability are present in Landsat data. For example, at some latitudes seasonal differences in climate substantially affect vegetation, resulting in quite different reflectance patterns from month to month. Unless care is taken, these changes in reflectance may be erroneously attributed to land-cover change. Because land-cover change is generally thought to act at temporal levels longer than several years, temporal sampling of Landsat data must be cognizant of these and other higher-frequency biogeophysical processes that also influence reflectance (figure 6.5).

All Landsat MSS and TM images acquired for a specific location in southern Indiana (see figure 6.2) are plotted in figure 6.6 using two temporal levels: the season by Julian date (day 1 through day 365) along the x-axis and the year along the y-axis (Nyerges and Green 2000). Only images with low cloud cover (less than 20 percent) are shown. This simple sampling matrix allows a researcher to select images

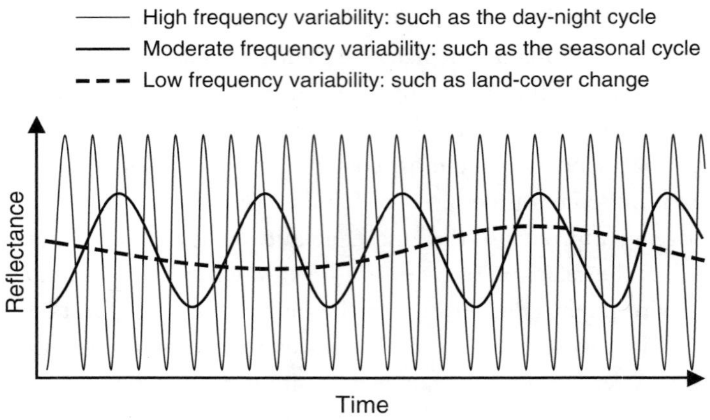

Figure 6.5
Various processes, including land-cover change, can affect reflectance in Landsat images. Processes may vary at different temporal frequencies. Changes in reflectance produced by other processes can confound those associated with land-cover change.

appropriate for investigating contrasting land-cover change questions: selecting images arranged in a vertical orientation allows the study of the human impact on forests across several decades while minimizing seasonal effects, whereas selecting images in a horizontal orientation would be appropriate for a study investigating seasonal effects on the landscape while minimizing the variability associated with land-cover change.

Other temporal considerations are also important. The researcher must take care to select images consistent with the temporal frequencies of the processes under study. For example, to capture the process of tropical swidden agriculture with a fallow cycle of three to five years would require a more frequent sampling of images than would be needed to capture timber harvesting cycles in a temperate forest with a rotation period of forty years. Siegal and Gillespie (1980) give some recommendations on the number of samples necessary to faithfully represent a sinusoidal wave, which can be thought to represent a given land-cover change process (see figure 6.5). They state that a "wave sampled twice per cycle is 'critically' sampled.... A wave sampled less than twice per cycle is 'undersampled' and cannot be reconstructed accurately from its sample points. If more than two measurements are made per cycle, the correct sine wave can still be fit to the data. In fact, the analyst may have greater confidence because of redundancy.... This situation is called 'oversampling'" (p. 149). Researchers of land-cover change must ask how many Landsat images are

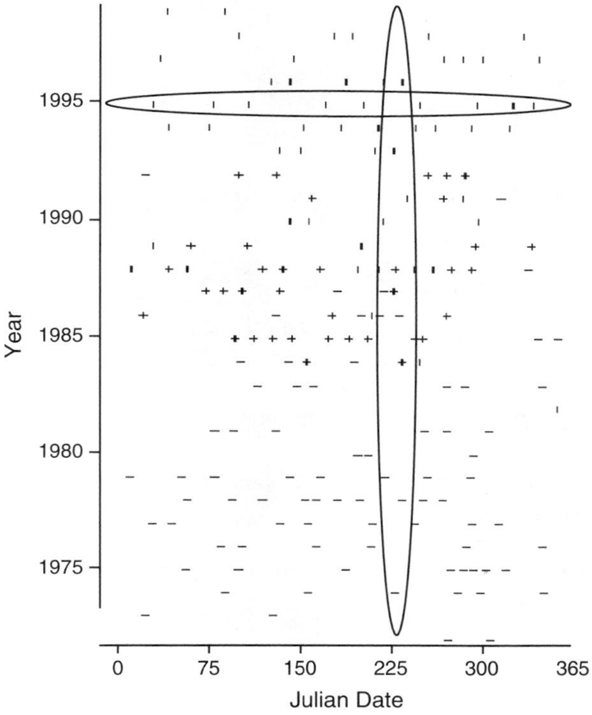

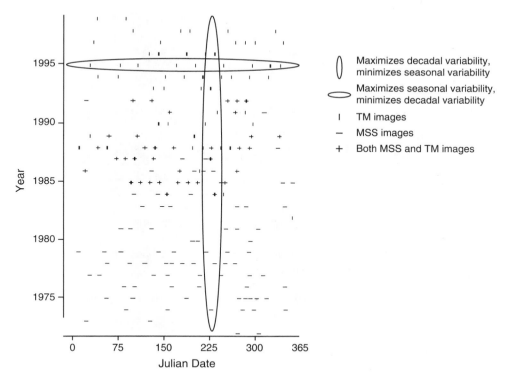

Figure 6.6
A sampling matrix diagram of available Landsat MSS and TM images (with cloud cover of less than 20 percent) for one location in Indiana. The matrix incorporates both seasonal variability (x-axis) and interannual variability (y-axis). Two contrasting sampling strategies are also shown.

required to critically sample a particular land-cover change process of interest, such as a deforestation episode, and realize that other higher-frequency (see figure 6.5) biogeophysical phenomena also may affect image reflectance.

To the extent possible, the effect of social and political events on land-cover change also should be considered (e.g., see chapter 10). We developed a remote-sensing timeline indicating Landsat images examined and significant political and climatic events (figure 6.7). Droughts and famine in southern Madagascar (Hoerner 1977; NDMC 1998; M. Brown 2000) are included in the timeline, as well as El Niño/Southern Oscillation (ENSO) events (Clay et al. 2002; CPC 2003). Some important national and global events (marked with crosses) in Malagasy history (M. Brown 2000) are also included on the timeline. Note that some of these events may

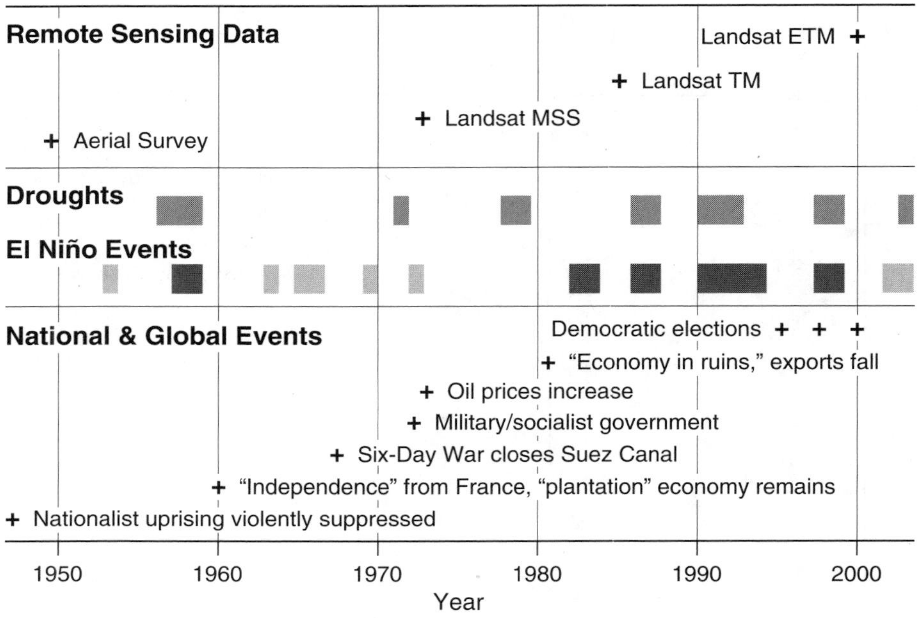

Figure 6.7
A Landsat sampling timeline for southern Madagascar with national political and climatic events that may affect land-cover change. Lighter shading indicates less severe El Niño event.

result in land-cover changes observed in remotely sensed imagery, while others may not be detected at all.

Minimizing Variability from Seasonal and Interannual Climate Effects

Numerous physical processes affect vegetation and its reflectance, sometimes in dramatic ways, but do not constitute land-cover change. Seasonal weather variations and interannual climatic variability are two such processes. Precipitation and temperature vary throughout the year in most terrestrial environments, and most vegetation responds to these seasonal differences. For example, a location in southern Madagascar (see figure 12.2) experiences wide differences in mean monthly precipitation and temperature (plate 3). The multispectral color composites in plate 3 show how the reflectance of various cover types within the location can change dramatically in association with plant phenological response to water availability. As a result, certain land-cover types are distinguishable during certain seasons. Land-cover change research needs to guard against misinterpreting these plant responses as land-cover change associated with human action. Misinterpretation of seasonal differences can be reduced by acquiring satellite images in the same season of each year (see figure 6.6). An approach of careful attention to average monthly rainfall and sampling at the same time of year may be sufficient to mitigate this problem in many terrestrial environments. However, interannual climatic variability also can be a problem in many environments where plant water availability, for example, at a given time in one year can be quite different at the same time in another year. Both temperature- and drought-induced foliage loss in deciduous forests are natural, recurring phenomena and are not "land-cover change" as typically defined. The forests remain there, but the foliage appears and disappears as a result of interseasonal (and sometimes, interannual) climatic variability. Thus the researcher must be careful not to mistakenly attribute either interseasonal or interannual climatic variability to land-cover change.

Reflectance from foliage varies among species both spatially and temporally. At least five factors may affect the reflectance from foliage: (1) species-specific differences in morphology, biochemistry, and nutrients; (2) seasonal phenological changes, particularly in deciduous forests in temperate climate; (3) episodic, seasonal, and interannual meteorological variations in precipitation, temperature, and solar radiation affecting soil water availability, as discussed above, and directly modifying the surface characteristics of the vegetation; (4) canopy density and structure as influenced by species composition and forest successional age; and (5) anthropogenic forest management practices.

Meteorological factors, particularly precipitation, can deviate significantly from climatic norms (figure 6.8 shows an example from Indiana). Tree species respond to wet and dry years by adapting their leaf physiology and morphology to seasonal and interannual variability in water availability (Kramer and Kozlowski 1979; NCDC 2004). Furthermore, the phenological response to climatic variability at growing season margins greatly influences annual net primary productivity in temperate forests (Davidson et al. 2002; Ehman et al. 2002a). Forest reflectance in southern Indiana appears to be controlled in part by species composition (Johnston et al. 1997) and in part by water availability between wet and dry years. Schweik (1998) has shown that color composites from Landsat images acquired in wet (1985) and dry (1972 and 1992) years reveal significant differences. In the wet year, forest reflectance appears to be greatly reduced in the near-infrared band. As these relationships are understood, meteorological variation, species variation, and

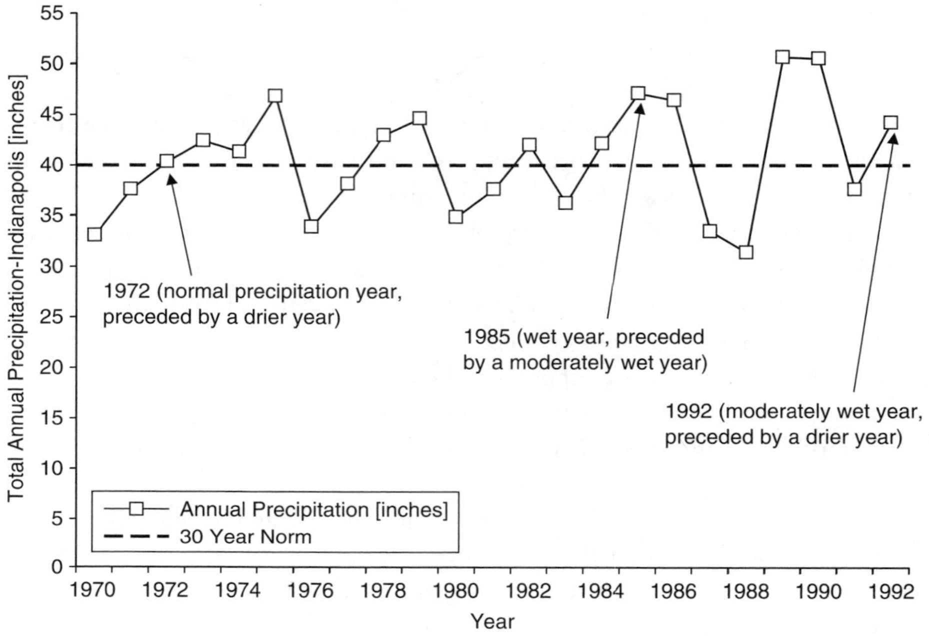

Figure 6.8
Significant deviations in annual precipitation from a thirty-year average can confound the identification of decadal-level land-cover changes.

variability in land management practices can yield a better understanding of land-cover change.

Minimizing Variability from Instrument, Illumination, and Atmosphere

A given Landsat scene is composed of a set of different images, or bands, each acquired at a different wavelength interval (see figure 6.1). Most MSS, TM, and ETM+ scenes are composed of four, seven, and eight individual bands, respectively. While each band from a Landsat scene represents a different wavelength interval (across the visible and infrared), each appears as a black-and-white image if displayed on a computer monitor individually, similar to a black-and-white aerial photo. Color to the human eye is only added to a Landsat scene through the process of constructing (in a computer) a color composite that builds a color image from three individual black-and-white images, each set to either blue, green, or red (the three main colors the human eye is sensitive to) (see plate 2). In this chapter, we de-

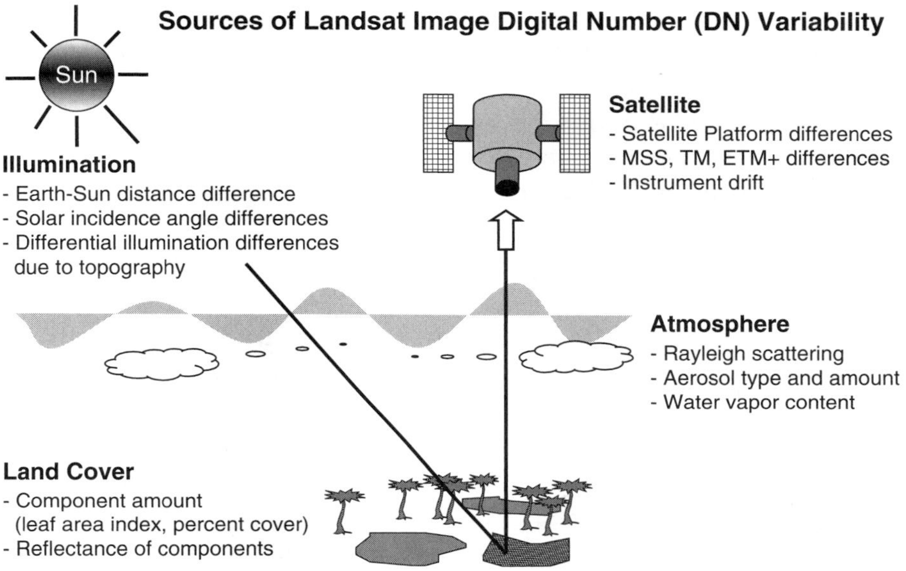

Figure 6.9
Landsat image digital numbers can be affected by multiple sources of variability. Other sources can confound the effects produced by land-cover change and need to be eliminated or minimized.

scribe two ways to construct color composites: (1) from three individual bands from one Landsat scene, creating a multispectral composite (top of plate 2); and (2) from three individual bands of similar wavelength from different Landsat scenes of the same location, creating a multitemporal composite (bottom of plate 2).

Each image band (middle of plate 2) from a Landsat scene is composed of an array or matrix (raster grid) of picture elements (pixels). Each pixel in a band has a brightness (from black to white) when displayed on a computer monitor. In the digital file that makes up the band, the brightness is represented by a numerical value from zero to 255, a value referred to as a digital number (DN). The DN value for each pixel is actually represented by an 8-bit number, or 1 byte, which contains 2^8 levels ranging from zero to 255. These arrays of DNs are what actually carry land-cover information present in a Landsat scene.

Unfortunately, along with any information on land cover, a multitude of other factors also can influence the value of these DNs. Figure 6.9 shows schematically many of the factors that can influence the DN value, including land cover. If the researcher of land-cover change can remove or minimize these other sources of image variability, such as atmospheric, illumination, or satellite instrument differences, any land-cover information present in the image can be more easily retrieved. Since land-cover change information must ultimately come from the comparison of multiple dates of Landsat scenes, many of the factors that contribute to this unwanted image variability relate to differences in the conditions under which each image was acquired and not in land cover itself. For example, any differences in the illumination and atmospheric conditions present when a Landsat scene is acquired should not be thought of as differences in land cover, even though they change image DN values.

How this non-land-cover–related variability is accommodated, whether qualitatively or quantitatively, depends on the user of the Landsat data and the resources and experience available to a particular project. Thus far in this chapter we have outlined how the land-cover change investigator can minimize much of this variability (in a sense, before it is introduced) by careful attention to spatial and temporal samplings as well as research design. We also have introduced a simple qualitative method, the multitemporal color composite, that mitigates much of this non–land-cover variability. The next three sections describe how non-land-cover–related variability can be eliminated or minimized using quantitative methods that involve more complex image processing of Landsat images.

Converting Landsat Digital Numbers to Reflectance Values

Researchers who use quantitative remote-sensing methods may find it advantageous to convert satellite image DNs to more comparable physical measures, such as surface reflectance values. The process of converting from DNs to reflectance values eliminates or minimizes many of the non–land-cover sources of variability shown in figure 6.9. Significant advances in computer technology and image analysis software now make these conversions possible, but they may still appear quite complicated to those less familiar with the new technology (as such, some readers may prefer to examine the next three sections at a later date).

Conversions typically involve three components, referred to in total as image restoration (Jensen 1996): (1) radiometric calibration, which transforms DNs to apparent at-sensor radiance values, adjusting for the response characteristics of the appropriate satellite sensor (see figure 6.9); (2) illumination corrections, which transform these radiance values to apparent at-sensor reflectance values, correcting for variation in illumination due to Earth-Sun-satellite geometry (Robinove 1982; Markham and Barker 1986; Hill 1991; Teillet and Fedosejevs 1995); and (3) atmospheric correction, which removes variability caused by the atmosphere, thereby transforming apparent at-sensor reflectance values to surface reflectance values (Ballew 1975; Chavez 1988, 1989, 1996; Teillet and Fedosejevs 1995). While transformation of satellite image DNs to surface reflectance values requires the additional image restoration steps above, the ultimate use of surface reflectance values often can allow more direct and robust comparisons of surface features across space and time. Each of these three steps is discussed below. We present a more detailed discussion of these steps in a CIPEC working paper (Green et al. 2002).

Radiometric Calibration

Radiometric calibration attempts to minimize the variance from two classes of variability (intra- and interinstrument differences) that can affect Landsat image DN values. Intrainstrument differences result from differences in the use of one sensor between satellite platforms; for example, while both Landsats 1 and 2 carried MSS sensors, the sensors were not exactly the same. The response of all scientific instruments, including remote-sensing sensors, may drift as a result of mechanical, optical, or electrical changes through time. Thome et al. (1994) have documented how the Landsat 5 TM sensor response changed through its lifetime. Interinstrument differences result from differences between Landsat sensors (MSS, TM, and ETM+) and usually are associated with improvements in sensor technology. Radiometric calibration attempts to adjust for intra- and interinstrument differences by using the known characteristics of how each instrument would respond to a known amount of light, specifically an instrument's gain (slope) and bias (intercept) values.

Illumination Corrections

A second class of variance in Landsat images results from differences in illumination when images are acquired. Unlike remote-sensing satellites that use radar or other active illumination technologies, most bands of Landsat images (except those acquired at longer, thermal infrared wavelengths; see figure 6.1) use the Sun to illuminate Earth's terrestrial surface. Solar irradiance into Earth's atmosphere varies as a function of Earth-Sun distance (d_{sun}). Earth-Sun distance changes along Earth's elliptical orbit. The flux of solar energy above the atmosphere decreases as a function of the square of the distance from Earth to the Sun. Thus, we can correct Landsat image DNs for this variability by using a factor of the square of d_{sun} (shown in figure 6.10) appropriate for the date the image was acquired.

Differences in solar illumination in Landsat images also are caused by variation in the solar zenith angle (θ_{sun}), which is the angle between a beam of sunlight and the zenith (the point directly overhead). The solar zenith angle varies as a function of

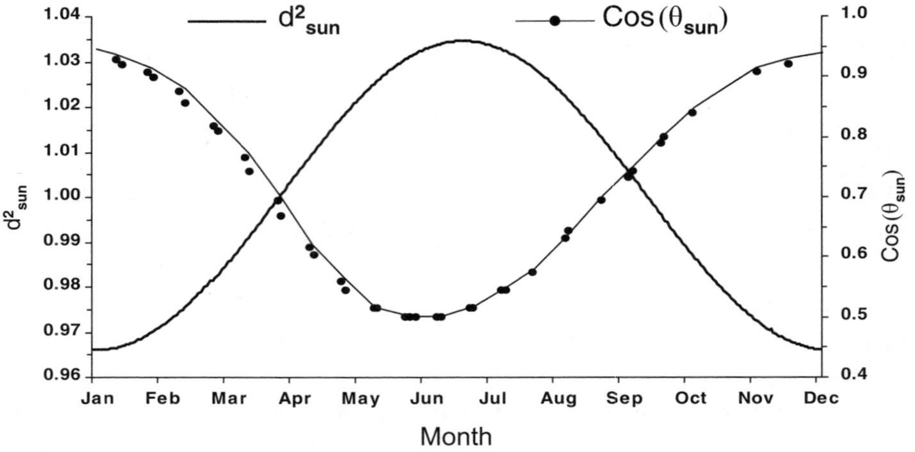

Figure 6.10
Solar insolation at the top of Earth's atmosphere varies inversely with the square of the Earth-Sun distance, which changes intra-annually. Solar insolation at Earth's surface varies with the cosine of the solar zenith angle, which changes seasonally, with latitude and time of day (the atmosphere and topography also affect it).

season, time of day, and latitude. In general, solar irradiance into Earth's atmosphere varies inversely with the cosine of the solar zenith angle. For example, figure 6.10 shows how Cos(θ_{sun}) varies throughout the year for a location in Indiana. The effect of radiometric calibration and illumination corrections on spectra acquired from the Landsat TM images are shown in figure 6.11. DN values (*a* in figure 6.11) have been converted to apparent at-sensor reflectance values (*b* in figure 6.11) for three contrasting land covers. DN values vary from zero to 255, and reflectance values vary between zero and one.

Atmospheric Corrections

The third class of variance in Landsat images results from differences in atmospheric conditions when images are acquired. The radiative and optical characteristics of Earth's atmosphere affect how light propagates through it. Variations in concentrations of radiatively active gases, water vapor, aerosols, and particulates can affect DN values and vary considerably across both space (from location to location) and time (the interval of time between image acquisitions). One effect of gases in the atmosphere, such as oxygen and nitrogen, is to scatter sunlight (called Rayleigh scattering), with more scattering at shorter wavelengths (see figure 6.1). This scattered

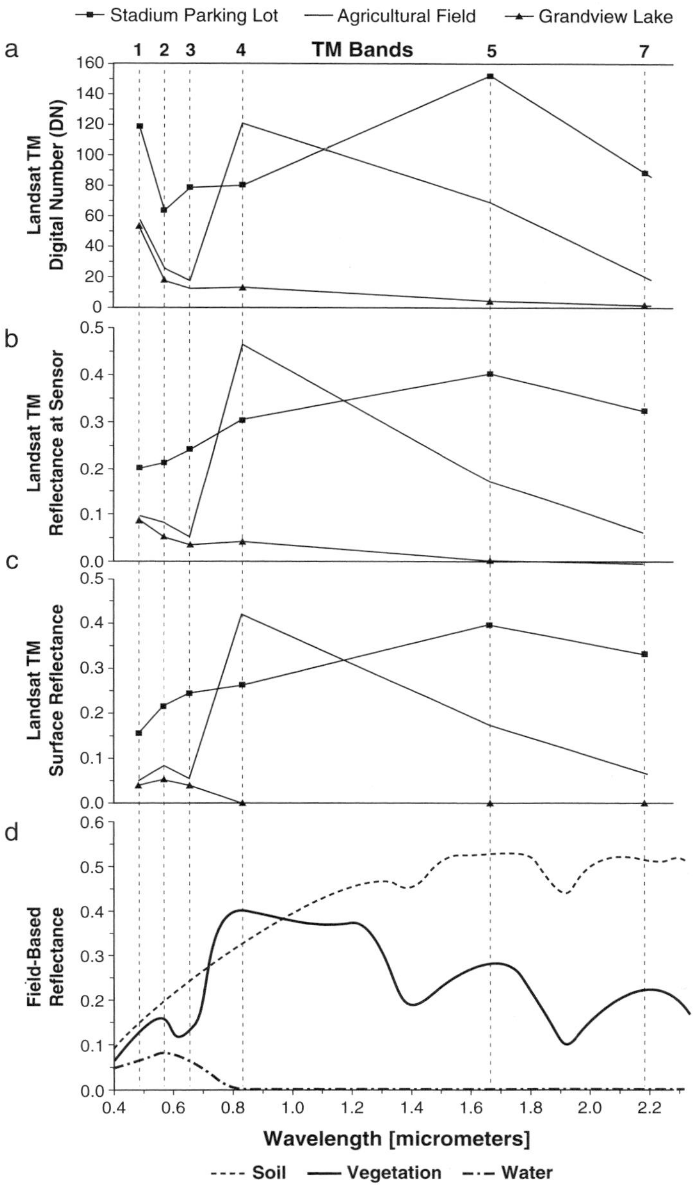

Figure 6.11
Landsat TM spectra of three contrasting types of land cover for successive levels of image restoration: Landsat image digital numbers (*a*); apparent at-sensor reflectance values (*b*) produced by radiometric calibration and illumination correction; surface reflectance values (*c*) produced by atmospheric correction. Field reflectance spectra (*d*) more closely match TM-derived values after image restoration procedures are applied.

light typically increases Landsat DN values in the visible bands, especially at blue wavelengths (TM band 1). Atmospheric corrections can be more difficult than the other corrections discussed above and, consequently, are not done in many image analyses.

Since the atmosphere tends to add brightness to an image, dark-target subtraction procedures may remove these first-order effects. Teillet and Fedosejevs (1995), however, have pointed out the limitations of these procedures. The effect of atmospheric correction on Landsat TM spectra is shown in figure 6.11. Atmospheric correction converts apparent at-sensor reflectance values (*b* in figure 6.11) to surface reflectance values (*c*), thereby minimizing the effects of atmospheric scattering. The relatively high values in TM bands 1 and 2 (*a* and *b*, respectively), caused by atmospheric scattering, have been reduced by atmospheric correction (*c*), thereby making these TM spectra much more similar to reflectance spectra acquired in the field with a portable spectrometer (*d*).

Different research designs (see figure 6.3) may require different types of image restoration steps. A Landsat image analysis that attempts to answer only research question 1 (What is the spatial extent and distribution of land cover at a specific location?) will not involve many comparisons across space or time because it only uses one Landsat scene acquired on one date. Thus, land-cover projects that deal with only one location and one image date will generally be much less sensitive to differences in sensors (only one is used), illumination (the image is acquired on one date), and atmospheric conditions (the atmosphere may be very similar within a single Landsat scene). If multiple images have been acquired within hours or even a few days of each other (*b* and *c*, respectively, in figure 6.3), the sensor response is unlikely to change, illumination should remain similar along the same row, and atmospheric conditions should remain reasonably consistent. Thus, for studies answering only research question 1, image analysis based on DNs alone may be quite satisfactory. In quantitative, multitemporal land-cover change analyses, such as the ones represented by research questions 2 and 3 in figure 6.3, particularly those spanning several years and involving several sensors and platforms, these time- and location-dependent sources of variance become important and typically are more likely to require conversion of DNs to surface reflectance values.

Strategies to Identify and Separate Biogeophysical and Human/Institutional Effects

At a given place and time, forests can be present or absent for strictly biogeophysical reasons, such as conditions in a wetland that prevent the establishment of woody plants. However, given sufficient biogeophysical conditions to allow the growth of forests in a certain place, they may still be absent because of human factors, such as those involved with clearing forest for agricultural production. Distinguishing between biogeophysical factors that influence the nature, composition, and productivity of a forest and the human processes and factors which may alter them, such as institutional arrangements, is a challenging task.

Researchers often tend to explain things based on their disciplinary expertise. For example, in an organization focused on the study of human dimensions of land-cover change, researchers may tend to interpret differences in the distribution of land cover as a result of human activities. Clearly, humans have made, and no doubt will continue to make, significant alterations in land cover. However, in conducting such analyses, it is critical not to overlook the influences of biogeophysical factors, such as climate, topography, soils, and nutrients, on forests (see chapter 5). Of course, the reverse is true as well for studies dominated by the physical sciences. For much of the remainder of this chapter we present two examples, one from Indiana and one from Nepal, which will illustrate strategies we have used to identify and separate biogeophysical and human/institutional factors that can affect the distribution of forests.

Indiana Example

While forests covered more than 85 percent of the land area in Indiana in presettlement times (*b* in plate 4), they were reduced to probably less than 5 percent in the early years of the twentieth century (see figure 3.4), but now forests cover more than 19 percent of the state (Evans et al. 2001a). Almost all of the current forest cover in Indiana today is secondary-growth vegetation (M. Davis 1996). As of 1992, agricultural row crops accounted for nearly 60 percent of Indiana's land cover (*c* in plate 4). Currently, only about 4 percent of the land area of the state is managed by state and federal agencies and private conservation groups. More than half of that area is managed by federal agencies, the three largest being the U.S. Forest Service (Hoosier National Forest), the U.S. Department of Defense (three large military bases), and the U.S. Army Corps of Engineers (land predominantly around large reservoirs). The Indiana Department of Natural Resources manages about 40 percent of state, federal, and private conservation areas in state forests, fish and wildlife refuges, and state parks. Local government agencies and private conservation groups manage less than 10 percent of state, federal, and private conservation lands.

In our study, we examined land-cover maps produced from Landsat satellite images, digital topographic data, and maps showing governance regimes (one aspect

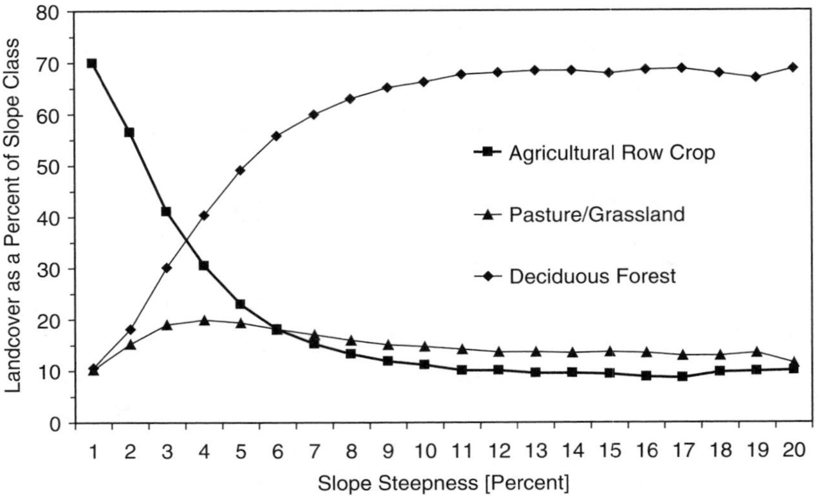

Figure 6.12
Land cover in Indiana in 1992 as a function of topographic slope gradient.

of the institutional landscape) to identify patterns in the distribution of forest land in Indiana. We found that both biogeophysical and institutional factors have contributed to the current distribution of the forests. Land-cover estimates for the state were made from classification of Landsat TM images (*c* in plate 4) processed by the Indiana GAP Analysis Project. Topographic relief values were calculated from 1:24,000 digital elevation models and compared to land cover (*a* in plate 4).

Topography is particularly important in influencing the present distribution of Indiana's forests. Figure 6.12 shows that much of the forest cover in Indiana is associated with areas of steeper topographic slopes (also compare *a* and *c* in plate 4). In the state as a whole, deciduous forest cover increases from 10 percent of flat land to more than 65 percent of steeper land (over 10 percent slope). In contrast, agricultural cropland decreases from 70 percent of flat land to about 10 percent of steeper land. Various state and federal agencies also manage land associated with contrasting topographic slopes (figure 6.13). While the USDA Forest Service manages land of relatively high relief, the U.S. Department of Defense and the Indiana Department of Natural Resources Division of Fish and Wildlife manage relatively flat land (see figure 6.13). By comparing the percent of forest present at a given slope we can identify areas that have significantly higher percentages of forest than the state as a whole. These anomalies are identified as local fluctuations from statewide patterns

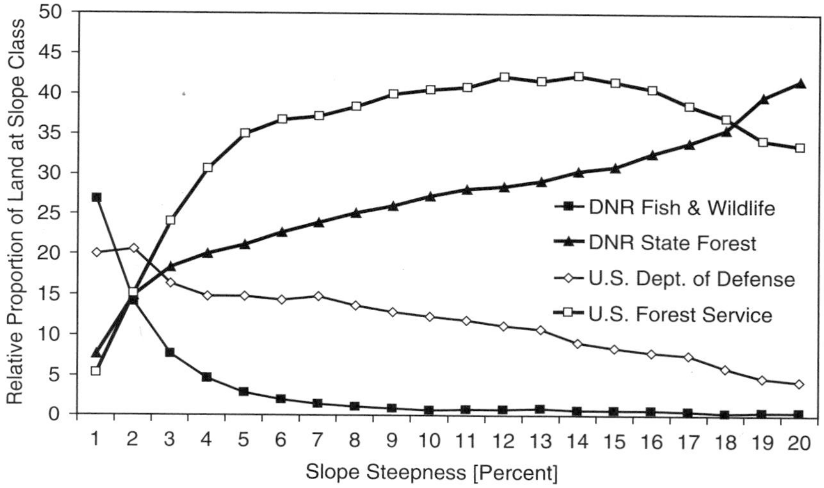

Figure 6.13
Percentage of land in Indiana managed by four government organizations as a function of topographic slope gradient. See text.

of forest distribution. Several areas with anomalously more forest are also associated with the boundaries of particular government institutions. Plate 4(*d*) shows the Crane Division, Naval Surface Warfare Facility, established in 1941 and managed by the U.S. Department of Defense. Plate 4(*e*) shows the Jefferson Proving Ground, an ordnance testing facility established in 1940, managed by the U.S. Department of Defense until decommissioned in 1995. Most of this property has been transferred to the management of the U.S. Fish and Wildlife Service. Both of these protected areas contain more forest than the surrounding private land. Plate 4(*f*) shows that many small forests are located on private lands. These forests are often woodlots located on private farm properties, and their distribution is related to private property boundaries (Donnelly 2004). Thus, when we take into account a major biogeophysical factor, such as topographic slope, we can easily identify anomalous forests associated with more strictly human factors, in this case institutional boundaries.

Nepal Example

We also have identified and studied areas of anomalous forests (see also chapter 12) in the context of Nepal (Schweik et al. 2003). In this study, we developed a simple model of deforestation using some of the drivers listed by Geist and Lambin (2001):

areas that were relatively flat, close to roads, and centers of population are more likely to be deforested. Using observations of land-cover change or stability identified using Landsat images (1989 and 2000), we focused on four land-cover change patterns of interest: (1) dense forest or vegetation present in 1989 and 2000; (2) agriculture in 1989 that changed to forest or vegetation in 2000; (3) areas of agriculture in 1989 that changed to forest or vegetation in 2000; and (4) areas of bare soil in 1989 that changed to forest or vegetation in 2000.

Using this forest anomalies approach, we took a sample across the landscape (see plate 8) by choosing sites that exhibited forest canopy regrowth or stability in areas where we would expect deforestation to have occurred. We then interviewed villagers and made field observations to determine why these forest anomalies exist. In one of the most interesting cases, we identified an innovative ecotourism initiative that was unknown to us prior to conducting the fieldwork, but had just been identified in an article in *Smithsonian* (Seidensticker 2002) as one of the premier ecotourism cases in all of Nepal. In this instance, the villagers had shifted from harvesting the forest for livelihood to allowing forest regrowth and promoting the forest (and the rhinos living within it) as a tourist attraction and conducting tours using elephant rides. This approach may lead to biased inferences in the causal variables, but interestingly, in qualitative research the bias appears to diminish the true causal effects of the explanatory variables of interest (King et al. 1994). In other words, if we find from a study that institutions appear to matter, then the true causal effects may be even greater than what we might conclude from an individual case. In addition, in the Nepal context, the approach to case selection also sampled independent variables, such as proximity to roads and population density, which lead to even more bias in causal inference (King et al. 1994). Under these circumstances, the analyst has to be cautious in making causal inferences; for example, we cannot definitively conclude that institutions made a difference in any particular case. However, we believe our Nepal study (Schweik et al. 2003) clearly shows that this approach can be quite fruitful in identifying interesting cases of forest management rather quickly. By first examining datasets that show land-cover change over large spatial extents and long temporal durations, such as a time series of Landsat images, and then targeting more detailed site-level studies on the observed broad patterns, we can rapidly focus on and identify particular institutional arrangements.

From this experience we believe that sampling (case selection) using a Landsat-based change analysis can help the researcher to generate and test hypotheses related to what factors influence deforestation and may help make theoretical arguments evolve more rapidly. This approach also may help the researcher identify interesting areas of study in locations where the land cover is changing rapidly in response to human activities. The theoretical refinements such case studies could provide could then be used to inform larger case selection strategies that may include random sampling and provide more variability in both dependent and independent variables, which could in turn lead to more definitive statements about the influence of independent variables of interest.

Sorting out the complex relationships between biogeophysical and human factors will never be straightforward because in reality they probably both coevolved through time. However, trying to understand the "causes and effects" of land-cover change can raise interesting new questions. Does a given type of institution actually determine the land cover, or, in contrast, do various types of institutions select and preferentially colonize particular kinds of land cover? For example, Sussman et al. (1994) suggest that parks and reserves in eastern Madagascar are preferentially and knowingly placed in areas of high topographic relief and that this biophysical factor may be chiefly responsible for the minimal deforestation in those parks and reserves. One also can make a similar case for the preferential acquisition of land by different government organizations, using some of our results from Indiana (see figure 6.13). After normalizing for physical factors such as topography, is land cover managed by state or federal government agencies significantly different from that of privately managed lands? Answers to such questions can be useful in evaluating whether certain forest habitats are either being protected or not on both public and private lands. The information gained may be very useful to forest management professionals and policy makers when evaluating current conservation policies and creating new plans to promote conservation of threatened forest habitat.

Conclusions

Remotely sensed images, such as those produced by the Landsat system of satellites, can provide crucial spatial and temporal information about land-cover change as well as a framework to help sample and integrate more detailed site-level field data, such as social interviews and ecological field measurements. However, it is important to minimize unwanted variability not directly related to land cover within the images by (1) giving careful attention to spatial and temporal sampling; (2) giving careful attention to seasonal and interannual climatic variability; and (3) incorporating techniques, such as radiometric calibration and illumination and atmospheric correction into land-cover change studies. Studies that employ multiple dates and locations may particularly benefit from the quantitative image-processing steps outlined in this chapter. Through such comparisons and with appropriate fieldwork, both biogeophysical and social processes can be examined in the broader context of land-cover change.

Internet Links

Center for International Earth Science Information Network. URL: http://www.ciesin.org/.

Landsat-7 Science Data User's Handbook. URL: http://ltpwww.gsfc.nasa.gov/IAS/handbook/handbook_toc.html.

Landsat 7 Homepage. URL: http://landsat7.usgs.gov/index.php.

Landsat 7 Gateway. URL: http://landsat.gsfc.nasa.gov/.

USGS Earth Explorer. URL: http://edcsns17.cr.usgs.gov/EarthExplorer/.

Earth Resources Observation Systems (EROS) Data Center. URL: http://edc.usgs.gov/.

Landsat Program. URL: http://geo.arc.nasa.gov/sge/landsat/landsat.html.

NASA Landsat Pathfinder Humid Tropical Deforestation Project. URL: http://www.geog.umd.edu/tropical/.

Orbital Tracking (J-Track) by Liftoff to Space Exploration, Marshall Space Flight Center. URL: http://liftoff.msfc.nasa.gov/.

Looking at Earth from Space, 40+ Years of NASA Earth Science. URL: http://www.earth.nasa.gov/history/index.html.

7

Human-Environment Research, Spatially Explicit Data Analysis, and Geographic Information Systems

Tom P. Evans, Leah K. VanWey, and Emilio F. Moran

Spatially explicit research methods have been advocated by a variety of disciplines in both the social (Bockstael 1996; Goodchild et al. 2000) and biophysical sciences (M. Turner et al. 1995). Land-cover change is explicitly a spatial process and is clearly affected by both social and physical processes. Thus it is natural to extend the advocacy of spatially explicit research in both the social and biophysical sciences to land-cover change research. Changes in land-cover pattern and composition are affected by factors as a function of proximity such as the expansion of urban areas and the spatial pattern of topography and soil nutrients. The impact of land-cover changes also is mediated by spatial relationships such as the loss of corridors between areas of species habitat or the impact of deforestation on soil erosion and downstream sediment. Geographic information systems (GIS) serve as a toolkit that can be used to manage and store spatial data, as well as provide tools to query and analyze integrated spatial datasets (Bolstad 2002; Lo and Yeung 2002), and have been used increasingly in studies of human-environment systems.

The method of connecting human actions to the landscape is particularly important for spatially explicit human-environment research. This operation is in part a function of the process under study and in part a function of data availability. A common method of implementing this linkage is to partition the landscape into discrete spatial units as defined by land ownership or land management boundaries. For example, parcel ownership boundaries might be used to link a household to an individual landholding (S. McCracken et al. 1999; E. Moran et al. 2003; Boucek and Moran 2004). Alternatively, a village boundary might be used to identify the area within which village residents alter the landscape (Crawford 2002; Walsh et al. 1999; Rindfuss et al. 2003). Land-cover characteristics then can be linked to social survey data collected at the household or community level. Spatial data analysis and GIS methods offer effective tools to enable this type of integration between people and the landscape (Walsh et al. 2003; Fox et al. 2003).

The purpose of this chapter is to introduce spatial data concepts and methods for linking human actions to landscape outcomes and to describe the challenges and pitfalls of spatially explicit data analysis for the study of land-use/land-cover change. Brief examples of common spatially explicit social and biophysical datasets are provided to introduce how different aspects of complex systems are represented in a GIS. We discuss how spatially explicit research data and methods can be used to explore the dynamics of complex human-environment systems. Among the issues addressed are questions of data representation and efforts to integrate data from disparate sources in a common data framework. The emphasis here is on land-cover change detection, analysis, and modeling, but the content is broadly applicable to other environmental processes.

Settlement Pattern and Spatial Representation of Land Ownership

A fundamental aspect of spatial analysis of land-cover change is the process by which human actions are linked to landscape outcomes. This linkage can be implemented at a variety of levels such as household, community, municipality, or region. At a local level, land ownership provides one means to link land-use decisions to outcomes on the landscape. However, the pattern of settlement and the types of land tenure determine the types of linkages which may be made and the amount of effort required to make those linkages. As a means of introducing how GIS can be used to integrate land-cover data to actors and land managers, the following sections describe experiences from research projects linking social survey data to land-cover changes. Each of the three study areas has a distinct settlement pattern and land tenure situation, and we have employed different approaches to data integration using GIS techniques. These research projects demonstrate the difficulties involved in creating a distinct linkage between land-cover change and individual social characteristics and their analytical potential. Here the focus is more on the structure and design of the research rather than on the specific analytical results, which are addressed in a later section. However, the diverse research settings of these examples convey the value to be gained from a GIS approach in developing a spatial linkage between actors and outcomes as well as the challenges encountered.

Altamira: Brazilian Amazon

Altamira, located in the Xingú Basin of the Brazilian Amazon, is an old riverine town that experienced government-directed large-scale colonization starting in 1971 (E. Moran 1976, 1981). Land was parceled into individual properties and

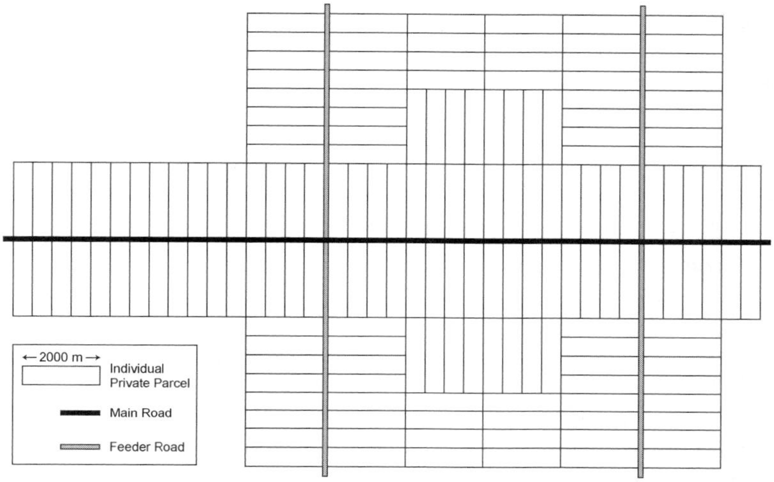

Figure 7.1
Hypothetical structure of land ownership pattern in Altamira, Brazil.

distributed to immigrants. Parcels are rectangular lots of 500 × 2000 m, with the 500-m boundary adjacent to the road to maximize the collective access for all parcels (see figure 7.1). This land settlement pattern has resulted in the well-documented "fishbone" pattern of settlement and deforestation found in many, but by no means all, parts of the Brazilian Amazon (E. Moran et al. 1994b). During the initial wave of colonization (circa 1971), each household was given a single parcel in exchange for little, if any, capital. Subsequent waves of colonization also have seen households allocated a single parcel, although as time passed land acquisition required more capital due to the emergence of a land market reflecting the area's development and farm improvements (e.g., buildings, pastures, plantations). Land consolidation has occurred in recent years, particularly in areas close to Altamira, the closest market town, as cattle ranchers purchase adjacent parcels to create large areas in which to graze their cattle. There is no evidence to date of land fragmentation in Altamira, despite the apparent absence of rules prohibiting the splitting of parcels.[1]

In terms of spatial data analysis, this situation provides a nearly ideal scenario for determining what social, institutional, and biophysical conditions result in particular land-use decisions and what landscape outcomes result from those land-use decisions. Because most landholders cultivate one parcel, there is a one-to-one linkage between the social unit of study and a partitioned space of the landscape. Therefore, household characteristics and decisions can be linked to specific landscape outcomes with relative ease in comparison to other land settlement arrangements. This is not to suggest that the task of connecting issues of spatial registration of the property grid to ensure accurate overlay of other datasets is a simple task (S. McCracken et al. 1999). Researchers used a series of hard-copy planimetric maps which were digitally scanned to produce image format files. These scanned maps were then georeferenced (also called rectified), tying the scanned map product to a defined spatial reference system consisting of a specified coordinate system, map projection, and datum. Once a series of datasets are in a common spatial reference system, they can be overlaid or integrated in a GIS. Property boundaries observed on the georeferenced planimetric maps were then digitized to create a vector dataset of polygons identifying the spatial extent of each distinct parcel. The construction of the property grid proved to be an intensive process, requiring substantial fieldwork over multiple field seasons to properly georeference the grid to a common coordinate system and map projection and correct errors in the existing base maps (S. McCracken et al. 1999). Once this process is completed, new satellite images can be routinely georeferenced and overlaid with the parcel boundaries. In other words, the parcel is a means to partition the other data layers and connect each landscape partition to a particular household actor.

Researchers conducted surveys of 402 landholders using two protocols focusing on land-use practices and demographic characteristics (S. McCracken et al. 1999, 2002b; Brondízio et al. 2002a; E. Moran et al. 2003). These surveys are capable of linking social and demographic characteristics to land-use practices by identifying specific cultivation practices, land-use activities, economic constraints (e.g., supply of labor/capital), and soil quality. When integrated with remotely sensed data, the surveys can link land-cover outcomes to land-use activities identified by the social survey. The social and demographic data provide insight into what led the landholder to pursue those land-use activities, whereas the satellite data provide an independent data source on land-cover change over a twenty-five-year period. Additional details of this effort may be found in the literature of Brondízio, S. McCracken, E. Moran, and their co-authors (Brondízio 1999; S. McCracken et al. 1999, 2002b; Brondízio et al. 2002a; E. Moran et al. 2003).

Santarém: Brazilian Amazon

The city of Santarém, located at the confluence of the Amazon and Tapajós rivers in the state of Pará in the Brazilian Amazon, is the third largest city in the Amazon with a population of more than 250,000. The study area includes rural areas to the

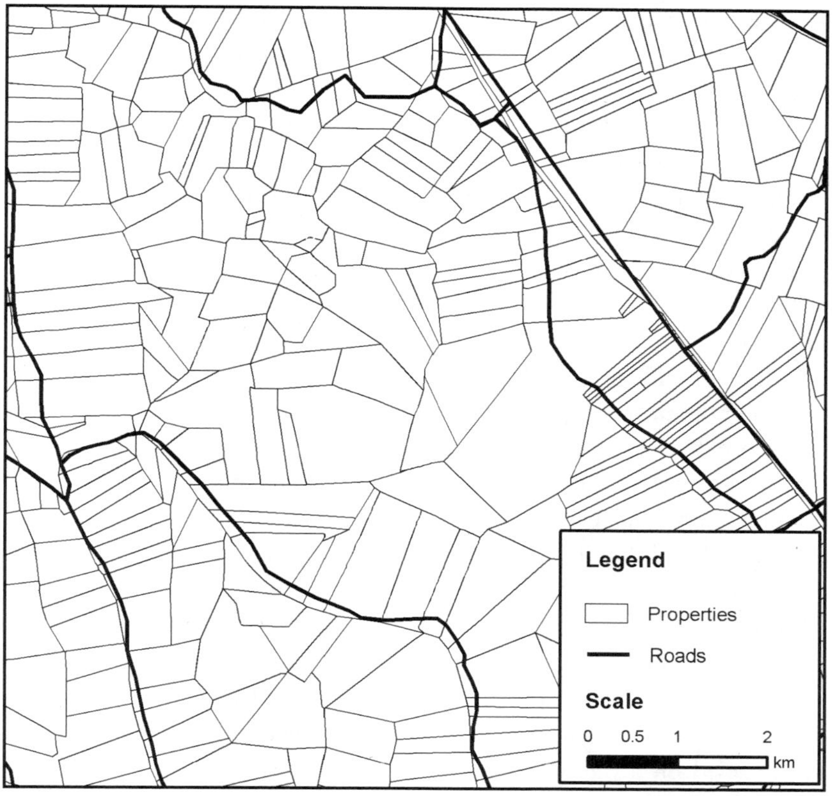

Figure 7.2
Example of land ownership pattern near Santarém, Brazil.

south of the city, bounded on the west by the Tapajós National Forest. In contrast to Altamira, colonists in the Santarém study area arrived over a relatively long period. Also, the spatial pattern of parcels is much less regular than the Altamira structure. Waves of settlers occupied the Santarém area from the 1930s until the 1970s. This heterogeneity in settlement timing is visible in the range of property sizes and shapes in our study area. Figure 7.2 shows a portion of the property grid that we obtained from the Brazilian National Institute of Colonization and Agrarian Reform (INCRA) and used for sampling in our fieldwork. Unlike the regular fishbone pattern seen in Altamira, the majority of the properties are of irregular shapes and sizes.

Santarém is currently undergoing changes in land use and urban/exurban development. The construction of (and current push to pave) BR-163, the highway linking

Santarém to the city of Cuiabá in the state of Mato Grosso, linked Santarém to an area of mechanized agriculture, higher land values, and higher levels of economic development. More recently, the United States–based multinational Cargill company sponsored the construction of a deep-water port in Santarém (opened in 2003) capable of loading soybeans onto oceangoing ships. These developments combine to make Santarém a very attractive area for growing soybeans. This has led to land consolidation and the expansion of mechanized agriculture in some parts of our study area and a dramatic increase in land values (some reports indicate an increase of 4000 percent). At the same time, the area is experiencing some concentration of settlement in selected areas along main highways. In these areas land fragmentation is associated with residential development.

The irregularity in the property grid, the long history of settlement, and the recent shifts in ownership patterns make linkages between people and land difficult in this study area. The irregularity of the shapes of properties means that corrections to the official property grid are difficult without taking global positioning system (GPS) points at all corners of each lot. The long history of settlement has led in some areas to the property grid from INCRA bearing little or no resemblance to the current division of land recognized by residents, or indeed to the division of land in the memory of any current residents. The recent consolidation and fragmentation similarly leads to problems with the INCRA property grid, as well as to sales and purchases of partial lots and noncontiguous lots. Landowners sometimes own one original parcel and have added on a piece of a neighboring lot and a lot down the street. These relations are further complicated by inheritance, with informal divisions of land occurring at different times from formal divisions. In addition to these difficulties of linking farmers and residents to their land within the GIS, virtually all of the owners of mechanized farms and many owners of nonmechanized farms do not reside on their lots or do not even reside anywhere in the region.

The complicated nature of linking landowners to their land leads to several problems. The difficulty of updating the property grid in the field has important implications for spatial analyses. Updating the entire property grid was not possible because of time and money constraints. During fieldwork in this region (described below) we focused on obtaining accurate boundaries for properties in our sample. This means that we cannot complete a meaningful regionwide analysis at the farm property level as was possible in Altamira (S. McCracken et al. 1999). Even for sample properties, several challenges arise. Owners sometimes must be linked to multiple noncontiguous pieces of land while often a single piece of land also must be linked to multiple households. Owners who do not reside on their lots are difficult to locate and collect data from. Thus some lots have incomplete information. More important, the type of information needed for different lots is different. The process of land-use decision making for a farmer with a small or medium operation who depends on household labor and is focused on household production is very different from the process of land-use decision making for a farmer with a large operation focused on profit and expansion. A single questionnaire cannot capture all of the relevant characteristics of landowners' determining changes in or between these two different types of agriculture.

Fieldwork in the summer of 2003 focused on the process of land-use decision making by family farmers. We selected a stratified random sample of properties from the INCRA property grid and collected information about the families living on them, or about the owners who had purchased them as part of their large landholdings. Household interview data were collected from 488 households living on 300 lots, and information was collected about 265 more lots with absentee landowners. These lots are linked to historical, remotely sensed data, spatially located road and topography data, and village locations in the GIS. These data allow analyses of the effects of household demographic and economic characteristics on land-use decisions (and vice versa) and analyses of the effects of past biophysical and human characteristics of the landscape on current land consolidation or fragmentation.

Monroe County, Indiana: The American Midwest

Monroe County, Indiana, located in the American Midwest, presents both similarities and contrasts to the Brazilian cases. Precolonial inhabitants had relatively little impact on the landscape, and large-scale land clearing did not occur until the first major wave of settlers arrived in the early 1800s. Land was surveyed according to the township and range system, which partitioned the landscape into 160-acre, square parcels which were allocated to individual settler households. This situation is somewhat analogous to the Altamira case in that parcels were originally of common size and dimension and, at the time of initial settlement, there was one household per parcel of land. In contrast to the case in Altamira where there is only a thirty-year history of settlement, Monroe County has experienced considerable parcelization during the 180 years since the initial major waves of settlement, and none of the originally demarcated parcels have retained their original boundaries (figure 7.3).

Monroe County and the State of Indiana experienced massive and steady deforestation from the time of initial settlement around 1810 to about 1920. Landholders

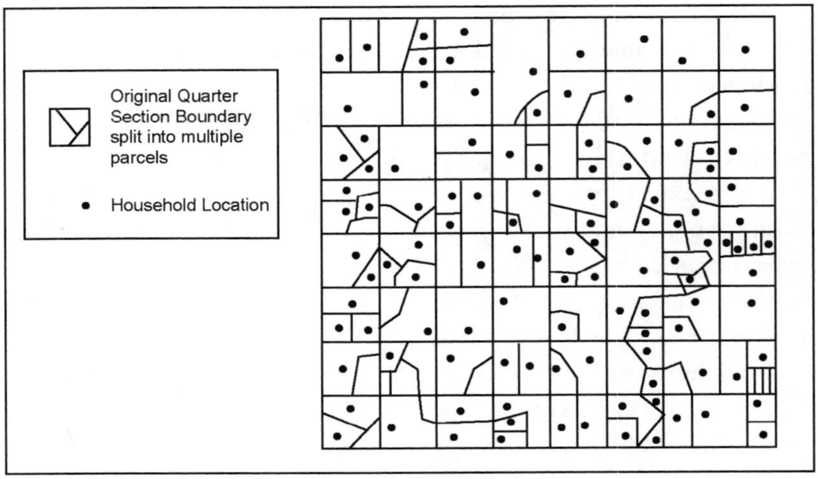

Figure 7.3
Hypothetical structure of land ownership pattern in Monroe County, Indiana.

reduced forest cover from nearly 100 percent in the precolonization period to approximately 5 percent by 1910—a rate not unlike what we have seen in the Brazilian Amazon for the past twenty-five years. Since then, forest cover has been gradually increasing due to state and federal acquisition of territory for managed forest land.[2] Areas that are marginal for agricultural production but were previously under cultivation are now changing into either forests or residential developments.

Community-level institutions play an important role in land-use management. However, an examination of policies does not give sufficient attention to landowner motivations and the role they play in land use and land management (Koontz 2001). In particular, landowners are sometimes motivated by factors such as aesthetics rather than maximizing profit (Koontz 2001). Macrolevel approaches in land-use/land-cover change studies are not well equipped to observe these microlevel processes but are well suited to identify the economic motivations driving land management in cases in which a homogeneous pattern of land use exists (e.g., forest to agricultural land use in Altamira). However, Monroe County presents a more heterogeneous land-use pattern (e.g., vacation homes, forest management areas, residential and suburban areas, commercial zones). A large number of Monroe County residents are professionals with nonfarm employment, and the management of their land is motivated as much by aesthetics as by the potential financial return to be gained from extractavist uses (Evans et al. 2001b).

In order to understand the mechanisms behind land-cover change in Monroe County, a multilevel and multifocus approach was adopted. The primary social unit of study is a household and the primary spatial unit of study is the parcel. However, these parcel-level land-cover assessments are integrated with U.S. Census Bureau block-group and tract-level data to examine the household/parcel-level land-cover changes within the context of a broader spatial extent. This parcel-level or local-level approach is particularly important for research questions related to forest fragmentation, forest structure, and biodiversity. Land cover on private parcels in Monroe County is characterized by a mosaic of forest, agriculture in rural areas, and an urban core comprised of the city of Bloomington and associated urban expansion. Contiguous forest patches sometimes span up to 100 individual parcels. Thus, focusing solely on the parcel level does not adequately explain the impact of landowner decisions and land-cover change on the spatial pattern and composition of forest as it relates to questions of species habitat.

The research design for this project consisted of household-level surveys of 250 landholders (of a total of approximately 10,000) in the county conducted in 1998 and 385 landholders in 2003. The surveys focused on land-use activities and motivations for those activities. Basic demographic data such as occupation, household composition, and educational attainment also were collected. This social survey was complemented with a rich spatial dataset including land parcel boundaries acquired in digital form from the county tax assessor's office.[3] The acquisition of this parcel boundary dataset was critical because it allowed us to make a reliable link between the social survey data and land-cover change in a particular location. In contrast to Altamira, parcel boundaries have become heavily fragmented compared to the boundaries initially established. Fragmentation occurs when landholders with multiple children split the parcel among their heirs and as farms are transformed into higher-density residential and commercial settlements.

Initial results showed a strong relationship between the land cover and topography (Evans et al. 2001b; Koontz 2001). Forested lands are located in areas with steep slopes, while agriculture and pasture lands are located in relatively flat areas. This conclusion seems natural, yet 100 years ago nearly the entire state was in agricultural production of some type, including steeply sloped areas. Thus the presence of forested land in areas of steep topography today can be attributed to changes in the social, economic, and institutional structures through time. In particular, the decreasing viability of agricultural production, a transforming labor economy, and the establishment of state- and federally managed lands have contributed to the increase in forest cover during the last century. Further analysis on this project is exploring the role of actor heterogeneity in landscape outcomes (Evans and Kelley 2004; Kelley and Evans under review) and the role of institutions in landowner decisions (York et al. in press).

Challenges of Spatially Explicit Land-Use/Land-Cover Change Research

The examples presented above have provided a context for a discussion of challenges faced by researchers using spatial data and analysis for the study of land-use/land-cover change. This section discusses particular challenges faced by researchers employing GIS to integrate social and biophysical data for the study of land-cover change. Human-environment relationships can be very complex, and developing and analyzing datasets to explore these relationships likewise can be fraught with methodological obstacles and challenges that must be overcome. The purpose of this section is to serve as a means of highlighting particularly important aspects of spatially explicit research and examples of how these challenges have been addressed.

Figure 7.4 represents the process of producing spatially explicit research results in the context of data issues and methodological decisions researchers must make. This process is of course not unique to spatially explicit data analysis but we use this diagram to frame the particular problems relevant to spatial analysis as they apply to land-use/land-cover change research. In this diagram, the upper triangle represents limitations imposed on research as a function of inadequacies in spatial data. These limitations include data availability, the scale at which data are available, and errors and uncertainty in spatial data. The issues represented in this figure are often interrelated. For example, spatial errors may be a product of the scale of the source data. Likewise, data availability is related to scale where a global, coarse-resolution dataset may be available but the use of that dataset presents analytical problems in finding relationships between phenomena. The center part of the diagram represents the decisions researchers make in selecting specific algorithms for producing results, how to represent data (e.g., vector vs. raster), and the decision of which scale to use for analysis. The following section elaborates on some of these issues as a way to present key challenges in spatially explicit land-use/land-cover change research.

Spatial Scale Issues

A fundamental aspect of both raster and data structures is the scale at which data are collected and represented in the GIS. The scale of a vector dataset determines the ability to represent curvature in line features. Scale in a raster dataset determines

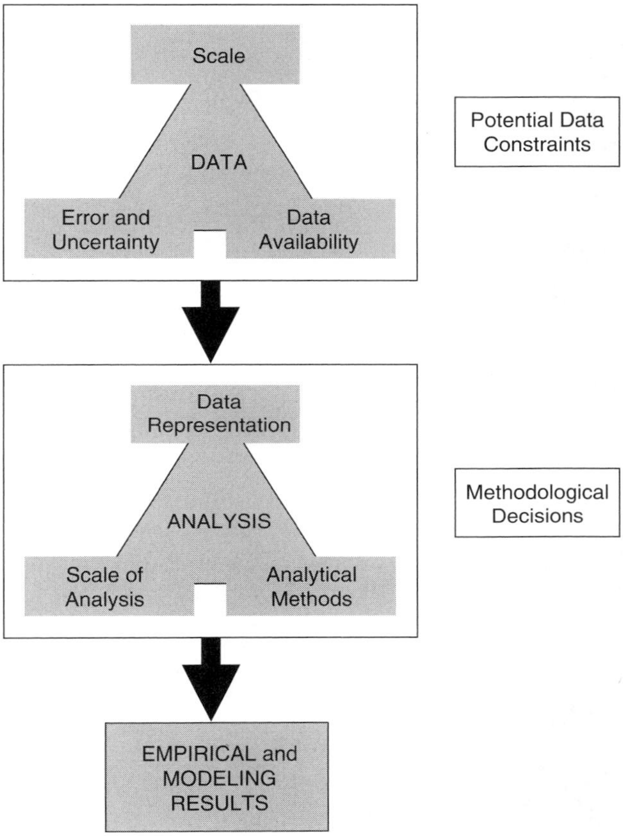

Figure 7.4
Research design in spatially explicit land-use/land-cover change analysis.

the cell size or minimum size area represented in the GIS. These scale issues are critical in assessing how spatial accuracy issues may bias results and must be considered in interpreting spatial data analyses.

The GIS analyst must consider the spatial extent of objects to be represented in the GIS when considering the appropriate cell size at which to depict those objects. An interesting characteristic of the vector and raster representations shown in figure 7.5 is that the total village area is relatively stable between the different representations. However, while the area of the vector and raster representations is similar, there are significant differences in the boundary extent referred to as errors of omission and commission. Some cells underrepresent the spatial extent of the village and

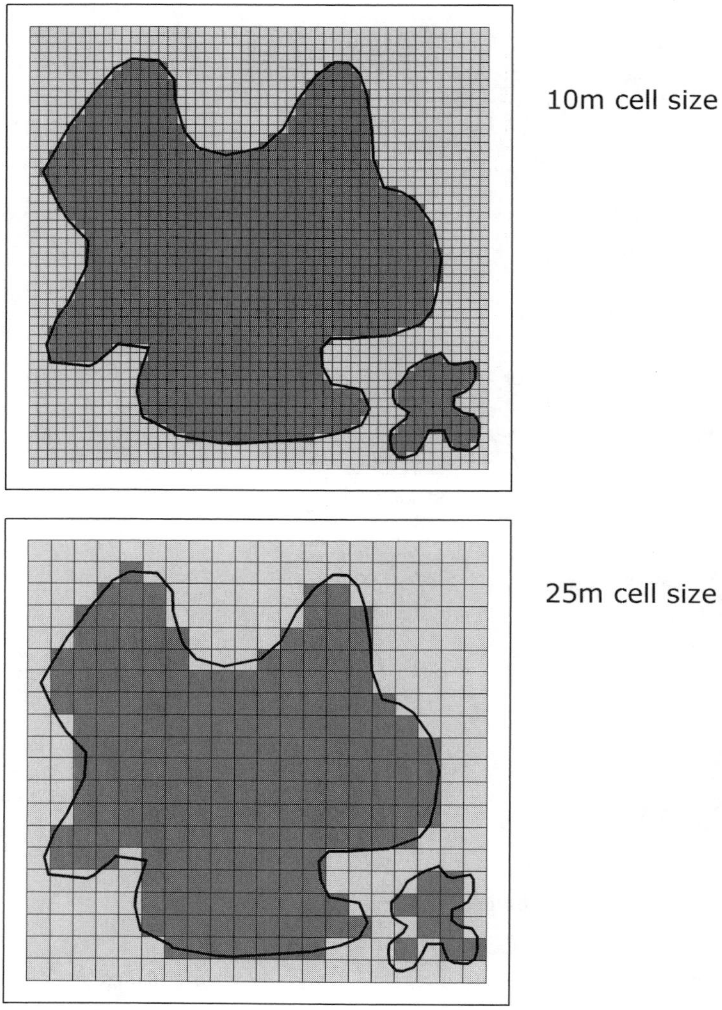

Figure 7.5
Vector and raster representations of hypothetical village boundaries at different cell sizes.

other cells overrepresent the spatial extent of the village. The magnitude of these errors of omission and commission is related to the object size and the cell size. A large object, such as a county 10 × 10 km in size, may exhibit relatively small errors of omission and commission in creating a raster representation from the vector representation (assuming a relatively small cell size such as 30 × 30 m cells or 50 × 50 m cells). That is, the ratio of area consisting of errors of omission and commission to the total size of the county is relatively small. However, with small objects, such as a parcel that is 100 × 100 m, the ratio of the area of errors of omission and commission to the total parcel area may be quite large. This is demonstrated by comparing the inconsistencies in the vector/raster boundaries of the large and small village boundaries seen in figure 7.5. The impact of cell size on the geographic object is a function of the size of the entity being represented. However, the small parcel will exhibit fewer spatial errors in conversion to a raster dataset with a very fine cell size such as 1 × 1 m.

Temporal Scale Issues

With all data collection methods, the timeliness of data collection is an important concern for land-use studies. Remotely sensed land-cover data are available at many closely spaced points over time (although cloud cover can complicate the construction of a dense time series). Government sources can provide data on population size and characteristics, data from agricultural censuses, and a host of indicators of the state of the economy. These indicators provide necessary data for analyses that take larger social units as their unit of analysis. They also provide important historical and contextualizing information for analysis at the individual or household level. However, data are not always available at the time of interest or with adequate temporal resolution. Population censuses most often are conducted on a decennial basis, with other government-run data collection happening at other intervals. The long periodicity of censuses and some other government data is problematic because dramatic and complex land-use changes can occur with greater frequency than the intervals of census data collections. Our three examples, and many other studies of human-environment interactions, used specially designed surveys to collect social data at the individual and household level. These provide the necessary spatial resolution, but surveys that are fielded only once do not allow us to examine the dynamic relationship between people and land use. Surveys that are fielded many times do allow us to examine these relationships, but these longitudinal surveys are rare because of their cost.

Data Availability Issues

While digital elevation model (DEM) data are available for the entire globe, they are often not available at an appropriate scale for exploring local-level land-cover change dynamics in many developing countries. The U.S. Geological Survey (USGS) produces DEM data products for the United States at a spatial scale of 30 m (i.e., the raster cell size is 30 m). A number of data providers publish global DEM data at various spatial resolutions (e.g., the National Geophysical Data Center GLOBE project [http://www.ngdc.noaa.gov/seg/topo/globel.shtml] and the U.S. Geological Survey GTOPO30 project [http://edcdaac.usgs.gov/gtopo30/gtopo30.asp]). The Shuttle Radar Topography Mission (http://srtm.usgs.gov/) soon may make available relatively high-resolution data (e.g., 30 m) for areas outside North and South America, but at this time most global DEM products are of relatively coarse resolution (1000 m). At this coarse resolution it is likely that the spatial variability of topography is misrepresented for many areas, which can lead to erroneous findings when integrated with finer-resolution land-cover data. The problem of two datasets available at different spatial scales is referred to as a "scale mismatch problem." The researcher risks biasing his or her analyses because of this scale mismatch. For example, in a study examining the relationship between land-cover change and topography using 1-km DEM data and 30-m Landsat Thematic Mapper (TM) data, important linkages may be missed because the resolution of the DEM is not sufficient to capture the precision of land-cover changes in heterogeneous environments. The advent of airborne-based LIDAR (Light Detection and Ranging) data presents an opportunity for DEM data to be rapidly collected at very high spatial scales (e.g., submeter). However, LIDAR data are not widely available for many areas of the world since LIDAR images are primarily acquired using airborne rather than satellite platforms at this time.

A particularly challenging data problem for studies of land-cover change is the availability of soils data. Soil characteristics and geology are very clearly related to the suitability of different areas for agricultural production and forest productivity. The primary problem with most soils datasets is that they often are not available at an appropriate scale to capture the spatial variability of soil characteristics necessary to integrate with other datasets. Soils data are usually acquired through polygonal-based data representing different soil characteristics using a specified soil classification system. In many areas, a 1:50,000- or 1:100,000-scale soil map produced from point sample data provides the best soils data available. While there are examples of remote-sensing methods used for the development of soils-related characteristics that would provide fine spatial resolution data, these products cannot approach the same amount of information (soil fertility, porosity, texture) as that obtained from field samples. Thus, the data availability of soils-related characteristics is a fundamental problem in land-cover change research. In cases where better information is needed to understand how the variability of soils characteristics affect land-use decision making, researchers may choose to collect field-based soils samples (E. Moran et al. 2000a, 2002b). However, the costs of such data collection and processing are prohibitive for many projects.

Social data availability presents different but equally important challenges for connecting human actions to landscape outcomes. The changes in land use and land cover in which we are interested are the direct result of decisions made by certain individuals or groups. In order to collect appropriate data and to conduct pertinent analyses, we must first identify the social unit of analysis. This requires initial knowledge of the study area. In particular, the researcher must understand the nature of property rights and decision making about crops. If land is collectively owned or managed by a community or by a subset of the community, this group or the institution (rules) set up for managing the land is the appropriate unit of analysis. If the land is owned and managed by a state or federal government, and local individuals and institutions have no decision-making authority, the state or federal decision-making body is the appropriate social unit for examining land-use decisions. Finally, if the land is owned and managed by individual landholders, the appropriate social unit of analysis is most often the household. Decisions are made by some subset of the members of the household, based on the needs and resources of the household. Even here, though, it is important to consider the possibility of rentals (where the individual/household renting the land has decision-making authority) and sharecropping arrangements (where the owner of the property maintains the decision-making authority).

Social Data Issues

Once the social unit of analysis is identified, the researcher must collect data on that unit. This is most often accomplished through the selection of a representative sample of these units, for example, households. The most difficult part of the sampling is identifying the population from which to draw the sample. The population is the set of units to which results can be statistically generalized. For example, in Altamira the sample was drawn from the population of lots in the study area. The significance of statistical results based on those data indicate whether a relationship is likely to be true for that population of lots and not for all of the households or people in the region. Alternatively, the Monroe County survey was conducted with a sample of landowners, meaning that statistical results generalize to the population of landowners and not to the population of lots or people (since multiple people reside on many lots but are not considered in the sampling, and single landowners own multiple lots that also are not considered in the sampling). Once the researcher decides what the group is to which statistical results should be generalizable, he or she can use standard sample selection methods given in research design or sampling texts (e.g., see Kish 1995; Singleton and Straits 1998; Babbie 2004).

For the analysis of land about which decisions are made by households or individuals, surveys often provide the only satisfactory means of collecting relevant data. These surveys are limited in their geographic scope and have a low likelihood of many observations across time. These limitations all stem from the expense of conducting surveys of any sort covering a sufficient number of households for statistical analysis, and from the added expense of conducting spatially explicit surveys including all factors relevant to land-use decisions. The primary costs of these data are not equipment costs. The expense of computers and GPS units is far below the cost of personnel time, including the time spent by researchers designing the survey and the time spent by enumerators in the field. For example, the data collection in Altamira involving interviews with household members and the collection of locational information about parcels of land took long enough that each team of enumerators was only able to complete surveys for two households per day. Given a goal of 500 households to provide the necessary statistical power, this comes to 250 team-days. With each team composed of two enumerators, a survey of this sort must find funding for 500 enumerator-days in addition to funding for travel, equipment, and time invested by the research team. Multiply this investment by the number of time points at which data should be collected to get a sense of change and land-cover dynamics and we have a very substantial cost.

Errors and Uncertainty in Spatial Data

Cell values in raster satellite data are classified to produce land-cover datasets. These raster datasets are characterized by a pixilated pattern associated with the cell geometry of the satellite platform (upper right in plate 5). The visual interpretation of aerial photography (upper left in plate 5) produces smooth polygonal boundaries (lower left in plate 5). Various errors are associated with each product. The *minimum mapping unit* (MMU) defines the smallest-size feature discriminated in a dataset. In satellite images MMU is defined by the cell size or spatial resolution of the satellite sensor. With visually interpreted aerial photography, the MMU is a product of what the interpreter is able to distinguish from the photos (which is affected by the spatial scale and quality of the photography).

Base maps, including transportation, rudimentary land cover, hydrology, and other common data layers, are often digitized to produce a fundamental set of data used to describe the context for land-use/land-cover change studies. When features from these base maps are digitized, the MMU is a product of the scale of the map (e.g., 1:24,000 or 1:50,000) and the features that were included when the map was constructed. For example, the map designers may have included every household location when producing the map but only added forest patches that are 100 × 100 m in size. Thus, the MMU for household features is different from the MMU for a forest, although the two features were derived from the same map product. It is critical to be aware of the MMU and how errors of omission might affect spatial analysis. For example, measures of landscape fragmentation and landscape connectivity are highly sensitive to the MMU. In many cases, such as the digitizing example of households and forest patches above, it is not always possible to identify a precise value for the MMU. At a minimum researchers should try to establish a conservative estimate of MMU that can be used in the interpretation of research results.

Spatial Data Representation

The advantages and disadvantages of raster and vector data structures are described in many introductory GIS texts (e.g., Bolstad 2002; Lo and Yeung 2002). In terms of land-use/land-cover change research the decision of what data structure to use largely depends on what analytical tools will be employed, how data will be integrated, and errors associated with transforming data between structures. Raster data structures are most suited to certain kinds of modeling, as discussed in chapter 8, particularly cellular automata and agent-based models. Raster data structures somewhat simplify the process of integrating or overlaying datasets (e.g., partitioning a raster land-cover dataset with parcel boundaries), and certain types of analyses, such as network analyses, are enabled specifically by vector data structures (e.g., see Entwisle et al. 1997). Most analyses can be conducted using a raster or vector approach, and errors are inherent in any spatial data analysis. Thus, it is the goal of the researcher to assess the errors associated with different approaches and to choose the method in which the errors are either minimized or best understood.

There are a variety of spatial operations that allow different types of data to be integrated. Collectively, these methods are called data transformations and refer to the spatial transformation of data between representations. For example, climate data collected at point locations can be transformed to an interpolated surface, transforming the data from a point representation to a surface (or raster) representation.

Likewise, population data collected at the community level (point data) can be interpolated to provide a continuous surface of population density (Walsh et al. 1999). These interpolated surfaces are typically generated from point population data representing some aggregate-level information such as villages, communities, or cities. Attributes of these point locations (e.g., village size) are used to interpolate values between point locations as a means of representing the impact or load of population on the landscape with the assumption that areas with many villages with high populations densely located will have a greater impact on the landscape than sparsely settled areas with few villages of small size. Such a population density (or distribution) surface can be overlaid with a land-cover change map to find the correlation between high population densities and zones of deforestation. However, interpolated surfaces do not always adequately represent the true distribution of phenomena affecting the landscape. The spatial distribution of point samples in part determines the quality and accuracy of interpolated surfaces and so data availability issues sometimes inhibit the ability to employ interpolation methods. Additionally, some variables do not lend themselves to interpolation. Examples include nominal data such as ethnicity or occupation.

Alternatively, a one-to-one or one-to-many linkage can be made between the social unit of observation (household, community) and the landscape associated with that spatial unit. A one-to-one linkage associates the social unit with a single partition of the landscape, such as a household, which resides on a single parcel of land. This type of one-to-one linkage is used in our Altamira example, in which a single landowner resides on a single parcel for which he is the sole decision maker. A one-to-many linkage associates the social unit of observation with multiple partitions of the landscape, as with a household that has several distributed landholdings in separate locations. We see this pattern in both our Santarém and our Monroe County examples. In these cases a small percentage of landowners own several noncontiguous parcels. In the Santarém area, a many-to-one linkage is also used for a portion of the properties. Multiple households reside on many of the parcels and share the work and produce of these areas.

All studies must make some compromises between spatial coverage, data collection costs, and data representation. Demographers typically collect data at the individual, household or community level. These data collection efforts may be samples or complete censuses of geographically defined areas. The availability of boundary measures can provide a sort of census of properties in a given area that can then be linked to remotely sensed and other spatially referenced data. Land-cover data are readily available as continuous surface data from satellite images and can be linked to these boundaries. Similarly, aggregate-level analyses (e.g., examining differences across counties or countries) primarily use publicly available data from censuses or other government data-collection programs. These data can be collected just as easily for the entire population of counties as for a sample of counties. However, when analyses require information about households, individuals, or other groups who do not make data publicly available, financial limitations usually require the use of sampling. The decision to use sampling strategies as opposed to a complete census in the collection of social survey data has important implications for how social and biophysical data are linked to land-cover change data using GIS tools. The noncontinuous nature of the resulting data hinders the estimation of and correction for spatial autocorrelation because of the patchy nature of the data. In addition, the use of a sample introduces the question of what to sample; researchers must decide between a sample that is representative of the landscape or one that is representative of the human population (or the population of relevant human actors).

Spatially Explicit Data Analysis

In GIS, the same dataset can be portrayed using different data structures, potentially changing the representation of that phenomenon. For example, topography can be represented in a raster-based DEM where each cell value identifies a single elevation value for that cell area. Alternatively, topography can be represented in a triangulated irregular network in which each triangular polygon represents a single slope angle and slope aspect surface. Likewise, data can be aggregated or resampled to different scale representations (i.e., aggregating a DEM with a 10-m cell size to a DEM with a 30-m cell size). The same analytical methods can produce varying results when using data at different spatial scales (Walsh et al. 1999). Thus, researchers have choices in the data structure used to represent their data in GIS as well as the scale or resolution of the data used for analysis.

Related to the task of selecting the data structure and scale/resolution for analysis is the choice of analytical method or algorithm. Distances between features can be measures using vector features (i.e., straight-line distance between a polygon representing household location and the point representing the location of the nearest market). Alternatively, that distance can be measured in a raster framework whereby a travel cost surface is produced in which each cell represents the travel cost to get from that location to a destination target. But distances and travel costs also can be measured using different representations. Straight-line distance is relatively easily calculated but is not always the most appropriate representation of travel cost or accessibility. An alternative approach is to measure distance along linear features representing road networks, which can produce dramatically different results compared to results from a straight-line distance (Entwisle et al. 1997).

Another example of how different methods can produce varying results is in the production of a slope dataset from a raster-based DEM. A common method used in many GIS software packages is to fit a plane to a 3×3 window of nine cell values to produce the slope value for the center cell. However, this is just one method of producing a slope dataset (Bolstad 2002). When researchers simply select the default method presented to a software user via a standard graphical user interface they risk missing important sensitivities present in their data. Over time, experience with GIS packages will help researchers become aware of the inadequacies of particular methods, but a bottom-line message to new GIS users is that a range of approaches can be employed to better understand data and thereby aid in the interpretation of results.

The selection of data structures, scale, and methods for analysis is holistic. The choice of data structure is related to what analytical methods will be employed, and the methods employed may be constrained by the data structure of available data. But because the data structure, scale/resolution, and methods used can affect spatial data analysis results, the best approach is to use a combination of analyses when possible. A reliance on a single analytical outcome produced from data at a specific scale of analysis risks missing important scale dependencies in data and systems or limitations of certain data structures for analysis.

Linking Human Actors to Landscape Outcomes

Ultimately, the goal of spatially explicit land-use/land-cover change research is to link human actions to landscape outcomes to anticipate future landscape changes and potentially design policies to ameliorate the negative consequences of those changes. But creating this linkage is a complicated task. The examples from Monroe County, Altamira, and Santarém describe projects where social survey data were linked to landscape partitions through the use of land ownership boundaries. Land ownership boundaries may already be available digitally as in these cases, though field verification of boundaries is necessary. For this field verification and for locating other features on the landscape, it is useful to have a method of identifying spatial locations in the field. A particularly useful tool for this process is the GPS device (Walsh et al. 2003). Field researchers conducting social surveys can geolocate survey respondents by using GPS devices, providing a mechanism to link specific household locations to areas on the landscape (E. Moran et al. 2003; Boucek and Moran 2004). Likewise, in cases where landholdings are separate from the household residence location, GPS devices can be used to identify the spatial locations of distributed landholdings (Rindfuss et al. 2002).

Once a specific household actor is associated with a specific landscape partition, it is still necessary to link actor decisions (and the motivation and process of making those decisions) to observed landscape outcomes. One mechanism to do this is to measure the spatial structure of landscapes through metrics describing the spatial pattern and composition of the landscapes (Walsh and Crews-Meyer 2002). The pattern and composition of a landscape is indicative of ecological function, and likewise the spatial pattern and composition of a landscape is indicative of the land-use decisions that produced that landscape. These land-cover characteristics can be used as inputs for models with various applications such as species habitat/biodiversity assessment and carbon emission/sequestration. Land-cover composition refers to the proportions of different land-cover types within an area and is particularly useful for questions of carbon sequestration models, which rely on the carbon cycling rates of different land-cover types. Land-cover pattern measures can be used to characterize the connectivity and fragmentation of a landscape which is related to land-use management and species habitat.

This type of linkage is particularly useful for land-use/land-cover change analysis because of the availability of satellite images, which provide a relatively inexpensive means of attaining complete data coverage for a large spatial area.[4] In addition, historical satellite images allow the pattern and composition of landscapes to be compared over time. Trends in measures of forest fragmentation and degradation can help identify the long-term implication of particular management practices on the landscape. Aerial photography, including declassified military images, can extend the temporal scale of study further. However, it should be noted that the different spatial resolution and format of data derived from Landsat TM (30-m spatial resolution), Landsat Multispectral Scanner (MSS) (80-m spatial resolution), and aerial photography (interpreted polygons) complicate comparison of metrics across these different data sources/products.

Confidentiality and Spatially Explicit Social Data

If spatial location measures were added to publicly available individual- and household-level data from multipurpose surveys, these data would become very useful for spatially explicit analysis of land use. These surveys have the funding to collect data from a sufficient number of households and across many regions, providing the statistical power to estimate both household and community/region effects. However, one of the strengths of these data—that they are made publicly available to research teams, obviating the necessity of extensive local knowledge and ties—increases the salience of confidentiality issues.

Data with exact spatial location measures exactly identify respondents in geographic space. Making these data publicly available would compromise research ethics and funding guidelines that state that respondents must be protected from any harm, including embarrassment or other emotional discomfort. If we collect all or even most of the data relevant to land-use decisions, and then enable any individual buying or otherwise accessing the data to link individuals to all of these data, we have failed in our obligation to protect our respondents. For example, strangers possessing information about children who have died, about types of land title, or about the employment or income histories of individuals will cause (at the very least) embarrassment or emotional discomfort in some respondents. Given a large enough sample, we can even imagine our respondents (and their neighbors who are likely to have similar characteristics) suddenly targeted by fertilizer marketing companies who possess extensive information on their land uses and their previous use of fertilizers. These problems are unlikely to happen in practice, but it is our responsibility as researchers to protect respondents from any harm that has a reasonable possibility of occurring.

These concerns with spatial locators in data extend to the presentation of results in papers or presentations. Maps of household locations can be easily used to find the identification of respondents and typically should be published only after substantial transformations (removing coordinate information, rotating or "mirror-imaging" depictions) have been used to mask the specific location of the map area depicted (Rindfuss 2002). In some situations it may not be possible to transform a map and still communicate the desired information, in which case researchers should opt to not present a spatial representation of the data. The ways of dealing with confidentiality in the presentation and dissemination of data vary from project to project and must be tailored to the goals of the research and the characteristics of the study area.

In the study of Santarém, the research team will eventually release the survey data to the public for its use. These data will have no locational or other identifying information, though they will have measures extracted from the GIS and linked to the survey records. In anticipation of this, the team designed rules for the display of data that will ensure that respondents cannot be identified in those public-use data. Because of the differences between the properties in their current size and shape (which exist only in our data) and their size and shape in the INCRA property grid (which is available to the public), researchers can display small portions of our property grid without any identifying features (road intersections, the edge of the national forest, the edge of the river) to demonstrate results. However, researchers cannot display our grid together with the original INCRA grid or any information locating our sampled areas in space. Specifically, the sample is clustered into 3 × 3 km cells to minimize travel time between interviews, and the location of these cells may never be displayed. This process is similar to releasing individual-level data without any community, school, or neighborhood data, on the assumption that it would be easy to figure out who particularly wealthy people were if you knew which neighborhood they lived in but not if you only knew that they lived somewhere in your county.

Data Documentation

An important component of the use of GIS- and remote-sensing–based data for the study of land-cover change is the proper documentation of datasets. Because of the cost of collecting geospatial data, data documentation or metadata provide a means to protect the investment placed in the collection and processing of those data. A poorly documented dataset can be easily misused, which can lead to serious errors in presenting results. Common items to document in land-cover change datasets include the spatial scale or cell size of satellite-derived land-cover data, the units for different attributes (feet, meters, miles, kilometers, etc.), and the data processing performed on a dataset (i.e., lineage). There are two primary standards for the documentation of metadata, one developed by the U.S. Federal Geographic Data Committee (FGDC 2003) and another developed by the International Organization for Standardization (ISO 2003). In practice, there are relatively minor differences between these two metadata standards and developments are underway to reconcile these differences. However, what is critical is to select a method of documenting geospatial data and implement that as part of data processing. Events such as staff turnover and data exchange present opportunities for the loss of important details regarding the proper use of a dataset. Metadata capture these important data aspects and allow for the appropriate use and application of spatial data.

Documentation is equally important in the reporting of data based on social surveys. Statistical results are only generalizable to the population from which a sample is drawn if that sample is a probability sample. Beyond that, if the sample is a stratified sample, inferences depend on weighting of the data to account for the complex sample design. Details about the sample design are necessary for other users of the data to avoid incorrect inferences and for readers of research to evaluate the claims based on the data. This reporting is particularly important for research on human-environment interactions, because some samples are drawn from a population of properties or are in some way a representation of the landscape, while some samples are drawn from the populations of individuals or households. In addition to details about the sample selection, researchers must report response rates to assess the quality of the sample and the inferences based on it.

Concluding Remarks

The ability of GIS to integrate social and biophysical data through a common spatial reference system provides a powerful analytical tool for the study of human-environment systems. Spatial data representation is a framework that can allow data from disparate sources to be analyzed in an integrated design, enabling key relationships to be explored in complex systems. However, because of the complexity of social and biophysical phenomena, the process of representing features in a GIS is often not straightforward. This chapter has described a series of challenges researchers are likely to encounter in the development and analysis of GIS-based datasets for the study of land-cover change. In particular, the examples and concepts described here demonstrate how it is important to understand how errors associated with spatial data representation can affect subsequent analysis of integrated datasets. All spatial datasets have some degree of error, thus it is important to be able to assess to what degree these errors affect results found from spatial data analysis. However, with an understanding of these errors, the integration of GIS and remote-sensing data presents an effective means of creating an analytical link between social and biophysical dynamics.

Notes

1. While no formal rules prohibiting parcelization of land have been found by researchers working in the study area, many landholders believe such laws do exist. This belief in part explains the lack of land fragmentation. Since land settlement in the Altamira region is relatively recent, it is possible that such land fragmentation will occur in the future as household heirs prefer to stay close to other family members rather than migrate to distant frontier areas.

2. These acquisitions are currently under timber production but the land-cover composition of these state- and federally managed lands represents the largest homogeneous forest areas in the state.

3. The data were in a format incompatible with the GIS software used by our research group and required significant processing in order to integrate with our other datasets. Acquiring these data in digital form was critical, however, as manual digitizing of these boundaries would have been a labor-intensive and error-prone pursuit.

4. For example, one Landsat TM scene covers approximately 185 × 170 km. Global-scale analyses utilize entire scenes, whereas images are usually subset to a portion of the scene for local-level studies to speed processing.

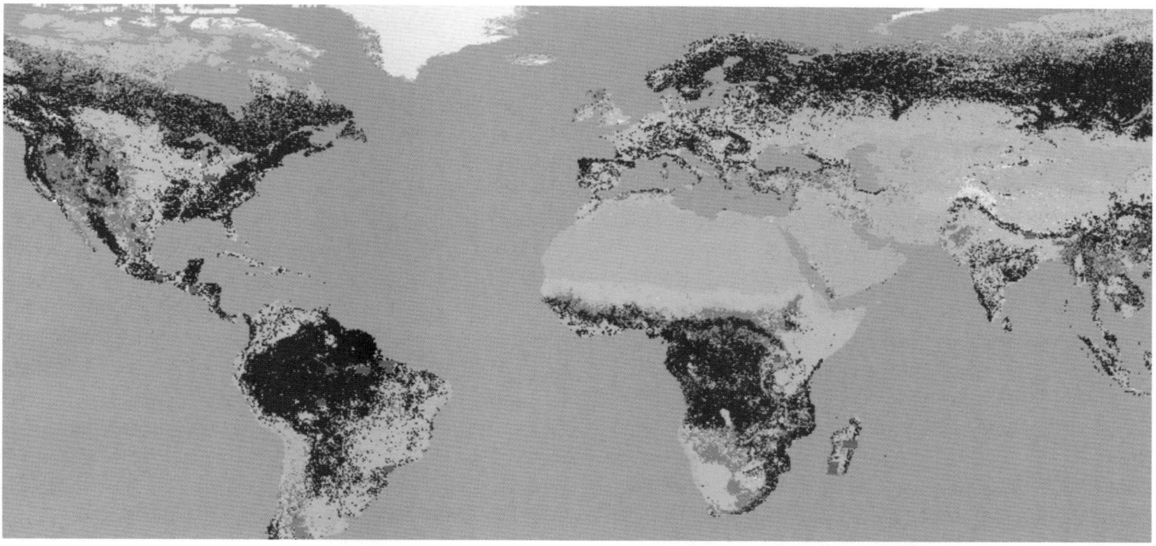

Plate 1 Earth's forests and CIPEC research locations. (Base map from the Global Vegetation Monitoring unit of the Institute for Environment and Sustainability [Ispra, Italy] website at http://www.gvm.jrc.it/glc2000/ProductGLC2000.htm.)

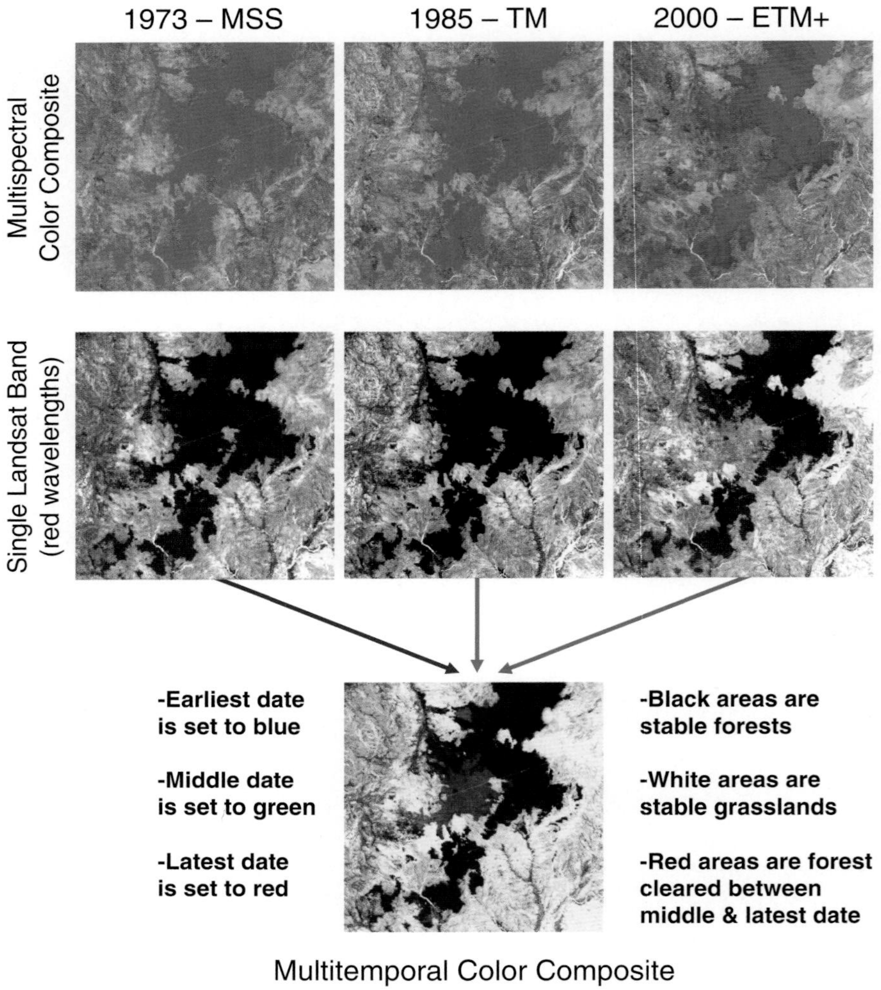

Plate 2 Examples of multispectral and multitemporal color composites generated from Landsat images. Images are 25 km wide and show the Zombitse Forest near Sakaraha, Madagascar.

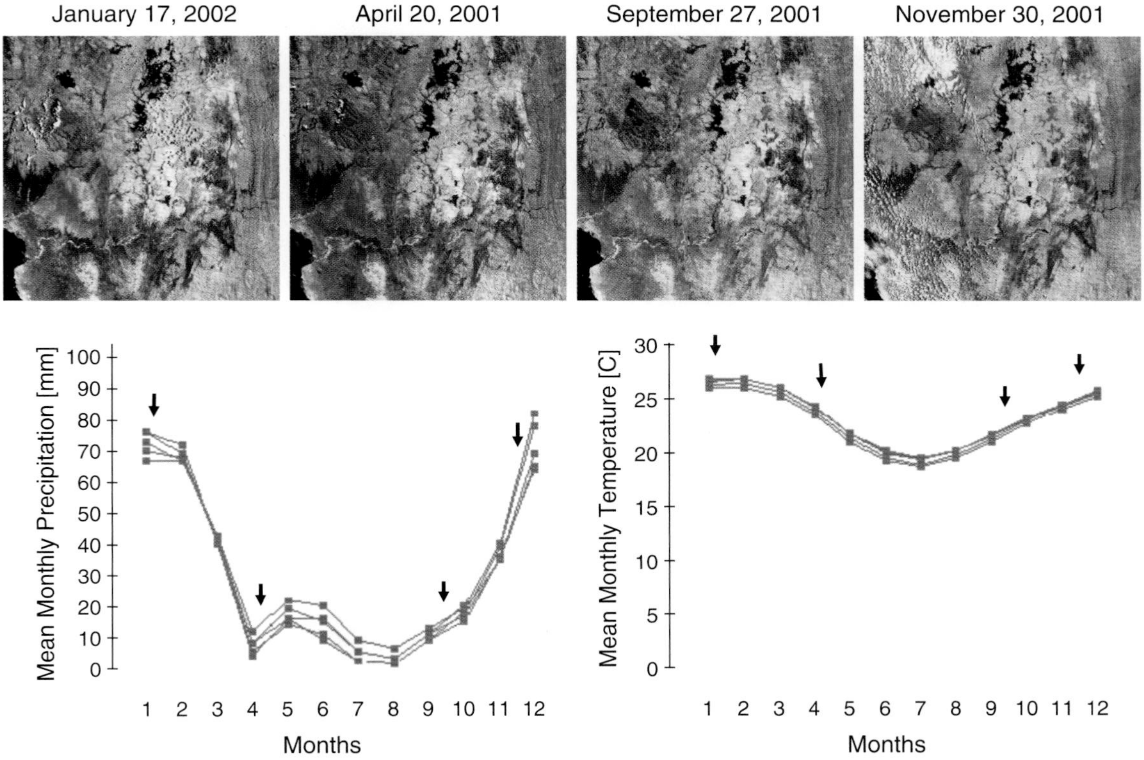

Plate 3 Four contrasting multispectral color composites from different seasons derived from Landsat Thematic Mapper images of southern Madagascar. These composites show how reflectance can change as plants respond to seasonal changes in water availability linked to precipitation.

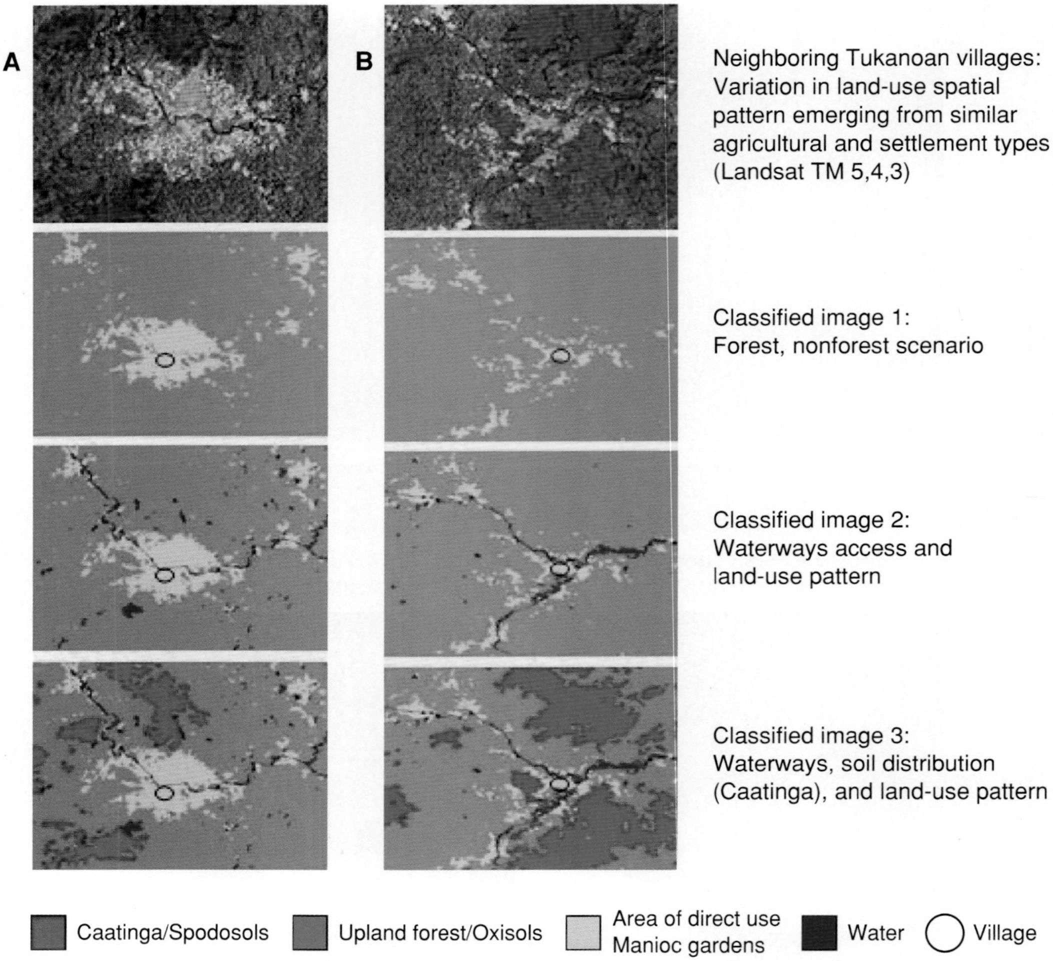

Plate 6 Variability in land-use patterns in Tukanoan indigenous communities, Vaupés region, Colombia. Neighboring Tukanoan villages in the Vaupés region present different spatial patterns of land use resulting from similar agricultural and settlement conditions. The role of soil distribution and waterways influencing the location of agricultural areas is highlighted through increasing detail of image classification. The village to the left shows crop areas immediate to the settlement, while the village to the right takes advantage of waterways to cope with the limited soil fertility surrounding the village. Different spatial configurations emerge. (Adapted from Castro and Brondízio 2000.)

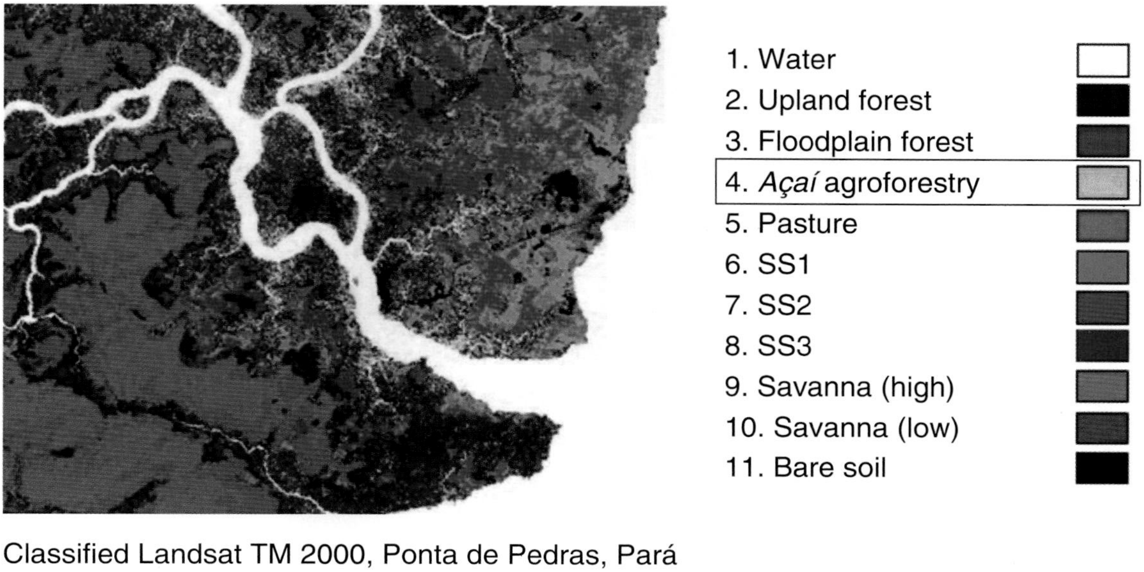

Plate 7 Discriminating intensively managed açaí agroforestry from floodplain forest. Intensive fieldwork allied with image analysis shows the possibility of discriminating agroforestry areas from unmanaged floodplain forest. If mapped together with floodplain forest, these large tracks of economic forests remain "invisible," as do their managers; once discriminated, this land-use class becomes the most significantly productive area of the region, actually corresponding to its top position in the regional economy. In the area represented here, intensively managed açaí agroforestry represents 12 percent of the total landscape, but close to 50 percent of the floodplain area. This example illustrates the sensitivity of remote-sensing data in portraying the regional economic reality. SS, secondary succession. (Adapted from Brondízio et al. 1996 and Brondízio 2004a, in press.)

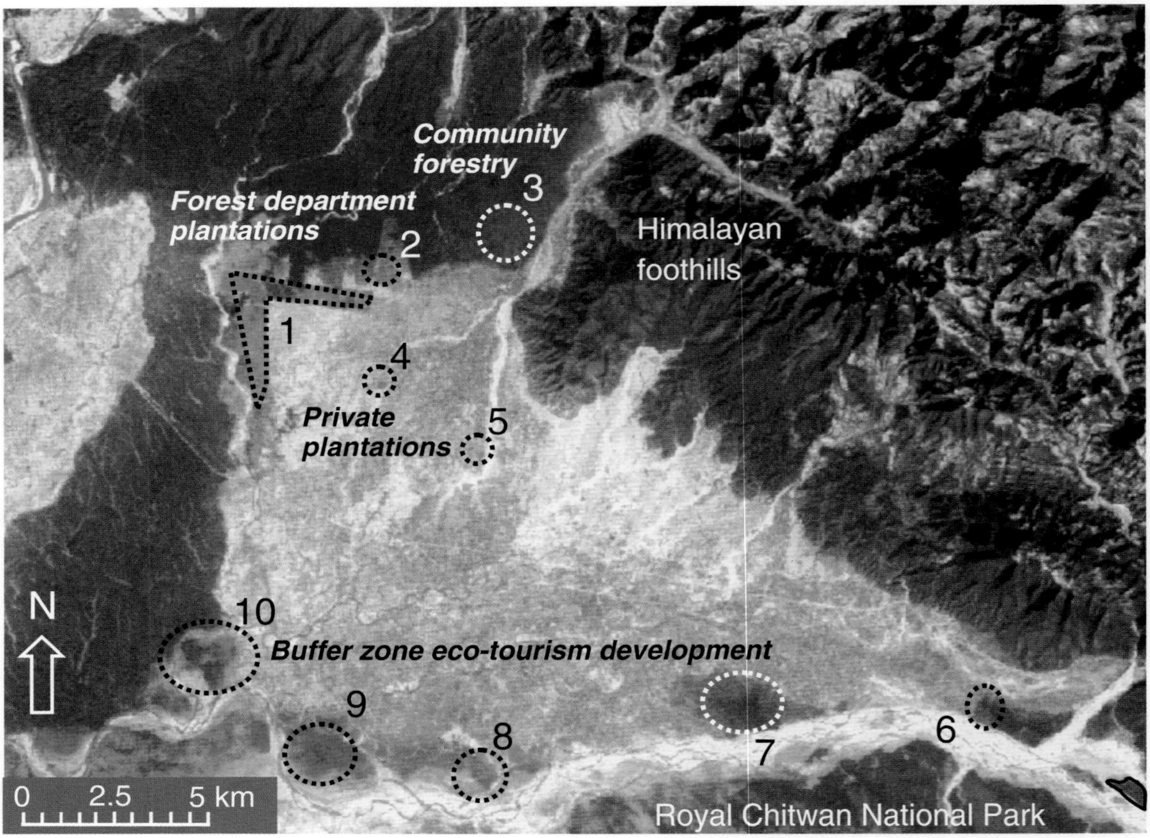

Plate 8 This multitemporal color composite of the Chitwan District of south-central Nepal was produced from Landsat images from 1976, 1989, and 2000: band 2 from a 1976 Multispectral Scanner scene as blue, band 3 from a 1989 Thematic Mapper scene as green, and band 3 from a 2000 Enhanced Thematic Mapper Plus scene as red. In this composite, forest loss is depicted in yellow or red, while forest regrowth is blue or green. Ten anomalous areas experiencing stability or regrowth of forest were identified and visited. They represent Forest Department plantations, community forests, private plantations, and comanaged buffer zone forests located adjacent to Royal Chitwan National Park.

8

Modeling Land-Use/Land-Cover Change: Exploring the Dynamics of Human-Environment Relationships

Tom P. Evans, Darla K. Munroe, and Dawn C. Parker

Empirical data analysis is an effective tool that can be used to test key linkages between social and biophysical drivers of land-cover change. Many land-cover change scientists have used this approach to make both theoretical and methodological contributions. In particular, linking social factors to landscape outcomes through the integration of household- and community-level social data with remotely sensed images has yielded important insights into how complex human-environment systems function. This type of analysis provides an effective tool to explore relationships between social and biophysical phenomena over a broad array of environmental conditions.

Many empirical analyses, however, are limited by the scope of existing data or the temporal and spatial resolution of those datasets. In addition, researchers are often limited in their analyses by the variables available in secondary datasets. Modeling approaches provide a means to further explore complex human-environment systems beyond the confines of existing data. While modeling efforts are more powerful with robust datasets to evaluate their fit to the real world, the model construction process alone sometimes can yield insights into complex systems that are not apparent from the interpretation of empirical analyses. In addition, if a diverse set of data is available at suitable temporal and spatial resolutions, modeling enables the use of alternative scenarios in the behavior of a system. For example, researchers might explore the impact of decreasing mortality and increasing population on resource use.

This chapter explores how modeling human-environment relationships can help researchers develop plausible explanations for land-cover change processes and how modeling methodologies can be incorporated into human-environment research.[1] An important point of modeling is that models need not be predictive to be useful to researchers. The process of developing models often provides new insights

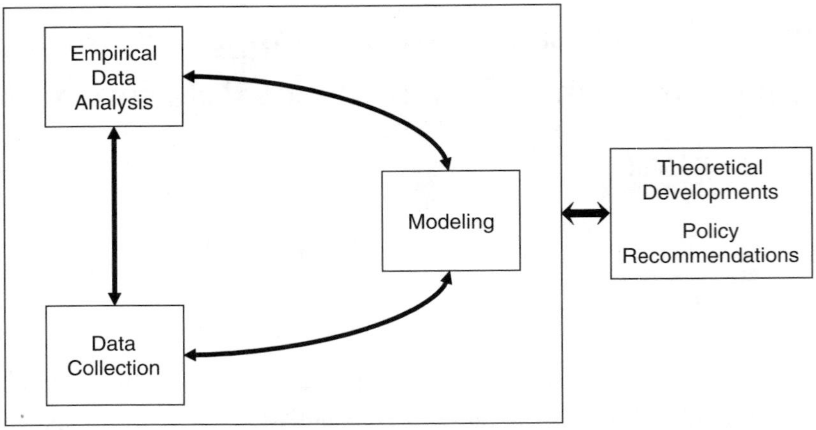

Figure 8.1
Research design integrating modeling into studies of land-use/land-cover change.

to complement empirically based research. In designing models, researchers must consider how each individual model component relates to other components in the system. This process of defining component relationships is a creative process. It is this creativity that can suggest lines of research that were formerly not considered. The insights gained from modeling can then be tested empirically. In this way, the combination of empirical data analysis and modeling can be a powerful research tool for researchers exploring complex systems. Empirical data analysis and data collection efforts can be informed by modeling activities and vice versa in an iterative process in which new research threads are explored by redesigning models and proposing new data collection efforts to support empirical data analysis (figure 8.1). The ultimate goal of this integrative research design is to make contributions to theory or potentially inform policy for a particular area of application.

This chapter presents three types of modeling approaches to show how different modeling methods can be applied to complex human-environment systems. The design of each of these models is in part a product of the project objectives and the disciplinary background of the model designers. Some differences between the three models described here are due to the different modeling methods used, and other differences are products of the model design process. The purpose of this comparison is to demonstrate what types of research questions can be addressed with different modeling methods and to illustrate how modeling can be incorporated into other research activities.

The Modeling Process

Models can be used to create a simplified structure of a complex system. All models are simplifications of reality, but by generalizing the components of a complex system, relationships between salient factors in these systems can be explored. Models are thus valuable analytical tools and can be used for a variety of different purposes in land-cover change research. In particular, models can be used to "(1) define and isolate a problem, (2) organize thought, (3) advance understanding of data or direct attention to relevant data yet to be gathered, (4) communicate ideas, (5) devise hypotheses and tests, and (6) make predictions" (Starfield and Bleloch 1986, 1; see also Winterhalder 2002).

These modeling objectives contribute to a variety of stages of typical research projects, including hypothesis generation, data collection, and interpretation of results. Another important application of modeling is the ability to explore alternative scenarios for a system, such as the impact of climate change on an alpine tree line or the impact of the introduction of family planning on population growth and, by extension, land-cover change. It is often not possible to validate the findings of these scenario-testing exercises fully, yet exploring these factors in a modeling exercise often yields insights that would not be apparent from empirical data analysis. It also can serve as a mechanism to get stakeholders and policy makers to initiate communication and consider previously unforeseen scenarios.

Land-cover change processes are rarely so simple that they can be deconstructed into the relationship between two or three main drivers. More commonly, land-cover change is the function of a broad set of factors that interact in complex ways, creating complicated feedbacks and relationships that are difficult to decipher. Modeling and the model construction/development process in particular are effective means of exploring the dynamics of a system and the interactions between components in complex systems. The understanding gained from the modeling process can be used to inform the design of survey instruments and future empirical data analysis. In particular, the process of model development itself can help researchers consider aspects of a system that constrain specific elements in a system.

Criticisms of models often focus on the application of models for predictive purposes. While there are many examples of effective predictive models (e.g., short-range weather forecasting), many of the modeling purposes listed above are related more to gaining understanding of how a system functions than for the development of a forecasting tool. This is not to suggest that model validation is not an important aspect of land-cover change modeling. On the contrary, researchers should strive to construct rich datasets for each model component at both high spatial and high temporal resolutions for the purpose of validating their models. There are several examples of literature related to validation of land-cover change outcomes from models (e.g., Pontius et al. 2003), and most modelers present some quantitative assessment of how well their model produces output that matches observed data. Less attention has been paid to validating the structure of land-cover change models.

It is often the case that the cost of data collection means that not all aspects of a model can be validated. In contrast to the example of effective forecasting models (e.g., weather forecasting), complex human-environment systems are not heavily instrumented. The resources necessary to provide a sufficient amount of data to validate all components of a model are beyond the scope of many modeling efforts. This does not mean that the development of complex models should not be attempted. Rather, it implies that the interpretation of modeling results should be carefully considered in the context of the quality of data that exist for validation. A complex model lacking robust validation can still serve to generate hypotheses or inform subsequent data collection efforts.

Critical Issues for Modeling Human-Environment Relationships

Here we introduce a series of key aspects related to the general process of modeling land-cover change, irrespective of the specific model approach used. These issues are fundamental components of model development that affect how dynamic interactions are represented in models. We briefly discuss aspects related to the architecture of models (especially temporal and spatial scale), as well as more mechanical issues such as how data availability affects data validation.

Spatial and Temporal Scales

Processes affecting land-use/land-cover change occur across multiple spatial and temporal scales of analysis. These processes are associated with a range of social and biophysical factors, and researchers from a variety of disciplines have acknowledged the importance of scale issues to their behavior (Gibson et al. 2000b; Evans et al. 2003). Climate change can be gradual, occurring over the course of decades or centuries and impacting large spatial extents. Smallholder decision making can result in very rapid land-cover changes within a very small spatial extent. The fact that land-cover change processes occur across spatial and temporal scales of analysis poses a series of problems and challenges for modelers of land-cover change

(Veldkamp and Fresco 1996; Walsh et al. 1999; Verburg and Chen 2000; Evans and Kelley 2004).

First, data availability issues may hinder the scope with which model components can be validated within a model. For example, climate data may be available over a relatively broad temporal extent but not with sufficient temporal or spatial resolution to adequately portray climate change within a model. Even if data are available, time and labor issues may make the processing of such data prohibitive (e.g., visual interpretation of historical aerial photography for large spatial extents). Second, computer processing limitations may make it impractical to run a model at a dense spatial or temporal resolution. Here there is a balance between extent and resolution. A coarse spatial scale model (e.g., 1-km resolution) with a large spatial extent (hundreds or thousands of kilometers) can require the same processing time as a fine-scale model (e.g., 30-m resolution) with a small spatial extent (tens of kilometers). Likewise a coarse temporal scale model (one-year time step) with a large temporal extent (hundreds of years) can require the same processing time as a fine-scale model (one-month time step) with a small temporal extent (ten years). There is a similar tradeoff between temporal scale/extent and spatial scale/extent. A coarse temporal scale model with a large spatial extent can require the same processing time as a fine temporal scale model with a small spatial extent. These tradeoffs are important aspects of the model design process.

Models are designed with a specific purpose/application in mind. To a certain extent this helps modelers decide how to construct a model at the most appropriate scale. These model objectives must be considered, however, in the context of data availability and data limitations. It is often the case that data limitations determine the scale at which a model can reasonably be validated. Thus, the modeler must consider model objectives in the context of data availability. One key characteristic of land-cover change models is the time required for processing, which is directly related to spatial scale of operation. Related to the issue of processing speed is the time step or temporal resolution of the model. While the relationship between time step and processing speed depends on the structure of the model, a model using a time step of one year might take twice the processing time of a model running with a two-year time step. On the other hand, a model running at 100-m spatial resolution might take four times the processing time of a model running at 200-m spatial resolution.

Another complication in the model design process is the possibility of a mismatch between different data sources, because human and bioecological systems are often represented quite differently in space. Economic variables, such as parcels, population, housing values, employment figures, and so on, are generally assigned to a particular administrative unit (with or without an explicit spatial reference). Often, the administrative units of particular variables are collected at different levels of aggregation, and one often has to scale up a model to the coarsest spatial unit. In contrast, environmental variables (such as soil or land cover) are often represented as a spatially continuous field.

Data Availability

One major obstacle to the development of effective land-cover change models is the availability of data and the limitations of available datasets for model validation. Ideally, data availability issues would not affect which elements are included in a model and how they are included. The realities of model development are, however, that data constraints must be considered. The integration of spatially disparate data sources can lead to significant spatial errors and various complications due to scale issues (Anselin 2001). Both temporal and spatial scale effects that confound the modeling process can result simply from measurement error alone (Elhorst 2001). These data issues affect the objectives that can be gained from modeling. For example, with a broad array of data available at fine spatial and temporal resolutions, a model can be developed with a higher level of confidence in its predictive power than a model developed in the absence of sufficient data for validation.

With modest amounts of data, a participatory modeling approach could be used in which key informants—experts and stakeholders—both inform the model and gain understanding that can help stakeholders with different positions find a place of compromise (e.g., Walters 1997; Barreteau and Bousquet 2000; Lynam et al. 2002). But modeling with only minimal data also can yield substantive results. Some modeling approaches, particularly those associated with complexity theory, are designed to explore key aspects of a system using highly abstract representations. These models have little or no predictive power but do provide insight into how systems function and how model representations can be used to explore fundamental or theoretical dynamics in a system in space and time (e.g., see http://www.brook.edu/SUGARSCAPE).

Lumpers vs. Splitters: Model Complexity

One fundamental aspect of model development is the decision of how much overall complexity to develop in a model. Models are often criticized because they oversimplify some aspects of a system. Researchers tend to add detail (or split) components of a model related to areas with which they are very familiar and simplify (or lump) components of a model with which they are less familiar. For example, a demographer might choose to add substantial detail to the social components of a model that explores the rate of deforestation in a frontier area. A forest ecologist modeling the same system may include relatively little detail in the social components (including human demographics) of a model but substantial detail in the forest regeneration component of the model. The forest ecologist might rightly criticize the forest regrowth component of the demographer's model and the demographer might criticize the sociodemographic component of the forest ecologist's model. This does not suggest that the most detailed model is always the best model.

A model should be as detailed as necessary to represent the dynamics of a system. Increasing the complexity of a model beyond that necessary to portray the key interactions in a system can complicate the interpretation of model results. It is difficult to track the dynamics of a highly detailed model, making such models prone to unexplainable outcomes. Thus, simple models are more easily interpreted, but simple models may not include sufficient complexity to represent the human-environment system in question. One approach is to add just enough complexity to represent the function of a system in the simplest possible way.

Modelers must make critical decisions regarding where to increase the amount of detail in a model and where to simplify components of a model. This is a particularly difficult pursuit with models developed by a team of multidisciplinary researchers. There is a tendency for each researcher to desire complexity or detail in his or her area of expertise and to suggest simplifying other components of the model. Thus, model development undergoes a series of negotiations between those wishing to split or add complexity to some component of a model and those wishing to lump or simplify that same model component. A model with a large number of components and interactions is more complex because it can be more difficult to trace the relationships affecting model outcomes when a model is highly detailed. Here the purpose of the model can be revisited as a way to guide where complexity is needed and where simplicity is allowable in a model.

Modeling Approaches for Land-Cover Change Analysis

This section describes three approaches for modeling land-cover change. The approaches discussed here (dynamic simulation models, agent-based models [ABMs], and statistical models) are by no means the only methods applicable to modeling land-cover change processes (see Agarwal et al. 2002 for a summary of representative models). Yet the models presented here do represent some of the diversity of approaches available to researchers. Each approach has its distinct advantages and disadvantages, and it should be stressed that there is no "correct" modeling approach. More important, each modeling approach is applicable to a different set of objectives behind the purpose of any one model. These advantages and disadvantages are discussed later in this chapter.

Dynamic Simulation Models

Dynamic simulation modeling provides a means by which land-cover change processes can be examined and different scenarios tested from a systems perspective (Costanza et al. 1993; Dale et al. 1993b; Voinov et al. 1999). These models can be calibrated and validated using a combination of primary data sources and the existing literature to develop a tool with which different simulations and scenarios may be tested. This section describes one example of a dynamic simulation model for land-cover change used to explore household decision making and land-cover change at the parcel level in Altamira, Brazil (Evans et al. 2001b). The purpose of the Altamira model was to identify those factors that are important components of the process of land-cover change and to test a variety of scenarios or conditions for their impact on land-cover change. While the long-term predictive ability of any model is limited for various reasons (such as unforeseen shocks to the system or dramatic changes in technology), dynamic models can provide considerable insight into the complex interactions operating to affect land-cover change. The Altamira model was designed to be run for durations on the order of approximately fifty years, incorporating multiple generations within households. The model simplifies many elements of land-cover change but includes enough complexity that important relationships between labor, resources, and land cover can be simulated.

In the Altamira model, each land-use activity was assigned a specific utility based on (1) the labor and economic resources available to the household and (2) the expected benefit from that land-use activity based on crop and cattle prices. The term "utility" is used to describe a mathematical function that expresses the preferences of land-use choices with respect to their perceived risk and expected financial return. Labor is allocated to specific land-use activities based on these relative utilities; landholders seek to maximize their financial income by allocating labor to those activities that they perceive will provide the greatest financial return on their labor investment. In other words, land-use systems chosen by the household are a product of the household decision-making structure of the model, rather than an input to the model itself.

The simulation is designed to be run for several decades using a one-year time step. Landholders can select multiple land-use decisions (e.g., cut primary forest for annual staple crop production or convert annuals to pasture) in one year, but there is only one decision-making round per year. At the beginning of the model run, the entire parcel is composed of mature forest simulating the settlement of this previously uncultivated area. Field data show that the majority of parcels in the Altamira study area only vary in size between approximately 90 and 110 hectares (ha), with most of them being 100 ha. A parcel size of 100 ha is used for the model runs presented here based on a 500 × 2000 m rectangular area characteristic of the settlement project. The model accommodates alternative parcel sizes by adjusting the initial size of mature forest at the beginning of the model run.

The model is organized into the following sectors representing the major processes affecting land-cover change: demography, household economics (finances and prices), land-use decision making, labor allocation, and institutions. Figure 8.2 shows a conceptual diagram describing how the main model components are related in the model structure. The interactions between each of these sectors result in specific land management decisions that affect the land-cover sector where the land-cover composition of the parcel is tracked. These land-cover decisions result in clearing of forest land, fallowing of agricultural land, and the transition from one type of agricultural production to another. These land-cover changes result in

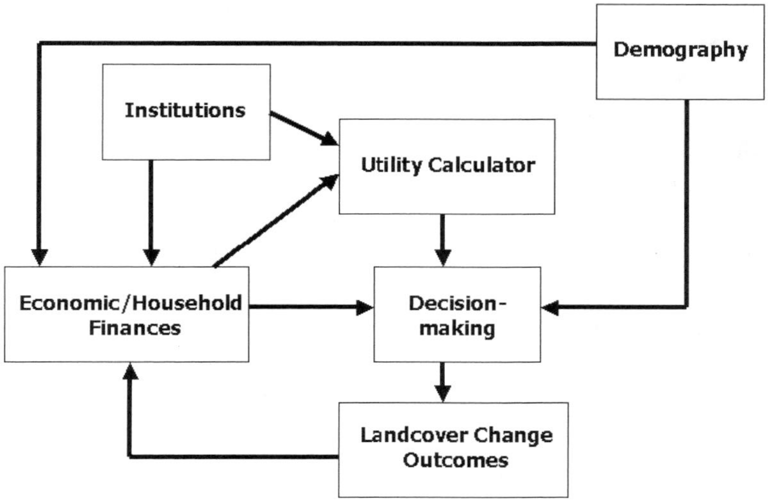

Figure 8.2
Overview of dynamic systems model components for Altamira, Brazil.

changes in the land-cover composition of the parcel. Land-cover class proportions are reported for the entire parcel and thus there is no representation of the land-cover pattern within the parcel (e.g., degree of fragmentation, number of patches). The model assumes that biophysical parameters, such as soil fertility, topography, and hydrography, are homogeneous within the parcel, which is a vast simplification of the Altamira landscape. However, subsequent model runs could be performed under scenarios of varying land suitabilities to explore the impact of land-use decisions on land-cover outcomes in more complex landscapes.

The model consists of a labor allocation framework whereby landholders invest labor and resources in specific activities to either maintain land already under one activity (e.g., perennial crop production) or convert area in one land use to another land use (e.g., the conversion of mature forest to annual crop production). While there is a clear distinction between land use and land cover in Altamira (e.g., successional forests can be used for either agroforestry or nontimber forest production or simply abandoned agricultural land), the model presented here has a one-to-one correspondence between each land-use activity and a corresponding land-cover class. The area in each land use is reported in single-year intervals, showing the land-cover composition over time and the types and proportions of land-cover transitions that have occurred during the model run. The model is run for an individual parcel given initial household composition, but multiple model runs using different household compositions can be aggregated to construct a regional-level perspective on land-cover change. In order to more properly model a regional-scale representation of land-cover change, various parcel characteristics affecting land use would need to be included, such as transportation accessibility measures and soil characteristics to represent the variable soil conditions in the Altamira study area. The performance of the model was evaluated using land-cover classifications for the Altamira study area derived from aerial photography from 1970, Landsat Multispectral Scanner (MSS) satellite data from 1978, and Landsat Thematic Mapper (TM) satellite images from 1985 and 1996 (see S. McCracken et al. 1999 and chapter 9).

The land-use choices of the household through time depend primarily on the household labor availability, the household's ability to hire wage laborers, and the prices of annual crops, perennial crops, and cattle. Adjusting model parameters allows the results of various scenarios to be compared, such as high- vs. low-human-fertility scenarios or changes in relative prices between crops and cattle. Dynamic systems modeling software allows for the construction of graphical user interfaces (GUIs) that can be employed to rapidly rerun models with new parameters for varying scenarios (e.g., low fertility, high fertility). Figure 8.3 presents the

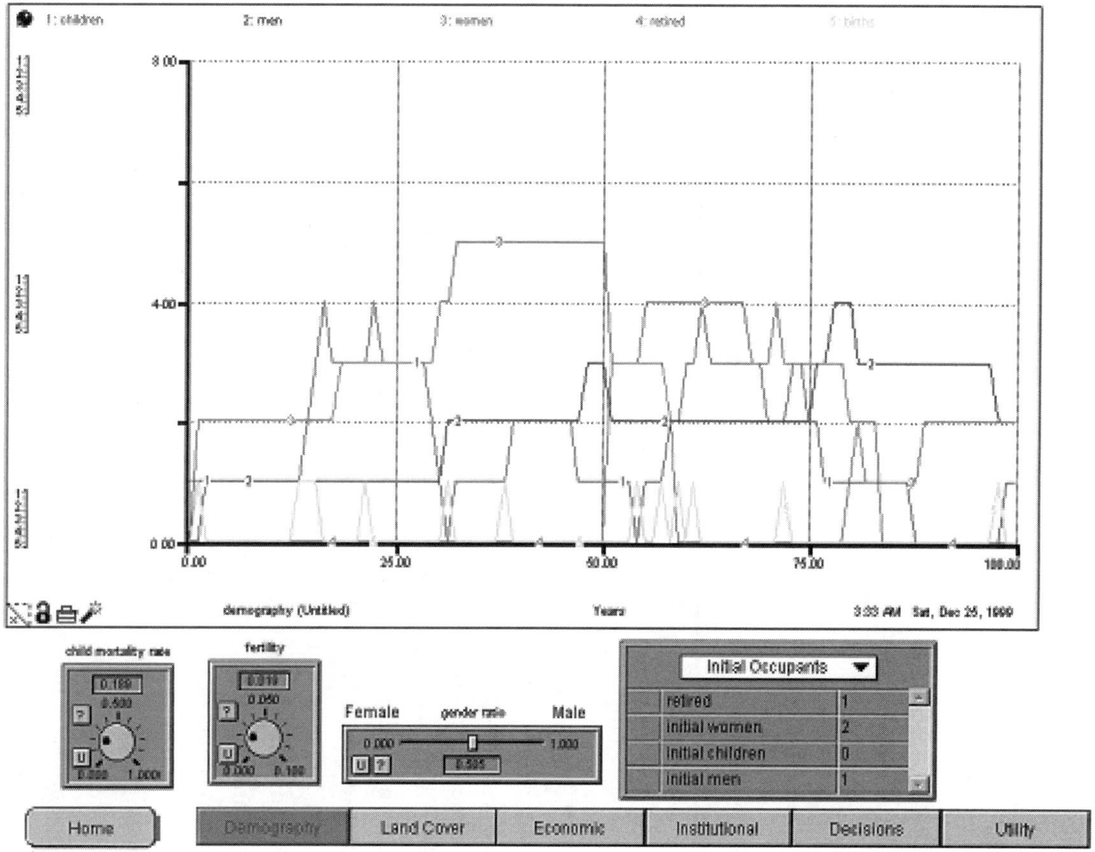

Figure 8.3
Demography sector and graphical user interface for dynamic systems model of Altamira, Brazil.

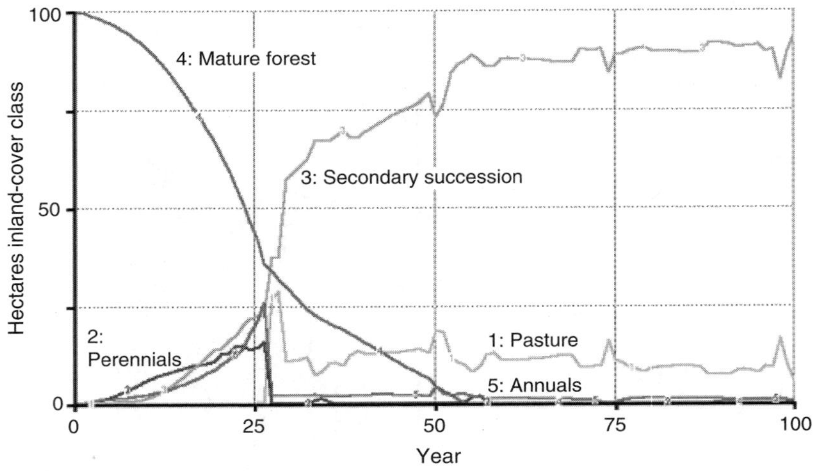

Figure 8.4
Dynamic systems model of Altamira, Brazil. Results for high-fertility scenario.

GUI for the demography component of the Altamira model. Land-cover composition over time can be observed for each of these model runs indicating the land uses conducted at each time point and, specifically, the ability of forest regrowth to keep pace with the degree of forest clearing for various agricultural activities.

Using a crude birth rate (CBR) of 40 (per 1000 total population), mature forest declines from 100 percent to zero percent in approximately forty-five to fifty years. Figure 8.4 shows the land-cover class compositions through a 100-year model run for a representative parcel in the high-fertility scenario with a low price for perennials and a moderate price for pasture. With a CBR of 11–16, which is more common in developed countries, 25 percent mature forest remains after sixty years for most model runs (figure 8.5), presumably as a result of the lack of labor available for the relatively high labor cost activity of clearing mature forest. Table 8.1 shows land-cover composition of the parcel for years zero through 50 in tabular form. The area of land under production (annuals, perennials, pasture) is greater under the high-fertility scenarios than in the low-fertility scenarios. It should be noted that the results of individual model runs vary. Some parcels in the high-fertility scenario actually exhibit low fertility due to the probabilistic nature of birth events in the model. However, the different scenarios can be compared by performing large sets of runs for the different scenarios, where individual model runs represent one parcel under a specific scenario. A comparison of the aggregate of these model runs shows

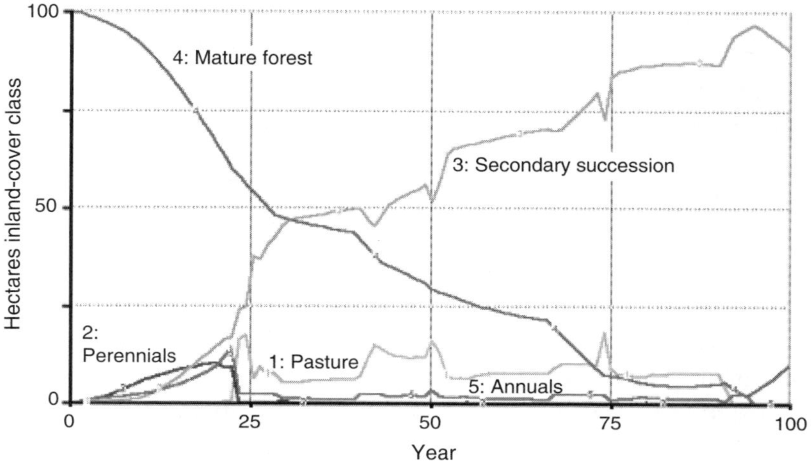

Figure 8.5
Dynamic systems model of Altamira, Brazil. Results for low-fertility scenario.

Table 8.1
Land-Cover Composition for Low-Fertility Model, Years 0–50

	Percentage of Parcel in Land-Cover Class				
Years	Secondary Succession	Pasture	Perennials	Mature	Annuals
0	0	0	0	100	0
5	0.27	0	1.8	96.83	1.1
10	1.52	0	5.78	90.39	2.31
15	7	0	8.5	79.63	4.88
20	14.63	0	10.03	66.06	9.28
25	37.69	6.16	0	54.14	2
30	46.69	5.12	0.22	47.12	0.84
35	48.54	5.69	0	45.09	0.69
40	49.66	6.51	0	41.82	2
45	52.27	11.8	0	34.35	1.57
50	51.73	15.87	0	29.27	3.13

a more rapid rate of deforestation under the high-fertility scenario compared to the low-fertility scenario.

What is critical to questions of biodiversity and carbon sequestration is the rate of deforestation occurring in the Brazilian Amazon, and the dynamics of forest regrowth. Figures 8.4 and 8.5 display the proportion of forest in different stages of regrowth in both fertility scenarios, showing that there is a gradual decline in mature forest and a gradual increase in the amount of forest in different successional stages. The rate of these land-cover changes and the proportion at different time points varies as a function of a variety of social, biophysical, and institutional factors, but the model does represent the mosaic of patches of forest at different stages of regrowth that follows settlement.

While this model attempts to construct a simplified model of land-use activities, the utility of this model as a predictive tool is understandably limited, particularly for long periods. At each time step, there is a probability that the model will misrepresent the actual behavior of that single household. Thus, as the model attempts to make predictions farther and farther into the future, the likelihood that the model represents the true land-cover composition of an individual parcel declines. However, this is not seen as a drawback to this method of research or to land-cover change modeling in general.

While the long-term predictive power for simulating a single specific household in Altamira is limited in this model, we believe that collectively the set of model runs is a very powerful tool that can be used to observe some interactions that affect land-cover change in the region. The utility of the model can be found in understanding the importance of different factors contributing to land-cover change more than as a tool to predict future land-cover composition. Additionally, it is not possible to foresee shocks to the system that may dramatically affect the interactions between sectors, such as natural disasters, changes in technology, and introduction of new crops or cultivars. Nevertheless, the model does represent a reasonable simulation of the process of land-use/land-cover change in Altamira. More recent research on the Altamira project includes the development of an ABM of land-cover change for this area (Lim et al. 2002).

Agent-Based Modeling

ABMs have their foundations in abstract representations of spatial interactions, usually based on a regular gridded spatial structure (D. Parker et al. 2003). The ability to explore these spatial interactions lends itself to the application to land-use/land-cover systems due to the prominence of spatial interactions such as spatial externalities and information diffusion in landscapes. In the land-use/land-cover change modeling community, there is growing interest in the application of ABMs or multi-agent systems models to the study of land-use/land-cover change phenomena (e.g., Gimblett 2001; Janssen 2002; D. Parker et al. 2002, 2003; Verburg et al. in press). An agent-based model of land-use/land-cover change (ABM/LUCC) consists of two key components. The first component is a cellular model that represents the landscape under study. The second component is an ABM that represents human decision making and interactions. An ABM consists of definitions of autonomous decision-making entities (agents), an environment through which agents interact, and a set of rules defining the relationship between agents and their environment and the sequencing of actions. Autonomous agents contain a set of rules that translate both internal and external information into updated states, decisions, or actions. In the context of an ABM/LUCC, an agent representing a land manager may combine individual knowledge and values with information on soil quality and topography (the biophysical landscape environment) and the land management choices of neighbors (the spatial social environment) to calculate a land-use decision.

ABMs have employed a range of models of human decision making, from the fully rational *Homo economicus* to simple heuristics. For ABM/LUCC models, the shared landscape, land markets, social networks, and resource management institutions may provide other important environments through which agent interactions occur. A detailed discussion of the components of an ABM/LUCC model, alternative models of human decision making, and further issues related to the development of these models are discussed in detail in D. Parker et al. 2003.

Abstract Agent-Based Models

A variety of examples of ABMs are being used to represent specific, stylized processes to examine alternative processes that may lead to emergent phenomena. Janssen and Ostrom (in press) use an ABM to examine the conditions under which a community of users of a common-pool resource may implement a rule to manage that resource. In their model, development of trust between agents plays a key role in determining whether or not the rule is implemented and enforced following implementation. In contrast to previous research, they find that agent heterogeneity need not be a barrier to successful implementation of the management rule, provided mutual trust evolves among the agents. Ongoing work by Center for the Study of Institutions, Population, and Environmental Change (CIPEC) colleagues Janssen and Ahn focuses on the testing of behavioral models, including learning models, on data from linear public-good experiments to develop a theoretically based, empirically tested ABM model for common-pool resource experiments. Hoffmann (2002; see also Hoffmann et al. 2002) uses an ABM environment to explore the evolution of norms. At a general level, his model demonstrates how autonomous agents can end up following the same rules of behavior in the absence of a central authority and explicit communication. In particular, he examines the role of "norm entrepreneurs" in norm emergence. He finds that while norm entrepreneurs are not always necessary for norm emergence, their effectiveness may depend on the complexity of the agent's environment.

The range of agent-based modeling activities demonstrates that ABMs can be applied to a spectrum of questions, from theoretical to empirical (D. Parker et al. 2002, 2003). Further, efforts at one end of the spectrum may effectively inform development of models at the other end. In other words, a range of ABMs with varying degrees of abstraction can be used as a suite of models to examine a system from more than one perspective. Likewise, agent-based modeling can complement other modeling techniques, such as interactive human experiments and statistical analyses.

An Agent-Based Model of Land-Cover Change in South-Central Indiana

Typical of much of the eastern United States, south-central Indiana experienced massive deforestation during the second half of the nineteenth century, followed by a period of gradual reforestation beginning in the early twentieth century and extending to the present day. However, while net reforestation has occurred, patterns of land-use change have been heterogeneous, with agricultural abandonment contributing to reforestation in some regions, and urban growth pressure contributing to deforestation in others (Munroe and York 2003). Heterogeneity among both biophysical (topography and soil quality) and socioeconomic (demographic and regional economic growth) factors appears to play an important role in observed patterns of deforestation and reforestation.

These heterogeneities suggest that modeling each agent identically would miss important dynamics of land management decisions and the spatial outcomes of those decisions. First, substantial heterogeneity exists among local decision makers with respect to goals, attitudes, and socioeconomic characteristics (Koontz 2001). Second, the biophysical environment is also heterogeneous, and this biophysical heterogeneity substantially impacts the potential success of particular land uses. The spatial distributions of social and biophysical factors are distinct and overlapping, creating a potentially diverse spatial mosaic of outcomes as differing decision-making strategies are applied across a varying landscape. Further, spatial interdependencies, such as diffusion of information about timber prices and soil erosion, may have a substantial influence on household decision making and subsequent impacts on landscape pattern. This complex combination of heterogeneity and spatial dependencies can be prohibitively difficult to represent using some modeling approaches. However, ABMs can successfully represent these relationships. The following paragraphs describe the research context of this agent-based modeling application and the modeling strategies employed to explore this system.

Much of south-central Indiana is characterized by nonglaciated, steeply sloped land of marginal quality for agricultural production. Subsequent to European settlement, these lands were quickly degraded, and for the most part, agricultural production has been abandoned as the region has become integrated with national markets. The region does produce high-quality hardwood timber, and nonindustrial private forestry remains an important economic activity. Land use in the region currently consists of a mix of urban/residential, agriculture, and forest land. Few full-time farmers remain, although many landowners practice both part-time farming and forestry. The region has experienced substantial urban growth pressure in recent years, and conversion of open land into both high- and low-density residential land use has been substantial. The ABM described here focuses solely on the rural landowner and therefore it treats demand for high-density residential conversion as exogenous.

As is the case in the development of any model, a tradeoff must be made between the benefits of abstraction and those of realistic representation of the system being modeled. In the case of an interdisciplinary model, this challenge is magnified due to the potentially high level of detail contributed by representatives of each discipline. The main argument for abstraction is one of transparency. Given a relatively stripped-down model, important causal mechanisms operating within the model may be more easily identified. However, historically, the majority of ABMs have lacked a strong empirical foundation. The model presented here draws on a rich foundation of empirical sources, including historical documents, discussions with local experts, survey data, and existing academic literature.

An important point of debate during project planning has been a strategy for model validation. This debate has been shaped by both competing philosophies of modeling and by anticipated data availability. The research group concluded that simple, heuristic ABMs that illustrate general trends and more detailed, empirically grounded models that produce detailed landscape outcomes are potentially useful. At the same time, it is apparent that data availability and quality are relatively sparse for the early frontier times and rich for the recent past. A prototype model was designed to qualitatively replicate temporal patterns of deforestation in the history of settlement of southern Indiana from the mid-nineteenth century to the present. Another model focuses on the period from 1939 to 1998. These foci imply different criteria for model validation for the two models.

The prototype version of this modeling effort was developed in C++ and is described in Hoffmann et al. (2002). The broad goal of the modeling effort is to build an ABM of rural landowner decision making from which both deforestation and reforestation emerge. In principle, the ideal model includes agent-agent, agent-economy, agent-political, and agent-environment interactions. As a first step, the prototype model focuses on agent-environment interactions and, in particular, on the influence of several economic and biophysical factors on the paths of deforestation and reforestation. The model demonstrates the sensitivity of this path to prices, tax rates, and slope. Two models of human decision making are employed. A variant of a fully rational economic agent calculates a utility-maximizing portfolio of land uses, and then implements changes in his or her current land use that move toward the economically optimal allocation. A boundedly rational agent calculates utility levels gained from each land use in the previous time period, and strives to increase those activities that previously resulted in increased utility levels. Each agent chooses among possible land uses: farming, fallow, forest regrowth, and timber harvesting. The utility of each is influenced by market prices; tax and subsidy rates; the agent's wealth, education, and risk preferences; variability in market prices and subsidies; and the productivity of the land. Land productivity is influenced by exogenous and endogenous biophysical factors, including slope and the duration of the land in either farming or fallow. Each agent owns a specified number of cells for the duration of the model, and there is no land market by which agents can move or acquire land within the study area.

A sensitivity analysis has been performed to explore whether the model produces simulated agents whose behavior qualitatively matches the historical agents under study. Sensitivity analysis demonstrates that agents react as expected to variations in price levels, price variance, slope, and diminishing marginal productivity due to continuously farming the same cells. The model also demonstrates temporal macropatterns that qualitatively match empirical patterns, as massive deforestation followed by slow reforestation occurs.

This general model framework has been extended to a new code set in Matlab that is built upon a richer foundation of empirical data to inform the model (Evans and Kelley 2004; Kelley and Evans under review). This model also uses households as agents that are associated with specific landscape partitions through land ownership boundaries. The land ownership parcels are aggregates of contiguous cells defining the spatial objects which can be manipulated by landowner agents. The basic decision-making process in the model defines landowner agents in terms of their preference parameters associated with the following land uses as defined by a labor allocation decision: pasture, forest, agricultural row crop, off-farm labor, and aesthetics. A last parameter used for calibrating the model is a spatial externality parameter that is an indicator of the spatial homogeneity of the landscape. A low value for this measure indicates a parcel with a very fragmented landscape with many discrete patches. A high value for this parameter indicates a highly homogeneous landscape with few small patches. This parameter is implemented in the model using a neighborhood function that affects where land-cover change transitions occur. This entire parameter set is fit for each agent/parcel to a time series of data representing land cover at the following time points: 1939, 1958, 1967, 1975, 1980, 1987, 1993, and 1998. The model is run iteratively, refitting each parameter to produce new model output and matching these modeled landscapes to the observed data using a percent forest landscape metric and a total landscape edge metric. Because different land-cover change outcomes are observed on different parcels, this modeling approach produces agents with heterogeneous parameter distributions representing the variability in landowner decision making (Evans and Kelley 2004).

An important aspect of this research is exploring the scale dependence of the models. This model has been run at cell resolutions from 60, 90, 120, 150, 240, 300, and 480 m. The results of these modeling runs indicate that the parameter distributions vary as a function of spatial resolution. In other words, the distribution of agent types varies depending on the resolution of the model run.

Both landscape composition and landscape pattern are important indicators of landscape function and have been found to be effective metrics for evaluating the correspondence between model landscapes and observed data (Hoffman et al. 2002; D. Parker and Meretsky 2004; Evans and Kelley 2004; Kelley and Evans under review). The overall performance of the model is evaluated based on comparisons of a series of landscape metrics representing both composition and pattern.

However, agreement between generated and empirically observed patterns may not necessarily imply that the model correctly reflects spatial processes present in a real-world landscape. Therefore, one important role for ABM/LUCC models is to formally link process to pattern though development of stylized theoretical models. Ongoing work uses a stylized theoretical ABM to examine the influence of spatial externalities, transportation costs, and endogenous distribution of land use on landscape pattern (D. Parker 1999; D. Parker and Meretsky 2002, 2004; D. Parker and Najlis 2003). This model has been used to demonstrate the possible emergence of inefficient patterns of production due to spatial externalities. It also has been used to formally map the relationship between model parameters and landscape metrics and to explore the possible nonlinear relationships that result.

Statistical Models

Statistical analysis has a number of advantages over other modeling approaches. In particular, statistical models can be used to derive strong, quantitative measures of the relationships among a set of variables, and to rank the relative influence of each. In addition, rigorous tests can be undertaken to falsify hypotheses. However, statistical approaches are less useful in cases where there are nonlinearities, path dependency, and other complex, emergent properties. Also, statistical analysis generally cannot assign causality, but rather only covariance. Finally, the data needed to develop a fully specified statistical framework may be unavailable or available only at levels of aggregation that would be unacceptable for inferring individual behavior. Thus, statistics are most helpful as one analytical approach to complement other empirical analyses. This section addresses the development of spatially explicit statistical models and their use in land-use/land-cover change modeling. Relevant issues include the extent of theoretical links with social sciences, institutional settings, and the appropriate scale of analysis.

A significant impediment to the development and advancement of statistical models of land-use/land-cover change is the issue of spatial complexity. Most conventional statistical techniques assume stationarity, or independence, in the distribution of a variable across space. In reality, many environmental and social variables related to land-use/land-cover change (including topography, soil, land cover, population) can exhibit significant spatial autocorrelation (Anselin 2001). In recent years, researchers have employed various techniques to correct for or filter spatial autocorrelation (for some examples of studies, see Mertens and Lambin 2000; G. Nelson et al. 2001; Munroe et al. 2002; Overmars et al. 2003).

Statistical Models for Land-Cover Change Analysis Irwin and Geoghegan (2001) argue that statistical land-use/land-cover change models provide a clear opportunity to link spatial and social science in a rigorous, quantitative manner. Most researchers break up the determinants of land use into two broad categories: proximate and ultimate driving forces. At a regional or landscape level, causal mechanisms include broader economic forces (price policies, wage trends) and intersectoral linkages, such as factor markets and trade (Coxhead et al. 2001; E. Moran et al. in press). At this landscape scale, one can answer questions appropriate to this level of analysis, such as, Does infrastructure development cause deforestation? Do markets cause deforestation? Can topography mitigate the impact of broader policies? (Munroe et al. 2002) Certain factors have been empirically observed to be related to land-use change; such as population density, infrastructure, and land tenure.

There is a clear link between land-cover change and underlying land uses. To explain land-cover change, particularly tropical deforestation, one must consider the proximate or immediate determinants of land use (B. Turner et al. 1995). Such factors include population size or density, technology, level of affluence, political structures, economic factors such as systems of exchange or ownership, and attitudes and values. Thus, land-cover change is in great part the realization of changing patterns in land use.

Two basic approaches to using statistical models in particular are consistent with the goals of human-environment research applications. The first is to link land cover with land use by modeling land cover, or land-cover changes, as a function of land use. This methodology has been used in household studies in Indiana (Koontz 2001) and Mesoamerica (Munroe et al. 2002). The most influential example of such a model was a study conducted by Chomitz and Gray (1996), which developed a latent variable model of land rent. The spatially explicit pattern of land cover is assumed to be a function of land-use incentives across the study region. One does not explicitly observe land rent, but it is assumed that relative returns to land use driven by infrastructure, topography, and land tenure variations (G. Nelson et al. 2001) generate, in equilibrium, a particular, spatially explicit pattern of land cover.

Second, statistical analysis can be a useful technique in an integrated, multiscale approach. Land-use change is a fundamentally local process, but it is nested in a structure of hierarchical decision making (E. Moran et al. in press). Statistical approaches can be a useful analytical link between regional-scale changes and the local (household) drivers of these changes. For example, a simple, spatially explicit regional model may posit land-cover change as a function of topography, infrastructure (e.g., roads), and institutional variation (e.g., national park and local administrative boundaries) (Munroe et al. 2002). The explained variation by these factors can illuminate the degree to which land-cover change is influenced by the enabling environment. Then, one can investigate on the ground regions where the statistical model explains less of the variation in observed land cover (i.e., by mapping regression residuals) to uncover more causal mechanisms at a household level that are not explained by the above factors. Regional statistical models also can serve as a bridge between local and national changes. For example, changes in policy can be built into the statistical model. G. Nelson et al. (2001) looked at the impact of road improvements on local land use. In this manner, the impact of reduced transportation costs on land-cover change in western Honduras was simulated (Munroe et al. 2002).

Statistical Analyses of Land-Use Change and Forest Cover in Indiana To identify the relevant factors associated with change in forested area, one can begin with a model of the returns to various other land uses (e.g., agriculture, urban) to estimate the opportunity cost of forest land. Ideally, one would be able to match changes in forest area to individual decision making, but due to data restrictions, this undertaking may be impossible, particularly over any significant period of time. Instead, in the forestry and agricultural economics literature, many models have been constructed at a county level, postulating that the observed changes in land use at the county level are the sum of individual landowner decisions.

Landowners choose an appropriate land use based on a variety of factors, including the profitability of that use (based on input and output prices) and individual preferences (considering factors such as the aesthetic value of forests). The ultimate usefulness of these aggregate models depends strongly on the empirical application and the relevant questions addressed by the research. Prior empirical examples include the prediction of future forest area (Mauldin et al. 1999; Ahn et al. 2000); the allocation of land to forestry over time, including timber and nontimber benefits (Parks and Murray 1994); estimating the amount and cost of carbon sequestration (Plantinga et al. 1999); and measuring the impact of agricultural land use on soil erosion (D. Miller and Plantinga 1999). Analysis in Indiana (Munroe and York 2003) builds on the above latent models of unobserved net benefits to land use, where the observed share of land uses at the county level is the sum of individual landowner decisions.

Though the coarse scale of the statistical analysis in Indiana was originally seen as a limitation, county-level analyses yielded the opportunity to consider driving factors of land-use change at a more regional level. Specifically, the hypothesis was tested that tradeoffs between forest and agriculture were likely to be a function of agricultural suitability, whereas tradeoffs between forest and urban land were more complex. Counties with better soil and flatter slopes were expected to have a greater share of agricultural land relative to forest. For urban land use, on the other hand, regional variations in employment and the value of land and the variation of resi-

Table 8.2
Selected Results for Econometric Analysis of Share of Agriculture-Forest and Urban-Forest Ratios of Land Use in Forty Southern Indiana Counties, 1967–1998

	Agriculture-Forest		Urban-Forest	
Variable	Coeff.	SE	Coeff.	SE
Constant			−0.5504	*−0.440*
Forest rent	0.0001	*−0.002*	0.0044	*−0.004*
Forest rent[a] slope	0.0033	*−0.017*	−0.0263	*−0.027*
LCC 1 & 2			0.0031	*−0.003*
Farm profits	0.6647	*−0.476*	1.3700	*−0.966*
Crop revenue	−1.1398	*−0.866*	2.5829[b]	*−1.191*
Population density	0.0005	*−0.001*	0.0016[c]	*0.000*
Median house value			0.0000	*0.000*
Variance in house value			−0.0323[a]	*−0.020*
LQ Tertiary/higher sector			−0.7570	*−0.501*

LCC, land-capability class; LQ, location quotient. *Source*: NRCS 2001.
[a] Significant at 90% level.
[b] Significant at 95% level.
[c] Significant at 99% level.

dential land values were important in explaining variations in the extent of forest area (Munroe and York 2003).

A set of nested models was developed to examine the variation in land-use shares at the county level as a function of known or hypothesized drivers of land-use rent, or profitability; variables were iteratively added to the model until no further explanatory power was gained. Selected results are presented in table 8.2. The study area covers forty southern Indiana counties in the Knobs, Lower Wabash, and Upland Flats units of the U.S. Forest Service, from 1967 to 1998.

Two regression equations—the ratio of agricultural land to forest area and the ratio of urban/developed land to forest area—were used to exhaustively represent land-use categories at the county level. These land-use ratios were regressed on key determinants of land-use profitability: forest and agricultural rent, measures of land quality, and drivers of urban land demand. Forest rent was modeled as the net present value of an infinite series of timber rotations, which are determined by stumpage prices and yield by species. Agricultural rent is determined by the net present value of a perpetual stream of annual crop and livestock revenues. Urban land use is defined as nonagricultural or nonforest use, including both industrial uses and residential purposes. The value of the urban land is reflected in direct competition to the other land uses, and was proxied by population density, median housing value and the variance in that value at the county level, and the percentage of employment in nonextractive sectors of the economy relative to the U.S. average (as measured by the location quotient, or LQ).

Panel techniques were used to account for structural differences among individual observations. We found that a fixed-effect formulation was best for the agriculture-forest share, whereas a random-effects formulation was most appropriate for modeling the tradeoff between urban and forest land. The interpretation of each model is that for the ratio of agriculture to forest, county-specific differences explain much of the variation across individuals, but for urban-forest changes, county-specific variations play out differently over time.

The profitability of forest land, as determined by the revenue streams defined above, was not a good predictor of the share of private forest at the county level. Instead, the drivers of agricultural profitability (farm profits, and crop revenues in the case of the urban-forest share) and urban land rent (population density and median housing value) were inversely related to the share of forest land. The forest rent variable was not significant in any of the models. This finding is contrary to applications of this model in other regions (e.g., see Ahn et al. 2000; Mauldin et al. 1999). One possible explanation for this difference is that nontimber forest land benefits are more important than timber profitability for nonindustrial private forest landowners, especially for the relatively small parcels common in Indiana.

Median house value was significant and positive, but mediated by variance in housing values. Thus, those areas with a higher median house value had higher shares of agriculture relative to forest, except for areas where the variance in housing values was quite substantial. The LQ variable was not significant, but its inclusion pulled down the magnitude of the housing value variable, indicating that areas with a greater concentration of tertiary and higher sectoral employment have less agricultural land. This finding indicates that areas with wealthier individuals and higher residential land values have a higher share of urban land use. We believe that increased urbanization and rural residential land conversion in southern Indiana is linked to changes in the regional labor market; namely, tertiary and quaternary sector job growth increases, and the effect of relatively wealthier individuals moving into rural areas.

Public policy suggests that the greatest threat to nonindustrial private forest land use in Indiana is residential land conversion. Our findings suggest that there is a complex interplay between the opportunity costs of agricultural and forest land in the face of increasing urbanization. Though declining farm profits may lead to residential conversion, this impact also is coupled with a decrease in forest cover. The insignificance of the forest rent may indicate that net benefits to forestry are undervalued relative to other uses. This finding suggests that one policy objective may be to protect forests on and around formerly agricultural land that becomes residential to minimize the impact of agricultural abandonment on forests.

Discussion: Complementing Empirical Analysis with Modeling

Each of these modeling methods is suited to different types of applications and data. And it should be noted that there are, of course, other modeling methods beyond those discussed in this chapter. For example, behavioral models and cellular automata models also have been used to explore land-cover change dynamics, but fundamentally, each modeling method has specific advantages and disadvantages. The dynamic systems model presented here for Altamira, Brazil, is nonspatial and thus does not allow complex spatial interactions to be incorporated into the model design and interpretation of results. However, there are ongoing efforts to integrate spatial interactions into dynamic models (e.g., Costanza and Voinov 2004; the FLORES model [http://simulistics.com/projects/flores/index.htm]).

Potential complementarities do exist between the three modeling approaches described here and other modeling approaches used elsewhere. Dynamic simulation models can be used to examine macroscale trends in coupled human and natural systems. Also, a dynamic simulation model of a household, such as the one presented here or the one described by Carpentier et al. (2000), could be used to develop an agent-based representation of a particular household. This approach has been taken by Berger (2001), who embeds a mathematical programming agricultural decision module into a multiagent system. Successful development of both dynamic and agent-based models requires an understanding of drivers of land-use/land-cover change at multiple scales. Statistical models can be used to develop this understanding and potentially can be used to estimate key parameters for dynamic or agent-based models. Finally, since many ABMs are stochastic, analysis of multiple model runs is required to draw general conclusions regarding model behavior. Statistical tools are essential for conducting this analysis. Thus, while data availability may dictate the use of one model over another in a particular case study, we wish to stress our conviction that alternative models should be viewed not as competitors, but as complements.

The modeling community is diverse and evolves quickly. New tools are rapidly developed that facilitate the modeling of certain dynamics and processes. However, because of the specifics of individual research locations, some models are designed for one location. This complicates the process of applying models to new areas, as well as the ease with which modelers can learn from the developments of their colleagues. The open-source approach is one means to address these obstacles (Schweik and Grove 2000). Broadly speaking, open-source models involve the publication of a model source code that is made available for use by other researchers. When modelers use a model code developed by another researcher, they are required to make any contributions or improvements to the original code available to the research community. Various web-based initiatives exist to facilitate these kinds of open-source projects such as SourceForge.net (http://sourceforge.net) and the Open Research System (http://www.open-research.org; see also Schweik 2001). While the publication of source code is not new to models of land-cover change, these community-based systems for sharing code are relatively recent developments and are well positioned to energize the development of open-source modeling projects. Two examples of current open-source modeling projects are the UrbanSim model (http://www.urbansim.org/) and the SLUDGE model (http://www.csiss.org/resources/maslucc/details.php?ID=20).

Many of these model objectives directly complement empirical data analysis and more traditional land-cover change analysis (see figure 8.1). In particular, models can be used to identify key factors that may be missing from an empirically based dataset, yet are important to the function of a system. For example, a number of researchers have used longitudinal survey data integrated with remotely sensed satellite images to explore the relationship between social factors such as population growth, institutions, and agricultural production to land-cover change. For these studies the success of the research is heavily reliant on the content covered by the questions included in the survey instrument. The omission of a key component, such as the impact of community-level institutions on land management, can severely hinder the final analysis of the system. Familiarity with the study area and survey pretests can be used to identify some of these key components, yet it is often not possible to predict the importance of any one given factor until after a survey has been conducted and the results analyzed. Researchers face difficult choices in trying to balance the need for a comprehensive survey with a desire to minimize the respondent burden for a particular survey instrument.

Conclusion

Modeling is an effective tool for researchers of land-cover change processes to explore the relationships between components of complex human-environment systems. While it can be argued that the most valuable models are those that are supported by robust datasets for model validation, there are other advantages to incorporating modeling into a research design beyond the development of a strictly validated model. The process of model development itself often leads to insights into the dynamics of land-cover change systems that may not have been apparent through empirical data analysis. Land-cover change models also can be used very effectively as a research tool to complement empirical data analysis. Even simple models can help generate hypotheses for the function of different drivers of land-cover change. Models also can be used to guide subsequent data collection efforts by suggesting content for survey instruments, field data forms, or new data collection efforts altogether (e.g., soil samples or climate data).

Modelers have a choice of different modeling approaches, each with specific advantages or disadvantages compared to other approaches. Limitations include those related to structure, scale, dynamics, and validation. The choice of modeling method should rely on a targeted set of research questions at the core of the research. In other words, the modeling method selected should be chosen based on the specific research questions that are to be explored. No single modeling framework is appropriate for all circumstances, and models should be developed in the context of the unique dynamics present in the study area in question. Likewise, it can be very effective to construct several models using diverse approaches and then compare the results from each model. The application of multiple modeling methods whose strengths complement each other can provide a rich context for analyzing a diverse array of processes in complex systems. This alleviates some of the pressure to select the ideal modeling approach. It is likely that insights can be gained from a variety of modeling approaches, particularly when applied in a research design leveraging data and results from traditional empirical methods.

Note

1. The agent-based work described in this chapter is the result of contributions from past and present members of the CIPEC modeling/biocomplexity team, including Jerome Busemeyer, Laura Carlson, Peter Deadman, Shanon Donnelly, Matthew Hoffmann, Hugh Kelley, Vicky Meretsky, Emilio Moran, Tun Myint, Robert Najlis, Elinor Ostrom, David Reeths, Jörg Rieskamp, James Walker, and Abigail York.

IV

Comparison: Generalizing from Case Studies

Comparative analyses represent an integral aspect of the study of human dimensions of global environmental change. While individual case studies can provide detailed information about interrelationships between human activities and environmental processes, comparative work allows researchers to test whether interrelationships and patterns found in one site reoccur across space and through time in multiple sites. Such research allows the identification of common patterns and processes and permits the testing of theories and hypotheses regarding forest change as well as the evaluation of policy.

Part IV presents five chapters that take a comparative approach to addressing the interrelationships between human dimensions, ecological/biophysical conditions, and processes of land-cover transformation. Four of the chapters focus on forest-cover change, while the fifth chapter (chapter 13) looks at trajectories of agricultural change. All of the chapters recognize, however, interrelationships between agricultural practices and forest cover. Agriculture may clear forests, imitate forests (agroforestry), or permit afforestation or regrowth (tree planting or field abandonment). The chapters underscore the benefits of using comparable methods of data collection and analysis. At the same time, the studies do not shrink from the challenges of comparative research.

Since each chapter focuses on a differing set of research questions relevant to the human dimensions of global change, a variety of specific approaches is presented. All of the studies except chapter 13 incorporate remote sensing and geographic information systems (GIS) in conjunction with field data to examine the interrelationships between human activities and land-cover/land-use change, particularly forest transformations. These chapters reflect comparable methods for processing remotely sensed data and collecting field data; they consistently emphasize that microlevel data and ground-truthing are necessary to interpret and contextualize remotely sensed data. By contrast, chapter 13 presents a meta-analysis based on secondary data sources in order to attain a larger sample size and analyze agricultural change across continents and through time.

In chapter 9, Eduardo Brondízio discusses the need for intraregional analysis in human dimensions research. Focusing on the Amazon basin, he presents three contrasting cases to illustrate that within any given region, there is likely to be a diversity of environmental, historical, and economic factors that mitigate against easy generalizations. Methods of remote sensing provide a fundamental means to depict regional land use, yet local-level details show a more complex set of relationships than remotely sensed data alone can assess. For example, the study cases reveal (1) that groups with similar cultures and economic activities may have different land-cover patterns; (2) that important differences in community-level land-use systems may exist, even across short distances, but such contrasts tend to be obscured in regional-level analyses (illustrating scale dependency in process-pattern linkages); (3) that changes in production systems through time might not be readily apparent with remotely sensed data; and (4) that deforestation trajectories vary at the household level with respect to period effects (such as variations in credit policy, inflation rates, and development programs), cohort effects, household age, and soil fertility. Brondízio argues that intraregional analysis provides a means to recognize the complexity of local circumstances that might otherwise confound regional research efforts. It also offers a means to identify consistently important variables in forest change, such as forms of access, land resource value, and human assets.

Catherine Tucker and Jane Southworth examine in chapter 10 contrasting patterns of forest-cover change in two sites with comparable forests in Guatemala and Honduras. Despite the relatively similar biophysical contexts and histories in which forest dominated the landscape, the two sites have markedly different deforestation histories. Analyses of remotely sensed data show that the Guatemalan site presents much less area in forest than the Honduran site; the contrast relates to different settlement histories, infrastructural constraints, and political-economic contexts. Drawing on extensive fieldwork data, the analysis focuses on the biophysical, institutional, and political-economic dimensions that contribute to highly dynamic patterns of forest change. Local and national institutions influence forest exploitation in these sites, and have periodically played important roles in constraining forest-cover change. Yet the institutional arrangements have shown recurrent weaknesses to enforce conservation principles when pressured by economic and political incentives for forest clearing. The results reveal that in these cases, deforestation is neither inevitable nor constant, but change processes may include periods of forest regrowth linked to economic and historical conditions. Such dynamism—in both forest change and institutions—rarely has been acknowledged in the literature on deforestation, yet it is likely to exist in other sites, and carries implications for policy design and implementation.

Chapter 11 by Dengsheng Lu, Emilio Moran, Paul Mausel, and Eduardo Brondízio presents a comparative study of biomass growth in three locations in the Amazon. Biomass change has critical implications for global climate change, since it speaks to carbon sequestration and net carbon emissions debates. Remote sensing offers a means to estimate biomass more efficiently than methods dependent on field measurements, yet tropical moist forests present difficulties for remote sensing of biomass due to their high species richness and complex stand structure. The authors test texture analysis as part of a suite of measures to estimate aboveground biomass and as a means to account for some of the complexity that characterizes the Amazon. The research acknowledges the relationships between biomass regrowth, land-use histories, and soil fertility. The histories of human occupation and prior land-use systems, in conjunction with site-specific biophysical characteristics, prove to be critical elements for the processes of biomass change. The results indicate that the accuracy of texture analysis relates to the nature of the vegetation structure and composition. The technique proves useful for estimating biomass change and thereby achieving a more precise understanding of land-cover changes in highly variable forest conditions.

In chapter 12, Jon Unruh, Harini Nagendra, Glen Green, Bill McConnell, and Nathan Vogt discuss research questions, challenges, and initial findings emerging from comparative research in Africa and Asia. While much of our comparative research focuses on the Western Hemisphere (chapters 9, 10, and 11), Africa and Asia represent notable contrasts in many of the human dimensions variables deemed critical for understanding forest-cover change. These variables include demographic conditions, institutional arrangements, histories of human settlement and colonization, and political-economic processes that impinge on forest change. Research findings for a site in Uganda have found a process of forest expansion on a grassland; the observed processes involve a different set of relationships from those reported by earlier researchers for West Africa. Such findings complement those of Brondízio in the Amazon, in that similar land-cover patterns may reflect fundamentally different sets of relationships. Further work to address complexity and refine theories of land-cover change is underway in Nepal, where researchers have developed methods to identify and study landscape anomalies. Particular interest has been given to identifying forest cover that exists in areas that are otherwise deforested or devoid of forest vegetation. The research into anomalies on the landscape has found institutional arrangements that protect forests. In addition to providing an overview of preliminary findings, the chapter defines major research questions for comparative research within Africa and Asia, and also points to the potential for cross-continental comparative analyses.

In chapter 13, Bill McConnell and Eric Keys conduct a meta-analysis of agricultural change in the tropics, encompassing case studies published in peer-reviewed journals and books. Through this approach, they are able to incorporate fine-scaled details, while including a large number of examples to achieve greater power of generalization than that obtainable with a limited number of case studies. The data collection coded 108 cases, with attention to biophysical, demographic, socioeconomic, and institutional variables. Interestingly, few case studies reported biophysical data; therefore analysis of the impacts of biophysical characteristics on agricultural change could not be evaluated. The results reveal intriguing differences across regions, but market demand and property-regime change appear frequently across sites and regions as factors associated with agricultural transformation. McConnell and Keys acknowledge the complexities of drawing a comparable sample from secondary sources that were not designed for comparative analysis. The lack of consistent data across sites limits the strength of the analyses; it is exactly this shortcoming that we address through the development of standardized research protocols. Yet the need for such meta-analyses as that employed in chapter 13 remains clear. On the one hand, they allow the inclusion of existing and historical sources that provide valuable information. On the other hand, they provide an alternative to the constraints of time and labor associated with collecting a large, global sample through use of a single, rigorously comparable methodology and a limited number of researchers.

All but one of the chapters (chapter 13) address the issue of forest regrowth. In Brazil, the growth of aboveground biomass relates to histories of land use and soil fertility. The latter appears to be the most important factor related to biomass at the location scale of analysis, but land-use differences explain more of the variance in sites studied. In Uganda, field abandonment has been a component in secondary successions on prior grasslands. Interestingly, field abandonment also has played a role in the intervals of forest regrowth in Honduras. In Honduras and Guatemala, periods of forest regeneration trends alternate with periods of deforestation, pointing to the dynamic nature of land-use change and people's relatively rapid responses to economic incentives and disincentives to deforest. In Nepal, a comparative analysis of three management regimes found that national parks had higher levels of biodiversity and biomass than national forests or community forests. Yet the fieldwork revealed that the forests transferred to communities by the government were initially in poorer condition than the areas retained as national forests or parks. Thus the evaluation of differing tenure regimes requires recognition of historical trends and conditions, especially when changes in tenure regimes have occurred.

Chapters 9 through 12 indicate that the widespread focus on deforestation needs to be complemented by analyses of forest regeneration and afforestation processes. If the goal is to find ways to mitigate deforestation, then it is also important to identify the circumstances in which forests endure, expand, and experience regrowth, especially when these apparently anomalous processes occur in the presence of factors typically associated with deforestation.

All of the chapters confront complexity in microlevel variation, and the concomitant implications for comparative analysis within or across levels and scales of analysis. Remotely sensed data provide an invaluable tool for cross-site comparisons of land-cover change, but also pose challenges for assessing variations in local conditions that may not be apparent at the scale of data collected by remote sensors. Therefore, fieldwork provides an integral element for interpreting and verifying remotely sensed data; only through data collected on the ground may researchers discover differences in histories, institutional arrangements, natural and human resources, and interactions of actors with each other that profoundly influence land-cover patterns and change trajectories. Chapters 9 through 12 indicate the strength of comparative research that results from the systematic integration of microlevel data with remotely sensed data and GIS, which facilitates the recognition of complexity and diversity in processes and patterns of land-cover change. Chapter 13 points to a complementary method that achieves a larger sample size by incorporating existing case studies. In this approach, the larger sample size permits broader generalizations than those resulting from the limited samples found in the other comparative analyses. By accounting for complexity and reaching toward larger sample sizes, our research efforts contribute to identifying the important variables and relationships that recur across sites.

Catherine M. Tucker

9

Intraregional Analysis of Land-Use Change in the Amazon

Eduardo S. Brondízio

One of the important aspects of research on the so-called *human dimensions of global environmental change*[1] is the understanding of intraregional variations in human-environment interactions.[2] This contribution reaches to the core of a research agenda marked by academic interdisciplinarity and policy concerns.[3] On one hand, it seeks to understand the interactions between households and communities and larger sociopolitical structures. On the other hand, it requires close attention to issues of the generalizability of models and the accuracy of data, since they aim to represent the social and environmental realities of a region. This chapter calls attention to the need for intraregional analysis in human-environment research, particularly land-use/land-cover change (LUCC) studies taking place in the Amazon region. Methodologically, the chapter focuses on the role of remote sensing in depicting regional land use, particularly on the implications of different forms of data resolution for revealing causal relationships related to environmental change and the relevance and limitations of these findings for regional development policy.

The popularization of the term *human dimensions* and LUCC research during the 1990s have brought together a diversity of theories, methods, and policy concerns to the study of human-environment interactions (NRC 1992, 1999a). They have emerged from the awareness of global environmental problems on one side and are linked to changes in the circulation of information and commodities on the other, and to the link among local, regional, and global issues (Arizpe 1996; E. Moran et al. in press). However, the diversity of perspectives in this kind of research, while embedded in the strength of disciplinary canons, presents challenges in terms of both defining which aspects of local and regional phenomena are relevant to the global environment (and vice versa) and discovering how to unite the various segments of the academic community and familiarize them with the different types and scales of scientific evidence needed to study these processes.

Few places on Earth have been so directly affected (politically and economically) as the Amazon region by issues relating to measurement and socioenvironmental analyses of LUCC. The challenge of incorporating intraregional diversity while considering the Amazon basin as a unified entity is not new, but in today's context it is one of great political and environmental import. Theoretical, methodological, and ideological differences underlie discrepancies in the estimation of rates of change and determination of agents of change. Further, prognostic model-building intended to inform policy has abounded since the region was depicted in the context of global environmental change scenarios (e.g., see Fearnside 1984; INPE 1988–2001; Goldenberg 1989; Skole and Tucker 1993; Nepstad and Uhl 2000; Laurence et al. 2001; Silveira 2001; Achard et al. 2002; Carvalho et al. 2002; Laurence and Fearnside 2002; Nepstad et al. 2002; Verissimo et al. 2002; Wood and Porro 2002).

A global perspective on environmental issues has placed regions such as the Amazon at the forefront of international conservation efforts and provided a sense of global entitlement to tropical forests. Directly or indirectly, this calls attention to national policies and local attitudes toward the regional environment, including issues of deforestation (Geores 2003). With the global environment at stake, human-environment research informing the analysis of LUCC in the Amazon is constantly faced with political and ethical considerations in defining causal relationships underlying environmental change and informing policy to alter or support particular forms of land use.

The focus on variables of global environmental relevance sometimes leads to disregard of local differences on the basis of their unmanageability or irrelevance. In this context, the main paradox of LUCC research is that the generalizations required to obtain a global perspective encompass details that matter to local people's livelihoods. Arguably, this is an oversimplified dichotomy of scale. For an interdisciplinary community such as that represented by human-environment research, however, these are issues that result in debates over research priorities, types of methodologies, and the nature of evidence emerging from different scales and fields of inquiry: How do local case studies inform the broader regional and global scenarios? Are these local variables and processes relevant to the global perspective? Which variables and processes are generalizable across all levels?

Remote sensing has been the single most important tool for LUCC analysis informing global environmental change research. In the Amazon, it provides the necessary spatial coverage, while presenting reasonable spatial resolution and a consistent dataset covering the post-1970 period, which has been characterized by high rates of demographic and environmental change. Despite its advantages, remote-sensing data alone present significant limitations to accomplishing land-use assessment tasks. These include limitations in temporal resolution to capture interannual land-use changes and in spatial and spectral resolutions that would allow a distinction to be made between subtle land-cover classes that are crucial to land-use interpretation (e.g., types of agriculture and agroforestry).[4]

In this context, remote sensing has the power to represent reality in several ways. It is a tool that privileges particular aspects of the land cover and often reveals the disciplinary background of its interpreters. Studying causal linkages underlying land-use change in the region puts different groups of people at the center of attention in the eyes of policy makers. How different groups are defined, represented, and interpreted underlie important components of future regional policies. From advanced very high resolution radiometer (AVHRR) images of fire spots since the 1980s, to time-series deforestation maps, to indigenous reserves surrounded by deforestation, remote-sensing data have been an important basis for mediation among the research community, policy makers, interest groups, and the public in general.

Building on case studies representing diverse sociocultural and environmental conditions, this chapter addresses some recurrent topics in the study of LUCC in the Amazon. Case studies are organized in order of increasing complexity, from isolated indigenous areas in the Rio Negro basin to riverine caboclo[5] communities near regional urban centers to colonization areas cutting across several municipalities (via the Transamazon highway). The chapter pays attention to issues of land-cover measurement, interpretation of land-use change, and land users as agents of change, as seen through the eyes of social scientists using remote-sensing data. The chapter builds a set of conceptual and empirical arguments for the importance of intraregional analysis in LUCC research. It uses strategies for integrating qualitative and quantitative evidence and illustrates their potential to overcome the methodological limitations of land-use research that relies on remote-sensing data for regional estimations of change.

The chapter is organized into three main sections. The first section is a threefold background section that aims to support the role of intraregional analysis in LUCC studies by discussing (1) the Amazon as a region, (2) land use as a unifying theme in research on human-environment interaction, and (3) the use of analytical strategies in LUCC research (driving forces and process-pattern). The second section presents empirical evidence based on case studies. The third and concluding section addresses the implications of LUCC research for the understanding of human dimensions of global environmental change.

Conceptual Considerations for Intraregional Analysis in LUCC Research in the Amazon

Amazônia as an Organic Entity and Its Regional Complexity

During the past thirty years, development projects, rural and urban population growth, and national and international market demands have been recognized as key underlying factors driving human-environment change in the Amazon (e.g., see E. Moran 1984a; Schmink and Wood 1984; Lena and Oliveira 1992; Dincao and Silveira 1994; Browder and Godfrey 1997; Kaimowitz and Angelsen 1998; Wood and Porro 2002). The increasing interaction among these processes has created a complex hierarchy of factors directly related to the study of land use, for instance, the compounding role of infrastructure, land value, land tenure arrangements, and regional markets. Furthermore, the future of the region continues to be highly influenced by macroprocesses of a geopolitical and economic nature, but now interacting with a far more complex set of conditions created during the past thirty years. Current examples include planned roads connecting the region to the Pacific Ocean (and, thus, to Asian markets), to the Guianas via the Amapá route, to the Caribbean via the Manaus-Caracas route, and to soybean export markets via the Cuiabá-Santarém route that links central Brazil to the new harbor in Santarém (figure 9.1).

While macrolevel socioeconomic processes continue to be important, the spread of change cannot be generalized because of the diversity of inter- and intraregional sociocultural variations, demographic dynamics, local social history, land tenure, economic arrangements, and environmental features of the landscape underlying land-use change (Brondízio in press). In addition, development programs and market opportunities often accentuate historical socioeconomic inequalities among regional populations, thus creating differential benefits and incentives for local communities and groups of individuals, with consequent diverse political, social, and environmental implications. For these and other reasons, attention to intraregional variability is and will be increasingly a premise of research aimed to represent the Amazon as a regional entity.

Considerable debate focuses on the fate of the Amazonian forests amid new economic development programs and the implications of the potential effects of these programs, for example, effects on the global environment in terms of the carbon budget. Treating the region as an entity, basinwide prognostic models of the impact of new development have generated important, though controversial and dramatic, scenarios for national policy discussion (Laurence et al. 2001; Silveira 2001; Carvalho et al. 2002; Laurence and Fearnside 2002; Nepstad et al. 2002). However,

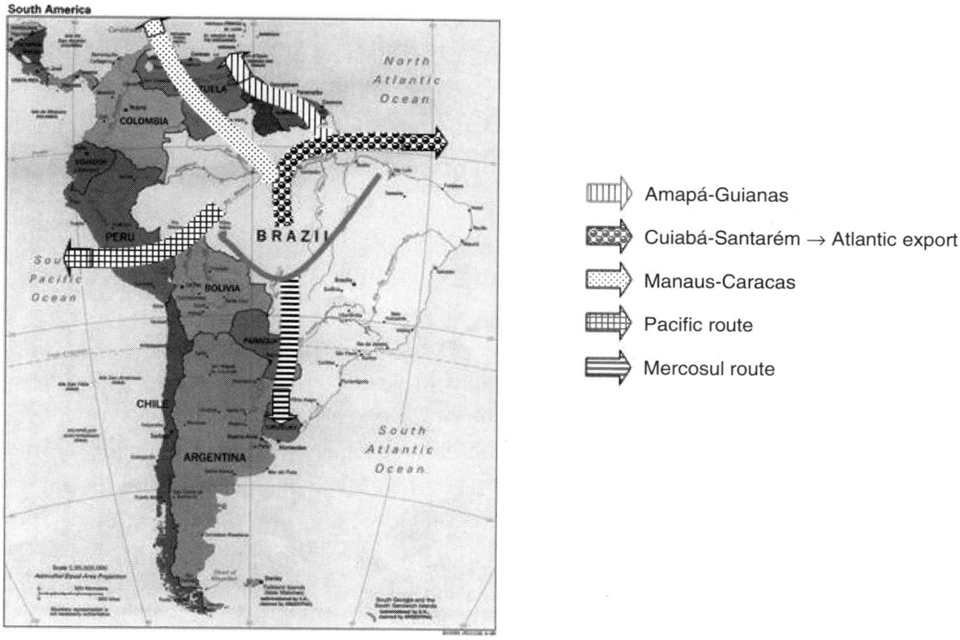

Figure 9.1
New routes and new markets in contemporary Amazônia. Existing and proposed new routes integrating Amazônia to regions and markets in the Americas, Asia, and Europe.

examples of the regional dynamics of development, including successful alternatives for frontier governance, call attention to a much more local level.

One of the most promising trends in frontier governance is the growing capacity of municipal governments for environmental and development planning. This trend is favored by Brazil's decentralization of many federal and state responsibilities to municipal (*municipio*) governments, which receive a larger share of the federal budget than in any other Latin American country. Through the G7 Pilot Program for Conservation of Brazilian rainforests, state and municipal governments are working together to strengthen local institutional capacity for environmental planning and regulation, while also learning how to integrate local stakeholders into the planning process. Although municipal governments' capacity for effective land-use planning and development is still highly variable, the overall trend is positive. The long-term economic and ecological vitality of the BR-163 corridor will depend on how well local governments are able to provide the social, economic, and legal infrastructure that local populations need, while managing the region's forest, soil, and water resources. (Nepstad et al. 2002, 631)

Nepstad and colleagues raise several issues relevant to LUCC research. Clearly, they call attention to the need to look at and consider intraregional complexity in the interpretation of regional trends. This brings up questions regarding how we assess, represent, and interpret the level of variability, as well as the political and economic strategies underlying land use within the region.

Striking a balance between these levels has been a key task for the LUCC research community in general and for understanding current and future land-use change in the region. While assessments based on generalization of the regional land-use reality may be useful for global carbon models, they are limited to inform policies that directly influence infrastructure, land tenure, incentives, and a multitude of other issues affecting local populations.

Land Use as a Converging Theme in Human-Environment Research

Land use has provided an integrative theme for global-level human-environment research for a number of reasons, but particularly because it offers a behavioral and measurable expression of human actions related to problems of local and global interest. In this context, land use refers to the purposes and intent of human activities that directly affect and are affected by the biophysical environment (B. Turner et al. 1994). By bringing together key elements underlying socioenvironmental change resulting from interactions among householders, communities, and regions, land use has provided a heuristic framework to articulate factors affecting and mediating the micro- and macrodimensions of social and environmental change.

Many precedents in the social and biophysical sciences support a convergence around land use within the context of analyzing human-environment interactions. Ecologically oriented anthropologists and geographers have moved toward scaling up their local unit of analysis due to the need to understand local agriculture and economy on a more encompassing regional scale (e.g., see Behrens et al. 1994; Wilkie 1987; Conant 1990; Guyer and Lambin 1993; Mertens et al. 2000; Nyerges and Green 2000; E. Moran and Brondízio 2001; Fox et al. 2003). Anthropology in general, and environmental anthropology in particular, share this task through an interest in agrarian studies, political ecology, and studies of consumption and markets. Second, ecological and biophysical sciences working at global and regional levels have perceived the need to scale down in order to understand the impact of local land-use strategies on macroprocesses such as biogeochemical cycles and climate (Dale et al. 1993a; Skole and Tucker 1993; NRC 1998).

In looking at comparative agrarian studies, Hunt (1995, 176–177) characterized this type of convergence of interests as pointing to key variables underlying the dynamics of human societies: the relationships between population, environment, food supply, technology, and productivity; the course of social change; and the nature of human decision making. In essence, these are some of the same questions underlying the study of land-use change at the global, regional, and local levels (NRC 1992; B. Turner et al. 1994). What differentiates current efforts to study LUCC from previous disciplinary approaches is their focus on developing an integrated, multiscale, and comparative approach to model and explain human behavior and interactions with the environment, and an awareness that no single theoretical model can account for this process. (For a more detailed discussion of this topic, see chapters 2 and 4.)

Amazonian land use, for instance, has been approached from different theoretical and methodological perspectives depending on the type of question and scale. Rural studies in the Amazon,[6] particularly those of peasant economy, have typically focused on the historical conditions defining the sociopolitical and economic relationships mediating communities and larger levels of organization. Highlighting the factors mediating these levels has contributed to our understanding of Amazonian rural development, including commodity production and economic cycles, labor arrangements, and control of capital. These are conditions which underlie different dynamics of land use in the region: from extractive booms and cattle ranching expansion to household-level agricultural intensification (e.g., see Schmink and Wood 1984; Bunker 1985; Nugent 1993; Chibnik 1994).

Several conceptual and empirical models explaining contemporary land use and deforestation have been developed, mostly at the mesolevel and macrolevel. Emphasis has been placed on demographic, political-economic, political-institutional, and infrastructure variables, such as population dynamics and migration, fiscal incentives and inflation, and colonization and political economy (Mahar 1988; Ozório de Almeida 1992; Pichón and Bilsborrow 1992; Wood and Skole 1998; S. McCracken et al. 1999; Walker et al. 2000; Laurence et al. 2001; Alves 2002).[7]

Most of our attention has been focused on addressing the challenges of linking farm- and regional-level studies of land-use change with emphasis on the articulation of survey research and time-series remote-sensing data. This work has aimed at integrating farm-level sociodemographic and economic processes, such as the domestic cycle, with regional-level events characterizing different periods of colonization (S. McCracken et al. 1999; Brondízio et al. 2002a; E. Moran et al. 2002a, 2003; Siqueira et al. 2003; Boucek and Moran 2004). The Center for the Study of Institutions, Population, and Environmental Change (CIPEC) also has contributed to various recent advances in the study of institutional factors affecting land use and regional development, notably issues of overlapping land tenure systems and forms of collective action and institutional arrangements. CIPEC researchers have addressed the role of incentives that lead individuals to create and maintain effective prescriptions that ultimately conserve or destroy natural resources in different land tenure systems (Castro 1999; Silva-Forsberg 1999; Futemma 2000; Batistella 2001; Futemma and Brondízio 2003). In this context, incentives for individuals to engage in different types of management systems are related to the characteristics of the resource managed, to the structure and organization of the group, and to the rules-in-use underlying the economic, political, and cultural system (E. Ostrom 1990).

In summary, the strength of land-use research in the region lies in the possibility of combining diverse disciplinary perspectives representing different theoretical and methodological approaches and levels of analysis. An intraregional perspective offers a point of intersection that allows one to build human-environment interaction research upon a legacy of land-use studies developed at both local and regional scales.

Analytical Strategies Based on an Integrative Framework

The diverse legacy of land-use studies has been dealt with in the recent LUCC literature through analytical strategies that could be called "integrative frameworks." Two prominent, interrelated analytical strategies could be labeled as "driving forces" and "process-pattern," both of which are based on the analysis of factors underlying land-use trajectories, with emphasis on rate, direction, and spatial patterns of land-cover change.

"Driving forces" is undoubtedly the most popular term within the LUCC literature of the past decade. It aims at establishing the relationship between the so-called underlying causes ("the initial conditions and 'fundamental' forces that underpin human action toward the environment") and proximate sources ("direct human activities affecting the biophysical environment") (Geist and Lambin 2001, 5–16; see examples in B. Turner et al. 1994, 1995; McConnell and Moran 2001). In most cases, underlying causes include broadly defined demographic, economic, technological, political, institutional, and sociocultural variables, while proximate sources refer to the set of transformation activities broadly defined as agricultural expansion, logging, and infrastructure development (Geist and Lambin 2001).

While heuristically important, the challenge has been to articulate different pathways and feedback mechanisms between underlying and proximate causes, given the variability of factors mediating them and the ambiguity of so-called underlying causes, which can be either local, global, or both (see Geist and Lambin 2001). For this reason, approaching these processes at an intraregional scale allows one to pay closer attention to local-specific processes interacting with macrolevel underlying conditions, and to consider historical particularities necessary to the understanding of land-use trajectories (Brondízio in press).

More recently, LUCC research has moved toward "process-pattern" approaches (e.g., see Mertens and Lambin 1997). The central idea of this framework is that perceived aggregated landscape patterns can be linked to factors underlying land-use patterns in a given area. This is an explicit attempt to connect what we observe regionally through remote sensing to the human activities behind land-use change. An underlying assumption is that social and economic factors (e.g., infrastructure, property regimes, and economic strategies) within a given environmental setting lead to the formation of predictable spatial patterns (e.g., spatial pattern of forest fragmentation and deforestation trajectories), which in turn feeds back to future land-use trajectories.

Figure 9.2 illustrates an example of this approach. While providing a useful framework for research design and hypothesis testing, it requires the organization

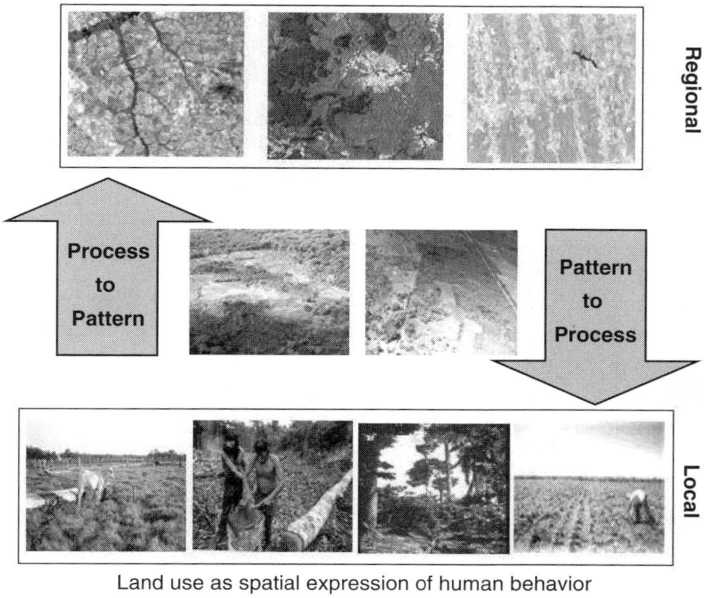

Figure 9.2
Idealized model of pattern and process linkages defining land cover. Schematic linkages between settlement, infrastructure, and land-use change at the local scale and emerging spatial patterns at larger regions as captured by remote-sensing data.

of land-use systems in the form of typologies, thus favoring variables of more prominence. For instance, it may require one to aggregate distinct land-use systems into broad land-cover classes and to disregard local variability in terms of land tenure, access to resources, and soil distribution, among others. Most datasets informing this type of analysis—remotely sensed data—have limited spatial and temporal resolutions to capture what farmers actually do on the ground. Thus, the emphasis on perceivable spatial patterns of the land's biophysical characteristics has serious implications for one's understanding of local economic strategies in forest and diverse agroforestry-based economies, as in the case of the Amazon.

Empirical Evidence for Intraregional Analysis in LUCC Research in the Amazon

The discussion above provides a conceptual basis for the importance of intraregional analysis in LUCC research. In this section, I provide empirical evidence from case studies in the Amazon. These examples aim to highlight aspects of our research strategies for integrating field and remote-sensing work, which are not covered by other chapters in this book, and to provide a critical perspective on the role of methodological tools in the interpretation of land use in the Amazon. Additional information regarding each research site is available in the literature cited in this chapter. Before proceeding to the case studies, it is relevant to highlight some underlying aspects of research methodology supporting these studies: image classification, vegetation inventory, and sampling procedures.

Methodological Background

Attention to detailed classification of secondary vegetation and soil has been important to several topics of our research. Baseline research on vegetation inventories and interviews about the use of fallow areas have provided support for image analysis and understanding of land-cover change. These include estimating rates of regrowth across areas of different land-use histories, mapping of different stages of secondary vegetation to characterize fallow cycles across different land-use systems, assessing the occurrence of economic species in fallow areas, and estimating aboveground biomass in landscapes characterized by different land-cover complexities (e.g., see Brondízio et al. 1996; E. Moran et al. 1996; J. Tucker et al. 1998).

Our work has contributed to understanding the effects of soil, age, and land-use history on rates of regrowth in the Amazon (E. Moran et al. 2000b, 2002a; Lu et al. 2002c; see also chapter 11). The structural characteristics of the vegetation directly influence spectral data and are key features used during image classification (Mausel

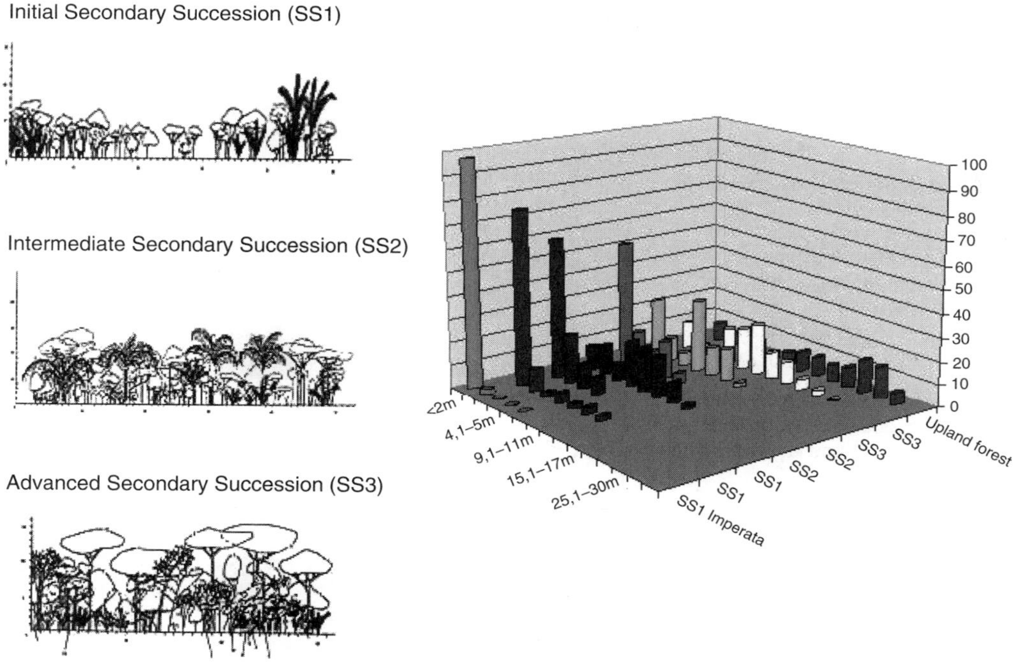

Figure 9.3
Secondary succession: classification key according to stand height in Marajó Island. A land-cover classification system based on differences in vegetation structure (derived from field inventories). Stages of secondary regrowth present distinctive vegetation structure in relation to canopy height, ground cover, and dominant life form. In this example, stages of secondary vegetation and upland forest are differentiated by the distribution of plants across height classes. This perspective on organizing a land-cover classification system provides useful information for interpreting spectral data used during image analysis and for linking estimates of aboveground biomass, from allometric equations to land-cover maps. (Adapted from Brondizio et al. 1996.)

et al. 1993; Brondízio et al. 1996; E. Moran et al. 2000b). Using this approach, we have been able to differentiate up to three stages of secondary succession, which has in turn allowed for a more detailed estimation of aboveground biomass and cycles of land use (figure 9.3). As part of this process we developed several methods of using remote-sensing images during land-use interviews and survey techniques to capture the farmers' perspectives on environmental management and land allocation (figure 9.4).

Although our image analysis includes standardized preprocessing techniques such as radiometric and atmospheric correction (see chapter 5; Green et al. 1998–2002;

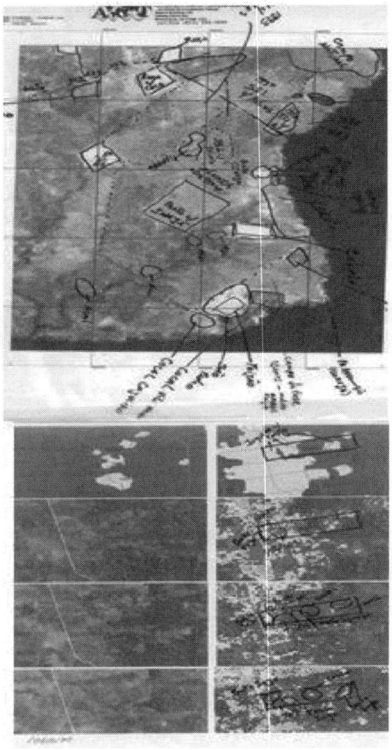

Examples of images used during interviews
Three stages of land-use interview using images:
1. Regional introduction and context
• Color composite: forest, soil, water, uses
• Landmarks and roads: locations, names
2. Feeder road and/or community
• Surroundings recognition
• Neighbors and land ownership
3. Farm lot
• Multitemporal changes
• Collecting ground information
• Accuracy assessment

Figure 9.4
Stages of interview using Landsat images. Three stages in which image printouts are used during interviews with farmers, moving from regional-scale images to surrounding farm lots. On the right are printouts showing notations derived from interviews. Every time an image printout is used for an interview, a copy of the image is left with the interviewee to keep. These, we have found, are kept, treasured, and discussed by farmers.

Lu et al. 2002b), classification procedures take into account the particularities of each area/image under investigation. In the Amazon, we have used a classification strategy based on image spatial-spectral stratification, aiming to account for intra-scene variation in land use, land cover, and physiographic compartments. This classification strategy starts with three main procedures. First, spatial pattern recognition is undertaken using two groups of parameters as guidelines. They are, specifically, the spectral and spatial parameters underlying variations in land-cover classes. Spectral data provide an initial indication of the main differences in terms of land-cover structure and environmental conditions. Spatially, we consider elements of contiguity and fragmentation, shape, and size of patches of the dominant land cover (e.g., patterns of forest cover) to differentiate intrascene variability of land-cover patterns.

It is fundamental to take into account existing variations in topography across a scene as part of the process of pattern recognition. Topography is a key landscape feature underlying variations in settlement pattern, land-use systems, and consequently, land-cover distribution. As a result, the scene is stratified, using an overlaying vector layer, into spatial compartments representing variations in spatial land-cover patterns, which are to be used to fine tune classification parameters across different parts of the scene, and to guide fieldwork.

Our second procedure aims to develop a level II classification system to account for intrascene distribution of classes. In this step, we organize a tentative hierarchical classification system that accounts for intrascene land-cover classes by combining visual and spectral analyses of multispectral images with literature, archive, fieldwork knowledge, and available ethnoecological information (such as using a calendar of agricultural and land-use activities). During our third step, land-cover classes are analyzed spectrally using training samples and unsupervised classification techniques. The structure and temporal dynamics of each land-cover class are analyzed to inform possible aggregation and adjustment of the classification system along with statistical analysis of spectral data. Classification is performed first at each subscene to account for site-specific classes, and then on the whole scene, if necessary, by aggregating particular classes to achieve a regional representation. What we gain through following these steps is the ability to map the distribution of land-cover classes at a regional scale that is also meaningful at the site-specific level (e.g., see Brondízio et al. 1994b).

By focusing on the discrimination of structural and spatial differences in land cover, such as stages of vegetation regrowth, this approach contributes to forms of land-cover assessment relevant to understanding underlying land-use processes. Figure 9.5 illustrates integration of field inventories and image data where we compare the role of land-cover classification detail for the estimation of aboveground biomass in two distinct landscapes in the Bragantina region of eastern Amazônia. One landscape is characterized by the dominance of forest and the other is dominated by different stages of secondary succession and agropastoral areas (J. Tucker et al. 2000). This figure shows a spatial perspective on the analysis presented in chapter 11. Land-cover classes representing structural characteristics (height classes, basal area, etc.) are discriminated during image classification. Five levels of aggregation of land-cover classification are presented and used for the calculation of aboveground

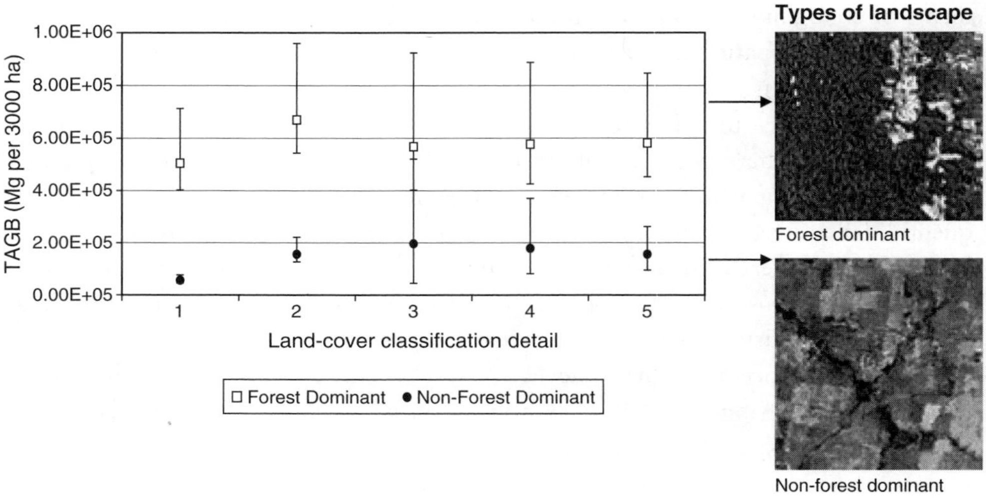

	Types of landscape and area of different land cover (ha)				Land-cover classification detail				
Land-cover class	**Forest dominant**	**Percent cover (%)**	**Non-forest dominant**	**Percent cover (%)**	**1**	**2**	**3**	**4**	**5**
Bare ground	261	8	161	5	X	X	X	X	X
Pasture	279	9	432	14	X				
SS1	215	7	887	28	X		X		
SS2	403	13	1214	39	X	X			
SS3	494	16	292	9	X			X	
Mature forest	1459	47	161	5	X	X	X		X

Figure 9.5
Estimating biomass in forest and nonforest landscapes at different levels of classification detail. This figure illustrates the effect of a land-cover classification system detail on the estimation of total aboveground biomass (TAGB) in different landscapes. Five scenarios of land-cover classification details are presented in the table. Biomass is calculated by applying allometric equations to vegetation inventory data representing each of the land-cover classes. Total biomass is calculated by multiplying the area of each land-cover class (for each classified landscape) by the estimated biomass in each class. Error bars in the figure (for each scenario) indicate the variation in estimation from different allometric equations. (Adapted from J. Tucker et al. 2000.)

biomass in the two landscapes represented in the figure. Available allometric equations appropriate to each land-cover class are used to calculate the aboveground biomass at each level of detail. Error bars indicate the variability in estimation among all the allometric equations used for each land cover present at a particular level of aggregation. This level of detail allows checking the sensitivity of classification details and types of allometric equations in landscapes of different land-cover complexities.

This analysis yields relevant findings for biomass estimation in the region. First, the forest and nonforest classification results in a significantly different biomass estimation when compared to more detailed classification systems. This is particularly true for the landscape dominated by secondary succession and agropastoral activities. On the other hand, it suggests that for a macroregional application, improvements in classification detail, by including more classes of secondary succession to the forest/nonforest dichotomy, yield an improved estimation of biomass similar to more detailed classification systems. Still, the example illustrates the variation in biomass estimation that results for landscapes within the same region. Our selection of these landscapes aims to represent the variability of spatial patterns within a region occupied by different types of colonization within the last 100 years. These scenarios represent the growing complexity of Amazonian landscapes.

Units of Analysis: Lots, Communities, and Settlements

Another area of methodological contribution to regional land-use studies is the integration of nested spatial units of analysis, such as farm lots, settlements, and region (see chapter 6). Colonization areas in the Amazon are dynamic landscapes because families arrive at different times. Thus, farm lots coexist in different stages of formation. In our research, two elements have been important in this type of analysis: temporal availability of data and nested units of analysis (farm lots, cohorts of farms, and the settlement landscape). Figure 9.6 illustrates the role of temporal resolution in capturing cycles of farm lot formation. Very different pictures emerge when a time series is assembled to account for narrow time intervals vis-à-vis two distant points in time. The combination of time-series remote-sensing data, property grid maps, and field surveys has provided us with an opportunity to look at LUCC at several levels, such as the colonization landscape, groups of farm lots (cohorts), and individual lots. Thus, data are sensitive to different time intervals in an area marked by dynamic land-use change, as in this colonization settlement. There is a great loss of information about the dynamics of change when the time intervals are more widely spaced than the cycles of land-use change taking place on the ground.

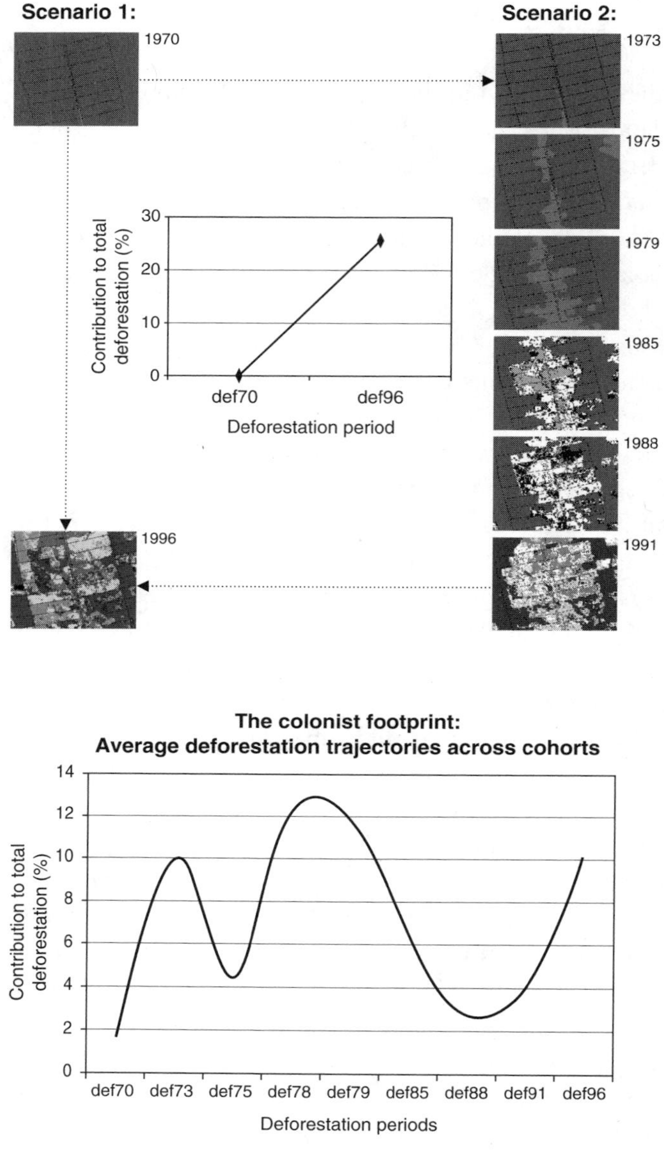

Figure 9.6
Temporal detail and the interpretation of trajectories. Gray areas represent deforestation events taking place during different years. This figure illustrates the role of multitemporal image availability in capturing the trajectory of deforestation in an area characterized by a dynamic occupation across a short period of time, such as a settlement region. To the left, images from two dates, twenty-six years apart, show overall deforestation for a particular group of farm lots; to the right, the same estimate is derived from eight different time intervals showing alternating pulses of deforestation related to stages of lot formation and regional economic conditions.

Of particular note is our development of an approach that permits querying at both landscape and farm-lot levels (S. McCracken et al. 1999, 2002a; Brondízio et al. 2002a; Evans and Moran 2002; E. Moran et al. 2002b). Previous work on an area of this size typically analyzed and described land-cover change from the perspective of the landscape, without addressing the differential and multiple land-use dynamics at the level of individual farms and households. We are the first research group to have carried out an overlay of a cadastral survey on a satellite time series with the goal of extracting property-level information from satellite data (E. Moran and Brondízio 1998; S. McCracken et al. 1999; Brondízio et al. 2002a). This effort is unique because of the very large spatial extent (3800 km^2), and the laborious fieldwork undertaken to ensure a high degree of accuracy in the overlay of the cadastral survey (over 90 percent accuracy). Overlaying a property grid onto remotely sensed time-series data permits examination of land-cover change at the level of households, the same level at which the demographic survey research occurs. Because these households live mostly on the property, there is a convenient one-to-one relationship between household and land that allows analyses to proceed expeditiously. To draw the sample for the survey research, we relied on satellite time series with the property grid overlay. This procedure allowed us to determine when a property was first occupied by a settler, thereby facilitating the definition of arriving cohorts to be followed through time.

Case Studies and Regional Variations: Implications for Methods and Theory in Land-Use Analysis

Cases are presented in order of increasing regional complexity. Figure 9.7 presents each of the study areas in relation to features of the larger Amazon basin, particularly roads, settlements, and proximity to urban areas.

Case 1: Variation in Land-Cover Patterns in Neighboring Indigenous Communities

The first example illustrates a sociocultural and environmental situation where the influence of external factors—urban markets, infrastructure—is relatively absent. The indigenous areas of Tukanoan-speaking populations are located in the Vaupés basin between Colombia and Brazil in northwestern Amazônia. The settlement pattern has been influenced by historical variations in regional migration and missionary occupation, as well as nucleation in village centers. The area is composed of large patches of nutrient-poor spodosols covered by Amazon caatinga (a vegetation characterized by sparse, short vegetation of distinct species composition) intermixed

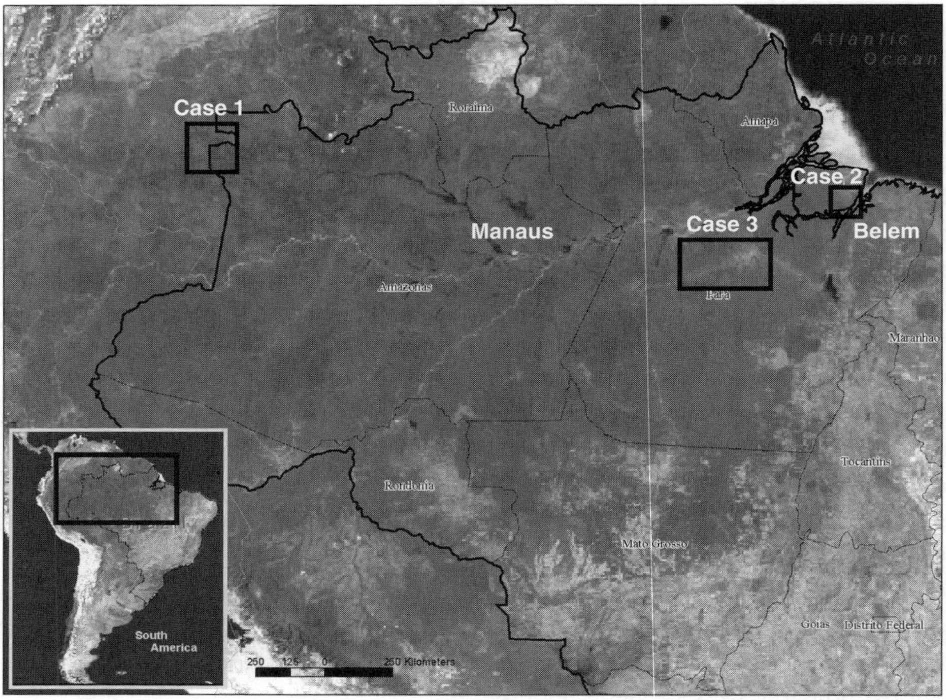

Figure 9.7
Map showing the regional context for each of the examples used in this chapter. Case 1: Yapu indigenous communities of the Vaupés basin. Case 2: Caboclo populations of the Amazon estuary. Case 3: Colonist populations of the TransAmazon highway.

with stretches of oxisols covered by dense upland forest. A manioc-based agricultural system characterized by long fallow cycles is the dominant land-use system in these communities. In this context, land-use choices are closely related to access to appropriate soils. Plate 6 shows two neighboring Tukanoan villages of relatively similar size (community *A* [left] and *B* [right]) (Castro et al. 2002). The puzzle presented here is simple: What explains the different spatial patterns of land cover in areas where similar sociocultural conditions and land-use systems are present?

Plate 6 presents a sequence of three classified images for each village representing different levels of detail of land-cover classes. First, the typical forest and nonforest scenario used in basinwide land-cover assessment is presented. At this level of detail, we can observe very different land-cover patterns, but the classification detail limits the analysis of factors explaining the distribution of forest and nonforest areas.

These spatial patterns, concentric (*A*) and dendritic (*B*), tend to appear as random in the landscape. When a class defining water is included, one can clearly see an association between access and opened areas for community B, but community A still presents little correlation between water access and opened areas. However, a clear pattern emerges after a fourth land-cover class is added that defines caatinga patches characterized by white sand and extremely nutrient-poor spodosols; the two communities differ in relation to their surrounding soil conditions. Whereas community B is surrounded by spodosols, community A is not. It is important to call attention to the fact that community B moved to this particular site because of missionary organization in previous decades (W. Wilson 1997; Castro et al. 2002). In summary, the history of settlement and the availability of proper soils allow community A to minimize the distance to their gardens by opening areas near their village center; whereas community B seeks appropriate soils by accessing areas via waterways. Consequently, even in the absence of roads, development projects, and private land tenure arrangements, among other factors, the same land-use system creates very different spatial patterns.

Evidence in This Case Supporting the Need for Intraregional LUCC Research First, dichotomous land-cover classifications hinder the understanding of intraregional variability and limit the linkages between land-use systems and spatial land-cover patterns. Land-use complexity is not a privilege of recently colonized areas, but is present throughout the Amazon, and this example serves as a cautionary tale for regional extrapolation and interpretation of deforestation patterns. As a second cautionary tale, this example illustrates the sensitivity of process and pattern linkages to the level of classification detail provided by remote-sensing data. Manipulation of classification detail can lead to different interpretations of forest fragmentation and spatial patterns. Third, the example also cautions against the use of generalized variables to predict future LUCC. Data limitations, for instance, regarding soil patchiness, as well as poor understanding of the role of different types of access (e.g., roads vs. waterways), need to be considered in any attempt to model factors influencing regional land-use change.

Case 2. Land-Use Trajectories in the Amazon Estuary

The study area is located in the estuarine region of the Amazon, on Marajó Island in the municipality of Ponta de Pedras, state of Pará (Brondízio et al. 1994a, 1996, 2002a; Brondízio 1999). During the past thirty years, development projects, government incentives, and market demand for locally produced food products have created different incentives and opportunities for estuarine communities. A long history of occupation and economic cycles based on extractivism has created variations in land tenure, social organization, and access to resources, markets, and the infrastructure. The case of the three populations presented here illustrates the diversity of land-use trajectories among communities located within similar distances to urban markets and having overall similar environmental settings (Brondízio et al. 1994a).

Population growth in urban Amazônia has created markets for regionally preferred food sources such as the açaí palm fruit (*Euterpe oleracea* Mart.), which is a regional staple food consumed by rural migrants living in urban centers.[8] Impressive intensification of the production system followed increasing market demand, thereby changing the regional economic profile. The growth of the açaí economy in the Amazon estuary provides a fascinating look at the linkage between external urban markets and rural land-use change (Brondízio et al. 2002b). First, this growth responded directly to the increase in staple food demand prompted by low-income urban population growth after 1970. Second, it responded to an increase in external demand prompted by the emergence of a national and international "gourmet food" market in the early 1990s.

Today, açaí fruit is the most important source of income for the vast majority of riverine households. In one Ponta de Pedras community, for instance, açaí represents 64 percent of household income generated from agricultural products (including rice, beans, and coconut) (POEMA 1994). The evolution of the açaí fruit economy in the past thirty years has created a complex structure of production, distribution, commercialization, and processing that is specialized and socially ranked (for a detailed description, see Brondízio 2004b; Brondízio et al. 2002b). Market demand has differentially influenced land users' decisions with regard to intensification depending on several factors affecting production. These include one's land tenure condition, proximity and access to markets, and access to resource areas. Thus, variation in market incentives and economic return among producers facing different constraints affects the rate, extent, and direction of land-use change and intensification within the estuarine region.

Building on existing knowledge and technology, the significant increase in fruit production has been a direct result of the management and planting of açaí palm agroforestry stands in areas of floodplain forest. Increasing market demand for staple food (açaí fruit) underlies land-use intensification in the Amazon estuary based on forest management and agroforestry techniques. Despite its high economic productivity and level of agroforestry manipulation, areas such as these are often treated as areas of extraction, and producers' work and management knowledge are disregarded (Brondízio 2004a). Contrary to a system based on extractivism, management and planting of açaí agroforestry requires clear input of specialized agricultural and forestry labor to maintain and increase crop stand productivity.

Management and planting strategies transform floodplain forest areas into açaí agroforestry, locally called *açaizais*—intensive areas of açaí fruit production. Paradoxically, the açaí production system is still regarded by politicians, academics, and the general public as a mere extractivist economy (Brondízio 2004a,b). This assertion is not only a result of the region's socioeconomic history, which is based on export-oriented extractivism and outside control of resources, but also of the way land-use systems are defined and represented (for a detailed discussion, see Brondízio and Siqueira 1997). The rigid boundary drawn between different food production systems has led to the characterization of forested areas, as in the case of agroforestry systems, as unproductive, or at best, under the category of agroextractivism. Consequently, it is common to see land-cover classification of the estuary that disregards açaí agroforestry as a land-use class, despite its position as the top land-use system in the region (plate 7). Elsewhere, we have argued for a reinterpretation of local agroforestry land-use systems as intensive and a change in the economic identity of local producers from extractivists to forest farmers (Brondízio 2004a; Brondízio and Siqueira 1997).

Evidence in This Case Supporting the Need for Intraregional LUCC Research First, this example shows the differential responses of local communities to regional market demand and development projects, thus resulting in diverse land-use systems even within short distances. Factors affecting these trajectories include variations in local land tenure arrangements, the availability of resources (e.g., floodplain forests for agroforestry management), and the social organization of local communities (e.g., cooperative arrangements to attract development projects). Second, the case illustrates the scale dependency of process-pattern linkages in land-use/land-cover analysis. While spatial land-cover patterns resulting from land-use activities are somewhat clear at the community level, these tend to disappear at the regional level due to variations in land-use systems and environmental characteristics (e.g., distribution of floodplain forests) across communities and settlements located at short distances from each other. Moreover, spatial land-cover patterns are influenced by certain land tenure arrangements, such as the size and shape of landholdings. Third, this example shows the potential for agricultural intensification based on local populations' ethnobotanical and ethnoecological knowledge. However, intensive production areas based on forest management tend to be disregarded in regional land-cover assessment if local-level, ethnographic work is not integrated into remote-sensing analysis. In this context, while açaí agroforestry represents the most significant land-use system in the estuarine area, a generalized classification system of land cover (see plate 7) in the area could actually ignore this production system, treating it as any other forest cover without regard for its important economic and social roles. The most important regional land-use systems may go unnoticed in maps and models, as would a whole social group managing these forest and agroforestry areas.

Case 3. Variations in Deforestation Trajectories at the Farm and Settlement Levels
The Altamira region along the Transamazon highway was one of most important focuses of the government colonization program during the 1970s (E. Moran 1973, 1981). Altamira grew from a small riverine town based on rubber collection into a booming town of 85,000 people due to agropastoral production (figure 9.8) stimulated by the Transamazon highway and associated colonization. The study

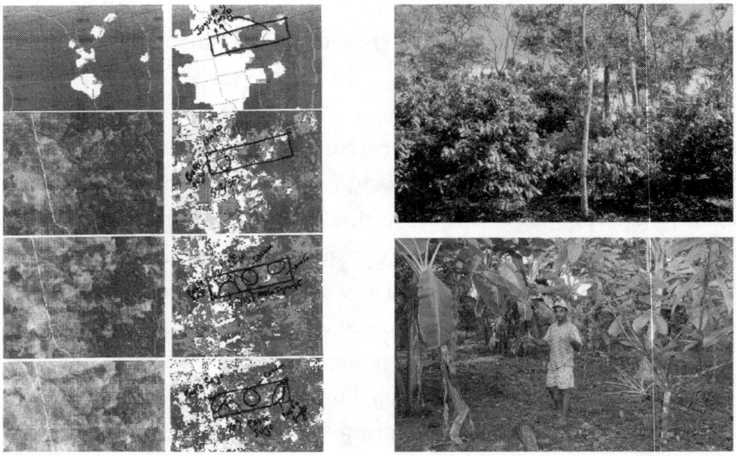

Farm lots between 1970 and 1991. Image printouts, derived from aerial photography and Landsat TM data, used for field interviews.

Farmer showing the location of agroforestry and cocoa areas classified as secondary vegetation.

Figure 9.8
Cocoa agroforestry classified as secondary succession. An image printout used during an interview with a colonist farmer showing notations necessary for classification accuracy assessment and area estimation. *Right*, a farmer shows an agroforestry area classified as abandoned land but which is actually in cocoa production.

area presented as an example here is defined by a group of approximately 3800 farm lots arranged according to different adjacent projects implemented by the National Institute of Colonization and Agrarian Reform (INCRA) during the past thirty years. It cuts across the municipalities of Altamira, Brasil Novo, and Medicilândia, in the state of Pará, and encompasses an area of about 355,000 ha, stretching approximately from Km 18 to Km 140 of the Transamazon highway west of the town of Altamira. The region is considered to have one of the most significant patches of the fertile alfisols, or *terra roxa estruturada eutrofica*, in the Brazilian Amazon. However, as colonists started to settle in, it became clear that the area consists of a patchwork of soil types, including less fertile oxisols and ultisols. Soil variations within and across farm lots have created differential conditions across colonist farms regarding agricultural productivity and land-use options (E. Moran 1981; N. Smith 1982; Fearnside 1986).

Available remote-sensing data since the 1970s (aerial photography and Landsat Multispectral Scanner [MSS] and Thematic Mapper [TM]) have allowed us to reconstruct the history of occupation of the study area (Brondízio et al. 2002a). We were able to stratify farm lots by time of arrival. In this study, we highlight the need to study land-use change on the frontier resulting from three main temporal effects: (1) period effects, such as fluctuations in migration, different credit policies, inflation, and so on; (2) cohort effects associated with the arrival and occupation of farm lots by groups of families; and (3) age effects associated with the transformation over time of households and their farms. Our work integrates two levels of analysis of deforestation trajectories: regional and cohort of farm lots. In both cases, deforestation trajectories are analyzed in relation to their distribution of events in different time periods (percent contribution of each period to total deforestation observed in 1996) (for details, see S. McCracken et al. 1999, 2002a,b; Brondízio et al. 2002a; E. Moran et al. 2002a; Siqueira et al. 2003).

Frontier occupation is an ongoing dynamic process whereby old settlers coexist with new ones, the latter being recent migrants or second-generation colonists taking over new lots. At this level of analysis, cohort and period effects underlie the process of deforestation. Fluctuations of deforestation rates after 1985 coincide with national-level economic indicators. Economic depression and inflation during the second half of the 1980s, as well as the withdrawal of cattle-ranching incentives, may explain the sharp decrease in deforestation rates perceived between 1985 and 1991. Moreover, the sharp increase in deforestation perceived in 1996 was likely associated with the economic stabilization and low inflation achieved after the *Plano Real* (the currency system established in 1994) was implemented and a return to credit incentives, now under the FNO (Fundo Nacional do Norte). At the cohort level, deforestation trajectories present a clear pattern across farm lots settled at different time periods. Pulses of deforestation associated with crop, pasture development, and secondary succession management mark these cycles of lot formation. Independent of cohort group, colonist farms show a developmental process associated with periods of establishment, expansion, and consolidation of land-use activities. The magnitude of these pulses of deforestation relates to the interaction between farmers' decisions (in the household sense) and regional period effects, such as changes in economic, institutional, and infrastructure conditions (e.g., credit, interest rates, road conditions) motivating or inhibiting a particular land-use behavior. We observe that intervals between pulses during stages of expansion and consolidation of a farm lot reflect processes of intensification and extensification of land-use activities, and relate to time of settlement, soil fertility in the lot, available household labor, and opportunities created by credit and markets—so-called period effects (S. McCracken et al. 2002b).

Whereas a significant positive correlation exists between time of settlement and deforestation, this is offset by the internal variability within cohorts, which is stronger than across cohorts (see Brondízio et al. 2002a for more detail). Such variability is even stronger in older cohorts, suggesting that variation in rate, extension, and direction of land-use change is probably associated with different trajectories in household economic strategies, composition, and farm production potential. Decisions regarding deforestation may be taken to seize a short-term opportunity, and not necessarily to focus on long-term investment.

This is the case, for instance, when a farmer allocates land to a particular crop to take advantage of a credit opportunity and later decides to discontinue the crop after the subsidy expires. As a result, large areas of secondary succession may appear. Differences in soil quality explain much of the variance in crop choice and farmer persistence on rural properties. Upon arrival, most colonists did not recognize the difference between alfisols and oxisols (E. Moran 1981). However, over the past twenty-five years, colonists have learned the difference. Today there is a clear association between the percentage of the property in alfisols and crop choice (E. Moran et al. 2002a).

In the region of Altamira, more than half (56 percent) of the households interviewed received credit at least once. Historical events clearly condition the variation and amount of credit allocated to different agricultural activities. An initial focus on annuals and perennials in the 1970s and early 1980s shifted to cattle ranching after 1991. During the 1990s, FNO was practically the sole credit program available to small farmers; although privileging cattle ranching, it mandated for the inclusion of a small area of some predefined perennials, which most of the time did not reflect the farmer's own crop preferences (E. Moran et al. 2002a). Credit to be used by the colonist farmer for the purchase of equipment generally has been unavailable and consistently low over the entire colonization period. According to most of the farmers we interviewed, this has been one of the main constraints on maintaining opened areas in production following their initial clearing. This shows the link between frontier farmers and regional and national economic and social policies.

Cocoa production by colonist farmers is an example of how national and international markets define land-use strategies among colonist farmers. Initially motivated by credit incentives, the total area under cocoa production in the region soared from zero to 13,000 ha in the late 1980s, Diseases such as witches' broom led to lower productivity and economic return, a trend accentuated by the decline in the international cocoa price. Combined, these factors were responsible for the abandonment of large areas of cocoa. More recently, however, cocoa price increases have motivated farmers to reclaim cocoa plantations by hiring off-farm labor or devising new land tenure arrangements, including sharecropping and leasing. Reclaiming cocoa areas has a direct impact on deforestation and pasture formation by shifting household labor allocation to existing open areas, while helping to generate income through the consolidation of farm lots, instead of by increasing deforestation. All these temporal and spatial dynamics, however, are not captured by Landsat data. The similarities between cocoa groves and secondary vegetation confound their spectral differentiation. For this reason, from a remote-sensing perspective, some of the most productive farm lots appear as abandoned (see figure 9.8). We have been able to overcome this problem, at least partially, by using farm-level field surveys, interviews with extension officers, and archival research.

Evidence in This Case Supporting the Need for Intraregional LUCC Research First, explanations of deforestation trajectories are a function of the level of analysis, as is the search for driving forces underlying these trends. Attention should be paid not only to regional dynamics but also to intraregional variability and differential conditions among colonist cohorts. Different trajectories are observed at the level of the colonization landscape, at the cohort level, and within cohorts. Whereas at the regional level, national colonization policies, the arrival of new colonists, and the national economy correlate with deforestation, farmers respond differently to these factors depending on the stage of farm formation, and on other factors such as labor, access to credit, agricultural prices, and the environmental endowment of their farms (e.g., soil fertility). Second, frontier areas challenge the application of conventional models of land-use intensification based on fallow cycles (such as Boserupian models) and factors of production, which are frequently used to explain the relationship between agropastoral systems and deforestation in other places (Futemma and Brondízio 2003). Colonist land use is characterized by cycles of farm formation that are marked by pulses of deforestation which vary in magnitude due to period effects. Farm lots go through cycles of establishment, consolidation, and expansion, what I called elsewhere "the colonist footprint" (Brondízio et al. 2002a). These processes, however, are characterized by high variation within farm cohorts resulting from differential rates, extents, and directions of land-cover change across farm lots. Third, the example shows the need to observe interannual cycles of deforestation if one aims to capture deforestation as a process of farm formation. Furthermore, the inability of remote-sensing data to capture important land-use activities, such as cocoa plantations, means there is a need for detailed field studies with farmers and within farm lots, as well as a need for archival research in regional institutions such as the cocoa research center, CEPLAC (Comissão Executiva de Produção da Lavoura Cacaueira). Farm lots that may be seen as failures from a remote-sensing classification that shows only secondary succession may actually turn out to be large cocoa production areas that are successes. Policies based solely on remotely sensed images, uninformed by detailed fieldwork, might be formulated that abandon these successful farms by road neglect and credit tightening. A clear understanding of cycles of farm formation can provide valuable insight that can better inform land-use policies to provide better support to colonist farmers during the consolidation period of their farm occupation. Understanding these processes will help focus more attention on the improvement of the existing infrastructure and will value local experiences to help existing farmers maintain forest stands in their lots by consolidating open areas.

Final Remarks: Complex Realities and LUCC Research in the Amazon

Emerging Intraregional Complexity Influencing LUCC in the Amazon

LUCC research offers a unique opportunity for understanding how micro- and macrolevels interact as a process, rather than dichotomously. Interpreting land use to include a critical understanding of local diversity, agrarian history, and commodity markets provides an opportunity for exciting and relevant research. Technically, this means coupling remote sensing and field tools by integrating ethnographic and survey methods, and by emphasizing the cross-training of social scientists and remote-sensing analysts in the region. Attention to local land-use systems and land-cover variations, forest management practices, and cycles of agricultural management will help to provide a regional picture that is much closer to reality. Remote sensing may represent the regional reality in several ways, for instance, in how it depicts productive land. By calling attention to local land-use practices and variations in land cover resulting from those practices, remote sensing may help to bring alternative forms of land use to the fore or, conversely, ignore land uses and users when presenting the region in maps and models (e.g., the agroforestry examples presented above).

Conceptually, an intraregional perspective on LUCC among Amazonian populations provides insight into the complexity of factors affecting social and environmental change in the region. Rather than creating unmanaged complexity for macroregional-level analysis, a better understanding of local diversity will highlight the different processes and the different needs faced by regional populations. Despite the complexity of land-use systems in the region, intraregional-level analyses have allowed us to find conditions that are common across sites, such as those defining forms of access, land resource value, and human assets underlying the rate and intensity of land-use change (Castro and Brondízio 2000).

A synthesis of the examples presented in this chapter illustrates this approach. First, different forms of access to resources exist in different combinations within the region as they relate to the infrastructure and the biophysical and institutional conditions mediating the interaction between people and the environment. On the one hand, roads and waterways link settlements, resources, and markets, while on the other hand, access is defined by the land tenure arrangements and social organizations that define rules and norms of resource ownership. Second, external markets, consumption needs, and economic interest all are factors influencing resource value that directly influences the rate, extent, and direction of LUCC in the region. In this sense, significant changes in regional land cover result, for instance, from price changes for forest and agropastoral products (e.g., açaí palm fruit), as well as from the dynamics of the regional land market (e.g., logging, clearing, pasture formation sequence). Finally, another group of factors can be defined as human assets; these include access to technology and available labor, as well as ethnobotanical and ecological knowledge to carry out particular activities; for instance, açaí agroforestry intensification in response to external markets or the ability of farmers to consolidate a farm lot in a colonization area without high rates of deforestation. Variations in ethnobotanical interpretations of the regional environment distinguish native Amazonians from recent colonists through their interpretation of the economic potential of forests vis-à-vis deforestation and conversion. On the other hand, the creativity of colonist farmers to develop new land-use systems—such as types of agroforestry—create new opportunities to couple forest and land-use management into rural development programs. These forms of land use should take the forefront of regional land-use analysis, thus helping to call attention to the need to improve the infrastructure and local livelihood conditions. The organization of these sets of factors may provide an alternative analytical strategy to capture variations in intraregional land-use change, while allowing forms of comparative interpretation useful for a broader regional picture.

Intraregional Analysis and Political Implications of LUCC Research

Extrapolating local dynamics to broader scales, and vice versa, underlies the conceptual, technical, and political developments of this research community. This requires a continuous balance of historical and ethnographic analyses explaining local conditions and patterns of human behavior expressed at larger spatial scales, as well as the macrolevel political economic forces underlying these regional changes. This is a prime task for social scientists involved in Amazonian research. The cases used in this chapter provide an example of how oversimplification of land-use/land-cover analysis can overlook the diversity of local human strategies resulting from micro- and macrolevel factors interacting historically in the Amazon (Brondízio in press). Common to many indigenous and peasant populations around the world, Amazonian rural communities tend to be invisible when it comes to getting their needs met, and highly visible when it comes to their impact on the environment. In part, this is the way the scientific community portrays and represents them, be they indigenous peoples, caboclos, or colonists.

When aggregating local land-use strategies to regional patterns, we tend to highlight "the problems," such as deforestation rates, and dismiss local solutions and coping strategies that actually point the way to alternatives, such as the examples of agroforestry systems illustrated in this chapter. Historically, Amazonian peasants tend to be characterized as having a lack of entrepreneurial spirit and being predisposed to extensive land-use practices and environmental degradation (Brondízio 2004a). Instead, more effort should be made to understand regional land-use strategies and deforestation as a result of the interplay of regional agrarian history, national political economy, and external market demand.

To some extent, LUCC as a research agenda has resulted in the placement of developing nations and rural landscapes at the forefront when compared to topics such as industrial emissions and consumption in developed nations, despite the latter's disproportionate contribution to global climate change. In this context, the current trend in modeling future scenarios of Amazonian land use has important political implications for the regional population. Modeling predictions have political consequences in negotiating the economics of global change at the international level—such as carbon emissions—and national and regional priorities of development policies. As the Amazon takes central stage in global change scenarios, the biggest challenge facing the LUCC research community in the Amazon is to balance the role of macrolevel and geopolitical forces vis-à-vis local environmental and historical conditions underling land-use change. Attention to intraregional land-use diversity is, therefore, key to minimizing misinterpretations and the long-term consequences of national and international policies for regional development. The potential academic and applied contribution of an internationally shared LUCC and human dimensions agenda rests on its commitment to understanding and prioritizing factors relevant to regional populations and development, at least as much as to the global environment. Failure to accomplish the former means failure to accomplish the latter.

Notes

1. The term *human dimensions of global environmental change* includes a broad range of research and policy topics, such as those related to industrial metabolism, health, poverty, economics, culture, and institutions, as well as studies of land-use change. When used in this chapter, the term refers mostly to the last-named, that is, the study of processes of human-environment interaction manifested in land-use change occurring at multiple temporal and spatial levels.

2. The term *intraregional* is used in this chapter as an analytical unit of research defined empirically to accommodate human populations and communities in relation to their biophysical, cultural, and institutional environment. Nested units of analysis can be defined according to one's research questions and regional conditions. For instance, rural communities in relation to a municipality, farm lots in relation to a settlement, one settlement in relation to a network of settlements, and communities in relation to a conservation unit. Biophysical units are also nested in this context, such as forest types within a watershed.

3. The case studies and examples in this chapter were developed as part of several research projects and field campaigns involving colleagues from the Anthropological Center for Training and Research on Global Environmental Change, the Center for the Study of Institutions, Population, and Environmental Change (CIPEC) at Indiana University, and collaborating Brazilian institutions such as Embrapa, Museu Paraense Emilio Goeldi, and INPE. The examples presented here benefit from research grants from the National Science Foundation (9100576, 9310049, 9521918), NICHD (9701386A), NASA (N005-334), NIGEC, and the McArthur Foundation through the Indiana Center on Global Change and World Peace. I am particularly thankful for the comments of William McConnell, Emilio Moran, Elinor Ostrom,

Andréa Siqueira, Michael Sauer, Fábio de Castro, Thomas Ludewigs, Ryan Adams, and Angelica Toniolo on earlier versions of this manuscript, to colleagues at CIPEC, the editorial work of Joanna Broderick, and figure compilation and printing support from Patti Torp, Scott Hetrick, Amanda Evans, Vonnie Peischl, Sarah Mullin, and Tarkan Kacmaz. An earlier version of this chapter was presented at the workshop "Globalization and the New Geographies of Conservation," organized by the Environment and Development Advanced Research Circle (EDARC) at the University of Wisconsin, Madison.

4. Only recently has remote sensing become part of the methodological toolkit of Amazonian social scientists, and to some extent ecological scientists and botanists. One of the earliest efforts in the social uses of remote sensing emerged not from the social sciences community, but from local political movements that were aware of its potential applications to land tenure and resource management issues (I. Brown and Stone 1989). Despite the wide application of remote-sensing data in the demarcation and monitoring of indigenous territories and different types of conservation areas (e.g., extractive reserves), integration of ethnographic work and remote sensing is still developing in the Amazon. Cultural ecologists have contributed for decades a rich and detailed ethnographic literature on land-use systems and forest management that is directly relevant to remote-sensing applications, but which is not always used by remote-sensing analysts. Examples include research focused on the ethnobotanical aspects of land use (Balée and Gely 1989; Balée 1994) and analysis of different aspects of swidden agriculture and agroforestry systems affecting spatial, temporal, and structural aspects of land cover (Beckerman 1983; Hiraoka 1985, 1989; Denevan and Padoch 1987; Balée and Posey 1989; Brondízio and Siqueira 1997). Furthermore, ethnographic work has contributed to regional-level land-use studies by taking into account the variability in local responses to external forces as well as the cultural and economic value of forest areas, variables which are relevant to land-use modeling.

5. The term *caboclo* is used in this chapter to refer to the native non-Indian population of the Brazilian Amazon, and is to some extent equivalent to the term "Ribereño" used in the Peruvian Amazonian floodplains (e.g., see Wagley 1953; E. Moran 1974). For a detailed discussion of the term, see Brondízio 2004a.

6. I use the term *rural studies* here to refer to various lines of research in anthropology, sociology, and geography concerned with rural development, sociocultural change, extractivism, and political ecology, mostly at meso- and microlevels.

7. Conceptual models supporting these analyses have included, for instance, the "central place" theory and Von Thünen approaches, particularly with the growing importance of urbanization in the region (Browder and Godfrey 1997). Boserupian analyses have been used to look at rates of regrowth, fallow cycle, and crop frequency in relation to population size, labor, technology, and land circumscription, mostly with emphasis on native peasant communities and Indian territories (Carneiro 1961; Shorr 1998; Scatena et al. 1996; Brondízio and Siqueira 1997; Futemma and Brondízio 2003). In colonization areas, applications of models of household cycles (e.g., Goody 1958, 1976) and labor arrangements to land-use analysis, including Chayanovian models, also have become increasingly used in studies focused on farm-level dynamics (Marquette 1998).

8. *Euterpe oleracea* Mart. is the main source of "heart of palm," also a top export product of the region.

10

Processes of Forest Change at the Local and Landscape Levels in Honduras and Guatemala

Catherine M. Tucker and Jane Southworth

Guatemala and Honduras experience the high rates of deforestation typical of many nations in Latin America (FAO 1993; Ascher 1995; Segura et al. 1997). These deforestation rates reflect aggregates to the national level and obscure important local variations in the rates and patterns of forest change. Local processes can include conservation, short- or long-term regrowth, and degradation or loss of forest area. This chapter explores the processes occurring in five forests in Guatemala and Honduras that represent a range of variation in forest management and different patterns in forest change through time. The sites are similar in vegetation structure, climatic patterns, and topography. The national levels manifest differences in economic policies and historical development of export crops, particularly coffee, but have similarities in their experiences with international commodity markets. The contexts surrounding the forests include factors frequently implicated in deforestation: population growth, market integration, agricultural intensification, and export crop expansion. Yet these forests do not consistently show deforestation as might be predicted. This chapter argues that the study of forest change requires attention to dynamic fluctuations and cyclical patterns, as well as dominant trends, if deforestation is to be mitigated.

Research Questions

In this chapter, we examine how forests have changed through time and the factors that appear to be most critical in the patterns observed for the study period, 1987–2000. The major independent variables of interest include community-level institutional arrangements for forest management, accessibility (elevation and slope), economic activities (especially commercial and subsistence agriculture), and the national policy context. The dependent variables of primary interest are total forest cover at single points in time for four Landsat Thematic Mapper (TM) satellite image dates (1987, 1991, 1996, 2000), trajectories of change in forest cover through time, and forest conditions as evaluated by foresters through fieldwork. The research teams recognize that soils, climate, and topography shape forest conditions. Therefore, we attempt to control for biophysical variables in the comparison by selecting forests of similar vegetation composition in fairly comparable environments. The study explores

- How has forest cover changed over time?
- What are the institutional dimensions that appear to be associated with forest-cover change?
- What are the economic activities that appear to be associated with forest-cover change?
- How have national policies impacted study communities' forest use and management?

Theoretical Foundations

The clearing of tropical forests has drawn a great deal of attention due to its implications for biodiversity, the global carbon cycle, degradation of ecosystems and environmental services, and the destruction of indigenous cultures (Hecht and Cockburn 1989; A. Anderson 1990; Shukla et al. 1990; Myers 1994). Nevertheless, identifying the major human drivers of deforestation in different geographic and historical contexts remains a challenge for researchers addressing the human dimensions of global environmental change (Geist and Lambin 2001). While studies of tropical deforestation have identified many factors that appear to be important, as yet no consensus has emerged as to the most important factors, or relationships among factors, that cause changes in forest cover. Indeed, the proximate causes of forest-cover change differ significantly across regions and countries (Imbernon 1999). If there is any consensus, it is a methodological one. Scholars now agree that interdisciplinary methods and perspectives are required to address the complex issues of deforestation and global environmental change. Therefore this research on processes of forest-cover change contributes to the efforts of integrating theoretical perspectives from multiple disciplines, including anthropology, economics, environmental sciences, geography, history, political science, and sociology.

In their meta-analysis of tropical deforestation, Geist and Lambin (2001) identify the most frequently noted proximate causes of deforestation: agricultural expansion, timber and fuel extraction, and expansion of infrastructure. The underlying factors that drive proximate causes include economic factors, policy and institutional factors, demographic processes, sociocultural characteristics and preferences, and technological change (Geist and Lambin 2001). Economic models of deforestation have failed to find any consistent relationships among macroeconomic factors, policies, and forest change (Kaimowitz and Angelsen 1998). Moreover, variables such as population growth appear to have contradictory influences; in some locales it appears to be correlated with *de*forestation, in other places with reforestation (regrowth) (Tiffen et al. 1994; Varughese 2000).

Institutional arrangements merit special attention in studies of forest change. Institutions, defined as rules-in-use, have the potential to limit forest exploitation or encourage it (see chapter 4). Effective land tenure institutions are widely recognized as fundamental to wise forest management. The relationship between property rights, economic development, and environmental destruction constitutes an important issue in the literature. Secure land rights may contribute to improved economic options and provide incentives for sustainable management of natural resources. Contrasting perspectives exist, however, as to which type(s) of property arrangements achieves these ends. Neoclassical economics and neoliberal perspectives view private and public property as the optimal forms of land tenure, based on an assumption that common property arrangements entail uncontrolled exploitation and lead to resource degradation (cf. Hardin 1968). Common-property scholars counter that this assumption derives from an erroneous interpretation of common property as open access (e.g., see Runge 1986, 624; McCay and Acheson 1987, 6–7; Berkes et al. 1989, 67–68; Molnar 1989, 96; E. Ostrom 1990). Open access refers to resources for which there are no defined property rights. In the absence of property rights, anyone can exploit the open-access resource freely, and degradation eventually results. By contrast, common property represents a form of private property in which members of a recognized group share rights of use (Bromley et al. 1992, 3–4; McKean and Ostrom 1995, 6).

Field studies have found that common-property regimes tend to provide more equitable access to, and distribution of, resources and yield lower costs than those needed to maintain a bureaucracy for managing, recording, and adjudicating land titles (Runge 1986). This has led to arguments (and in a few nations, policy initiatives) for protecting and fostering common-property arrangements and community forestry as the preferred approach for achieving an equitable, cost-effective, and potentially sustainable form of resource management (cf. Rangan 1997). The development of effective common-property institutions, however, requires that the users of the shared resources be motivated to manage them sustainably. Gibson (2001) argues that effective common-property institutions will develop only under conditions of dependence and scarcity; otherwise, users will not care if the resource endures or disappears. While these factors may be necessary, they are unlikely to be adequate to encourage the formation of effective institutions. Attributes of the users (such as trust, reciprocity, and reputation) shape whether or not people are willing and able to cooperate at the level needed to create and maintain common-property institutions (E. Ostrom 1998a). Elinor Ostrom (2001) points out that the benefits of forming and maintaining institutions must be expected to outweigh the costs of organization, and that people must have a level of trust and shared understanding to reach agreements and attain compliance. Attributes of the resource also contribute to the potential for effective institutional arrangements; for example, if a resource is severely degraded, or if availability is highly unpredictable, its protection is unlikely to generate benefits adequate to satisfy a whole group of users (E. Ostrom 2001).

The emergence of effective institutions for sustainable resource management poses a challenge not only for jointly held property but also for individual private and public property (NRC 2002). Whatever the property system, the development and persistence of sustainable management practices is likely to be related to a number of other variables, such as market pressures, policy incentives, wages, land values, and systems of production, as well as personal constraints and priorities. Comparative studies indicate that no single type of tenure will consistently assure specific environmental outcomes or necessarily promote sustainable resource management (Rangan 1997; C. Tucker 1999; Dietz et al. 2003). In many cases, government policies have contributed to deforestation. Detrimental elements have included timber contracting arrangements and pricing structures, land tenure and titling laws, cattle-ranching subsidies, and road-building programs (Repetto and Gillis 1988; Browder 1989; Hecht 1989; Binswanger 1991; Utting 1993; Deacon 1995). In this comparative study of Guatemala and Honduras, the relationships between traditional property regimes and policy transformations bear particular relevance.

Guatemala and Honduras have both implemented policies that tend to support private tenure over communal tenure, and promote export crop production over production of staple crops for food security. The study sites, however, preserve a notable proportion of their forests as common property. Many of these forests lie on marginal, topographically complex areas, with few productive alternative uses. Several studies have found that communal ownership often occurs on marginal land (Netting 1982, 1993). Thus the preservation of communal forests within these sites suggests adaptation to local environmental conditions, as well as the possibility that local government arrangements have been able to mediate national policy initiatives to meet local traditions and practices. This further implies that national policies have permitted some flexibility for local management decisions. The presence of benign or supportive national policies appears to be a key aspect in the endurance and success of common-property arrangements (McKean and Ostrom 1995). In both Guatemala and Honduras, recent policies have devolved certain rights over natural resource management to the municipal level. At the same time, extreme climate events (e.g., Hurricane Mitch) and market shocks, particularly volatility in coffee prices, have challenged national and local governments to respond effectively with limited financial resources and personnel.

Methods

Site Selection

Site selection proceeded by identifying *municipios* (similar to U.S. counties) that were comparable in terms of biophysical conditions and fell within the same footprint of a satellite image. To be included in the analysis discussed here, the municipios had to be free of cloud cover in the satellite images. Within each municipio, at least two forests and one settlement were selected as focuses for the study. The study aimed to minimize variation in biophysical conditions so observed changes could be related directly to human rather than environmental factors. To examine the role of tenure in forest management, sites were selected so that both communal (common property) and private ownership would be represented.

Fieldwork in Communities

Fieldwork in the study sites involved interdisciplinary methods to collect sociocultural, economic, institutional, and biophysical data. Teams composed of researchers from the natural and social sciences used protocols developed by the International Forestry Resources and Institutions (IFRI) research program to obtain comparable data in each of the sites (see E. Ostrom and Wertime 2000). Through interviews and participatory rural appraisal activities with residents, local officials, and representatives of organizations active in the study regions, researchers obtained information on forest use and management, economic conditions, policy impacts, patterns of forest use, and the institutional arrangements related to forest management.

Forest Mensuration

The teams conducted forest mensuration in each of the study forests during fieldwork in 1997 and 1998, with the assistance of experienced botanists and local people serving as plant identifiers. As described more thoroughly in chapter 5, forest plots were randomly selected following a random number generation procedure for determining coordinates for points on forest maps. In each forest plot, researchers identified species, measured tree height and diameter at breast height (dbh), and obtained geographic coordinates with a global positioning system (GPS) unit. Plot characteristics were recorded, including the slope, aspect, elevation, presence of erosion, evidence of livestock, and indication of insect infestation.

Teams made observations of land cover and land use to classify remotely sensed images. The training sample observations identified areas that represented the variety of land covers in the region (e.g., mature *Pinus-Quercus* forest, secondary succession *Pinus-Quercus* forest, grassland/pasture, clearing/agriculture) that could be identified as distinct land-cover patches on satellite images. Each of these classes was later defined as either forest or nonforest (typically agricultural uses).

The examination of forest conditions based on forest mensuration provides detailed, ground-level information. Forest mensuration data are limited by representing a single point in time, and even with repeat visits the method is time- and labor-intensive. In order to follow changes in forest area through time, the use of remote-sensing techniques prove more efficient.

Processing and Analysis of Landsat TM Images

Analysis of satellite images (see chapter 6) offered the primary source of quantitative estimates of land cover over the thirteen-year interval that constituted the study period. Landsat 5 TM images were obtained for 1987, 1991, 1996, and 2000. Each image was selected from the month of March because it corresponds to the end of the dry season, when agricultural fields can be easily distinguished from forests, and cloud cover tends to be minimal. Geometric rectification of the 1996 image was carried out using 1:50,000-scale maps and the nearest-neighbor resampling algorithm, with a root mean square error of less than 0.5 pixel (<15 m). Using a similar procedure, the rectified 1996 image served as the basis to rectify the 1987, 1991, and 2000 images. An overlay function verified that the images overlapped precisely across the three image dates. Following rectification, calibration procedures corrected for sensor drift and other differences, such as variations in the solar angle and atmospheric conditions. Without such calibration, change detection analysis may evaluate differences at the sensor level rather than changes at Earth's surface.

Training sample data were used to determine the land-cover classes on the ground and then train the satellite images to recognize them. Classes for agriculture, young fallows (approximately one to three years), pasture, clearings, and settlements, as well as a negligible area in water, were aggregated to create a nonforest class. This class is predominantly agriculture, but for the purposes of our research questions, the definition of nonforest best represents the land cover. Forest was defined as having a canopy closure of 25 percent or greater, based on forest plots from fieldwork. Land-cover maps of forest and nonforest cover for 1987, 1991, 1996 and 2000 were derived by independent, supervised classification of the four Landsat images, using a Gaussian maximum likelihood classifier. Only two cover classes (forest, nonforest) were used to simplify the change analysis and modeling procedure (see also Southworth et al. 2002; Nagendra et al. 2003).

With classification accuracies exceeding 85 percent for all four dates, classified images generally agreed visually with actual land cover and with the very distinct spectral signatures of each class. Following classification, change detection analysis was undertaken. Change detection is a technique used to determine the change between two or more time periods of a particular region or for a particular land cover by providing quantitative information on spatial and temporal distribution. It offers an important tool for monitoring and managing natural resources (Macleod and Congalton 1998). In addition, fieldwork in March 2000 verified the land-cover trajectories of 100 randomly selected locations, based solely on either visual inspection of tree size and age, and other factors, or a combination of visual analysis and interview data. This field verification provides added confidence in the change analyses and the underlying classifications. This is important, as the error across each land-cover classification is additive in the creation of change grids. In this study, the field verification and accurate registration procedures in which overlay accuracy was verified served to minimize potential errors in the forest/nonforest classification procedure.

Changes in land cover were detected using an image grid addition technique. Analyses of four images across three intervals (1987–1991, 1991–1996, 1996–2000) were conducted to measure land-cover changes for each forest. These analyses resulted in four possible classes for each interval: forest (unchanged), deforestation (forest to nonforest), regrowth (nonforest to forest), and nonforest (unchanged). This postclassification grid analysis led to a newly classified image incorporating information from all images (Mertens and Lambin 1997) and producing a categorical map—a change image. This image is associated with a change matrix that gives the area for each class and its changes during the period. At the municipal level, an additional change analysis was conducted across three images (1987, 1991, 1996) to produce a new image with eight possible classes. Change

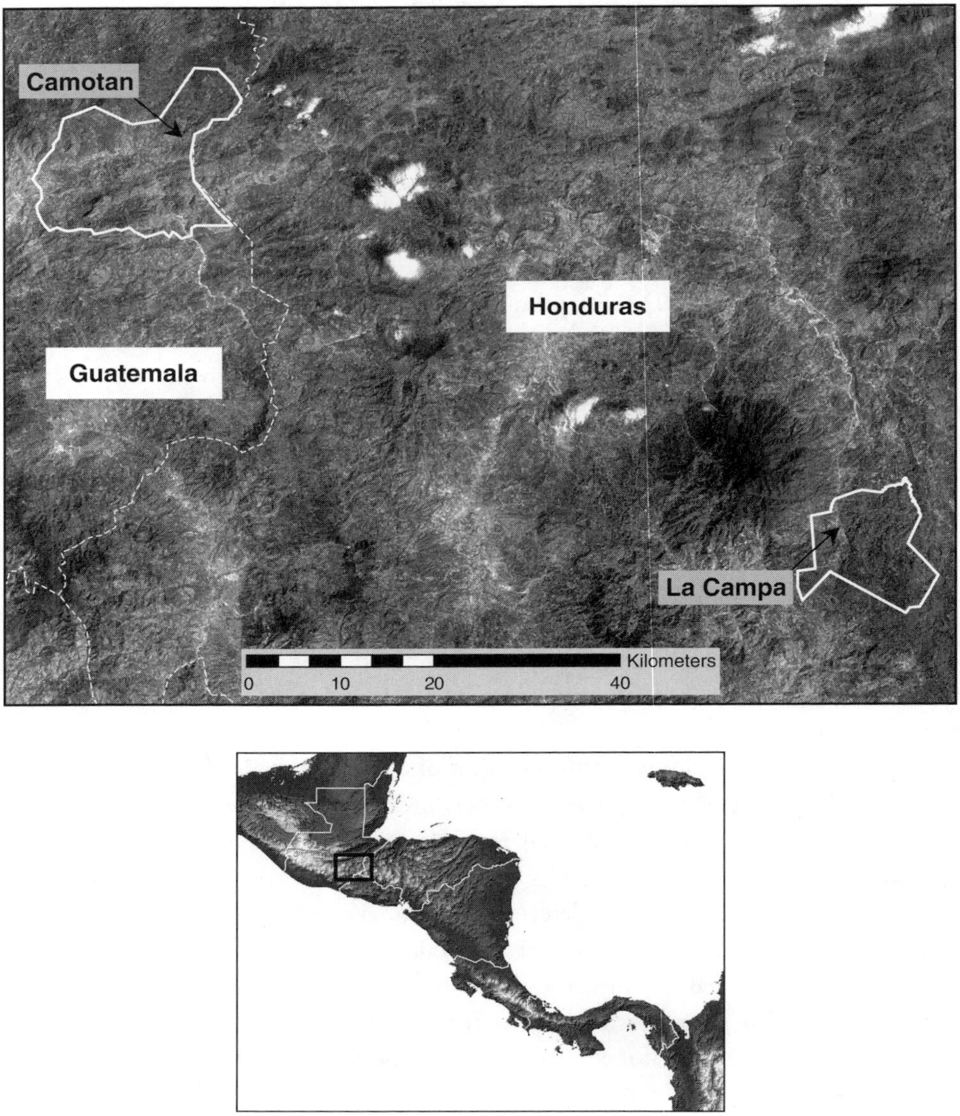

Figure 10.1
Guatemalan and Honduran study sites.

data for the forest and municipal levels allow comparison of change processes across these levels of analysis.

Overview of the Sites

Two municipios are the focus for this analysis: Camotán in eastern Guatemala and La Campa in western Honduras (figure 10.1). Both Camotán and La Campa met the criteria of having private and communal forest ownership, which permitted contrasting the influence of tenure regimes. The institutional arrangements associated with private and communal management varied across the sites. Despite efforts to find highly comparable biophysical contexts, we found the nature of the landscape and the distribution of forests involved variation in average elevation, slope, temperature, and precipitation, which influence the species composition and biodiversity (table 10.1). The study forests chosen in the municipios nevertheless contain pine-oak forests with similar vegetation structure located on topographically complex terrain.

Camotán

The research in Camotán focused on a private farm, known as Tachoche, with a large forest, and the village of Tesoro, which shared a communal forest with an adjacent community and several other small villages (figure 10.2). The villagers had formally designated Tesoro Community Forest only two years before the fieldwork (and some of the boundaries remained in flux), but the area had been used as a village woodlot for generations. Fifty years ago, most of the municipio remained in forest, but most of it has since been cleared for agriculture as families have grown and immigrants have arrived from Honduras. Residents traditionally depend on subsistence production of maize and beans, but the primary economic activity is now coffee production, which expanded with road building and good prices through the early 1990s. Coffee incomes permitted growers to gain material goods (trucks, stone houses) and reduce their dependence on the forest. People mainly cook with gas or deadwood from their coffee plantations instead of harvesting firewood from the communal forest. Few residents use the forest, although individuals occasionally harvest timber for personal use (e.g., house construction). Tachoche experienced a change in ownership in the late 1980s and markedly expanded coffee production and timber extraction. The owners clear the forest by section, and replant clearings with pine. Since the change in ownership, the villagers have respected the private property limits.

Table 10.1
Biophysical Characteristics of Study Site Forests

	Forest Name				
	Camotán, Guatemala		La Campa, Honduras		
	Tachoche	Tesoro Community Forest	La Campa Private Forests	La Campa Communal Forest	Resin Tappers' Zone
Tenure type	Private	Communal	Private	Communal	Communal
Forest size (ha)[b]	369.6[a]	524.6	48.6	383.8	236.3
Species richness (woody plants)	31[c]	17	9	7	13
Mean annual temperature (°C)	23	23	20	20	20
Mean annual precipitation (mm)	2000	1740	1300	1300	1300
Mean slope (degrees) (*SD*)	29 (*8.3*)	26 (*6.6*)	19 (*6.5*)	18 (*9.0*)	20 (*7.1*)
Mean elevation (mean sea level) (*SD*)	953 (*103.7*)	943 (*93.6*)	1214 (*41.2*)	1233 (*32.7*)	1374 (*42.5*)

[a] Based on the area of the entire property, as the proportion devoted to forest did not have a specified boundary.
[b] Based on geographic information system (GIS) coverages of boundaries derived from fieldwork; the resulting forest area within the GIS coverage tended to differ from the forest area estimated by respondents.
[c] Based on identification of woody plants to the species level. Fifteen woody plants, including small saplings, could not be identified. They were not ascertained to be different species and therefore are not counted.

La Campa

The municipio of La Campa, in western Honduras, contains eight villages and the municipal center (Centro Urbano, similar to a county seat). The research focused on three forest areas: (1) a large communal forest, La Campa Communal Forest, comprised of two areas under identical management rules and used by residents of Centro Urbano and two neighboring villages; (2) a private forest area composed of four small (2–19 ha), adjacent private forests, La Campa Private Forests, held by individuals who follow similar management practices; and (3) a forest parcel, Resin Tappers' Zone, granted in 1994 to a newly formed resin tappers' cooperative (figure 10.3). The majority of the municipio's population depends on subsistence production of maize and beans, but coffee production expanded during the 1990s. Coffee expansion has been associated with road improvements (La Campa did not have a

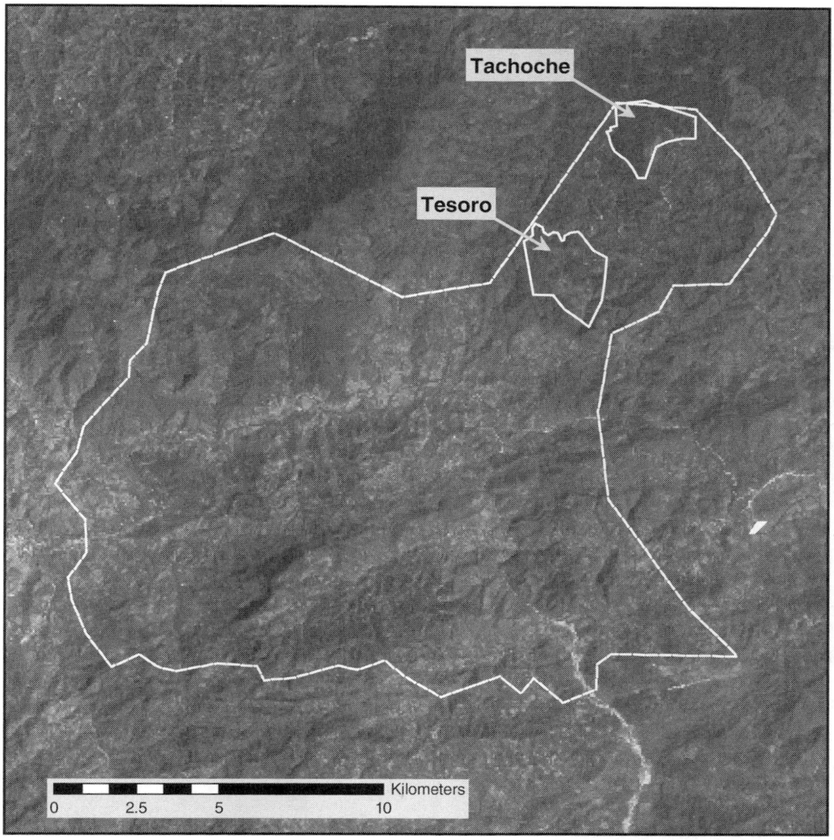

Figure 10.2
Study forests in the *municipio* of Camotán, Guatemala.

road into the coffee-producing highlands until 1993), agricultural extension programs, and national subsidies. People depend on communal forests for firewood, timber for construction, and pasture for livestock. The private forest owners, most of whom also produce coffee on separate parcels, have fenced off the land to serve as pasture for their livestock, and they rarely harvest timber or firewood from their land.

Comparison of Study Forest Characteristics and Institutions

Important differences, as well as similarities, exist between the study forests. Tachoche receives the highest average annual rainfall and has a higher average

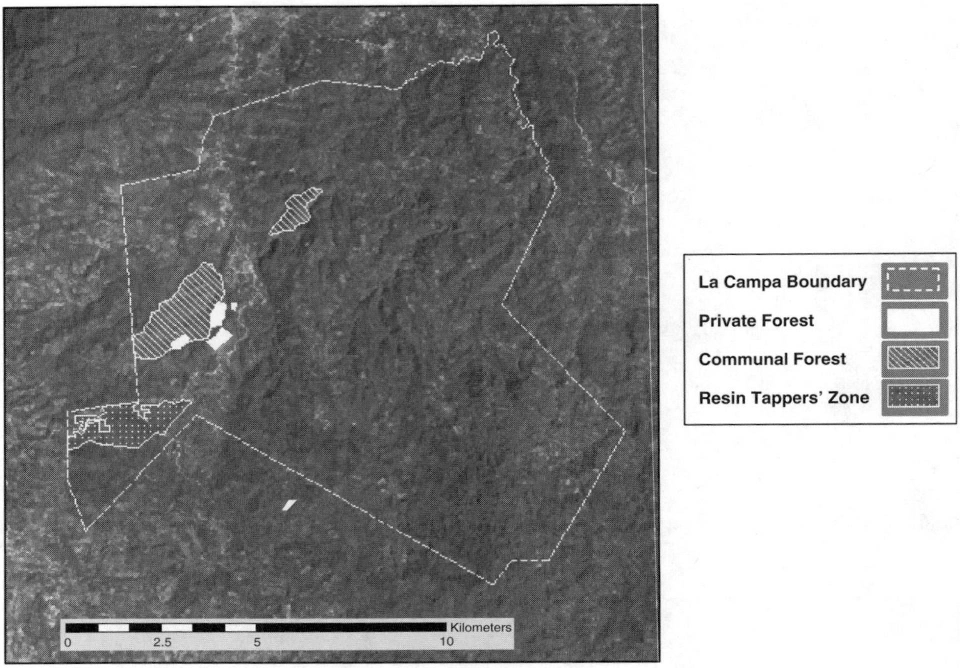

Figure 10.3
Study forests in the *municipio* of La Campa, Honduras.

temperature than the other forests (see table 10.1). Accordingly, it is not surprising that Tachoche supports the greatest species richness of woody plants in the study. Tesoro Community Forest, which lies close to Tachoche, receives slightly less rainfall and has the second highest species richness. The forests studied in La Campa are adjacent and do not differ noticeably in rainfall or temperature. Camotán's forests have steeper average slopes and lower average elevations in contrast to those of La Campa. In terms of accessibility, the gentler slopes may facilitate access, as do nearby roads.

The forests have strong similarity in terms of dominant species—pine (*Pinus oocarpa*) dominates, followed by oak (*Quercus* spp.)—with the exception of Tachoche, in which another pine (*P. maximinoi*) is the secondary dominant species (table 10.2). In terms of basal area, however, the forests differ notably: Tachoche and Tesoro Community Forest have much higher basal areas than any of La Campa's forests. In comparison, La Campa Private Forests have higher basal areas than La Campa Communal Forest and the Resin Tappers' Zone. The forests also

Table 10.2
Species Dominance and Basal Area of Study Forests

	Forest Name				
	Camotán, Guatemala		La Campa, Honduras		
	Tachoche	Tesoro Community Forest	La Campa Private Forests	La Campa Communal Forest	Resin Tappers' Zone
Total basal area (m^2/ha)	27.43	24.57	15.04	10.13	11.72
Dominant species	*Pinus oocarpa*	*P. oocarpa*	*P. oocarpa*	*P. oocarpa*	*P. oocarpa*
Dominant tree basal area (m^2/ha)	9.08	21.13	12.05	8.50	8.42
Relative dominance (m^2/ha)	0.39	0.88	0.92	0.92	0.91
Secondary dominant tree	*P. maximinoi*	*Quercus crispifolia*	*Quercus sapoetaefolia*	*Q. sapoetaefolia*	*Q. sapoetaefolia*
Secondary dominant basal area (m^2/ha)	6.92	2.16	0.64	0.36	0.75

Table 10.3
Study Forests' Mean Values for Crown Cover, Tree Diameter at Breast Height, and Tree Height

	Forest Name				
	Camotán, Guatemala		La Campa, Honduras		
	Tachoche	Tesoro Community Forest	La Campa Private Forests	La Campa Communal Forest	Resin Tappers' Zone
Mean crown cover (%) (*SD*)	38 (*22.3*)	27 (*15.3*)	30 (*24.2*)	22 (*15.6*)	24 (*20.3*)
Mean tree[a] dbh[b] (cm) (*SD*)	25 (*14.8*)	26 (*13.5*)	22 (*11.7*)	20 (*11.4*)	19 (*8.7*)
Mean tree height (m) (*SD*)	16 (*6.5*)	15 (*5.4*)	14 (*4.5*)	12 (*5.7*)	13 (*5.6*)

[a] Trees are defined as having a minimum diameter at breast height of 10 cm.
[b] dbh, diameter at breast height, measured 137 cm above the ground.

differ in terms of crown cover, mean tree dbh, and mean tree height; in all of these dimensions, Camotán's forests have higher mean values (table 10.3). This suggests in general that Camotán's forests present better general forest conditions.

Fieldwork observations indicate that Camotán's forests are subject to lower levels of human exploitation than La Campa's forests. These observations are supported by La Campa forest plot data indicating the presence of livestock and erosion, which can influence forest degradation and may imply human presence. All of the forests except Tachoche had high levels of livestock presence, based on the number of plots that had signs of livestock. La Campa's communal and private forests revealed the most intense grazing pressure—100 percent and 95.2 percent of all plots, respectively, had signs of livestock (table 10.4). Erosion appeared most severe in Tesoro Community Forest, followed by La Campa Communal Forest and the Resin Tappers' Zone. The notable differences between forests with notably similar biophysical conditions indicate that institutional arrangements and associated patterns of use represent important dimensions in the study forests' conditions.

Institutional arrangements of particular importance to the municipios include rules for forest use, the activities of local governance bodies, and the user groups' relationships among themselves and with government entities. All of the study forests have land titles, whether owned communally or privately. The private forest owners in La Campa have private holdings specified under communal village titles,

Table 10.4
Signs of Forest Degradation

	Forest Name				
	Camotán, Guatemala		La Campa, Honduras		
	Tachoche	Tesoro Community Forest	La Campa Private Forests	La Campa Communal Forest	Resin Tappers' Zone
Total no. of plots	40	40	21	20	21
Percent (%) of plots with erosion (No. of plots)	0 (0)[a]	47.5 (19)	4.8 (1)	30 (6)	28.6 (6)
Percent (%) of plots with evidence of livestock (No. of plots)	0 (0)[a]	57.5 (23)	95.2 (20)	100 (20)	52.4 (11)

[a] Based on 39 of 40 plots due to missing data.

and owners must cooperate with the relevant village council. In practice, tenure security exists uniformly in La Campa. Tachoche has a legally recognized private title under Guatemalan law.

Approaches in forest management differ markedly within as well as across tenure regimes. Tachoche exploits its forest on a large scale and plants pine stands to supply its onsite sawmill. Private forest owners in La Campa use their forests principally for grazing, but they respect municipal rules restricting commercial forest activities. Tesoro Community Forest is used primarily for harvesting timber for household construction at low levels of exploitation. In contrast, La Campa Communal Forest experiences a high level of firewood extraction for cooking and tempering of artisanal pottery.

The communal forests in the study vary in the degree to which rules limit residents' forest exploitation (table 10.5). The community of Tesoro has not created and enforced many rules to constrain forest harvesting; however, the forest appears to experience a low level of exploitation since most of the population obtains firewood from their coffee fields. The owner and manager of Tachoche must follow a forest management plan approved by Guatemala's National Forestry Institute, yet they have considerable latitude in deciding many issues regarding forest harvesting, construction of infrastructure, and use of fire. La Campa has enforced rules that prohibit commercial exploitation of forests, with the exception of the permission

Table 10.5
Forest Rules and Enforcement

	Forest Name			
	Camotán, Guatemala		La Campa, Honduras	
	Tachoche[a]	Tesoro Community Forest	La Campa Private Forests	La Campa Communal Forest
Rules exist to govern uses	Yes[b]	Yes	Yes[c]	Yes
Rules govern maintenance/ improvement	Yes[b]	No	No	No
Rules govern infrastructural changes	No[d]	Yes	No	Yes
Rules govern use of fire	No[d]	Yes	Yes[c]	Yes
Rules govern types of seeds that may be planted	Yes[e]	No	No	No
Rules limit wild game that may be taken	No	No	No	Yes
Rules are enforced	Unclear	Yes	Variable	Variable

[a] The presence of municipal or higher-level government rules constrains this private owner's uses, but private owners may change self-imposed management principles at will, without sanction.
[b] The owner must follow an officially approved management plan.
[c] La Campa's municipal rules require permission to set fires, and prohibit residents from harvesting timber for commercial sale.
[d] The owner and manager make decisions jointly but are free of external regulations.
[e] The owner and manager must consult with the National Forestry Institute (INAB).

granted to the resin tappers' cooperative to use one section of the communal forest. The resin tappers' cooperative must follow a management plan approved by the semiautonomous Honduran National Forest Development Corporation (COHDEFOR) that specifies the number and size of trees that can be tapped. They, and other La Campa residents, also may harvest deadwood for firewood and graze livestock in the zone. The zone is more than 4 km from most households, so it is under less pressure for firewood exploitation and livestock grazing. La Campa's municipal council attempts to control exploitation of live trees by charging residents for extraction of trees for household construction. It also fines residents of adjacent municipios whose cattle cross borders into the communal forests. Even so, the municipal council does not consistently enforce its rules prohibiting transformation of communal forest to privately claimed land. Perhaps most important for forest conditions, there are no

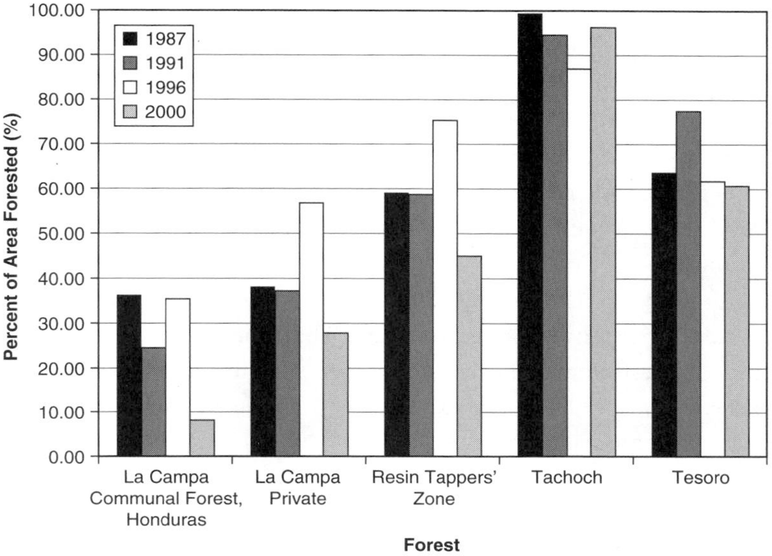

Figure 10.4
Total forest area actually forested by date.

limits on the quantity of firewood that households may harvest. Since La Campa Communal Forest is located within a kilometer of the municipal seat, it is the source for the majority of firewood and the destination for most livestock. Despite concerns over forest degradation, residents use this forest with few constraints, and the forest data indicate that this forest has poorer conditions than the others.

Results of Forest-Change Analysis

Theory suggests that deforestation is likely to occur in areas with weaker institutions, such as La Campa Communal Forest, which is also easily accessible. Tachoche's and La Campa's private forests appear to offer stronger institutions in terms of prohibiting outsiders from exploiting the resources. In both sites, neighbors usually respect private forest boundaries, even though the owners have limited ability to sanction trespassers. The results provide some support for theoretical predictions, yet also indicate that the reality is more complex than theory anticipates.

The analyses of the classified images for each image date (1987, 1991, 1996, 2000) show that the forests experienced different trends in cover change. Figure 10.4 indicates the percentage of the total area actually forested for each of the four dates. The percentage of total area in forest fluctuates through time rather than following a linear trend. La Campa Communal Forest experienced the most dramatic fluctuations. With 36 percent of its area in forest cover in 1987, it experienced a loss in forest cover from 1987 to 1991, a gain in forest cover from 1991 to 1996, and an astonishing loss in forest from 1996 to 2000, such that only 8.1 percent of the area remained in forest in 2000. Other forests experience less drastic fluctuations but still show intervals of regrowth as well as declines in forest cover. Tachoche presents the least overall variation.

The three interval analyses (1987–1991, 1991–1996, 1996–2000) provide further insight into the change processes (figure 10.5). The change classes show that both regrowth and deforestation occurred simultaneously during those intervals. Indeed, all of the forests except Tachoche experienced notable regrowth and deforestation during each two-date image interval.

Discussion of Forest-Change Results for Sites Studied

The fluctuations in forest cover suggest that short-term changes in forest users' strategies occur through time, as users adjust to transient political, economic, or social pressures, and perhaps climatic events. Moreover, some forest uses and transformations have cyclical patterns, such as fallow cycles and slash-and-burn agriculture (cf. Munroe et al. 2002). The changes in the two-date intervals imply that notable changes occurred in the climate, policy environment, or institutional arrangements. In particular, the 1987–1991 data seem to be an exception to subsequent years. Fieldwork data from La Campa suggest several events are related to the processes seen in La Campa Communal Forest. In 1987, a major forest fire in the communal forest caused a notable loss in forest cover (the burn scar is visible in the 1987 image); the burned area experienced regrowth through 1996. A major political event—the expulsion of COHDEFOR from the area in 1987—also contributed to the deforestation in La Campa Communal Forest during the 1987–1991 interval. The expulsion resulted from residents' anger and organized protests against COHDEFOR, which had granted numerous permits to regional sawmills that severely overexploited communal forests. In return, La Campa had received only token payments, and COHDEFOR had severely fined residents for forest use related to their limited commercial activities.

Following 1987, the municipal council granted people areas in communal forest for personal use, which had been prohibited by COHDEFOR. Although the council and residents strongly opposed logging by outsiders, they were eager to regain full

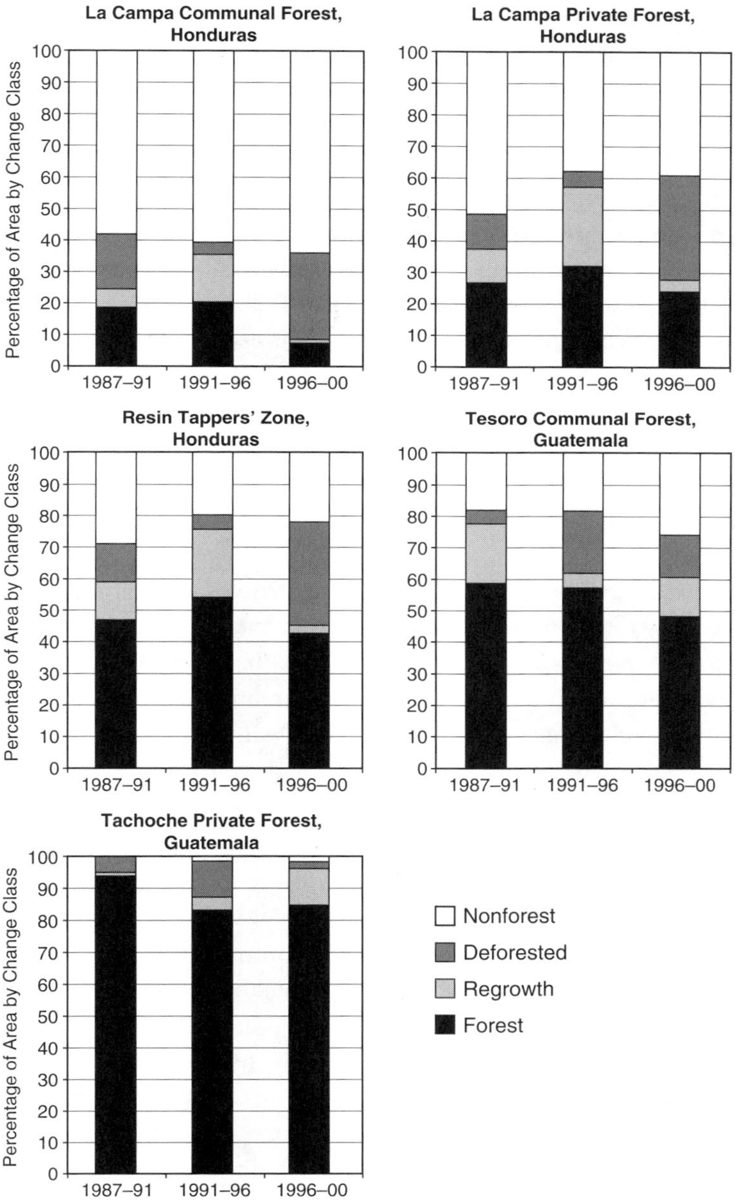

Figure 10.5
Forest transformation by time interval.

use of their communal forests, which had been severely curtailed under COHDEFOR. The freedom to claim new land encouraged some households to clear areas in La Campa Communal Forest and the section designated in 1994 as the Resin Tappers' Zone. By 1996, however, some of these fields and pastures had reverted to fallow. The land had low productivity, and the more affluent farmers sold livestock to fund export coffee production in the higher elevations. Similarly, the regrowth noted in La Campa Private Forests for 1991–1996 appears to be associated with a general decrease in the number of cattle owned by these more affluent households (one of which sold off all but 20 head of a 300-head herd), in order to concentrate resources in coffee planting. In Guatemala, the people of Tesoro hired forest guards beginning in 1998 to prevent outsiders' incursions and harvesting. The regrowth seen for the forest suggests that the guards may have helped to reduce trespassing and harvesting by nonresidents.

Results of Forest-Change Analysis at the Municipal Level

Processes of forest change can vary by scale of analysis. While patterns of use in study forests can be readily linked to institutional arrangements, the factors that influence forest change at coarser scales may be less obvious. In order to understand the broader processes within which the study forests are situated, we conducted an analysis of forest change at the municipal levels. This analysis does not include the 2000 image. It focuses on an analysis of forest cover for three of the image dates (1987, 1991, 1996) and a time-series analysis of change classes, which indicate the status of each pixel through time. These two analyses presented different perspectives. Looking at the amount of forest cover for each of the images suggests that the forest cover is relatively stable through the study period. Camotán retains just over a third of its total land in forest across the three-date image analysis (table 10.6). The data seem to imply that very little forest-cover change occurred over the nine-year study interval.

The time-series analysis revealed a much more dynamic picture. In Camotán 28.5 percent of the area experienced a switch between forest and nonforest status over the three image dates (table 10.7). This suggests that farmers are actively clearing and fallowing land for short intervals. The areas that remain under permanent forest cover (forest in each of the images) tend to lie on steep slopes and at higher elevations, while areas that remain cleared (mainly for agriculture and settlements) are at lower elevations and near roads. Another interesting facet of the analysis was the contrast between the Honduran and the Guatemalan municipios. While just over

Table 10.6
Percentages of Forest Cover by *Municipio* (1987, 1991, 1996)

Image Date	Camotán, Guatemala Forest (%)	La Campa, Honduras Forest (%)
1987	63.7	64.0
1991	77.5	63.0
1996	61.7	67.5

Table 10.7
Change-Trajectory Classes by *Municipio* (1987–1991–1996)

Change Class	Camotán, Guatemala (%)	La Campa, Honduras (%)
f–f–f	21.16	47.92
f–n–f	5.67	7.19
n–f–f	5.13	6.16
n–n–f	5.96	6.70
f–f–n	1.84	5.26
f–n–n	3.92	3.65
n–f–n	2.78	3.67
n–n–n	53.55	19.88

f, forest; n, nonforest.

20 percent of Camotán remained as stable forest over the three image dates, almost half of La Campa's land was in stable forest.

Discussion of Results of Municipal-Level Forest-Cover Analysis

Several factors appear to contribute to the contrast in forest cover between Camotán and La Campa. Guatemala, for the most part, has been producing coffee for the market for a longer period than La Campa, and Camotán appears to have had better roads, which have benefited coffee producers for several decades. Permanent agricultural fields appear to be well established in Camotán, while La Campa has been experiencing agricultural intensification only recently, with a transition from swidden agriculture to extended field production with chemical inputs and ox-drawn plows. Population growth may have occurred more rapidly in Guatemala, but recent demographic data are lacking for Honduras. Additionally, La Campa's land offers less area suitable for agriculture due to the prevalence of cliffs and rocky slopes, and a lower average precipitation than Camotán.

The municipal level of analysis presents several contrasts and parallels with the forest-level analyses. Perhaps most interesting is that the 1987–1991–1996 time-series analysis shows that La Campa municipio experienced a forest regrowth trend, and this was mirrored for that same time frame by forest regrowth within the study forests. While part of the regrowth in La Campa Communal Forest can be attributed to regeneration following the 1987 fire, the regrowth occurring more broadly in the municipio evidently reflects abandonment of marginal agricultural fields associated with the adoption of modern soil conservation methods, chemical fertilizers, and plowing (Southworth and Tucker 2001). Through the 1990s, coffee expansion clearly impacted the highland forests of La Campa. Subsequent to the period covered by the municipal-level image analysis, a precipitous drop in international coffee prices evidently slowed the planting of new fields. Fieldwork observations and interviews conducted in 2000 and 2002 revealed that farmers were reducing investments in coffee. Larger coffee producers, unable to rely solely on family labor, were leaving coffee to rot in the fields because the cost of labor exceeded coffee's market price. In this situation, it is not yet clear whether farmers are clearing more forest to plant alternative crops, replacing coffee with another crop, adopting off-farm strategies to mitigate the consequences of volatile coffee prices, or waiting to see if coffee prices improve. The impact of coffee price volatility on land-cover change in La Campa is a focus of current work to include more recent images in the 1987–1991–1996 municipal-level analysis.

National Policies and Deforestation

Both Guatemala and Honduras have experienced difficulties in designing policies that promote wise forest management. In part, the design and implementation of policies have created contradictions. In Guatemala, the responsibilities for forest protection and enforcement have been divided among several government entities and programs that are not always clear in terms of their exact responsibilities (Suazo et al. 1997). Enforcement of forest laws has had a checkered history. Honduras has experienced similar shortcomings in the enforcement of forest laws. COHDEFOR has experienced several major reorganizations and continues to suffer from a poor reputation among farmers. In addition, the National Agricultural Institute (INA) promotes transformation of forest lands to agriculture under enabling legislation that contradicts forest policy. COHDEFOR, with a smaller budget and limited political resources, has been unable to reverse INA decisions in recourse to judicial processes, even when protected areas are at stake.

In the past decade, both nations devolved certain rights over natural resource management to the municipal level. In Honduras, an early study of the policy implications of the devolution of rights indicated that the overall effects should be favorable for wise management (ESA Consultores 1993). In Guatemala, decentralization of forest management since 1996 has included programs to provide national institutional support for municipal forest management (Larson 2003). The results of these changes are not yet clear. The costs and benefits of forest exploitation are now borne to a greater extent by the municipios, many of which have few resources or the experience to manage forests. These policy impacts, as they differ or run parallel across the two nations, require further research and analysis.

The Role of Coffee Production

Guatemala has been more successful than Honduras in promoting coffee production, and this appears to be a factor in the state of forest transformation in our comparison of Honduran and Guatemalan study sites. Coffee is currently the most important export crop produced in each of the study sites, but it has been important in the Guatemalan sites for a longer time. While many processes have influenced deforestation through time, Guatemala's coffee production has been intertwined with forest transformation since the mid-1800s. Coffee production in Guatemala has been linked to the expropriation of communal lands, expansion of road networks, integration of the national economy with international markets, and increasing inequities in the distribution of land and wealth. These processes have in turn been implicated in deforestation. Guatemala's success in promoting coffee production relates in part to favorable environmental conditions, particularly its rich volcanic soils, and the accessibility of some of its finest coffee-growing lands to urban markets and ports. More notably, the social relations of labor and land tenure patterns proved amenable to transformations that favored large-scale coffee production (R. Williams 1994).

Interestingly, Camotán falls in the department (state) of Chiquimula, a region of eastern Guatemala that presented greater difficulties for coffee expansion, including less fertile soils, greater distance from ports and urban markets, and persistence of communal lands. A low population density and labor scarcity apparently contributed to the difficulties of coffee production in this region through the mid-1900s. With population growth and improving roads, coffee became the most important market crop for the region during the latter half of the twentieth century. Yet in contrast to the rest of the country, where the large coffee growers dominate production, smallholders dominate in Chiquimula, as they have since the late 1800s (R. Williams 1994, 65).

Honduras has faced obstacles to coffee expansion that contrast with the Guatemalan experience. Honduras proved less favorable for coffee production. It had a smaller population, its soils tended to be more weathered and less fertile, and regions suitable for coffee production were for the most part located in mountains far from ports and markets (the department of Choluteca was an exception; it had easy access to a port and a larger labor pool; thus coffee production expanded more readily than in the rest of the nation) (R. Williams 1994). But perhaps more important, the liberal policies that swept Central America in the late 1800s followed a different path in Honduras than in Guatemala. The Honduran government did not enact legislation that directly attacked common property (Lapper and Painter 1985, 19). Instead, the government encouraged commercial agriculture by granting public lands to municipios that requested land for production, and it sold public lands to private individuals who promised to plant export crops. Common properties and private titles expanded most rapidly in areas where coffee production took hold (R. Williams 1994, 93–94). Honduran coffee production has remained in the control of smallholders, many of whom still produce coffee on communal lands, as is the case in La Campa.

Concluding Discussion

In nations with such high rates of deforestation, the study of these forests through time shows that deforestation is not necessarily a uniform trend in all forests. The forests included in this study are in relative proximity, yet their patterns vary. Forest management decisions play a large role in determining forest conditions, and in these forests the institutional arrangements provide leeway for management and use decisions that may include clearing. As a result, the rules-of-use and tenure regime do not appear to be as important in shaping the patterns of change as economic and political factors. Thus, Tesoro Community Forest experienced fluctuations, but only a minor reduction in total forest cover occurred over the thirteen-year period despite a context of relatively weak institutions. In this case, users had preferred alternatives to forest products, and began a process of strengthening institutions through the hiring of forest guards. Tachoche, which had strict management rules, experienced deforestation between 1987 and 1996. Timber harvesting decisions had evidently led to clearing in certain areas, but by 2000, reforestation efforts on logged areas had helped to compensate for lost forest cover. In La Campa, it appears that weak institutions permitted periods of high forest exploitation, while changing economic conditions shaped pressures on forests for transformation to pasture and possibly agriculture.

The Guatemalan study sites reveal a notable percentage of productive land in coffee and less than a third of their land in forest. By contrast, La Campa's coffee plantations cover less than 5 percent of its territory, while over 60 percent of its land is in forest, at least through 1996. La Campa's potential for coffee expansion is high, and many current coffee growers have fenced land in highland forests with plans to eventually plant coffee. Yet the crisis in coffee prices that began in the late 1990s currently represents a negative incentive for investment in coffee.

The Guatemalan municipio may represent a more advanced stage of the process occurring in La Campa, in which forest clearing slows as land suitable for transformation to agriculture becomes scarcer and forests retreat to the steepest, least productive areas. Thereafter, forest cover remains relatively unchanged, although temporary uses amenable to the marginal lands lead to dynamic switching between forest and nonforest covers. The dynamism observed in the landscape represents the most intriguing dimension of this research. Future efforts will involve additional fieldwork and satellite image analysis to further investigate these patterns and their drivers. If we are to understand the factors causing deforestation, then we also must understand the temporary and dynamic dimensions of forest-cover change, as well as sustained trends of expansion, conservation, and degradation. Can local institutions and national policies be designed to encourage forest protection before forests decline to a minimal level defined by local landscapes and economies? Or will forest transformation be inevitable until the costs exceed the possible benefits of transformation?

11

Comparison of Aboveground Biomass across Amazon Sites

Dengsheng Lu, Emilio F. Moran, Paul Mausel, and Eduardo Brondízio

The future of carbon emissions may be the largest source of uncertainty in climate scenarios. While fossil fuel emissions may account for a significant part of global carbon emissions, tropical deforestation and the fires associated with it make up a considerable proportion of total emissions, and make estimating even current emissions difficult. Part of the problem lies in the magnitude of tropical forest clearing, the isolation of many of the areas where deforestation is taking place, and the difficulty of arriving at accurate estimates of the total area deforested. In the 1980s it was believed that carbon emissions from fossil fuels were 5.5 ± 0.5 gigatons per year (Gt/yr) in contrast to $1.7 \pm$ Gt/yr from land use, but there was greater uncertainty over the latter number. Much of the "missing carbon" in estimates of carbon pools came from the land component. Likewise, estimates of the carbon sink have high degrees of uncertainty, and what proportion comes from secondary forest regrowth is largely unknown except for some small areas that have been carefully studied. To overcome these uncertainties it is particularly important to understand patterns and processes of land-use change as they affect net emissions, to understand past and current trajectories of land use, and to have strategies in place to monitor future changes in land use that are amenable to rapid assessment of net emissions and sequestration of carbon.

One useful way to proceed is to develop approaches for estimating biomass changes in land cover using remotely sensed data. A number of studies have provided useful approaches for estimating biomass, and thus carbon, related to loss from deforestation and subsequent use of fire to remove the vegetation for agropastoral activities. Our work on human-environment relationships, linking as it does biophysical with social science approaches to understand changes in forest ecosystems, has routinely developed methods to integrate time-series satellite digital data with field measurements that provide a foundation for developing accurate approaches to biomass and carbon estimation. Linking remote sensing to actual land cover is a challenge. We have tried to address this challenge by intensive field studies and vegetation and biomass measurements.

This chapter illustrates some methods for estimating carbon and biomass in ways that take into account significant variability in the sensitivity of different measurements. While it would be ideal to use a universal method to estimate biomass, our research shows that differences of vegetation structure lead to some indices being accurate in one type of canopy structure and less accurate in other types.

Many methods for aboveground biomass (AGB) estimation that have been used (Gillespie et al. 1992; Overman et al. 1994; Roy and Ravan 1996) include complete harvesting or destructive sampling, allometric equations, conversion of tree volume to AGB, remote-sensing techniques, and geographic information systems (GIS) techniques (Lu 2001). Destructive sampling requires complete harvesting of all biomass within the plots, followed by drying and weighing (Klinge et al. 1975). This approach is time-consuming and costly, but it provides accurate results. Allometric equations are often derived from the precise destructive sampling data. Many models have been developed based on various combinations of diameter at breast height (dbh), tree height, and wood density through linear or nonlinear regression models (Jordan and Uhl 1978; Saldarriaga et al. 1988; Uhl et al. 1988; Overman et al. 1994; B. Nelson et al. 1999). Once an allometric equation is established, it can be used for inventories of stand biomass quickly and nondestructively. However, the equations tend to reflect the specific characteristics of the area sampled and are rarely applicable universally. Conversion of tree volume to AGB can save time and cost because large datasets of tree volumes are available from regional or national forest inventories. These inventory data can be used for estimation of AGB (S. Brown et al. 1989; S. Brown and Lugo 1992).

Remote-sensing techniques have many advantages over other methods, including repetitive data acquisition, synoptic views, potentially lower cost, and a digital format amenable to computer processing. These make remotely sensed data the primary source for AGB estimation of large areas, especially in areas of difficult access. In recent years remote-sensing techniques have become more prevalent in estimating AGB (R. Nelson et al. 1988, 2000; J. Franklin and Hiernaux 1991; Leblon et al. 1993; Steininger 2000; Lu et al. 2002a). If ancillary data such as soil data, topographic data, and climate data are available, GIS technology can integrate them with remote-sensing data to improve AGB estimation. S. Brown et al. (1992) used GIS technology to produce a forest biomass map for peninsular Malaysia, and Iverson et al. (1992) used GIS to estimate total biomass and biomass density of the tropical forests in South and Southeast Asia.

Most previous AGB estimations using remote-sensing data focused on coniferous forest because of its simple species composition and homogeneous stand structure (Hussin et al. 1991; Hame et al. 1997; Kurvonen et al. 1999). Because of its complex stand structure and rich species composition, AGB estimation research has rarely been conducted successfully in a large area of moist tropical forest. Although many vegetation indices have been developed and applied in AGB estimation (G. Anderson et al. 1993; Bannari et al. 1995), there is little understanding about which vegetation index is best related to AGB in a given study area and how different biophysical characteristics affect the vegetation index and AGB relationships (Lu 2001). Also, rarely has research involved the study of textures for AGB estimation. Texture measures that have been developed (Haralick et al. 1973; Haralick 1979; Irons and Petersen 1981; Kashyap et al. 1982; He and Wang 1990) were mainly used for land-use/land-cover classification using remote-sensing data (D. Gordon and Phillipson 1986; S. Franklin and Peddle 1989; Jakubauskas and Price 1997). Texture can be an important factor in improving AGB estimation accuracy, but many uncertainties remain: What types of texture measures are appropriate to extract AGB information? What size of moving window for selected texture measures can most effectively extract AGB information? This chapter focuses on developing appropriate AGB estimation models by testing vegetation indices and textures in the Amazon basin as well as exploring how different biophysical characteristics affect the AGB estimation.

Study Areas

Three study areas in Brazil—Altamira, Bragantina, and Ponta de Pedras—were selected for this research (figure 11.1). They have different soil conditions, land-use history, landscape complexity, vegetation growth rates, stand structures, and human activities. The Altamira study area is located along the Transamazon highway in the Brazilian state of Pará. The city of Altamira and the Xingú River anchor the eastern edge of the study area. With the construction of the Transamazon highway in 1970, incoming population and older caboclo settlers from earlier rubber eras claimed land along the new highway and legalized their land claims (E. Moran 1973, 1981). Early settlement was driven by geopolitical goals and political economic policies that aimed at production of staples like rice, corn, and beans. The region has experienced a gradual shift to a more diverse set of land uses. Cocoa, sugar cane, and black pepper have been added to the staple crops. The dominant native types of vegetation are mature moist forest and liana forest. Nutrient-rich alfisols, as well

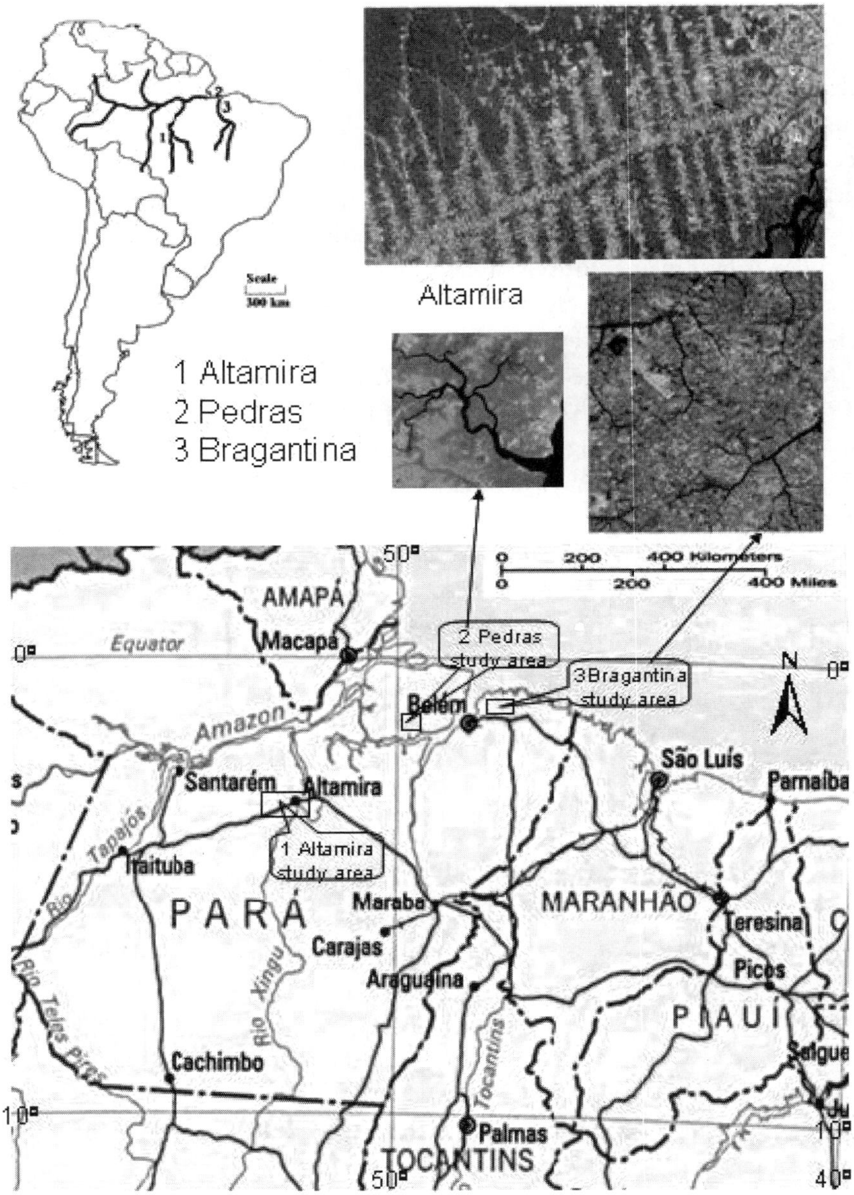

Figure 11.1
Locations of the study areas.

as nutrient-poor ultisols and oxisols, can be found in this area. The Altamira area has experienced high rates of deforestation and secondary succession associated with implementation of agropastoral projects. Annual rainfall in Altamira is approximately 2000 mm and is concentrated from late October through early June. Average temperature is about 26°C.

The Bragantina study area is located within the state of Pará. The vegetation in this region is composed mostly of pasture and cropland, secondary growth forest (*capoeira*), flooded forests (*igapó*), and a few remaining areas of dense forest. At the beginning of the twentieth century, almost 1 million hectares of dense tropical rain forest covered the Bragantina region; however, less than 2 percent of the forest remained by 1960. Heavy occupation of this region has transformed the landscape into a mosaic of secondary vegetation (J. Tucker et al. 1998). Currently, secondary succession in all stages of regrowth dominates the landscape. The main agricultural products are passion fruit (*maracujá*), manioc, rice, corn, beans, and oil palm. The soils in this area are dominated by nutrient-poor oxisols and ultisols. Land use has gone through several phases, and today the dominant form is short-fallow swidden cultivation and pasture development. Cycles of secondary growth and cultivation have been common for decades (E. Moran et al. 2000a). Annual rainfall ranges from 2200 to 2800 mm with a dry period from July through November. The average annual temperature is 25° to 26°C.

The Ponta de Pedras study area (hereinafter referred to as Pedras) is located in the estuarine region of the Amazon on Marajó Island in the state of Pará. It is a transitional region between two macroenvironments: the dense floodplain forests to the west and the natural savanna grasslands to the northeast. The savanna grasslands are the most prominent features in this study area. The vegetation has complex structure and is rich in palms. The forest presents uniform stratification consisting of large trees with canopy emergents reaching up to about 35 m with a sparse herbaceous layer (Brondízio et al. 1994b, 1996). The human population of this region is found in small urban centers or scattered along the river banks. For local people, the açaí palm (*Euterpe oleracea*) is the most important plant species in this environment because of its significant contribution to household food intake and its economic value in the regional market. Crop cultivation includes manioc (*Manihot esculenta*) gardens, beans, and rice, but it is restricted to small areas (see chapter 9). Pedras has been occupied historically by caboclo populations, mainly devoted to agroforestry activities in the floodplain and swidden agriculture in the uplands, although pasture and mechanized agriculture can be found in the upland oxisols.

The annual average temperature is approximately 27°C, and rainfall is about 3000 mm per year with a dry season from May through November.

Methods

Field Data Collection

A nested sampling strategy, organized by region, site, plot, and subplot, was employed to inventory vegetation data. The region represented the study area that included all sample sites. Sites varied in size according to the land-use activity previously in place and were selected for plot sampling to represent a particular age class and previous land-use history. The first step for sampling was to visit each site to assess the homogeneity of the land-use patterns. In particular, we wanted to assess whether the site had the same land-use history and if parts of it were not affected by other disturbances, such as accidental fire, plant removal, and so on. The sizes of sites ranged from a minimum of 2 ha (e.g., swidden agricultural area) to several hundred hectares (a mature forest). The number of sites for field survey was chosen based on the stratified random fashion using Landsat Thematic Mapper (TM) classification images. Once a site was selected and demarcated for sampling, plots were randomly located along one or more transects and subplots were located randomly inside the plots. In general, ten plots (10 × 15 m for each plot) in each site were allocated, and one randomly selected subplot (5 × 2 m for each subplot) was nested within each plot. Plots were used to inventory trees, and subplots were used to inventory saplings, seedlings, and herbaceous species. In each plot, all individual trees with a dbh greater than 10 cm were identified and measured for dbh, stem height (the height of the first major branch), and total height. In the subplot, all saplings (dbh between 2 and 10 cm), seedlings (dbh <2 cm), and herbaceous vegetation (percent of ground cover) were identified and counted. The diameter and total height were recorded for all individual trees with dbh between 2 and 10 cm. At each site, soil samples were collected at 20-cm intervals to a depth of 1 m, resulting in five sets of measurements for each sample site. Soil samples were analyzed at soil laboratories in Belém, Brazil, for chemical and physical properties. Table 11.1 summarizes the data collected and used in this chapter.

Calculation of Aboveground Biomass

An Oracle-based database was developed to store and manage the vegetation inventory data, soil data, and land-use history information. The Amazon information sys-

Table 11.1
Field-Inventoried Data and Thematic Mapper Images Used in This Research

	Altamira	Bragantina	Pedras
No. of			
Sites	20	18	14
Plots[a]	131	126	81
Subplots	239	215	187
Trees	1572	989	1527
Saplings	744	1085	1060
Seedlings	9593	13,461	7129
Soil samples	20	18	14
Year of field data collection	1992, 1993	1994, 1995	1992, 1993
Acquisition date of TM images	7/20/1991	6/21/1994	7/22/1991
Other data collected: land-use history, topographic maps, etc.			

TM, Landsat Thematic Mapper.
[a] Some sites of initial succession stage did not have trees with dbh greater than 10 cm; thus no plots were allocated in those sites.

tem software was developed using Visual Basic language to analyze the vegetation stand parameters. In this research, two models were selected for individual vegetation biomass estimation. Equation (1) (B. Nelson et al. 1999) was used to calculate biomass for trees and saplings with dbhs less than 25 cm, and equation (2) (Overman et al. 1994) was used to calculate biomass for trees with dbhs greater than or equal to 25 cm. Equation (3) was used to calculate AGB (kg/m^2).

$$\ln(DW1) = -2.5202 + 2.1400 * \ln(\mathrm{D}) + 0.4644 * \ln(\mathrm{H}) \tag{1}$$

$$\ln(DW2) = -3.843 + 1.035 * \ln(\mathrm{D}^2 * \mathrm{H}) \tag{2}$$

$$\mathrm{AGB} = \left(\sum_{i=1}^{m} DW1_i + \sum_{j=1}^{n} DW2_j\right)\bigg/\mathrm{PA} + \left(\sum_{k=1}^{s} DW1_k\right)\bigg/\mathrm{SPA}, \tag{3}$$

where ln is the natural logarithm, D is dbh (cm), H is total height (m), $DW1$ is individual tree or sapling biomass (kg) when D is less than 25 cm, $DW2$ is the individual tree biomass when D is greater than or equal to 25 cm, m is the total tree number when D is 10 to 25 cm within a plot, n is the total tree number when D is greater than or equal to 25 cm within a plot, and s is the total sapling number when D is 2 to 10 cm within a subplot area. PA and SPA are the total plot area and subplot area (m^2) in a site, respectively.

Image Preprocessing

Accurate geometric rectification and atmospheric calibration are two important aspects in image preprocessing (see Chapter 6). In this research, the images (see table 11.1 for acquisition dates) were geometrically rectified into Universal Transverse Mercator (UTM) projection using control points taken from topographic maps of 1:100,000 scale. A nearest-neighbor resampling technique was used and a root-mean-square error of less than 0.5 pixel was obtained for each TM image. The TM images collected have very good quality, without any clouds in the study areas, and the terrains are relatively flat. Hence, the atmospheric effects can be regarded as uniform. Because atmospheric data and the images could not be acquired for the same dates, some advanced atmospheric calibration software, such as 6S, was difficult to use for this study. However, an improved image-based dark object subtraction (DOS) model was valuable for atmospheric correction of historical TM images in the Amazon basin (Lu et al. 2002b). During radiometric calibration using the DOS model, gain and offset for each band and sun elevation angle were obtained from the image header file. The path radiance was identified based on clear water for each band. The atmospheric transmittance values for visible and near-infrared bands were derived from Chavez (1996) and were averages for each spectral band derived from radiative transfer code. For middle infrared bands, the atmospheric transmittance was set to 1. The surface reflectance values fall within the range of 0 to 1. For convenience of data analysis, the reflectance values were rescaled to the range of 0 to 100 by multiplying 100 for each pixel.

Development of Vegetation Indices and Textures

After geometric rectification and atmospheric correction, vegetation indices were calculated separately for each study area. Four types of vegetation indices were grouped and used: (1) simple ratio: TM 4:3, TM 5:3, TM 5:4, and TM 5:7; (2) normalized vegetation indices: NDVI (normalized difference vegetation index), ND53, ND54, ND57, and ND32; (3) complex vegetation indices: ARVI (atmospherically resistant vegetation index), ASVI (atmospheric and soil vegetation index), SAVI (soil adjusted vegetation index), MSAVI (modified soil adjusted vegetation index), and GEMI (global environmental monitoring index); and (4) linear image transformation: VIS123, MID57, albedo, KT (tasseled cap) transform, and PCA (principal components analysis). In addition to the TM bands and different vegetation indices, four types of texture measures—mean Euclidean distance (MED), variance, skewness, and kurtosis—were tested in this research. Different texture measures com-

Table 11.2
Vegetation Indices Used in This Research

Vegetation indices		Formula
Simple ratio	TM 4:3	TM 4/TM 3
	TM 5:3	TM 5/TM 3
	TM 5:4	TM 5/TM 4
	TM 5:7	TM 5/TM 7
Normalized vegetation indices	NDVI	(TM 4 − TM 3)/(TM 4 + TM 3)
	ND53	(TM 5 − TM 3)/(TM 5 + TM 3)
	ND54	(TM 5 − TM 4)/(TM 5 + TM 4)
	ND57	(TM 5 − TM 7)/(TM 5 + TM 7)
	ND32	(TM 3 − TM 2)/(TM 3 + TM 2)
Complex vegetation indices	ARVI	(NIR − 2 RED + BLUE)/(NIR + 2 RED − BLUE)
	ASVI	$((2NIR+1)-\sqrt{(2NIR+1)^2-8(NIR-2RED+BLUE)})/2$
	SAVI	$\frac{NIR-RED}{NIR+RED+L}(1+L)$
	MSAVI	$((2NIR+1)-\sqrt{(2NIR+1)^2-8(NIR-2RED)})/2$
	GEMI	$\xi(1-0.25\xi)-\frac{RED-0.125}{1-RED}$
		Where $\xi=\frac{2(NIR^2-RED^2)+1.5NIR+0.5RED}{NIR+RED+0.5}$
Linear image transform	VIS123	TM 1 + TM 2 + TM 3
	MID57	TM 5 + TM 7
	albedo	TM 1 + TM 2 + TM 3 + TM 4 + TM 5 + TM 7
	KT1	0.304TM1 + 0.279TM2 + 0.474TM3 + 0.559TM4 + 0.508TM5 + 0.186TM7
	KT2	−0.285TM1 − 0.244TM2 − 0.544TM3 + 0.704TM4 + 0.084TM5 − 0.180TM7
	KT3	0.151TM1 + 0.197TM2 + 0.328TM3 + 0.341TM4 − 0.711TM5 − 0.457TM7
	PC1	The constants for the principal
	PC2	component (PC) are similar to those
	PC3	for the tasseled cap (KT) transform, but they are dependent on the given images of the study areas.

Table 11.3
Texture Measures Used in This Research

Texture measures	Formula	Notes
Mean Euclidean distance (first order)	$\frac{\sum(\sum_{\lambda}(X_{c\lambda} - X_{ij\lambda})^2)^{1/2}}{n-1}$	$X_{ij\lambda}$ is DN value of spectral band λ and pixel (i, j) of a multispectral image.
Variance (second order)	$\frac{\sum(X_{ij} - M)^2}{n-1}$	$X_{c\lambda}$ is DN value for spectral band λ of a window's center pixel.
Skewness (third order)	$\frac{\sum(X_{ij} - M)^3}{(n-1)V^{3/2}}$	X_{ij} is DN value of pixel (i, j). M is the mean of the moving window,
Kurtosis (fourth order)	$\frac{\sum(X_{ij} - M)^4}{(n-1)V^2}$	where $M = \frac{\sum X_{ij}}{n}$.
		V is variance.
		n is number of pixels in a window.

DN, digital number.

bined with different window sizes (3×3, 5×5, 7×7, 9×9, and 15×15) for each TM band were tested. Descriptions of formulas associated with the selected vegetation indices and texture measures are provided in tables 11.2 and 11.3, respectively.

Integration of Image Variables and Vegetation Inventory Data

In this research, all the sample data had accurate coordinates that were provided by global positioning system (GPS) devices and geometrically rectified TM color composites during the fieldwork. These sample data were linked to image variables to extract the mean spectral and textural values for each sample site. For each site, AGB was aggregated from ten plots and ten subplots. A 3×3 window was used to extract the mean value of spectral response or texture for each site. Pearson's correlation coefficient was used to analyze such relationships. Using AGB as a dependent variable and remote-sensing variables such as TM bands, vegetation indices, and textures as independent variables, multiple regression models were used to establish the relationships between AGB and remote-sensing variables.

The critical step is to find the most important independent variables so the combination of multiple independent variables can provide the best estimation results. The coefficient of determination (r^2) is an indicator that is used to determine whether a regression model is good or not. Stepwise regression analysis is used to find the best independent variable combination.

Impacts of Biophysical Environments on Aboveground Biomass Estimation

Tree species composition, forest stand structures and associated canopy shadows, and vegetation vigor are regarded as the main factors affecting vegetation reflectance (Lu 2001). Soil conditions, including soil fertility, influence vegetation growth and AGB accumulation rates (E. Moran et al. 2000b; Lu et al. 2002c). The biomass growth rate (kg/m^2 per year) of successional forests for each site was calculated based on the biomass density and vegetation age. The soil fertility was evaluated by a soil evaluation factor (SEF), which was developed based on soil chemical components such as calcium, magnesium, potassium, aluminum, and organic matter (Lu et al. 2002c). A higher SEF value is a proxy to indicate higher soil fertility. Soil fertility, biomass growth rate, and land-use history from the three study areas were used to explore the impact of different biophysical conditions on the AGB estimation.

Results

Aboveground Biomass Estimation

Linear regression models were developed based on integration of vegetation inventory data and remote-sensing variables. Table 11.4 provides a comparison of the best regression models identified according to a single TM band, a single vegetation index, a single texture, and a combination of different image bands. TM 5 was identified as the best single band because it has the highest regression coefficient in Altamira and Pedras, and TM 4 was the best band in Bragantina. In Altamira, vegetation indices slightly improved relationships between AGB and spectral signatures, while textures significantly improved the regression coefficient. However, in Bragantina and Pedras neither vegetation indices nor textures improved the regression coefficients. In Altamira, variance with TM 2 and the 9×9 window was the best texture measurement, while in Bragantina it was variance with TM 5 and the 15×15 window and in Pedras it was kurtosis with TM 3 and the 5×5 window. Table 11.4 also implies that a single TM band, a single vegetation index, or a single texture does not have a sufficiently high regression coefficient to develop an AGB estimation model. Therefore, it is necessary to seek two or more independent variables to improve estimation performance.

Table 11.4
Comparison of Regression Coefficients among Different Models

		Altamira		Bragantina		Pedras	
		Ind. Var.	R	Ind. Var.	R	Ind. Var.	R
Single variable	TM	TM 5	0.627	TM 4	0.837	TM 5	0.826
	VI	ND54	0.635	KT1	0.835	MID57	0.822
	Text	VARtm2_9	0.841	VARtm5_15	0.551	KUtm3_5	0.702
Combination of multiple variables	TM & text	TM 5 + VARtm2_7	0.874	TM 4 + SKtm4_9	0.883	TM 7 + KUtm3_5	0.865
	VI & text	KT1 + VARtm2_9	0.878	PC2 + VARtm5_15	0.851	MID57 + KUtm3_5	0.864

Ind. Var., independent variable; R, regression coefficient; VI, vegetation index; text, texture.

Stepwise regression analysis indicates that if the independent variables consist of two or more TM bands, two or more vegetation indices, combinations of TM bands and vegetation indices, or two or more textures, the regression coefficients are not significantly improved in multiple regression models. Only the combination of TM bands or vegetation indices with textures can improve the regression coefficients shown in table 11.4, because (1) high correlations exist between spectral responses and between textures or (2) very weak relationships exist between AGB and selected vegetation indices or textures. However, spectral and textural information are complementary. For example, in Altamira the TM bands and vegetation indices are not strongly correlated with AGB, but some specific textures, such as VARtm2_9 (variance combined with TM 2 and a 9 × 9 window), are strongly correlated with AGB. In Bragantina, spectral signatures (e.g., TM 4) have strong correlations with AGB, but textures do not. The identification of the role of textures in AGB estimation is particularly valuable because it offers an effective method for improving model performance based on the image itself.

Table 11.5 summarizes the best regression models used for AGB estimation in the selected study areas. The beta value provided a means of measuring the relative changes in variables on a standard scale. It indicated how much change in the dependent variable was produced by a standardized change in one of the independent variables when the others were controlled. The beta values confirmed that texture was more important in Altamira than in Bragantina. It was also valuable in improving model performance in Pedras. Visually comparing AGB estimation results with TM 5-4-3 color composites indicated that a high AGB corresponds to more mature vegetation growth stages. For example, those areas where AGB was greater than 20 kg/m^2 were dominated by mature forest. Different successional forests had AGBs ranging from 0 to 20 kg/m^2.

Table 11.5
Models for Aboveground Biomass Estimation in Selected Study Areas

Study Area	Regression Models	R	Beta Value
Altamira	122.288 – 1.078*KT1 – 128.913*VARtm2_9	0.878	−0.28 (sp), −0.72 (txt)
Bragantina	64.037 – 1.651*TM 4 + 1.405*SKtm4_9	0.883	−0.76 (sp), 0.29 (txt)
Pedras	65.239 – 10.189*TM 7 – 3.816KUtm3_5	0.865	−0.58 (sp), −0.42 (txt)

R, regression coefficient; sp, spectral variables such as KT1 and TM 4 in the models; txt, texture variables used in the models.

Impacts of Biophysical Characteristics on Aboveground Biomass Estimation

The analysis described above indicates the need for separate AGB estimations for different study areas when each area has significantly different biophysical characteristics (e.g., forest stand structure, soil condition, land-use history), because they influence the reflectance captured by optical sensors. Physical and human-driven factors directly or indirectly influence the vegetation characteristics. For example, terrain aspect and slope affect sun illumination and moisture distribution which directly influence plant photosynthesis and AGB accumulation; different soil types have different physical structures and nutrient components that directly influence vegetation growth; and climate conditions, especially precipitation distribution, are important factors in vegetation vigor and distribution. Different human activities, such as road construction, selective logging, mining, and population pressure on forest resources, also influence vegetation area loss, disturbance, or fragmentation. The biophysical characteristics created by these factors affect vegetation reflectance values captured by remote-sensing sensors by influencing vegetation stand structures, species composition, and vegetation vigor, resulting in different relationships between AGB and remote-sensing variables. Table 11.6 summarizes the effects of biophysical characteristics on AGB and TM data relationships in the selected study areas.

In Altamira, because of the overall high soil fertility and relatively short land-use history, vegetation growth is fast, developing complex stand structures and species composition in a relatively short time. Conversely, poor soil conditions and a long

Table 11.6
Effects of Biophysical Characteristics on Aboveground Biomass and Thematic Mapper Data Relationships

Characteristics	Altamira	Pedras	Bragantina
Overall soil fertility	***	**	*
Land-use history	*	***	***
Vegetation stand structures	***	***	**
Vegetation species composition	***	***	**
Significance of correlations between AGB and			
(1) TM bands	*	**	***
(2) Vegetation indices	*	**	***
(3) Textures	***	**	*

AGB, aboveground biomass.
Note: The higher number of asterisks indicates higher soil fertility, or longer land-use history, or more complex stand structures, or richer species, or more significant correlation.

land-use history in Bragantina result in a slow vegetation growth rate and relatively less complex stand structures and species composition. Such different biophysical characteristics lead to different relationships between AGB and image data. Better understanding of such relationships is valuable in determining the remote-sensing variables that are most appropriate to use for AGB estimation or vegetation classification in a given study area. For example, in a study area with slower vegetation growth rates, *spectral signatures* are important in AGB estimation, while in a study area like Altamira the importance of *textures* in improving AGB estimation performance is significant.

Figure 11.2 illustrates the change in soil fertility with soil depth in different succession stages in the selected study areas. Altamira has much higher SEF values in different successional stages than Pedras and Bragantina. Bragantina has the lowest SEF values. Figures 11.3 and 11.4 show the soil fertility and successional forest biomass growth rate relationships at various depths from the soil surface. The three selected study areas have very different soil fertilities and associated biomass growth rates. Altamira has the highest biomass growth rate and soil fertility value, and Bragantina has the lowest. Earlier work also confirmed that the soil condition is an important factor in succession growth rates (E. Moran and Brondízio 1998; J. Tucker et al. 1998; E. Moran et al. 2000a,b). Figure 11.5 indicates that at the same fallow age Altamira has more AGB than Pedras and Bragantina in different successional stages. This trend is especially obvious at older ages.

Our field studies involve lengthy interviews with farmers to reconstruct land-use history. We use schedules of annual shifts in land use and remotely sensed images to further aid the memory of the participant during the interview. These conversations have led to very precise accounting of land-cover changes. In Bragantina, specific types of land-use history on nutrient-poor oxisols and ultisols induce slow vegetation growth rates, but in Altamira, a relatively short land-use history in nutrient-rich and clay-rich alfisols is one of the factors leading to high vegetation growth rates. Pedras has a faster vegetation growth rate than Bragantina due to a combination of relatively better soil conditions and longer fallow cycles when compared with Bragantina. Earlier work has shown that previous land use has a significant impact on later land cover, including biomass change through time (Uhl 1987; Dantas 1988; Brondízio et al. 1996; E. Moran et al. 1996, 2000b). Biomass regrowth is fast if an area is cut and burned but never planted (Dantas 1988). Biomass accumulation is fast if an area is manually cleared and planted for a short period and then abandoned. In mechanized areas, not only is regrowth of biomass slow but the composition of vegetation will be much different from the original

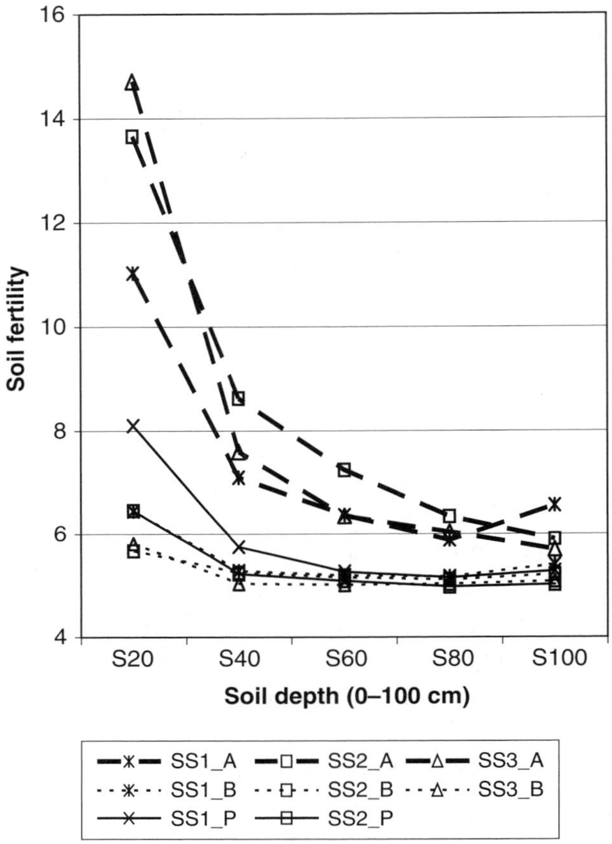

Figure 11.2
Comparison of soil fertility in Altamira (A), Bragantina (B), and Pedras (P). SS1, initial secondary succession; SS2, intermediate secondary succession; SS3, advanced secondary succession.

vegetation. Thus, land use is a major determinant in both the species composition of biomass and in its rate of regrowth.

Selective logging varies in its impact, but mortality rates of surrounding vegetation can be high despite removal of only small amounts of biomass. More important, selective logging results in accumulation of dead biomass, thereby increasing the flammability of forest during dry episodes or from nearby burning of pastures. Studies suggest that in areas where both farming and selective logging are taking place, as much as 60 percent of the burned areas are a result of unintentional fires (Cochrane and Schulze 1998; Nepstad et al. 1999; Sorrensen 2000).

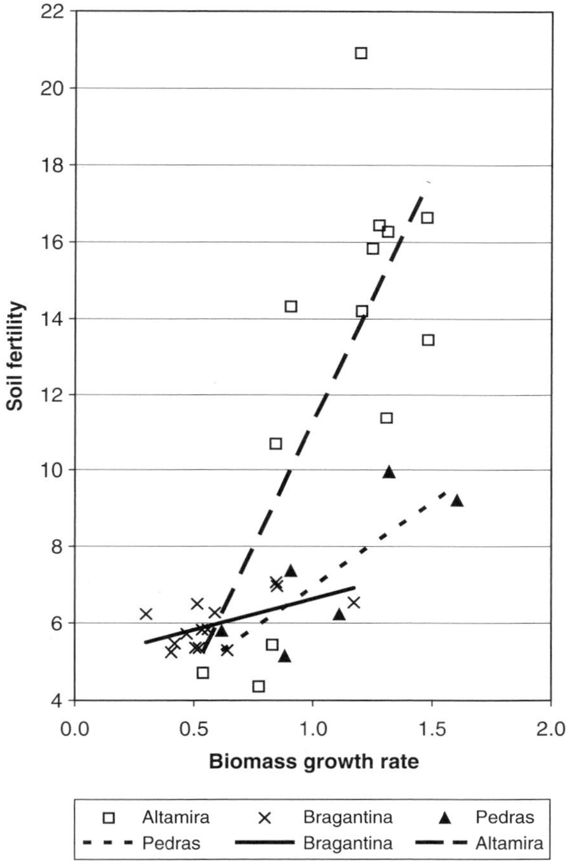

Figure 11.3
Relationships between soil fertility and successional forest biomass growth rate (kg/m^2 per year) at the soil surface (0–20 cm).

Table 11.7 provides a comparison of secondary succession forest stand structures among selected study areas. Although the AGB amounts in selected sample sites are similar, the successional forest age and density vary greatly because of their different soil conditions and land-use histories. Comparing tree dbh and height distributions, Altamira has more complex, multilayered stand structures with different dbh and height distributions, while Bragantina has more trees dominating the canopy. This indicates that Altamira is likely to present more canopy shadowing. A marked shadow problem in Altamira is an important factor in reducing the relationships between AGB and remote-sensing spectral responses. Conversely, it enhances the

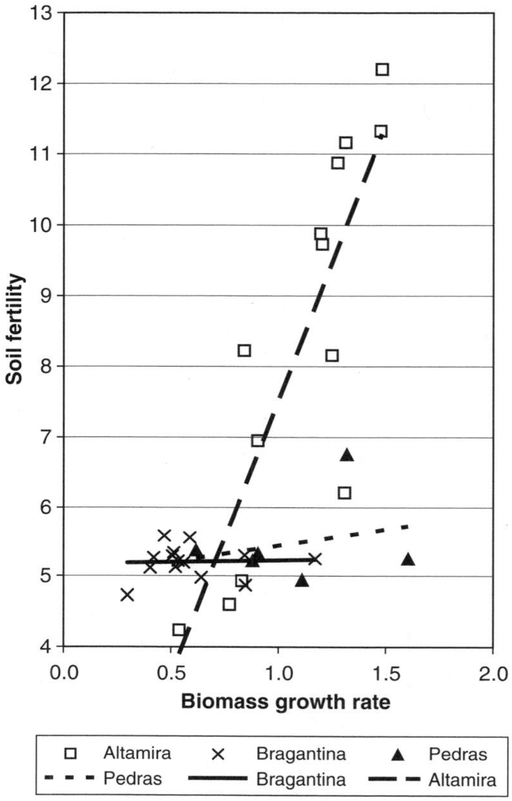

Figure 11.4
Relationships between soil fertility and successional forest biomass growth rate (kg/m^2 per year) at 20–40 cm depth from soil surface.

relationships between AGB and texture. Bragantina has less shadow, resulting in a high correlation between AGB and spectral responses, but has a lower correlation between AGB and texture.

In addition to the vegetation stand structure and species composition, vegetation density is also an important factor affecting AGB estimation. For example, when recently fallowed sites (two sites with one-year vegetation age in Altamira and two sites with two- and three-year vegetation ages in Bragantina) were excluded, the regression coefficients were improved and overall estimation biases were significantly decreased. This implies that the younger initial secondary successional forests (SS1) are the main cause of estimation bias. This is because saplings and seedlings dominate SS1 vegetation, which lacks obvious stratification of stand structure. Texture

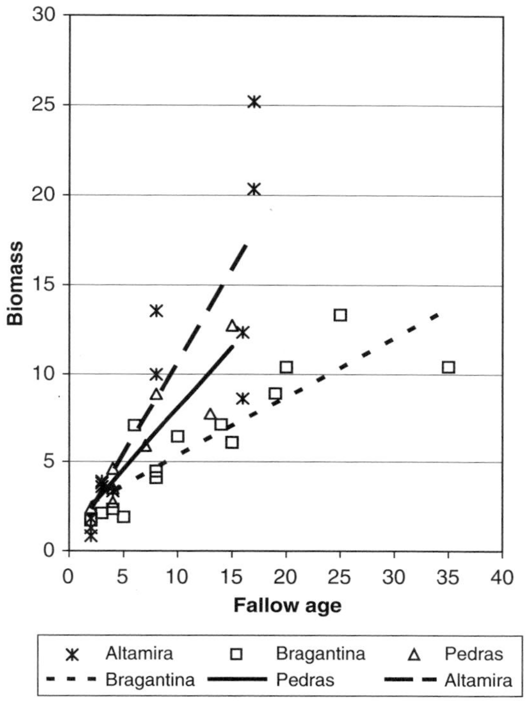

Figure 11.5
Relationships between successional forest biomass (kg/m^2 per year) and fallow age (years).

measures cannot effectively extract AGB texture information from SS1 vegetation reflectance. Another reason is that younger SS1 vegetation is not sufficiently dense to cover the ground; the information captured by the sensor is a mixture of soil and vegetation. The soil color, moisture, and mineral composition can significantly influence the reflectance of these SS1 sites. This leads to wide reflectance ranges of SS1 vegetation that result in low correlations between SS1 vegetation reflectance and SS1 biomass. Although some vegetation indices such as SAVI and MSAVI can reduce the influence of soil conditions, they are only weakly correlated with AGB because they use near-infrared (TM 4) and red (TM 3) bands, which are weakly correlated with AGB (Lu 2001).

Discussion

Different authors have arrived at different conclusions about the relationships between AGB and TM spectral responses as a result of the impact of different

Table 11.7
Distribution of Tree Diameter at Breast Height and Height among Different Successional Forests

Characteristic		Site No.					
		A013	P001	B006	A011	P004	B024
Age (yr.)		10	13	19	10	15	25
AGB (kg/m^2)		8.297	7.712	8.927	13.118	12.742	13.347
Tree density (no./ha)		6300	12027	7813	11067	7433	2300
Tree dbh distribution (tree density and percentage)	<10 cm	5600 (88.89%)	11594 (96.40%)	7400 (94.71%)	10200 (92.17%)	6786 (91.30%)	1800 (78.26%)
	10–20 cm	573 (9.10%)	347 (2.88%)	327 (4.18%)	740 (6.69%)	447 (6.01%)	273 (11.88%)
	20–30 cm	127 (2.01%)	87 (0.72%)	87 (1.11%)	67 (0.60%)	127 (1.70%)	133 (5.8%)
	>30 cm				60 (0.54%)	73 (0.99%)	93 (4.68%)
Tree height distribution (tree density and percentage)	<10 m	5954 (94.50%)	11833 (98.39%)	6873 (87.97%)	10533 (95.36%)	7000 (94.17%)	1860 (80.86%)
	10–15 m	227 (3.60%)	193 (1.61%)	940 (12.03%)	453 (4.10%)	333 (4.48%)	153 (6.66%)
	>15 m	120 (1.90%)			60 (0.54%)	100 (1.35%)	287 (12.47%)

A, Altamira; P, Pedras; B, Bragantina; AGB, aboveground biomass; dbh, diameter at breast height.
Note: Percentages show the percent of tree density in a certain dbh or height group within the total tree density.

biophysical features. For example, the correlation between AGB and near-infrared wavelength may be positive (Spanner et al. 1990), negative (Ripple et al. 1991; Danson and Curran 1993), or flat (J. Franklin 1986; Peterson et al. 1987) because of increased canopy shadowing with larger stands and decreased understory brightness (soil brightness) due to biomass increase (Horler and Ahern 1986; Spanner et al. 1990; Roy and Ravan 1996). Shadowing probably plays an important part in the response of all bands to change in wood volume (Ardo 1992) and is thought to be at least as important as canopy water content in determining the shortwave infrared response (Horler and Ahern 1986; Cohen and Spies 1992). Lu (2001) analyzed the relationships between TM spectral responses and AGB in Amazon basin sites and found that such relationships vary depending on the characteristics of the study areas. In an area like Altamira, with complex forest stand structure, TM spectral responses were not strongly correlated with AGB; band TM 5 had the relatively strongest relationship. In a study area like Bragantina with a relatively simple stand structure, TM spectral responses, especially TM 2, TM 4, and TM 5, were strongly correlated with AGB.

Although many vegetation indices have been developed and used for classification or AGB estimation (G. Anderson et al. 1993; Eastwood et al. 1997), not all vegetation indices are significantly correlated with AGB. Also, the conclusions about the vegetation indices and AGB relationships vary in previous research, depending on the data used and the characteristics of the study areas. F. Hall et al. (1995) found that NDVI was not a reliable predictor of biophysical parameters for the dominant coniferous species of boreal forests. Sader et al. (1989) found that NDVI differences were not detectable for successional forests older than approximately fifteen to twenty years. Biomass differences in young successional tropical forests were also not detectable using NDVI. Huete et al. (1997) indicated that NDVI saturated over forested areas and was sensitive to canopy background reflectance change. Boyd et al. (1996) found weak correlations between NDVI and biophysical properties in tropical forests. Lu (2001) analyzed and compared twenty-three vegetation indices in three study areas of the Amazon basin with different biophysical conditions. Three categories of vegetation indices can be roughly grouped according to their relationships with AGB (Lu 2001): (1) Vegetation indices that have stable and strong relationships with AGB are somewhat independent of biophysical features and can be used in different study areas. Such vegetation indices include KT1, PC1, MID57, and albedo. (2) Vegetation indices that have strong relationships with AGB are appropriate for use in a study area like Altamira with complex forest stand structures. Such vegetation indices are ND54, TM 5:4, and KT3. (3) Vegetation indices that have weak relationships with AGB are not appropriate for use in forest biomass research. They include most complex vegetation indices (e.g., ASVI and ARVI), NDVI, and the simple ratios that include TM 3 band (e.g., TM 5:3, TM 4:3).

To date, rarely has research focused on the use of texture in improving AGB estimation, especially for tropical successional and mature forests. Our research indicates that texture is a very important factor in improving model performance and that its importance depends on the forest stand characteristics. In practice, it is difficult to find an appropriate texture that is strongly correlated with AGB because only some textures with specific window size and image band can effectively extract AGB texture information. Purely textural information is often not sufficient to establish a model for estimating AGB with high accuracy. To effectively capture texture information, selection of an appropriate window size is very important. In theory, there should be an optimal combination of window size, image band, and texture measures to best extract textural information, but no one has found the optimal combination yet. More detailed research on extraction of texture information is needed.

Landsat TM data mainly capture the canopy information, instead of individual tree information, due to limited spatial resolution. Because of relatively low radiometric resolution (8 bit in TM data), similar stand structures, and effects of canopy shadows, mature forest often has digital number (DN) value saturation problems, although the mature forest biomass in different sites varies significantly due to different soil conditions and terrain effects. Spectral responses cannot distinguish biomass differences of mature forests in different sites; however, texture signatures have the potential to better extract biomass information. Some advanced techniques, such as linear spectral mixture analysis, can decompose the mixture spectra into different proportions of selected components and have the potential to improve biomass estimation performance (F. Hall et al. 1995; Peddle et al. 1999). Other sensor data, such as radar and hyperspectral data, probably can provide new insights into biomass estimation. Some high-resolution data such as IKONOS and Lidar data also have the potential to estimate biomass with higher accuracy, thereby providing a means to validate the results derived from TM images.

As previously indicated, physical and human driving factors can directly or indirectly affect vegetation growth rate, vegetation vigor, and species composition, thereby affecting the reflectance values that are captured by remote-sensing sensors. Therefore, a complex model that can integrate different data sources (e.g., soil and terrain data) and remotely sensed data will provide a method to estimate biomass with higher accuracy. Such a complex model is best developed through integration of GIS, remote sensing, and modeling techniques. There is a possibility that these kinds of models could be transferred directly to different study areas for biomass estimation and to multitemporal images for biomass change detection when the radiometric and atmospheric corrections are implemented. Researchers will have to pay more attention to developing such a complex model in the future.

Conclusions

Timely and accurate AGB estimation and AGB change across large areas is valuable for better understanding of land-cover changes. Remote sensing provides the best source for AGB estimation of a large area, especially for those areas where access is difficult. This research demonstrated that AGB can be estimated using Landsat TM data through integration of field inventory data and image data. Using multiple regression models has proved to be a useful approach for AGB estimation using remote-sensing variables in areas much larger than those defined by sample sites. These models take advantage of remotely sensed data (digital data format, synoptic view, etc.) to update the AGB distribution image and AGB statistical data in a timely manner. This is especially important in moist tropical areas such as the Amazon due to the difficulty in gathering ground-truthed data representative of a large area. In a study area with a complex forest stand structure, selection of an appropriate texture is very important for improving model performance. In contrast, in a study area with relatively simple forest stand structures, textures are less important than spectral signatures. The effectiveness of a texture in models is greatly dependent on vegetation stand structure. This finding, that a model comprised of spectral and textural signatures provides better AGB estimation performance, is valuable. It is useful for selecting appropriate spectral and textural signatures for developing estimation models in other study areas.

Vegetation vigor, species composition, stand structure, and associated canopy shadows are important factors in AGB estimation using remotely sensed data. Physical factors (e.g., soil fertility and types, terrain slope and aspect, climate conditions) and human-driven factors (e.g., decisions related to land use) can directly or indirectly influence vegetation characteristics. It is important to recognize the impact of differences in the biophysical features of different study areas on AGB estimation. Caution must be taken when AGB estimation models are transferred to multitemporal TM images for monitoring AGB change or cross-scene TM image for AGB estimation of a large area.

12

Cross-Continental Comparisons: Africa and Asia

Jon Unruh, Harini Nagendra, Glen M. Green, William J. McConnell, and Nathan Vogt

The research in the Western Hemisphere reported in this book has allowed for a cohesive program with a focus on forest ecosystems and has produced a sizable body of findings on human-environment interactions in forests in the Americas. Africa and Asia present different sets of challenges to understanding how human societies interact with forest resources. Significantly greater population densities exist in parts of Asia, and significantly different institutional environments can be found locally in both continents. In 2000, the Center for the Study of Institutions, Population, and Environmental Change (CIPEC) expanded its research work to sites in Asia and Africa, building on a rich array of preexisting institutional and biophysical information available from the International Forestry Resources and Institutions (IFRI) research teams working in these regions. This chapter examines the opportunities and challenges of research in Africa and Asia as compared to research in the Americas with respect to land tenure, land-cover change history, population characteristics, and other factors that impact human-environment interactions.

We selected sites in countries in eastern and southern Africa and South Asia where considerable work already had been accomplished by the IFRI research program (see chapter 4): Uganda, Madagascar, Nepal, and India. Research in these IFRI sites previously had focused on field data collection, and we expanded the scope of inquiry to include a spatially explicit dimension using geographic information systems (GIS) and remote sensing. Use of these tools followed the techniques developed for our other locations (see chapters 1, 3, 6, and 7).

A time-series analysis, combining the detailed information a community-level study provides with the synoptic spatial and temporal perspectives of remotely sensed data, offers a more comprehensive evaluation of forest change. With this in mind, we used global positioning system (GPS) units to locate the specific forests in which the earlier field research had taken place and integrated forest plot information with a Landsat image analysis to evaluate changes in forest cover under different governance regimes (Nagendra 2002; Sussman et al. 2003; McConnell et al. 2004; Nagendra et al. 2004). Integrated research of this kind provides a more robust approach for answering the often complex and multidisciplinary questions associated with forest change.

While researchers who work with a mix of remote sensing, GIS, and field data to study land-cover change would like to initiate all aspects of a study at the same time and in optimal locations, often either the fieldwork or the remote-sensing and GIS work is already underway, and the other aspect must be added. Such is the situation in our Africa and Asia research, and while incorporating preexisting work offers obvious advantages, it also entails certain challenges. Initiating research in field sites in most developing countries comes with significant costs associated with establishing local contacts and creating mutually beneficial institutional relationships. Other political, institutional, infrastructural, social, and cultural challenges range from the local to the national and require significant time, effort, and finances to learn and manage. The ability to leverage preexisting research arrangements, relationships, and knowledge, however, can offer worthwhile advantages in time savings and reduced financial outlay.

We have learned valuable lessons in linking preexisting work to new research (see chapter 6). Much of IFRI's pre-CIPEC field program for collection of information on local institutional arrangements and forest conditions was initiated before the widespread availability and affordability of handheld GPS receivers. The lack of spatial georeferencing can make direct integration of these field data particularly challenging. Sites selected for studying the impact of institutions on resource conditions are frequently constructed around specific resources and how communities access and use them. The IFRI fieldwork, which forms the foundation of our research in Asia and Africa, is locally descriptive and hence represents relatively small areas, frequently ranging from tens to hundreds of hectares. As explained in chapter 6, CIPEC primarily has relied on Landsat images, whose footprint is much larger (see figure 3.7) and covers an area of more than 3000 ha. These contrasting spatial extents pose a challenge with regard to how the two different kinds of data can inform each other. Overcoming this challenge constitutes an important aspect of studies that incorporate both social and biogeophysical datasets collected across multiple extents and durations (see chapter 9 for a discussion of intraregional comparison methods). An "ethnography of landscape" approach (Nyerges and Green 2000), based on the combination of detailed field studies with the spatial and temporal synoptic view offered by remote sensing, offers great potential for the study of forest distribution over large areas (Nagendra and Gadgil 1999; Nagendra 2001; Green et al. 2004).

The specific challenges we have faced in building on prior research analyses include determining whether forests and communities included in the earlier work are representative of a larger spatial area and assessing how processes acting in the broader area covered by satellite images can influence the character of institutions and forests studied in the earlier work. We addressed these challenges in our study countries using different approaches. For our African studies, the matching of prior field sites and satellite images took advantage of the clustering of IFRI sites in Uganda and Madagascar (figures 12.1 and 12.2) such that a single Landsat location (see chapter 6) encompassed multiple sites. In Asia, given the wide variation in topography within our study areas in the sub-Himalayan regions of Nepal and India, the sites were deliberately not clustered and chosen to include a wide range of topography, forest-cover types, and biophysical and social conditions (plate 8 and figure 12.3).

The combination of GPS location information and the volume of detailed vegetative description contained in the site-specific data added significant value to the

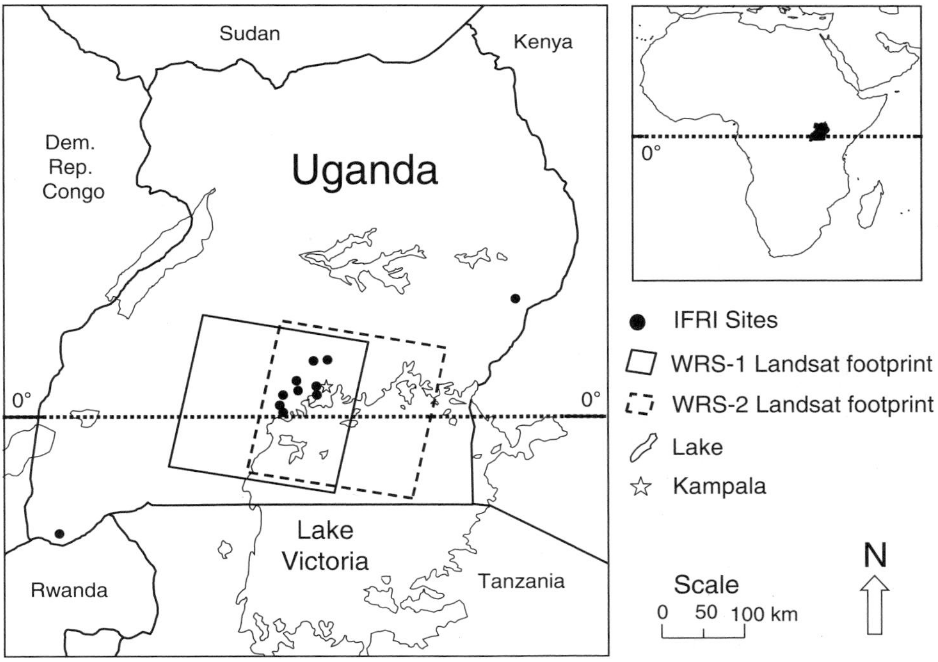

Figure 12.1
Place map of Uganda showing our Landsat study location, which covers the majority of the previously collected IFRI sites.

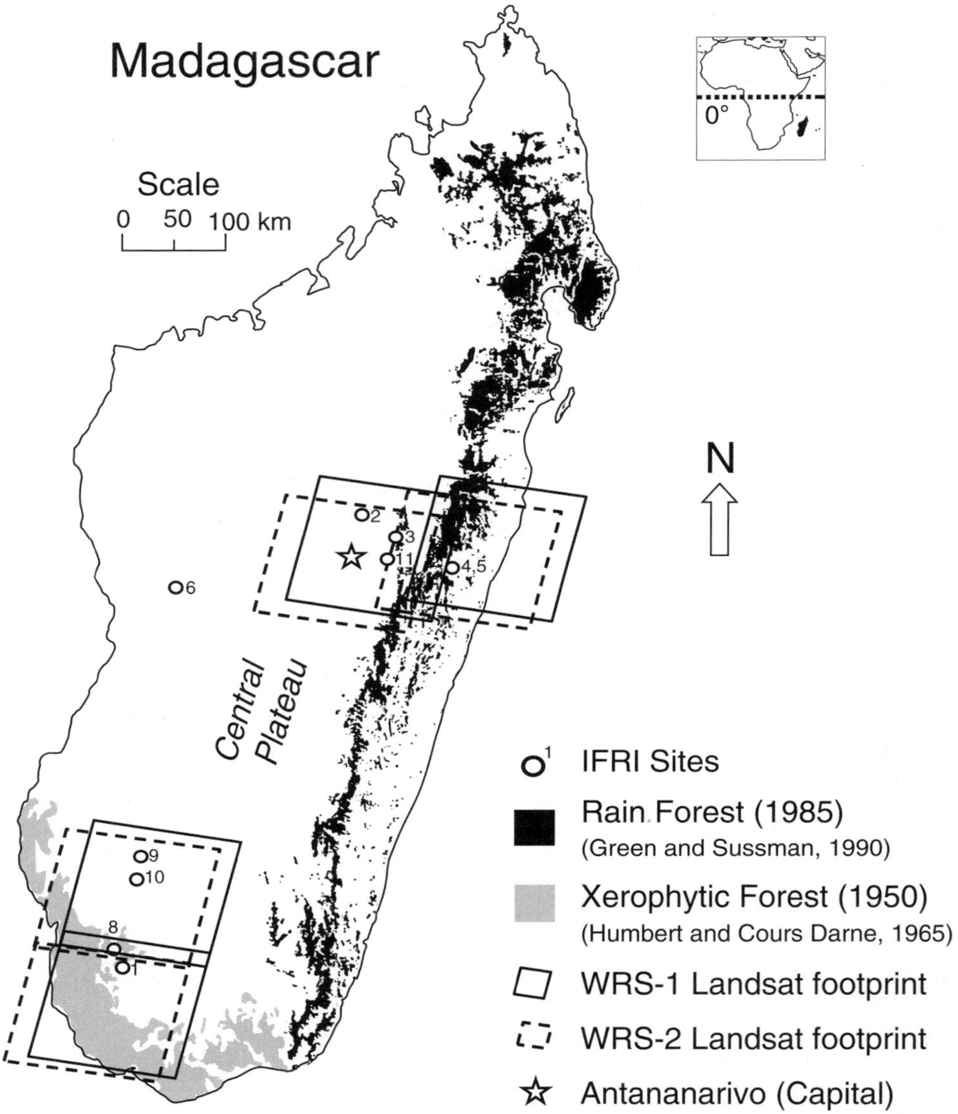

Figure 12.2
Place map of Madagascar showing two forest types: tropical moist forest as of 1985 (Green and Sussman 1990) and southern tropical dry forest (Humbert and Cours Darne 1965). Prior IFRI sites are present in several concentrated areas that are covered by two Landsat study locations.

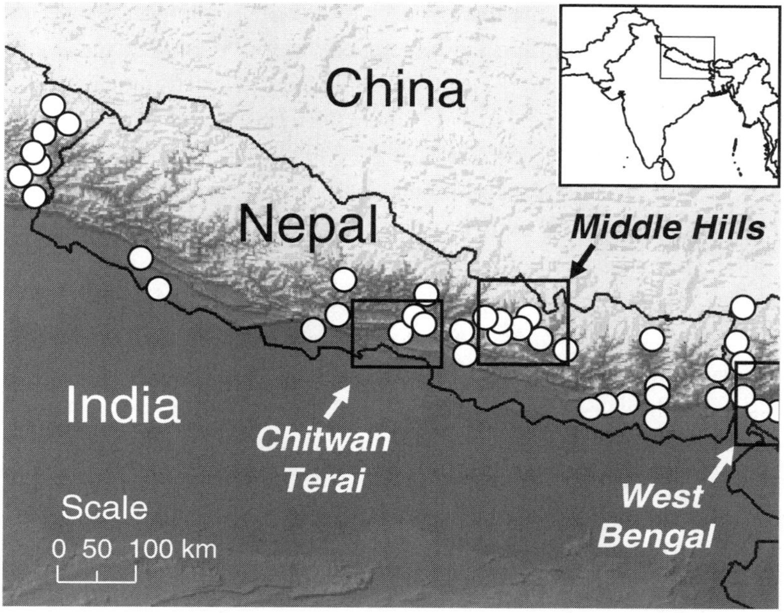

Figure 12.3
Place map of Nepal and bordering regions. Base image shows elevation where brighter tones are higher areas of the Himalayan Mountains and the Tibetan plateau. Circles represent preexisting IFRI sites; boxes show study areas covered by Landsat time-series images.

training samples used for analysis of the satellite images. While the earlier sites do not cover the full extent of the satellite images, they nonetheless provide an important entry into understanding the processes underway in the broader area, facilitating research into how local social and environmental characteristics affect the larger area and vice versa.

Research Themes and Initial Findings in Africa and Asia

Challenging the Conventional Wisdom on Land-Cover Change: The Population-Degradation Narrative

At the continental scale, Africa and Asia are characterized by very long human occupations—much longer than the Americas—and by very rapid population growth. Human-environment dynamics in Africa and Asia may thus appear to support a Malthusian connection between rapidly growing population and declining resources (see chapter 2), because forest cover is declining on both continents, while population growth rates are among the highest ever recorded. While policies rooted in assumptions of pervasively degrading landscapes due to population growth and unsustainable land use persist, recent studies have challenged a strictly linear causal relationship between them (B. Turner et al. 1993a; Batterbury and Taylor 1998; Angelsen and Kaimowitz 1999; Place and Otsuka 2000; Lambin et al. 2001; Lee and Barrett 2001; Reenberg 2001; McConnell 2002a; Nagendra and Agrawal 2004). A growing body of empirical evidence has challenged the conventional wisdom relating population increases to resource degradation, and specific case studies in Africa point to a landscape that has apparently been historically misread (Tiffen et al. 1994; Leach and Mearns 1996; McCann 1997; Gray 1999).

While the countries in which our research has been undertaken—Uganda, Madagascar, Nepal, and India—saw rapid population growth in the late twentieth century, the histories of our specific research sites reveal the significance of major migration events before, and subsequent to, European colonization. Madagascar was only settled from Indonesia around 1500 to 2000 years ago—much later than North America, first colonized by humans at least 10,000 years ago. "Stone Age" peoples in Uganda were displaced as the area was settled by "Iron Age" agriculturalist Bantu peoples from an area near present-day Nigeria only 2500 years ago.

While urban grain-growing civilizations have been documented in the Indian subcontinent since 5300 B.P., there have been successive waves of migration from different countries into India and Nepal, which continues today. There was considerable movement of ethnicities, religions, and cultures in these areas, with possibly multiple waves of deforestation and reforestation, occurring over millennia. As discussed later in the chapter, the eradication or control of diseases, including malaria and trypanosomiasis, have enabled migration into areas previously sparsely inhabited, with significant implications for forest cover.

Africa Perhaps the most well-known case of misread landscapes was documented by Fairhead and Leach (1996) in an analysis of historical aerial photographs and contemporary satellite images. Their study documented expanding forests near Kissidougou, Guinea, along a portion of the Guinea savanna-forest boundary in West Africa. Detailed land-cover histories were linked to specific land-use practices in and around village centers. Forest patches in this landscape were shown to represent anthropogenic afforestation, *not* the remnants from pervasive degradation of prior continuous forest cover as had been previously assumed. Such findings are important because they challenge the dominant paradigm established in colonial-era narratives of nearly ubiquitous African environmental degradation at the hands of local populations. Their findings also support models developed by Posey (1985), who documented similar anthropogenic forest production among the Kayapó of central Brazil. In a recent study, Nyerges and Green (2000) have contributed to this discussion by examining forest-cover change in the Kilimi area of northwestern Sierra Leone, in another part of the Guinea savanna-forest boundary. They found that while areas of forest-cover expansion do exist, the dominant land-cover change process documented by Fairhead and Leach (1996)—forest island growth from changing soil structure and fertility, seed import, and fire protection—is not universal. In South Asia, there is similar debate over evidence pointing to widespread deforestation in the sub-Himalayas, where tragic consequences (landslides and floods) often are predicted (Ives and Messerli 1989).

The debate in the literature reflects CIPEC's findings in parts of the Western Hemisphere, including Mesoamerica (see chapter 10) and Indiana (see chapters 6, 7, and 8). Similar to our Mesoamerican sites (C. Tucker et al. 2004), the long periods of human occupation and coexistence with forests in Africa, together with the variety of production systems, do not appear to fit easily into notions of either a pervasively degrading or a pervasively reforesting landscape. Instead, the landscapes are patchworks of loss *and* gain of woody biomass. As such, what are the aggregate influences, what is the aggregate direction, and, given African histories of landscape occupation, what is the appropriate time from which to begin measuring these losses and gains? CIPEC's research into these questions as they apply to Africa (and to Asia), linked with work on land-cover change in the Western Hemisphere, can contribute to a more robust understanding of the spatial and temporal forest changes.

In Uganda, we observed the long-term stability of gazetted forest reserves (forests owned by the government that are not designated as national parks) located in the West Mengo (Mpigi) region (see the online supplement to Dietz et al. 2003). Their boundaries have long been recognized and enforced and have been remarkably stable since the first aerial photographs were taken in 1955. The long-term stability of forest boundaries and cover in the forest reserves is explained primarily by the persistence of well-demarcated and enforced boundaries, continued government intolerance of conversion to agriculture, assignment of local forest rangers to implement and enforce forest department management goals (practices maintained by the postcolonial government), and the rapid canopy closure after stem removal. The poor drainage of the soils in the forest reserves also helps discourage conversion to agriculture without major technological investment. Recent increases in illegal harvesting, however, may undercut this long-term stability (Vogt 2003; Banana et al. under review).

We also observe in portions of Uganda human-forest interactions that have led to an advance of trees onto an edaphic grassland savanna, but under a mechanism different from that observed in West Africa (Vogt et al. under review). Our study covers part of Bugala Island, located within Lake Victoria. Until a few decades ago, the island was largely uninhabited due to the presence of tsetse flies, the transmitters of trypanosomiasis. Since 1980, the island has experienced a sustained increase in the number of farmers, new construction of villages and schools, and a variety of new agricultural endeavors.

We documented the advance of woody plants into grasslands (due to changing grassland utilization) and a subsequent increase in woody biomass on the agricultural landscape by combining Landsat-derived color composites with field observations. A 1995 Landsat Thematic Mapper (TM) multispectral color composite was draped over a 30-m digital elevation model (in *a* in figure 12.4). The forest-nonforest boundaries as of 1955 also are shown. In this figure, the presence of grassland is indicated by bright tones, and the forest is darker (with the darkest areas indicating recent grass burns). The figure shows that forest expanded into grassland between 1955 and 1995. An oblique aerial photograph (*b*), taken in 2001 at approximately 500 ft above ground, reveals that woody plants have continued to expand into the savanna since 1995. If past trends continue, one would expect areas with many individual small trees (*b* in figure 12.4) to be colonized by continuous forest at some date in the future.

Forest loss in Madagascar (see figure 6.4) has been well documented in both the eastern moist tropical forests (Green and Sussman 1990) and in the dry tropical forests of the south (Sussman et al. 2003), but the proposition that Malagasy forests are universally in decline has been challenged in recent years, as research reveals recent examples of increases in tree cover on the island's central plateau. For example, Kull (1998) and McConnell (2001), using aerial photographs, have found evidence of proliferation of fruit orchards and other woody species in the highlands since the 1960s, while Bertrand (1999) has documented the expansion of fuel wood plantations around the capital, Anatanarivo. Our analysis of time-series Landsat images at several IFRI sites in eastern Madagascar shows that pine, eucalyptus, cinchona, and acacia forests were found to have exhibited great dynamism (expansion and loss) over the past several decades.

Similarly, analyses of remotely sensed images and field observations in southern Madagascar show that the dry forests (see figure 12.2) have not undergone uniform change throughout the area (Clark et al. 1998; Sussman et al. 2003). While many

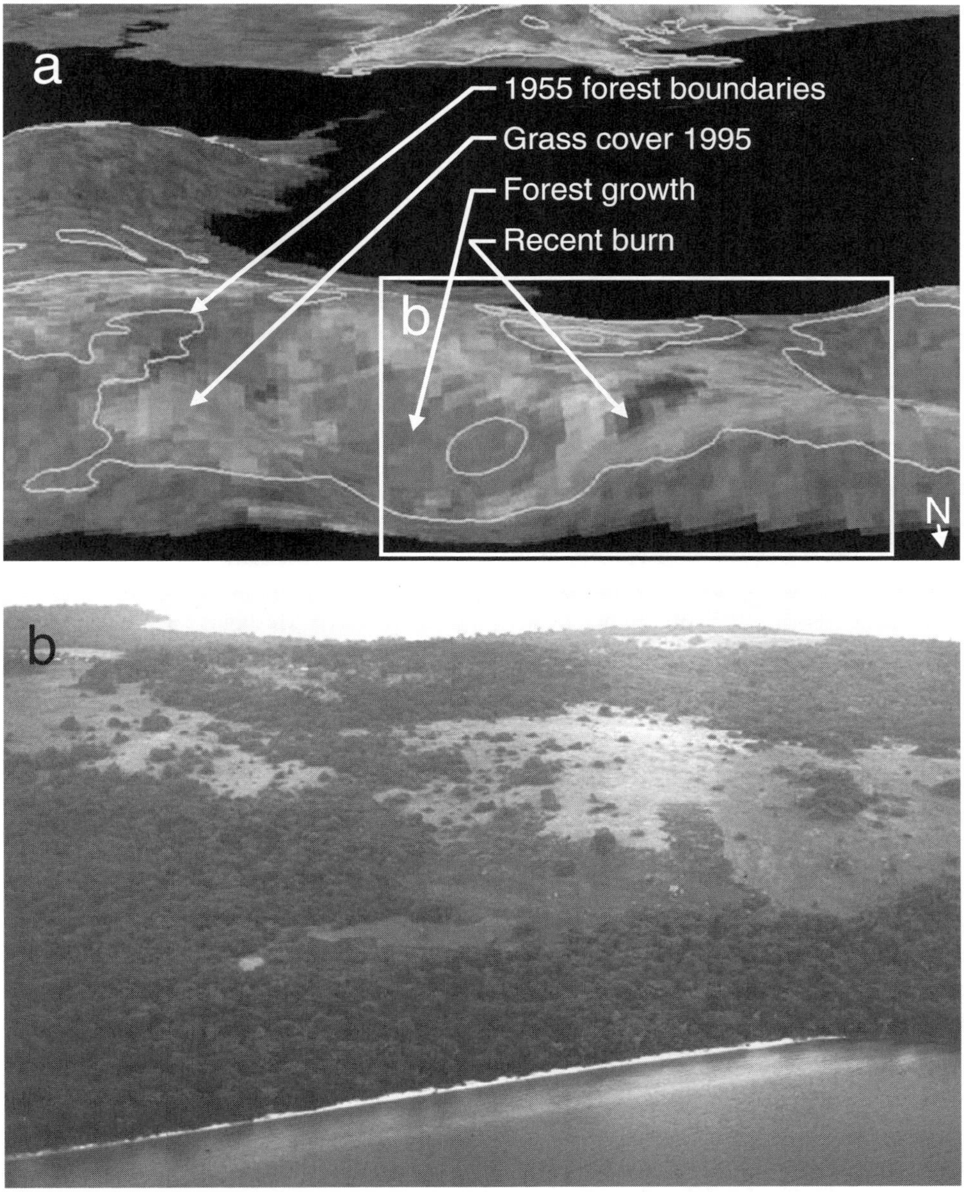

Figure 12.4
Bugala Island, Uganda: (*a*) An oblique projection of a digital elevation model draped with a Landsat multispectral composite acquired in 1995 and lines marking the forest-nonforest boundaries as of 1955. (*b*) An aerial photograph showing a similar area in 2001. These products show continued woody plant growth expanding into savanna.

forest stands have remained virtually unchanged, others have undergone massive clearing. A large number of small, circular, forested stands surrounded by cleared agricultural land on the southeastern coast of Madagascar were observed in Landsat images from 1973, 1985, and 1999. They range in size from 300 to 400 m in diameter, each covering from 7 to 13 ha (Clark et al. 1998). Multitemporal color composites show that many of these stands have not experienced significant change since 1973, and comparison with maps based on aerial photographs taken around 1950 shows that the boundaries have remained virtually unchanged during the past fifty years (Sussman et al. 2003). Further, the patches probably have existed without change for the past 300 years, because Robert Drury, who was shipwrecked there in 1701, mentions them in his journal (Drury [1729] 1970).

Dry forest clearings appear to be associated with a range of land-cover change processes, such as subsistence agriculture, commercial charcoal harvesting for a domestic urban market, and commercial agriculture for an export market (Green et al. 2004). Field observations and interviews show that the spatial and temporal patterns of these three processes are significantly different. Qualitative analysis based on interpretation of multitemporal color composites (e.g., see plates 2 and 8) indicates that clearing for subsistence agriculture in southern Madagascar has increased in the last fifty years and is not associated directly with proximity to major roads. In contrast, clearing for charcoal for cooking fuel began in the early 1970s and is associated with major roads and a nearby town. Forest clearing for corn production destined for export as cattle feed is a more recent phenomenon (since 1980), has progressed rapidly, and has occurred closer to the nearby coastal port than other types of clearing. Another short-lived deforestation episode (see plate 2) was associated with the arrival of subsistence farmers fleeing an area affected by drought (see figure 6.7). Our work also reveals the fragile nature of these dry forests (Sussman et al. 2003; Green et al. 2004)—once cut, many convert to secondary grassland.

While the various interpretations of African landscapes contribute to the development of a general understanding about how landscapes function over long periods of time and across large spatial extents, our work points out that multiple mechanisms of land-cover change acting concurrently and coevolving are more likely than a few pervasively operating mechanisms such as those described by Malthus ([1803] 1989) and Fairhead and Leach (1996). The incredible range of conditions, both social and biogeophysical, on the African continent has led to numerous, different mechanisms operating simultaneously. Policy approaches intended to address human-environment relationships will need to engage this diversity.

Asia In the sub-Himalayan region of Nepal, an intense, thirty-year debate has focused on "the theory of Himalayan degradation." Central to this debate is Huang's (1979) dramatic assertion that caught the attention of the world: Nepal had lost half its forest cover between 1950 and 1980, and unless steps were taken, there would be no accessible forests by the year 2000. Despite this alarming prediction, large parts of Nepal are still forested several years after 2000, and there is much evidence of recent reforestation (Ives and Messerli 1989). Even so, deforestation continues in accessible areas, indicating that critical gaps in knowledge exist and more studies are needed to examine land-cover change over larger areas, across a range of biophysical and ecological environments, and covering temporal durations of several decades.

Our initial analysis, in the plains and middle hills of Nepal (see figure 12.3), indicates that much deforestation has occurred since the late 1950s. In the plains, scholars have pointed to the successful efforts of the World Health Organization, the U.S. Agency for International Development, and the Nepali government to combat malaria during the late 1950s as a major cause of migration into the area from India and from the middle hills of Nepal (Bista 1991). The efforts did reduce the number of malaria infection reports, from 2 million cases a year in the 1950s to fewer than 2500 in 1968 (Jha 1993, 37). Government agencies widely publicized the successful malaria eradication program in the middle hills regions. Many land-hungry families migrated south and some families migrated north from India under resettlement programs sponsored by international donors (K. Moran 1991). The population of the Terai was estimated to grow tenfold within a decade of malaria eradication (HMG/N 1984). Even with substantial migration to the south, however, population in the middle hills also has increased substantially since the 1950s.

While substantial deforestation has been observed in many locations, we also have detected significant reforestation as well. Thus, it appears that the sub-Himalayan region is a shifting mosaic of forest loss and gain. Careful interpretation of this diversity is needed. Drawing on methods developed and used in our Mesoamerica research (Southworth et al. 2002; Nagendra et al. 2003; see also chapter 10), we find that differences in land-use/land-cover change in our Asian study sites are related to the social, institutional, and biogeophysical differences between these areas (Schweik et al. 2003; Nagendra and Schweik 2004). Our research in Indiana (see chapter 6) and Honduras (Southworth and Tucker 2001; Munroe et al. 2002; Southworth et al. 2002; see also chapter 10) has shown that surviving forests tend to be located on steeper slopes, at higher elevations, and in less accessible areas than those forests that have suffered loss. Specifically, the topography in the middle hills is much more rugged and presents far greater challenges to human movement, forest protection, and agriculture compared to the topography of the plains (see figure 12.3). In the Nepal Terai, landholdings and communities tend to be larger than those in the middle hills. Communities constitute a mix of indigenous lowland inhabitants and immigrants from the middle hills, in contrast to the relatively homogeneous inhabitants of the hill forest communities.

Our examination of the conventional wisdom concerning the fate of forests in Africa and Asia reveals pictures of considerable complexity and contributes to debunking the simplistic, Malthusian view often persisting from the colonial era. The next section describes our efforts to explain the differential role of institutions in shaping patterns of forest-cover change in these regions.

Forest Governance: Ethnic Identity, Land Tenure, Conservation, and Decentralization

Having determined that forest-cover change is not unidirectional and that observed dynamics cannot be explained simply by population pressure, our research has sought to explain the role of institutional factors in our study sites in Africa and Asia. Two fundamental, and related, differences in the experiences of European colonization and in the contemporary role of ethnic identity lead us to expect different contexts of forest governance in our Africa and Asia research sites than we have found in the Americas.

While Asia, Africa, and the Western Hemisphere all experienced colonialism, the timing, character, and outcomes of colonial occupation were quite different. At the time of independence from European rule in the Western Hemisphere, the European influence was dominant, and those countries continued to be governed by European descendants. In contrast, indigenous populations were, and continue to be, much more numerous in both Asia and Africa, and the postcolonial era saw a stronger mix of native and European cultures. In Africa, European constructs have been taken and used in African ways, and countries are governed by Africans. In parts of South Asia, including India, the culture and governance also remain Asian, but with a significant European bureaucratic logic. Nepal, with the exception of parts of the Terai, was never occupied or colonized by Europeans; however, the Nepali forest bureaucracy interacts extensively with the Indian Forest Service, and many Nepali foresters were trained in India.

Identity plays a large and pervasive role in land use in Africa and Asia, and operates in significantly different form than in the Americas. Ethnic identities in particular, but religious, geographic, and economic identities as well, often are much stronger than national identities in Africa and Asia. A. Smith (1988) noted that "the ethnic 'self' remains the fundamental territorial 'self' in Africa" (p. 78). And in many cases the existence of ethnic, religious, geographic, or other identities to which primary attachments persist can be based on connections to land, home area, or territory (Unruh 1998). Dislocation from home areas via conflict or food shortage can result in a relative rise in the influence of identity-based attachments to land, especially if there is an identity component to the dislocation event, and destination locations for migrants become problematic for reasons involving identity (Ibrahim 1998). Notions of identity also can involve land claim justifications based on earlier historical occupation. Migrants can then seek out such areas as destination locations, supported by oral histories that can be traced back through time into mythologies about how various peoples came to exist in an area and in the world (Comaroff and Roberts 1977). Such justification can gain renewed strength during dislocation and migration, and the pursuit of a return to historical lands or territory—from which groups were expelled or departed, recently or long ago—can become a priority in a migration event (Unruh 2003). In some cases, such a situation can be seen as a singular opportunity to regain historical lands. In such a context the viability of institutions for rational management of forest resources can be extremely problematic, as various groups, including the state, vie for control of areas and resources.

In many parts of Africa and Asia, customary tenure continues to shape land-use practices, sometimes in tenuous balance with formal, state-sanctioned land rights. At the same time, the effectiveness of major investments in the creation and maintenance of conservation areas in both continents has been questioned. Both of these issues are intertwined with efforts to decentralize control of forest resources. Our research examined (1) different institutional arrangements as mediated by the relationships between customary and formal tenure regimes; (2) the relationship between local community use of forest products and conservation objectives; (3) local attempts to devolve rights from the formal domain to the customary; and (4) the conditions, constraints, and opportunities that ecotourism can provide in the management of forests.

Africa In the Mpigi District in Uganda, boundaries of gazetted forests have long been recognized and enforced, and have been remarkably stable. Agreements between the British colonial government and the regents of the Buganda Kingdom in 1900 and 1907 established a process to register private land parcels, referred to as *mailo* land, as well as the gazetted forests. In the 1930s and 1940s, the gazetted forest reserve boundaries were demarcated with earth cairns and the traditional boundary tree or shrub planted at each cairn. Relevant mailo owners and traditional administrators were present during the process of demarcation to ensure agreement on the locations of the gazetted reserve boundaries. Since the 1930s, the Ugandan Forest Department has periodically remarked these boundaries. Conversion of gazetted forest reserves to other purposes is consistently prosecuted even though some charcoal harvesting in small areas may be tolerated by government officials (Vogt 2003). A study comparing IFRI field measures obtained from nine forests in the Mpigi District in 1995 with similar measures obtained in 2000 after a major reduction in the local staff of the forest department, however, did reveal deterioration in biomass, basal area, and stem density due to increased levels of tree harvesting (Banana et al. under review).

Expanding forest cover on Bugala Island is also closely linked to institutional factors. The explanation for the advance of agriculture into grasslands, while nearby forests exhibit less clearing, is found in the differences in land tenure between the two categories of land. While both categories are mailo land (customarily based), significant enforcement exists in the form of rules against the clearing of forest for agriculture, while similar rules protecting grasslands are not enforced nearly as strictly. The observed agricultural encroachment has resulted, and with it trees have spread into the grassland (see figure 12.4).

In Madagascar, preservation of parks is a national priority due to global interest in certain fauna species, particularly lemurs (Sussman et al. 2003), and a number of changes in national policy seem to have played a significant role through time. In the eastern moist tropical forest of Madagascar, our analyses have demonstrated the effectiveness of the Mantadia National Park in halting deforestation, while nearby forests continued to be cleared for agriculture (McConnell 2002a,b; McConnell et al. 2004). Subsequent examination of other forms of forest governance revealed mixed success in preventing forest conversion. A Landsat image time-series analysis suggests that variable rates of change are related to the history of national forest policy and the resulting enforcement activities. The studied forests that are favorably located for generating tourist revenue or have enjoyed substantial external investment appear to have stable or growing forested areas compared to private forests and to more distant government forests in which fewer resources are available.

The many isolated stands of tropical dry forest, mentioned earlier, in the southern part of Madagascar appear to be protected by local institutions (see the online supplement to Dietz et al. 2003). Landsat multitemporal color composites and aerial photographs reveal that many of these forests have enjoyed this protection for at least fifty years (Green et al. 2004). Referred to as *fady* or taboo forests, local Antandroy peoples have maintained several hundred forest remnants as sacred areas (Elmqvist 2004) that often protect grave sites. Engström (2001) found more than 1400 of these forest patches evenly distributed throughout the area, but they covered only 4 percent of the total area in the author's analysis. Drury ([1729] 1970) mentioned the sacred grave sites of this region in his journal. Thus, these sacred forests may have been respected by the local people and protected by communal institutions for more than 300 years.

Asia In large parts of Nepal and India, the protected areas have remained relatively well forested in the face of increasing population pressure. Data from three IFRI sites in the Chitwan District provided us with information on seven forest patches in three different institutional categories: (1) a protected area (the Royal Chitwan National Park), (2) national forests, and (3) areas recently handed over to local users as community forests. All seven forest patches are dominated by *Shorea robusta*, an important tropical moist deciduous hardwood tree. A total of 69 forest sample plots had been laid out in the community forests, 102 plots in national forests, and 45 plots in the national park (see chapters 4 and 5 for a description of plots in IFRI research). Analysis of the forest plot data revealed that, on average, vegetation density and species diversity in the community forests in the heavily populated Terai region were lower than in the national forests, which in turn were in poorer condition than the forests within comanaged buffer zones at the edges of the national park (Nagendra 2002). Research conducted in the middle hills, however, has documented community forests in much better condition (Varughese and Ostrom 2001). The high levels of biodiversity and biomass found in the protected national park were not surprising, given the manpower and external resources available for preserving the area from human use. Without the same levels of manpower and resources, it is doubtful other areas of the Terai could expect similar results. The fact that areas in poorer condition are handed over to local communities to be managed as community forests (while the forests with greater vegetation density and biodiversity are retained by the forest department as national forests under their control) signify the largely top-down nature of these reforms and may indicate a lack of devolution of power to local communities.

In recent years, buffer-zone development projects near protected areas in Nepal and India have sought to provide economic benefits to the local communities through ecotourism, but there is a lack of empirical examination of the effect of these innovative approaches on forest regeneration. However, our image analysis (see plate 8) in the Nepal Terai demonstrates that these policies have led to a dramatic increase in forest cover in the buffer zone of the Royal Chitwan National Park during the past decade (Schweik et al. 2003; Nagendra and Schweik 2004).

For the Chitwan District, an initial proof-of-concept methodology was developed and evaluated to locate reforestation anomalies where effective institutions of forest management have impacted forest regrowth significantly. Our methodology combines deforestation theory with satellite image change analysis to identify forest patches that are inconsistent with forest patterns observed across a larger spatial extent (see also an example from Indiana in chapter 6). Based on CIPEC research on processes leading to deforestation in Honduras (Nagendra et al. 2003), an analysis of deforestation literature, and our knowledge of the landscape, we identified elevation and distance from roads as two variables that are significantly associated with forest cover in the study area. A multitemporal color composite derived from three nearly cloud-free Landsat images from 1976 (Multispectral Scanner), 1989 (TM), and 2000 (Enhanced Thematic Mapper Plus) were examined together with a GIS database on roads and a visual estimation of topography to identify ten forest anomalies (blue and green areas in plate 8). Many of these areas had maintained or regenerated tree cover between 1989 and 2000 despite their locations in areas at low elevation and their proximity to roads (Schweik et al. 2003).

A rapid field reconnaissance was undertaken to determine which of these forest anomalies exhibit interesting management innovations. The anomalies we identified fall into three institutional categories: (1) state government command and control, (2) profitable private plantations, and (3) common-property community management. While both state protection and private plantations have the potential to promote regrowth and generate resources, they are, by their very nature, not necessarily equitable forms of resource sharing. Thus, the most interesting of these, from the perspective of identifying common-pool resource institutions that have potential for sustainable and equitable management, are several forest patches adjoining the Royal Chitwan National Park (see plate 8). These patches fall within the buffer-zone community forestry program and are managed by the forest user communities that derive income from ecotourism (Schweik et al. 2003). We selected one of these forest patches for detailed field study, and it turned out to be a major case of community forestry and a premier ecotourism initiative that we were not aware of until we undertook this analysis. However, further field research and interviews with user groups indicated that this particular forest management approach is being implemented in a fairly top-down manner.

This methodology allows us to sample a diverse array of land-use/land-cover change patterns and institutional regimes. Thus, we are able to quickly identify areas that have potentially important institutional configurations and to more thoroughly document those institutional arrangements using field studies. Since we know the anomalies do not follow broader deforestation patterns, such as those associated with proximity to roads and population growth dynamics, this finding lends strong support to the hypothesis that institutional arrangements can have significant influence in shaping land-cover change. This methodology also can help to quickly generate or refine hypotheses on what types of institutional arrangements lead to which patterns of land-cover change and, in turn, could facilitate studies using random sampling approaches that provide more variation in dependent and independent variables.

Among developing countries, Nepal has become an enthusiastic leader in setting conservation goals and priorities and experimenting with participatory systems of forest governance (Agrawal et al. 1999). CIPEC research examining the effect of these policies on forest-cover change has enabled us to compare our findings with ongoing analyses of decentralization in a very different context in Bolivia and Guatemala.

Before the mid-1950s, traditional practices of forest management were prevalent in the middle hills of Nepal. The Nationalization Act of 1957 brought all forested land under government ownership. As in many other developing countries, the process of nationalization in Nepal converted many limited-access, community-controlled forests to open-access resources (NRC 1986). This loss of ownership by local communities resulted in increased levels of deforestation in several national forests. Subsequent forest acts have attempted to return some degree of ownership and control of forest resources to the people. By 1999, over 620,000 ha of forest area had been handed over to 8500 forest user groups. The most vigorous implementation of these policies has been in the middle hills, where 83 percent of community forests are located (Chakraborty 2001). In contrast, only 17 percent of all community forests are located in the Nepal Terai, and doubts have been expressed about the feasibility of expanding community forestry in this region (Schweik 2000). Problems of implementing community forestry are mostly related to differences in the topography and history of settlement between the Terai and the middle hills. While the middle hills have supported local populations for centuries, the Terai has experienced extensive in-migration since the eradication of malaria in the 1960s, and recent deforestation has resulted (Schweik et al. 1997; Matthews et al. 2000). Relatively low forest resource usage prior to the 1960s minimized the need for traditional systems of forest protection, and the challenge for community forestry in the Terai now is to support the creation of new institutions of community forest management that can manage effectively with the increased demand.

The contrast between the relationship of recent migrants to the forest and indigenous users' perceptions of the forest (also seen in other CIPEC sites in Africa and the Americas with long histories of indigenous use)—as a living resource with spirits, gods, and a variety of resources to be used but also protected for future generations—has led to significant conflicts. The conflict over land between the various ethnic groups that have moved to the Terai from the middle hills and the indigenous, long-term residents of the region, such as the Tharus, was substantial. Families who had lived in the region for centuries, but had not registered their land under new legislation, were evicted from the traditional homesteads and villages (Jha 1993).

Our research in Nepal has thus enabled us to gauge the extent to which these approaches toward decentralization actually have been implemented on the ground and to evaluate their effectiveness. While the Nepal government has developed innovative programs of community-based forest management, concerns have been raised about the actual levels of devolution. Although several studies argue that community forestry has been successful in improving the conditions of the people and forests in the Nepal middle hills (Gautam et al. 2002; also summarized in Chakraborty 2001), the effectiveness of community forestry in the Nepal Terai is being questioned (Schweik 2000). With forest users and the Nepali government taking opposite sides, the debate would benefit from careful empirical evaluation.

In contrast to Nepal, decentralization of forest management via the Joint Forest Management program in India has involved far less devolution of power (Agrawal and Ostrom 2001; Sundar et al. 2001). The existence of IFRI sites in similar biophysical and ecological regimes in the sub-Himalayan regions of India and Nepal sets the initial agenda for comparative analysis of decentralization policies in these two countries. With over fifty IFRI sites in the sub-Himalayan region of South Asia, the incorporation of remotely sensed time-series analyses will allow us to carry out a careful empirical examination of the outcome of policies of decentralization on local institutions and forest-cover change.

Lessons from the Africa and Asia Work

CIPEC's research in Africa and Asia demonstrates that forest loss is NOT an inevitable result of population growth. At our sites in Uganda, Madagascar, India, and

Nepal, we find institutional regimes assuring the stability, and even expansion, of forest cover despite rapid population growth at the national level. We find significant deforestation events often associated with specific biophysical and social factors. While the number and distribution of our studies do not enable us to offer general propositions about forest dynamics, they do contribute to a growing understanding of the topic that appears headed toward a coherent framework of understanding.

Several different institutional regimes provide evidence of successful governance of forest resources in our study sites, including management regimes rooted in ethnic traditions, as well as state-sponsored (and internationally assisted) conservation regimes, especially when local communities are given the opportunity to benefit from tourism-based revenues. A number of cases have been identified as successfully managed private forest plantations, at least as judged by the stability or expansion of tree canopy over time. By contrast, large forest resources held under the centralized control of national agencies with insufficient resources, and thus inadequate monitoring of forest boundaries, appear in many cases to have been subject to considerable loss of forest cover. These findings underline the importance of careful examination of comanagement arrangements that take advantage of not only professional expertise and external resources but also of the ability of local communities to assure the monitoring and maintenance of forest resources.

Future Directions of CIPEC Research in Africa and Asia: Social Phenomena Different from Those in the Western Hemisphere and Their Interaction with Forest Use

An issue of particular importance in future research in Africa and Asia is the conflict and resulting displacement of people. It is our intention to pursue this issue in our ongoing research in these regions.

Conflict and Refugees

In recent decades, refugees have become a significant aspect of African land-cover and institutional change, and complicate research on the interaction of institutions and forest-cover and environmental change. Postindependence conflict, drought, floods, and famines have produced ongoing forced dislocations in Africa (Unruh 1993) not comparable in magnitude or character with events in the Western Hemisphere. While the dislocated people who cross international borders are labeled as refugees and qualify for international assistance and are often settled in organized camps or settlements, the number of internally dislocated people is often much higher and the latter are rarely resettled in any organized fashion. The differences in terms of land-cover change and change in institutions are large (Unruh 1993; Unruh and Lefebvre 1995). First, migrations due to forced dislocation disrupt resource use at both source and destination locations, with influences on institutions and land-cover change. E. Ostrom et al. (1999) make the point that if resource users are added rapidly, such as through migration, local communities and migrants will not share similar understandings of resources and resource use and access.

Second, how refugees settle in destination areas can have a significant influence on land-cover change. Different patterns can emerge from modes of settlement, including (1) in refugee camps or other concentrated areas, (2) in scattered locations within the host community, or (3) scattered in a wide rural area in and around the host area. Concentrated settlement of migrants for reasons of security, humanitarian concern, or resource availability can encourage forms of resource use that are more competitive and contentious (Unruh 1993, 1995b; Ghimire 1994), and lead to spatially acute forms of resource degradation (land, fuel wood, timber, water, etc.) (Unruh 1993; McGregor 1994). Decisions about where government and donors locate concentrations of refugees are rarely made with local community consultation, compensation, or coordination, especially with regard to how land is accessed and used.

Settlement of refugees in a more dispersed fashion within a local community results in differentiated approaches to land-cover change. While a good relationship (ethnic, religious, economic, etc.) between host and refugee populations may result in secure access to land-based resources (K. Wilson 1992) and more rational and conservative land resource use, this is frequently difficult to achieve. Refugees can derive their own forms of land claim and access in reaction to rules of exclusion by local communities or exclusion from the institutions which facilitate an equitable place in the local (host) land tenure system (Unruh 1993, 1995a). Such alternative forms of claim and access can frequently result in land being cleared purely for the sake of claim. Often local rules of exclusion are constructed and enforced with regard to refugees in an attempt by the local community to avoid resource degradation and a "tragedy of the commons" scenario. Such exclusion often can be facilitated by the weak position of refugees vis-à-vis local communities (socially, economically, and politically) (Ghimire 1994). However, with resource needs and desperation frequently high among refugees, alternative ways, reasons, and legitimacy can quickly be configured in reaction to exclusion, competition, and confrontation with local communities (Unruh 2003). Where refugees are able to engage local (host) resource access and use arrangements, subsets of local rules—special rules that provide limited rights for refugees—can be set up.

In Asia, the influx of refugees from political conflicts, famines, and floods, although far less in the India-Nepal context when compared to Africa, nonetheless pose significant challenges to the study of land-cover change. For instance, a significant influx of political refugees from Bhutan has placed additional pressure on already scarce forest resources in the east-west Nepal-India border areas. The tragic violence that has erupted in Nepal during the last decade is creating a new generation of homeless people, many of whom have migrated out of the rural areas to Kathmandu.

The influence of conflict and security issues on environmental change constitutes a significant domain of study. Conflict and insecurity, especially in Africa, operate in such a pervasive and ongoing fashion as to profoundly disrupt the human ecology of millions of people over very large areas (O. Bennett 1993; Unruh 1995a,b, 2002). The forces of conflict, insecurity, and resource degradation in such disruptions operate in mutually reinforcing ways (Homer-Dixon 1990; Unruh 1993, 1995b, 2003). Because few civil institutions can endure the stresses of armed conflict (E. Ostrom et al. 1999), much of the environmental repercussions from conflict and insecurity can be linked to institutional breakdown, malfunction, and absence, as well as attempts to impose alternative ways of ordering access and use of land resources. For example, the recent violent conflicts in Nepal have had an adverse impact on forest and animal conservation, with increased illegal timber extraction and smuggling, and wildlife poaching. Apart from the institutions of resource use that are directly affected, repercussions on economies, migration, food security, law, and the activities of the international community also affect local to national institutions and systems of resource use and claim. The role of conflict and insecurity in environmental change is likely to become more prominent in the future, given the general recognition that future instability will often be manifest as low-intensity conflicts within, rather than between, nations, with the origins of conflict buried deep within the aggravating problems of inequitable access to resources, including, and often especially, land resources (Creveld 1991; Homer-Dixon 1991; Crocker and Hampson 1996; Sahnoun 1996; Unruh 2001, 2003).

Conclusion

As work in Asia and Africa proceeds, we envision the challenge of the expansion to provide valuable lessons for the conduct of significant aspects of human-environment interactions research. The need to tie remote sensing to preexisting, local-level field research in a way that the two are able to bring more meaning to each other reflects in significant ways the realities of pursuing such research. Opportunities to bring either remote sensing to preexisting field research, or the reverse, will in all likelihood be more frequent in human-environment interactions research, as this is more cost- and time-effective than initiating new research that combines these two aspects from the beginning. We see this as a significant contribution of the Africa and Asia work. In this regard borrowing from other approaches, such as that described for meta-analysis in chapter 13, may provide significant utility.

The different local contexts, histories, and social issues in Africa and Asia, compared to the Western Hemisphere, provide an important opportunity to extend our research on human-environment linkages to these different continents. How the processes of settlement and movement, as well as the constraints and opportunities of different economic, political, and cultural conditions, become manifest with regard to land-cover change will provide important insights into the fundamentals of processes, as well as highlight differences and similarities in potential policy approaches. The initial work in Africa and Asia demonstrates that there is substantive variation between countries and regions based on differences in history and in local socio-economic, political, and biophysical contexts. This hints at the different approaches that are needed in the policy domain regarding workable arrangements for resource management, development, and participation in global efforts at mitigating the effects of global environmental change.

13

Meta-Analysis of Agricultural Change

William J. McConnell and Eric Keys

A variety of approaches have been used to assess the causes behind observed spatio-temporal patterns of land-use change. These efforts have largely been focused on a few key outcomes, such as the removal of forest cover, agricultural change, and urban expansion. Of course these processes are closely related, as conversion to agricultural uses accounts for a significant portion of forest loss. A wide range of contextual and causal factors, both slow-moving and "triggers," have been analyzed from both the biophysical and socioeconomic realms to explain the location and pace of such change. Such efforts generally follow one of two approaches: (1) broad cross-sectional techniques and (2) fine-scale case studies. Intermediate analyses that combine the richness of case studies with the power of generalization gained from larger samples are rarer. This chapter explores the advantages and disadvantages of this intermediate approach and presents results from one such effort, focused on trajectories of agricultural change in the tropics based on the comparative analysis of existing case study literature.

The study of agricultural change constitutes a significant portion of the research in human-environment relations described in chapter 2, and can largely be situated within the theoretical frameworks outlined therein. The fundamental questions driving agricultural change research concern the ability of societies to produce sufficient agricultural products under changing conditions, such as land scarcity related to demographic growth, or environmental change. Whether from a neo-Malthusian or Boserupian stance, scholars have explored the conditions under which new agricultural practices are devised and diffused, focusing variously on environmental, technical, financial, sociocultural, and other sets of constraints and opportunities faced by farmers.

The IPAT formulation described in chapter 2 suggests the panoply of right-side factors (population, affluence, technology) addressed. Each of these has been unpacked in the literature into a broad range of variables. The simplification of the left-side term (impact) is particularly problematic in the study of agricultural change. Scholars from different disciplines studying agricultural systems around the world have focused on a wide variety of outcomes, usually increases in inputs (land, labor, capital, technology) or outputs (production per unit of time per unit of input). The multiphasic response to population pressure has been a bulwark of agricultural change studies exploring why some production increases are achieved through the adoption of irrigation, animal traction, or new cultivars, while others are marked by stagnation, degradation, and impoverishment. Structural explanations have been a mainstay of agricultural change research, implicating external, often financial, factors that impede innovation or adoption in some situations or encourage it in others. The analysis described in this chapter constitutes a structured, comparative approach to discern the relative importance of these causal factors.

Local Case Studies and National Cross-Sectional Analysis

In-depth case studies capture a wealth of detail about fairly geographically restricted areas, striving to understand precisely what land change occurred as well as the context and the particular factors, events, or triggers that accounted for the observed changes. A century of investment has been made in field studies along these lines by anthropologists, geographers, sociologists and others. Such research is generally conducted against the background of existing theories of land change, presented in chapter 2. In many instances this approach has been adopted in order to test theories explicitly. While this may allow for the confirmation or refutation of such theories at particular locales, the very strength of the approach—the tailoring of the inquiry to specific local conditions—works against its use for general theory development. Since it requires a huge investment in research in situ, only a small number of studies can be carried out (typically as dissertations). Opposing arguments claim, sometimes justifiably, that the places studied are unique and that results therefore cannot be extrapolated. The utility of these one-dimensional critiques is limited, however, as the most common outcome of them is the claim that the human-environment processes under study are simply too complex to support robust generalization.

At the broadest scale, the whole earth may be studied by using, of necessity, coarse units of analysis. The growing availability of national-level data on both types of variables—dependent (land change) and independent (e.g., demographic or economic change)—means that such results are becoming ever more robust (Rudel 1989; Rudel and Roper 1996, 1997). Nevertheless, several major weaknesses attend this approach. Most important, gross aggregation of patterns at the national, decadal scale masks much of the interesting variation in both dependent and independent variables. So, while some parts of a country may be undergoing substantial deforestation, another region may experience forestation (see chapter 10). Conflating these processes and their causes weakens the resulting analysis. Moreover, the datasets upon which such analyses are carried out are known to suffer from lack of comparability (e.g., in the definition of forest) and from low reliability (e.g., population censuses of varying, and often unknown, reliability).

The limitations of each of these approaches have led scholars to explore a middle ground that shares the benefits of both, while minimizing their weaknesses. Two techniques are possible for comparative analyses that are broad enough to support generalization, but fine enough to capture key variability. The first is to conduct a set of standardized case studies, wherein a common set of variables is collected at a representative sample of locales, according to common protocols that can support inferential statistical modeling. This approach has been successfully applied to land-change questions in work aimed at identifying regions at risk of environmental change (Kasperson et al. 1995) and at exploring the relationship between population growth and agricultural change (B. Turner et al. 1993a; Tri-Academy 2001). The development of a fresh set of in-depth case studies focused on forest-cover dynamics is at the heart of all cases in this book. The comparative analyses in part IV identify the role of particular factors in shaping land-change trajectories across research sites, where other factors may be held constant. As described in those chapters, the approach is quite time-consuming and expensive; as the area of interest expands it becomes increasingly difficult to hold other factors constant.

The complementary approach described here—the systematic comparison of case studies in the literature—can illuminate the factors that have been found important in different cases, and specify the ways in which these factors have traditionally been studied at different times, in different regions, and from the perspectives of different disciplines. This can help place the in-depth case studies in a broader context and provide key information for the design of future research that will be amenable to comparative analysis.

Comparative Analysis of Extant Case Studies: The Approach

Colleagues in the Workshop in Political Theory and Policy Analysis (hereinafter Workshop) pursued an exemplary approach in exploring the conditions under which irrigation systems and inshore fisheries are managed (Tang 1992, 1994; Schlager

1994; Lam 1998). These studies reviewed documents pertaining to hundreds of irrigation works and fisheries in numerous countries, resulting in the development of a database amenable to the analysis of institutional conditions associated with successful outcomes. A similar approach was adopted in recent meta-analyses of case studies of tropical deforestation and desertification (Geist and Lambin 2001, 2004).

Several methodological issues arise in this type of meta-analysis, including the definition and selection of cases, the specification and coding of variables, and the analysis of the resulting database. There is no hard-and-fast rule for identifying the universe of case studies to be used in a particular meta-analysis. This entails a crucial issue: the choice of a unit of analysis. The Workshop study concerned small- to medium-scale irrigation systems, about which very little had been formally published, and the work was therefore based on a combination of published papers and gray literature (project documents, such as field reports). In the Workshop study, the autonomous irrigation system provided a relatively discrete, and therefore convenient, unit of analysis. On the other hand, the tropical deforestation study (Geist and Lambin 2001, 2002) chose instead to select cases from peer-reviewed literature, and identified cases from the citation index of the Institute for Scientific Information (ISI 2003).

We applied this approach to the study of agricultural change and began by following the meta-analysis method developed by Geist and Lambin. While the use of their method assures a high level of quality in the cases used, it severely limits the case study population to articles in the ISI database. In order to identify a sufficient number of cases, the universe of cases was expanded to include articles located through other indexes, such as JSTOR (http://www.jstor.org/, subscription required) and AGRICOLA (http://agricola.nal.usda.gov/), and books. Both the tropical deforestation and agricultural change meta-analyses were restricted to subnational studies in the tropics. Many of the articles selected presented more than one case, conducting their own comparative analysis of as many as seventeen cases. In total, 108 cases were coded. These are listed under Coded Cases at the end of this chapter, and their geographic distribution is shown in figure 13.1.

In his writing on the practice of comparative analysis in the social sciences, Ragin (1987, 2000) addresses the process of scoping, casing, or "constituting" populations: "The researcher's specification of relevant cases at the start of the investigation is often nothing more than a working hypothesis that the cases initially selected are in fact alike enough to permit comparative analysis. In the course of the research, the investigator may decide otherwise and drop some cases, or even

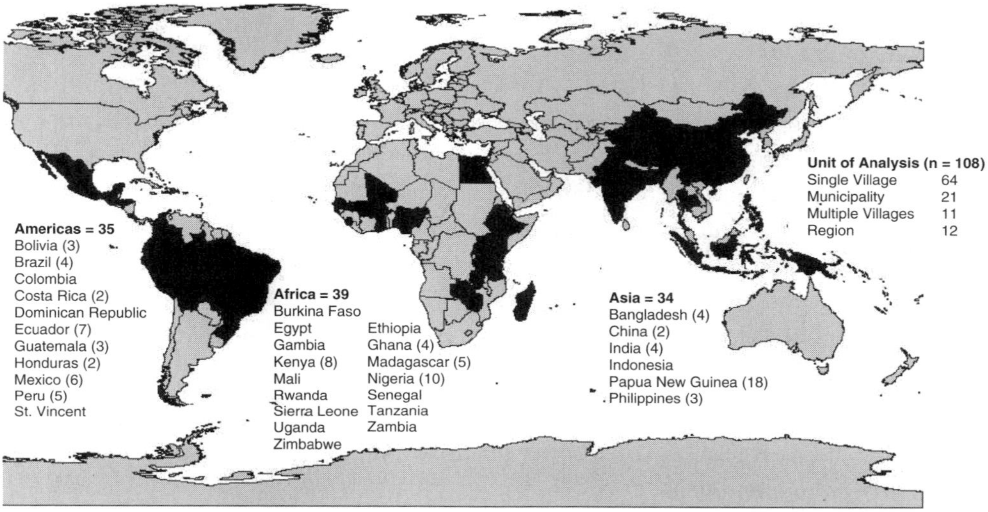

Figure 13.1
Geographic distribution of coded cases.

whole categories of cases, because they do not appear to belong with what appear to be the core cases" (2000, 57–58).

Ragin argues that such flexibility, while anathema to variable-oriented research approaches, is crucial to the comparative-case mode of inquiry that embraces a continuous dialogue between ideas and evidence. The crux of the matter is the determination of the outcome of interest—the dependent variable. In this respect the meta-analysis cannot build a control group according to a standard practice of statistical analysis, since case studies are rarely published about land change that did not occur (though some cases were identified that sought to understand why change failed to occur despite the presence of theoretically sufficient conditions). In the tropical deforestation study, Geist and Lambin (2001, 2002) sought cases analyzing net losses of forest cover according to a very broad definition that included both the conversion of forest to some other cover type and various modifications of forest cover (degradation).

While the distinction between conversion and modification is problematic, the definition of the dependent variable in a study of agricultural change is vastly more complex. All agricultural systems are dynamic, and tropical farming, which often relies on highly variable rainfall and other factors, is notoriously so. Defining a threshold at which a farming system may be considered to have undergone a substantial change is quite difficult, even if the focus is on a specific dimension, say production per unit area per unit time. In fact, a wide range of measures of agricultural change have been developed in the literature, focusing not only on output but also on input type and intensity, commercial orientation, and so on. Indeed, the literature faces internal contradictions based on whether agricultural intensity is measured as an input or as an output. One prominent approach is to measure the frequency of cultivation, which is the converse of fallow period. A field that is under crops for one year, followed by three years of fallow, is said to be used at an intensity of 25 percent.

In order to record the information presented on the change in the dependent variable, we tracked various aspects of change in the production system, including

- size of landholdings;
- type of land used (e.g., upland, bottom land/swamp);
- production (qualitative);
- production quantity (quantitative);
- land intensity, or the frequency of cultivation on a parcel;
- production mix, including cultivars and livestock;
- production techniques (e.g., intercropping);
- mechanical technology;
- chemical technology;
- water management;
- labor; and
- other capital requirements.

Once the outcome has been defined and the cases selected, the collection of information on causal factors (independent variables) can begin. The agricultural change literature provides strong theoretical foundations for hypothesizing the importance of a range of causal factors, both biophysical and human. In the relatively young field of land-cover change, reference is often made to such factors as driving forces, borrowing the language of atmospheric and other physical sciences. This usage (terminology) may be problematic, however, as a given factor (e.g., precipitation) may be observed to directly cause change in one case (e.g., drought causing the adoption of irrigation), while existing as a general context in others (e.g., interannual variability influencing cropping strategies). Although it may not be found to have triggered a change in a particular case, the state of that factor is an important part of the context within which the production system exists and should therefore be retained. The biophysical variables recorded in this study include

- biome (rain forest, desert, alpine, etc.);
- topography (general characterization, elevation range, and steepness);
- precipitation (annual means and variability);
- water bodies (presence and proximity); and
- soil conditions (fertility, structure, erosion).

More than a dozen human and social variables were identified and grouped as follows:

Demographic	Socioeconomic and Cultural	Institutions
Population size and growth	Religion and ethnicity	Property regimes
Population density and distribution	Education	Market demand
Population composition	Market access	Government or nongovernment organization (NGO) policy or program
Settlement and migration	Standard of living	Water program
	Social structure	Income-affecting program
	Off-farm income or food	Infrastructure

Information on each of these independent variables was recorded in abbreviated form into a database, and subsequently coded as one of three states:

1. An important factor in causing the observed outcome
2. Not an important factor in causing the observed outcome
3. Absent

The analysis of the coded database was guided by a search for patterns in the articulated importance of causal variables. Ragin (2000) advocates the analysis of configurations of conditions (conjunctures of causation), rather than the standard practice of treating variables as interchangeable factors capable of acting independently. In our study of agricultural change, the database was first queried for the frequency of authors' assignment of importance of each independent variable—simply the proportion of cases in which a given variable is coded as an important factor in the observed change in the agricultural system. The database is then subjected to multiple, iterative cross-tabulation to reveal the frequency of occurrence of clusters, or configurations, of variables. Like the biophysical factors presented above, each of the social variables (e.g., population, market, property regimes) represents a cluster

Table 13.1
Outcome Details by Region

	Pan-Tropical		Africa		Americas		Asia	
Outcomes	N=108	%	N=39	%	N=35	%	N=34	%
Crop mix	71	66	29	74	28	80	14	41
Production	67	62	23	59	29	83	15	44
Land intensity	67	62	26	67	16	46	25	74
Labor inputs	51	47	16	41	23	66	12	35
Chemical inputs	48	44	18	46	13	37	17	50
Water management	46	43	12	31	9	26	25	74
Landholdings	42	39	18	46	18	51	6	18
Techniques	37	34	10	26	10	29	17	50
Mechanical inputs	36	33	11	28	4	11	21	62
Land used	34	31	12	31	14	40	8	24

Note: Multiple counts are possible; percentages relate to the total of cases (*N*) for the region.

of factors too numerous to code individually. Details about the specific processes included in these clusters are provided in the next section.

Major Findings

Pan-Tropical Patterns

The production systems studied were judged to have undergone substantial changes in the overwhelming majority of the cases reviewed. Three cases involved a failure to intensify, including failure to adopt agroforestry (Browder and Pedlowski 2000), failure to irrigate (Johnson 1986), and the acquisition of new bottom lands (Bebbington 2000). Of the changes observed in the production systems, somewhat less than half involved some form of water management, usually irrigation or rain-water harvesting (table 13.1). About two-thirds of the cases involved an increase in production, usually some combination of increased frequency of cultivation and changes in cultivars or livestock, or both. While these three aspects of production systems often occurred together, multiple configurations were recorded. The adoption and increased use of various factors of production were reported as follows: labor and chemical inputs were adopted in roughly half of the cases. In an additional one-third of the cases, farmers adopted some mechanical technology or other farming technique (e.g., intercropping), or shifted their production to different types of land (e.g., bottom lands previously used for pasture or uncultivated), or a combi-

Table 13.2
The Importance of Sociocultural Factors

	Important	Not Important	Absent
Population factors			
Population numbers/density	70	22	16
Population composition	8	12	88
Settlement/migration	34	41	33
Household factors			
Religion/Ethnicity	7	41	60
Education	21	11	76
Market access	58	18	32
Standard of living	48	32	28
Off-farm employment	30	28	50
Institutional factors			
Property regime	65	34	9
Market demand	69	11	28
Government/NGO policy	55	24	29
Water provision program	16	0	92
Income-affecting program	36	14	58
Infrastructure program	33	10	65

NGO, nongovernment organization.
Note: Total number of cases is 108; multiple counts are possible.

nation of these. Regional variations in these patterns are reported in the sections below.

In terms of the causal factors attributed to these changes by the original authors, the results largely followed expectations (table 13.2). Agricultural change theory would lead us to expect population pressure and market demand to be the key causal factors in engendering land-use intensification. Indeed, each of these was listed as important in roughly two-thirds of the observed cases. These two factors operated in tandem in nearly half of the cases. Other demographic variables described in the cases, including original settlement patterns and migration, occurred about half as often as population growth or density and almost always in conjunction with these variables. Another variable, population composition, was mentioned in twenty cases and noted as important in fewer than half of those. Finally, the related variables—the religious and ethnic backgrounds of studied peoples—were mentioned in roughly half the cases, but were very rarely noted as important factors in the intensification process.

Population emerged as a strong cause of change in only two-thirds of the cases, which undermines its universal, explanatory use by researchers. In fact, many authors explicitly stated that the goal of their studies was to challenge the primacy of population as a causal factor and to either dispel or moderate the power often accorded this single factor. It is especially noteworthy that sixteen of the cases (roughly one-eighth) provided no information at all on population.

Market demand was mentioned by case authors (as important or not important) more often than population as a causal variable. This presence may be an artifact of sampling strategies and is discussed later in this chapter. A separate variable—improved market access—was found to be important less frequently than market demand and usually co-occurred with it. The eleven cases where market access did not co-occur with demand imply that there was improved access to a largely unchanged market in terms of demand. A related variable, standard of living, was important less often than market access but when present occurred almost always in conjunction with market access. A possible linkage also was discovered between market access and the availability of off-farm employment, which was judged important in less than one-third of all cases.

A set of nonmarket institutional variables also emerged as frequently as other important causes and included property regimes and policies and programs of the government or NGOs. Property regimes were important causes in almost as many cases as population or market and were mentioned (as important or not important) more frequently. Government and NGO policies were somewhat less frequently important than property regimes. Information was recorded specifically on water provision programs, income-affecting programs, infrastructure, and education. Of these factors, income and infrastructure programs were important in roughly one-third of the cases, followed by water and education programs.

The relatively weak role attributed to biophysical factors was surprising (table 13.3). Soil conditions—mainly declining fertility, but also erosion—were cited in

Table 13.3
The Importance of Biophysical Factors

	Important	Not Important	Absent
Precipitation variation	30	30	48
Watercourse/water body	23	35	50
Soil properties	43	27	38

Note: Total number of cases is 108; multiple counts are possible.

less than half of the cases, and precipitation variation in less than one-third. Information also was coded for general climatic and topographic conditions, including the presence of water courses and water bodies, for the purpose of analyzing the broader biophysical context of the production systems.

The configuration analysis explained in the previous section revealed a high co-occurrence was found in the primary causes—population and market—in forty-four, or almost half, of the coded cases. This pair was joined almost always by property regimes or policy, or both. In the few cases where neither population nor market was judged important, property regimes or policy, individually or together, filled the explanatory void. In four cases, none of these causes was deemed important. No substantial clusters of secondary (weak) variables could be identified, which is not surprising because even in a presence/absence formation a small number of variables yields a huge number of possible configurations (e.g., eight variables yield 2^8, or 256 configurations). Thus the potential configurations far exceed the number of cases. This picture changes when the dataset is broken down by region, as discussed below.

Sub-Saharan Africa

The bulk of the thirty-nine African cases involved a change of cultivars and livestock without any explicit change in water management. Gains in productivity were seen to be coming from more frequent use of the land, that is, reduction in length of fallows (table 13.4). Land-use changes largely consisted of three dynamics. Farmers used farmland more frequently (decreasing fallow time); shifted from mainly consumption-oriented production of staple foods toward the adoption of cash crops like peanuts and cotton, and especially tree crops such as coffee, tea, palms, and vanilla; and switched from rain-fed production to small-scale irrigation, in the form of urban and kitchen gardening. The adoption of high-yield varieties, particularly maize, was seen in several cases and resulted in increased output. Finally, changes in livestock practices, including replacement of grazing with cropping and intensive stabling (zero grazing), also were seen.

In terms of the causes of these changes, a cluster of population growth and market demand, along with property regime changes or other government policies were important in more than half the cases (see table 13.4). In another cluster where population was not important, market demand and property regime or other government policies accounted for one-third of the cases. Notably, property regimes were important in thirty-one of the African cases. In almost half of the cases the change in

Table 13.4
Outcomes and Causes in African Cases ($N = 39$)

Outcomes		Causes	
Crop mix	29	Population numbers/density	24
Production	23	Population composition	4
Land intensity	26	Settlement/migration	16
Labor inputs	16	Religion/ethnicity	1
Chemical inputs	18	Education	3
Water management	12	Market access	27
Landholdings	18	Standard of living	19
Techniques	10	Off-farm employment	11
Mechanical inputs	11	Property regime	31
Land used	12	Market demand	33
		Government/NGO policy	28
		Water provision program	4
		Income-affecting program	13
		Infrastructure program	17

Note: Multiple counts are possible.

property rights was a shift from customary, communal control of land to some form of individual, private, or quasi-private land tenure, including cadastres and land registration. The renting and leasing of land also was frequently an important factor, and several cases involved commoditization, commercialization of land, or land speculation, while consolidation, expropriation, proletarianization, and sharecropping also were cited. Single cases of land redistribution and the protection of land in perpetuity by a church, such as the cases in Ethiopia (Benin and Pender 2001) and Ghana (Maxwell et al. 1999), respectively, were found as well.

Other government and NGO policies were said to play important roles in twenty-eight of the African cases, particularly the state's role in marketing produce and the diminution of that role following structural adjustment. Assistance with gaining access to inputs by both the state and by NGOs was frequently cited, particularly the provision of credit, especially through village associations. Other frequently cited policy variables included agricultural extension programs involving the dissemination of high-yield crop varieties and livestock stabling and soil and water conservation techniques. In at least one case in Africa (Tiffen et al. 1994), the absence of any noteworthy government program spurred land users to undertake intensified cultivation. Other government policies mentioned include fertility reduction, road improvement, and nature conservation.

Box 13.1
Returning to Diverse Land Uses

At the onset of colonial domination in Sierra Leone farmers were discouraged from farming floodplains as they had done historically. Instead, colonial policy encouraged farmers to move to uplands that were beset with thinner soils and lower agricultural productivity. At the end of the colonial period farmers returned to former methods of cropping but were confronted with population growth that had occurred during the colonial period from in-migration and from natural means. Property regimes were enacted that allowed native-born farmers first and best access to land in the bottoms and the uplands. Because of the increased access to lowland soils yields of rice increased dramatically. Market access also has improved, mediated by the arrival of middlemen who control the rice market economy. Intensification has taken the form of increased cash cropping and access to new lands. While agriculture has indeed brought more land under cultivation, it also has increased the amount of labor per unit area. (Adapted from Richards 1987)

Latin America

The minor role of water management in agricultural production system changes was even more striking in the thirty-four cases from the Americas (table 13.5). Here, the range of cultivars adopted was quite broad, reflecting the diversity of biomes and climate types found in the inhabited American tropics. Among the major crops mentioned in this broadened repertoire of crops were bananas and potatoes, followed by alfalfa and watermelons, and finally coffee, black pepper, garlic, jalapeño peppers, bitter and sweet manioc, onion, peanuts, sesame, soy beans, tobacco, and tomatoes. Other aspects of the production systems changed concurrently, with increases in cattle production (including dairy) and beekeeping mentioned several times. Increases in the frequency of cultivation (decreasing fallow length) were less frequent than in Africa or Asia and may in part reflect the crowded nature of the American highlands where many of the cases were established. In these zones, much of the cropping had already reached 100 percent or higher intensity, and the ability to increase frequency was limited if not impossible. In these cases, change took the form of adoption of yield-increasing technology or wholesale shifts in agricultural strategies. At the other end of the spectrum for the Americas are cases in lowland areas with relatively low population density and difficult access to markets. In these cases, fallow length was probably not reduced because of the relative expense in improving land quality through soil and water conservation measures in the face of pristine or near-pristine lands to cultivate.

Table 13.5
Outcomes and Causes in Latin American Cases ($N = 35$)

Outcomes		Causes	
Crop mix	28	Population numbers/density	22
Production	29	Population composition	3
Land intensity	16	Settlement/migration	12
Labor inputs	23	Religion/ethnicity	5
Chemical inputs	13	Education	14
Water management	9	Market access	21
Landholdings	18	Standard of living	20
Techniques	10	Off-farm employment	15
Mechanical inputs	4	Property regime	15
Land used	14	Market demand	25
		Government/NGO policy	16
		Water provision program	5
		Income-affecting program	15
		Infrastructure program	12

Note: Multiple counts are possible.

Fewer clusters of causal variables were found in the cases from the Americas than in those from Africa (see table 13.5). The cluster of population, market, and property or government policy was less pronounced in this region, occurring in only one-third of the cases. Government and NGO policies were, on the whole, less important in the Americas than in Africa. Notably, the state's withdrawal (or divestment) from the agricultural sector, often linked to the implementation of structural adjustment programs, was even more evident here than in Africa. This withdrawal included the retraction of both price subsidies (e.g., for maize) and reduced input subsidies. Likewise, currency devaluations and market liberalization were noted to have led to rapid increases in the cost of inputs, particularly agrochemicals.

Agricultural extension efforts were credited with the adoption of new crops, such as cocoa, rubber, coconut and improved pasture, as well as mechanical technology (tractors), credit (marketing cooperatives and soft loans), and infrastructure (roads and small-scale irrigation). Specific government policies included fines for leaving fields fallow (Peru) and nature conservation and import controls. Likewise, NGOs were credited with the provision of capital and knowledge (e.g., in limiting erosion on hillsides and green manure application). In one Latin American case, liberation theology was cited as important, as religious NGOs were trying to help agricultural technology production. In another case, missionaries also served as educators to na-

Box 13.2
Crop Diversification in Costa Rica

Smallholders in Costa Rica confronted changing market dynamics by engaging in varied markets. Initially engaged in cattle rearing and dairying, farmers in the humid lowlands of Costa Rica began to add diversified, higher-risk cash crops to their economic portfolios as wealth allowed them to diversify and sell more ground crops to markets. The farmers chose to engage in relatively high-risk cash crops in addition to maintaining low-risk cattle production and risk-reducing subsistence production on their land. They intensified their labor input to their land for higher returns per land area although perhaps not per unit labor. In addition, farmers garnered increased cash from off-farm employment activities focused on large landholdings near their homes. This infusion of cash allowed the farmers to invest in risky cash crops. The farmers behave in a hybrid subsistence/market mode. Intensification will apparently continue in lowland Costa Rica in a start-stop manner. (Adapted from Schelhas 1996)

tive peoples, who developed new preferences for consumer goods previously foreign to their communities.

Property regimes were causal factors considered in virtually all (94 percent) of the cases from the Americas but were important in only half of those cases. As in the African cases, the privatization of landholdings is the dominant process evoked, though in the Americas, partial privatization was at least as prominent as fully private holdings, including the use of deeds or titles. The system of communal tenure in Mexico contributed strongly to these findings. Nationalization and land reform were more frequently mentioned in this region, though still in fewer than one-fifth of the cases. Renting and borrowing land and land sales were each reported in a small number of cases. Finally, squatting, sharecropping, and land consolidation were found in isolated cases. The lack of importance of land reform in the Americas is interesting and upon first inspection counterintuitive. Between the 1940s and 1980s land reform was a major factor driving Latin American government policy, and a number of notable successes of these programs exist. Perhaps access to at least some land in Latin America is now taken as a status quo and has become less thought of as a cause of change. Many researchers in Latin America may see property regimes, in their varied and diverse forms, as a preexisting condition, much as they consider soil and climate factors.

Latin America was the only region in which a change in labor input played an important role, appearing in more than two-thirds of the cases. In some cases, reference was made to increased labor requirements associated with aging fields, but new labor-intensive tasks, such as those associated with terracing, were mentioned more often. In particular, authors discussed the issue of labor bottlenecks created in the adoption of new crops, such as chilies (Yucatán), or other practices, such as bee-keeping (also in the Yucatán) or green manure application. In one case, labor availability was said to have declined as populations temporarily migrated to cities or plantations to work seasonally. These arrangements are particularly problematic as new, more labor-intensive crops are introduced in the region. They may however, be foregoing the opportunity cost of their home-based labor for the perception of much greater income in other locales.

East/Southeast Asia

It was unsurprising that three-fourths of the cases in Asia involved water management as part of the process of agricultural change—more than twice as often as in the other two regions (table 13.6). Asia has the longest record of continuous large-scale irrigated agriculture in the tropics. While increased frequency of cultivation was nearly as strong as in Africa, changes in cultivars appeared to be much less frequent in this region, as in Latin America. We could not see a trend in change of cultivars partly because few cases reported such a change, and partly because there

Table 13.6
Outcomes and Causes in Asian Cases ($N = 34$)

Outcomes		Causes	
Crop mix	14	Population numbers/density	24
Production	15	Population composition	1
Land intensity	25	Settlement/migration	6
Labor inputs	12	Religion/ethnicity	1
Chemical inputs	17	Education	4
Water management	25	Market access	10
Landholdings	6	Standard of living	9
Techniques	17	Off-farm employment	4
Mechanical inputs	21	Property regime	19
Land used	8	Market demand	11
		Government/NGO policy	11
		Water provision program	7
		Income-affecting program	8
		Infrastructure program	4

Note: Multiple counts are possible.

were so many different cultivars being adopted. As expected, the adoption of high-yield varieties, especially rice, was particularly strong in this region, often accompanied by increased use of chemical inputs. It is in this region that the impact of the Consultative Group on International Agricultural Research and green revolution technologies was most dramatically demonstrated. Other crops mentioned include American taro, beans, cotton, okra, Job's tears, maize, manioc, millet, mustard, peanuts, sesame, soy beans, squash, sweet potatos, and taro. Notably, the intensification of forest product collection and the adoption of agroforestry practices were rather high in this region and included bananas, cashews, coconuts, coffee, fruit, pepper, and rubber. Livestock were mentioned very rarely, but the adoption of mechanical inputs was markedly higher in this region where animal traction and tractors are much more common than in Africa and probably Latin America. In a few cases, especially Papua New Guinea, livestock were seen as an impediment to crop-based intensification, because they frequently damaged crops and interfered with cropping practices.

The co-occurrence of population and market demand operated differently in the Asian cases than in the other cases (see table 13.6). This variation is due in part to the large number of cases garnered from Papua New Guinea from the late 1950s through the 1970s, a period of this region's relative isolation from wider market forces and government programs. Furthermore, the authors of these studies did not record information for market demand or government programs, perhaps because there was little variance in community experience along these lines. When information on market access and demands was present, in India and the Philippines, access to nearby markets and changing urban market tastes spurred notable changes in the types of crops farmed and the land-cover intensity of these crops (Leaf 1987; Eder 1991).

The studies in Papua New Guinea, however, did yield very rich data relative to outcomes. In the remainder of the Asian cases, fewer than one-third were subject to the population, market, and institutional cluster found in other regions. Another cluster is found in Bangladesh where only one of the major hypothesized causal variables—population—seemed to play a role. In the remaining cases (excluding Papua New Guinea), related but different variables, such as increased market access, social differentiation, and infrastructure programs, were key factors. Property regimes were deemed important factors in 59 percent of the Asian cases, placing it squarely between Africa and the Americas. Interestingly, fully 15 percent of the cases failed to consider property regimes—more than twice as many as in the other regions. Much less detail was provided in cases about property regimes, especially in the multiple cases culled from P. Brown and Podolefsky's (1976) comparative analysis, which constituted half of the cases for this region.

In the Asian cases outside Papua New Guinea, government and NGO programs figured in two-thirds of the cases. Some of these cases included broad national policies, such as China's Open Door policy, or tax policies favoring industrialization, market intervention, and even tax policy favoring coconuts and rubber over rice. More often cited were direct agricultural policies, such as import quotas, rice reserve requirements, and rice premiums, and the encouragement of soybean production, subsidies for market vegetables, and irrigation credits. Conservation policies, including reforestation and the prohibition of swidden cultivation, also were mentioned, as were the construction of roads and, of course, a range of irrigation infrastructure (dams, levees, tube wells). Credit and other financial programs were largely absent in this region, and in only one case was an NGO (Summer Institute of Linguistics) mentioned as carrying out agricultural extension.

Box 13.3
Hyperintensification in Bangladesh

High population density and improved market access have encouraged the intensification of agriculture in Bangladesh. Five villages in the Bengal basin studied by B. Turner and Ali (1996) exhibited extremely high population densities (ranging from 301 to 1466 people per square kilometer). The population densities in this region in fact show signs of increasing. During the period under study, the government of Bangladesh improved market access through road building and the control of rivers to enable more reliable river transport. While all of the study sites reported increased productivity, those closest to markets or benefiting from infrastructure programs reported the highest increases in productivity. Increasing productivity mirrored rapidly growing populations. Testing the theories of Boserup (1965), the authors conclude that intensification was induced by external structural factors (the market and infrastructure) and internal demographic factors (population). The case of Bangladesh in some ways is extraordinary but may point to the future for the most crowded areas of the world. Farmers there have been able to increase their labor input and add the benefits of new crop varieties to increase production. Cropping frequencies in excess of 100 percent existed in most of the villages, with two villages approaching 300 percent, or three crops per year per area. In the village of Khazanagar, for example, cropping intensity grew from 213 percent to 234 percent while land productivity grew from 5001 kg/ha per year to 5196 kg/ha per year. While the point of stagnation may be approaching, it has yet to be reached. (Adapted from B. Turner and Ali 1996)

Discussion

Early explanations of differential economic development hinged largely on the role of the opportunities and constraints afforded societies by the biophysical environment in which they arose. In its extreme, and perhaps most persuasive, form *environmental determinism* left little room for human agency and cultural choice, and its excesses left the social sciences shy of invoking biophysical factors in explaining human conditions for the remainder of the twentieth century. The study of human-environment relations has instead turned to the enumeration and operationalization of variables that describe these behavioral and cultural factors. It appears that the pendulum may have swung a bit too far, however.

One of the most striking findings of the meta-analysis presented above is the dearth of biophysical information found in the case studies. Almost one-third of the cases could not be coded for even simplistic precipitation categories (humid, subhumid, semiarid, arid). Information on soil properties was likewise lacking in more than one-third of the cases and, when provided, was often of a very cursory nature, rarely referring, for example, to a recognized pedological system. While general topographic information was more frequently provided, many studies lacked elevation values. It is likely that a great deal of information was collected but not reported, due either to limitations on the length of articles in peer-reviewed journals or to the perceived unimportance of biophysical factors. Either way, the lack of information, and its inconsistency when provided, precludes systematic analysis of the role of biophysical context in the process of agricultural change.

The meta-analysis reveals that the testing of neo-Malthusian and Boserupian propositions concerning the role of population growth, and the implied land constraint, has been the major preoccupation of the study of agricultural change. Many of the studies reviewed here set out explicitly to examine these propositions, and all possible relations were identified: sometimes population growth led to a land constraint and to the mining of soil resources, increasing investment in labor despite declining marginal returns; sometimes the land constraint led to technomanagerial shifts that raised production apace with consumption needs; but sometimes such shifts occurred in the absence of a severe land constraint. So population clearly does not work in a universal, or unmediated, fashion. But in order to know what effect population growth is having, one needs to know how it is growing. In sixteen of the cases (15 percent), codable information could not be found on whether population growth or density, or both were important factors, and, as in the biophysical factors discussed above, when information was provided, it was rarely in a form that would enable rigorous, comparative analysis (e.g., population per square kilometer). Other key demographic information, such as age structure (dependency ratio) or sex ratio, was even more frequently missing. Other fundamental information on religion, ethnicity, education, and standard of living also was disappointingly rare.

The other main factor proposed to explain agricultural change is market demand, implying a desire for cash to procure goods and services not available on the farm. This either could lead to an increase in production using the present technomanagerial system, with more inputs per unit area per unit of time, or could lead to a shift to a new system, with new crops, new techniques, or any of myriad production inputs. Again, many studies reviewed here found new or increased market demand closely implicated in the observed shift in the production system, and this comes as no surprise. Once again, while qualitative information was frequently provided, rarely did it come in a form permitting broad, systematic comparison (e.g., farm-gate price of a specified product, along with an exchange rate).

The finding that demographic and economic factors do not work in an unmediated fashion is by no means novel, and begs the question of the effects of mediating sociocultural and institutional factors. There is considerably less agreement in this realm, since the possible relevant dimensions of a single cluster of factors, say government programs, are effectively unlimited. For example, the provision of irrigation infrastructure is a fairly small subset of government interventions affecting agricultural systems, yet there are innumerable irrigation technologies introduced by a range of government agencies, NGOs, and international aid agencies through a range of different mechanisms, such as loans and grants. Thus each instance of government assistance with the adoption of irrigation technology is practically unique, and changes in access to credit and the provision of transportation infrastructure may be even less susceptible to standardization, and thus to comparative analysis.

The cases reviewed here do exhibit a certain coherence in the treatment of social and institutional factors grouped under the heading of property regime dynamics. The main processes found important were the consolidation of landholdings, and the reverse process of land redistribution, as well as the shift from communal, traditional systems to formal, state-sanctioned regimes. The processes, and the language used to describe them, were found to vary substantially by region, as would be expected given their very different historical experiences of colonization and postcolonial social change.

While many of the variables considered here could be treated as either "causes" shaping agricultural trajectories, or as "outcomes" of particular sets of agricultural practices, one particularly intractable set of factors, in this sense, were coded under the headings "social structure" and "standard of living." In many cases, such factors differentiated individuals or communities that enjoyed opportunities not available to others and could thus be construed as "causal," yet were clearly related to the success of the agricultural enterprise, and should therefore be considered "outcomes" inasmuch as they both explain why change occurred, and describe the results of that change.

Several interrelated dimensions emerged, often expressed in economic terms. For example, the gender dimensions of agricultural change were quite strong in the African cases, where women were frequently seen exploiting new opportunities for market gardening, while in the cases from Latin America this was generally the domain of men. Class issues, often related to property regimes, arose in all three regions, as discussed above. The underlying processes, however, took rather different forms in the various regions, with caste issues evoked in India (Leaf 1987), forced labor and slavery in Colombia (Taussig 1978) and Brazil (Brondízio and Siqueira 1997), and the legacy of colonial ethnic favoritism in Kenya (F. Bernard 1993). Such historically rooted structural differentiation yields to comparative analysis with great difficulty, however, even when a common theoretical and methodological approach has been taken, which is certainly not true in the set of cases analyzed here.

Conclusions

The range of information presented in the case studies varied widely. As discussed above, many did not provide basic geographic data (e.g., topography, soils, climate) while others neglected information on population, cropping technology, market demand, and government policy. It is abundantly clear that there is no widely accepted protocol for carrying out field studies about agricultural change, despite long-standing calls for standardization. An edited volume based on papers first prepared in the late 1980s suggested minimum datasets for climatic, pedological, demographic, and other sets of variables (E. Moran 1995). This call for the collection of minimum-standard datasets was echoed in *Land-Use and Land-Cover Change Science/Research Plan* (B. Turner et al. 1995).

In seeking to understand the apparent lack of standards, one can look to the academic mode of research. First and foremost, academic research rewards innovation and ingenuity. Repeating others' studies is frowned upon because repeating previous work is seen as noninnovative, even in cases where different results are found. A repeat methodology even in a different locale is not attractive to researchers, presumably because it does not yield new answers to old questions. Furthermore, within the academy, there are divergent ideas about what is worthy of research. Candidate causes for change range from the international economy to individual perceptions of how land should be used. With this range of causal variables, the researcher must focus on those deemed important by his or her discipline. Research questions posed by each discipline also have changed as the disciplines position themselves for research funding and intellectual importance.

The systematic treatment of social (institutional) factors is close at hand, evidenced by a lively discussion of the crucial dimensions, or design principles, of institutional regimes used by communities that successfully manage common-property resources over time (E. Ostrom 1990; Agrawal 2002). Widespread use of analytical frameworks, such as Institutional Analysis and Design (McGinnis 1999), would improve the comparability of case studies, and thus the ability to develop and test hypotheses based on their results. Greater standardization of data collection on other social variables also may be feasible. A number of equity issues, such as economic, class, and gender differentiation, have been the subject of the development of qualitative and quantitative data collection techniques that seem to be gaining currency in studies of rural agrarian societies. For example, the use of household wealth ranking to elucidate the range of social and economic means within a community is a staple of so-called rapid, or participatory, rural appraisal (Chambers 1980; Conway 1986; J. McCracken et al. 1988). Likewise, suites of tools for the systematic analysis of gender dimensions of rural communities are widespread (Rocheleau et al. 1996). Several organizations and programs doing research in human-environment interactions, including the Center for the Study of Institutions, Population, and Environmental Change (CIPEC), the International Forestry Resources and Institutions (IFRI) program (see chapter 4), and the Carolina Population Center, have begun to share data protocols in the ongoing effort to promote such standardization (see http://www2.eastwestcenter.org/environment/lucclink/papers.htm).

Field methods reflect the academic orientation and the abilities of the researchers carrying out a study. If the researcher comes from a discipline that has long ignored the importance of culture in human society, it is not surprising that this researcher should be ill-equipped to investigate culture, even if she or he notes its importance. Other problems for data acquisition arise in the availability of relevant data for a particular research problem. In some countries much of the basic data used in land-use change studies, such as population and agricultural data, are unreliable or unavailable. The research costs associated with creating such data are beyond the means of all but the largest of social science projects. Indeed, the "big science" model common in the physical and natural sciences has been difficult to apply in the social sciences, because the latter traditionally have been funded at a considerably lower level (e.g., 3 percent of the global change budget). Alternative methods to generate these data should be created and may include innovative and nonthreatening methods of data sharing.

Two crucial issues arise in the collection and analysis of comparable information in land-change studies. As discussed in chapter 3, the scale of inquiry affects both the level of detail and the general nature of a study and in part predetermines the type of data deemed important. For example, a regional study could make great use of population and national economic policy as an explanatory variable for noted changes. At the village level, however, it may become clear that cultural transformation caused by contact with the outside world is more appropriate. Another important cause of change at local levels that does not act as importantly at coarser scales of research is household life cycle (E. Moran et al. 2002b; Vance and Geoghegan 2004). This is a quandary for future research on cases of land-use/land-cover change that must be confronted by the global change community. How can one rectify important drivers of change at one scale that are apparently unimportant at another? Academic research questions occur at different scales that are frequently discipline dependent.

In addition to these issues of spatial scale, there are clearly issues related to the temporal, or historical, scale of analysis. Contemporary studies are valuable in that they promise to collect comparative data. Furthermore, the causal processes vary from place to place and using similar datasets for different places allows robust testing of predominant theories. Deeper historical studies also are valuable for understanding the range of factors that can condition change, providing information on the necessary preconditions for current change (Redman 1999; Haberl et al. 2001). Care must be taken, however, as deeper historical cases frequently exhibit less useful data than more recent cases in terms of cross-sectional comparisons. Also, research that attempts to delve back into history is difficult because it relies on data more fragmentary than contemporary research.

Future Directions

The meta-analysis presented above used each case "as is." It is likely that in many of the cases reviewed, the authors actually possess much of the information found lacking in the review, and that this information was omitted largely due to space restrictions in the journals. If so, the editors and reviewers of the journals concerned bear some responsibility for these omissions. It might prove fruitful to pursue data completion for a case study area from other work by the same or different authors, through extrapolation from other places thought to be similar, or through interpolation from synoptic data. The use of websites to provide more complete data access is promising. Another approach is to commission case studies using standardized sets of variables—such work has yielded interesting results in the past, but the effort required is not trivial (see, e.g., B. Turner et al. 1993a; Tri-Academy 2001). The new generation of land-based research currently being designed under the aegis of the International Geosphere-Biosphere Programme and the International Human Dimensions Programme on Global Environmental Change could be crucial in fostering detailed regional analyses that yield to comparative analysis.

We do not suggest that all future land-change studies should conform to a global-change science paradigm or protocol. The importance of disciplinary inquiry remains paramount in the academy, and there is little sign that this importance is waning, despite innovative, interdisciplinary programs. Nor is the disciplinary structure of the academy less important than it used to be. Indeed, as technology improves, disciplines are better positioned to ask more meaningful and deeper questions. However, to be useful for comparisons, baseline data should be provided to address the following:

- Biophysical data: What are the relevant biophysical constraints and boons to cultivation in the region?
- Area: What is the extent of the region under consideration?
- Population: What is the population density or total population for that area?
- Property institutions: Is decision making affected by the way land is held?
- Markets: Are the land users substantially involved in market institutions beyond their control?
- Policy: Is the region subject to policies that affect land use?

This baseline data collection should not preclude the application of disciplinary questions and, indeed, will serve to make these specific questions hold up to outside scrutiny.

Judging from a comparative analysis of case studies it becomes clear that generalizing human and social phenomena (behavior) at any level is problematic. The hypothesized major causal variables—market, population, property regime, and policy—are important in most of the cases. This can be seen as encouraging for future policy analyses. By investigating these factors it becomes possible to capture most of the action in trajectories of agricultural change. The comparative analysis does not, however, yield country- or region-specific policy suggestions and great care should be taken when attempting to compare disparate cases. The directionality of the relationships between causal variables is multiple: high market demand can encourage investment in landesque capital, or it can spur the degradation of geographically dispersed resources. Our study contributes to a growing literature of meta-analysis, and to land-change science in general. To the degree that the recommendations above are taken to heart, research should provide increasingly sound understanding of the processes and outcomes of land dynamics.

Coded Cases

Barlett, P. F. 1976. Labor Efficiency and the Mechanism of Agricultural Evolution. *Journal of Anthropological Research* 32:124–140.

Batterbury, S., and N. Taylor. 1998. Zarma Livelihoods and African Environmental History: Studying Social and Environmental Change in the 20th Century in South-West Niger. Presented at the Association of American Geographers Annual Meeting, Boston, March 26–29.

Bebbington, A. 2000. Reencountering Development: Livelihood Transitions and Place Transformations in the Andes. *Annals of the Association of American Geographers* 90(3): 495–520.

Benin, S., and J. Pender. 2001. Impacts of Land Redistribution on Land Management and Productivity in the Ethiopian Highlands. *Land Degradation and Development* 12(6):555–568.

Benjaminsen, T. A. 2001. The Population-Agriculture-Environment Nexus in the Malian Cotton Zone. *Global Environmental Change* 11:283–295.

Bernard, F. E. 1993. Increasing Variability in Agricultural Production: Meru District, Kenya, in the Twentieth Century. In *Population Growth and Agricultural Change in Africa*, ed. B. L. Turner II, G. Hyden, and R. Kates, 80–113. Gainesville: University Press of Florida.

Boyd, D. J. 2001. Life without Pigs: Recent Subsistence Changes among the Irakia Awa, Papua New Guinea. *Human Ecology* 29(3):259–282.

Briggs, J. 1991. The Peri-Urban Zone in Dar es Salaam, Tanzania: Recent Trends and Changes in Agricultural Land Use. *Transactions of the Institute of British Geographers* 16(3):319–331.

Brondízio, E. S., and A. D. Siqueira. 1997. From Extractivists to Forest Farmers: Changing Concepts of Agricultural Intensification and Peasantry in the Amazon Estuary. *Research in Economic Anthropology* 18:233–279.

Browder, J. O., and M. A. Pedlowski. 2000. Agroforestry Performance on Small Farms in Amazonia: Findings from the Rondonia Agroforestry Pilot Project. *Agroforestry Systems* 49(1):63–83.

Brown, P., and A. Podolefsky. 1976. Population Density, Agricultural Intensity, Land Tenure, and Group Size in the New Guinea Highlands. *Ethnology* 15:211–238.

Carney, J. 1993. Converting the Wetlands, Engendering the Environment: The Intersection of Gender with Agrarian Change in the Gambia. *Economic Geography* 69(4):329–348.

Conelly, W. T. 1992. Agricultural Intensification in a Philippine Frontier Community: Impact on Labor Efficiency and Farm Diversity. *Human Ecology* 20(2):203–223.

Conelly, W. T., and M. S. Chaiken. 2001. Intensive Farming, Agro-Diversity, and Food Security under Conditions of Extreme Population Pressure in Western Kenya. *Human Ecology* 28(1):19–51.

Coomes, O. T., F. Grimard, and G. J. Burt. 2000. Tropical Forests and Shifting Cultivation: Secondary Forest Fallow Dynamics among Traditional Farmers of the Peruvian Amazon. *Ecological Economics* 32(1):109–124.

Cruz, M. 1999. Competing Strategies for Modernization in the Ecuadorean Andes. *Current Anthropology* 40(3):377–383.

Doolittle, W. E. 1984. Agricultural Change As an Incremental Process. *Annals of the Association of American Geographers* 74(1):124–137.

Drescher, A. W. 1996. Urban Microfarming in Central Southern Africa: A Case Study of Lusaka, Zambia. *African Urban Quarterly* 11(2–3):210–216.

Eder, J. F. 1991. Agricultural Intensification and Labor Productivity in a Philippine Vegetable Gardening Community: A Longitudinal Study. *Human Organization* 50(3):245–255.

Ewell, P. T., and D. Merrill-Sands. 1987. Milpa in Yucatan: A Long-Fallow Maize System and Its Alternatives in the Maya Peasant Economy. In *Comparative Farming Systems*, ed. B. L. Turner II and S. B. Brush, 95–129. New York: Guilford.

Fisher, M. G., R. L. Warner, and W. A. Masters. 2000. Gender and Agricultural Change: Crop Livestock Integration in Senegal. *Society and Natural Resources* 13(3):203–222.

Ford, R. E. 1993. Marginal Coping in Extreme Land Pressures: Ruhengeri, Rwanda. In *Population Growth and Agricultural Change in Africa*, ed. B. L. Turner II, G. Hyden, and R. Kates, 145–186. Gainesville: University Press of Florida.

George, P. S., and S. Chattopadhyah. 2001. Population and Land Use in Kerala. In *Growing Populations, Changing Landscapes: Studies from India, China, and the United States*, ed. Tri-Academy Panel (Indian National Science Academy, Chinese Academy of Sciences, and U.S. National Academy of Sciences), 79–105. Washington, DC: National Academy Press.

Godoy, R., D. Wilkie, and J. Franks. 1997. The Effects of Markets on Neotropical Deforestation: A Comparative Study of Four Amerindian Societies. *Current Anthropology* 38(5):875–878.

Goldman, A. 1993. Agricultural Innovation in Three Areas of Kenya: Neo-Boserupian Theories and Regional Characterization. *Economic Geography* 69(1):44–71.

Gray, L. C., and M. Kevane. 2001. Evolving Tenure Rights and Agricultural Intensification in Southwestern Burkina Faso. *World Development* 29(4):573–587.

Grossman, L. S. 1993. The Political Ecology of Banana Exports and Local Food Production in St. Vincent, Eastern Caribbean. *Annals of the Association of American Geographers* 83(2):347–367.

Guillet, D. 1987. Agricultural Intensification and Deintensification in Lari, Cloca Valley, Southern Peru. *Research in Economic Anthropology* 8:201–224.

Gumbo, D. J., and T. W. Ndiripo. 1996. Open Space Cultivation in Zimbabwe: A Case Study of Greater Harare, Zimbabwe. *African Urban Quarterly* 11(2–3):210–216.

Guyer, J., and E. F. Lambin. 1993. Land Use in an Urban Hinterland: Ethnography and Remote Sensing in the Study of African Intensification. *American Ethnologist* 95:836–859.

Henrich, J. 1997. Market Incorporation, Agricultural Change, and Sustainability among the Machigueuga Indians of the Peruvian Amazon. *Human Ecology* 25(2):319–351.

Hopkins, N. S. 1987. Mechanized Irrigation in Upper Egypt: The Role of Technology and the State in Agriculture. In *Comparative Farming Systems*, ed. B. L. Turner II and S. B. Brush, 223–247. New York: Guilford.

Humphries, S. 1993. The Intensification of Traditional Agriculture among the Yucatec Maya Farmers: Facing Up to the Dilemma of Livelihood Sustainability. *Human Ecology* 21(1):87–102.

Johnson, S. H., III. 1986. Agricultural Intensification in Thailand: Complementary Role of Infrastructure and Agricultural Policy. In *Irrigation Investment, Technology, and Management Strategies for Development*, ed. W. K. Easter, 111–127. Boulder, CO: Westview.

Kammerbauer, J., and C. Ardon. 1999. Land Use Dynamics and Landscape Change Pattern in a Typical Watershed in the Hillside Region of Central Honduras. *Agriculture, Ecosystems, and Environment* 75(1/2):93–100.

Kasfir, N. 1993. Agricultural Transformation in the Robusta Coffee/Banana Zone of Bushenyi, Uganda. In *Population Growth and Agricultural Change in Africa*, ed. B. L. Turner II, G. Hyden, and R. Kates, 41–79. Gainesville: University Press of Florida.

Keese, J. R. 1998. International NGOs and the Land Use Change in a Southern Highland Region of Ecuador. *Human Ecology* 26(3):451–468.

Kull, C. A. 1998. Leimavo Revisited: Agrarian Land-Use Change in the Highlands of Madagascar. *Professional Geographer* 50(2):163–176.

Kunstadter, P. 1987. Swiddeners in Transition: Lua' Farmers in Northern Thailand. In *Comparative Farming Systems*, ed. B. L. Turner II and S. B. Brush, 130–155. New York: Guilford.

Laney, R. 2000. Disaggregating Induced Intensification for Land-Change Analysis: A Case Study from Madagascar. *Annals of the Association of American Geographers* 92(4):702–726.

Leaf, M. J. 1987. Intensification in Peasant Farming: Punjab in the Green Revolution. In *Comparative Farming Systems*, ed. B. L. Turner II and S. B. Brush, 248–275. New York: Guilford.

Martin, S. 1993. From Agricultural Growth to Stagnation: The Case of the Ngwa, Nigeria, 1900–1980. In *Population Growth and Agricultural Change in Africa*, ed. B. L. Turner II, G. Hyden, and R. Kates, 302–323. Gainesville: University Press of Florida.

Maxwell, D., W. O. Larbi, G. M. Lamptey, S. Zakariah, and M. Armar-Klemesu. 1999. Farming in the Shadow of the City: Changes in Land Rights and Livelihoods on Peri-Urban Accra. *Third World Planning Review* 21(4):373–391.

Mortimore, M. 1993. The Intensification of Peri-Urban Agriculture: The Kano Close-Settled Zone, 1964–1986. In *Population Growth and Agricultural Change in Africa*, ed. B. L. Turner II, G. Hyden, and R. Kates, 358–400. Gainesville: University Press of Florida.

Netting, R. McC., G. D. Stone, and M. P. Stone. 1993. Agricultural Expansion, Intensification and Market Participation among the Kofyar, Jos Plateau, Nigeria. In *Population Growth and Agricultural Change in Africa*, ed. B. L. Turner II, G. Hyden, and R. Kates, 206–249. Gainesville: University Press of Florida.

Nichols, D. L. 1987. Risk and Agricultural Intensification During the Formative Period in the Northern Basin of Mexico. *American Anthropologist* 89(3):596–616.

Okoth-Ogendo, H. W. O., and J. O. Oucho. 1993. Population Growth and Agricultural Change in Kisii District, Kenya: A Sustained Symbiosis? In *Population Growth and Agricultural Change in Africa*, ed. B. L. Turner II, G. Hyden, and R. Kates, 187–205. Gainesville: University Press of Florida.

Ortiz, R. 1998. Cowpeas from Nigeria: A Silent Food Revolution. *Outlook on Agriculture* 27(2):125–128.

Padoch, C., E. Harwell, and A. Susanto. 1998. Swidden, Sawah, and In-Between: Agricultural Transformation in Borneo. *Human Ecology* 26(1):3–20.

Richards, P. 1987. Upland and Swamp Rice Farming Systems in Sierra Leone: An Evolutionary Transition? In *Comparative Farming Systems*, ed. B. L. Turner II and S. B. Brush, 156–187. New York: Guilford.

Robbins, P. 2001. Tracking Invasive Land Covers in India, or Why Our Landscapes Have Never Been Modern. *Annals of the Association of American Geographers* 91(4):637–659.

Rudel, T. K., D. Bates, and R. Machinguiashi. 2002. Ecologically Noble Amerindians? Cattle Ranching and Cash Cropping among Shuar and Colonists in Ecuador. *Latin American Research Review* 37(1):144–159.

Schelhas, J. 1996. Land Use Choice and Change: Intensification and Diversification in the Lowland Tropics of Costa Rica. *Human Organization* 55(3):298–306.

Shidong, Z., L. Jiehua, Z. Hongqi, Z. Yi, Q. Wenhu, L. Zhiwu, Z. Taolin, L. Guiping, Q. Mingzhou, and J. Leiwen. 2001. Population, Consumption, and Land Use in the Jitai Basin Region, Jiangxi Province. In *Growing Populations, Changing Landscapes: Studies from India, China, and the United States*, ed. Tri-Academy Panel (Indian National Science Academy, Chinese Academy of Sciences, and U.S. National Academy of Sciences), 179–205. Washington, DC: National Academy Press.

Shidong, Z., Z. Yi, B. Wanqi, L. Jiehua, Q. Wenhu, Z. Taolin, L. Guiping, Q. Mingzhou, and J. Leiwen. 2001. Population, Consumption, and Land Use in the Pearl River Delta, Guangdong Province. In *Growing Populations, Changing Landscapes: Studies from India, China, and the United States*, ed. Tri-Academy Panel (Indian National Science Academy, Chinese Academy of Sciences, and U.S. National Academy of Sciences), 207–230. Washington, DC: National Academy Press.

Shively, G. E. 2001. Agricultural Change, Rural Labor Markets, and Forest Clearing: An Illustrative Case from the Philippines. *Land Economics* 77(2):268–284.

Shorr, N. 2001. Early Utilization of Flood-Recession Soils As a Response to the Intensification of Fishing and Upland Agriculture: Resource-Use Dynamics in a Large Tikuna Community. *Human Ecology* 28(1):73–107.

Shriar, A. J. 2001. The Dynamics of Agricultural Intensification and Resource Conservation in the Buffer Zone of the Maya Biosphere Reserve, Peten, Guatemala. *Human Ecology* 29(1):27–48.

Sierra, R., F. Rodriguez, and E. Losos. 1999. Forest Resource Use Change during Early Market Integration in Tropical Rain Forests: The Huaorani of Upper Amazonia. *Ecological Economics* 30:107–119.

Taussig, M. 1978. Peasant Economics and the Development of Capitalist Agriculture in the Cauca Valley, Colombia. *Latin American Perspectives* 5(3):62–91.

Tiffen, M., M. Mortimore, and F. Gichuki. 1994. Population Growth and Environmental Degradation: Revising the Theoretical Framework. In *More People, Less Erosion*, ed. M. Tiffen, M. Mortimore, and F. Gichuki, 261–274. West Sussex, UK: Wiley.

Turner, B. L., II, and A. M. S. Ali. 1996. Induced Intensification: Agricultural Change in Bangladesh with Implications for Malthus and Boserup. *Proceedings of the National Academy of Sciences of the United States of America* 93(25):14984–14991.

Vashishtha, P. S., R. K. Sharma, R. P. S. Malik, and S. Bathla. 2001. Population and Land Use in Haryana. In *Growing Populations, Changing Landscapes: Studies from India, China, and the United States*, ed. Tri-Academy Panel (Indian National Science Academy, Chinese Academy of Sciences, and U.S. National Academy of Sciences), 107–144. Washington, DC: National Academy Press.

Vermeer, D. E. 1970. Population Pressure and Crop Rotational Changes among the Tiv of Nigeria. *Annals of the Association of American Geographers* 60(2):299–314.

Wiegers, E. S., R. J. Hijmans, D. Herve, and L. O. Fresco. 1999. Land Use Intensification and Disintensification in the Upper Canete Valley, Peru. *Human Ecology* 27(2):319–339.

Zweifler, M. O., M. A. Gold, and R. N. Thomas. 1994. Land Use Evolution in Hill Regions of the Dominican Republic. *Professional Geographer* 46(1):39–53.

V

Epilogue

14

New Directions in Human-Environment Interactions and Land-Use/Land-Cover Research

Emilio F. Moran

The research presented in this book represents one important line of research on human-environment interactions: land-use/land-cover change, particularly focusing on human interactions with forest ecosystems. There are many other important topics that have gained salience in the last few years, such as urbanization, industrial transformations, institutional dimensions of global change, and environmental security (http://www.ihdp.uni-bonn.de/). Many of the findings, theoretical contributions, and methodological advances we have presented apply broadly to the entire field of human-environment interactions, sometimes also known as human dimensions of global change. This is a fast-moving area of research. The priorities are changing quickly as progress is made and new questions, methods, and theories come to the fore.

In chapters 1 and 2, the authors reviewed the way the field came into being in the last decade, and what theories and methods were available to tackle the then-prominent questions. In subsequent chapters, authors explored these interactions using both case study and comparative approaches. In this epilogue, a review of emerging new questions and approaches is undertaken with a view to informing the community what we, and many other colleagues, feel are some of the more urgent questions and approaches that are likely to take center stage in the coming decade and beyond. The issues raised are partly a result of the work presented in the book, and partly a result of our reflections on where we need to go as a global environmental change research community. Like any attempt to project into the future, our effort is sure to overlook some new directions that are either not currently foreseen or that we missed, despite our best efforts to be comprehensive.

Issues of Methodological Integration

In the past decade, global change research has advanced scientific capacity by moving in the direction of standardized protocols and methodologically integrative methods. From an earlier era when each area of science acted independently, the nature of contemporary science calls for ever-growing degrees of integration. This integration is sometimes restricted to areas within single disciplines (e.g., interactions between molecular and evolutionary biologists or between cultural and biological anthropologists). Less common, but more along the lines of what needs to happen routinely in the future, is joint collaborative work between scientists from whatever areas of science are needed to tackle the challenges posed by our rapidly changing planet: atmospheric sciences, community and population ecology, forestry, soil science, anthropology, geography, political science, economics, and biogeochemistry, to name but a few. Scientists in these areas would have to collaborate in understanding terrestrial ecosystem dynamics in an integrative science framework. Can this work? If we believe that the collective wisdom of scientists is any indication, the future of environmental research clearly points in this direction.

Two ambitious efforts that have sought to define the integrative research agenda in human-environment studies for the coming decade were led by panels called together by the National Research Council: *Grand Challenges in Environmental Sciences* (NRC 2001) and *Human Dimensions of Global Environmental Change: Research Pathways for the Next Decade* (NRC 1999a), also called, for short, the *Pathways* book. *Grand Challenges* is a much briefer book than *Pathways*, focusing as it does less on summarizing what was accomplished in the last decade, and more simply on explaining why some areas of research were picked and what directions might most profitably be followed for each research area selected. *Pathways* is a superb synthesis of the advances of the past decade, and chapter 7 on the human dimensions is a first-rate summary of the state of knowledge in a topic of central interest to readers of this book. One red thread running through these two expert reports, and several others such as the recommendations for environmental research made by the National Science Board (NSB 2000), is the necessity of ensuring that environmental research in the future must integrate the theories and methods of the natural, biological, and social sciences if progress is to be made in the years ahead. While this assertion is hard to argue with, it is rarely practiced. The traditions of compartmentalized science departments and the challenges to collaborative research among communities of scientists speaking different languages, using different methods and sampling techniques, and taking up different assumptions present many difficulties to the course charted by these expert panels. Yet it is a challenge that must be undertaken.

One of the advances made in this past decade is the recognition by the entire community of scientists that human activities now constitute a dominant feature of

Earth's system dynamics. Whereas we spoke a decade ago that urban systems were the only ones that were human-dominated, it is increasingly recognized today that virtually all of Earth's ecosystems, and the planet at large, are human-dominated (Vitousek et al. 1997). Whether we look at the contribution of human activities to the nitrogen cycle, or the contribution to the atmosphere of carbon, human activities often account for at least half of the total, and this role is increasing at a rapid pace. But how might we undertake such a complex task? Fortunately, some scientists from the natural, biological, and social sciences have recognized this challenge and are taking steps to develop new approaches.

Two other recent efforts by the community are worthy of note: the National Science Foundation's *Complex Environmental Systems: Synthesis for Earth, Life and Society in the 21st Century* (NSF 2003) and the International Geosphere-Biosphere Programme's *The Land Project: A Science Plan and Implementation Strategy for Integrated Research on Coupled Human-Environment Systems on Land* (IGBP 2003). The latter is an effort to bring together scientists from the natural, biological, and social sciences working on the terrestrial ecosystems of Earth and to address major questions in an integrative science approach. In defining the central questions, they give priority to defining questions in human-environment terms with a focus on how human society depends on ecosystem goods and services, how human activities impact this provisioning and under what conditions vulnerabilities ensue for either human or natural systems, and to identify in ever more precise ways who the agents of change are, what the magnitude of impacts might be, and what may be done to improve the feedback processes between environmental systems and human systems. The National Science Foundation's synthesis identified coupled human and natural systems research, coupled biological and physical systems research, and the interactions of people and technology as particularly promising critical areas for the next decade. Coupled human and natural systems research looks at the interaction at diverse temporal and spatial scales, uses models to integrate these dimensions, and focuses on issues such as land resources and the built environment, human health and the environment, water resources, and environmental services. The coupled biological and physical systems research agenda focuses on biogeochemical cycles (Schlesinger 1997), climate variability (NRC 1999b), and biodiversity (Tilman 1999) and ecosystem dynamics (Vitousek et al. 1997). The role of technology is critical to our future, but developments need to be focused more on new technologies that protect and improve the environment, that respond promptly to natural hazards and risks experienced by human systems and ecosystems, and that are integrated into knowledge of how we make decisions under uncertainty and how institutions operate to mobilize people to act favorably toward the ecosystems upon which they depend.

In the past decade we have made good progress, as evident in this book and other publications (NRC 1998, 1999b; Matson et al. 1998; S. McCracken et al. 2002a; Fox et al. 2003), in beginning to implement an integrated study of people and environment. We are well posed as a scientific community to make further advances in the coming decades. During the first phase of the International Geosphere-Biosphere Programme, the Earth system was divided into its component parts and its processes studied. In phase 2, currently underway, the Earth system has been put back together with insights from the past decade's worth of research, and processes are now being studied at a regional scale in an integrative science fashion. This has been done by looking at key interactions between land-based systems, ocean-based systems, and atmospheric-based systems. Such a perspective allows examination of whole interactions and interactions in the interphase (such as coastal areas which thereby become the focuses of the interaction between land and ocean). This perspective also allows one to focus on particularly critical points of interaction such as the interactions between megacities and the atmosphere, which allow one to focus on understanding the emissions of various gases from dense urban settlements and their impact on the urban microclimate and precipitation pattern, downwind impacts on the surrounding landscape, and the selective pressure felt by some species in such an environment. Social scientists have similar, but not equivalent, ways of partitioning the world and the research: rural vs. urban, one country vs. another, less developed countries vs. more developed countries. In the years ahead we need to find a common framework that cuts across the natural and social sciences' ways of dividing the world into meaningful research units. The current way of partitioning the world keeps the physical and social sciences from working together more effectively.

One significant source of pressure, and advances, in this area comes from the ever-growing sophistication of observational systems that routinely collect data worldwide. Programs such as Landsat, which since 1972 has provided routine coverage of Earth's land cover, have provided a superb historical archive of digital data that allows for sophisticated comparisons. Over the years, the spatial resolution of these satellite-based sensors has improved. A diverse array of satellites have been launched into orbit since that time that provide ever-growing capabilities for analysis at a variety of spatial and temporal scales—MODIS, AVIRIS, GOES, and many others. These high-atmosphere sensors complement the extensive array of ocean-based buoys that have resulted in our current sophisticated understanding of changes in the oceans' temperatures. We have thus improved our capacity to predict

ENSO events and other climatic anomalies that have a profound impact on human livelihoods through higher or lower precipitation. A growing array of instrumented towers—Fluxnet towers—are now present, not just in the United States (Ameriflux, available at http://public.ornl.gov/ameriflux/) but across the globe (with more than 270 already up and operating), and coordination around the world is moving toward a growing capacity to share the data generated by these towers which are capable of measuring a broad array of ecosystem processes at very fine temporal resolution. Building research around these towers and extending their spatial and temporal coverage will be one important way to make best use of fine temporal resolution data by increasing their spatial relevance.

While no comparable worldwide system of observation of social dynamics is currently available, there is some progress here too. The most common sources of observational systems for social dynamics are the decadal censuses carried out by many countries. Unfortunately, these censuses are not uniform in either method or content. This results in very uneven data being reported, and countries vary in their capability to analyze the data and ensure their comparability. Through global change research we have begun to create regional human-environment observational systems (e.g., the Human-Environment Regional Observatory, or HERO) that are beginning to put order into the current cacophony of data, and they have done so by linking environmental and social data. HERO (see website at http://hero.geog.psu.edu/index.jsp) is a network of researchers using web-based videoconferencing, electronic Delphi tools for collective discussion and decision making, shared notebooks and databases, and interactive maps and graphs to stay in close collaboration across a number of regions that offer contrasts in human-environment dynamics. The researchers are seeking ways to make regional comparisons address global change issues. In the coming decades a lot needs to be done to further bring into line the quality of the natural sciences' data for Earth, with precise measurements and observations of social dynamics so that integrative modeling of human-environment interactions can be undertaken at a variety of scales. The advances will need to come from the kind of integrative science that National Research Council and National Science Foundation panels have suggested must come into existence, and from confronting the challenges of such integrative science.

Issues of Scale

During the past decade, we have grown accustomed to giving attention to issues of scale—particularly temporal and spatial scales—in understanding human-environment interactions (see chapters 2 and 4). While considerable advances have been made (e.g., see Gibson et al. 1998, 2000b) a lot remains to be done. We still do not clearly understand, for example, why a process that explains most of the variance at one scale largely disappears as an explanatory factor at another (E. Moran and Brondízio 1998). Is it because that variable is not important at the other scale, or is it a result that data for that variable are not as available at another scale? Do we have a difference in explanation, or a difference in data quality or availability? (Walsh et al. 1999).

The problem of scale is particularly challenging in the social sciences, since, as noted above, the quality of the observations decreases as one moves from the local to the national to the global scale. The patchiness of Earth presents considerable challenges to issues of scale. People tend to be concentrated in settlements, yet their impact, or footprint, can be felt very far away. How do we quantify the impact of a human population in a Japanese city on a forest in the Philippines or Brazil, from which the Japanese population derives considerable wood products? The tradition of place-based research in both ecology and the social sciences, particularly in local places, has given us valuable insights into the interactions between species and of species with their immediate environment and the feedback processes that help explain their adaptive behavior to the opportunities and constraints they face. Yet this very tradition is challenged by the ever-growing recognition that many species, including the human species, must keep an eye out for resources not only in their local environment but also in environments very far away. It is generally understood that negative feedback is the primary way in which we adjust to normal changes. In cases where our resources are drawn from faraway places, rather than our immediate environment, are the feedback mechanisms different? Or are they absent due to the disconnect of consumption with places that we are unable to do much about? Is this a case of spatial mismatch between dependent and independent variables? How do the characteristics of those feedbacks affect decisions made in the next year or decade for using those resources? What are the lag times in feedback processes at different spatial distances between people and the resources they use?

There is a great deal we can learn from advances in spatial health research where it has been common to deal with phenomena that appear at one scale, but which disappear at a finer scale. This has been particularly intriguing in health research on the relationship between inequality and health which found that countries with greater economic inequalities were associated with lower levels of general health, but that at a variety of scales these inequalities could disappear. Studies of neighborhoods, in contrast to nations, resulted in clearer associations between inequality and health status (Kawachi and Kennedy 2002; Kawachi and Berkman 2003). Openshaw et al. (1988) also addressed this issue with reference to the concept of the modifiable unit area in working within geographic information systems (GIS) in health applications.

Continued attention to how we can keep spatial and temporal scales in mind and resolve the uncertainties we currently experience in understanding processes at different scales of analysis will continue to shape science in the years ahead. This is as it should be since this challenge affects all the sciences, and our ability to make decisions that are scale-informed, rather than misinformed and destructive of those ecosystems.

Issues of Comparison

One way to cope with the challenges of integrative science and scale is to turn to comparative research for help in the interim. Comparative research can be of two kinds, as we have seen in part IV of this book. It can use existing studies and derive from them some metrics for comparison (see chapter 13), using methods such as meta-analysis. It also can be designed from the outset as a comparative dataset, which requires that a large set of studies be undertaken using similar methods and protocols for data collection to ensure comparability of results. The latter yields better results, but is limited, from both a financial and human resources perspective, in the number of case studies it can undertake. The former might be able to have a larger set of cases at much lower cost, but it is unlikely that the cases were collected with the same goals or protocols and thus have many gaps in data (e.g., the lack of soils and environmental data in the cases examined in chapter 13).

During the coming decade, we will need major investments in systematic studies of cases using ever more standardized methods that reflect the needs of the research community and of society. The growing expectation of society that the research paid for by taxpayers ought to be available to society at large will gradually lead the research community to identify what data can be ethically shared with society, and these data will be standardized since the data are not useful otherwise. Thus, whether a study is conducted by a municipality or a state agency, or is federally funded, a growing pressure will exist to archive data centrally. Further pressure will also be brought to bear to ensure that the data are articulated at a variety of temporal and spatial scales, and that each one constitutes added value—rather than paying for the same or similar research several times. The use of the data, or data mining, will create further pressures to streamline data collection and make the data contribute to national, state, and local priorities.

This process will not be easy. There is a long tradition of not sharing data with the public in a timely fashion, and of the importance of publishing in advancing the careers of researchers. Nor is there a tradition of investing the resources of research in the development of robust metadata products that facilitate the use and access to such data by others. Yet the future is relatively clear in this regard: researchers will need to share their data in a timely fashion, they will be expected to provide detailed metadata for such data, and the data will be subjected to ever-growing inspection for its contribution to a variety of objectives. Already, an organization like the National Science Foundation, whose charge is largely to promote the advancement of basic science, has taken into account not just the scientific merit of research, but also its societal relevance and impact in making its funding decisions. Other agencies, more applied in nature, have long held research and data production to standards of usability and require depositing those data in ways that benefit the entire community.

Issues of Institutions and Governance

In chapter 4 and elsewhere in this book, readers have come to appreciate the importance of institutions to the management of resources. This is one of the top priorities of the Committee on Grand Challenges in the Environmental Sciences (NRC 2001), and in several other expert panels. A recent state-of-the-art assessment of our understanding of common-property institutions found a lot of progress in the past two decades, and many challenges to undertake in the decade ahead (NRC 2002). For most of human history, institutions evolved locally in response to local needs. As our environmental crises have become global, however, institutions created to address broad-scale problems, as well as finer-scale ones, have proliferated. For example, 20,000 water management units operate in the United States alone to provide rules for water rights. Yet, very little is known about how these local institutions vary in their capacity to adapt successfully to changes in the resource or in the policies that make them possible. There is a challenge ahead to develop a sufficient understanding of different institutions and their responses to change so that institutional design choices can be based on empirically grounded knowledge. We need, particularly, studies on how institutions vary in their capacity to adapt to variability: Can lessons from studies of institutional adaptability in areas with traditionally high environmental variability be drawn on to adjust institutions to areas only now experiencing this degree of variability due to climate change?

One particularly promising research area for the future is understanding how global environmental goods, such as ozone, atmospheric carbon dioxide, and oceans can be governed given the previously unregulated nature of these global common-pool resources. Both global agreements and national and local implementation are required, yet very little experience in how to do this effectively exists. Research needs to focus on how different combinations of policy instruments and monitoring systems can be put in place that can ensure an effective incentive structure at local, national, and global scales.

Issues around the Cycling of Carbon and Nitrogen

One of the most critical dimensions of contemporary global change research has centered on carbon accounting: understanding the carbon emissions, the stored sinks of carbon, and closing the accounts by finding out why there is a very large pool of carbon unaccounted for. However, as we move between local/regional models and global models we discover that the accounting problem is far more serious than is routinely acknowledged. At global scale, and using very coarse grid cells for modeling, there is a lot of carbon unaccounted for, and very large data gaps. What is less recognized is that at local to regional scales the problem is magnified further because there is great diversity of capacity to measure these carbon sources and sinks from place to place on Earth. Europe and the United States have reasonable accounts for the near past, but for much of Earth the estimates are based on a very limited number of studies in a very small number of locations, which are extrapolated spatially to much larger areas than may be justified. This quickly becomes evident when working at regional and local scales. Thus, a challenge for the decades ahead is to increase capacity globally to monitor carbon emission and sequestration, as well as establish the magnitude of pools, so that future global and regional models are based on robust measurements and less on estimates and backcasting. Considerable resources are being invested in the first decade of the twenty-first century to improve our understanding of the carbon cycle, and it is a research priority worldwide. Biogeochemical cycles have been ripe for further study, but today greater attention is being paid to how human activities affect these cycles and how actions might be taken to ensure that our actions do not undermine the fundamental capacity of those systems to provide us with goods, such as water, sustain biodiversity, and maintain a stable rather than wildly fluctuating climate. The U.S. Carbon Cycle Science Plan (USGCP 1999) constitutes just one of many such efforts being undertaken across the globe (cf. the Global Carbon Project at http://www.globalcarbonproject.org/) to provide improved understanding of the magnitude and distribution of carbon sources and sinks; the effects of past, present, and future land-use change; how these sources and sinks change at seasonal to centennial time scales; and what the impact of these changes in carbon sources and sinks means to the Earth system.

Only recently has it become clear that models of forest carbon sequestration, such as TEM, Century, PnET, MEL, and others, are highly sensitive to the effects brought about by export of nutrients in dissolved organic forms, and that they need to be revised to incorporate such dynamics (Perakis and Hedin 2002). Such incorporation is currently prohibited by our poor understanding of how inorganic and organic nutrient losses vary across landscapes as a function of major factors thought to influence ecosystem biogeochemical cycles. To advance our understanding of what might be the landscape-level controls on nutrient-carbon interactions (particularly nitrogen and phosphorus on the operation of these cycles) we need a better understanding of the patterns of hydrologic nitrogen and phosphorus losses. These must, in turn, be linked to indices of terrestrial nutrient cycling and stocks across soil types and intensities of land use. How the nitrogen and phosphorus stocks and fluxes enter and exit a given ecosystem is expected to have very large consequences for the productivity of those ecosystems, and to the fate of carbon in those systems.

This research theme should not be seen purely in atmospheric terms. There is considerable literature emerging on environmentally significant consumption from the social sciences that can and should be related to issues of carbon emission and sequestration; and of course, as we have seen earlier, institutions and governance of international agreements of carbon emissions and goals by nations also are closely related to what happens to carbon. Human patterns of consumption have everything to do with carbon emissions from fossil fuels: automobile use, the size of homes (currently becoming larger, thereby requiring more heating and cooling than the smaller homes of the past) associated with affluence, and even food consumption (consumers expect food from anywhere in the world without regard for the energy costs of transporting it). Linking these human demands, institutional regulation, and patterns of land use to the carbon cycle will go a long way in advancing our understanding of these dynamic processes.

Issues of Biodiversity and Conservation

An even higher priority for the coming decades is being assigned by the scientific community to understanding the regulatory and functional consequences of biological diversity, and how we can best sustain this diversity. It is said frequently that today we face the risk of a great mass extinction comparable to only a couple of other events in Earth's geological history. While we seem to value biodiversity, it is not at all clear how much biodiversity is necessary to sustain the ecosystems on which we depend. To understand this relationship we need to understand the fundamental controls on biological diversity present in nature; we need to understand how much alteration can take place without damage to the services provided by ecosystems; and we need to understand how to integrate conservation with human uses. Much of the negative impact of humans on biodiversity is not "intentional" but rather the result of single actions (e.g., agricultural development and food production) that have unintended consequences in the form of transforming forests into plowed fields devoid of the species that lived in the forest.

To advance research in this area we need to use new techniques for assessing biodiversity from incomplete sampling and use tools such as remote sensing to examine ecosystem characteristics and monitor the rapid changes that can occur in the habitat conditions that sustain biodiversity. We need to develop a process-based theory of biological diversity at a variety of spatial and temporal scales. We need to tighten scientific explanation with regard to the relationship of diversity to ecosystem functioning, including experiments with manipulated diversity and quasi-experiments that examine patterns of human activities and their impact on biodiversity. We need a lot of research on techniques for managing habitats that include people but still operate as integral systems even if reduced in spatial scale from their earlier, and much larger, geographic extent. Changes in agriculture and in settlement patterns across the world affect biogeochemical cycles through changes in land cover. We need to understand the feedback from these changes on biodiversity and on the biogeochemical cycles that sustain those systems. In short, how do we create or manage sustainable natural systems, with people as a part of them, that operate in such a way that the goods and services of natural systems are still provided, biodiversity is sustained, and extinction rates are reduced to a minimum? This is a tough challenge for research, but one that we overlook at our peril.

Issues of Vulnerability and Sustainability

It remains to be seen to what extent human populations can begin to put a priority on ensuring the sustainability of Earth's natural systems by realizing how vulnerable we are by not conserving them. We already see evidence of how many people suffer across the world from the destruction of habitats and exposure to famine, lack of access to water, and other losses of environmental goods and services. Considerable efforts are underway to advance our understanding of vulnerabilities, both natural and human (see NAS 2003). Vulnerability is the degree to which a system is likely to experience harm due to exposure to a hazard. In environmental terms, it refers to the vulnerability of human systems and ecosystems to local-to-global environmental changes. This is an important area since it synthesizes in a number of ways all of the concerns we have about the consequences of environmental changes taking place on the planet. It is concerned with the sensitivity of the coupled human-environment system to multiple stresses and the resilience or adaptability of the system to handle multiple stresses.

In the years ahead, we must improve our capacity to characterize these stresses, understand their interactions with and consequences on different parts of ecosystems and human systems, and identify where and who is most likely to be vulnerable. This means having a more robust system for identifying differential exposure to these stresses (magnitude, sequencing, and combinations that are particularly stressful), to understand enough about the resilience of human and natural systems to have predictive capability with regard to their sensitivity to multiple stresses, and ultimately to enhance the resilience of human and natural systems through interventions that reduce the risk of extinction or losses that bring about irreversible changes in the human-environment system (Kates and Parris 2003; Parris and Kates 2003).

One of the most notable changes taking place that increases vulnerability is climate change and the growing frequency of extreme weather events. One of the challenges here is the consideration of different temporal and spatial scales in assessing these impacts, and developing and testing techniques for modifying, creating, and managing habitats that can sustain biological diversity and human activities within a healthy environment. These tasks become viable only if we undertake further research on climate variability by increasing our capacity to predict extreme events, and to ready ourselves for interannual and decadal changes in climate. This will require attention to how and why humans respond, or not, to information about these upcoming events and at what level of spatial and temporal detail such information is likely to affect human behavior and reduce human and ecosystem vulnerabilities to these fluctuations. Climate variability is ineluctably linked to changes in water availability—thus the importance of improving hydrologic forecasting. Floods, droughts, sedimentation, and other processes affect terrestrial and aquatic ecosystems, human settlement, and the integrity of human-environment systems (B. Turner et al. 2003).

These are, in turn, affected by how changes in the environment, in climate, and in hydrology affect human health and the spatial and temporal distribution of infectious diseases and their evolution. Research that improves our capacity to predict where and when such events will occur can lay the foundations for preparedness and reduction of vulnerability, particularly if efforts also are made to improve human understanding and capacity to respond to this information. Another source are disturbances coming from the human system, such as broad-scale development efforts and natural resources exploitation that open up previously unaffected systems to rapid change, without careful attention to the characteristics of those systems and their vulnerabilities. The last remaining wildlife refuge areas, and protected areas, are always under threat of being opened up for resource use by political and economic interests, despite their importance. Making sure that the contributions of those areas to human welfare are well established provides a foundation for their protection, even if it cannot always guarantee it. Attention to stakeholders, and their vulnerabilities, may be of growing importance in reducing the vulnerability of human and natural systems, and protecting biodiversity and biogeochemical cycles. After all, it is the human population that ultimately decides when and where to transform the landscape for its benefit (Cash et al. 2003).

Population and Environment Issues

Last, but always first on most people's lips as a cause of global environmental change, is the role of population in environmental change. While there is no question that the demands of the human population on the physical environment are a major cause of the changes we see around us, it is hardly sheer numbers alone that explain this impact. Affluent populations have a disproportionate impact on the environment compared with less affluent peoples—thus, the importance of evaluating both population and consumption as joint contributors to the overall human impact (NRC 1997). In fact, there is evidence that stewardship sometimes improves with increased density: as resources become scarce, wasteful behavior is restrained by community or social rules restricting access to resources.

During the coming decades we can expect that the scientific analysis of population and environment interactions will emerge as a distinct field of study (Lutz et al. 2002). To advance this new field of study, research will need to be explicit and sophisticated in how it measures both population and environmental variables. In the past, studies have tended to be strong on one side and weak on the other. This can be corrected by implementation of the sorts of integrative studies mentioned in the first section of this chapter, with strong representation of demographers, environmental scientists and modelers, and other scientists whose expertise is appropriate to the questions being asked. While such approaches are likely to be case study specific, it is through ensuring their interdisciplinarity that we can advance the field, as long as the community is in communication about standards of measurement that ensure eventual comparison across a diverse set of cases. Advances also can be expected by focusing on specific mechanisms, whether populational or environmental, that seem to mediate these dynamics. Population and environment studies will need to develop more sophisticated theoretical models to advance this area of research. Another sure way to improve the chances of having this work take place is to make sure the work speaks to the concerns of stakeholders. Population and environment encapsulate many of the concerns raised in earlier sections of this chapter: the need for integrative approaches across the physical and social sciences; the importance of scale in explanation and causality; the need for comparisons on which to hang integrative case studies; the impact of people on carbon cycling and biodiversity (and vice versa); and the key role of human institutions in mediating the relationships of people to the environment, particularly their vulnerabilities to it or their resilience.

A Final Word

The above issues present a very broad agenda for the global change community, and a great challenge: the integrative study of human-environment dynamics. The work presented in this book reflects some of the progress that has been made in this direction, with authors from Earth system science and social science working together to address questions that are inherently interdisciplinary. Yet our universities are still organized very much along disciplinary lines, and the professional reward system still favors disciplinary approaches over interdisciplinary ones.

One of the lessons our research group has learned from the past several years of carrying out this work is that one can sustain disciplinary rigor and develop interdisciplinary skills at the same time. While there are surely other ways to achieve this, it might be useful to share how we went about it. First, the process cannot be hurried, but can be assumed from the outset to require time and lots of good will on the part of the majority of disciplinary partners. In our case, it took well over a year and a half of extended meetings, nearly each week at the outset, to begin to lay out the assumptions we were working from. Second, it required a willingness to learn new theories and methods. We did this by creating theory and method groups, wherein members selected key theories and methods that underlie the approach of the discipline represented, and each week we assigned the group to read one or two key examples that used that theory or method, and discussed what each offered to the research questions we were addressing. This allowed us to evaluate the merits and appropriateness of each and to decide whether it would be a part of our approach. Third, we took over a year and a half to develop protocols for research that could be applied across our sites, while still allowing some site-specific components to be present. This helped overcome the "my site is different" syndrome common to many case study–oriented scientists, as it allowed standardization of both important variables across sites and site-specific variables or information sensitive to site variability. Fourth, ensuring that field teams had people from across the disciplines working together led to very valuable dialogue during field data collection, and resulted in mutual respect and discussions on how to integrate the data being collected across the social and biophysical sciences. And last, to ensure that these efforts were institutionalized, it was very important that senior members of the effort work toward changing the system of rewards in the university. This can be accomplished only if senior scientists' work holds to the highest scholarly standards of their disciplines and demonstrates the validity and rigor of interdisciplinary scientific work; if the younger scientists' work does the same; and if the process of hiring and promotion is restructured to promote an ideology in which the quality of the research, and not its disciplinarity, is valued the most. This can take many forms, but one which we found to be particularly valuable was in hiring for given lines of research (e.g., land use, institutions, demography, GIS, remote sensing), inviting at least three disciplines, and sometimes up to five, to take part in the search. This had two benefits: (1) it provided a mechanism for different disciplines to put forth their best candidates, and (2) it led to mutual respect and competition for faculty positions. Because hiring was always done with the approval of the disciplinary unit in which the faculty person would be housed, the departments were pleased to participate. But by having an interdisciplinary search committee make the first cuts and the final decisions, it ensured that the best scientist would be hired from a diverse pool, and that that person would contribute the most to the research effort of the center. In our experience this approach has led to increasing cooperation between departments, and a tremendous growth in good will among units. We made sure that we did not have quotas for given units and that those units that were likely to have a supply of candidates for the given area of interest were invited to take part. The fact that our faculty members have been of interest to other universities since their appointments is a measure of the quality that resulted from this process. A further benefit is that the faculty has developed curricula that mix disciplinary rigor and interdisciplinarity across units, thereby achieving a critical role of the center—to enrich the curriculum with courses that are of more than individual disciplinary interest.

The next step for us, and for many in the community, is to carry this perspective to the undergraduate curriculum and to K–12 schools so that addressing environmental issues is a truly holistic effort, backed by an integrative science dedicated to uncovering the pathways to a sustainable society.

Glossary

actor Any unit that makes decisions with respect to a particular land use (e.g., a company that makes decisions about what to do on its land, a household that makes decisions about its land use).

afforestation (vs. reforestation) Ecologists often do not differentiate between afforestation and reforestation. Afforestation refers to increasing forest lands in the absence of human effort. Reforestation refers to increasing forest lands primarily by means of human effort such as tree planting.

agent-based model A disaggregated simulation model in which decision-making actors, such as landowners or institutional actors, are represented as autonomous objects. Simulation outcomes are determined through sequenced interactions between these autonomous agents and their environment. In contrast to analytical mathematical models, outcomes emerge through individual decisions and interactions between agents, rather than being imposed as a set of equilibrium conditions.

agricultural intensification The process of increasing the agricultural inputs (labor, fertilizer, insecticide, herbicide) or shortening the fallow length to increase the yield on a given piece of land. This is in contrast to agricultural *ex*tensification, in which previously uncultivated lands are brought into cultivation to increase production for a given group of people.

alfisols Moderately leached forest soils that have relatively high native fertility. These soils are well developed and contain a subsurface horizon in which clays have accumulated. They are mostly found in temperate humid and subhumid regions of the world. The combination of generally favorable climate and high native fertility allows alfisols to be very productive soils for both agriculture and silviculture. Patches are found also in the humid tropics, such as the Amazon basin.

allometric equation An equation that uses known size or mass measurements to estimate related unknown measurements; for example, an estimation of the biomass of a tree using an equation based on the **dbh** (q.v.) and height of that tree.

basal area of a stand The sum of the basal area of each of the tree species occurring in the stand. Units typically are square meters of stem area per hectare.

basal area of a tree species The sum of the cross-sectional area, measured at **dbh** (q.v.), of all stems of a tree species within a given stand. Units typically are square meters of stem area per hectare.

behavioral economics A contemporary approach in economics that examines individual behavior in a variety of exchange, coordination, bargaining, trust, and dilemma situations, frequently in experimental laboratories, rather than relying exclusively on analytical models based on a single model of short-term maximization of utility.

biomass The mass of living and nonliving biological tissues, usually measured per unit area. *Total biomass* includes the aboveground and belowground mass, such as trees, shrubs, vines, roots, dead plants, and leaf litter.

broad-scale In terms of space, broad-scale processes (or datasets) encompass geographically large spatial extents (or coarser resolutions). In terms of time, broad-scale processes (or datasets) designate long-lived phenomena (or long sampling intervals). For example, the cutting of the primary forest in the eastern United States is a fine-scale phenomenon, but it may eventually affect half a continent and take several hundred years.

caboclo The native non-Indian population of the Brazilian Amazon.

calibration The process of comparing an instrument's measurements with a standard or known input.

change detection The process of identifying differences in the state of an object or phenomenon by observing it at different times.

change detection image A difference image generated by digitally comparing images acquired at different times.

collective action The process of obtaining an outcome that requires the inputs of two or more actors.

collective-choice rules Rules that define who is eligible and the decision rules that will be used in making policy-level choices in legislative, administrative, or judicial settings.

common-pool resources Resources that are subject to depletion and for which exclusion of users is difficult.

common-property regimes A form of property in which joint owners share governance and management decisions and rights of access to a resource.

community (1) Social scientists refer to a community as the relationships between a group of individuals who interact on a regular basis and the meanings associated with these relationships. Thus, a sociology department is a community with shared ideas and values composed of individuals interacting regularly. Or we can refer to a virtual community of individuals interacting on the Internet. (2) Natural scientists refer to a community as a group of living things that occupy the same space at the same time. Community is often prefixed by a name that describes the major biota (e.g., temperate forest community, desert shrub community, benthic invertebrate community, etc.).

dbh Diameter at breast height. The diameter of a tree stem (the bole) measured at 137 cm above ground level.

digital elevation model (DEM) A raster set of elevations, usually spaced in a uniform horizontal grid.

duration The length or period of time (either short or long) that some process operates or state exists, or the length of time during which a dataset is collected. For example, "the drought lasted for eighteen months," or "the Landsat image series had a duration of thirty-one years."

dynamic simulation model A systems modeling approach with explicit representations of the dynamic interactions among entities.

economically rational In contemporary economics, *rational behavior* means choices made by an individual in light of complete information about the situation the individual is in and the likely choices of others made to achieve the highest level of utility feasible in that situation.

economies of scale In production processes that require a substantial initial investment in factories, equipment, and other physical infrastructure, the marginal costs of producing outputs is reduced, the larger the scale of operations (the more product produced with a fixed investment) up to some limit.

ecosystem product In the economic sense, a "good" is anything that anyone wants or needs. Ecosystems products are goods produced by natural, rather than human, means such as food, fiber, building materials, oxygen, clean water, and so on.

ecosystem service Processes involved in producing ecosystem products, including photosynthesis, decomposition, pollination, filtration, weather processes, flood control, erosion protection, and so on.

emergent property A property of a system which is evident at one level of inquiry but not evident at lower levels of organization. Single cells are not capable of thought, but if they organize into a nervous system and combine with other cells organized into other systems, thought becomes possible at the level of the whole organism.

endogenous Information or conditions that are determined within the system under study; the output of a modeling effort. For example, land-use choices are generally a key endogenous output of land-use models.

equilibrium (1) In ecology, a *static equilibrium* refers to a constant state in which a particular condition would persist indefinitely unless disturbed. This definition regards disturbance as exogenous to this system. As our understanding of disturbance has improved, ecologists now use the concept of *dynamic equilibrium* in which the proportions of different biota may be somewhat constant but change over time as disturbances disrupt biotic communities, changing structure and composition to some new arrangement which may then, over time, return to an earlier configuration. (2) In economics, an equilibrium is the outcome, if one exists, that occurs when all participants choose their best strategies in a market or other institutional arrangement.

evapotranspiration The annual sum of the water evaporated to the atmosphere from the soil and other surfaces plus the water transpired by plants.

exogenous Information or conditions that are determined outside the system under study. For example, climate change is considered to be exogenous in most fine-scale land-use studies.

extent The total geographic area covered by a certain land cover, process, or dataset. For example, "the forest extent was over 100 ha," or "half the extent of the forest was cleared."

externality A positive or negative outcome from transactions that affect individuals other than those directly involved in the transaction. Examples: pollution is a negative externality from the production and exchange of private goods; economic productivity is a positive externality from private investments in education.

fine-scale In terms of space, fine-scale processes (or datasets) encompass geographically small areas of analysis, that is, small extents (or finer-image resolutions). In terms of time, fine-scale processes (or datasets) designate short-lived phenomena (or short sampling intervals). For example, an individual farmer cutting a single tree is a fine-scale phenomenon; it may affect an area of less than 100 m^2 and may take only an hour.

gazetted forests Forests owned by the government of Uganda that are not designated as national parks.

general equilibrium model (GEM) A macromodel that focuses on the broad properties of a national economic system at equilibrium.

geographic information system (GIS) A computer-based system to aid in the collection, maintenance, storage, analysis, output, and distribution of spatial data and information.

geometric rectification The process whereby an image is "warped" to fit a grid or map projection. Ground control points with known geographic coordinates are found on both a map and in the raw sensor data and submitted to the computer for processing. The transformation embeds the geographic coordinates onto the satellite data and converts the data to overlay a known grid.

global positioning system (GPS) A satellite-based system used to find the locational coordinates of a receiver unit on Earth's surface in a specified coordinate system. GPS applications include navigation, field data collection, and route finding.

institutional analysis Methods and approaches for analyzing institutional arrangements, including their characteristics and processes of development and change.

Institutional Analysis and Development (IAD) framework An approach for analyzing the major dimensions and interrelationships that shape institutional functions and processes. It presents a set of elements that are common to any type of institutional analysis at multiple levels.

institutions The formal and informal (unwritten) rules that specify the actions that an individual in a particular situation may, must, or must not undertake. Rules encompass the information available and the likely consequences of the actions, as well as specifying who is responsible for monitoring conformance.

International Forest Resources and Institutions (IFRI) research program An interdisciplinary, comparative methodology for investigating the social and biophysical factors that influence forest conditions, and shape resource use and management through time. The program incorporates ten protocols that address socioeconomic, demographic, and biophysical variables, as well as institutional dimensions that may influence relationships among people, forests, and institutions.

landscape trajectory The direction (deforestation or reforestation) that a landscape takes over time.

land tenure system The system of rules about rights to use land, ownership of land, and rights to the products of the land.

liana A woody climbing plant with a stem diameter of 2 to 10 cm.

location quotient (LQ) A commonly used statistic to measure regional concentration, defined as the ratio of shares of employment in a given sector of the regional economy to employment in that sector of the state or national economy.

maximum-likelihood classifier A classification decision rule based on the probability that a pixel belongs to a particular class. The basic equation assumes that these probabilities are equal for all classes, and that the input bands have normal distributions.

metadata "Data about data." They describe the content, quality, condition, and other characteristics of data. Metadata help a person to locate and understand data.

minimum mapping unit (MMU) The size of the smallest feature represented in a spatial dataset for a particular feature class. An example is a land-cover dataset where a minimum threshold size for a forest polygon is defined at the time of image interpretation.

norms Culturally specific ideas about behavior that is appropriate in a particular situation.

open access A resource or area that has no effective owner or rules-in-use to control access. This may include areas such as "paper parks" for which legislation is written and ownership is designated, but which are not recognized in practice.

open source A system of software licensing in which software code is made available to a broader community with rights to modify and further distribute the code.

oxisols Very highly weathered soils that are found primarily in the intertropical regions of the world. Most of these soils are characterized by extremely low native fertility, resulting from very low nutrient reserves, high phosphorus retention by oxide minerals, and low cation exchange capacity. Most nutrients in oxisol ecosystems are contained in the standing vegetation and decomposing plant material.

parcel A tract or area of land usually identified by an organization as being owned by a single entity (e.g., individual or household) and identifiable by distinct spatial boundaries.

patch A relatively homogeneous area of vegetation. The degree of homogeneity required will vary with the scale of interest and the nature of the interested party. A mountain lion hunting deer will likely regard a meadow as homogeneous, whereas the deer will regard it as being composed of edible and inedible plants which may, themselves, constitute patches within the meadow.

raster A two- or three-dimensional data matrix. One of two main data structures used in GIS and remote sensing (see also **vector**). Raster data structures use a gridded set of cells to represent spatial features. Cells are of uniform dimensions, and each cell has a specific value. Cell values can represent the existence of a water feature (0 or 1), surface elevation (in meters), or population density (people/km^2).

relative dominance The basal area of a tree species divided by the total basal area of the stand. Often used as an estimate of the proportion of biomass that a species contributes to stand structure, measured as a percentage of the basal area represented by a species relative to the total basal area of all species in a stand.

resilience In ecology, the ability of an ecosystem to undergo disturbance and return to its predisturbance condition. Most grasslands are resilient to fire because although aboveground foliage is burned, undamaged belowground vegetation allows these communities to recover.

resolution The smallest spatial unit (area) that makes up a dataset. Usually defined as the length of one side of a cell in a raster representation of a dataset, each unit or cell, or picture element (pixel). Usually the cells are square, arranged in a rectilinear grid, and of a constant size. For example, "the image had a resolution of 29.5 m."

robustness The maintenance of some desired system characteristics despite fluctuations in the behavior of its component parts or its environment.

rules-in-use Rules that are recognized and practiced. These may include both formal rules that are written, and informal or customary rules that are known and may have evolved over time.

sampling frequency The smallest temporal unit at which a dataset was acquired. Also called sampling interval, time step, or rate of occurrence. For example, "the sampling frequency of the IFRI study was five years."

spatial metrics Measurements that quantify the spatial pattern and composition of geographic areas.

spatial reference system The datum, coordinate system, and map projection of a spatial dataset.

stand A group of trees growing in a specific locale and having sufficient uniformity in species composition, area, density, and other spatial arrangements to be distinguishable from adjacent stands.

strategic actor An actor that evaluates all of the strategies available and chooses the one that is judged most likely to get the outcome preferred by the actor.

structure The relationships between individuals and between organizations created by humans. For example, the transportation network that links various places in a country is a structure, as is the set of social relationships linking the members of a government.

swidden agriculture Shifting agriculture in which users change the fields they cultivate frequently, with more land fallow than in cultivation at any one time.

textural analysis of soil Measurement of the particle size distribution of a soil as percents of sand, silt, and clay. These properties influence soil characteristics such as soil structure, bulk density, infiltration rate, water-holding capacity, and cation exchange capacity.

texture The pattern of intensity variations in an image.

texture measure An approach or formula used to calculate texture.

time-series analysis An approach using remote sensing to analyze change over time by layering satellite images taken at different times. Also referred to as multitemporal analysis.

topology In GIS, the spatial relationships between objects. Topological properties include adjacency, connectivity, contiguity, and containment.

training sample A field observation used to refer to (1) a selected cluster of pixels representative of a specific land cover in a remotely sensed image and (2) the actual land cover observed on the ground for that location.

traverse A prescribed, repeatable method for locating sampling points in field research.

ultisols Strongly leached, acid forest soils with relatively low native fertility. These soils have a subsurface horizon in which clays have accumulated, often with strong yellowish or reddish colors resulting from the presence of iron oxides. They are found primarily in humid temperate and tropical areas of the world, typically on older, stable landscapes. Because of the favorable climate regimes in which they are typically found, ultisols often support productive forests but are poorly suited for continuous agriculture without the use of fertilizer and lime.

vector One of two main data structures used in GIS and remote sensing (see also **raster**). Vector data structures represent spatial objects as points, lines, and polygons constructed from sets of x,y-coordinates.

vegetation composition Usually, the species composition of the vegetation of a particular community or at a particular site.

vegetation structure Usually, the layers of vegetation (e.g., understory, shrub, understory tree, canopy tree) or the plant growth forms (herbaceous, shrub, single-stem tree, multistem tree) of a particular community or at a particular site.

window size The size of a moving window, which is often used in texture analysis or spatial filtering. Processing is done by mathematic calculation using the pixels in a moving window. When selecting the size, odd numbers are often used. Common window sizes are 3×3, 5×5, and 7×7.

References

Aber, J. D., and J. M. Melillo. 2001. *Terrestrial Ecosystems*, 2d ed. San Diego: Academic Press.

Achard, F., H. D. Eva, H.-J. Stibig, P. Mayaux, J. Gallego, T. Richards, and J.-P. Malingreau. 2002. Determination of Deforestation Rates of the World's Humid Tropical Forests. *Science* 297:999–1002.

Agarwal, C., G. M. Green, J. M. Grove, T. P. Evans, and C. M. Schweik. 2002. *A Review and Assessment of Land-Use Change Models: Dynamics of Space, Time, and Human Choice*. CIPEC Collaborative Report No. 1. USFS Publication GTR-NE-297. Joint publication by the Center for the Study of Institutions, Population, and Environmental Change at Indiana University–Bloomington and the U.S. Department of Agriculture (USDA) Forest Service. Burlington, VT: USDA Forest Service Northeastern Forest Research Station. URL: http://www.srs.fs.usda.gov/pubs/viewpub.jsp?index=5027.

Agrawal, A. 1995. Population Pressure = Forest Degradation: An Oversimplistic Equation? *Unasylva* 181:50–58.

———. 1996. The Community vs. the Market and the State: Forest Use in Uttarakhand in the Indian Himalayas. *Journal of Agricultural and Environmental Ethics* 9(1):1–15.

———. 2000. Small is beautiful, but is large better? Forest Management Institutions in the Kumaon Himalaya, India. In *People and Forests. Communities, Institutions, and Governance*, ed. C. C. Gibson, M. A. McKean, and E. Ostrom, 57–85. Cambridge, MA: MIT Press.

———. 2002. Common Resources and Institutional Sustainability. In *The Drama of the Commons*, ed. E. Ostrom, T. Dietz, N. Dolšak, P. C. Stern, and E. U. Weber, 41–85. Washington, DC: National Academy Press.

Agrawal, A., C. Britt, and K. Kanel. 1999. *Decentralization in Nepal: A Comparative Analysis*. Oakland, CA: ICS Press.

Agrawal, A., and C. Gibson. 1999. Enchantment and Disenchantment: The Role of Community in Natural Resource Conservation. *World Development* 27:629–649.

Agrawal, A., and E. Ostrom. 2001. Collective Action, Property Rights and Decentralization in Resource Use in India and Nepal. *Politics and Society* 29(4):485–514.

Ahn, S. E., A. J. Plantinga, and R. J. Alig. 2000. Predicting Future Forestland Area: A Comparison of Econometric Approaches. *Forest Science* 46:363–376.

Alavi, S. M. Z. 1965. *Arab Geography in the Ninth and Tenth Centuries*. Aligarh, India: Department of Geography, Ali-garh Muslim University.

Alchian, A. 1950. Uncertainty, Evolution, and Economic Theory. *Journal of Political Economy* 58:211–221.

Allen, T. F. H., and T. W. Hoekstra. 1992. *Toward a Unified Ecology*. New York: Columbia University Press.

Alves, D. S. 2002. An Analysis of the Geographical Patterns of Deforestation in the Brazilian Amazon in the Period 1991–1996. In *Deforestation and Land Use in the Amazon*, ed. C. H. Wood and R. Porro, 95–106. Gainesville: University Press of Florida.

Anderies, J. M., M. A. Janssen, and E. Ostrom. 2004. A Framework to Analyze the Robustness of Institutions in Social-Ecological Systems. *Ecology and Society* 9(1):18 [online]. URL: http://www.ecologyandsociety.org/vol9/iss1/art18.

Anderson, A. 1990. Deforestation in Amazonia. In *Alternatives to Deforestation: Steps toward Sustainable Use of the Amazon Rain Forest*, ed. A. Anderson, 3–23. New York: Columbia University Press.

Anderson, G. L., J. D. Hanson, and R. H. Haas. 1993. Evaluating Landsat Thematic Mapper Derived Vegetation Indices for Estimating Above-Ground Biomass on Semiarid Rangelands. *Remote Sensing of Environment* 45:165–175.

Andersson, K. P. 2003a. *Can decentralization save Bolivia's forests? An Institutional Analysis of Municipal Forest Governance*. CIPEC Dissertation Series, No. 9. Bloomington: Center for the Study of Institutions, Population, and Environmental Change (CIPEC), Indiana University.

———. 2003b. What motivates municipal governments? Uncovering the Institutional Incentives for Municipal Forest Governance in Bolivia. *Journal of Environment and Development* 12(1):5–27.

Angelsen, A., and D. Kaimowitz. 1999. Rethinking the Causes of Deforestation: Lessons from Economic Models. *World Bank Research Observer* 14(1):73–98.

Anselin, L. 2001. Spatial Effects in Econometric Practice in Environmental and Resource Economics. *American Journal of Agricultural Economics* 83:705–710.

Ardo, J. 1992. Volume Quantification of Coniferous Forest Compartments Using Spectral Radiance Record by Landsat Thematic Mapper. *International Journal of Remote Sensing* 13:1779–1786.

Arizpe, L., ed. 1996. *The Cultural Dimensions of Global Change: An Anthropological Approach*. Paris: UNESCO.

Arizpe, L., M. P. Stone, and D. C. Major. 1994. Rethinking the Population-Environment Debate. In *Population and the Environment: Rethinking the Debate*, ed. L. Arizpe, M. P. Stone, and D. C. Major, 1–9. Boulder, CO: Westview.

Arnold, J. E. M., and J. G. Campbell. 1986. Collective Management of Hill Forests in Nepal: The Community Forestry Development Project. In *Proceedings of the Conference on Common Property Resource Management, April 21–26, 1985*. Publication of the National Research Council (NRC). Washington, DC: National Academies Press. Available from National Academies Press library at nrclib@nas.edu.

Ascher, W. 1995. *Communities and Sustainable Forestry in Developing Countries*. San Francisco: ICS Press.

Babbie, E. R. 2004. *The Practice of Social Research*, 10th ed. Belmont, CA: Thomson/Wadsworth. Includes CD-ROM and InfoTrac.

Baland, J.-M., and J.-P. Platteau. 1996. *Halting Degradation of National Resources: Is there a role for rural communities?* Oxford: Clarendon Press.

Baldocchi, D. D., R. Valentini, S. Running, W. Oechel, and R. Dahlman. 1996. Strategies for Measuring and Modeling Carbon Dioxide and Water Vapour Fluxes over Terrestrial Ecosystems. *Global Change Biology* 2:159–168.

Balée, W. 1994. *Footprints of the Forest: Ka'apor Ethnobotany, the Historical Ecology of Plant Utilization by an Amazonian People*. New York: Columbia University Press.

Balée, W., and A. Gely. 1989. Managed Forest Succession in Amazonia: The Ka'apor Case. *Advances in Economic Botany* 7:129–158.

Balée, W., and D. Posey, eds. 1989. *Resource Management in Amazonia: Indigenous and Folk Strategies*. Vol. 7 of Advances in Economic Botany. New York: New York Botanical Garden.

Ballew, G. I. 1975. *A Method for Converting Landsat 1 MSS Data to Reflectance by Means of Ground Calibration Sites*. Stanford Remote Sensing Lab Technical Report SRSL 75-5. Stanford, CA: Stanford University.

Banana, A., and W. Gombya-Ssembajjwe. 2000. Successful Forest Management: The Importance of Security of Tenure and Rule Enforcement in Ugandan Forests. In *People and Forests: Communities, Institutions, and Governance*, ed. C. C. Gibson, M. A. McKean, and E. Ostrom, 87–98. Cambridge, MA: MIT Press.

Banana, A., N. Vogt, W. Gombya-Ssembajjwe, and J. Bahati. Under review. Decentralization, Local Governance, and Forest Conditions: The Case of Forests in Mpigi District of Uganda. *World Development*.

Bannari, A., D. Morin, F. Bonn, and A. R. Huete. 1995. A Review of Vegetation Indices. *Remote Sensing Reviews* 13:95–120.

Barbier, E. B. 2000. Links between Economic Liberalization and Rural Resource Degradation in the Developing Regions. *Agricultural Economics* 23(3):299–310.

Barford, C. C., S. C. Wofsy, M. L. Goulden, J. W. Munger, E. H. Pyle, S. P. Urbanski, L. Hutyra, S. R. Saleska, D. Fitzgerald, and K. Moore. 2001. Factors Controlling Long- and Short-Term Sequestration of Atmospheric CO_2 in a Mid-Latitude Forest. *Science* 294:1688–1691.

Barnes, B. V., D. R. Zak, S. R. Denton, and S. H. Spurr. 1998. *Forest Ecology*. New York: Wiley.

Barreteau, O., and F. Bousquet. 2000. SHADOC: A Multi-Agent Model to Tackle Viability of Irrigated Systems. *Annals of Operations Research* 94:139–162.

Batistella, M. 2001. *Landscape Change and Land-Use/Land-Cover Dynamics in Rondônia, Brazilian Amazon*. CIPEC Dissertation Series, No. 7. Bloomington: Center for the Study of Institutions, Population, and Environmental Change (CIPEC), Indiana University.

Batterbury, S. P. J., and A. Bebbington. 1999. Environmental Histories: Access to Resources and Landscape Change. *Land Degradation and Development* 10:279–289.

Batterbury, S., and N. Taylor. 1998. Zarma Livelihoods and African Environmental History: Studying Social and Environmental Change in the 20th Century in South-West Niger. Presented at the Association of American Geographers Annual Meeting, Boston, March 26.

Bebbington, A. 2000. Reencountering Development: Livelihood Transitions and Place Transformations in the Andes. *Annals of the Association of American Geographers* 90(3):495–520.

Becker, C. D. 1999. Protecting a Garũa Forest in Ecuador: The Role of Institutions and Ecosystem Valuation. *Ambio* 28(2):156–161.

Becker, C. D., and R. Leon. 2000. Indigenous Forest Management in the Bolivian Amazon: Lessons from the Yuracaré People. In *People and Forests: Communities, Institutions, and Governance*, ed. C. C. Gibson, M. A. McKean, and E. Ostrom, 163–192. Cambridge, MA: MIT Press.

Beckerman, S., ed. 1983. Does the swidden ape the jungle? *Human Ecology* 11(2):1–12.

Begon, M., J. L. Harper, and C. R. Townsend. 1996. *Ecology*. Oxford: Blackwell Science.

Behrens, C. A., M. G. Baksh, and M. Mothes. 1994. A Regional Analysis of Bari Land Use Intensification and Its Impact on Landscape Heterogeneity. *Human Ecology* 22(3):279–316.

Benin, S., and J. Pender. 2001. Impacts of Land Redistribution on Land Management and Productivity in the Ethiopian Highlands. *Land Degradation and Development* 12(6):555–568.

Bennett, J. 1969. *Northern Plainsmen: Adaptive Strategy and Agrarian Life*. Chicago: Aldine.

Bennett, O., ed. 1993. *Greenwar: Environment and Conflict*. London: Panos Institute.

Berger, T. 2001. Agent-Based Spatial Models Applied to Agriculture: A Simulation Tool for Technology Diffusion, Resource Use Changes, and Policy Analysis. *Agricultural Economics* 25(2–3):245–260.

Berkes, F., D. Feeny, B. J. McCay, and J. M. Acheson. 1989. The Benefits of the Commons. *Nature* 340:91–93.

Berkes, F., and C. Folke. 1998. *Linking Social and Ecological Systems*. Cambridge, UK: Cambridge University Press.

Bernard, F. E. 1993. Increasing Variability in Agricultural Production: Meru District, Kenya, in the Twentieth Century. In *Population Growth and Agricultural Change in Africa*, ed. B. L. Turner II, G. Hyden, and R. Kates, 80–113. Gainesville: University Press of Florida.

Bernard, H. R. 1995. *Research Methods in Anthropology: Qualitative and Quantitative Approaches*, 2d ed. Walnut Creek, CA: Altamira.

Bertrand, A. 1999. La Dynamique Séculaire des Plantations Paysannes d'Eucalyptus sur les Hautes Terres Malgaches (The Secular Dynamics of the Country Plantations of Eucalyptus on the Malagasy Highlands). *African Studies Quarterly* 3(2):art4 [online (in French)]. URL: http://web.africa.ufl.edu/asq/v3/v3i2a4.htm.

Bierregaard, R. O., Jr., R. Mesquita, T. E. Lovejoy, and C. Gascon. 2001. *Lessons from Amazonia: The Ecology and Conservation of a Fragmented Forest*. New Haven, CT: Yale University Press.

Bilsborrow, R. E. 1987. Population Pressure and Agricultural Development in Developing Countries: A Conceptual Framework and Recent Evidence. *World Development* 15:183–203.

Bilsborrow, R. E., and D. L. Carr. 2001. Population, Agricultural Land Use and the Environment in Developing Countries. In *Tradeoffs or Synergies? Agricultural Intensification, Economic Development and the Environment*, ed. D. R. Lee and C. B. Barrett, 35–56. Cambridge, MA: CABI Publishing.

Bilsborrow, R. E., and H. W. O. O. Ogendo. 1992. Population-Driven Changes in Land-Use in Developing-Countries. *Ambio* 21:37–45.

Binswanger, H. 1991. Brazilian Policies That Encourage Deforestation in the Amazon. *World Development* 19(7):821–829.

Birch, T. W. 1996. *Private Forest-Land Owners of the United States, 1994*. Resource Bulletin NE-134. Radnor, PA: Northeastern Forest Experiment Station, USDA Forest Service.

Bista, D. H. 1991. *Fatalism and Development: Nepal's Struggle for Modernization*. Hyderabad, India: Orient Longman.

Bohn, H., and R. T. Deacon. 2000. Ownership Risk, Investment, and the Use of Natural Resources. *American Economic Review* 90(1):526–550.

Bockstael, N. E. 1996. Modeling Economics and Ecology: The Importance of a Spatial Perspective. *American Journal of Agricultural Economics* 78(5):1168–1180.

Bolstad, P. 2002. *GIS Fundamentals: A First Text on Geographic Information Systems*. White Bear Lake, MN: Eider Press.

Boserup, E. 1965. *The Conditions of Agricultural Growth*. Chicago: Aldine.

———. 1981. *Population and Technological Change: A Study of Long-Term Trends*. Chicago: University of Chicago Press.

———. 1983. The Impact of Scarcity and Plenty on Development. *Journal of Interdisciplinary History* 14:383–407.

———. 1990. *Economic and Demographic Relationships in Development*. Baltimore: Johns Hopkins University Press.

Boucek, B., and E. F. Moran. 2004. Inferring the Behavior of Households from Remotely Sensed Changes in Land Cover: Current Methods and Future Directions. In *Spatially Integrated Social Science*, ed. M. F. Goodchild and D. G. Janelle, 23–47. Spatial Information Systems series. New York: Oxford University Press.

Boyd, D. S., G. M. Foody, P. J. Curran, R. M. Lucas, and M. Hónzak. 1996. An Assessment of Radiance in Landsat TM Middle and Thermal Infrared Wavebands for the Detection of Tropical Forest Regeneration. *International Journal of Remote Sensing* 17:249–261.

Braudel, F. 1973. *The Mediterranean and the Mediterranean World in the Age of Philip II*, 2 vols. New York: Harper & Row.

Breckle, S.-W. 2002. *Walter's Vegetation of the Earth: The Ecological Systems of the Geo-Biosphere*. New York: Springer-Verlag.

Bromley, D. W., D. Feeny, M. McKean, P. Peters, J. Gilles, R. Oakerson, C. F. Runge, and J. Thomson, eds. 1992. *Making the Commons Work: Theory, Practice, and Policy*. San Francisco: ICS Press.

Brondízio, E. S. 1999. Agroforestry Intensification in the Amazon Estuary. In *Managing the Globalized Environment: Local Strategies to Secure Livelihoods*, ed. T. Granfelt, 88–113. London: IT Publications.

———. In 2004a. Agriculture Intensification, Economic Identity, and Shared Invisibility in Amazonian Peasantry: Caboclos and Colonists in Comparative Perspective. *Culture and Agriculture* 26(1–2):1–24.

———. In 2004b. From Staple to Fashion Food: Shifting Cycles, Shifting Opportunities and the Case of *Açaí* Fruit (*Euterpe oleracea* Mart.) of the Amazon Estuary. In *Working Forests of the American Tropics: Management for Sustainable Forests?*, ed. D. Zarin, 339–365. New York: Columbia University Press.

———. In press. Footprints of the Past, Landscapes of the Future: Historical Ecology and the Analysis of Land Use Change in the Amazon. In *Time and Complexity in the Neotropical Lowlands: Studies in Historical Ecology*, ed. W. Balée and C. Erikson. New York: Columbia University Press.

Brondízio, E. S., S. D. McCracken, E. F. Moran, D. R. Nelson, A. D. Siqueira, and C. Rodriquez-Pedraza. 2002a. The Colonist Footprint: Toward a Conceptual Framework of Land Use and Deforestation Trajectories among Small Farmers in the Amazonian Frontier. In *Deforestation and Land Use in the Amazon*, ed. C. H. Wood and R. Porro, 133–161. Gainesville: University Press of Florida.

Brondízio, E. S., E. F. Moran, P. Mausel, and Y. Wu. 1994a. Land Use Change in the Amazon Estuary: Patterns of Caboclo Settlement and Landscape Management. *Human Ecology* 22(3):249–278.

———. 1996. Land Cover in the Amazon Estuary: Linking of the Thematic Mapper with Botanical and Historical Data. *Photogrammetric Engineering and Remote Sensing* 62:921–929.

Brondízio, E. S., E. F. Moran, A. D. Siqueira, P. Mausel, Y. Wu, and Y. Li. 1994b. Mapping Anthropogenic Forest: Using Remote Sensing in a Multi-Level Approach to Estimate Production and Distribution of Managed Palm Forest (*Euterpe oleracea*) in the Amazon Estuary. *Proceedings of the ISPRS Commission VII Symposium* 30(7a):184–191.

Brondízio, E. S., C. Safar, and A. D. Siqueira. 2002b. The Urban Market of *Açaí* Fruit (*Euterpe oleracea* Mart.) and Rural Land Use Change: Ethnographic Insights into the Role of Price and Land Tenure Constraining Agricultural Choices in the Amazon Estuary. *Urban Ecosystems* 6(1–2):67–98.

Brondízio, E. S., and A. D. Siqueira. 1997. From Extractivists to Forest Farmers: Changing Concepts of Caboclo Agroforestry in the Amazon Estuary. *Research in Economic Anthropology* 18:234–279.

Brookfield, H. C. 1972. Intensification and Disintensification in Pacific Agriculture: A Theoretical Approach. *Pacific Viewpoint* 13:30–48.

Browder, J., ed. 1989. *Fragile Lands of Latin America: Strategies for Sustainable Development*. Boulder, CO: Westview.

Browder, J. O., and B. Godfrey. 1997. *Rainforest Cities: Urbanization, Development, and Globalization of the Brazilian Amazon*. New York: Columbia University Press.

Browder, J. O., and M. A. Pedlowski. 2000. Agroforestry Performance on Small Farms in Amazonia: Findings from the Rondonia Agroforestry Pilot Project. *Agroforestry Systems* 49(1):63–83.

Brower, L. P. 1999. Biological Necessities for Monarch Butterfly Overwintering in Relation to the Oyamel Forest Ecosystem in Mexico. In *1997 North American Conference on the Monarch Butterfly (Morelia, Mexico)*, ed. J. Hoth, L. Merino, K. Oberhauser, I. Pisanty, S. Price, and T. Wilkinson, 11–28. Montreal, Canada: Commission for Environmental Cooperation.

Brower, L. P., G. Castilleja, A. Peralta, J. Lopez-Garcia, L. Bojorquez-Tapia, S. Diaz, D. Melgarejo, and M. Missrie. 2002. Quantitative Changes in Forest Quality in a Principal Overwintering Area of the Monarch Butterfly in Mexico, 1971–1999. *Conservation Biology* 16(2):346–359.

Brown, I. F., and T. Stone. 1989. Using Satellite Photography for Grassroots Development in Amazonia. *Cultural Survival Quarterly* 13(1):35–38.

Brown, M. 2000. *A History of Madagascar*. Cambridge, UK: Damien Tunnacliffe.

Brown, P., and A. Podolefsky. 1976. Population Density, Agricultural Intensity, Land Tenure, and Group Size in the New Guinea Highlands. *Ethnology* 15:211–238.

Brown, S., A. J. R. Gillespie, and A. E. Lugo. 1989. Biomass Estimation Methods for Tropical Forests with Applications to Forest Inventory Data. *Forest Science* 35:881–902.

Brown, S., L. R. Iverson, and A. E. Lugo. 1992. Land-Use and Biomass Changes of Forests in Peninsular Malaysia from 1972 to 1982: A GIS Approach. In *Effects of Land Use Change on Atmospheric Carbon Dioxide Concentration: Southeast Asia As a Case Study*, ed. Y. H. Dale, 117–143. New York: Springer-Verlag.

Brown, S., and A. E. Lugo. 1992. Aboveground Biomass Estimations for Tropical Moist Forests of the Brazilian Amazon. *Interciencia* 17:8–18.

Bruner, A. G., R. E. Gullison, R. E. Rics, and G. A. B. da Fonseca. 2001. Effectiveness of Parks in Protecting Tropical Biodiversity. *Science* 291(5501):125–128.

Bunker, S. G. 1985. *Underdeveloping the Amazon: Extraction, Unequal Exchange, and the Failure of the Modern State*. Urbana: University of Illinois Press.

Butzer, K. 1990. A Human Ecosystem Framework for Archeology. In *The Ecosystem Approach in Anthropology: From Concept to Practice*, ed. E. F. Moran, 91–130. Ann Arbor: University of Michigan Press.

Camerer, C. 1998. Bounded Rationality in Individual Decision-Making. *Experimental Economics* 1:163–183.

———. 2003. *Behavioral Game Theory: Experiments in Strategic Interaction*. Princeton, NJ: Princeton University Press.

Canterbury, G. E., T. E. Martin, D. R. Petit, L. J. Petit, and D. F. Bradford. 2000. Bird Communities and Habitat as Ecological Indicators of Forest Condition in Regional Monitoring. *Conservation Biology* 14(2):544–558.

Carneiro, R. L. 1961. Slash-and-Burn Cultivation among the Kuikuru and Its Implications for Cultural Development in the Amazon Basin. In *The Evolution of Horticultural Systems in*

Native South America: Causes and Consequences, ed. J. Wilbert, 47–67. Antropológica Suppl. 2. Caracas: Sociedad de Ciencias Naturales La Salle.

Carpentier, C. L., S. A. Vosti, and J. Witcover. 2000. Intensified Production Systems on Western Brazilian Amazon Settlement Farms: Could they save the forest? *Agriculture, Ecosystems and Environment* 82(1–3):73–88.

Carvalho, G., D. Nepstad, D. McGrath, M. del C. Vera Diaz, M. Santilli, and A. C. Barros. 2002. Frontier Expansion in the Amazon: Balancing Development and Sustainability. *Environment* 44:34–45.

Cash, D. W., W. C. Clark, F. Alcock, N. M. Dickson, N. Eckley, D. H. Guston, J. Jager, and R. B. Mitchell. 2003. Knowledge Systems for Sustainable Development. *Proceedings of the National Academy of Sciences of the United States of America* 100(14):8086–8091. URL: http://www.pnas.org/cgi/content/full/100/14/8086.

Castro, F. de. 1999. *Fishing Accords: The Political Ecology of Fishing Intensification in the Amazon*. CIPEC Dissertation Series, No. 4. Bloomington: Center for the Study of Institutions, Population, and Environmental Change (CIPEC), Indiana University.

Castro, F. de, and E. S. Brondízio. 2000. The role of ecological patchiness in forest fragmentation patterns: The Upper Negro River case. Poster presented at the First International Open Science Meeting of the Large Scale Biosphere-Atmosphere Experiment in Amazonia, CNPq, INPE, NASA, Belém, Pará, Brazil, June 21–26.

Castro, F. de, M. C. Silva-Forsberg, W. Wilson, E. Brondízio, and E. Moran. 2002. The Use of Remotely Sensed Data in Rapid Rural Assessment. *Field Methods* 14(3):243–269.

Chakraborty, R. N. 2001. Stability and Outcomes of Common Property Institutions in Forestry: Evidence from the Terai Region of Nepal. *Ecological Economics* 36:341–353.

Chambers, R. 1980. *Rapid Rural Appraisal: Rationale and Repertoire*. IDS Discussion Paper no. 148. Brighton, UK: Institute of Development Studies (IDS), University of Sussex.

Chapela, G., and D. Barkin. 1995. *Monarcas y Campesinos: Estrategia de Desarrollo Sustentable en el Oriente de Michoacán*. Mexico City: Centro de Ecología y Desarrollo.

Chapin, F. S. III, P. A. Matson, and H. A. Mooney. 2002. *Principles of Terrestrial Ecosystem Ecology*. New York: Springer-Verlag.

Chase-Dunn, C. 1998. *Global Formation: Structures of the World Economy*. Lanham, MD: Rowman and Littlefield.

Chavez, P. S., Jr. 1988. An Improved Dark-Object Subtraction Technique for Atmospheric Scattering Correction of Multi-Spectral Data. *Remote Sensing of Environment* 24:450–479.

———. 1989. Radiometric Calibration of Landsat Thematic Mapper Multispectral Images. *Photogrammetric Engineering and Remote Sensing* 55:1285–1294.

———. 1996. Image-Based Atmospheric Corrections: Revisited and Improved. *Photogrammetric Engineering and Remote Sensing* 62(9):1025–1036.

Chayanov, A. V. [1925] 1966. *The Theory of Peasant Economy*. Trans. C. Lane and R. E. F. Smith. Ed. D. Thorner, R. E. F. Smith, and B. Kerblay. Homewood, IL: Richard D. Irwin for American Economic Association.

Chesnais, J.-C. 1992. *The Demographic Transition: Stages, Patterns and Economic Implications*. New York: Clarendon.

Chibnik, M. 1994. *Risky Rivers*. Tucson: University of Arizona Press.

Chomitz, K. M., and D. A. Gray. 1996. Roads, Land Use, and Deforestation: A Spatial Model Applied to Belize. *World Bank Economic Review* 10(3):487–512.

Clark, C. D., S. M. Garrod, and M. Parker Pearson. 1998. Landscape Archeology and Remote Sensing in Southern Madagascar. *International Journal of Remote Sensing* 19:1461–1477.

Clay, E., L. Bohn, and E. Blanco de Armas. 2002. Climatic variability and southern Africa. Summary of presentation to the Southern African Crisis Meeting, ODI, July 10, 2002. URL: http://www.odi.org.uk/Food-Security-Forum/docs/ejc.pdf.

Climate Prediction Center (CPC). 2003. Cold and Warm Episodes by Season. URL: http://www.cpc.ncep.noaa.gov/products/analysis_monitoring/ensostuff/ensoyears.html.

Coale, A. J., and S. C. Watkins. 1986. *The Decline of Fertility in Europe*. Princeton, NJ: Princeton University Press.

Cochrane, M. A., and M. D. Schulze. 1998. Fire as a Recurrent Event in Tropical Forests of the Eastern Amazon: Effects on Forest Structure, Biomass, and Species Composition. *Biotropica* 31:2–16.

Cohen, W. B., and T. A. Spies. 1992. Estimating Structural Attributes of Douglas Fir/Western Hemlock Forest Stands from Landsat SPOT Imagery. *Remote Sensing of Environment* 41:1–17.

Coleman, J. A. 1990. *Foundations of Social Theory*. Cambridge, MA: Harvard University Press.

Comaroff, J. L., and S. A. Roberts. 1977. The Invocation of Norms in Dispute Settlement: The Tswana Case. In *Social Anthropology and Law*, ed. I. Hamnet. London: Academic Press.

Commoner, B. 1972. *The Closing Circle*. New York: Knopf.

Conant, F. P. 1990. 1990 and Beyond: Satellite Remote Sensing and Ecological Anthropology. In *The Ecosystem Approach in Anthropology*, ed. E. F. Moran, 357–388. Ann Arbor: Michigan University Press.

Connell, J. H., and M. D. Lowman. 1989. Low-Diversity Tropical Rain Forests: Some Possible Mechanisms for Their Existence. *The American Naturalist* 134:88–119.

Conway, G. 1986. *Agroecosystem Analysis for Research and Development*. Bangkok: Winrock International Institute.

Costanza, R., R. d'Arge, R. de Groot, S. Farber, M. Grasso, B. Hannon, K. Limburg, S. Naeem, R. O'Neill, J. Paruelo, R. Raskin, P. Sutton, and M. van den Belt. 1997. The Value of the World's Ecosystem Services and Natural Capital. *Nature* 387(6230):253–260.

Costanza, R., and A. Voinov, eds. 2004. *Landscape Simulation Modeling: A Spatially Explicit, Dynamic Approach*. New York: Springer-Verlag.

Costanza, R., L. Wainger, C. Folke, and K.-G. Mäler. 1993. Modeling Complex Ecological Economic Systems: Toward an Evolutionary, Dynamic Understanding of People and Nature. *BioScience* 43:545–555.

Coward, E. W., Jr. 1979. Principles of Social Organization in an Indigenous Irrigation System. *Human Organization* 38:28–36.

Coxhead, I., A. Rola, and K. Kim. 2001. How do national markets and price policies affect land use at the forest margin? Evidence from the Philippines. *Land Economics* 77(2):250–267.

Crawford, T. W. 2002. Spatial Modeling of Village Functional Territories to Support Population-Environment Linkages. In *Linking People, Place and Policy: A GIScience Approach*, ed. S. J. Walsh and K. A. Crews-Meyer, 91–111. Boston: Kluwer.

Creveld, M. van. 1991. *The Transformation of War*. New York: Free Press.

Crocker, C., and F. O. Hampson. 1996. Making Peace Settlements Work. *Foreign Policy* 104:54–71.

Croissant, C. 2001. Spatial Patterns of Forest Cover within Urban, Urban-Fringe, and Rural Areas of Monroe County, Indiana. *Proceedings of ASPRS 2001, St. Louis, Mo., April 23–27*, 3–20. Bethesda, MD: American Society for Photogrammetry and Remote Sensing.

Cross, A. F., and W. H. Schlesinger. 1999. Plant Regulation of Soil Nutrient Distribution in the Northern Chihuahuan Desert. *Plant Ecology* 145:11–25.

Curtis, P. S., P. J. Hanson, P. Bolstad, C. Barford, J. C. Randolph, H. P. Schmid, and K. B. Wilson. 2002. Biometric and Eddy-Covariance Based Estimates of Annual Carbon Storage in Five Eastern North American Deciduous Forests. *Agricultural and Forest Meteorology* 113(1–4):3–19.

Dahlman, C. 1980. *The Open Field System and Beyond: A Property Rights Analysis of an Economic Institution*. Cambridge, UK: Cambridge University Press.

Daily, G. S., S. Alexander, P. R. Ehrlich, L. Goulder, J. Lubchenco, P. A. Matson, H. A. Mooney, S. Postel, S. H. Schneider, D. Tilman, and G. M. Woodwell. 1997. Ecosystem Services: Benefits Supplied to Human Societies by Natural Ecosystems. *Issues in Ecology* 2:1–16.

Dale, V. H., R. V. O'Neill, M. Pedlowski, and F. Southworth. 1993a. Causes and Effects of Land-Use Change in Central Rondônia, Brazil. *Photogrammetric Engineering and Remote Sensing* 59(6):997–1005.

Dale, V. H., F. Southworth, R. V. O'Neill, A. Rose, and R. Frohn. 1993b. Simulating Spatial Patterns of Land-Use Change in Rondonia, Brazil. In *Some Mathematical Questions in Biology*, ed. R. H. Gardner, 29–56. Providence, RI: American Mathematical Society.

Dales, J. H. 1968. *Pollution, Property and Prices: An Essay in Policy-Making and Economics*. Toronto: University of Toronto Press.

Danson, F. M., and P. J. Curran. 1993. Factors Affecting the Remotely Sensed Response of Coniferous Forest Plantations. *Remote Sensing of Environment* 43:55–65.

Dantas, M. 1988. Studies on succession in cleared areas of Amazonian rain forest. Ph.D. diss. Oxford University, Oxford.

Dasgupta, P., and G. M. Heal. 1979. *Economic Theory and Exhaustible Resources*. Cambridge, UK: Cambridge University Press.

Davidson, E. A., K. Savage, P. Bolstad, D. A. Clark, P. S. Curtis, D. S. Ellsworth, P. J. Hanson, B. E. Law, Y. Luo, K. S. Pregitzer, J. C. Randolph, and D. Zak. 2002. Belowground Carbon Allocation in Forests Estimated from Litterfall and IRGA-Based Soil Respiration Measurements. *Agricultural and Forest Meteorology* 113:39–51.

Davis, K. 1963. The Theory of Change and Response in Modern Demographic History. *Population Index* 29:345–366.

Davis, M. B. 1996. *Eastern Old-Growth Forests: Prospects for Rediscovery and Recovery*. Washington, DC: Island Press.

Deacon, R. T. 1994. Deforestation and the Rule of Law in a Cross-Section of Countries. *Land Economics* 70(4):414–430.

———. 1995. Assessing the Relationship between Government Policy and Deforestation. *Journal of Environmental Economics and Management* 28(1):1–18.

Debinski, D. M., and R. D. Holt. 2000. A Survey and Overview of Habitat Fragmentation Experiments. *Conservation Biology* 14:342–355.

Demsetz, H. 1967. Toward a Theory of Property Rights. *American Economic Review* 62:347–359.

Denevan, W., and C. Padoch, eds. 1987. *Swidden-Fallow Agroforestry in the Peruvian Amazon*. Vol. 5 of Advances in Economic Botany. New York: New York Botanical Garden.

Devlin, R. A., and R. Q. Grafton. 1998. *Economic Rights and Environmental Wrongs*. Cheltenham, UK: Edward Elgar.

Dietz, T., N. Dolšak, E. Ostrom, and P. C. Stern. 2002. The Drama of the Commons. In *The Drama of the Commons*, ed. E. Ostrom, T. Dietz, N. Dolšak, P. C. Stern, S. Stonich, and E. U. Weber, 3–35. Washington, DC: National Academy Press.

Dietz, T., E. Ostrom, and P. C. Stern. 2003. The Struggle to Govern the Commons. *Science* 302:1907–1912. URL: http://www.sciencemag.org/cgi/reprint/302/5652/1907.pdf (subscription required).

Dincao, M. A., and I. M. Silveira, eds. 1994. *A Amazônia e a crise da modernizacao*. Belém, Brazil: Editora do Museu Paraense Emilio Goeldi.

Donnelly, S. 2004. *Linking Landscape Pattern to Social Process: A Multi-Scale Analysis of Farm Woodlots in Northern Indiana*. CIPEC Working Paper CWP-04-02. Bloomington: Center for the Study of Institutions, Population, and Environmental Change (CIPEC), Indiana University. URL: http://www.ucgis.org/summer03/studentpapers/shanondonnelly.pdf.

Doornbos, M., A. Saith, and B. White. 2000. Forest Lives and Struggles: An Introduction. *Development and Change* 31:1–10.

Douglas, M. 1986. *How Institutions Think*. Syracuse, NY: Syracuse University Press.

———. 1992. *Risk and Blame: Essays in Cultural Theory*. New York: Routledge.

Drury, R. [1729] 1970. *Madagascar; or Robert Drury's Journal, during Fifteen Years Captivity on That Island*. Reprint, Westport, CT: Greenwood.

Eastwood, J. A., M. G. Yates, A. G. Thomson, and R. M. Fuller. 1997. The Reliability of Vegetation Indices for Monitoring Saltmarsh Vegetation Cover. *International Journal of Remote Sensing* 18:3901–3907.

Eder, J. F. 1991. Agricultural Intensification and Labor Productivity in a Philippine Vegetable Gardening Community: A Longitudinal Study. *Human Organization* 50(3):245–255.

Ehleringer, J. R., and C. B. Field. 1993. *Scaling Physiological Processes: Leaf to Globe*. London: Academic Press.

Ehman, J. L., W. Fan, J. C. Randolph, J. Southworth, and N. T. Welch. 2002a. An Integrated GIS and Modeling Approach for Assessing the Transient Response of Forests of the Great Lakes Region to a Doubled CO_2 Climate. *Forest Ecology and Management*

155(1–3):237–255. URL: http://www.sciencedirect.com/science/journal/03781127 (subscription required).

Ehman, J. L., H. P. Schmid, C. S. B. Grimmond, J. C. Randolph, P. J. Hanson, C. A. Wayson, and F. D. Cropley. 2002b. An Initial Intercomparison of Micrometeorological and Ecological Inventory Estimates of Carbon Sequestration in a Mid-Latitude Deciduous Forest. *Global Change Biology* 8:575–589.

Ehrhardt-Martinez, K. 1998. Social Determinants of Deforestation in Developing Countries: A Cross-National Study. *Social Forces* 77:567–586.

Ehrhardt-Martinez, K., E. M. Crenshaw, and J. C. Jenkins. 2002. Deforestation and the Environmental Kuznets Curve: A Cross-National Investigation of Intervening Mechanisms. *Social Science Quarterly* 83:226–243.

Ehrlich, P. R., and A. H. Ehrlich. 1991. *Healing the Planet: Strategies for Resolving the Environmental Crisis*. Reading, MA: Addison Wesley.

Elhorst, J. P. 2001. Dynamic Models in Space and Time. *Geographical Analysis* 33(2):119–140.

Ellis, R., and M. Thompson, eds. 1997. *Culture Matters: Essays in Honor of Aaron Wildavsky*. Boulder, CO: Westview.

Elmqvist, T. 2004. The Forgotten Dry Forest of Southern Madagascar. *Plant Talk* 35(January):29–31.

Engström, A. 2001. Demography of *Didierea trollii* and analysis of forest fragmentation in southern Madagascar. Masters thesis, Department of Systems Ecology, Stockholm University, Sweden.

Entwisle, B., R. R. Rindfuss, S. J. Walsh, T. P. Evans, and S. R. Curran. 1997. Geographic Information Systems, Spatial Network Analysis, and Contraceptive Choice. *Demography* 34:171–188.

ESA Consultores. 1993. *El impacto de las políticas de ajuste estructural sobre el medio ambiente en Honduras* (The Impact of Structural Adjustment Policies on the Environment in Honduras). Tegucigalpa, Honduras: Postgrado Centroamerica en Economía, Universidad Nacional Autónoma de Honduras.

Evans, T. P., G. M. Green, and L. Carlson. 2001a. MultiScale Analysis of Landcover Composition and Landscape Management of Public and Private Lands in Indiana. In *GIS and Remote Sensing Applications in Biogeography and Ecology*, ed. A. C. Millington, S. J. Walsh, and P. E. Osborne, 271–287. Boston: Kluwer.

Evans, T. P., and H. Kelley. 2004. Multi-Scale Analysis of a Household Level Agent-Based Model of Landcover Change. *Journal of Environmental Management* 72(1–2):57–72.

Evans, T. P., A. Manire, F. de Castro, E. Brondízio, and S. McCracken. 2001b. A Dynamic Model of Household Decision Making and Parcel-Level Land Cover Change in the Eastern Amazon. *Ecological Modelling* 143(1–2):95–113.

Evans, T. P., and E. F. Moran. 2002. Spatial Integration of Social and Biophysical Factors Related to Landcover Change. In *Population and Environment: Methods of Analysis*, ed. W. Lutz, A. Prskawets, and W. C. Sanderson, 165–186. *Population and Development Review*, suppl. to vol. 28. New York: Population Council.

Evans, T. P., E. Ostrom, and C. Gibson. 2003. Scaling Issues in the Social Sciences. In *Scaling in Integrated Assessment*, ed. J. Rotmans and D. S. Rothman, 75–106. Integrated Assessment Studies Series, ed. P. Martens and J. Rotmans. Lisse, the Netherlands: Swets & Zeitlinger.

Fairhead, J., and M. Leach. 1996. *Misreading the African Landscape: Society and Ecology in a Forest-Savanna Mosaic*. African Studies Series, no. 90. New York: Cambridge University Press.

Fearnside, P. M. 1984. ¿A floresta vai acabar? *Ciência Hoje* 2(10):42–52.

———. 1986. *Human Carrying Capacity of the Brazilian Rainforest*. New York: Columbia University Press.

Federal Geographic Data Committee (FGDC). 2003. Geospatial Metadata Standards. URL: http://www.fgdc.gov/metadata/meta_stand.html. Accessed January 2003.

Ferretti, M., R. Bussotti, E. Cenni, and A. Cozzi. 1999. Implementation of Quality Assurance Procedures in the Italian Programs of Forest Condition Monitoring. *Water, Air, and Soil Pollution* 116:371–376.

Foiben-Taosarintanin'i Madagasikara (FTM). 1985. *1:6,000,000 Scale Climate Map of Madagascar*. Antananarivo, Madagascar: Institut Géographique et Hydrographique National de Madagascar. URL: http://www.dts.mg/ftm/framecontact.htm.

Food and Agriculture Organization of the United Nations (FAO). 1993. *Forest Resources Assessment 1990: Tropical Countries*. Rome: author. URL: http://www.ciesin.org/docs/002-471/002-471.html.

Forman, R. T. T. 1995. *Land Mosaics: The Ecology of Landscapes and Regions*. Cambridge, UK: Cambridge University Press.

Fox, J. 1993a. Forest Resources in a Nepali Village in 1980 and 1990: The Positive Influence of Population Growth. *Mountain Research and Development* 13(1):89–98.

———, ed. 1993b. *Legal Frameworks for Forest Management in Asia: Case Studies of Community/State Relations*. Occasional Papers of the Program on Environment, no. 16. Honolulu: East-West Center.

Fox, J., R. R. Rindfuss, S. J. Walsh, and V. Mishra, eds. 2003. *People and the Environment: Approaches for Linking Household and Community Surveys to Remote Sensing and GIS*. Dordrecht, the Netherlands: Kluwer.

Frank, A. G. 1967. *Capitalism and Development in Latin America: Historical Studies of Chile and Brazil*. New York: Monthly Review Press.

Franklin, J. 1986. Thematic Mapper Analysis of Coniferous Forest Structure and Composition. *International Journal of Remote Sensing* 7:1287–1301.

Franklin, J., and P. Y. H. Hiernaux. 1991. Estimating Foliage and Woody Biomass in Sahelian and Sudanian Woodlands Using a Remote Sensing Model. *International Journal of Remote Sensing* 12:1387–1404.

Franklin, S. E., and D. R. Peddle. 1989. Spectral Texture for Improved Class Discrimination in Complex Terrain. *International Journal of Remote Sensing* 10:1437–1443.

Freden, S. C., and F. Gordon Jr. 1983. Landsat Satellites. In *Manual of Remote Sensing*, ed. R. N. Colwell, 517–570. Falls Church, VA: American Society of Photogrammetry.

Futemma, C. 2000. *Collective Action and Assurance of Property Rights to Natural Resources: A Case Study from the Lower Amazon Region, Santarém, Brazil.* CIPEC Dissertation Series, No. 6. Bloomington: Center for the Study of Institutions, Population, and Environmental Change (CIPEC), Indiana University.

Futemma, C., and E. S. Brondízio. 2003. Land Reform and Land-Use Changes in the Lower Amazon: Implications for Agricultural Intensification. *Human Ecology* 31(3):369–402.

Futemma, C., F. de Castro, M. C. Silva-Forsberg, and E. Ostrom. 2002. The Emergence and Outcomes of Collective Action: An Institutional and Ecosystem Approach. *Society and Natural Resources* 15:503–522.

Gautam, A. P., E. L. Webb, and A. Eiumnoh. 2002. GIS Assessment of Land Use/Land Cover Changes Associated with Community Forestry Implementation in the Middle Hills of Nepal. *Mountain Research and Development* 22:63–69.

Geertz, C. 1963. *Agricultural Involution*. Berkeley: University of California Press.

Geisler, C., and G. Daneker. 2000. Introduction. In *Property and Values: Alternatives to Public and Private Ownership*, ed. C. Geisler and G. Daneker, xiii–xvii. Washington, DC: Island Press.

Geist, H. J., and E. F. Lambin. 2001. *What Drives Tropical Deforestation? A Meta-Analysis of Proximate and Underlying Causes of Deforestation Based on Subnational Case Study Evidence*. LUCC Report Series, no. 4. Louvain-la-Neuve, Belgium: LUCC International Project Office, International Geosphere-Biosphere Programme. URL: http://www.geo.ucl.ac.be/LUCC/pdf/LUCC%20Report%20-%20Screen.pdf.

———. 2002. Proximate Causes and Underlying Driving Forces of Tropical Deforestation. *BioScience* 52(2):143–150.

———. 2004. Dynamic Causal Patterns of Desertification. *BioScience* 54(9):817–829.

Gentry, A. H. 1992. Tropical Forest Biodiversity: Distributional Patterns and Their Conservational Significance. *Oikos* 63:19–28.

Geores, M. E. 2003. The Relationship between Resource Definition and Scale: Considering the Forest. In *The Commons in the New Millennium: Challenges and Adaptation*, ed. N. Dolšak and E. Ostrom, 77–97. Cambridge, MA: MIT Press.

Ghimire, K. 1994. Refugees and Deforestation. *International Migration* 32:561–569.

Gibson, C. C. 2001. Forest Resources: Institutions for Local Governance in Guatemala. In *Protecting the Commons: A Framework for Resource Management in the Americas*, ed. J. Berger, E. Ostrom, R. B. Norgaard, D. Policansky, and B. D. Goldstein, 71–90. Washington, DC: Island Press.

Gibson, C. C., and C. D. Becker. 2000. A Lack of Institutional Demand: Why a Strong Local Community in Ecuador Fails to Protect Its Forest. In *People and Forests: Communities, Institutions, and Governance*, ed. C. C. Gibson, M. A. McKean, and E. Ostrom, 135–162. Cambridge, MA: MIT Press.

Gibson, C. C., and T. Koontz. 1998. When "Community" Is Not Enough: Institutions and Values in Community-Based Forest Management in Southern Indiana. *Human Ecology* 26(4):621–647.

Gibson, C. C., and F. E. Lehoucq. 2003. The Local Politics of Decentralized Environmental Policy in Guatemala. *Journal of Environment and Development* 12(1):28–49.

Gibson, C. C., F. E. Lehoucq, and J. T. Williams. 2002. Does privatization protect natural resources? Property Rights and Forests in Guatemala. *Social Science Quarterly* 83:206–225.

Gibson, C. C., M. A. McKean, and E. Ostrom, eds. 2000a. *People and Forests: Communities, Institutions, and Governance*. Cambridge, MA: MIT Press.

Gibson, C. C., E. Ostrom, and T. K. Ahn. 1998. *Scaling Issues in the Social Sciences*. IHDP Working Paper, no. 1. Bonn, Germany: International Human Dimensions Programme (IHDP).

———. 2000b. The Concept of Scale and the Human Dimensions of Global Change: A Survey. *Ecological Economics* 32(2):217–239.

Gibson, C. C., J. T. Williams, and E. Ostrom. In press. Local Enforcement and Better Forests. *World Development*.

Gillespie, A. J. R., S. Brown, and A. E. Lugo. 1992. Tropical Forest Biomass Estimation from Truncated Stand Tables. *Forest Ecology and Management* 48:69–87.

Gimblett, H. R., ed. 2001. *Integrating Geographic Information Systems and Agent-Based Modeling Techniques for Understanding Social and Ecological Processes*. Oxford: Oxford University Press.

Glacken, C. 1967. *Traces on a Rhodian Shore*. Berkeley: University of California Press.

Goldenberg, J., ed. 1989. *Proceedings of the Symposium Amazônia: Facts, Problems, and Solutions*. University of São Paulo, São Paulo, Brazil, July 31–August 2.

Goodchild, M. F., L. Anselin, R. P. Appelbaum, and B. Herr-Harthorn. 2000. Toward Spatially Integrated Social Science. *International Regional Science Review* 23(2):139–159.

Goody, J. 1958. *The Developmental Cycle in Domestic Groups*. Cambridge Papers in Social Anthropology, no. 1. Cambridge, UK: Cambridge University Press for the Department of Archaeology and Anthropology.

———. 1976. *Production and Reproduction: A Comparative Study of the Domestic Domain*. New York: Cambridge University Press.

Gordon, D. K., and W. R. Phillipson. 1986. A Texture Enhancement Procedure for Separating Orchard from Forest in Thematic Mapper Imagery. *International Journal of Remote Sensing* 8:301–304.

Gordon, H. S. 1954. The Economic Theory of a Common-Property Resource: The Fishery. *Journal of Political Economy* 62:124–142.

Gorte, R. W. 2002. Forest Ecosystem Health: An Overview. In *Encyclopedia of Global Change: Environmental Change and Human Society*, ed. A. S. Goudie, 243–250. Oxford, UK: Oxford University Press. Reprint of Congressional Research Service Report no. RS20822, 2001.

Goudie, A. S., ed. 2002. *Encyclopedia of Global Change: Environmental Change and Human Society*. Oxford, UK: Oxford University Press.

Grant, J. P. 1994. *The State of the World's Children*. Oxford: Oxford University Press for UNICEF.

Gray, L. 1999. Is land being degraded? A Multi-Scale Investigation of Landscape Change in Southwestern Burkina Faso. *Land Degradation and Development* 10:329–343.

Green, G. M., ed. 1998–2002. *CIPEC Remote Sensing Lab Manual.* Bloomington: Center for the Study of Institutions, Population, and Environmental Change (CIPEC), Indiana University. Contact cipec@indiana.edu for password.

Green, G. M., C. M. Schweik, and M. Hanson. 2002. *Radiometric Calibration of LANDSAT Multi-Spectral Scanner and Thematic Mapper Images: Guidelines for the Global Change Community.* CIPEC Working Paper CWP-02-03. Bloomington: Center for the Study of Institutions, Population, and Environmental Change (CIPEC), Indiana University.

Green, G. M., and R. W. Sussman. 1990. Deforestation History of the Eastern Rain Forests of Madagascar from Satellite Images. *Science* 248:212–215.

Green, G. M., R. W. Sussman, S. P. Sweeney, I. Porton, O. L. Andrianasolondraibe, and J. Ratsirarson. 2004. *Stability in a Convolving Mosaic of Land-Cover Change Episodes: Conservation by Sacred Forests in Southwestern and Southern Madagascar.* CIPEC Working Paper CWP-04-04. Bloomington: Center for the Study of Institutions, Population, and Environmental Change (CIPEC), Indiana University.

Greenhood, D. 1964. *Mapping.* Chicago: University of Chicago Press.

Grove, J. M., C. M. Schweik, T. P. Evans, and G. M. Green. 2002. Modeling Human-Environmental Systems. In *Geographic Information Systems and Environmental Modeling*, ed. K. C. Clarke, B. E. Parks, and M. P. Crane, 160–188. Upper Saddle River, NJ: Prentice Hall.

Gunderson, L. H., and C. S. Holling. 2002. *Panarchy: Understanding Transformations in Human and Natural Systems.* Washington, DC: Island Press.

Guyer, J. I., and E. F. Lambin. 1993. Land Use in an Urban Hinterland: Ethnography and Remote Sensing in the Study of African Intensification. *American Anthropologist* 95(4):839–859.

Haberl, H., S. Batterbury, and E. Moran. 2001. Using and Shaping the Land: A Long-Term Perspective. *Land Use Policy* 18:1–18.

Hägerstrand, T., and U. Lohm. 1990. Sweden. In *The Earth as Transformed by Human Action*, ed. W. C. Clark, B. L. Turner II, R. W. Kates, J. Richards, J. T. Mathews, and W. Meyer, 605–622. Cambridge, UK: Cambridge University Press.

Hall, F. G., Y. E. Shimabukuro, and K. F. Huemmrich. 1995. Remote Sensing of Forest Biophysical Structure Using Mixture Decomposition and Geometric Reflectance Models. *Ecological Applications* 5:993–1013.

Hall, P. G. 1966. *Von Thünen's Isolated State.* Oxford: Pergamon Press.

Hall, P. A. and R. C. R. Taylor. 1996. Political Science and the Three New Institutionalisms. *Political Studies* 44:936–957.

Hame, T., A. Salli, K. Andersson, and A. Lohi. 1997. A New Methodology for the Estimation of Biomass of Conifer-Dominated Boreal Forest Using NOAA AVHRR Data. *International Journal of Remote Sensing* 18:3211–3243.

Hanink, D. M. 1997. *Principles and Applications of Economic Geography.* New York: Wiley.

Hanson, P. J. 2001. Elements of a deciduous forest carbon cycle. Miscellaneous drawing. Environmental Sciences Division, Oak Ridge National Laboratory, Oak Ridge, TN 37831.

Haralick, R. M. 1979. Statistical and Structural Approaches to Texture. *Proceedings of the IEEE* 67:786–804.

Haralick, R. M., K. Shanmugam, and I. Dinstein. 1973. Textural Features for Image Classification. *IEEE Transactions on Systems, Man and Cybernetics* SMC-3(6):610–620.

Hardin, G. 1968. The Tragedy of the Commons. *Science* 162:1243–1248.

Harrison, G. A., and H. Morphy, eds. 1998. *Human Adaptation*. New York: Berg.

Hart, T. B., J. A. Hart, and P. G. Murphy. 1989. Monodominant and Species-Rich Forests of the Humid Tropics: Causes for Their Co-Occurrence. *The American Naturalist* 133:613–633.

Hayes, T. 2004. *Parks, People, and Forest Protection: An Institutional Assessment of the Effectiveness of Protected Areas*. CIPEC Working Paper CWP-04-01. Bloomington: Center for the Study of Institutions, Population, and Environmental Change (CIPEC), Indiana University.

He, D. C., and L. Wang. 1990. Texture Unit, Textural Spectrum and Texture Analysis. *IEEE Transactions on Geoscience and Remote Sensing* 28:509–512.

Hecht, S. 1989. The Sacred Cow in the Green Hell: Livestock and Forest Conversion in the Brazilian Amazon. *The Ecologist* 19(6):229–234.

Hecht, S., and A. Cockburn. 1989. *The Fate of the Forest*. London: Verso.

Hill, J. 1991. A Quantitative Approach to Remote Sensing: Sensor Calibration and Comparison. In *Remote Sensing and Geographical Information Systems for Resource Management in Developing Countries*, ed. A. S. Belward and C. R. Valenzuela, 97–110. Brussels: European Coal and Steel Community, European Economic Community, and European Atomic Energy Community.

Hiraoka, M. 1985. Zonation of Mestizo Riverine Farming Systems in Northeast Peru. *National Geographic Research* 2(3):354–371.

———. 1989. Agricultural Systems on the Floodplains of the Peruvian Amazon. In *Fragile Lands of Latin America*, ed. J. O. Browder, 75–101. Boulder, CO: Westview.

His Majesty's Government/Nepal (HMG/N). 1984. *National Commission on Population, Inter-regional Migration in Nepal: Problems and Prospects*. Kathmandu, Nepal: author.

Hoerner, J. M. 1977. L'eau et l'agriculture dans le sud-ouest de Madagascar. *Madagascar Revue de Géographie* 30:63–104.

Hoffmann, M. 2002. Entrepreneurs and the Emergence and Evolution of Social Norms. In *Proceedings of Workshop 2002: Agent-Based Simulation 3*, ed. C. Urban. Erlangen, Germany: SCS European Publishing House.

Hoffmann, M., H. Kelley, and T. P. Evans. 2002. Simulating Land-Cover Change in Indiana: An Agent-Based Model of De/Reforestation. In *Complexity and Ecosystem Management: The Theory and Practice of Multi-Agent Systems*, ed. M. A. Janssen, 218–247. Cheltenham, UK: Edward Elgar.

Holland, J. H., and H. Mimmaugh. 1995. *Hidden Order: How Adaptation Builds Complexity*. Reading, MA: Addison-Wesley.

Holling, C. S. 1973. Resilience and Stability of Ecological Systems. *Annual Review of Ecology and Systematics* 4:1–23.

Homer-Dixon, T. F. 1990. *Environmental Change and Violent Conflict.* Occasional Paper, no. 4. Cambridge, MA: International Security Studies Program, American Academy of Arts and Sciences.

———. 1991. On the Threshold: Environmental Changes As Causes of Acute Conflict. *International Security* 16(2):76–116. URL: http://www.library.utoronto.ca/pcs/thresh/thresh1.htm.

Hopfenberg, R. 2003. Human Carrying Capacity Is Determined by Food Availability. *Population and Environment* 25(2):109–117.

Horler, D. N. H., and F. J. Ahern. 1986. Forestry Information Content of Thematic Mapper Data. *International Journal of Remote Sensing* 7:405–428.

Houghton, J. T., Y. Ding, D. J. Griggs, M. Noguer, P. J. van der Linden, X. Dai, K. Maskell, and C. A. Johnson. 2001. Climate Change 2001: The Scientific Basis. Contribution of Working Group I to the Third Assessment Report of the Intergovernmental Panel on Climate Change (IPCC). URL: http://www.grida.no/climate/ipcc_tar/wg1/index.htm.

Huang, Y. 1979. *Nepal: Development Performance and Prospects.* A World Bank Country Study. Washington, DC: South Asia Regional Office, World Bank.

Huete, A. R., H. Q. Liu, K. Batchily, and W. van Leeuwen. 1997. A Comparison of Vegetation Indices over a Global Set of TM Images for EOS-MODIS. *Remote Sensing of Environment* 59:440–451.

Humbert, H., and G. Cours Darne. 1965. *Carte internationale du tapis végétal: Madagascar, 1:1,000,000* (International Chart of the Vegetation Carpet: Madagascar, 1:1,000,000). *Travaux Section Scientifique et Technique.* Hors série no. 6. Pondicherry, India: Institut Français de Pondichéry.

Hunt, R. C. 1995. Agrarian Data Sets: The Comparativist's View. In *The Comparative Analysis of Human Societies: Toward Common Standards for Data Collection and Reporting*, ed. E. F. Moran, 173–189. Boulder, CO: Lynne Rienner.

Hussin, Y. A., R. M. Reich, and R. M. Hoffer. 1991. Estimating Slash Pine Biomass Using Radar Backscatter. *IEEE Transactions on Geoscience and Remote Sensing* 29:427–431.

Ibrahim, F. 1998. Editorial: Identities in Sub-Saharan Africa. *GeoJournal* 46:77–78.

Imbernon, J. 1999. A Comparison of the Driving Forces behind Deforestation in the Peruvian and Brazilian Amazon. *Ambio* 28(6):509–513.

Indiana Department of Natural Resources (IDNR). 1997. *Annual Report.* Indianapolis, IN: author.

Innes, J. L., and R. C. Boswell. 1990. Reliability, Presentation, and Relationships among Data from Inventories of Forest Condition. *Canadian Journal of Forestry Research* 20:790–799.

Instituto Nacional de Pesquisas Espaciais (INPE). 1988–2001. *INPE Deforestation Reports, 1988–2001.* São José dos Campos, Brazil: Diretoria de Observacao da Terra, Instituto Nacional de Pesquisas Espaciais. URL: http://www.inpe.br/.

International Geosphere-Biosphere Programme (IGBP). 2003. *The Land Project: A Science Plan and Implementation Strategy for Integrated Research on Coupled Human-Environment*

Systems on Land. Presented at the Open Science Conference on "Global Change and the Terrestrial Human-Environment System (Land Core Project)," Morelia, Mexico, December 1–4.

International Organization for Standardization (ISO). 2003. *ISO/TC 211*, Geographic Information/Geomatics. URL: http://www.isotc211.org/. Accessed January 2003.

Irons, J. R., and G. W. Petersen. 1981. Texture Transform of Remote Sensing Data. *Remote Sensing of Environment* 11:359–370.

Irwin, E. G., and J. Geoghegan. 2001. Theory, Data, Methods: Developing Spatially Explicit Economic Models of Land Use Change. *Agriculture, Ecosystems and Environment* 85:7–23.

ISI Web of Knowledge: Transforming Research. 2003. URL: http://isi1.isiknowledge.com/portal.cgi. Accessed June 2003.

Iverson, L. R., S. Brown, A. Prasad, H. Mitasova, A. J. R. Gillespie, and A. E. Lugo. 1992. Use of GIS for Estimating Potential and Actual Forest Biomass for Continental South and Southeast Asia. In *Effects of Land Use Change on Atmospheric Carbon Dioxide Concentration: Southeast Asia As a Case Study*, ed. Y. H. Dale, 67–116. New York: Springer-Verlag.

Ives, J. D., and B. Messerli. 1989. *The Himalayan Dilemma: Reconciling Development and Conservation*. London: United Nations University and Routledge.

Jackson, M. T. 1997. *The Natural Heritage of Indiana*. Bloomington: Indiana University Press.

Jakubauskas, M. K., and K. P. Price. 1997. Empirical Relationships between Structural and Spectral Factors of Yellowstone Lodgepole Pine Forest. *Photogrammetric Engineering and Remote Sensing* 63:1375–1381.

Janssen, M. A., ed. 2002. *Complexity and Ecosystem Management: The Theory and Practice of Multi-Agent Systems*. Cheltenham, UK: Edward Elgar.

Janssen, M. A., and E. Ostrom. In press. Adoption of a New Regulation for the Governance of Common-Pool Resources by a Heterogeneous Population. In *Inequality, Collective Action and Environmental Sustainability*, ed. J. M. Baland, P. Bardhan, and S. Bowles. Princeton, NJ: Princeton University Press.

Jarvis, P. G. 1993. Prospects for Bottom-Up Models. In *Scaling Physiological Processes: Leaf to Globe*, ed. J. R. Ehringer and C. B. Field, 115–126. San Diego: Academic Press.

Jensen, J. R. 1996. *Introductory Digital Image Processing: A Remote Sensing Perspective*. Upper Saddle River, NJ: Prentice Hall.

Jensen, J. R., and M. E. Hodgson. 2004. Remote Sensing of Selected Biophysical Variables and Urban/Suburban Phenomena. In *Geography and Technology*, ed. S. D. Brunn, S. L. Cutter, and J. W. Harrington Jr., 109–154. Dordrecht, the Netherlands: Kluwer.

Jet Propulsion Laboratory (JPL). 2003. The Shuttle Radar Topography Mission. URL: http://www2.jpl.nasa.gov/srtm/.

Jha, H. B. 1993. *The Terai Community and National Integration in Nepal*. Kathmandu, Nepal: Centre for Economic and Technical Studies.

Johnson, S. H., III. 1986. Agricultural Intensification in Thailand: Complementary Role of Infrastructure and Agricultural Policy. In *Irrigation Investment, Technology, and Management Strategies for Development*, ed. W. K. Easter, 111–127. Boulder, CO: Westview.

Johnston, J. J., D. R. Weigel, and J. C. Randolph. 1997. Satellite Remote Sensing—An Inexpensive Tool for Pine Plantation Management. *Journal of Forestry* 95(6):16–20.

Jordan, C. F., and C. Uhl. 1978. Biomass of a "Terra Firme" Forest of the Amazon Basin. *Oecologia Plantarum* 13:387–400.

Kaimowitz, D., and A. Angelsen. 1998. *Economic Models of Tropical Deforestation: A Review*. Bogor, Indonesia: Center for International Forestry Research.

Kashyap, R. L., R. Chellappa, and A. Khotanzad. 1982. Texture Classification Using Features Derived from Random Field Models. *Pattern Recognition Letters* 1:43–50.

Kasperson, J. X., R. E. Kasperson, and B. L. Turner II. 1995. *Regions at Risk: Comparisons of Threatened Environments*. New York: United Nations University Press.

Kates, R. W., and T. M. Parris. 2003. Long-Term Trends and a Sustainability Transition. *Proceedings of the National Academy of Sciences of the United States of America* 100(14):8062–8067. URL: http://www.pnas.org/cgi/reprint/100/14/8062.pdf.

Kawachi, I., and L. Berkman, eds. 2003. *Neighborhoods and Health*. New York: Oxford University Press.

Kawachi, I., and B. Kennedy. 2002. *The Health of the Nations*. New York: New Press.

Kelley, H., and T. P. Evans. Under review. The Relative Influence of Landowner and Landscape Heterogeneity in an Agent-Based Model of Land Use. *Journal of Economic Dynamics and Control*.

King, G., R. O. Keohane, and S. Verba. 1994. *Designing Social Inquiry: Scientific Inference in Qualitative Research*. Princeton, NJ: Princeton University Press.

Kirk, D. 1996. Demographic Transition Theory. *Population Studies* 50:361–387.

Kish, L. 1995. *Survey Sampling*. Wiley Classics Library edition. New York: Wiley.

Klinge, H., W. A. Rodriguez, E. Brunig, and E. J. Fittkau. 1975. Biomass and Structure in a Central Amazonian Rain Forest. In *Tropical Ecological Systems*, ed. F. B. Golley and E. Medina, 115–122. Berlin: Springer-Verlag.

Koestler, A. 1973. The Tree and the Candle. In *Unity through Diversity*, ed. N. D. Rizzo, 287–314. New York: Gordon & Breach.

Kohler, H. P. 2000. Fertility Decline As a Coordination Problem. *Journal of Development Economics* 63:231–263.

Kolstad, C. D. 2000. *Environmental Economics*. Oxford: Oxford University Press.

Kolstad, C. D., and D. Kelly. 2001. Malthus and Climate Change: Betting on a Stable Population. *Journal of Environmental Economics and Management* 41:135–161.

Koontz, T. M. 2001. Money Talks—But to Whom? Financial v. Non-Monetary Motivations in Land Use Decisions. *Society and Natural Resources* 14:51–65.

———. 2002. *Federalism in the Forest: National versus State Natural Resource Policy*. American Governance and Policy series. Washington, DC: Georgetown University Press.

Kramer, P., and T. Kozlowski. 1979. *Physiology of Woody Plants*. New York: Academic Press.

Krugman, P. 1995. *Development, Geography, and Economic Theory*. Cambridge, MA: MIT Press.

Kubin, E., H. Lippo, and J. Poikolainen. 2000. Heavy Metal Loading. In *Forest Condition in a Changing Environment—The Finnish Case*, ed. E. Malkonen, 60–71. Dordrecht, the Netherlands: Kluwer.

Kull, C. A. 1998. Leimavo Revisited: Agrarian Land-Use Change in the Highlands of Madagascar. *Professional Geographer* 50(2):163–176.

Kurvonen, L., J. Pulliainen, and M. Hallikainen. 1999. Retrieval of Biomass in Boreal Forests from Multitemporal ERS-1 and JERS-1 SAR Data. *IEEE Transactions on Geoscience and Remote Sensing* 37:198–205.

Lam, W. F. 1998. *Governing Irrigation Systems in Nepal: Institutions, Infrastructure, and Collective Action*. Oakland, CA: ICS Press.

Lambin, E. F., B. L. Turner II, H. J. Geist, S. Agbola, A. Angelsen, J. W. Bruce, O. Coomes, R. Dirzo, G. Fischer, C. Folke, P. S. George, K. Homewood, J. Imbernon, R. Leemans, X. Li, E. F. Moran, M. Mortimore, P. S. Ramakrishnan, J. F. Richards, H. Skånes, W. Steffen, G. D. Stone, U. Svedin, T. Veldkamp, C. Vogel, and J. Xu. 2001. The Causes of Land-Use and Land-Cover Change: Moving Beyond the Myths. *Global Environmental Change* 11(4):261–269.

Lansing, J. S., and J. N. Kremer. 1993. Emergent Properties of Balinese Water Temple Networks: Coadaptation on a Rugged Fitness Landscape. *American Anthropologist* 95:97–114.

Lapper, R., and J. Painter. 1985. *Honduras: State for Sale*. London: Latin American Bureau (Research and Action) Ltd.

Larson, A. 2003. Decentralisation and Forest Management in Latin America: Towards a Working Model. *Public Administration and Development* 23:211–226.

Laurance, W. F., and R. O. Bierregaard Jr. 1997. *Tropical Forest Remnants: Ecology, Management, and Conservation of Fragmented Communities*. Chicago: University of Chicago Press.

Laurence, W. F., M. A. Cochrane, S. Bergen, P. M. Fearnside, P. Delamonica, C. Barber, S. D'Angelo, and T. Fernandes. 2001. The Future of the Brazilian Amazon. *Science* 291(5503):438–442.

Laurence, W. F., and P. Fearnside. 2002. Issues on Amazonian Development. *Science* 295:629–631.

Leach, M., and R. Mearns. 1996. *The Lie of the Land*. Oxford: The International African Institute and James Currey.

Leaf, M. J. 1987. Intensification in Peasant Farming: Punjab in the Green Revolution. In *Comparative Farming Systems*, ed. B. L. Turner II and S. B. Brush, 248–275. New York: Guilford.

Leblon, B., H. Granberg, C. Ansseau, and A. Royer. 1993. A Semi-Empirical Model to Estimate the Biomass Production of Forest Canopies from Spectral Variables. Part 1: Relationship between Spectral Variables and Light Interception Efficiency. *Remote Sensing Reviews* 7:109–125.

Lee, D. R., and C. B. Barrett. 2001. *Tradeoffs or Synergies? Agricultural Intensification, Economic Development and the Environment*. Wallingford, UK: CABI.

Lena, P., and A. Oliveira, eds. 1992. *Amazônia: A fronteira agrícola 20 anos depois* (Amazônia: An agricultural frontier after 20 years). Belém, Brazil: Edicoes CEJUP.

Levin, S. A. 1998. Ecosystem and the Biosphere as a Complex Adaptive Systems. *Ecosystems* 1(5):431–436.

Libecap, G. 1989. *Contracting for Property Rights*. New York: Cambridge University Press.

———. 1995. The Conditions for Successful Collective Action. In *Local Commons and Global Interdependence: Heterogeneity and Cooperation in Two Domains*, ed. R. O. Keohane and E. Ostrom, 161–190. London: Sage.

Lim, K., P. Deadman, E. Moran, E. Brondízio, and S. McCracken. 2002. Agent-Based Simulations of Household Decision Making and Land Use Change near Altamira, Brazil. In *Integrating Geographic Information Systems and Agent-Based Modeling Techniques for Understanding Social and Ecological Processes*, ed. H. R. Gimblett, 277–310. Oxford, UK: Oxford University Press.

Lisle, D. de. 1978. Effects of Distance Internal to the Farm: A Challenging Subject for North American Geographers. *Professional Geographer* 30:278–288.

Livi Bacci, M. 2001. *A Concise History of World Population*. Malden, MA: Blackwell.

Lo, C. P., and A. Yeung. 2002. *Concepts and Techniques of Geographic Information Systems*. Upper Saddle River, NJ: Prentice-Hall.

Loucks, O. L. 1992. Forest Response Research in NAPAP: Potentially Successful Linkage of Policy and Science. *Ecological Applications* 2:117–123.

Lu, D. 2001. Estimation of forest stand parameters and application in classification and change detection of forest cover types in the Brazilian Amazon basin. Ph.D. diss., Indiana State University, Terre Haute.

Lu, D., P. Mausel, E. S. Brondízio, and E. Moran. 2002a. Above-Ground Biomass Estimation of Successional and Mature Forests Using TM Images in the Amazon Basin. In *Advances in Spatial Data Handling*, ed. D. Richardson and P. van Oosterom, 183–196. New York: Springer-Verlag.

———. 2002b. Assessment of Atmospheric Correction Methods for Landsat TM Data Applicable to Amazon Basin LBA Research. *International Journal of Remote Sensing* 23(13):2651–2671.

Lu, D., E. Moran, and P. Mausel. 2002c. Linking Amazonian Secondary Succession Forest Growth to Soil Properties. *Land Degradation and Development* 13:331–343.

Ludwig, D., B. Walker, and C. S. Holling. 1997. Sustainability, Stability, and Resilience. *Conservation Ecology* 1(1):article 7 [online]. URL: http://www.consecol.org/vol1/iss1/art7/.

Lugo, A. E. 1988. Estimating Reductions in the Diversity of Tropical Forest Species. In *Biodiversity*, ed. E. O. Wilson, 58–70. Washington, DC: National Academy Press.

Lundquist, J. E., and J. S. Beatty. 1999. A Conceptual Model for Defining and Assessing Condition of Forest Stands. *Environmental Management* 23:519–525.

Lutz, W., W. C. Sanderson, and A. Wils. 2002. Conclusions: Toward Comprehensive Population-Environment Studies. *Population and Development Review* 28(Suppl.):225–250.

Lynam, T., F. Bousquet, C. Le Page, P. d'Aquino, O. Barreteau, F. Chinembiri, and B. Mombeshora. 2002. Adapting Science to Adaptive Managers: Spidergrams, Belief Models, and

Multi-Agent Systems Modeling. *Conservation Ecology* 5(2):article 24 [online]. URL: http://www.consecol.org/vol5/iss2/art24.

Maass, A., and R. L. Anderson. 1986. *... And the Desert Shall Rejoice: Conflict, Growth and Justice in Arid Environments*. Malabar, FL: R. E. Krieger.

Macleod, R., and R. Congalton. 1998. A Quantitative Comparison of Change Detection Algorithms for Monitoring Eelgrass from Remotely Sensed Data. *Photogrammetric Engineering and Remote Sensing* 64(3):207–216.

Mahar, D. J. 1988. *Government Policies and Deforestation in the Brazilian Amazon Region*. Washington, DC: World Bank.

Malthus, T. R. [1803] 1989. *An Essay on the Principle of Population*. Reprint with the variorums of 1806, 1807, 1817, and 1826. Ed. P. James. Cambridge, UK: Cambridge University Press.

March, J. G., and J. P. Olsen. 1984. The New Institutionalism: Organizational Factors in Political Life. *American Political Science Review* 78:734–749.

Markham, B. L., and J. L. Barker. 1986. Landsat MSS and TM Post-Calibration Dynamic Ranges, Exoatmospheric Reflectances and At-Satellite Temperatures. *EOSAT Technical Notes* 1:3–8.

Marquette, C. 1998. Land Use Patterns among Small Farmer Settlers in the Northeastern Ecuadorian Amazon. *Human Ecology* 26(4):573–598.

Mason, K. O. 1997. Explaining Fertility Transitions. *Demography* 34:443–454.

Massey, D. S., J. Arango, G. Hugo, A. Kouaouci, A. Pellegrino, and J. E. Taylor. 1993. Theories of International Migration: A Review and Appraisal. *Population and Development Review* 19:431–466.

Matson, P., R. Naylor, and I. Ortiz-Monasterio. 1998. Integration of Environmental, Agronomic, and Economic Aspects of Fertilization Management. *Science* 280:112–115.

Matthews, S. A., G. P. Shivakoti, and N. Chhetri. 2000. Population Forces and Environmental Change: Observations from Western Chitwan, Nepal. *Society and Natural Resources* 13:763–775.

Mauldin, T. E., A. J. Plantinga, and R. J. Alig. 1999. Determinants of Land Use in Maine with Projections to 2050. *Northern Journal of Applied Forestry* 16:82–88.

Mausel, P., Y. Wu, E. Moran, and E. Brondízio. 1993. Spectral Identification of Succession Stages Following Deforestation in the Amazon. *Geocarto International* 8:61–72.

Maxwell, D., W. O. Larbi, G. M. Lamptey, S. Zakariah, and M. Armar-Klemesu. 1999. Farming in the Shadow of the City: Changes in Land Rights and Livelihoods in Peri-Urban Accra. *Third World Planning Review* 21(4):373–391.

Mayr, E. 1982. *The Growth of Biological Thought: Diversity, Evolution, and Inheritance*. Cambridge, MA: Harvard University Press.

McCann, J. C. 1997. The Plow and the Forest: Narratives of Deforestation in Ethiopia, 1840–1992. *Environmental History* 2(2):138–159.

McCay, B. J., and J. M. Acheson. 1987. Human Ecology of the Commons. In *The Question of the Commons: The Culture and Ecology of Communal Resources*, ed. B. J. McCay, and J. M. Acheson, 1–36. Tucson: University of Arizona Press.

McConnell, W. J. 2001. Why and How People and Institutions Matter beyond Economy. *International Geosphere-Biosphere Programme Newsletter* 47:20–22.

———. 2002a. Madagascar: Emerald Isle or Paradise Lost? *Environment* 44(8):10–22.

———. 2002b. Misconstrued Land Use in Vohibazaha: Participatory Planning in the Periphery of Madagascar's Mantadia National Park. *Land Use Policy* 19(3):217–230.

McConnell, W. J., and E. F. Moran, eds. 2001. *Meeting in the Middle: The Challenge of Meso-Level Integration*. LUCC Report Series, no. 5. Bloomington, IN: Land Use and Cover Change (LUCC) Focus 1 Office of the International Geosphere-Biosphere Programme.

McConnell, W. J., S. P. Sweeney, and B. Mulley. 2004. Physical and Social Access to Land: Spatio-Temporal Patterns of Agricultural Expansion in Madagascar. *Agriculture, Ecosystems, and Environment* 101(2–3):171–184.

McCracken, J., J. Pretty, G. Conway. 1988. *An Introduction to Rapid Rural Appraisal for Agricultural Development*. London: International Institute for Environment and Development.

McCracken, S., B. Boucek, and E. Moran. 2002a. Deforestation Trajectories in a Frontier Region of the Brazilian Amazon. In *Linking People, Place, and Policy: A GIScience Approach*, ed. S. Walsh and K. Crews-Meyer, 215–234. Dordrecht, the Netherlands: Kluwer.

McCracken, S., E. S. Brondízio, D. Nelson, E. F. Moran, A. D. Siqueira, and C. Rodriguez-Pedraza. 1999. Remote Sensing and GIS at the Farm Property Level: Demography and Deforestation in the Brazilian Amazon. *Photogrammetric Engineering and Remote Sensing* 65(11):1311–1320.

McCracken, S. D., C. A. M. Safar, and G. M. Green. 1997. Deforestation and Forest Regrowth in Indiana, 1860–1990. Presented at the Annual Meeting of the Population Association of America, Washington, DC, March 26–28.

McCracken, S. D., A. D. Siqueira, E. F. Moran, and E. S. Brondízio. 2002b. Land Use Patterns on an Agricultural Frontier in Brazil: Insights and Examples from a Demographic Perspective. In *Deforestation and Land Use in the Amazon*, ed. C. H. Wood and R. Porro, 162–192. Gainesville: University Press of Florida.

McGinnis, M., ed. 1999. *Polycentric Governance and Development: Readings from the Workshop in Political Theory and Policy Analysis*. Ann Arbor: University of Michigan Press.

McGregor, J. 1994. Climate Change and Involuntary Migration: Implications for Food Security. *Food Policy* 19(2):120–132.

McKean, M. A. 1982. The Japanese Experience with Scarcity: Management of Traditional Common Lands. *Environmental Review* 6:63–88.

———. 1992a. Management of Traditional Commons Lands (*iriaichi*) in Japan. In *Making the Commons Work: Theory, Practice, and Policy*, ed. D. W. Bromley, D. Feeny, M. McKean, P. Peters, J. Gilles, R. Oakerson, C. F. Runge, and J. Thomson, 63–98. San Francisco: ICS Press.

———. 1992b. Success on the Commons: A Comparative Examination of Institutions for Common Property Resource Management. *Journal of Theoretical Politics* 4(3):247–282.

———. 2000. Common Property: What is it, what is it good for, what makes it work? In *People and Forests: Communities, Institutions and Governance*, ed. C. C. Gibson, M. A. McKean, and E. Ostrom, 27–56. Cambridge, MA: MIT Press.

McKean, M. A., and E. Ostrom. 1995. Common Property Regimes in the Forest: Just a Relic from the Past? *Unasylva* 46(1):3–15.

McLaughlin, S., and K. Percy. 1999. Forest Health in North America: Some Perspectives on Actual and Potential Roles of Climate and Air Pollution. *Water, Air, and Soil Pollution* 116:151–197.

Meffe, G. K., and C. R. Carroll. 1997. *Principles of Conservation Biology*. Sunderland, MA: Sinauer.

Mensing, D. M., S. M. Galatowitsch, and J. R. Tester. 1998. Anthropogenic Effects on the Biodiversity of Riparian Wetlands of a Northern Temperate Landscape. *Journal of Environmental Management* 53(4):349–377.

Merino, L. 1999. Reserva Especial de la Biósfera Mariposa Monarca: Problemática general de la region (The Monarch Butterfly Special Biosphere Reserve: The General Problem of the Region). In *1997 North American Conference on the Monarch Butterfly*, ed. J. Hoth, L. Merino, K. Oberhauser, I. Pisanty, S. Price, and T. Wilkinson, 239–247. Montreal: Commission for Environmental Cooperation.

Mertens, B., and E. Lambin. 1997. Spatial Modelling of Deforestation in Southern Cameroon: Spatial Disaggregation of Diverse Deforestation Processes. *Applied Geography* 17(2):143–162.

———. 2000. Land-Cover–Change Trajectories in Southern Cameroon. *Annals of the Association of American Geographers* 90:467–495. URL: http://www.geo.ucl.ac.be/LUCC/MODLUC_Course/PDF/E.%20Lambin.pdf.

Mertens, B., W. D. Sunderlin, O. Ndoye, and E. F. Lambin. 2000. Impact of Macroeconomic Change on Deforestation in South Cameroon: Integration of Household Survey and Remotely Sensed Data. *World Development* 28(6):983–999.

Meyer, W. B., and B. L. Turner II. 1992. Human Population Growth and Global Land-Use/Land-Cover Change. *Annual Review of Ecology and Systematics* 23:39–61.

Miller, C., and D. L. Urban. 2000. Modeling the Effects of Fire Management Alternatives on Sierra Nevada Mixed-Conifer Forests. *Ecological Applications* 10:85–94.

Miller, D. J., and A. J. Plantinga. 1999. Modeling Land Use Decisions with Aggregate Data. *American Journal of Agricultural Economics* 81:180–194.

Moguel, P., and V. M. Toledo. 1999. Biodiversity Conservation in Traditional Coffee Systems of Mexico. *Conservation Biology* 13(1):11–21.

Molnar, A. 1989. *Community Forestry: Rapid Appraisal*. Rome: Food and Agriculture Organization of the United Nations.

Monteith, J. L. 1977. Climate and the Efficiency of Crop Production in Britain. *Philosophical Transactions of the Royal Society of London. Series B: Biological Sciences* 281:227–294.

Moran, E. F. 1973. Transamazon: Long Road to a Nation's Riches. *Modern Government* November–December:30–38.

———. 1974. The Adaptive System of the Amazonian Caboclo. In *Man in the Amazon*, ed. C. Wagley, 136–159. Gainesville: University Press of Florida.

———. 1976. *Agricultural Development along the Transamazon Highway*. Center for Latin American Studies Monograph Series. Bloomington: Center for Latin American Studies, Indiana University.

———. 1981. *Developing the Amazon*. Bloomington: Indiana University Press.

———. 1984a. Colonization in the Transamazon and Rondonia. In *Frontier Expansion in Amazonia*, ed. M. Schmink and C. H. Wood, 285–303. Gainesville: University Press of Florida.

———. 1984b. Limitations and Advances in Ecosystems Research. In *The Ecosystem Concept in Anthropology*, ed. E. F. Moran, 3–32. Washington, DC: American Association for the Advancement of Science.

———. 1990. Levels of Analysis and Analytical Level Shifting: Examples from Amazonian Ecosystem Research. In *The Ecosystem Approach in Anthropology: From Concept to Practice*, ed. E. F. Moran, 279–308. Ann Arbor: University of Michigan Press.

———. 1992. Amazonian Deforestation: Local Causes, Global Consequences. In *Proceedings of the International Conference on Human Ecology: Human Responsibility and Global Change, Göteborg, June 9–14, 1991*, ed. L. Hansson and B. Jungen, 54–67. Göteborg, Sweden: Section of Human Ecology, University of Göteborg.

———. 2000. *Human Adaptability: An Introduction to Ecological Anthropology*, 2d ed. Boulder, CO: Westview.

Moran, E. F., ed. 1995. *The Comparative Analysis of Human Societies: Toward Common Standards for Data Collection and Reporting*. Boulder, CO: L. Rienner.

Moran, E. F., and E. S. Brondízio. 1998. Land-Use Change after Deforestation in Amazônia. In *People and Pixels: Linking Remote Sensing and Social Science*, ed. D. Liverman, E. F. Moran, R. R. Rindfuss, and P. C. Stern, 94–120. Washington, DC: National Academy Press.

———. 2001. Human Ecology from Space: Ecological Anthropology Engages the Study of Global Environmental Change. In *Ecology and the Sacred: Engaging the Anthropology of Roy A. Rappaport*, ed. M. Lambek and E. Messer, 64–87. Ann Arbor: University of Michigan Press.

Moran, E. F., E. S. Brondízio, and P. Mausel. 1994a. Secondary Succession. *National Geographic Research and Exploration* 10(4):458–476.

Moran, E. F., E. Brondizio, P. Mausel, and Y. Wu. 1994b. Integrating Amazonian Vegetation, Land-use, and Satellite Data. *BioScience* 44(5):329–338.

Moran, E. F., E. S. Brondízio, and S. D. McCracken. 2002a. Trajectories of Land Use: Soils, Succession, and Crop Choice. In *Deforestation and Land Use in the Amazon*, ed. C. H. Wood and R. Porro, 193–217. Gainesville: University Press of Florida.

Moran, E. F., E. S. Brondízio, S. McCracken, A. Siqueira, D. Nelson, and C. Rodriguez-Pedraza. 2002b. The Colonist Footprint: Toward a Conceptual Framework of Land Use and Deforestation Trajectories among Small Farmers in the Amazonian Frontier. In *Deforestation and Land Use in the Amazon*, ed. C. H. Wood and R. Porro, 133–161. Gainesville: University Press of Florida.

Moran, E. F., E. S. Brondízio, J. M. Tucker, M. C. Silva-Forsberg, I. Falesi, and S. D. McCracken. 2000a. Strategies for Amazonian Forest Restoration: Evidence for Afforestation in Five Regions of the Brazilian Amazon. In *Amazônia at the Crossroads: The Challenge of Sustainable Development*, ed. A. Hall, 129–149. London: Institute for Latin American Studies, University of London.

Moran, E. F., E. S. Brondízio, J. M. Tucker, M. C. Silva-Forsberg, S. D. McCracken, and I. Falesi. 2000b. Effects of Soil Fertility and Land Use on Forest Succession in Amazônia. *Forest Ecology and Management* 139(1–3):93–108.

Moran, E. F., S. McCracken, and E. S. Brondízio. 2001. The Developmental Cycle of Domestic Groups and Its Impact on Deforestation and Land Use in the Amazon. Presented at the Population Association of America 66th Annual Meeting, Washington, DC, March 29–31.

Moran, E. F., E. Ostrom, and J. C. Randolph. In press. Ecological Systems and Multitier Human Organization. In *UNESCO Encyclopedia of Life Support Systems*. Oxford: EOLSS Publishers.

Moran, E. F., A. Packer, E. S. Brondízio, and J. Tucker. 1996. Restoration of Vegetation Cover in the Eastern Amazon. *Ecological Economics* 18:41–54.

Moran, E. F., A. D. Siqueira, and E. S. Brondízio. 2003. Household Demographic Structure and Its Relationship to Deforestation in the Amazon Basin. In *People and the Environment: Approaches for Linking Household and Community Surveys to Remote Sensing and GIS*, ed. J. Fox, R. Rindfuss, S. Walsh, and V. Mishra, 61–89. Dordrecht, the Netherlands: Kluwer.

Moran, K. 1991. *Partnership for Development: 40 Years of American Assistance*. Washington, DC: United States Agency for International Development.

Muller, P. O. 1973. Trend Surfaces of American Agricultural Patterns: A Macro-Thünen Economy. *Geographical Analysis* 24:228–242.

Munroe, D. K., J. Southworth, and C. M. Tucker. 2002. The Dynamics of Land-Cover Change in Western Honduras: Exploring Spatial and Temporal Complexity. *Agricultural Economics* 27(3):355–369.

Munroe, D. K., and A. York. 2003. Jobs, Houses and Trees: Changing Regional Structure, Local Land-Use Patterns, and Forest Cover in Southern Indiana. *Growth and Change* 34(3):299–320.

Myers, N. 1994. Tropical Deforestation: Rates and Patterns. In *The Causes of Tropical Deforestation*, ed. K. Brown and D. W. Pearce, 27–40. Vancouver: University of British Columbia Press.

Myers, N., and J. Kant. 2001. *Perverse Subsidies: How Tax Dollars Can Undercut the Environment and the Economy*. Washington, DC: Island Press.

Nagendra, H. 2001. Using Remote Sensing to Assess Biodiversity. *International Journal of Remote Sensing* 22(12):2377–2400.

———. 2002. Tenure and Forest conditions: Community Forestry in the Nepal Terai. *Environmental Conservation* 29:530–539.

Nagendra, H., and A. Agrawal. 2004. More People, More Trees? Examining Community Forestry in Nepal's Terai. *IHDP UPDATE: Newsletter of the International Human Dimensions Programme on Global Environmental Change* 01/2004:13. URL: http://www.ihdp.uni-bonn.de/html/publications/publications.html.

Nagendra, H., and M. Gadgil. 1999. Biodiversity Assessment at Multiple Scales: Linking Remotely Sensed Data with Field Information. *Proceedings of the National Academy of Sciences of the United States of America* 96(16):9154–9158.

Nagendra, H., and C. M. Schweik. 2004. Forests and Management: A Case Study in Nepal Using Remote Sensing and GIS. In *100 Geographic Solutions to Saving Planet Earth: Association of American Geographers Centennial Volume*, ed. B. Warf, K. Hansen, and D. Janelle, 391–396. Boston: Kluwer.

Nagendra, H., J. Southworth, and C. M. Tucker. 2003. Accessibility as a Determinant of Landscape Transformation in Western Honduras: Linking Pattern and Process. *Landscape Ecology* 18(2):141–158.

Nagendra, H., J. Southworth, C. M. Tucker, M. Karmacharya, B. Karna, and L. A. Carlson. 2004. Monitoring Parks through Remote Sensing: Studies in Nepal and Honduras. *Environmental Management* Online First publication. URL: http.//www.springerlink.com (subscription required).

National Academy of Sciences (NAS). 2003. Mapping Economic and Environmental Vulnerabilities. *Proceedings of the National Academy of Sciences of the United States of America* 100(14):8059–8091. URL: http://www.pnas.org/content/vol100/issue14/index.shtml.

National Climatic Data Center (NCDC). 2004. URL: http://www.ncdc.noaa.gov/oa/ncdc.html.

National Drought Mitigation Center (NDMC). 1998. Reported Drought-Related Effects of El Niño for November 1997. URL: http://www.drought.unl.edu/index.htm.

National Research Council (NRC). 1986. *Proceedings of the Conference on Common Property Resource Management, April 21–26, 1985*. Washington, DC: National Academies Press. Available from National Academies Press library at nrclib@nas.edu.

———. 1992. *Global Environmental Change: Understanding the Human Dimension*, ed. P. C. Stern, O. Young, and D. Druckman. Washington, DC: National Academy Press.

———. 1994. *Science Priorities for the Human Dimensions of Global Change*. Washington, DC: National Academy Press.

———. 1997. *Environmentally Significant Consumption: Research Directions*, ed. P. C. Stern, T. Dietz, V. W. Ruttan, R. H. Socolow, and J. L. Sweeney. Washington, DC: National Academy Press.

———. 1998. *People and Pixels: Linking Remote Sensing and Social Science*, ed. D. Liverman, E. F. Moran, R. R. Rindfuss, and P. C. Stern. Washington, DC: National Academy Press.

———. 1999a. *Human Dimensions of Global Environmental Change: Research Pathways for the Next Decade*. Washington, DC: National Academy Press.

———. 1999b. *Making Climate Forecasts Matter*. Washington, DC: National Academy Press.

———. 2001. *Grand Challenges in Environmental Sciences*. Report from the Committee on Grand Challenges in Environmental Sciences. Washington, DC: National Academy Press.

———. 2002. *The Drama of the Commons*, ed. E. Ostrom, T. Dietz, N. Dolšak, P. C. Stern, S. Stonich, and E. Weber. Washington, DC: National Academies Press. URL: http://www.nap.edu/books/0309082501/html/.

National Science Board (NSB). 2000. *Environmental Science and Engineering for the 21st Century: The Role of the National Science Foundation*. Report no. NSB 00-22. Arlington, VA: National Science Foundation.

National Science Foundation (NSF). 2003. *Complex Environmental Systems: Synthesis for Earth, Life and Society in the 21st Century*. Report from the Advisory Committee for Environmental Research and Education. Arlington, VA: National Science Foundation.

Nelson, B. W., R. Mesquita, J. L. G. Pereira, S. G. A. de Souza, G. T. Batista, and L. B. Couto. 1999. Allometric Regression for Improved Estimate of Secondary Forest Biomass in the Central Amazon. *Forest Ecology and Management* 117:149–167.

Nelson, G. C., V. Harris, and S. Stone. 2001. Deforestation, Land Use and Property Rights: Evidence from Darien, Panama. *Land Economics* 77:187–205.

Nelson, R. F., D. S. Kimes, W. A. Salas, and M. Routhier. 2000. Secondary Forest Age and Tropical Forest Biomass Estimation Using Thematic Mapper Imagery. *BioScience* 50:419–431.

Nelson, R. F., W. Krabill, and J. Tonelli. 1988. Estimating Forest Biomass and Volume Using Airborne Laser Data. *Remote Sensing of Environment* 24:247–267.

Nepstad, D., D. McGrath, A. Alencar, A. C. Barros, G. Carvalho, M. Santilli, and M. del C. Vera Diaz. 2002. Frontier Governance in Amazonia. *Science* 295(5555):629–632.

Nepstad, D., A. Moreira, and A. Alencar. 1999. *Flames in the Rain Forest: Origins, Impacts, and Alternatives to Amazonian Fire*. Brasilia, DF: Pilot Program to Conserve the Brazilian Rain Forest, United States Agency for International Development (USAID/Brazil).

Nepstad, D., and C. Uhl. 2000. Amazonia at the Millennium. *Interciencia* 25(3):159–164.

Netting, R. McC. 1976. What Alpine Peasants Have in Common: Observations on Communal Tenure in a Swiss Village. *Human Ecology* 4(2):135–146.

———. 1980. *Balancing on an Alp*. New York: Cambridge University Press.

———. 1982. Territory, Property, and Tenure. In *Behavioral and Social Science Research: A National Resource*, Part 2, ed. R. McC. Adams, N. J. Smelser, and D. J. Treiman, 446–502. Washington, DC: National Academy Press.

———. 1986. *Cultural Ecology*. Prospect Heights, IL: Waveland.

———. 1990. Links and Boundaries: Reconsidering the Alpine Village an Ecosystem. In *The Ecosystem Approach in Anthropology*, ed. E. F. Moran, 229–245. Ann Arbor: University of Michigan Press.

———. 1993. *Smallholders, Householders: Farm Families and the Ecology of Intensive, Sustainable Agriculture*. Stanford, CA: Stanford University Press.

Nordlund, G. 2000. Emissions, Air Quality and Acidifying Deposition. In *Forest Condition in a Changing Environment—The Finnish Case*, ed. E. Malkonen, 49–59. Dordrecht, the Netherlands: Kluwer.

North, D. C. 1990. *Institutions, Institutional Change and Economic Performance*. New York: Cambridge University Press.

Nugent, S. 1993. *Amazonian Caboclo Society: An Essay on Invisibility and Peasant Economy*. Oxford: Oxford University Press.

Nyerges, A. E., and G. M. Green. 2000. The Ethnography of Landscape: GIS and Remote Sensing in the Study of Forest Change in West African Guinea Savanna. *American Anthropologist* 102(2):271–289.

Oakerson, R. J. 1992. Analyzing the Commons: A Framework. In *Making the Commons Work: Theory, Practice, and Policy*, ed. D. W. Bromley, D. Feeny, M. McKean, P. Peters, J. Gilles, R. Oakerson, C. F. Runge, and J. Thomson, 41–59. San Francisco: ICS Press.

O'Kelly, M., and D. Bryan. 1996. Agricultural Location Theory: von Thünen's Contribution to Economic Geography. *Progress in Human Geography* 20:457–475.

Olson, M. 1965. *The Logic of Collective Action.* Cambridge, MA: Harvard University Press.

Openshaw, S., A. Craft, M. Charlton, and J. Birch. 1988. Investigation of Leukaemia Clusters by Use of a Geographical Information Analysis Machine. *Lancet* 6:272–273.

Ostrom, E. 1990. *Governing the Commons: The Evolution of Institutions for Collective Action.* New York: Cambridge University Press.

———. 1992. *Crafting Institutions for Self-Governing Irrigation Systems.* San Francisco: ICS Press.

———. 1998a. A Behavioral Approach to the Rational Choice Theory of Collective Action. *American Political Science Review* 92(1):1–22.

———. 1998b. The International Forestry Resources and Institutions Research Program: A Methodology for Relating Human Incentives and Actions on Forest Cover and Biodiversity. In *Forest Biodiversity in North, Central and South America, and the Caribbean: Research and Monitoring*, ed. F. Dallmeier and J. A. Comiskey, 1–28. Vol. 21 of Man and the Biosphere series. New York: Parthenon.

———. 1999. Coping with Tragedies of the Commons. *Annual Review of Political Science* 2:493–535.

———. 2001. Reformulating the Commons. In *Protecting the Commons: A Framework for Resource Management in the Americas*, ed. J. Burger, E. Ostrom, R. B. Norgaard, D. Policansky, and B. D. Goldstein, 17–41. Washington, DC: Island Press. Reprint from *Swiss Political Science Review* 6(1):29–52.

Ostrom, E., J. Burger, C. B. Field, R. B. Norgaard, and D. Policansky. 1999. Revisiting the Commons: Local Lessons, Global Challenges. *Science* 284(5412):278–282.

Ostrom, E., R. Gardner, and J. Walker, eds. 1994. *Rules, Games, and Common-Pool Resources.* Ann Arbor: University of Michigan Press.

Ostrom, E., and J. Walker. 2003. *Trust and Reciprocity: Interdisciplinary Lessons from Experimental Research.* New York: Russell Sage Foundation.

Ostrom, E., and M. B. Wertime. 2000. International Forestry Resources and Institutions Research Strategy. In *People and Forests: Communities, Institutions, and Governance*, ed. C. C. Gibson, M. A. McKean, and E. Ostrom, 243–268. Cambridge, MA: MIT Press.

Ostrom, V. 1999. Polycentricity. In *Polycentricity and Local Public Economies. Readings from the Workshop in Political Theory and Policy Analysis*, ed. M. McGinnis, 52–74. Ann Arbor: University of Michigan Press.

Overman, J. P. M., H. J. L. Witte, and J. G. Saldarriaga. 1994. Evaluation of Regression Models for Above-Ground Biomass Determination in Amazon Rainforest. *Journal of Tropical Ecology* 10:207–218.

Overmars, K., G. H. J. de Koning, and A. Veldkamp. 2003. Spatial Autocorrelation in Multi-Scale Land Use Models. *Ecological Modelling* 164:257–270.

Ozório de Almeida, A. L. 1992. *The Colonization of the Amazon*. Austin: University of Texas Press.

Parker, D. C. 1999. *Landscape Outcomes in a Model of Edge-Effect Externalities: A Computational Economics Approach*. SFI Publication 99-07-051. Santa Fe, NM: Santa Fe Institute. URL: http://www.santafe.edu/sfi/publications/Working-Papers/99-07-051.pdf.

Parker, D. C., T. Berger, and S. M. Manson, eds. 2002. *Agent-Based Models of Land-Use/Land-Cover Change: Report and Review of an International Workshop, October 4–7, 2001, Irvine, California*. LUCC Report Series, no. 6. Bloomington: Focus 1 Office of the International Geosphere-Biosphere Programme and the International Human Dimensions Programme on Global Environmental Change, Indiana University. URL: http://www.indiana.edu/~act/focus1/ABM_Report6.pdf.

Parker, D. C., S. M. Manson, M. A. Janssen, M. J. Hoffmann, and P. Deadman. 2003. Multi-Agent Systems for the Simulation of Land-Use and Land-Cover Change: A Review. *Annals of the Association of American Geographers* 93(2):316–340.

Parker, D. C., and V. Meretsky. 2002. Empirical Tests Based on Emergent Landscape Properties: Linking Multi-Agent Systems Models to Data. Presented at the Association of American Geographers Annual Meeting, Los Angeles, March 19–23.

———. 2004. Measuring Pattern Outcomes in an Agent-Based Model of Edge-Effect Externalities Using Spatial Metrics. *Agriculture, Ecosystems, and Environment* 101(2–3):233–250.

Parker, D. C., and R. N. Najlis. 2003. Using Multi-Agent System Models to Link Spatial Externalities and Landscape Fragmentation: A "Pseudo-Inductive" Analysis. Presented at Framing Land Use Dynamics, Utrecht University, the Netherlands, April 16–18. URL: http://networks.geog.uu.nl/conference/abstracts.html.

Parker, G. R. 1997. The Wave of Settlement. In *The Natural Heritage of Indiana*, ed. M. T. Jackson, 369–382. Bloomington: Indiana University Press.

Parks, P. J., and B. C. Murray. 1994. Land Attributes and Land Allocation: Nonindustrial Forest Use in the Pacific Northwest. *Forest Science* 40:558–575.

Parris, T., and R. Kates. 2003. Characterizing a Sustainability Transition: Goals, Targets, Trends, and Driving Forces. *Proceedings of the National Academy of Sciences of the United States of America* 100(14):8068–8073. URL: http://www.pnas.org/cgi/content/abstract/100/14/8068.

Peddle, D. R., F. G. Hall, and E. F. LeDrew. 1999. Spectral Mixture Analysis and Geometric-Optical Reflectance Modeling of Boreal Forest Biophysical Structure. *Remote Sensing of Environment* 67:288–297.

Perakis, S. S., and L. O. Hedin. 2002. Nitrogen Loss from Unpolluted South American Forests Mainly via Dissolved Organic Compounds. *Nature* 415:416–419.

Perz, S. G. 2001. Household Demographic Factors as Life Cycle Determinants of Land Use in the Amazon. *Population Research and Policy Review* 20:159–186.

Peters, B. G. 1999. *Institutional Theory in Political Science: The "New Institutionalism."* Washington, DC: Pinter.

Peterson, D. L., M. A. Spanner, S. W. Running, and K. B. Teuber. 1987. Relationship of Thematic Mapper Simulator Data to Leaf Area Index of Temperate Coniferous Forests. *Remote Sensing of Environment* 22:323.

Pfister, C., and P. Messerli. 1990. Switzerland. In *The Earth as Transformed by Human Action*, ed. W. C. Clark, B. L. Turner II, R. W. Kates, J. Richards, J. T. Mathews, and W. Meyer, 605–622. Cambridge, UK: Cambridge University Press.

Pichón, F., and R. Bilsborrow. 1992. Land Use Systems, Deforestation and Associated Demographic Factors in the Humid Tropics: Farm-Level Evidence from Ecuador. In *Population and Deforestation in the Humid Tropics*, ed. R. Bilsborrow and D. Hogan, 175–207. Paris: International Union for the Scientific Study of Population.

Pickett, S. T. A., and P. S. White. 1985. *The Ecology of Natural Disturbance and Patch Dynamics*. Orlando, FL: Academic Press.

Place, F., and K. Otsuka. 2000. Population Pressure, Land Tenure, and Tree Resource Management in Uganda. *Land Economics* 76(2):233–251.

Plantinga, A. J., T. Mauldin, and D. J. Miller. 1999. An Econometric Analysis of the Cost of Sequestering Carbon in Forests. *American Journal of Agricultural Economics* 81:812–824.

Pontius, R. G., A. Agrawal, and D. Huffaker. 2003. Estimating the Uncertainty of Land-Cover Extrapolations while Constructing a Raster Map from Tabular Data. *Journal of Geographical Systems* 5(3):253–273.

Posey, D. A. 1985. Indigenous Management of Tropical Forest Ecosystems: The Case of the Kayapó Indians of the Brazilian Amazon. *Agroforestry Systems* 3:139–158.

Powell, W. W., and P. J. DiMaggio. 1991. *The New Institutionalism in Organizational Analysis*. Chicago: University of Chicago Press.

Programma Pobreza e Meio Ambiente na Amazônia (POEMA). 1994. *Pobreza e meio ambiente na amazonia Belém*. Pará, Brazil: Universidade Federal do Pará.

Ragin, C. C. 1987. *The Comparative Method: Moving beyond Qualitative and Quantitative Strategies*. Berkeley: University of California Press.

———. 2000. *Fuzzy Set Social Science*. Chicago: The University of Chicago Press.

Raitio, H. 2000. Weather Conditions during 1980–1995 and Tree Damage Directly Attributable to Weather. In *Forest Condition in a Changing Environment—The Finnish Case*, ed. E. Malkonen, 41–48. Dordrecht, the Netherlands: Kluwer.

Rangan, H. 1997. Property vs. Control: The State and Forest Management in the Indian Himalaya. *Development and Change* 28:71–94.

Rea, A. M., T. Ijichi, and G. P. Nabhan. 1997. *At the Desert's Green Edge: An Ethnobotany of the Gila River Pima*. Tucson: University of Arizona Press.

Reams, G. A., and C. E. Peterson, Jr. 1992. Evaluating Changes in Forest Condition Potentially Related to Acidic Deposition: An Example Using Red Spruce. *Forest Ecology and Management* 51:5–16.

Redman, C. L. 1999. *Human Impact on Ancient Environments*. Tucson: University of Arizona Press.

Reenberg, A. 2001. Agricultural Land Use Pattern Dynamics in the Sudan-Sahel: Towards an Event-Driven Framework. *Land Use Policy* 18:309–319.

Repetto, R. 1989. Economic Incentives for Sustainable Production. In *Environmental Management and Economic Development*, ed. G. Schram and J. J. Warford, 69–86. Baltimore: Johns Hopkins University Press.

Repetto, R., and M. Gillis, eds. 1988. *Public Policies and the Misuse of Forest Resources.* Cambridge, UK: Cambridge University Press.

Richards, P. 1987. Upland and Swamp Rice Farming Systems in Sierra Leone: An Evolutionary Transition? In *Comparative Farming Systems*, ed. B. L. Turner II and S. B. Brush, 156–187. New York: Guilford.

Riitters, K. H., B. E. Law, R. C. Kucera, A. L. Gallant, R. L. DeVelice, and C. J. Palmer. 1992. A Selection of Forest Condition Indicators for Monitoring. *Environmental Monitoring and Assessment* 20:21–33.

Rindfuss, R. R. 2002. Conflicting Demands: Confidentiality Promises and Data Availability. *IHDP Newsletter UPDATE* 2/02:1–4. URL: http://www.ihdp.uni-bonn.de/html/publications/update/IHDPUpdate02_02.html. Accessed June 2003.

Rindfuss, R. R., B. Entwisle, S. J. Walsh, P. Prasartkul, Y. Sawangdee, T. W. Crawford, and J. Reade. 2002. Continuous and Discrete: Where They Have Met in Nang Rong, Thailand. In *Linking People, Place and Policy: A GIScience Approach*, ed. S. J. Walsh and K. A. Crews-Meyer, 7–37. Boston: Kluwer.

Rindfuss, R. R., S. J. Walsh, V. Mishra, J. Fox, and G. P. Dolcemascolo. 2003. Linking Household and Remotely Sensed Data: Methodological and Practical Problems. In *People and the Environment: Approaches for Linking Household and Community Surveys to Remote Sensing and GIS*, ed. J. Fox, R. Rindfuss, S. Walsh, and V. Mishra, 1–30. Dordrecht, the Netherlands: Kluwer.

Ripple, W. J., S. Wang, D. L. Isaacson, and D. P. Pairre. 1991. A Preliminary Comparison of Landsat Thematic Mapper and SPOT-1 HRV Multispectral Data for Estimating Coniferous Forest Volume. *International Journal of Remote Sensing* 12:1971–1991.

Robinove, C. J. 1982. Computation with Physical Values from Landsat Digital Data. *Photogrammetric Engineering and Remote Sensing* 48(5):781–784.

Rocheleau, D. E., B. P. Thomas-Slayter, and E. Wangari. 1996. Gender and Environment: A Feminist Political Ecology Perspective. In *Feminist Political Ecology: Global Issues and Local Experiences*, ed. D. E. Rocheleau, B. P. Thomas-Slayter, and E. Wangari, 3–26. New York: Routledge.

Root, T. L., and S. H. Schneider. 1995. Ecology and Climate: Research Strategies and Implications. *Science* 269:334–341.

Rosenzweig, M. R., and K. I. Wolpin. 1985. Specific Experience, Household Structure, and Intergenerational Transfers: Farm Family Land and Labor Arrangements in Developing Countries. *Quarterly Journal of Economics* 100:961–987.

Roy, P. S., and S. A. Ravan. 1996. Biomass Estimation Using Satellite Remote Sensing Data: An Investigation on Possible Approaches for Natural Forest. *Journal of Bioscience* 21:535–561.

Rudel, T. K. 1989. Population, Development and Tropical Deforestation: A Cross-National Study. *Rural Sociology* 54(3):327–338.

Rudel, T. K., D. Bates, and R. Machinguiashi. 2002. A Tropical Forest Transition? Agricultural Change, Out-Migration, and Secondary Forests in the Ecuadorian Amazon. *Annals of the Association of American Geographers* 92(1):87–102.

Rudel, T. K., M. Perez-Lugo, and H. Zichal, 2000. When Fields Revert to Forest: Development and Spontaneous Reforestation in Post-War Puerto Rico. *Professional Geographer* 52(3):386–397.

Rudel, T. K., and J. Roper. 1996. Regional Patterns and Historical Trends in Tropical Deforestation, 1976–1990: A Qualitative Comparative Analysis. *Ambio* 25(3):160–166.

———. 1997. The Paths to Rain Forest Destruction: Crossnational Patterns of Tropical Deforestation, 1975–90. *World Development* 25(1):53–65.

Runge, C. F. 1986. Common Property and Collective Action in Economic Development. *World Development* 14(5):623–635.

Sader, S. A., R. B. Waide, W. T. Lawrence, and A. T. Joyce. 1989. Tropical Forest Biomass and Successional Age Class Relationships to a Vegetation Index Derived from Landsat TM Data. *Remote Sensing of Environment* 28:143–156.

Sahnoun, M. 1996. Managing Conflict after the Cold War. *Horn of Africa Bulletin* 8(3):1,35.

Saldarriaga, J. G., D. C. West, M. L. Tharp, and C. Uhl. 1988. Long-Term Chronosequence of Forest Succession in the Upper Rio Negro of Colombia and Venezuela. *Journal of Ecology* 76:938–958.

Samuelson, P. A. 1983. Thünen at Two Hundred. *Journal of Economic Literature* 21:1468–1488.

Sandler, T. 1995. Collective Action and Tropical Deforestation. *International Journal of Social Economics* 24(7–9)741–760.

Sassen, S. 1988. *The Mobility of Labor and Capital: A Study in International Investment and Labor Flow*. Cambridge, UK: Cambridge University Press.

Saugier, B., J. Roy, and H. A. Mooney. 2001. Estimating of Global Terrestrial Productivity: Converging toward a single number? In *Terrestrial Global Productivity*, ed. J. Roy, B. Saugier, and H. A. Mooney, 543–557. San Diego: Academic Press.

Scatena, F., A. Walker, A. Homma, C. Conto, C. Ferreira, R. Cavalho, A. Rocha, A. Santos, and P. Oliveira. 1996. Cropping and Fallowing Sequences of Small Farms in the "Terra Firme" Landscape of the Brazilian Amazon: A Case Study from Santarém, Pará. *Ecological Economics* 18:29–40.

Schelhas, J. 1996. Land Use Choice and Change: Intensification and Diversification in the Lowland Tropics of Costa Rica. *Human Organization* 55(3):298–306.

Schelhas, J., and R. Greenberg. 1996. *Forest Patches in Tropical Landscapes*. Covela, CA: Island Press.

Schlager, E. 1990. Model specification and policy analysis: The governance of coastal fisheries. Ph.D. diss., Indiana University, Bloomington.

———. 1994. Fishers' Institutional Responses to Common-Pool Resource Dilemmas. In *Rules, Games and Common-Pool Resources*, ed. E. Ostrom, R. Gardner, and J. Walker, 247–265. Ann Arbor: University of Michigan Press.

———. 1997. A Response to Kim Quaile Hill's "In Search of Policy Theory." *Policy Currents* 7(June):14–15.

Schlesinger, W. 1997. *Biogeochemistry: An Analysis of Global Change*, 2d ed. San Diego: Academic Press.

Schmink, M. 1994. The Socioeconomic Matrix of Deforestation. In *Population and the Environment: Rethinking the Debate*, ed. L. Arizpe, M. P. Stone, and D. C. Major, 253–276. Boulder, CO: Westview.

Schmink, M., and C. H. Wood, eds. 1984. *Frontier Expansion in Amazonia*. Gainesville: University Press of Florida.

Schweik, C. M. 1996. *Social Norms and Human Foraging: An Investigation into the spatial Distribution of* Shorea robusta *in Nepal*. FAO Working Paper in Forest Trees and People Programme, Phase II series. Rome: Food and Agriculture Organization of the United Nations.

———. 1998. *The Spatial and Temporal Analysis of Forest Resources and Institutions*. CIPEC Dissertation Series, No. 2. Bloomington: Center for the Study of Institutions, Population, and Environmental Change (CIPEC), Indiana University.

———. 2000. Optimal Foraging, Institutions, and Forest Change: A Case from Nepal. In *People and Forests: Communities, Institutions, and Governance*, ed. C. C. Gibson, M. A. McKean, and E. Ostrom, 99–134. Cambridge, MA: MIT Press.

———. 2001. *Open Research System: A System to Support Environmental Research Collaboration*. URL: http://www.open-research.org.

Schweik, C. M., K. R. Adhikari, and K. N. Pandit. 1997. Land-Cover Change and Forest Institutions: A Comparison of Two Sub-Basins in the Southern Siwalik Hills of Nepal. *Mountain Research and Development* 17(2):99–116.

Schweik, C. M., and G. M. Green. 1999. The Use of Spectral Mixture Analysis to Study Human Incentives, Actions and Environmental Outcomes. *Social Science Computer Review* 17(1):40–63.

Schweik, C. M., and J. M. Grove. 2000. Fostering Open-Source Research via a World Wide Web System. *Public Administration and Management: An Interactive Journal* 5(4):article 2 [online]. URL: http://www.pamij.com/00_5_4.html.

Schweik, C. M., H. Nagendra, and D. R. Sinha. 2003. Using Satellite Imagery to Locate Innovative Forest Management Practices in Nepal. *Ambio* 32(4):312–319. Available at http://www.bioone.org/pdfserv/i0044-7447-032-04-0312.pdf (subscription to BioOne required).

Schweik, C. M., and C. Thomas. 2002. Using Remote Sensing for Evaluating Environmental Institutions: A Habitat Conservation Planning Example. *Social Science Quarterly* 83(1):244–262.

Scientific News in Washington. 1888. *Science* 12:169–171.

Scott, A. D. 1955. The Fishery: The Objectives of Sole Ownership. *Journal of Political Economy* 63:116–124.

Segura, O., D. Kaimowitz, and J. Rodriguez, eds. 1997. *Políticas forestales en Centroamérica: Análisis de las restricciones para el desarrollo del sector forestal* (Forest Policies in Central America: Analysis of Restrictions on the Development of the Forestry Sector). San Salvador, El Salvador: Instituto Interamericano de Cooperación para la Agricultura.

Seidensticker, J. 2002. Tiger tracks. *Smithsonian* 32(10):62–69.

Seto, K. C., and R. K. Kaufmann. 2003. Modeling the Drivers of Urban Land Use Change in the Pearl River Delta, China: Integrating Remote Sensing with Socioeconomic Data. *Land Economics* 79(1):106–121.

Shorr, N. 1998. Agricultural intensification in a large Tikuna community on the floodplain of the upper Brazilian Amazon. Ph.D. diss., Indiana University, Bloomington.

Shukla, J., C. Nobre, and P. Sellers. 1990. Amazon Deforestation and Climate Change. *Science* 247:1322–1325.

Siegal, B. S., and A. R. Gillespie. 1980. *Remote Sensing in Geology*. New York: Wiley.

Silva-Forsberg, M. C. 1999. *Protecting an Urban Forest Reserve in the Amazon: A Multi-Scale Analysis of Edge Effects, Population Pressure, and Institutions*. CIPEC Dissertation Series, No. 3. Bloomington: Center for the Study of Institutions, Population, and Environmental Change, Indiana University.

Silveíra, J. P. 2001. Development of the Brazilian Amazon. *Science* 292:1651–1654.

Simon, H. 1985. Human Nature in Politics: The Dialogue of Psychology with Political Science. *American Political Science Review* 79:293–304.

———. 1997. *Models of Bounded Rationality: Empirically Grounded Economic Reason*. Cambridge, MA: MIT Press.

Singer, J. W. 2000. Property and Social Relation: From Title to Entitlement. In *Property and Values: Alternatives to Public and Private Ownership*, ed. C. Geisler and G. Daneker, 3–19. Washington, DC: Island Press.

Singleton, R. A., and B. C. Straits. 1998. *Approaches to Social Research*, 3d ed. New York: Oxford University Press.

Siniarska, A., and F. Dickinson. 1996. *Annotated Bibliography in Human Ecology*. Delhi, India: Kamla-Raj Enterprises.

Siqueira A. D., S. McCracken, E. S. Brondízio, and E. F. Moran. 2003. Women in a Brazilian Agricultural Frontier. In *Gender at Work in Economic Life*, ed. G. Clark. Society for Economic Anthropology Monograph series, no. 20. Walnut Creek, CA: Altamira.

Siy, R. Y., Jr. 1982. *Community Resource Management: Lessons from the Zanjera*. Quezon City: University of the Philippines Press.

Skelly, J. M. 1989. Forest Decline versus Tree Decline—The Pathological Considerations. *Environmental Monitoring and Assessment* 12:23–27.

Skole, D., and C. Tucker. 1993. Tropical Deforestation and Habitat Fragmentation in the Amazon: Satellite Data from 1978 to 1988. *Science* 260(5116):1905–1910.

Skole, D., and B. L. Turner II. 1995. *Land Use and Land Cover Change Science Plan*. Joint publication of the International Geosphere-Biosphere Programme (Report no. 35) and the Human Dimensions of Global Environmental Change Programme (Report no. 7). Bonn, Germany/Stockholm: International Human Dimensions Programme (IHDP)/International Geosphere-Biosphere Programme.

Smith, A. D. 1988. Toward Geography of Peace in Africa: Re-Defining Substate Determination Rights. In *Nationalism, Self Determination and Political Geography*, ed. R. J. Johnston, D. B. Knight, and E. Kofman, 70–86. New York: Croom Helm.

Smith, N. 1982. *Rainforest Corridors: The Transamazon Colonization Scheme*. Berkeley: University of California Press.

Skole, D., and C. J. Tucker. 1993. Tropical Deforestation and Habitat Fragmentation in the Amazon: Satellite Data from 1978 to 1988. *Science* 260:1905–1910.

Sorrensen, C. L. 2000. Linking Smallholder Land Use and Fire Activity: Examining Biomass Burning in the Brazilian Lower Amazon. *Forest Ecology and Management* 128:11–25.

Sousa, W. P. 1984. The Role of Disturbance in Natural Communities. *Annual Review of Ecology and Systematics* 15:353–391.

Southworth, J., H. Nagendra, and C. M. Tucker. 2002. Fragmentation of a Landscape: Incorporating Landscape Metrics into Satellite Analyses of Land Cover Change. *Landscape Research* 27(3):253–269.

Southworth, J., and C. M. Tucker. 2001. The Roles of Accessibility, Local Institutions, and Socioeconomic Factors Influencing Forest Cover Change in the Mountains of Western Honduras. *Mountain Research and Development* 21(3):276–283.

Spanner, M. A., L. L. Pierce, D. L. Peterson, and S. W. Running. 1990. Remote Sensing of Temperate Coniferous Leaf Area Index: The Influence of Canopy Closure, Understory Vegetation, and Background Reflectance. *International Journal of Remote Sensing* 11:95–111.

Spies, T. A., and M. G. Turner. 1999. Dynamic Forest Mosaics. In *Maintaining Biodiversity in Forest Ecosystems*, ed. M. L. Hunter, 95–160. Cambridge, UK: Cambridge University Press.

Starfield, A. M., and A. L. Bleloch. 1986. *Building Models for Conservation and Wildlife Management*. New York: Macmillan.

Steffen, W., A. Sanderson, P. D. Tyson, J. Jager, P. A. Matson, B. Moore III, F. Oldfield, K. Richardson, J. J. Schellnhuber, B. L. Turner II, R. J. Wasson. 2004. *Global Change and the Earth System: A Planet under Pressure*. IGBP Book series. Berlin: Springer-Verlag.

Steininger, M. K. 2000. Satellite Estimation of Tropical Secondary Forest Above-Ground Biomass Data from Brazil and Bolivia. *International Journal of Remote Sensing* 21:1139–1157.

Steward, J. 1938. *Basin-Plateau Aboriginal Sociopolitical Groups. Bureau of American Ethnology Bulletin 120*. Washington, DC: Smithsonian Institution.

———. 1955. *Theory of Culture Change*. Urbana: University of Illinois Press.

Stommel, H. 1963. Varieties of Oceanographic Experience. *Science* 139:572–576.

Suazo, J. N., I. Walker, M. Ramos, and S. Zelaya. 1997. Políticas Forestales en Honduras (Forest Policies in Honduras). In *Políticas forestales en Centroamérica: Análisis de las restricciones para el desarrollo del sector forestal* (Forest Policies in Central America: Analysis of Restrictions on the Development of the Forestry Sector), ed. O. Segura, D. Kaimowitz, and J. Rodríguez, 231–265. San Salvador, El Salvador: Instituto Interamericano de Cooperación para la Agricultura.

Sundar, N., R. Jeffery, and N. Thin. 2001. *Branching Out: Joint Forest Management in India*. Oxford: Oxford University Press.

Sussman, R. W., G. M. Green, I. Porton, O. L. Andrianasolondraibe, and J. Ratsirarson. 2003. A Survey of the Habitat of *Lemur catta* in Southwestern and Southern Madagascar. *Primate Conservation* 19:32–57.

Sussman, R. W., G. M. Green, and L. K. Sussman. 1994. Satellite Imagery, Human Ecology, Anthropology and Deforestation in Madagascar. *Human Ecology* 22(3):333–353.

Szreter, S. 1996. *Fertility, Class and Gender in Britain, 1860–1940*. New York: Cambridge University Press.

Tang, S. Y. 1992. *Institutions and Collective Action: Self-Governance in Irrigation*. San Francisco: ICS Press.

———. 1994. Institutions and Performance in Irrigation Systems. In *Rules, Games and Common-Pool Resources*, ed. E. Ostrom, R. Gardner, and J. Walker. Ann Arbor: University of Michigan Press.

Taussig, M. 1978. Peasant Economics and the Development of Capitalist Agriculture in the Cauca Valley, Colombia. *Latin American Perspectives* 5(3):62–91.

Teillet, P. M., and G. Fedosejevs. 1995. On the Dark Target Approach to Atmospheric Correction of Remotely Sensed Data. *Canadian Journal of Remote Sensing* 21(4):374–387.

Thomas, F. 1925. *The Environmental Basis of Society*. New York: Century.

Thome, K. J., S. F. Biggar, D. I. Gellman, and P. N. Slater. 1994. Absolute-Radiometric Calibration of Landsat-5 Thematic Mapper and the Proposed Calibration of the Advance Spaceborne Thermal Emission and Reflection Radiometer. In *International Geoscience and Remote Sensing Symposium '94*, 2295–2297. Los Alamitos, CA: Institute of Electrical and Electronics Engineers.

Tiffen, M., M. Mortimore, and F. Gichuki. 1994. *More People, Less Erosion: Environmental Recovery in Kenya*. New York: Wiley.

Tilman, D. 1999. Ecological Consequences of Biodiversity: A Search for General Principles. *Ecology* 80:1455–1474.

Tocqueville, A. de. [1840] 1945. *Democracy in America*. Reprint of *Democracy in America: Part the Second: The Social Influence of Democracy*, trans. H. Reeve, as revised by F. Bowen, further corrected and edited with introduction, editorial notes, and bibliographies by P. Bradley. New York: Knopf.

Tri-Academy Panel on Population and Land Use (Indian National Science Academy, Chinese Academy of Sciences, and U.S. National Academy of Sciences), eds. 2001. *Growing Populations, Changing Landscapes: Studies from India, China, and the United States*. Washington, DC: National Academies Press. URL: http://www.nap.edu/books/0309075548/html/.

Tucker, C. M. 1999. Private vs. Communal Forests: Forest Conditions and Tenure in a Honduran Community. *Human Ecology* 27(2):201–230.

———. 2004. Community Institutions and Forest Management in Mexico's Monarch Butterfly Reserve. *Society and Natural Resources* 17(7):569–587.

Tucker, C. M., D. K. Munroe, J. Southworth, and H. Nagendra. 2004. Trading Spaces: Following the Impact of Forest-Coffee Conversions on Honduran Livelihoods. *IHDP UPDATE: Newsletter of the International Human Dimensions Programme on Global Environmental Change* 01/2004:14–15. URL: http://www.ihdp.uni-bonn.de/html/publications/publications.html.

Tucker, J. M., E. S. Brondízio, F. de Castro, and E. Moran. 2000. A multi-level approach to a comparative analysis of biomass estimation in eastern Amazônia. Unpublished manuscript of the Anthropological Center for Training and Research on Global Environmental Change, Indiana University, Bloomington.

Tucker, J. M., E. S. Brondízio, and E. F. Moran. 1998. Rates of Forest Regrowth in Eastern Amazônia: A Comparison of Altamira and Bragantina Regions, Pará State, Brazil. *Interciencia* 23(2):64–73.

Turner, B. L., II, and A. M. S. Ali. 1996. Induced Intensification: Agricultural Change in Bangladesh with Implications for Malthus and Boserup. *Proceedings of the National Academy of Sciences of the United States of America* 93(25):14984–14991.

Turner, B. L., II, G. Hyden, and R. Kates, eds. 1993a. *Population Growth and Agricultural Change in Africa: Studies from Densely Settled Areas of Sub-Saharan Africa*. Gainesville: University Press of Florida.

Turner, B. L., II, R. E. Kasperson, P. A. Matson, J. J. McCarthy, R. W. Corell, L. Christensen, N. Eckley, J. X. Kasperson, A. Luers, M. L. Martello, C. Polsky, A. Pulsipher, and A. Schiller. 2003. A Framework for Vulnerability Analysis in Sustainability Science. *Proceedings of the National Academy of Sciences of the United States of America* 100(14):8074–8079. URL: http://www.pnas.org/cgi/content/full/100/14/8074.

Turner, B. L., II, W. B. Meyer, and D. L. Skole. 1994. Global Land-Use/Land-Cover Change: Toward an Integrating Study. *Ambio* 23(1):91–95.

Turner, B. L., II, R. H. Moss, and D. L. Skole, eds. 1993b. *Relating Land Use and Global Land-Cover Change: A Proposal for an IGBP-HDP Core Project*. Joint publication of International Geosphere-Biosphere Programme (Report no. 24) and Human Dimensions of Global Environmental Change Programme (Report no. 5). Stockholm: Royal Swedish Academy of Sciences.

Turner, B. L., II, D. L. Skole, S. Sanderson, G. Fischer, L. Fresco, and R. Leemans, eds. 1995. *Land-Use and Land Cover Change Science/Research Plan*. IGBP Report no. 35 and IHDP Report no. 7. Stockholm: International Geosphere-Biosphere Programme (IGBP); Bonn, Germany: International Human Dimensions Programme on Global Environmental Change (IHDP). URL: http://www.ihdp.uni-bonn.de (click on Publications, then IHDP Report Series).

Turner, M. G., G. J. Arthaud, R. T. Engstrom, S. J. Hejl, J. Liu, S. Loeb, and K. McKelvey. 1995. Usefulness of Spatially Explicit Population Models in Land Management. *Ecological Applications* 5(1):12–16.

Turner, M. G., R. H. Gardner, and R. V. O'Neill. 2001. *Landscape Ecology in Theory and Practice: Pattern and Process*. New York: Springer-Verlag.

Uhl, C. 1987. Factors Controlling Succession Following Slash-and-Burn Agriculture in Amazônia. *Journal of Ecology* 75:377–407.

Uhl, C., R. Buschbacher, and E. A. S. Serrao. 1988. Abandoned Pastures in Eastern Amazônia. I. Patterns of Plant Succession. *Journal of Ecology* 76:663–681.

United States Geological Survey (USGS). 1979. *Landsat Data Users Handbook*. Sioux Falls, SD: EROS Data Center.

———. 1984. *Landsat 4 Data Users Handbook*. Sioux Falls, SD: EROS Data Center.

———. 2003. *Landsat 7 Science Data Users Handbook*. URL: http://ltpwww.gsfc.nasa.gov/IAS/handbook/handbook_toc.html.

United States Global Change Program (USGCP). 1999. *A U.S. Carbon Cycle Science Plan*. Report of the Carbon and Climate Working Group. Washington, DC: author.

United States National Resources Conservation Service (NRCS). 2001. *State Soil Geographic Database (STATSGO)*. Washington, DC: author, United States Department of Agriculture.

Unruh, J. D. 1993. Refugee Resettlement on the Horn of Africa: The Integration of Host and Refugee Land Use Patterns. *Land Use Policy* 10:49–66.

———. 1995a. Agroforestry, Reforestry and the Carbon Problem: The Role of Land and Tree Tenure. *Interdisciplinary Science Reviews* 20:215–228.

———. 1995b. Post-Conflict Recovery of African Agriculture: The Role of "Critical Resource" Tenure. *Ambio* 24:343–350.

———. 1998. Land Tenure and Identity Change in Postwar Mozambique. *Geojournal* 46:89–99.

———. 2001. Postwar Land Dispute Resolution: Land Tenure and the Peacekeeping Process in Mozambique. *Journal of World Peace* 18:3–30.

———. 2002. Poverty and Property Rights in the Developing World: Not As Simple As We Would Like. *Land Use Policy* 19:275–276.

———. 2003. Land Tenure and Legal Pluralism in the Peace Process. *Peace and Change: A Journal of Peace Research* 28(3):352–377.

Unruh, J. D., and P. A. Lefebvre. 1995. A Spatial Database Approach for Estimating Areas Suitable for Agroforestry in Africa. *Agroforestry Systems* 32:81–96.

Utting, P. 1993. *Trees, People and Power: Social Dimensions of Deforestation and Forest Protection in Central America*. London: Earthscan.

Vance, C., and J. Geoghegan. 2004. Modeling the Determinants of Semi-Subsistent and Commercial Land-Uses in an Agricultural Frontier of Southern Mexico: A Switching Regression Approach. *International Regional Science Review* 27(3):326–347.

Van der Dussen, K. 1998a. Condo Owners to be Sued over Cutting of Trees near Lake. *Bloomington Herald-Times*, 7 May.

———. 1998b. County Sues over Cutting of Trees near The Pointe. *Bloomington Herald-Times*, 22 July.

———. 2002a. Pedigo Bay Faces More Fines over Tree Cutting. *Bloomington Herald-Times*, 18 May.

———. 2002b. Lakeside Residents Face Fines for Tree Cuts. *Bloomington Herald-Times*, 18 September.

Varughese, G. 1999. Villagers, bureaucrats and forests in Nepal: Designing governance for a complex resource. Ph.D. diss., School of Public Affairs and Environmental Sciences and Department of Political Science, Indiana University, Bloomington.

———. 2000. Population and Forest Dynamics in the Hills of Nepal: Institutional Remedies by Rural Communities. In *People and Forests: Communities, Institutions, and Governance*, ed. C. C. Gibson, M. A. McKean, and E. Ostrom, 193–226. Cambridge, MA: MIT Press.

Varughese, G., and E. Ostrom. 2001. The Contested Role of Heterogeneity in Collective Action: Some Evidence from Community Forestry in Nepal. *World Development* 29(5):747–765.

Veldkamp, T., and L. O. Fresco. 1996. CLUE-CR: An Integrated Multi-Scale Model to Simulate Land Use Change Scenarios in Costa Rica. *Ecological Modelling* 91:231–248.

Ventocilla, J., H. Herrera, and V. Núñez. 1995. *Plants and Animals in the Life of the Kuna*, trans. E. King. Austin: University of Texas Press.

Verburg, P. H., and Y. Chen. 2000. Multiscale Characterization of Land-Use Patterns in China. *Ecosystems* 3:369–385.

Verburg, P. H., P. Schot, M. Dijst, and A. Velkamp. In press. Land-Use Change Modeling: Current Practice and Research Priorities. *GeoJournal*.

Verissimo, A., M. A. Cochrane, and C. Souza Jr. 2002. National Forests in the Amazon. *Science* 297:1478.

Visser, S. 1982. On Agricultural Location Theory. *Geographical Analysis* 14:167–176.

Vitousek, P. M. 1993. Global Dynamics and Ecosystem Processes: Scaling Up or Scaling Down? In *Scaling Physiological Processes: Leaf to Globe*, ed. J. R. Ehleringer and C. B. Field, 169–177. San Diego: Academic Press.

Vitousek, P. M., H. A. Mooney, J. Lubchenco, and J. M. Melillo. 1997. Human Domination of Earth's Ecosystems. *Science* 277:494–499.

Vogt, N. 2003. *Understanding the Long-Term Stability of West Mengo (Mpigi) Forest Reserve Boundaries*. CIPEC Working Paper CWP-03-02. Bloomington: Center for the Study of Institutions, Population, and Environmental Change (CIPEC), Indiana University.

Vogt, N., J. Bahati, J. Unruh, G. M. Green, A. Banana, W. Gombya-Ssembajjwe, and S. P. Sweeny. Under review. Untangling Mechanisms of Land-Cover Change: A Rapid, Policy-Relevant Analysis of Human-Environment Interactions at the Forest-Grassland Interface in Uganda. *Land Degradation and Development*.

Voinov, A., R. Costanza, L. Wainger, R. Boumans, F. Villa, T. Maxwell, and H. Voinov. 1999. The Patuxent Landscape Model: Integrated Ecological Economic Modeling of a Watershed. *Environmental Modelling and Software* 14:473–491.

Wade, R. 1994. *Village Republics: Economic Conditions for Collective Action in South India*. San Francisco: ICS Press.

Wagley, C. 1953. *Amazon Town: A Study of Man in the Tropics*. New York: Macmillan.

Walker, R. T., and A. K. O. Homma. 1996. Land Use and Land Cover Dynamics in the Brazilian Amazon: An Overview. *Ecological Economics* 18:67–80.

Walker, R. T., E. F. Moran, and L. Anselin. 2000. Deforestation and Cattle Ranching in the Brazilian Amazon: External Capital and Household Processes. *World Development* 28(4):683–699.

Wallerstein, I. 1974. *The Modern World-System*. San Diego: Academic Press.

Walsh, S. J., and K. A. Crews-Meyer, eds. 2002. *Linking People, Place, and Policy: A GIScience Approach*. Boston: Kluwer.

Walsh, S. J., T. P. Evans, B. L. Turner II. 2003. Population-Environment Interactions with an Emphasis on LULC Dynamics and the Role of Technology. In *Geography and Technology*, ed. S. D. Brunn, S. Cutter, and J. W. Harrington Jr., 491–519. Dordrecht, the Netherlands: Kluwer.

Walsh, S. J., T. P. Evans, W. F. Welsh, B. Entwisle, and R. R. Rindfuss. 1999. Scale Dependent Relationships between Population and Environment in Northeastern Thailand. *Photogrammetric Engineering and Remote Sensing* 65(1):97–105.

Walters, C. 1997. Challenges in Adaptive Management of Riparian and Coastal Ecosystems. *Conservation Ecology* 1(2):article 1 [online]. URL: http://www.consecol.org/vol1/iss2/art1.

Waring, R. H. 1983. Estimating Forest Growth and Efficiency in Relation to Canopy Leaf Area. *Advances in Ecological Research* 13:327–354.

Webber, M. J. 1973. Equilibrium of Location in an Isolated State. *Environment and Planning* 5:751–759.

Wei, Y. D. 2002. Multiscale and Multimechanisms of Regional Inequality in China: Implications for Regional Policy. *Journal of Contemporary China* 11:109–124.

Welch, W. P. 1983. The Political Feasibility of Full Ownership Property Rights: The Cases of Pollution and Fisheries. *Policy Sciences* 16:165–180.

Wernstedt, F. L. 1972. *World Climatic Data*. Lemont, PA: Climate Data Press.

Whitford, H. N. 1901. The Genetic Development of the Forests of Northern Michigan: A Study in Physiographic Ecology. *Botanical Gazette* 31:289–325.

Whittaker, R. H. 1975. *Communities and Ecosystems*, 2d ed. New York: Macmillan.

Whittaker, R. H., and G. E. Likens. 1975. The Biosphere and Man. In *Primary Productivity of the Biosphere*, ed. H. Lieth and R. H. Whittaker, 305–328. Berlin: Springer-Verlag.

Wilkie, D. 1987. Cultural and Ecological Survival in the Ituri Forest: The Role of Accurately Monitoring Natural Resources and Agricultural Land Use. *Cultural Survival Quarterly* 11(2):72–74.

Williams, M. 1989. *Americans and Their Forests: A Historical Geography*. Cambridge, UK: Cambridge University Press.

———. 2003. *Deforesting the Earth: From Prehistory to Global Crisis*. Chicago: University of Chicago Press.

Williams, R. G. 1994. *States and Social Evolution: Coffee and the Rise of National Governments in Central America*. Chapel Hill: University of North Carolina Press.

Wilson, E. O. 1988. *Biodiversity*. Washington, DC: National Academies Press.

———. 2002. *The Future of Life*. London: Little, Brown.

Wilson, K. 1992. Enhancing Refugees' Own Food Acquisition Strategies. *Journal of Refugee Studies* 5(3/4):226–247.

Wilson, W. M. 1997. Why bitter cassava (*Manihot esculenta* Crantz)? Productivity and perception of cassava in a Tukanoan Indian settlement in the northwest Amazon. Ph.D. diss. University of Colorado, Boulder.

Winterhalder, B. 1994. Concepts in Historical Ecology: The View from Evolutionary Ecology. In *Historical Ecology*, ed. C. Crumley, 17–41. Santa Fe, NM: School of American Research Press.

———. 2002. Models. In *Darwin and Archaeology: A Handbook of Key Concepts*, ed. J. P. Hart and J. E. Terrell, 201–223. Westport, CT: Bergin & Garvey.

With, K., and A. King. 1999. Dispersal Success on Fractal Landscapes: Consequence of Lacunarity Thresholds. *Landscape Ecology* 14:73–82.

Wood, C. H., and R. Porro, eds. 2002. *Deforestation and Land Use in the Amazon*. Gainesville: University Press of Florida.

Wood, C. H., and D. Skole. 1998. Linking Satellite, Census, and Survey Data to Study Deforestation in the Brazilian Amazon. In *People and Pixels: Linking Remote Sensing and Social Sciences*, ed. D. Liverman, E. F. Moran, R. R. Rindfuss, and P. C. Stern, 70–93. Washington, DC: National Academies Press.

World Resources Institute, United Nations Environment Programme, United Nations Development Programme, and World Bank (WRI et al.). 2000. *A Guide to World Resources 2000–2001: People and Ecosystems: The Fraying Web of Life*. Washington, DC: World Resources Institute.

Wu, J., and O. L. Loucks. 1995. From Balance of Nature to Hierarchical Patch Dynamics: A Paradigm Shift in Ecology. *Quarterly Review of Biology* 70:439–466.

York, A. M., M. A. Janssen, and E. Ostrom. In press. Incentives Affecting Decisions of Non-Industrial Private Forest Landowners about Using Their Land. In *International Handbook of Environmental Politics*, ed. P. Dauvergne. Cheltenham, UK: Edward Elgar.

Young, O. 1999. *The Effectiveness of International Environmental Regimes: Causal Connections and Behavioral Mechanisms*. Cambridge, MA: MIT Press.

———. 2002a. A Note from the Chair. *IDGEC News* 5:3. Published by Institutional Dimensions of Global Environmental Change, Dartmouth College, Hanover, NH.

———. 2002b. *The Institutional Dimensions of Environmental Change: Fit, Interplay and Scale*. Cambridge, MA: MIT Press.

Index